CRITICAL SURVEY
OF
LONG FICTION

CRITICAL SURVEY
OF
LONG FICTION

English Language Series

REVISED EDITION
Nai-Sar

6

Edited by
FRANK N. MAGILL

SALEM PRESS
Pasadena, California   Englewood Cliffs, New Jersey

SECOND PRINTING

∞ The paper used in these volumes conforms to the
American National Standard for Permanence of Paper
for Printed Library Materials, Z39.48-1984.

Library of Congress Cataloging-in-Publication Data
Critical survey of long fiction. English language series/
  edited by Frank N. Magill. — Rev. ed.
      p.   cm.
    Includes bibliographical references and index.
    1. English fiction—Dictionaries. 2. American
fiction—Dictionaries. 3. English fiction—
Bio-bibliography. 4. American fiction—
Bio-bibliography. 5. Novelists, English—
Biography—Dictionaries. 6. Novelists, American—
Biography—Dictionaries.
I. Magill, Frank Northen, 1907-
PR821.C7   1991
823.009′03—dc20   91-19694
ISBN 0-89356-825-2 (set)   CIP
ISBN 0-89356-831-7 (volume 6)

PRINTED IN THE UNITED STATES OF AMERICA

LIST OF AUTHORS IN VOLUME 6

CRITICAL SURVEY
OF
LONG FICTION

V. S. NAIPAUL

Born: Chaguanas, Trinidad; August 17, 1932

Principal long fiction

The Mystic Masseur, 1957; *The Suffrage of Elvira*, 1958; *Miguel Street*, 1959; *A House for Mr. Biswas*, 1961; *Mr. Stone and the Knights Companion*, 1963; *The Mimic Men*, 1967; *In a Free State*, 1971; *Guerrillas*, 1975; *A Bend in the River*, 1979; *The Enigma of Arrival*, 1987.

Other literary forms

V. S. Naipaul is a rarity among writers in that he enjoys equal recognition for his novels and for his works of nonfiction. Indeed, had Naipaul never published a novel, his works of nonfiction would in themselves be sufficient to assure his reputation as a major writer. As a writer of nonfiction, Naipaul has specialized in a distinctive blend of travelogue, reportage, and auto-biography, offering penetrating accounts of regions as diverse as his native Trinidad, India (the home of his ancestors and the subject of several of his books), Africa, and the American South.

Naipaul is a prolific writer, and, as a journalist and fiction editor for *New Statesman*, he wrote a considerable number of articles, book reviews, and short stories for a variety of magazines both in the United States and the United Kingdom. Most of these have not been collected in any form.

Achievements

"He began to write in London in 1954. He has followed no other profession" is Naipaul's own crisp author's note to the Penguin editions of his books. In *Naipaul: An Introduction to His Work*, Paul Theroux points out that Naipaul had no other occupation, held no job other than being a full-time writer. He is a man completely dedicated to his art. It is interesting to note that the characters Ganesh (*The Mystic Masseur*), Biswas (*A House for Mr. Biswas*), Ralph Kripal Singh (*The Mimic Men*), and Mr. Stone (*Mr. Stone and the Knights Companion*) are writers and that they participate in the "thrilling, tedious struggle with the agony and discouraging, exhilarating process of making a book." Naipaul looks upon his travels as essential to his writing, and he travels extensively. He considers such wanderings as essential to sustaining his life as a writer and to releasing his imagination from familiar, deadening scenes.

Starting his career as a comic interpreter of Trinidad society, Naipaul has gradually moved to becoming an interpreter of global issues and convulsions of culture. *The Mystic Masseur*, his first novel, had a regional cast and flavor while *In a Free State*, written fourteen years later, has an international cast.

His landscapes have shifted from the alleys and lanes of Miguel Street to East Africa, French Africa, South America, and India. From the Dickensian comedy and irony of *A House for Mr. Biswas*, he has moved to probing the heart of universal darkness in *Guerrillas* and *A Bend in the River*. This growth and development as a serious novelist involved with human concerns is one of Naipaul's major achievements.

Naipaul has received wide critical attention. He is the subject of a number of full-length critical studies and innumerable articles. His books have received front-page reviews; and Irving Howe has called him "the world's writer, a master of language and perception, our sardonic blessing." Elizabeth Hardwick considers the sweep of Naipaul's imagination and the brilliant fictional frame it encompasses unique and without equal in contemporary literature. Paul Theroux considers him to be superior to Albert Camus in his treatment of the theme of displacement. To Alfred Kazin, Naipaul is the perfect example of the novelist as thinker, and "the most compelling master of social truth." Michael Thorpe, in a brief study of Naipaul, calls him Joseph Conrad's heir as a political novelist. Critics and students of Naipaul place him in the company of such masters of fiction as Joseph Conrad—intensely admired by Naipaul—and Graham Greene.

In his nonfiction writing, Naipaul has proven himself adept at the scholar's meticulous research, and in his travelogues he displays the journalist's ability for brilliant reportage coupled with the novelist's ability for narrative skill and dramatization of human concerns.

In all his work, Naipaul confirms his stature as a writer of uncompromising standards and values, of relentless inquiry and tough judgment, thereby establishing him as one of the foremost masters of contemporary fiction.

Biography

Vidiadhar Surajprasad Naipaul, a third generation West Indian of East Indian ancestry, was born in Lion House—which is reincarnated as Hanuman House in his fourth novel, *A House for Mr. Biswas*—into a Hindu Brahmin family in Chaguanas in Central Trinidad, on August 17, 1932.

Naipaul grew up in a large Indian joint family with a brother, five sisters, and more than fifty cousins. Such a family, according to Naipaul, was "a microcosm of the authoritarian state" where power was supreme and growing up in such an atmosphere provided the seamy aspects of human behavior.

Naipaul's father, Seepersad Naipaul, was a correspondent for *The Trinidad Guardian* and an avid reader of Charles Dickens. He was also the author of *Gurudeva and Other Indian Tales* (1943, 1946), a collection of short stories. Naipaul used this book as one of his models to discover "the trick of writing." He was very close to his father, and in the love story of a father and son in his first major novel, *A House for Mr. Biswas*, he distills this affection and tenderness for his father. Even so, Naipaul, while talking about his childhood in Trinidad (*The Listener*, September 7, 1972), described his father as "a defeated man," who, like Mr. Biswas, felt alienated from the hierarchy of the family and solaced himself with "easy contempt."

Naipaul spent about two years at Chaguanas Government School. His father had attended the same school about twenty years earlier when it was the Canadian Mission School. In 1938, when his father was transferred to the capital city, Port of Spain, Naipaul transferred to Tranquillity Boys' School. He distinguished himself and won a free place at the prestigious Queens Royal College, where he studied for six years, specializing in French and English. The school features in three of his novels, and Naipaul wrote an article to the *Queens Royal College Chronicle* for 1948. It was a discussion of W. Somerset Maugham's first novel, *Liza of Lambeth* (1897), and it explores the origins of Maugham's skills as a novelist. Maugham's study of slum life in *Liza of Lambeth* fascinated Naipaul and in his third novel, *Miguel Street*, he explored the same theme.

Naipaul developed a great urge to get out of Trinidad, and in his book of travel essays about the West Indies, *The Middle Passage*, he describes this passionate obsession to leave the tropical island of his birth. Even after he left, his biggest nightmare was the dream that he had returned to Trinidad. He left Trinidad when he was seventeen and entered University College, Oxford, in the middle of 1950, where, after four years, he took a degree in English. While he was at Oxford, his father died. After graduation in 1955, Naipaul married Patricia Ann Hale and settled in London.

Naipaul worked as editor of the B.B.C. *Caribbean Voices* program and served as fiction reviewer on the staff of the *New Statesman* until 1961. From May, 1950, to May, 1960, he reviewed as many as sixty-one novels. He does not think very highly of these reviews and none has been included in *The Overcrowded Barracoon and Other Articles*, where he reflects negatively on his eight-year stay in London and fears that a continued London stay would lead to his own sterility.

To overcome this fear of sterility, Naipaul undertook travels, first to Trinidad for seven months, his first visit home and then to India for a year to research his cultural heritage. The Trinidad visit resulted in *The Middle Passage* and the India visit produced *An Area of Darkness*. It was also during his India travels, while in Kashmir, that Naipaul wrote his first novel about London, *Mr. Stone and the Knights Companion*, which won the Hawthornden Prize. Despite this literary productivity, the travels only fueled Naipaul's restlessness and intensified his sense of displacement and his difficulty in summoning a positive response to London. This mood of "being physically lost" is brilliantly articulated in Naipaul's next novel, *The Mimic Men*, which was completed in Uganda. The novel was awarded the W. H. Smith Prize.

Four years later, in 1971, Naipaul seemed to break out of his state of detachment by signing a petition in support of the birth of Bangladesh. This active commitment clearly marks a new trend in Naipaul's works, such as his nonfiction *The Loss of El Dorado*. A historical study of Trinidad, meticulously researched, it was selected by *Time* magazine as one of the ten best nonfiction books of the year in 1969.

In a Free State, Naipaul's next book, won England's highest literary award, the Booker Prize. Naipaul's realization that homelessness is not merely an Indian or West Indian trait but a universal feature of the modern world is eloquently expressed in the series of linked stories that make up the book. In *Guerrillas*, named by *The New York Times* as the best novel of 1975, and *A Bend in the River*, Naipaul attempts to portray "the ordeals and absurdities of living in the third world." Travels again took him out of London to visit Ayatollah Khomeini's Iran, General Zia's Pakistan and two other Muslim nations, Indonesia and Malaysia. The result of these seven months of travel was *Among the Believers*, a journalistic report on the new Islamic energy sweeping these nations. Naipaul continues to write and travel widely from his home in the English countryside.

Analysis

"The novel is my main delight," says V. S. Naipaul; in a brief prefatory note to *The Return of Eva Perón, with The Killings in Trinidad* (1980), however, he states that when a novel does not offer itself to him, he travels and turns to nonfiction. In *India: A Wounded Civilization* (1977), Naipaul calls the novel a form of social inquiry. In *An Area of Darkness* (1964), Naipaul insists that the novel must be concerned with the conditions of men and respond to the here and now. To him, the novel in its finest form is indistinguishable from truth. It is important to keep these comments in mind when studying Naipaul's novels.

Naipaul grew up in the multiracial society of Trinidad, peopled by migrants from four continents. He was a part of a joint Hindu family with its rigid, clannish, and suffocating atmosphere. Naipaul was an alien in the midst of other aliens. He observed how the various migrant groups, including his own, attempted to maintain their own identity. They failed to do so because they were uncertain about what constituted their identity. They were either unaware of their cultural background or had a romantic fantasy about their past. When they were unable to latch on to their ethnic identity, they often rejected their past and attempted to adapt the identity of their colonial masters, acquiring in the process a hodgepodge of pseudo-Westernization. Ganesh in *The Mystic Masseur* is a classic example; East Indian by tradition, Trinidadian by birth, he sets out as a champion of Hinduism, but when that fails, he swings to the other extreme. He changes his name from Ganesh Ramsumair to G. Ramsay Muir, Esq., M.B.E., completely rejecting his past.

The pseudo-Westernization that Naipaul's characters pursue is in itself symtomatic of their rootlessness. This theme of displacement and the consequences of such displacement, comically absurd at first, later tragic, is a major theme in Naipaul's works. Naipaul himself desperately wanted to escape from Trinidad when he was young; yet, when he moved to London, he was a stranger in search of a tradition, feeling the burden of his double displacement from India and Trinidad. In order to resolve the dilemma and find a resting place for his imagination, Naipaul undertook a voyage of self-discovery to India. He journeyed to the very village from which his ancestors had migrated to Trinidad. Instead of clarifying the past, the trip thrust him into the heart of an area of darkness; the trip was a complete failure and broke his life in two. On his return to England, he had to confront his own emptiness, a sense of dark negation. Naipaul unflinchingly distills these personal experiences of his life into his novels. Possibly no other contemporary author, with the possible exception of Albert Camus, is so quintessentially the voice of exile and alienation.

Naipaul's three early novels, *The Mystic Masseur*, *The Suffrage of Elvira*, and *Miguel Street* belong to his apprentice years. The novels are comedies of Trinidadian manners, and Naipaul uses satire and irony in portraying the Trinidad of "crazy people." Ganesh Ramsumair "the great belcher" whose rise "from laughing-stock to success" with his political poster "A vote for Ganesh is a vote for God," in *The Mystic Masseur*, and Surujpat "Pat" Harbans, in *The Suffrage of Elvira*, with its political theme and setting in Elvira "the smallest, most isolated and most neglected of the nine counties of Trinidad," and the colorful cannery-row-type Caribbean characters in *Miguel Street* all belong to the rootless, homeless, nomadic migrant world of Naipaul. In satirizing them, Naipaul reveals a Dickensian influence on his work.

Naipaul began writing as a satirist of his society, but to him the novel is a form of social inquiry as well. He is also a serious thinker; thus, in presenting his gallery of misfits and nomadic exiles, he also probes into the ethos of the half societies in which they drift. They are the debris from wounded civilizations. Trinidad, India, French Africa, and Latin America are not romantic lands of primitive innocence, but rather they are harsh and inhospitable, barbaric and cruel, and very different from the images of the slick travel brochures. Naipaul uncompromisingly portrays the "ordeals and absurdities of living in new 'third world' countries."

A House for Mr. Biswas is Naipaul's first serious work, the book in which he discovered "the trick of writing." Dickensian in approach, it meticulously and leisurely chronicles one man's obsession with establishing his identity. Mohun Biswas' desire to own a house in order to give himself a physical and spiritual home is a universal feeling. In *A House for Mr. Biswas*, Naipaul has moved from the regional character portraits of his early novels to a universal theme.

The novel's mood is serious and the comic tone is muted. Events are seen from Biswas' point of view as the reader follows his trials and tribulations within the Tulsi family and his attempts to be a writer. Biswas is modeled upon Seepersad Naipaul, Naipaul's father. Although Naipaul has protested that the work is not autobiographical, the love story between Biswas and his son at the heart of the novel echoes the affection Naipaul and his father had for each other.

Naipaul's narrative style parallels the story line: lyrical when describing the environment and short and crisp when expressing the frustrations and disappointments of Biswas. Social history, characterization, comedy, and the sense of tragedy all blend in the novel, making it that rare thing, "a novel indistinguishable from truth."

Mr. Stone and the Knights Companion, written during Naipaul's visit to Kashmir, India, in the early 1960's, has a completely English setting. In the character of Mr. Stone, Naipaul again echoes his theme of rootlessness and the feeling of emptiness. Mr. Stone, a former colonial, has returned to England and faces an identity crisis. His immediate environment seems hostile to him and his colonial memories are secondhand. The novel is concerned with the three years before his mandatory retirement at sixty-five, when Mr. Stone is faced with a sense of insecurity and is apprehensive about the approaching emptiness of life, the "experience of nothingness, an experience of death." Mr. Stone's attempt to avoid this emptiness is the novel's central theme.

Mr. Stone decides to establish a commune for old men and thus is born the idea of the Knights companions. He wants to give old men like himself something to do. He perfects the idea by writing about it, and the act of writing gives him deep satisfaction. Passages describing Mr. Stone going to his study and wrestling with the challenge of writing with full concentration are some of the most forceful passages in the novel.

The project on which he works so devotedly is taken away by Bill Whymper, a colleague. Whymper has a knack for "licking things into shape." Insensitive to the human concern for old age, which had motivated Mr. Stone's proposal, he turns Stone's idea into a slick public relations project. Mr. Stone is heartbroken and inwardly rages with anger, yet, totally alienated, he is unable to share it with anyone. Gradually, Mr. Stone calms down and stoically takes consolation from merely having survived.

The Mimic Men, in the form of fictional autobiography, is the story of Ranjit "Ralph" Kirpal Singh, a forty-year-old Indian from the West Indies. It is Naipaul's darkest novel, and Ralph Kirpal Singh expresses the unrelieved mood and feeling of emptiness even more intensely than Mr. Stone. *The Mimic Men* is also one of Naipaul's most complex novels; there is no real chronological sequence. Closeted in an old hotel in London, Kirpal Singh writes the story of his life, attempting to establish a sense of order of the four periods of his life, "student, householder, and man of affairs, recluse." His opinions and remembrance of events are episodic and constantly shifting, depending on the intensity of his feelings. He alternates between images of fantasy and reality as he moves from India to London and back to Isabella, the West Indian island where he grew up. Like Naipaul, Kirpal Singh also is drawn to London. In London, his marriage to Sandra, an English girl, does not succeed. He returns to Isabella where he is successful in real estate and runs for political office. All these "actions" are, he perceives, "roles" that he is playing, imitating others. He has become one of the mimic men. They are absurd; he is absurd and, he concludes, "shipwrecked." He wants to escape again, this time "to a place unknown, among people whose lives and even language" he need never enter. The best he could do is escape to an old hotel.

Kirpal Singh is *the* Naipaul man: educated, sophisticated, complex, forever conscious of his physical and spiritual rootlessness. He echoes Naipaul's own belief that one cannot return to an ordered harmony or hope for magical moments of tranquillity. One must accept what one has, since the pursuit of illusions is the absurd role of mimic men.

In a Free State, which contains a short novel—a series of interconnected stories—and two fragments of a travel diary, marks an important stage in Naipaul's career. After its publication, Naipaul described the novel as a "rather final statement" of the themes he had already exhausted.

In a Free State presents five different kinds of wandering, represented by a group of international characters. They are all in middle passage—in a free state—yet they are not truly free in that they do not belong in the countries they are in and are unable to belong in the countries from which they come. The very title is indicative of the aimless drift of contemporary aliens. The varied characters in the book include an Indian in America ("one out of many"); a displaced Indian from the West Indies ("tell me who to kill"); a West Indian in London; and an Englishman and Englishwoman in Africa ("In a free state").

The prologue ("The Tramp at Piraeus") and the epilogue ("The Circus at Luxor") of the work make an important statement about Naipaul himself. In the prologue, a tramp is harassed by a fat Egyptian student, an incident watched by Naipaul. In the epilogue, when a group of Arab beggar boys are whipped by another Arab boy for a group of Italians to photograph, Naipaul rebels and puts a stop to it. His action represents the quality missing in his characters in *In a Free State*; they have surrendered and resigned without any attempt at protest. The writer, however, must protest against injustice and remind the world of its responsibility to humanity.

Guerrillas was written "in five months of controlled frenzy." *Guerrillas*, like *In a Free State* and *A Bend in the River*, realistically presents "the ordeals and absurdities of living in the third world." The title is ironic because none of the major characters in the novel engages in any revolutionary action. There is pretension to guerrilla activity, which results in a murder as a result of sexual shame. The words of "revolutionary" Jimmy Ahmed, "when everybody wants to fight there's nothing to fight for. Everybody wants to fight his own little war, everybody is a guerrilla," placed as epigraph to the novel, summarize the philosophic core of the book.

Jimmy Ahmed is another one of Naipaul's rootless heroes. He is half-black and half-Chinese, and even his name is assumed, an imitation of the black Muslims, and so he has no authentic identity whatsoever. Michael de Freitas, alias Michael X, the Trinidadian black power leader who was hanged for murder, is the inspiration for Jimmy Ahmed.

Jimmy Ahmed's fantasy is to be the true hero. He lives in an imaginary world, talking much about revolutionary guerrilla activity and thereby play acting in much the same way Kirpal Singh did in *The Mimic Men* and the various characters do in *In a Free State*. Jimmy, who has fled from England, where he had been involved in a rape case, has an army made up of slum rejects; his attempt at a peaceful commune is pathetic.

Peter Roche, a white South African who had been tortured and imprisoned because of his opposition to the apartheid regime, and Roche's girl friend, Jane, one of those "liberals who come flashing their milk white thighs and think they're contributing to the cause," travel to Jimmy's commune to help him. All three are homeless, and yet none of them really trusts the other or is committed to any cause, but each of their pretensions to guerrilla activity gives them a needed escape, a façade.

The city of the emerging Caribbean island is bristling with political corruption and greedy men from multinational corporations. Naipaul is brilliant in evoking the locale, "a place at the end of the world, a place that had exhausted its possibilities." He captures the smell and substance of the third world with its irritations, bureaucracy, and nightmarish fantasies. The city reaches its breaking point, and when it snaps, anger and violence take over. The trio—Jimmy, Peter, and Jane—are jolted from their fantasy and what results is one of the harshest sexual violations in contemporary literature, followed by Jane's brutal murder.

In *Guerrillas*, Naipaul demonstrates how far he has traveled from the Dickensian irony and comedy of *The Mystic Masseur* and from the regionalism of Trinidad to the global universal tragedy of rootlessness.

A Bend in the River is set in Africa, and the country could resemble either Zaire under General Mobutu Sese Seko or Uganda. It is an Africa with Colonial vestiges, the same terrain Conrad had explored in *Heart of Darkness* (1902). The story is told by Salim, a young Indian shopkeeper from the East Coast of Africa. Salim is an outsider, the quintessential Naipaul hero, an exile in a damaged land. Salim's ancestors came from Northern India, and Salim has traveled to the interior of the country, about a thousand miles from the capital, to set up a shop "at a bend in the great river," a place "where the future had come and gone." The novel describes approximately seven years in his life, during which time he carries on his modest trade in pencils, copy-books, toothbrushes, and pots and pans. He keeps to himself, limiting his wanderings to "flat, shop, club, bar, the river embankment at sunset."

Independence comes to the country, and it emerges from its own past. In spite of all the trappings of modern civilization—tall buildings, schools and universities, long radio broadcasts by the Big man who's now elected himself for life—the country has a hard time becoming a part of the contemporary world.

It is this absurd, violent, corrupt, twilight world that Naipaul sketches in *A Bend in the River*. The capital has the Big man with his army, sorcery, and terrorism, while in the bush lurk the guerrillas of the Liberation Army and the ghosts of an ancestral past. In Salim's town at the bend of the river are refugees, impoverished Africans, and corrupt officials, who are anxious and nervous about the bloodshed that preceded independence.

Each character in the novel contributes to the tension and the rage: Raymond, the French scholar who was once a close adviser to the Big man, "the Big man's white man"; Metty, "someone of mixed race," Salim's lifelong servant whose relations with Salim disintegrate because he no longer gets the traditional protection from his master; Father Huisman, the Belgian priest who collects African tribal masks which are decaying, reflecting the world from where they come; Yvette, Raymond's wife, who has an affair with Salim, which makes him say "I felt blessed and remade"; and Ferdinand, son of a woman from the bush, a student who vociferously repeats the Big man's sayings of national pride.

Salim's shop is confiscated as part of the Big man's radicalization and given to citizen Theotime, who hires Salim as his manager. Then Salim is arrested and imprisoned and released by Ferdinand, who sums up what is happening in this attempt to impress order on disorder: "We're all going to hell, and every man knows this in his bones. . . . Everyone wants to make his money and run away. But where?" He answers that question cryptically by saying, "The bush burns itself. But there is no place to go."

To make the darkness even more intense, Naipaul creates an incident in the novel where Salim visits his friend Nazruddin in London, before his decision to leave Africa. Nazruddin tells Salim that people are stampeding, everyone—Argentines, Chinese, blacks, Koreans—"All of them are on the run. They are frightened of the fire. You musn't think it's only Africa people are running from." Thus, rootlessness and wandering become worldwide.

In 1987, Naipaul published *The Enigma of Arrival*, his first novel in almost a decade. In several ways this book marked a change of direction for Naipaul. Set primarily in Wiltshire, England, and spanning the period from 1950 to 1984, *The Enigma of Arrival* is by far Naipaul's most autobiographical novel. The protagonist, like Naipaul himself, is a middle-aged writer, a native of Trinidad who came to England on a scholarship to study at the University of Oxford. Like Naipaul, too, he has settled in the English countryside. Indeed, so close are the parallels between author and protagonist that some reviewers wondered why Naipaul had published the book as a novel. In its reflective tone and its relative lack of novelistic incident, *The Engima of Arrival* could easily be mistaken for a memoir.

Nevertheless, Naipaul chose to treat his experience at one remove by casting it in the form of a novel. His reflections on his Wiltshire neighbors, his memories of his early years in England, and his account of a return to Trinidad for a memorial service after the death of his sister—these quietly developed scenes sound a note that is new in Naipaul's work: a sense of reconciliation, of serenity even, growing out of an awareness of the endless cycles of life and death. In the English countryside, it seems, Naipaul has found a vision which is central to the Indian heritage that he left behind.

K. Bhaskara Rao

Other major works

SHORT FICTION: *A Flag on the Island*, 1967.

NONFICTION: *The Middle Passage: Impressions of Five Societies—British, French and Dutch—in the West Indies and South America*, 1962; *An Area of Darkness: An Experience of India*, 1964; *The Loss of El Dorado: A History*, 1969; *The Overcrowded Barracoon and Other Articles*, 1972; *India: A Wounded Civilization*, 1977; *The Return of Eva Perón, with The Killings in Trinidad*, 1980; *Among the Believers: An Islamic Journey*, 1981; *Finding the Center: Two Narratives*, 1984; *A Turn in the South*, 1989; *India: A Million Mutinies Now*, 1990.

Bibliography

Cudjoe, Selwyn R. *V. S. Naipaul: A Materialist Reading*. Amherst: University of Massachusetts Press, 1988. A fellow Trinidadian but of black descent, Cudjoe understandably takes a negative stance with regard to Naipaul's work, attacking him for his racist views. He also employs psychoanalytical references to explain Naipaul's literary characters and the man himself. A strong counterpart to the praise given Naipaul by many British critics.

Morris, Robert K. *Paradoxes of Order: Some Perspectives on the Fiction of V. S. Naipaul*. Columbia: University of Missouri Press, 1975. A slim volume (105 pages) that gives particular emphasis to *The Mimic Men*. Offers some interesting religious background on Naipaul, and the influence of his Hindu upbringing on his work.

Nightingale, Peggy. *Journey Through Darkness: The Writing of V. S. Naipaul*. New York: University of Queensland Press, 1987. A thorough examination of the major writings of Naipaul, covering his background and core themes in both his fiction and nonfiction. A scholarly work, yet quite readable. Includes an extensive bibliography until 1984.

Thorpe, Michael. *Writers and Their Work: V. S. Naipaul,* edited by Ian Scott-Kilvert. Essex, England: Longman, 1976. A slim volume relating the non-fiction to autobiographical elements in Naipaul's novels, eight of which are analyzed here. Selected bibliography.

Walsh, William. *V. S. Naipaul.* New York: Barnes & Noble, 1973. This small volume nevertheless manages to analyze eleven works of Naipaul until 1971. Special emphasis is given to *A House for Mr. Biswas.* Includes quotes from Naipaul's novels and a bibliography. Contains a chapter on various critics' responses to Naipaul.

R. K. NARAYAN

Born: Madras, India; October 10, 1906

Principal long fiction

Swami and Friends, 1935; *The Bachelor of Arts*, 1937; *The Dark Room*, 1938; *The English Teacher*, 1945 (also known as *Grateful to Life and Death*, 1953); *Mr. Sampath*, 1949 (also known as *The Printer of Malgudi*, 1957); *The Financial Expert*, 1952; *Waiting for the Mahatma*, 1955; *The Guide*, 1958; *The Man-Eater of Malgudi*, 1961; *The Sweet-Vendor*, 1967 (also known as *The Vendor of Sweets*); *The Painter of Signs*, 1976; *A Tiger for Malgudi*, 1983; *Talkative Man: A Novel of Malgudi*, 1987; *The World of Nagaraj*, 1990.

Other literary forms

In addition to his novels, R. K. Narayan has published a number of volumes of short stories. The title of his first collection of short stories, *Malgudi Days* (1941), is also the title of a later collection, published by Viking in 1982. Other collections include *Dodu and Other Stories* (1943), *Cyclone and Other Stories* (1944), *An Astrologer's Day and Other Stories* (1947), *Lawley Road* (1956), *A Horse and Two Goats and Other Stories* (1970), *Old and New* (1981), and *Under the Banyan Tree and Other Stories* (1985). Two autobiographical works are *My Days* (1974), which covers four decades of Narayan's career as a writer, and *My Dateless Diary* (1960), a journal of his travels through America. "Gods, Demons and Modern Times," a talk given at Columbia University in 1972, is collected together with tales from Indian mythology in *Gods, Demons and Others* (1964). Narayan has also published translations of *The Ramayana* (1972) and *The Mahabharata* (1978). During the war years, he edited *Indian Thought*, and his weekly newspaper "middles" were collected in *Next Sunday* (1960). Harvey Breit's stage adaptation of *The Guide* only incurred Narayan's displeasure. Despite his attempt to withhold permission for production, *The Guide* opened on Broadway in March, 1968, and was subsequently made into a motion picture.

Achievements

On January 18, 1982, Narayan was inducted into the American Academy of Arts and Letters. Though he received a similar honor in India from the Sahitya Academy (Literary Academy), it was not without debate. Could a South Indian writer who had never stirred outside his home region, who was writing in English rather than his own mother tongue, whose fiction was not concerned with lofty nationalistic issues, actually be worthy of a literary prize? Indeed, it is to Narayan's credit that he has continued to write in English. His writing is neither imitative nor experimental. Never feeling compelled to work within the boundaries of large literary or nationalistic trends, Narayan has not found it necessary to vary the English language or to describe moments of nationalistic history as a means of establishing his identity. Joycean word-coinage, attempts to introduce the rhythms of various Indian languages in his English style, or the use of Indian-English dialect are not Narayan's tools. It is through character description and his characters' world-views that Narayan expresses a distinctly Indian sensibility. For him, Standard English is the most effective medium for conveying this sensibility. He finds English so opaque that it can take on the "tint of any country."

Thus, Narayan's bilingual situation has never been a handicap. It has provided him with the means to know and use English while keeping him in touch with his own roots and cultural wisdom. It has kept him aware of English literary history, yet his style does not show "the marks of a labored acquisition." On the contrary, it reflects the English language in its "process of transmutation," as Narayan has described the adoption of English in India. Most of Narayan's characters speak and use the sort of Standard English Narayan himself would speak in India. Occasionally, an Indian-English idiom reflects a character's situation.

Narayan's consistent use of Standard English is, more often than not, appropriate to the circumstances of his fiction. Swami and his cricket-playing cohorts, reading the Mssrs. Binn's catalog of cricket hats, are not likely to be speaking in a native language, nor are the boys educated at Albert Mission college. In *The Guide*, Raju, providing instruction to Velan the villager, is not likely to be speaking English or Indian English, yet his Tamil is best translated into straightforward, crisp, Standard English. Thus, Narayan does not provide any superfluous Tamil lilt to the English prose of these passages. The characters and situations are more than sufficient expressions of Indianness.

Narayan has been widely criticized for being immune to the stylistic experimentation other commonwealth writers seem to have found necessary. He has also been criticized for the very sentence structure for which Ernest Hemingway has been praised. In his *A Human Idiom* (1964), Professor William Walsh, while admiring Narayan's style for "its pure and easy flow," finds it lacking in the "adventitiously injected" energy that "marks the writing of the West Indians." A number of Indian critics have objected that Narayan's prose seems oblivious to the tradition of English literary style. What they mean is that it lacks a "Macaulayan amplitude of phrase." Narayan's distance from the centers where the language is changing and developing is seen as yet another handicap to the development of his style.

Such criticism fails to recognize Narayan's supreme achievement as an Indian writer in English: his refusal to heed critical stereotypes and his development of an individual style based on his understanding of the process of the English language's transmutation in India. By his rejection both of an overt Indian idiom and of a self-conscious literary English, Narayan is able to maintain his unobtrusive authorial stance. His style is far from monotonous; it often changes pace to reflect action and character. Both in *The Guide* and in *The Painter of Signs*, it reflects the breathlessness with which the action takes place, but slows down as it reflects moments of repose in the consciousness of his characters.

By using his simple sentence constructions, Narayan is able to bend the English language to describe suitably the languorous quality of South Indian life. Ironically, he achieves this effect with short, crisp, Hemingwayesque sentences with simple variations on the subject-object construction. While for Hemingway this technique yields "sparse and muscular prose" which conveys the American character, in Narayan's prose it conveys a certain effeteness, even "lackadaisicalness" characteristic of the Indian's ordinary life and daily conversation.

In elevating ordinary life through style, character, and situation, Narayan's fiction is like a prism that reflects a many-colored Indianness. Ignoring the obvious means of providing his work with an Indian identity, Narayan focuses instead on quintessential situations in which Indian character develops. "Episode and escapade," "moment and mood," in their peculiarly Indian contexts of a belief in destiny, astrology, and arranged marriages, give Narayan's fictional locale, Malgudi, its own postge stamp that says, "In India we trust."

Biography

Rasipuram Krishnaswami Narayan was born in Madras on October 10, 1906. During his early years he was reared by his grandmother in Madras. Very early in his autobiography, *My Days*, he records his dislike of education, of the mission schools, of the British colleges, and of his short-lived adventure as a schoolteacher. All these experiences permeate his writing and have become the subject matter of his fiction. His literary education was predominantly Victorian in flavor. Francis Palgrave's *Golden Treasury* (1861), Sir Walter Scott, and reading William Shakespeare aloud were its staples. In 1933, he fell in love with a woman whom he married only after great difficulties because their horoscopes would not match; she died of typhoid in 1939. The trauma of this loss, the inability to come to terms with his fate, and the effort to defy his destiny led to Narayan's interest in purported communication with the dead, the inspiration of *The English Teacher*. A feeling of helplessness in the face of destiny takes sometimes comic and sometimes tragic turns throughout Narayan's work.

Commissioned by the Dewan of Mysore, Narayan wrote a travel book on Mysore. After several years of writing for *The Hindu* and other journalistic experiences, Narayan began publishing *Indian Thought*, a quarterly of literature, philosophy, and culture. Not until October, 1956, did Narayan travel outside the boundaries of the three-city area of Madras, Mysore, and Coimbatore. He went to Berkeley, California, on a Rockefeller Foundation grant to write a novel, *The Guide*. Subsequently, he has visited the United States several times, while continuing to live and write in Mysore.

Analysis

The common man in his passage toward self-knowledge, in his sometimes comic and sometimes tragic struggle against destiny, is the subject of R. K. Narayan's fiction. Narayan's recurring preoccupations are universal, but they are given form in an intensely particularized fictional world, as palpable and idiosyncratic as William Faulkner's Yoknapatawpha. The reality of Narayan's Malgudi is established in his first novel, *Swami and Friends*.

With *Swami and Friends*, the Malgudi town became reality. Lawley extension was laid out at a perfect distance from the Sarayu river, just enough distance to be comfortable for the Westernized Indian and the British Sahibs. The railway station made civilized connections possible, while an old trunk road wound through the forest. It is through following the trunk road and spending a night out in the cold that Swami comes to an understanding of himself. He makes the passage from innocence to experience, very much like Mark Twain's Huck Finn. British and Indian critics have compared him to Richmal Crompton's William and Jennings, both very young British school boys, who through several volumes fail to mature. It is the universal experience of childhood, the process of "growing up" that *Swami and Friends* captures and yet Swami's misadventures are played out in uniquely Indian settings. The cricket games and cricket bat catalogs are as Indian and real to the bicultural situation as grandmother, the monkey, and mango chutney.

In another work, the teenage years become a time of learning and realization; and Chandran, in *The Bachelor of Arts*, learns about the importance of success and failure. Though this success and failure are centered around seemingly trivial issues—the passing of college examinations, the winning of college elections, and the gaining of attention from the opposite sex—these situations are tremendously important in the life of the Indian college student. At the same time, however, they are infused with the general human yearning for success at any cost, the debating of the ethics of such situations, and the human fear of failure. Each little question of conscience holds its own cathartic tragicomedy. Narayan's preeminence among Indian writers in English lies in his ability to capture moments in time, as much a part of his reader's life as they are of the life of his characters, and to depict both the comic and tragic aspects of those moments.

The English Teacher or *Grateful to Life and Death* describes the existential moments through which almost any individual faces the "eternal now." The Malgudi adolescent moves to the householder stage, yet cannot procure the woman whom he loves in marriage: the horoscopes do not match. The astrologers will not give their consent. The English teacher, however, is able to persuade the astrologer that the girl's horoscope has some adverse stars that might cancel out those in the boy's horoscope. He then triumphantly brings his wife home to an idyllic happiness, a happiness that reigns despite an unsuccessful teaching career and returned manuscripts.

Yet every individual must face the disparity between "man's hope" and "man's fate." The Karmic wheel turns, and the English teacher is helpless in the face of merciless fate, in this case, typhoid. Intensely personal, it is a private tragedy of the "felt experience"—the tragedy that no human being can fully accept. In his refusal of his destiny, the English teacher attempts to transcend his fate. His struggle against death and his eventual acceptance of it takes the form of efforts to communicate with the dead. While this second half of the novel seems melodramatic and purposeless, it is the "still point" on which Narayan's philosophy of man turns and is developed in his later novels. The ring of cosmic laughter surrounds the English teacher's struggles against that external force that "moves" and "mates" and "slays."

The struggle against man's destiny in this uniquely personal, human, small, and yet heroic way pervades *The Guide*, *The Financial Expert*, *The Vendor of Sweets*, and *The Painter of Signs*.

Railway Raju in *The Guide* is clearly an individual caught on the wheel of fortune. Raju starts out attempting to be as successful as his father with a magazine stand in the Malgudi Railway station; he also has a side business in tours of Malgudi, the caves, the Mempi Hills, and the Source of the Sarayu for tourists. On one such tour, he falls in love with a professor's dancer-wife, gives her shelter to escape from her boring husband, and eventually, foolishly falls into a trap devised by the professor. Raju ends up in the Malgudi jail accused of forgery.

Upon his release from prison, accident and his fortune confer on him the important position of a holy man. Raju, who knows himself well as a foolhardy scoundrel, makes every attempt to shun this position. Hungry as he is though, in return for gifts of food from the villagers, he gives them the words of wisdom he had learned from his mother's bedtime stories and from the magazines and books he had read at his magazine stand. When famine returns and rages through Malgudi and the surrounding villages, a chance conversation with the village idiot leads Raju to undertake a fast to bring on the rains. This happens while Raju himself is yearning for a particular Indian delicacy—"bondas." While on the one hand he wants to ask for food, he finds himself trapped. Raju attempts to be honest and describe to Velan, the villager, his ordinary humanness. "Greatness," however, cannot be revoked. Furthermore, a television crew from California is photographing the last days of the fast of this mahatma or great soul. "Have you always been a yogi?" asks the reporter. "Yes, more or less," Raju replies.

Raju does his penance, his yoga, and moves toward the self-knowledge of a Sanyasi. The question remains whether his penance is real or merely a form of self-delusion. As the dancer's manager, he had attained a new-found importance that ended in a crushing fall. Perhaps he is to meet a similar fall from his Swamihood. Through all his adventures, even his last, Raju had been painstakingly honest. Is Narayan's ironic vision saying something about the power of delusion? It is in that last scene, where the fasting Raju/Swami sinks to his knees and believes that his fast has in fact caused it to rain in the hills, that the reader feels the fall of a great man—an ordinary, common man, struggling against destiny.

In *The Guide*, readers hear "cosmic laughter" not only at the individual's struggle against his fate but also at the setting in which the struggle takes place. In a sense, Malgudi has lost its innocence; the changing destiny, its sudden growth, has brought it only famine and criminals. It is no longer the Malgudi of Swami and his friends, of cricket fields, of the Lawley extension bungalows, and "the club." In *The Dark Room*, corruption slowly begins to appear in Malgudi. By the time of *The Guide*, technology has worked its evil magic. Yet, underneath the crust of technology, change, and evil, the essence of Malgudi remains the same. The people remain innocent, gullible, and incapable of acting against their destinies.

The rise and fall of the "fortunes" of *The Financial Expert*, Margayya, follows more closely the classic tragic pattern. In fact, critics have often seen its five chapters as the five parts in an Elizabethan tragedy. Narayan's vision, however, does not permit him a "tragic hero." Margayya seems more and more of a buffoon as he is driven by his blind passion for money; and Narayan's readers continue laughing with him as he shows what fools mortals can be. The disparity between Margayya's "hope" and his "fate" is a wide chasm, and Margayya is a man continually on the brink of an abyss. He begins as a small-time moneylender working under a banyan tree across from an established bank. The bankers try to drive him away so that he will not take the villagers' business, but Margayya persists. An astrologer has told him that the goddess Lakashmi will be kind to him if certain *pujas* are carried out. When he comes in contact with Dr. Pal, who has the manuscript of a sex manual, he seizes the opportunity to make more money. With the aid of a publisher, he markets this supposed book on "domestic harmony."

Margayya invests all his energy and affection and hope in his son Balu. He works hard to provide for him the best opportunities in the hope of having a highly educated, supportive son. Yet the more Margayya gives his son—the best schools and the best clothes—the more recalcitrant Balu becomes. He is unable to pass his high school exam; he falls into a life of lust and debauchery with Dr. Pal; and Margayya appears more and more to be a blundering fool. Both Balu and Margayya see themselves as "men of consequence." An attempt to support their style of living, more particularly Balu's debauchery, results in financial difficulties, and Balu begins to demand his share of his father's wealth.

When Margayya discovers that Dr. Pal is responsible for his son's corruption, a hostile exchange of words follows. To avenge himself, Dr. Pal spreads a rumor that Margayya is insolvent. His investors demand the return of their investments, which leaves Margayya without any money. Yet, he has it in him to consider his beginnings, whereas his son does not. Balu refuses to go back to his father's humble origins. With his hopes for wealth dashed, Margayya goes back to being the financial expert under the banyan tree. Like other Narayan characters, he has come the full circle of his destiny.

Among this portrait gallery of Malgudiwalas who have kept their "trysts" with their destinies are Jagan, the "vendor of sweets," and Raman, "the painter of signs," in *The Painter of Signs*. Their destinies lock them in a battle with modernity and change. With the flow of time, Malgudi has grown far beyond the limits of Lawley extension and even the central cooperative land mortgage bank. Computers, the story writing machine that Jagan's son wants to develop, and the family planning clinic that Daisy develops, have become part of this growing, bustling city.

Incapable of controlling the changes that surround him, Jagan, the vendor of sweets, also finds himself disappointed by his son of whom he expected so much. Yet the reader questions how fair it is for Jagan to expect his Americanized son, who holds an M.B.A., to follow in the footsteps of Jagan's Gandhism and to sit at his sweetshop. It is Jagan, whose Gandhism would not let him permit his wife to take aspirin, who remains the absurd focus of this tragicomic situation. Raman, the painter of signs, whose hope is to marry Daisy, the independent manager of the family planning clinic, is left similarly baffled. Daisy evades him in much the same way as the concept of an independent woman eludes him. The passionate tiger, prowling under the bullock cart on the desolate trunk road where the female government official must travel to spread the enlightenment of family planning, is surprised to find not only that the modern woman is quick to escape but that she is also willing to spend the night on a high tamarind tree branch. In the same way, the modern woman is puzzled and unable to come to terms with the barren woman villagers who must visit the swami on the hill in order to bear children.

While their changing destinies continue to thwart them, Malgudiwalas remain essentially innocent. Their tragedy is in the bewilderment at their fate, and Malgudi remains a very accurate microcosm of the socio-political scene in contemporary India.

Much of Narayan's success as a novelist lies in his ability to capture the tragicomedy of the human situation. Like F. Scott Fitzgerald, Narayan appeals to two different audiences—the popular and the literary elite—with only one difference, he appeals to the literary elite outside his country. The Indian literary elite generally do not go beyond Narayan's undecorated English and structured plots to experience his celebration of moment and character. These so-called literary mistakes, however, lead to his popularity with the popular audience in India and the literary elite abroad. Graham Greene, who first championed Narayan's cause, referred to him as the "Indian Chekhov." In *My Days*, Narayan records that a rumor circulated in Mysore in which W. Somerset Maugham, during a visit, wanted to meet the great Indian novelist, and no one in Mysore's bureaucracy could think of who it could be. Such is the dichotomy of Narayan's reception.

Appellations such as the "Indian Chekhov" and the "Indian Jane Austen" fall short of Narayan's achievement. He is *the* "Indian Narayan," as Indian as William Faulkner is American. His concern is the heroic quality of the ordinary Indian individual's struggle with his destiny, as it is portrayed through personal, seemingly trivial experiences. This is what makes Narayan's fiction "moral art."

Feroza Jussawalla

Other major works

SHORT FICTION: *Malgudi Days*, 1941, 1982; *Dodu and Other Stories*, 1943; *Cyclone and Other Stories*, 1944; *An Astrologer's Day and Other Stories*, 1947; *Lawley Road: Thirty-two Short Stories*, 1956; *Gods, Demons and Others*, 1964; *A Horse and Two Goats and Other Stories*, 1970; *Old and New*, 1981; *Under the Banyan Tree and Other Stories*, 1985.

NONFICTION: *Mysore*, 1944; *My Dateless Diary*, 1960; *Next Sunday: Sketches and Essays*, 1960; *My Days*, 1974; *Reluctant Guru*, 1974; *A Writer's Nightmare: Selected Essays, 1958-1988*, 1988.

TRANSLATIONS: *The Ramayana: A Shortened Modern Prose Version of the Indian Epic*, 1972; *The Mahabharata: A Shortened Prose Version of the Indian Epic*, 1978.

Bibliography

French, Warren. "R. K. Narayan." In *Contemporary Novelists*, edited by James Vinson. New York: St. Martin's Press, 1982. Reviews the success of Narayan in his tales of the imaginary community of Malgudi. According to French, the Malgudi stories can be read both as character studies and as an inner process from "fanaticism to serenity." A marvelous introduction to Narayan, albeit in contracted form; nothing extraneous here.

Mukerji, Nirmal. *The World of Malgudi: A Study of the Novels of R. K. Narayan*. Ph.D. dissertation. Ann Arbor, Mich.: University Microfilms, 1973. Analyzes and evaluates the achievement of Narayan as a novelist, with particular emphasis on the author's fictional world of the Malgudi, but including other novels. Written from an Indian's cultural perspective, this readable and insightful study is a useful resource.

Raizada, Harish. *A Critical Study of R. K. Narayan*. New Delhi: Young Asia Publications, 1969. A standard-type critical study, chronicling Narayan's life and novels. The book is peppered with extracts from Narayan's writing, set off in denser type for easy reading. The most interesting chapter is the last in which Raizada explores Narayan's characteristics as a writer. Bibliography.

Ram, Atma, ed. *Perspectives on R. K. Narayan*. Indo-English Writers Series 3. Ghaziabad, India: Vimal Prakashan, 1981. A collection of essays on Narayan, all new except for one reprint. Preface by Warren French. Some interesting views on Narayan's writing, such as Lakshmi Holstrom's study of women characters in the novels and Rameshwar Gupta's "The Gandhi in Narayan." Select bibliography. A valuable resource on Narayan.

Walsh, William. *R. K. Narayan: A Critical Appreciation*. London: William Heinemann, 1982. A thoughtful, comprehensive criticism of Narayan's writings, from his early novels to his mature works. A definitive work, thorough and accessible; the writing is a delight, the transitions smooth, and happily free from jargon. Select bibliography.

GLORIA NAYLOR

Born: New York, New York; January 25, 1950

Principal long fiction
The Women of Brewster Place: A Novel in Seven Stories, 1982; *Linden Hills*, 1985; *Mama Day*, 1988.

Other literary forms
In 1986, Gloria Naylor wrote a column, *Hers*, for *The New York Times* and published a work of nonfiction, *Centennial*. She has also written a number of screenplays, short stories, and articles for various periodicals. She is known primarily, however, for her novels.

Achievements
Enjoying both critical and popular acclaim, Naylor's work has reached a wide audience. *The Women of Brewster Place* won the 1983 American Book Award for best first novel and was later made into a television miniseries. Naylor's other awards include a National Endowment for the Arts Fellowship in 1985 and a Guggenheim Fellowship in 1988.

Surveying the range of black life in America, from poor ghetto to affluent suburb to Southern offshore island, Naylor's work examines questions of black identity and, in particular, celebrates black women. In the face of enormous problems and frequent victimization, black women are shown coping through their sense of community and their special powers. Male readers might find less to cheer about in Naylor's work, as she writes from a feminist perspective, but her depictions of courage, community, and cultural identity have universal appeal.

Biography
The oldest child of black parents who had migrated from Mississippi, Gloria Naylor was born and reared in New York City. After graduation from high school, she spent seven years as a missionary for the Jehovah's Witnesses in New York, North Carolina, and Florida. She eventually found missionary life too strict, but her original zeal apparently carried over into her later feminism. Although her writings are not religious, a fundamentalist pattern of thinking still pervades them. She tends to separate her characters into the sheep and the goats (mostly men), the saved and the damned, with one whole book, *Linden Hills*, being modeled after Dante's *Inferno* (c. 1320).

In high school Naylor read widely in the nineteenth century British novelists, but later in a creative writing course at Brooklyn College she came across the book that influenced her most—*The Bluest Eye* (1970), by the black American novelist Toni Morrison. The example of Morrison inspired Naylor to write fiction and to focus on the lives of black women, who Naylor felt were underrepresented (if not ignored) in American literature. Naylor began work on *The Women of Brewster Place*, which was published the year after her graduation from Brooklyn College with a B.A. in English. By that time, Naylor was studying on a fellowship at Yale University, from which she received an M.A. in Afro-American studies in 1983.

Naylor's background and literary achievements won for her numerous invitations for lectureships or other appointments in academia. She has held visiting posts at George Washington University, the University of Pennsylvania, Princeton University, New York University, Boston University, Brandeis University, and Cornell University. She continues, however, to make her home in New York City.

Analysis

White people do not appear often and are certainly never featured in the work of Gloria Naylor. Yet their presence can be felt like a white background noise, or like the boulevard traffic on the other side of the wall from Brewster Place. White culture is simply another fact of life, like a nearby nuclear reactor or toxic waste dump, and the effects of racism and discrimination are omnipresent in Naylor's work. Against these stifling effects her characters live their lives and try to define their sense of black identity, from the ghetto women of Brewster Place to the social climbers of Linden Hills to the denizens of Willow Springs, a pristine Southern island relatively untouched by slavery and segregation.

Naylor writes about these settings and characters in a romantic mode that sometimes verges on the melodramatic or gothic. The influence of her earlier reading—such authors as Charlotte and Emily Brontë, Charles Dickens, William Faulkner, and Morrison—is apparent. The settings have heavy but obvious symbolic meanings, some derived from literary references: Brewster Place is a dead-end street, Linden Hills is a modern version of Dante's Hell, and Willow Springs recalls the magical isle of William Shakespeare's *The Tempest* (1611). The weather and numerous details also carry symbolic freight, almost as much as they do for such an emblematic writer as Nathaniel Hawthorne. In addition to literary influences, the symbolism seems to draw on Hollywood, particularly Hollywood's Gothic genre, horror films; for example, in *Linden Hills* the character Norman Anderson suffers from attacks of "the pinks"—imaginary blobs of pink slime—while the rich undertaker Luther Nedeed locks his wife and child away in the basement.

These two examples also show, in an exaggerated fashion, how Naylor's characters fit into the romantic mode. Her characters tend to go to extremes, to be emotional and obsessive, or to have a single trait or commit a single act that determines their whole life course. While being rather one-dimensional and melodramatic, they nevertheless linger in the memory. Such is the case with Luther Nedeed, who represents Satan in *Linden Hills*, and with the old conjure woman Miranda "Mama" Day, who represents Satan's usual opposition in the scheme of things.

In Naylor, this scheme of things illustrates how she has transferred her former missionary fervor, along with the framework of religious thought, over into her feminism. Luther Nedeed's behavior is only the most sensational example of men's cruelty to women in Naylor's work; he has a large following. On the other hand, the mystical ability of Mama Day, the Prospero of women's liberation, to command the forces of nature and the spirit world is only the most sensational example of women's special powers in Naylor's thinking. Even the women of Brewster Place demonstrate these powers through their mutual love and support, enabling them to triumph over devastating personal tragedies and demeaning circumstances.

Naylor's men are another story: if not outright demons or headed that way, they seem to lack some vital force. Even the best men are fatally flawed— they are subject to "the pinks," are addicted to wine, or have a weak heart. Failing at key moments, they are useful only as sacrifices to the feminine mystique. A prime example is the engineer George Andrews of *Mama Day*, who, for all his masculine rationality and New York smarts, does not know how to handle, significantly, a brooding hen.

Naylor began fulfilling her commitment to make black women more prominent in American fiction with *The Women of Brewster Place*, subtitled *A Novel in Seven Stories*. The seven stories, featuring seven women, can be read separately, but they are connected by their setting of Brewster Place and by characters who carry over from one story to another (at least by brief mention). The women arrive on the dead-end street by different routes that exhibit the variety of lives of black women, but on Brewster Place they unite into a community.

The middle-aged bastion of Brewster Street is Mattie Michael, who over the course of her life was betrayed by each of the three men she loved—her seducer, her father, and her son. She mothers Lucielia Louise Turner (whose grandmother once sheltered Mattie) when Ciel's abusive boyfriend destroys her life. In addition, Mattie welcomes her close friend Etta Mae Johnson, who also once gave Mattie refuge. Etta Mae is a fading beauty who has used men all of her life but is now herself used by a sleazy preacher for a one-night stand. The other women featured are the young unwed Cora Lee, a baby factory; Kiswana Browne, an aspiring social reformer who hails from the affluent suburb of Linden Hills; and Lorraine and Theresa, two lesbians seeking privacy for their love.

Few men are in evidence on Brewster Place, and these few inspire little confidence. C. C. Baker and his youth gang lurk about the alleyway and, in the novel's brutal climax, rape Lorraine. The crazed Lorraine in turn kills the wino Ben, the old janitor who earlier had befriended her.

As these scenes suggest, Brewster Place is located in a ghetto plagued by social ills. The women must face these on a daily basis in addition to their personal tragedies and dislocations. Instead of being overcome by their sufferings, however, the women find within themselves a common fate and a basis for community. They gain strength and hope from their mutual caring and support. Besides their informal support system, they form a block association to address larger problems. The ability of women to unite in such a community inspires admiration for their courage and their special powers.

The community feelings of Brewster Place, from which the women gain a positive sense of identity, somehow make the ghetto's problems seem less awesome, paradoxically, than those of Linden Hills, an affluent suburb. If Brewster Place is a ghetto, Linden Hills is a hell. Naylor underlines this metaphor by deliberately modeling her novel *Linden Hills* after Dante's *Inferno*. Linden Hills is not a group of hills, but only a V-shaped area on a hillside intersected by eight streets. As one travels down the hill, the residents become richer but lower on the moral scale. Lester and Willie, two young unemployed poets who perform odd jobs for Christmas money (they are the modern counterparts of Vergil and Dante), take the reader on a guided tour.

The residents of Linden Hills have sold out for affluence: they suffer from a loss of black identity, or soul, as the result of adopting white attitudes, compromising their personal loyalties, and denying their kinship with other blacks. Lester's sister Roxanne deems black Africans in Zimbabwe unready for independence; one young executive, Maxwell Smyth, encourages another, Xavier Donnell, no longer to consider Roxanne as a prospective corporate bride; and Dr. Daniel Braithwaite has written the authorized twelve-volume history of Linden Hills without making a single moral judgment. Other sellouts are more personal: the young lawyer Winston Alcott leaves his homosexual lover to marry respectably and Chester Parker is eager to bury his dead wife in order to remarry.

Significantly, Linden Hills is ruled over by men. The archfiend himself is Luther Nedeed, the local undertaker and real estate tycoon who occupies the lowest point in Linden Hills. Speaking against a low-income housing project planned for an adjacent poor black neighborhood, Nedeed urges outraged Linden Hills property owners to make common cause with the racist Wayne County Citizens Alliance. Most damning of all, however, is that Nedeed disowns his own wife and child and imprisons them in an old basement morgue; the child starves, but the wife climbs up to confront the archfiend on Christmas Eve.

It is clear that, while examining problems of middle-class black identity in *Linden Hills*, Naylor has not overlooked the plight of black women. In *Mama Day*, Naylor returns to a more celebratory mood on both subjects. The setting of *Mama Day* is a unique black American culture presided over by a woman with even more unique powers.

The coastal island of Willow Springs, located off South Carolina and Georgia but belonging to no state, has been largely bypassed by the tides of American history, particularly racism. The island was originally owned by a white man, Bascombe Wade, who also owned slaves. Bascombe married Sapphira, one of his slaves, however, who bore their seven sons. In 1823 Bascombe freed his other slaves and deeded the island to them, his sons, and their respective descendants in perpetuity (the land cannot be sold, only inherited). Bascombe was more or less assimilated, and a black culture grew up on the island that was closely tied to the land, to the culture's beginnings, and to African roots. In other words, Willow Springs is definitely a mythical island—a tiny but free black state flourishing unnoticed under the nose of the Confederacy. Naylor underlines the island's mythic qualities by drawing parallels between it and the magical isle of *The Tempest*.

If Prospero presides over Shakespeare's island, then Prospero's daughter, Miranda "Mama" Day (actually a great-granddaughter of the Wades), presides over Willow Springs. Known and respected locally as an old conjure woman, Mama Day is a repository and embodiment of the culture's wisdom. In particular, she is versed in herbs and other natural phenomena, but she also speaks with the island's spirits. Mama Day uses her powers to heal and aid new life, but other island people who have similar powers are not so benevolent. One such person is Ruby, who stirs her knowledge with hoodoo to kill any woman who might take her man.

Unhappily, Mama Day's grandniece Cocoa, down from New York on a visit with her husband George, arouses Ruby's jealousy. By pretending to be friendly, Ruby is able to give Cocoa a deadly nightshade rinse, scalp massage, and hairdo. Just as a big hurricane hits the island, Cocoa begins to feel the effects of the poison. George, an engineer, native New Yorker, and football fan, works frantically to save Cocoa, but he is overmatched. With his urbanized, masculine rationality, he cannot conceive of what he is up against or how to oppose it. Suffering from exhaustion and a weak heart, he is eventually killed in an encounter with a brooding hen.

Meanwhile, Mama Day has been working her powers. She confronts Ruby in a conjuring match, good magic versus bad magic, just as in Mali's oral epic tradition of the thirteenth century ruler Sundjata and in other traditions of modern Africa. Ruby is destroyed by lightning strikes, and Cocoa is saved. It is too late for George the doubter, however, who learns about the mystical powers of women the hard way.

Mama Day provides Naylor's most advanced statements of her favorite themes, the assertion of black identity and the celebration of black women. There is much about her work that might ultimately prove self-limiting, mainly her doctrinaire feminism and her tendency to write in broad, sweeping gestures. Yet these same features give her work a mythic quality that is

undeniably powerful. Naylor has obviously taken a few magical hints from
Mama Day.

Harold Branam

Bibliography

Bell, Bernard W. *The Afro-American Novel and Its Tradition*. Amherst: University of Massachusetts Press, 1987. This literary history of the Afro-American novel does not treat Naylor, but it is useful for background on the Afro-American novel's roots, developments, and contemporary forms and themes. Includes a brief section on the women's movement and its influence on black women writers.

Braxton, Joanne M., and Andrée Nicola McLaughlin, eds. *Wild Women in the Whirlwind: Afro-American Culture and the Contemporary Literary Renaissance*. New Brunswick, N.J.: Rutgers University Press, 1990. This wide-ranging collection of critical articles brings the cultural history of black women's writing up to the 1980's. Barbara Smith's article "The Truth That Never Hurts: Black Lesbians in Fiction in the 1980's" discusses the section of *The Women of Brewster Place* entitled "The Two," but other articles also bear indirectly on important themes in Naylor.

Carby, Hazel V. *Reconstructing Womanhood: The Emergence of the Afro-American Woman Novelist*. New York: Oxford University Press, 1987. While this book includes nothing on Naylor, it is good background reading. Tracing black women's writing from early slave narratives through the first two major black women novelists in the early twentieth century, it provides a cultural history that reveals the forces and assumptions that black women faced.

Gates, Henry Louis, Jr. "Significant Others." *Contemporary Literature* 29 (Winter, 1988): 606-623. Gates responds to Homans' article (listed below), taking issue with Luce Irigaray's feminist theories as too abstract, ideological, and limiting and with Homans' interpretation of *Linden Hills* based on Irigaray. Bristling with learned allusions and contemporary critical terminology, Gates calls for rejection of sexual binarism and allegory and more consideration of the complexities of class, age, and race.

Homans, Margaret. "The Women in the Cave: Recent Feminist Fictions and the Classical Underworld." *Contemporary Literature* 29 (Fall, 1988): 369-402. Homans bases her reading of *Linden Hills*, specifically the wife-in-the-basement episodes, on the feminist theory of Luce Irigaray in *Speculum of the Other Woman* (1974; Ithaca, N.Y.: Cornell University Press, 1985). Irigaray interprets the visit to the underworld in Vergil's *Aeneid* (c. 29-19 B.C.) and Plato's image of the cave in his *Republic* (fourth century B.C.) as classical versions of men's control over reproduction in an androcentric culture. Homans sees the story of Willa Nedeed in *Linden*

Hills as a modern feminist version of the myth.

Naylor, Gloria, and Toni Morrison. "A Conversation." *The Southern Review* 21 (Summer, 1985): 567-593. In this recorded conversation, Naylor visits her role model, Toni Morrison, whose novel *The Bluest Eye* (1970) had the deepest influence on her. Their conversation ranges over men, marriage, the inspiration for their various books, how they went about writing them, and the characters in them. Naylor says that she tried in *The Women of Brewster Place* not to depict men negatively and thought that she had succeeded.

NGUGI WA THIONG'O

Born: Kamiriithu village, near Limuru, Kenya; January 5, 1938

Principal long fiction
Weep Not, Child, 1964; *The River Between*, 1965; *A Grain of Wheat*, 1967; *Secret Lives*, 1974; *Petals of Blood*, 1977; *Caitaani Mutharaba-Ini*, 1980 (*Devil on the Cross*, 1982); *Matigari ma Njiruungi*, 1986 (*Matigari*, 1989).

Other literary forms
In addition to the above novels, Ngugi wa Thiong'o has published a collection of short stories, *Secret Lives and Other Stories* (1975). He has written numerous plays, including *The Black Hermit* (1962), *This Time Tomorrow: Three Plays* (1970; includes *The Rebels*, *The Wound in My Heart*, and *This Time Tomorrow*), *The Trial of Dedan Kimathi* (1974, with Micere Githae-Mugo), *Ngaahika Ndeenda* (1977, with Ngugi wa Mirii; *I Will Marry When I Want*, 1982), *Maitu Njugira* (1982, with Ngugi wa Mirii; *Mother, Sing for Me*, 1986).

Ngugi's commitment to his political responsibility as a writer has expressed itself in numerous works of social and literary criticism, including *Homecoming: Essays on African and Caribbean Literature, Culture, and Politics* (1972), *Writers in Politics* (1981), *Detained: A Writer's Prison Diary* (1981), *Decolonising the Mind: Resistance to Repression in Neo-Colonial Kenya* (1983), and *Writing Against Neocolonialism* (1986). In the 1980's he pursued his interest in African-based educational curricula by recasting stories of the Mau Mau resistance, many of which had appeared in his novels, as works for children, written first in his native Kikuyu and later translated into English.

Achievements
With the publication of his first three novels, Ngugi quickly established himself as the major East African writer of the anglophone literary movement that began in Africa in the late 1950's and early 1960's. This anglophone literary school, which must be distinguished from the preceding romantic francophone movement called "Negritude" because of its different political assumptions and its stress on realism, coincided with the bitter political and at times military struggle and the eventual achievement of independence by most African countries under British colonial rule. Given the political situation, this literary movement was naturally preoccupied with assessing the impact of colonialism and defining independent and syncretic African cultures. With a handful of other African writers, Ngugi stands out as a literary pioneer in this movement. His systematic examination of the manner in which indigenous cultures were destroyed by colonialism has distinguished him from many

of his colleagues, while his depiction of these cultures' attempts to reconstitute themselves has made him unique. His refusal to divorce literature from politics and his acerbic portrayal of corruption in independent Kenya—first in *Petals of Blood* and then in his play, *Ngaahika Ndeenda*, which was considered more dangerous by the government because it was performed in an indigenous language—earned him the wrath of the political leaders and a year in prison without a trial.

Ngugi has also been concerned with the implications entailed in the use of English language by African writers, and he has supplemented his theoretical reflections by switching to Kikuyu as his primary literary language. Ngugi is widely recognized as Africa's foremost revolutionary writer and is one of the world's most read African writers.

Biography

Ngugi wa Thiong'o, who was known as James Thiong'o Ngugi until 1970, was born in 1938 near Limuru, in a Kikuyu area of Kenya. He received a varied education, alternating between mission schools and an institution that was part of the Independence Schools Movement, aimed at preparing Kenya's young people for freedom from British rule. The outbreak of the Mau Mau war briefly disrupted Ngugi's education and had a profound impact on his family; his brother Walter fought with the Mau Mau, and his parents were detained as subversives. Ngugi's experiences of the war left a lasting impression on him and became the basis of his first three novels. In 1955, he transferred again to a missionary school, the Alliance High School. His literary career blossomed rapidly once he entered Makerere University in Kampala, Uganda, in 1959. He soon became editor of *Penpoint*, a literary journal, and was graduated with honors.

In 1964, Ngugi published his first novel, which soon won two prizes, one from the 1965 Dakar Festival of Negro Arts and one from the East African Literature Bureau. After working for the *Daily Nation*, a leading newspaper, he attended graduate school at the University of Leeds in England and then returned to become a lecturer at University College, Nairobi. In 1969, he resigned from this position in sympathy with a student strike and taught for a period at Northwestern University in the United States. He returned to University College and continued to teach there until 1977, when he was imprisoned for his political views.

Released from prison in December, 1978, Ngugi returned to teaching and to involvement in a theater group. This group, however, was banned by Kenyan authorities in 1982, and Ngugi, anticipating further restrictions of his artistic freedom, fled to self-imposed exile in London.

Analysis

Ngugi's fiction, like that of many contemporary African novelists, is highly political: it portrays the traumatic transition from colonized culture to an independent African society. His novels illustrate with unmatched clarity the problems created by this period of rapid change. Superior European technology introduced into Africa at the turn of the century undercut traditional cultural values, and colonial domination (denunciation of indigenous cultures and religions, appropriation of native lands, and forced labor) led to a disintegration of indigenous societies. The major themes of Ngugi's novels derive from his characters' attempts to overcome the confusion caused by the peripeteia of values and to reintegrate and revitalize their new syncretic culture. Faced with the drastic dissolution of his family in the Mau Mau war from 1952 to 1958, Njoroge, the protagonist of *Weep Not, Child*, tenaciously adheres to his beliefs in education and messianic deliverance in a vain attempt to maintain some cohesion in his life. Waiyaki, the hero of *The River Between*, believing that he is the new messiah, also attempts in vain to reunite the Christian and traditional Kikuyu factions of his village. While both novels are truncated *Bildungsroman*, in which the education of the heroes is incomplete, *A Grain of Wheat* is experimental in form: The novel's meaning is available not through the character and experiences of a single protagonist but through the complex interrelationships of five major and many minor characters. Yet the theme remains the same: the attempt of a Kikuyu village to reintegrate itself and to reorder its priorities after it has been devastated by the Mau Mau war. *Petals of Blood*, set in postcolonial Kenya, once more depicts a group of peasants who are trying to fashion a meaningful life for themselves in the context of economic exploitation by the new black leaders of the country.

Ngugi's preoccupation with this theme is best understood in the historical context of the conflict between the Kikuyus and British colonizers that culminated in the Mau Mau war of 1952 and that was provoked by three important factors: the economic and cultural effects of land appropriation, the importance of education for the Kikuyus and consequently the impact of its deprivation, and the messianic fervor that characterized Kikuyu politics at the time. All of Ngugi's novels are focused on various combinations of these three factors, and his repeated concern with these issues is largely determined by his traumatic experiences during the war.

When the British settled in Kenya, large areas of the best arable land were expropriated from the Kikuyus (who were then crowded into reserves) and given, at little or no cost, to English syndicates, investors, and farmers. Piecemeal appropriation of Kikuyu land was finally systematized by the 1921 court ruling that all land, even that which had been put aside for "reserves," was owned by the British government, and the natives were thus considered squatters on land they had owned for generations. In exchange for squatting "rights," the Kikuyus had to provide 180 days of free labor per annum. Such manipulation, along with coercive tax laws and punitive raids, put a tremendous pressure on the Kikuyus and eventually led to the Mau Mau war. Although independence was achieved in 1962, the war was a bitter experience for the Kikuyus because they were quite divided—some fought for and some against the British.

While being deprived of their land, the Kikuyus focused their attention on education, only to find themselves once more at odds with the colonial government, which, with the aim of promoting agricultural and vocational training, limited African education to the primary level and prohibited the use of English as the medium of instruction. The Kikuyus, however, preferred liberal, humanistic secondary education because it permitted access to civil service jobs and, more important, because English was the language of technology and power. They reasoned, quite accurately, that mastery of English was crucial for their nationalistic aspirations. The Kikuyus responded by mercilessly taxing themselves in order to build their own schools, only to have them shut down repeatedly by the government. This struggle continued until the outbreak of the Mau Mau war, when all Kikuyu schools were closed for several years.

The final factor important for appreciating Ngugi's fiction is the prediction by Mugo wa Kibiro, a Kikuyu prophet, that a messianic leader would come to deliver the tribe from colonial bondage. Jomo Kenyatta, the leader of the independence movement and the first president of Kenya, skillfully used this prophecy to coalesce the social and religious sentiments of the Kikuyu around himself during the Mau Mau war. Hence the atmosphere at that time was charged by powerful contradictory feelings: fear, uncertainty, bitterness, and despair produced by colonial oppression were balanced by fervent feelings of loyalty, sacrifice, and elation resulting from messianic expectations and the hopes of independence, freedom, and recovery of the land.

At the age of fifteen, Ngugi was caught up in this historical and emotional drama. Its effects on him were profound. He had experienced extreme poverty and thus clearly sympathized with the economic and political predicament of the peasants. At the age of ten or eleven he witnessed the forced evacuation of Kikuyu farmers from their land. As they were being moved, they sang about their hopes of reclaiming their property and about their educated children who might attain this goal some day. Ngugi's memory of this scene explains his preoccupation with the war: "They sang of a common loss and hope and I felt their voice rock the earth where I stood literally unable to move." Ngugi's burden was exacerbated by the closing of schools. Young Kikuyus were being exhorted to master Western knowledge and use it as a weapon of liberation, but the political and military crises blocked access to education and therefore to the possibility of leadership. This deprivation was rendered even more painful by the sustained messianic fervor which reemphasized the role of leadership. This, then, was the nexus of forces that composed the sociopolitical and religious ambience in which Ngugi reached maturity. Yet because he was so young when he began writing, his early fiction shows an imperfect understanding of his predicament. His first two novels graphically depict his entanglement in the peripeteia of values, whereas his third and fourth novels, written after a study of Frantz Fanon's psychopolitical analysis of colonialism, show a sudden and clearer understanding of the ambiguities and contradictions of colonial society.

Set in Kenya in the 1940's and 1950's and ending in the midst of the Mau Mau war, *Weep Not, Child* is Ngugi's most autobiographical novel; Njoroge, its child protagonist, is about the same age as Ngugi would have been at that time. The novel is an anticlimactic, truncated *Bildungsroman* in that it follows the development of a child into adolescence but does not adequately resolve the question of what precisely has been learned by the hero.

The novel rapidly and cogently focuses on Njoroge's preoccupation with education and messianism. Ngotho, Njoroge's father, is confused and emasculated by his inability to comprehend and resist the appropriation of his land by an English settler named Howlands, and consequently the family begins to disintegrate, reflecting in a microcosm the general social fragmentation. The family's burden passes to Njoroge, who is fortunate enough to be receiving a formal education (which annually consumes the wages of two brothers). When Njoroge graduates into secondary school, the entire village contributes to his tuition, and thus the hero is transformed from the "son of Ngotho to the son of the land." Thus he begins to feel that through his education he will become a great leader. Kenyatta's imprisonment further fuels his grandiose fantasies: he even envisions himself as the new messiah. His self-image, however, remains insubstantial. His love of "education" is abstract: he does not care for particular subjects, nor does his vision encompass specific goals or projects. His messianic delusions are equally empty, and his egocentric world crumbles as soon as he is confronted with the reality of the war. When his father dies from severe torture and castration, when his brothers are either imprisoned or killed, and when he too is tortured in spite of his innocence, his illusions are shattered. Finally, the girl he loves rejects him, and he attempts suicide but is easily dissuaded by his mother. The novel ends with his recognition that he is a coward.

The rapid descent from the height of self-importance to the nadir of self-negation is enacted against the backdrop of a society in violent turmoil, which Ngugi depicts in effective detail. The complex social entanglements and contradictions—the different political views and the conflict between generations within Ngotho's family, the enmity between Ngotho and Jacobo, whose loyalty to the British is rewarded with wealth and political power, the mixture of fear, hatred, and respect that Howlands harbors for Ngotho because he has occupied the latter's land, the Englishman's desire to torture and kill Ngotho which leads to the retaliatory murder of Howlands by Ngotho's son, Howlands' contempt for Jacobo's collaboration, Njoroge's love for Mwihaki, Jacobo's daughter, and his brief friendship with Howlands' son—as well as the descriptions of torture and summary executions by the British and the Mau Mau, create a powerful microcosmic picture of a whole society being ripped apart by economic and political conflict. The novel brilliantly depicts the trauma and the ambiguities of a revolution. Yet Njoroge's actual experience is not derived from active involvement in this upheaval; rather, he functions as a passive, reluctant witness. His experience is that of a highly suggestible and solitary adolescent who easily internalizes the hopes, frustrations, and anguish of his society and then soothes his own trauma with self-aggrandizing fantasies.

The violence and trauma to which Njoroge is subject only partially account for the oscillation of his self-image. The rest of the explanation lies in the peripeteia of values that engulfs the hero and the narrator. Njoroge's early subscription to English values includes a naïve belief in biblical messianic prophecies which supplement the Kikuyu myth. As a self-styled messiah, he attempts to soothe the fears of a "*weeping child.*" Thus his attitude to others exactly parallels the narrator's depiction of Njoroge as the weeping child. This profound sympathy and parallelism between the narrator's and the hero's views underscores the complete absence of irony in Ngugi's portrayal of Njoroge.

The denouement of the novel also confirms this underlying problem. Without any justification, Njoroge assumes all the guilt of the trauma suffered by several families and accuses the girl he loves of betraying him before he tries to commit suicide. Thus, he is still following the model of Christ, of a messiah who assumed all human guilt, was betrayed, and then turned into a scapegoat. By allowing his hero to transform his self-image from that of a savior to that of a scapegoat, Ngugi allows him to retain his original egocentricity. This essential continuity in Njoroge's characterization testifies to the powerful influence of Christianity on Ngugi himself. If Njoroge's fantasies are a product of the sociopolitical and religious factors in this specific colonial situation, then the ambiguity in the narrative attitude to Njoroge can be ascribed to the same forces. In the final analysis, it is Ngugi's inability to define adequately his stand toward these factors that is responsibile for the narrative ambiguity. The novel, then, can be seen simultaneously as a portrayal *and* a product of the peripeteia of values. The persistence of this confusion led Ngugi to a reworking of the same issues in his next novel.

The plot of *The River Between*, set in the late 1920's and 1930's, is centered once more on a combination of education and messianism, while the subplot examines the clash of values through the emotionally and culturally charged controversy over female circumcision. The geographical setting is allegorical: the events take place in the "heart and soul" of Kikuyu land and culture among the communities on two ridges ranged on either side of the river Honia (which means "Regeneration" in Kikuyu). Both ridges, Kameno and Makuyu, claim to be the source of Kikuyu culture, but as the novel progresses, Kameno, home of the Kikuyu prophet Mugo wa Kibiro and his descendant Waiyaki, the novel's protagonist, becomes the base for those who want to retain the purity of Kikuyu culture, whereas Makuyu becomes the home of those who have converted to Christianity and have renounced various "evil" aspects of their original tradition. The ensuing conflict thus becomes emblematic of the problems of peripeteia experienced by the entire culture. Characterization, too, is stylized to reflect this antagonism between the desire for cultural purity and the desire to abrogate traditional values.

Among the older generation, which provides the secondary characters, the opposition is embodied in Chege and Joshua. Chege, Waiyaki's father, a minor prophet embittered by the people's disregard for his claims, is realistically aware of the specific cultural and technological superiority of European society and thus, in spite of inherent dangers, commands his son to attend the missionary school and master Western knowledge without absorbing its vices. He is simultaneously concerned with preserving Kikuyu purity and with ensuring its survival through the absorption of clearly efficacious aspects of Western culture. On the other hand, Joshua, a zealous convert who has become a self-righteous, puritanical minister, renounces Kikuyu culture as dirty, heathen, and evil. He has entirely dedicated himself to his own and other people's salvation through Christianity. Ngugi balances these static and absolute oppositions with the dynamic and relativistic attitudes of their children, Waiyaki and Joshua's two daughters, Muthoni and Nyambura, who attempt in their different ways to synthesize the two cultures.

The poignant and touching subplot depicts Muthoni's disastrous attempt to combine what she considers to be the best aspects of both cultures. Even though her parents will not permit her to undergo circumcision because the Church has forbidden this most important rite of purification and rebirth in Kikuyu culture, Muthoni decides that she must be circumcised. By becoming a circumcised Christian she hopes to combine the two cultures within herself. Unfortunately, an infection contracted during the ceremony kills Muthoni. In addition to radicalizing the two factions, her apostasy and death reveal the more profound problems of cultural transition. The fact that her notion of womanhood is predicated on circumcision shows that peripeteia involves not only physical and social but ontological changes; specific modifications of a culture become meaningless unless the entire cultural gestalt is altered to accommodate particular infusions. Waiyaki sees Muthoni as a sacrifice to the clash of cultures, and when he falls in love with her uncircumcised sister, Nyambura, the subplot is deftly woven into the main plot—Waiyaki's attempt to become a messiah and an educator.

Unlike *Weep Not, Child*, where the messianic possibility is entirely confined to Njoroge's fantasies, *The River Between* presents it as an actual, unambiguous fact: while Waiyaki is still a child, his "mission" to master Western knowledge and unite the Kikuyus is revealed to him. When, along with many other students, he resigns from the Christian mission school, he gets his chance to fulfill his destiny. With the help of the people and his colleagues he establishes an independent Kikuyu school which flourishes and thus earns him the respect befitting a messiah; by successfully mediating between the English and Kikuyu cultures and by making the positive aspects of the former available to the latter, he seems to have fulfilled the prophecy. His success, however, is short-lived. Jealousy and political ambition spur a faction from Kemano to accuse him of treason and spiritual contamination because he loves an uncircumcised woman. Since he is unwilling to renounce Nyambura, Waiyaki is forced to relinquish his leadership, and his personal fate remains ominously ambiguous at the end of the novel.

The River Between is a better *Bildungsroman* than Ngugi's first novel because Waiyaki does realize that he is a product of the peripeteia of values and that cultural synthesis is an ambiguous, complex, and even dangerous undertaking. Yet, this education of the hero is not sufficient to save the novel from the confusion caused by a double narrative intention. Overtly, the narrator clearly intends to present Waiyaki as a man constantly concerned with communal welfare, yet the rhetoric of Waiyaki's contemplation demonstrates that he is entirely engrossed in his own messianic potentiality: all his dealings with people always revert to questions about his status and leadership. Furthermore, the divine source of his authority, by providing him with *transcendent* knowledge, severs him from the Kikuyu to the extent that his vision of the future, and actions based on that vision, need not rely on mundane familiarity with the people's social and political desires.

The major problem of the novel is that Ngugi seems unable to decide whether to treat his protagonist as a real messiah or whether to portray him as a character whose prophetic calling is a self-delusion: Waiyaki is simultaneously subjected to divine surety and human fallibility. At the end of the novel, Ngugi seems to sympathize with two incompatible feelings—with Waiyaki's decision to choose a personal relationship over communal obligation, a private cultural synthesis over a larger social synthesis, and with the people's decision to protect their culture by sacrificing a promising individual. The persistent ambiguity about Waiyaki and the final recourse to scapegoating, which resembles so closely the pattern of grandiose self-delusion and vindication through persecution in *Weep Not, Child*, reveal once more that *The River Between* is a product of subjective anxiety. Waiyaki's insight into the anxiety caused by the peripeteia of values is applicable to the novel as a whole. According to him this anxiety can cause a man to cling fanatically to whatever promises security. For Waiyaki and Ngugi, messianism provides that security. If one considers Ngugi's predicament at the age of fifteen, when he internalized the social preoccupation with education, leadership, and messianism, one can see that the ambiguity and the ambivalence of *The River*

Between are a literary transformation of his own traumatic experience.

Before writing his next novel, *A Grain of Wheat*, Ngugi studied Frantz Fanon's *The Wretched of the Earth*, which unmistakably altered his understanding of the psychological and cultural changes that take place in the process of anticolonial revolutions. The view that education and messianism are panaceas is entirely displaced by a clear and deep comprehension of the way out of the psychological bind produced by colonial subjugation. In *A Grain of Wheat*, Ngugi is still concerned with the reintegration of Kikuyu society, but his method has changed drastically. Instead of focusing on a single protagonist Ngugi uses five major characters, Mugo, Karanja, Kihika, Gikonyo, and Mumbi, and a host of minor ones in order to contrast different kinds of personal isolation, love, and sympathy for others, and then he orchestrates a complex pattern wherein some characters move from isolation to community, some move in the opposite direction, while still others remain relatively static. By contrasting and interweaving these movements, Ngugi creates a polyphonic novel in which the experience of social regeneration and communal cohesiveness lies not in the awareness of any single character but in the interactions between various individuals and in the reader's experience of these interactions.

The novel's plot concerns an intriguing search for the traitor who betrayed Kihika, a leader of the Mau Mau guerrillas. The war is over, and, just prior to independence day, Kihika's comrades emerge from the forests in order to seek the traitor. The search, however, is really a vehicle for investigating various characters' motives and actions during the war that has destroyed the village of Thabai. The actual time encompassed by the novel is only six days, but through retrospection the reader is allowed to experience the whole Mau Mau revolution and even the prerevolutionary childhood of the protagonists as well as the mythic past of the Kikuyus. The multiplicity of viewpoints through which one is led to understand the characters conveys admirably Ngugi's notion that an organic community can be apprehended only through its historical and interpersonal interactions.

Ngugi's investigation of patterns of isolation and communality is focused on four males and one female. Two men, Mugo and Karanja, are motivated by an almost pathological desire for isolation and two, Kihika and Gikonyo, are deeply dependent on their different views of communality. Mugo, deprived of human warmth since childhood, attempts in vain to avoid all involvement. His isolation is repeatedly shattered, first by Kihika, who is seeking shelter from the colonial soldiers and whom Mugo betrays, and then by the whole village of Thabai, which, having mistaken Mugo for a supporter of Kihika and a staunch patriot, ironically invites him to become the village chief on independence day. While Mugo gradually journeys from isolation to social integration, Karanja moves in the opposite direction. In order to remain with Mumbi, who had earlier rejected him for Gikonyo, Karanja joins the colonial police when Gikonyo is sent to a concentration camp. His collaboration with the British naturally earns him the enmity of the entire village, which expels him on independence day. While Karanja betrays the community as an abstract entity in order to remain with a specific woman, Kihika abandons his pregnant lover in order to become a guerrilla fighter and plays an important part in winning the freedom of his society. In contrast to Kihika, Gikonyo has always been dependent on concrete relationships with his mother and Mumbi. His personality and the very meaning of existence crumble when he is forcibly isolated from them. He confesses his involvement with the Mau Mau so that he can return to his village, only to find when he arrives that Mumbi has given birth to Karanja's child.

Ngugi explores these labyrinthine relationships with great skill. The retrospections, juxtapositions, and multiple interpretations of events, and the gradual, interrupted revelation of the truth represent in a concrete and poignant manner the actual reintegration of a community that has been destroyed. Ngugi's main objective, admirably realized, is to show that strength in one character can be a weakness in another and that what is constructive and desirable at one stage in a community's history is harmful at another—that all forms of fortitude and lapses are necessary for social cohesion. Even Mugo's betrayal performs a vital function in the end. His confession of the betrayal fits into the pattern of complementary wills which is essential for the cohesion of a community. Thus, where Kihika's callousness toward individuals may be undesirable in itself, its reverse, his concern for abstract humanity, proves invaluable for the freedom of his country. Where Kihika's self-sacrifice, in spite of its eventual usefulness, causes a great deal of pain to the community (because of his assassination of a British District Officer, Thabai is burnt to the ground), Mugo's self-sacrifice, through his confession, is ultimately soothing. It comes to symbolize the depth of misunderstanding and the renewal of honest and open communication.

In a different manner, Kihika and Gikonyo form a complementary unit that is equally vital for the society. Kihika's disregard for the individual and concern for people in general are balanced by Gikonyo's lack of concern for an abstract conception of community, his betrayal of the Mau Mau covenant, and his powerful desire for concrete individual relations with Mumbi and his mother. Whereas Kihika's attitude is necessary for society's struggle to free itself, Gikonyo's attitude is necessary for its survival. Similarly, even Karanja's defection can be seen as a complementary necessity because he is responsible for keeping Mumbi alive while the rest of the men are either guerrillas hiding in the forests or prisoners in the camps. People are thus tied to one another in ways that they themselves fail to understand. By focusing on these interconnections, Ngugi demonstrates that relationships between individuals are more important than individual character.

The vast bulk of *A Grain of Wheat* represents the reintegration of Thabai through keen and accurate realism, but in order to emphasize that he is depicting the entire Kikuyu culture, Ngugi resorts to symbolism at the end of the novel. Gikonyo and Mumbi clearly symbolize the mythic ancestors of their society, Kikuyu and Mumbi. Gikonyo feels that his "reunion with Mumbi would see the rebirth of a new Kenya." In light of this symbolism, Karanja's protection of Mumbi and Mugo's confession, which is responsible for the reunion of Gikonyo and Mumbi, become significant contributions to their society. Finally, the iconography—a father, a pregnant mother, a child, a field ready for harvest, and a stool that Gikonyo intends to carve and present to Mumbi as a gift of reconciliation—implies the regeneration of community that is so central to all of Ngugi's fiction. The formal structure of *A Grain of Wheat*, a perfect emblem of an actual viable society, and Ngugi's definition of community make this a unique novel in African fiction.

Toward the end of *A Grain of Wheat* there are signs that after political "independence" has been won the struggle between British colonizers and Africans, which has dominated the country and the novel, will be displaced gradually by a conflict between the native political-economic elite and the peasants, who will be disinherited once again. *Petals of Blood*, set in independent Kenya in the mid-1970's, examines in depth the problem that Ngugi's previous novel has accurately predicted. In *Petals of Blood*, Kenya is drastically, perhaps too schematically, divided between the rich capitalists, portrayed as two-dimensional, greedy, conniving predators, and their peasant victims, depicted as complex individuals who become prey to a modern world they cannot control. The problem with this dichotomy is that the opposition between the poor and the rich lacks any dramatic tension because the latter are shallow characters minimally and symbolically represented through their expensive automobiles, lavish parties, and deceptive contracts. Thus, even though Ngugi's portrayal of the economic and political situation in Kenya is broadly accurate it is not entirely convincing.

The center of *Petals of Blood* is a powerful, fecund woman, Wanja, a prostitute who is many things to the different men arranged around her like petals of blood. If the novel is read as an allegory, she can be seen as the protean substance of Kenya, which entices the lechery of the capitalists and sustains and inspires the resistance of the peasants. Kimeria, one of the three successful entrepreneurs in the novel, seduces her while she is a teenager and then abandons her only to lust after her again when she has become the successful madam of a house of prostitution. Munira, an introspective, religious schoolteacher, is initially liberated from his repressions through her, but, after his guilt has overwhelmed him, he sees her as an incarnation of Satan. Karega, a young, nascent revolutionary, has an idyllic affair with her and finds in her the inspiration for his rebellion. Finally, Abdulla, a crippled Mau Mau warrior, treats her as a comrade and eventually fathers the child that she has desired throughout the novel.

The plot of *Petals of Blood* is similar to a Charles Dickens plot in its labyrinthine relationships and its reliance on coincidence. Ostensibly, the novel is a detective story; it begins with the arrest of three major characters, Munira, Abdulla, and Karega, who are under suspicion for the murder of three wealthy directors of the Theng-eta Breweries, Kimeria, Chui, and Muzigo. After being ignored for the vast bulk of the novel, the mystery is suddenly solved at the end by Munira's admission that he set fire to Wanja's brothel, in which the directors were trapped. The relations between characters are revealed in an equally sudden and summary fashion, with the result that the plot becomes a mere vehicle for the political substance of the novel—a detailed examination of the manner in which the rightful inheritance of the peasants and idealists has been stolen from them. Once more this is accomplished through a series of retrospective scenes that reveal the past in the light of the present struggle. The peasants undertake an epic journey to Nairobi, the capital city, in order to confront their parliamentary representative, who has in fact ignored and even tried to plunder his constituency. The climax of this spatial journey—that is, the confrontation in the city— allows the peasants to understand the economic opposition between them and the new African elite, but through the various personal and communal stories told by the peasants to one another during their journey, they also realize that they are a part of a temporal "journey"—that they are the current embodiment of a long historical tradition. As Karega says, "The history that he had tried to teach as romantic adventures, the essence of black struggle apprehended in the imagination at the level of mere possibilities, had tonight acquired immediate flesh and blood."

Petals of Blood is at its best when it explores the lives and sensibilities of these people. Through Munira and Karega, Ngugi shows the radically different effects of quite similar causes. Both are expelled from Siriana high school at different times (they are a generation apart) for leading student strikes. Whereas the resultant shock and confusion experienced by Munira turns into depression and later into a pathological preoccupation with spiritual purity, the initial confusion felt by Karega is gradually displaced by an increasingly clear understanding of his place in the sociopolitical system of the country and eventually turns into a radical opposition to the new elite. Thus Munira treats people such as Wanja or Abdulla as mere objects of his lust or indifference, whereas Karega sees them as subjects whose personal histories make him aware of his own predicament and potential. The novel makes a dramatic distinction between individuals lost in their own subjectivity and those who through circumstances, personal courage, and fidelity are able to understand themselves in terms of an objectively determined social and political reality.

Unfortunately, Ngugi's sensitive representation of the inner lives of his politically oppressed characters is not matched by an equally sensitive management of the novel's structure. The caricature of the capitalists and the plot's reliance on brief, mechanical coincidences deprive the novel of a demonstrated and felt struggle between the exploiters and the exploited. Instead of using viable fictive embodiments of oppressive forces, Ngugi relies heavily on discursive delineation of capitalist exploitation. At times, the novel sounds like a leftist pamphlet. In contrast to *A Grain of Wheat*, where Ngugi's political concerns are perfectly interlocked with a well-wrought and ingenious structure, *Petals of Blood* is overwhelmed by the writer's sensitive and moving depiction of the peasants' lives and by his justified anger over callous exploitation and broken promises.

Devil on the Cross, Ngugi's sixth novel, is another passionate denunciation of postcolonial abuses. Written on stolen bits of toilet paper during his year in prison, *Devil on the Cross* features, again, several protagonists—mostly peasants—who are grievously wronged by the corrupt politicians and bureaucrats of modern Kenya. With this novel and the nonfiction works that followed, Ngugi solidified his commitment to a revolutionary African literature—outraged, combative, and uncompromising.

Abdul R. JanMohamed

Other major works

SHORT FICTION: *Secret Lives and Other Stories*, 1975.

PLAYS: *The Black Hermit*, 1962; *This Time Tomorrow: Three Plays*, 1970 (includes *The Rebels*, *The Wound in My Heart*, and *This Time Tomorrow*); *the Trial of Dedan Kimathi*, 1974 (with Micere Githae-Mugo); *Ngaahika Ndeenda*, 1977 (with Ngugi wa Mirii; *I Will Marry When I Want*, 1982); *Maitu Njugira*, 1982 (with Ngugi wa Mirii; *Mother, Sing for Me*, 1986).

NONFICTION: *Homecoming: Essays on African and Caribbean Literature, Culture, and Politics*, 1972; *Writers in Politics*, 1981; *Detained: A Writer's Prison Diary*, 1981; *Barrel of a Pen: Resistance to Repression in Neo-Colonial Kenya*, 1983; *Decolonising the Mind: The Politics of Language in African Literature*, 1986; *Writing Against Neocolonialism*, 1986.

Bibliography

Carter, Steven R. "Decolonization and Detective Fiction: Ngugi wa Thiong'o's *Petals of Blood." Clues: A Journal of Detection* 1 (Spring/Summer, 1987): 101-126. This analytic article tackles the issues of capitalism, neocolonialism, foreign narrative forms, and detective fiction in the novel. Includes notes.

Killam, G. D. *An Introduction to the Writings of Ngugi*. London: Heinemann, 1980. A good starting point for the study of Ngugi, with a biographical outline, an introduction, individual chapters devoted to one title, a bibliography, and an index.

_____. "Ngugi wa Thiong'o." In *The Writing of East and Central Africa*. London: Heinemann, 1984. The three parts of this volume contain chapters surveying writing in six countries, chapters on genres, and chapters on individual authors. A useful study for those who wish to understand authors in these contexts. Includes an index.

Moore, Gerald. "Ngugi wa Thiong'o: Towards Uhuru." In *Twelve African Writers*. Bloomington: Indiana University Press, 1980. The introduction provides a quick overview of issues in studying African literature. The twelve authors, selected for their longevity as writers, are appraised individually and comparatively. Contains references, a bibliography of primary sources, a suggested reading list, and an index.

Palmer, Eustace. "Negritude Rediscovered: A Reading of the Recent Novels of Armah, Ngugi, and Soyinka." *The International Fiction Review* 8 (1981): 1-11. This discussion of the concept of Negritude pays particular attention to three works: Wole Soyinka's *Season of Anomy*, Ngugi's *Petals of Blood*, and Ayi Kwei Armah's *Two Thousand Seasons*. Includes notes.

Shyam, Jai. "Plights of Contemporary Life in Recent African Fiction." *The Arizona Quarterly* 42 (Autumn, 1986): 248-260. This scholarly article discusses the alienating results of Western individualism in African society as depicted in novels by four writers. Ngugi's *Petals of Blood* is discussed.

Sicherman, Carol. *Ngugi wa Thiong'o: A Bibliography of Primary and Secondary Sources, 1957-1987*. London: Hans Zell, 1989. A treasure for the scholar, with citations of Ngugi's works in the original languages, manuscripts and other unpublished material, translations, secondary sources, undated material, nonprint media, and indexes of authors, editors, translators, titles, interviews, and subjects. Includes a brief introduction and preface.

ANAÏS NIN

Born: Paris, France; February 21, 1903
Died: Los Angeles, California; January 14, 1977

Principal long fiction

House of Incest, 1936; *Winter of Artifice*, 1939; *Winter of Artifice: Three Novelettes*, 1945 (contains *Winter of Artifice*, "Stella," and "The Voice"); *This Hunger*, 1945; *Cities of the Interior: A Continuous Novel*, 1959 (contains *Ladders to Fire*, 1946, *Children of the Albatross*, 1947, *The Four-Chambered Heart*, 1950, *A Spy in the House of Love*, 1954, *Solar Barque*, 1958); *Seduction of the Minotaur*, 1961; *Collages*, 1964.

Other literary forms

Anaïs Nin published numerous volumes of perceptive literary criticism. Highly acclaimed, her first book of nonfiction, *D. H. Lawrence: An Unprofessional Study*, appeared in 1932. In 1968, near the end of her career, she wrote *The Novel of the Future*, partly as an attempt to explain the literary philosophy that inspired her innovative fiction. In 1976, a collection of her essays appeared, entitled *In Favor of the Sensitive Man and Other Essays*. During the last decade of her life, Nin was extremely active as a public speaker; her lectures, seminars, and interviews have been edited by Evelyn J. Hinz and published as *A Woman Speaks* (1975).

Nin's published short stories, like her criticism, span her career. The most distinguished collection is *Under a Glass Bell and Other Stories* (1944). Her apprentice writing is available in another collection, *Waste of Timelessness and Other Early Stories* (1977), while two volumes of erotica were published after Nin's death: *Delta of Venus* (1977) and *Little Birds* (1979).

In addition to her works of fiction and criticism, Nin's extensive diary has been published. Edited from a vast manuscript, this autobiographical work has appeared in two series. The first series, entitled *The Diary of Anaïs Nin*, comprises seven volumes which have appeared periodically since 1966. The second series contains two volumes, *Linotte: The Early Diary of Anaïs Nin, 1914-1920* (1978) and *The Early Diary of Anaïs Nin: Volume Two, 1920-1923* (1982).

Achievements

Nin's achievement in literature is of two distinct kinds: artistic and sociological. Strongly influenced by Arthur Rimbaud, Marcel Proust, and D. H. Lawrence, Nin conceived of and developed a uniquely personal approach to style and structure that places her within the modernist tradition as it evolved in the French literature of the early decades of the twentieth century. Nin persisted in articulating, refining, and extending an avowedly "feminine" ideal of the novel; this resulted in lyrical novels in which the imagistic manner of the poet is fused with the psychological penetration of the novelist. In her treatment of character, of time and of space, Nin belongs with such writers as Virginia Woolf, Djuna Barnes, and Anna Kavan.

Nin's sociological importance is related to her intention to create a specifically "feminine" novel in which the emphasis is on the evocation of feeling, and to portray as deeply and as honestly as possible an authentically female emotional experience. In this respect, her achievement may be compared with that of Woolf, Dorothy Richardson, Marguerite Duras, and a number of French writers, including Annie LeClerc, Hélène Cixous, Monique Wittig, and Julia Kristeva.

The audience for Nin's novels is smaller than for either her diary or her collections of erotica. As the diary has increased Nin's audience, it has also brought her fiction to the attention of well-qualified critics and scholars, many of whom have been able to interpret it in ways that make it more accessible to a general readership trained on the conventions of realism. Considering the climate of growing respect for and interest in Nin's novels, it seems that her reputation as a literary artist is now securely established.

Biography

On February 21, 1903, Anaïs Nin was born in Paris, the oldest child of musicians Joaquin Nin and Rosa Culmell-Nin. Her parents' marriage was turbulent, and in 1913, Joaquin Nin deserted his family at Archachon, France. The following year, Rosa Culmell-Nin transported her daughter and two sons, Thorvald and Joaquin, to the United States. For some years, they lived in New York City and in Queens, actively participating in the lively Cuban community there, many of whose members were musicians. Nin has recorded this period of her life in *Linotte: The Early Diary, 1914-1920*. What stands out most poignantly is her inconsolable grief at the loss of her father and her intense worship of her mother. At this time, Nin's aspiration to become an artist of one sort or another strongly manifested itself, and her account of her adolescence is a rich study of the formative years of an artist.

In 1918, Nin left school in order to manage the household for her mother, who worked for Lord and Taylor's as a special buyer for the Cuban clientele, and in 1923, Nin married Hugh P. Guiler (known as an engraver and filmmaker under the name of Ian Hugo). As a young married woman, Nin lived in France. Marriage caused her to experience intense conflicts which she has described and analyzed in her diary. During those years, as in adolescence, Nin continued to write, and in 1932, she published her first book, *D. H. Lawrence: An Unprofessional Study*. This work brought about the explosive friendship with Henry and June Miller which she describes in the first published diary. Nin and Miller maintained a relationship until Nin's death.

In Paris during the 1930's, Nin embarked upon a lifelong devotion to psychotherapy. Her therapeutic relationship with the reknowned Viennese psychoanalyst Otto Rank is recounted in the first volume of *The Diary of Anaïs Nin*. An independent, original and forceful thinker whose special area of interest was the artist, Rank was of great assistance to Nin in the fulfillment of her artistic aspirations. His influence on her was so persuasive that for a time she actually considered making a living as a lay psychoanalyst. For a few months in 1934, she lived in New York and assisted Rank with his practice. In 1935, however, she resumed her literary work and returned to France to rejoin her husband, but with the outbreak of World War II, she again returned to the United States. This move in 1939 was to become permanent. It was not easy for Nin to give up her "romantic life" in Paris, as she called it, and her difficulty understanding Americans' disdain for the arts is a recurrent theme of her diary in the 1940's and 1950's.

Throughout her life, Nin maintained many friendships with writers and other artists. Among her friends and acquaintances were Lawrence Durrell, Robert Duncan, James Merrill, and Kenneth Patchen; performers Canada Lee, Josephine Premice, and Louise Rainer; Caresse Crosby, proprietor of the Black Sun Press; composer Edgar Varèse and his wife the translator Louise Varèse; collage artist Janko Varda; and the owner of the influential Gotham Book Mart, Frances Steloff. Even though Nin had widespread contacts among writers and artists in New York City and on the West Coast, she experienced continual frustration in the publishing world. On the whole, editors and critics were either hostile to her work or simply ignored it. The breakthrough of this period was the acceptance by Alan Swallow, founder of the famed Swallow Press then located in Denver, Colorado, of the five works that constitute *Cities of the Interior: A Continuous Novel*. For many years, Nin was an underground literary figure with a small but enthusiastic following.

In 1966, Nin's status changed suddenly; she had already published all her fiction, the last book, *Collages*, appearing in 1964. When Harcourt Brace and World, with The Swallow Press, brought out the first volume of *The Diary of Anaïs Nin*, Nin quickly became a public figure. Because the content of the work expressed the feelings of many women who were experiencing deep evolutionary changes in their own lives, Nin involuntarily became a spokesperson for the women's movement. She achieved the "dialogue with the world" for which she had longed since childhood.

During the remaining years of Nin's life, individual volumes of her diary continued to appear, and Nin, although viewed as controversial by leaders of the women's movement, received considerable public acclaim. Traveling throughout the United States, she gave hundreds of talks at colleges and universities and undertook trips to various countries, including Sweden and Bali. In 1970, she was awarded the French Prix Sévigné, and in 1974, she was elected to the National Institute of Arts and Letters. Nin's books have been translated into all the major Western languages as well as Serbo-Croatian and Japanese.

Analysis

It was natural that Anaïs Nin should grow up desiring to be an artist. Her father was a friend of Gabriele D'Annunzio. Before Nin's parents separated, their household was filled with the aura of the *fin de siècle* symbolist movement. The symbolists' ideas about art had a decisive and lasting influence on Nin, although she greatly transformed the influences she absorbed in the process of adapting them to the expressive needs of her own temperament.

Like the symbolists, Nin believed that phenomena possess hidden meanings, significances that escape most people. The artist's task is to penetrate surfaces to reveal the truths they conceal. "The symbol," she wrote, "is an acknowledgement of the emotional and spiritual content of every act and every object around us." Equipped with heightened perception and expressive talent, the artist can interpret the vast confusing world of phenomena, revealing essences in a world of masks and misleading surfaces. Nin described a story as "a quest for meaning."

With the symbolists, too, and with the later surrealists, Nin shared a positive attitude toward dream and fantasy. Her books are poetic defenses of her belief in the unconscious as a source of the visions and imaginary experiences that complement verifiable reality, compensating for its limitations and endowing it with the richness of mental play that "reality" is not capable of providing. Nin stressed the positive aspects of fantasy in order to balance what she perceived as American society's mistrust, fear, and even condemnation of any sort of activity that is not directly productive in a materialistic way.

Nin's literary aspiration was formidable; she wanted to express passionately and powerfully that of which others were not aware, or if they were, could not express because they did not possess a creative medium. Throughout her life, Nin was searching for "another kind of language, the inspirational, which is one that penetrates our unconscious directly and doesn't need to be analyzed or interpreted in a cerebral way. It penetrates us in the way that music does, through the senses." That is why Nin, like so many other twentieth century writers, borrowed as widely as possible from the nonverbal arts. "My only structure," she wrote, "is based on three forms of art—painting, dancing, music—because they correspond to the senses I find atrophied in literature today."

Inspired by many artists, including Claude Debussy, Paul Klee, her friend Janko Varda, Richard Lippold, Jean Tinguely, Edgar Varèse, and many others, Nin looked not so much to poets (although Arthur Rimbaud influenced her style as well as her ideas), as to those novelists who were masters of a lyrical style: to D. H. Lawrence, to Jean Giradoux, Pierre Jean Jouve, Djuna Barnes, and, above all, to Marcel Proust. Nin's approach to the novel was that of a poet with a heightened and highly developed sense of language. Oliver Evans, who wrote the first book-length study of her work, called Nin "one of the best imagists writing in this country today." The image was her indispensable medium of expression; free association, which she learned to trust as a patient in psychotherapy, became the process through which she allowed literary structures to emerge. Always, Nin's subject was the self in its evolution, especially the self in relationships with others; her perspective was always psychological (she called psychology her "philosophy" and psychoanalysis her "school"), though her books do not demonstrate any particular school of psychoanalytical thought.

Dispensing with conventional plots and with the framework of linear chronology, Nin portrayed her characters in a series of "shots" that derive their power from the carefully selected detail of their imagery. Her language, never purely decorative, is metaphorical in a truly organic sense. It is the language of lyrical poetry; the essence is compressed into a few words or phrases. Nin does not describe, she interprets, and in the act of interpretation, she re-creates her subjects. To know Nin's characters, the reader, too, must interpret their action, their gestures, look beneath the surfaces.

Free association creates its own unique structures. Nin's writing is filled with patterns that are natural and spontaneous, having emerged from the associative flow of images. The form of her books is organic. Repetitions, inversions, and superimpositions are artfully arranged into significant patterns. Increasingly in Nin's later prose, readers will discover improvisatory flights in which images are treated as are themes in jazz. Fluency, fluidity, a sense of motion as well as continuity are what Nin sought in her fiction, an orchestration of a great many elements into a composition that moves through time horizontally and vertically at the same instant, an orchestration that expresses emotion with sensuousness and with emotional power that are impossible, she believed, to achieve in conventional realistic fiction.

House of Incest is not, technically speaking, a novel, but it is pertinent as being the source, as Nin herself said, of all her later fiction. *House of Incest* is the earliest and most extreme example of her "symphonic writing." It also introduces the essential questions of her lifelong exploration of the problem of reconciling human love with the needs of ever-evolving, mobile people, always in the process of transformation, growing through the process of change.

A prose poem, *House of Incest* was envisioned by Nin as a woman's version of Rimbaud's famed confession, *Une Saison en Enfer* (1873, *A Season in Hell*). She wrote the book between 1932 and 1936 when she was intensely involved with psychotherapy, and it is composed entirely of dreams that have been cut, altered, polished, and artfully arranged to express an agonizing journey into the psyche of the nameless first-person narrator. Her suffering is caused by the sundering of feeling from sensuality, of emotion from sexuality, of body from soul. *House of Incest* is filled with images of fragmentation and mutilation.

Like *A Season in Hell*, Nin's prose poem is a confession. The narrator yearns to express her pain and to confess that even when she imagines that she loves another, it is only a projection of herself. In the other, then, she loves only herself. The "house" of the title refers to the self, perhaps specifically to the body; "incest" suggests the sterility of feeling imprisoned inside this self, unable to transcend its boundaries through the supreme act of loving another.

Two types of "incest" are suggested by the book's two personae, both of whom strongly attract the narrator. They are Sabina, lush, sensuous and irresponsible, freely engaging in sex without emotional commitment; and Jeanne, an aristocrat with a crippled leg, a woman who "strangles" her guitar when she tries to make it produce music. Jeanne is hopelessly in love with her brother. The emotional damage caused by such an inverted fixation is explored in Nin's later works, "The Voice," *Winter of Artifice*, and "Under a Glass Bell" (from the story collection with the same title).

The extreme difficulty of achieving a stable, committed love while continuing to "turn and change" is at the center of all Nin's novels. A positive resolution appears only in the later books, *Seduction of the Minotaur* and *Collages*, both of which are lighter in tone than earlier works. Nin's passionate advocacy of love, all forms of love, suggests an affinity between her work and that of the surrealists. In this respect and also in the great importance placed upon the unconscious and the dream, Nin is an ally of surrealism. At the same time, her methods of writing were opposed to those stated emphatically by André Breton in his famous manifestos and by other surrealist poets. (In *The Novel of the Future*, Nin took up the question of the relationship of her writing to surrealism, perhaps because so often her work has been erroneously labeled surreal.)

Winter of Artifice comprises three "novelettes" (Nin's term): "Stella," *Winter of Artifice*, and "The Voice." Written in 1944 when Nin was planning a series of interconnected novels and struggling with the psychological problems of the woman artist, "Stella" explores the failure of connection between a woman's personal life and her work; this failure is caused by a neurosis that is unchallenged. As a movie star, Stella is much more glamorous, vital, self-assured, and daring than in private life (her "mask" may be said to dominate her "self"). The contrast is so great that when Stella sits in the audience watching one of her own films, she is never recognized. The most important object in her apartment is a "very large, very spacious Movie Star bed of white satin," which she usually occupies alone. The connection that Nin sought between the personal life and the artistic expression of this life does not occur for Stella. Like others, she has been damaged by her childhood, but she has done nothing to repair this damage. Because Stella "did not grow," Nin decided not to include her as one of the major characters in *Cities of the Interior*. Viewed as a psychological portrait of a narcissist, however, "Stella" is an insightful piece of work, and it is brilliantly expressed.

When evaluated exclusively as art, "The Voice" is one of Nin's most original and daring pieces. It is both an extended portrait of a kind and self-neglectful psychotherapist (perhaps suggested by Otto Rank), and an animated essay or exposition of ideas through a seemingly random selection of characters and incidents. "The Voice" is a virtuoso piece that spins off from contrasting motions: soaring, plummeting, floating, sinking, spiraling, rushing and flowing; it is an excellent example of Nin's deft way of translating characters and incidents into imagery. The center of this active world is a psychoanalyst's office located in a skyscraper. Tortured New Yorkers, The Voice's patients include Djuna (who becomes one of the principals in *Cities of the Interior*), a young violinist who wishes to be released from lesbianism; Mischa, a cellist whose emotions are paralyzed; and Lilith, who suffers from frigidity. The Voice himself falls in love with Lilith, the only one of his patients who can see beyond her own needs to the hungers of the man whose voice is so comforting to the others. As in Nin's later books, Djuna plays the role of comforting confidante to both parties in this impossible dream of love between analyst and patient.

Winter of Artifice is perhaps the most "musical" of Nin's works; it is also among the most courageous in its subject: an adult daughter's flirtation and near-union with the handsome, seductive father who abandoned her when she was a child. The theme is "musique Ancienne," to quote Nin, the Oedipal temptation told from the point of view of the highly intelligent yet vulnerable daughter. *Winter of Artifice* was begun in 1933, when Nin started therapy with Rank, and was completed in 1939, the year of Rank's death.

The novelette is organized in thirteen "movements." A climax of emotional and erotic yearning occurs in the sixth, central movement. From this excruciating height of desire, the work subsides into a slower rhythm and a sadder tone. Eventually, *Winter of Artifice* becomes a solo for the daughter. When she sees her father's "feminine-looking" foot, she imagines that it is really her foot and that he has stolen it. Now she understands that he would like to steal her youth and her capacity for action, her mobility. "Tired of his ballet dancing" (formal, traditional movements), the daughter symbolically reclaims her foot and, with it, her ability to flee from the dangers of the attraction: *"Music runs and I run with it."*

The five novels found in the final version of *Cities of the Interior*, Nin's "continuous novel" are *Ladders to Fire, Children of the Albatross, The Four-Chambered Heart, A Spy in the House of Love*, and *Seduction of the Minotaur*. They were first published individually during the 1940's and 1950's. Entries in Nin's diary indicate that she began writing *Ladders to Fire* in 1937; she made substantial revisions as late as 1962. *Seduction of the Minotaur*, which was published individually in 1961, was begun in 1938 and expanded in 1958 to include *Solar Barque*. Alan Swallow, a pioneer among small-press publishers, brought out the five novels under their collective title in 1959. When it was first published, *Cities of the Interior* had been growing for twenty years. An extraordinary work, it displays a brilliance of conception, a mastery of image and metaphor, and a refinement of structural technique that make it the equal of many better-known modern masterpieces.

The title, *Cities of the Interior: A Continuous Novel*, suggests the timeless scope of this work. The "cities" are both ancient and modern. Nin set out to excavate the buried "cities" or the psychic worlds of her three main characters: Lillian, Djuna, and Sabina. The idea of "continuity," however, is more complex. It suggests that *Cities of the Interior* is an "open" work, like certain modern sculptures that extend into and penetrate the space which surrounds them, interacting with their setting.

This multifaceted work is not set apart from life, not carved out of it, not bounded by the conventions of classically written fiction with its concluding "resolution." "Cities of the Interior" remains "open" to the addition of new parts and to the rearrangement of its five basic novel units. The individual books are entirely self-contained. As Nin uses the word, "continuous" does not mean "to be continued." It does not refer to linear progressive time. There is no fixed starting point and no concluding point. The books have been bound—because books, seemingly, must be bound—in the order in which they were written.

A reader can begin with any one of the five volumes and move to the other four in any order, losing no essential connections. In short, the five novels of *Cities of the Interior* are interchangeable in the total composition, which can be viewed as a type of mobile, an innovation in fiction inspired by the example of modern sculpture. Nin's characters are totally immersed in the flow of internalized psychic time, in the patterns of their own growth. One of the main figures in *Collages* quotes the Koran, saying, "Nothing is ever finished." The French philosopher Henri Bergson, whose ideas influenced a number of modern novelists, including Proust, stated the concept of personal evolution succinctly and elegantly: "If matter appeared to us as a perpetual flowering, we should assign no termination to any of our actions." To Nin, life does indeed appear as a "perpetual flowering," In *Cities of the Interior*, she has selected and expressed significant relationships and states of feeling in the ever-changing, continuous process of growth. Life, as distinct from existence, is possible only for those who can accept mutability, knowing that while change promises growth, it also demands inevitable loss.

Lillian's development spans *Cities of the Interior*, opening and closing the work when it is read in conventional sequence. The first part of *Ladders to Fire* describes "This Hunger," Lillian's ravenous need for love. Spontaneous, impetuous, unsure of her physical attractiveness, and compulsively generous, she gives up her career as a pianist so that she can support her lover's ambition to paint, but this sacrifice does not bring her the loyalty and security she desires. Jay repays Lillian's devotion by having affairs with other women.

The most threatening of Lillian's rivals is Sabina. The relationship between these two women is the most compelling in the novel and a superb example of Nin's brilliance at unmasking psychological motivations. When Lillian attempts to stop Sabina's pursuit of Jay by overwhelming the other woman with friendship, she discovers that she, too, is powerfully attracted to Sabina. For different reasons, both women are angry at Jay: Lillian because he has neglected her; Sabina because he would like to conquer her. The two women form an alliance against him. After dancing together in a working-class tavern, they go to Sabina's room to make love, but they discover that it is not sensuality they are seeking in each other so much as an exchange of feminine qualities. They both feel a "mysterious craving . . . to become each other."

During the dazzling party scene with which *Ladders to Fire* closes, Lillian commits "invisible hara-kiri" with an outburst of harmful self-criticism. It is clear to the reader that she has grown, that her anger at herself is partly an expression of this growth, and that she will soon end her unsatisfying relationship with Jay.

A delicate, playful book, with an undercurrent of sadness, *Children of the Albatross* traces a theme that is familiar in French literature but something of a novelty in the United States: the initiation of a young man by an older woman. Djuna, in her late twenties, becomes involved with Paul, seventeen. The other "children" of the novel's title are their friends, young gay men who meet with Paul and Djuna in her "house of innocence and faith." Here, they dance, paint, and play, celebrating their love of freedom from responsibility. The young men and Djuna are drawn together by their mutual fear of tyrannical, authoritarian fathers. For Djuna, this figure is represented by the cruel and lecherous watchman who terrified her when she was a child living in an orphanage. The positive creative act of evoking a counter-world to erect against the conventional and materialistic values of the "fathers" ignites sympathy among the rebellious "children."

From the start of *Children of the Albatross*, it is clear that Djuna's affair with Paul will be brief and will provide her with little emotional sustenance. Predictably, Paul's family disapproves of her, not only because she is "older" but also because she is a dancer. A crucial dream in which Djuna imagines herself as Ariadne predicts that after she has guided Paul safely through the passage from adolescence to early manhood, she will be abandoned. At the novel's end, Paul embarks upon an exciting journey to India, leaving Djuna behind. Feeling empty and dissatisfied, she searches the unexplored "cities" of her self. She begins to seek a fuller emotional life with a more mature partner.

In *The Four-Chambered Heart*, Nin explores the psychological complexity of a woman's involvement with a married man. Romantically ensconced in a houseboat on the Seine are Djuna and Rango, a tempestuous vagabond, so she imagines. Their relationship is initially enthralling but ultimately frustrating; both parties are weighed down by responsibilities to demanding hypocondriacs: he to his wife, Zora; Djuna to her father. Heavy rains force the lovers to move their houseboat up and down the river. Like their relationship, the boat does not "go anywhere"; it merely plies its way back and forth over the same area.

Djuna and Rango's passion attains its height in the novel's first thirty pages. After that, there is conflict and threatened violence. Zora makes a bizarre attempt to kill Djuna. Rango comes to the boat very late one night and falls into a heavy depressed sleep. Djuna, desperate to initiate a change of some sort, rips up floor boards in a wild attempt to sink the boat. It is swept down the river; everyone survives, though not in the same form. A fisherman rescues a doll from the water with a joke about its having tried to commit suicide. The doll is a comment on Djuna's passivity with regard to her own life and to the image of conventional femininity that she has been struggling to maintain, at the expense of her "true" self. It is time for her to move beyond the static situation she experiences with Rango, to give up the illusion of her generosity toward Zora, and to recognize and accept the negative qualities she has been "acting out" through Rango. Djuna must grow.

In *A Spy in the House of Love*, Sabina is portrayed as a glamorous woman seeking to express herself as "Don Juana." Married to a fatherly, indulgent man, she is free to fulfill her desire for adventure, which she experiences through relationships with men. Each of Sabina's partners embodies an aura, a sense of place, an ambience that lies waiting for her exploration and participation. There is the opera star Philip; he represents "Vienna before the war." There is Mambo, a black musician transplanted to Greenwich Village from a Caribbean island. There is John, a former aviator who has been grounded because of uncontrollable anxiety. Finally, there is Donald, a gay man who returns Sabina's maternal love with an irresistibly flattering letter-portrait of her idealized self. This balances the grossly sexual and cruel portrait given to her by her former lover, Jay, a painter.

A Spy in the House of Love is a musical novel both in style and structure. There is a prelude in which Sabina invites the detection of her "crime" (experiencing sex without feeling) by phoning a "lie detector." There is a coda in which Djuna, Sabina's consoling friend, plays a late Beethoven quartet to soothe and heal the dejected Don Juana. The body of the novel is a series of variations on the central theme: Sabina's attempt to live through her relationships with men who—so she deludes herself into believing—have far more exciting lives than she herself has. Each man is associated with a particular type of music, while Igor Stravinsky's "Firebird" is said to be Sabina's "unerring musical autobiography."

At once the most mature in theme and the most resplendent in imagery among Nin's novels, *Seduction of the Minotaur* takes up the story of Lillian.

She has developed considerably since *Ladders to Fire*. Now a jazz performer instead of an interpreter of the classics, Lillian journeys to Mexico, imagining that she has finally freed herself from everything that imprisoned her in the past.

Traveling alone, Lillian meets a series of men, each of whom becomes a teacher or guide of sorts, revealing something of great significance in her own circuitous passage through the labyrinth of the self. The most engaging of these figures is Dr. Hernandez, a male version of Ariadne. He helps Lillian to see that she is not yet as free as she has imagined, wisely telling her that "we live by a series of repetitions until the experience is solved, understood, liquidated." The monster Lillian confronts is a "masked woman," the part of herself that she has previously been unwilling to recognize.

In Lillian's journey to Mexico and her confrontation with herself, Nin creates a living dream simultaneously in the past, present, and future. The meaning of freedom is not flight, as Sabina imagines, but commitment. If a woman can discover and love the many aspects of one man, she can be fulfilled with a single love. Lillian learns to see her husband Larry, from whom she has been separated, as a complex, multidimensional person. This discovery brings a new excitement, a forgiveness, the grace of understanding to her feelings about him. Because she untangles the knots in her own past, Lillian rediscovers the love of her husband. Thus, there is reconciliation instead of separation.

A more ambitious and a deeper book than its easy surface and gentle humor suggest, *Collages* is composed of nineteen short blocks of prose, showing once again Nin's preference for constructed rather than narrated fiction. *Collages* begins and ends with the same passage. Its circular structure encloses twenty-two characters portrayed in a wide variety of quickly sketched settings. The cement that binds these colorful elements into a composition is Renate, a woman artist who "makes her own patterns." She weaves in and out of the lives of the others, bringing inspiration not only to her paintings but also to her friends.

Collage art is shown to work magic transformations. In this book, Nin once again stresses the many ways in which dream and fantasy enrich life. There is an intense relationship, for example, between a young woman and a raven. An elderly man feels closer to seals than to human beings; he finally develops the courage to renounce people in order to live with the animals he loves. A gardener pretends to be a millionaire in order to fulfill his dream of financing a literary magazine. A woman whose husband has rejected her for a younger woman replaces him with an exotic phantom lover. In *Collages*, imagination is sovereign.

The healing power of genuine relationships is shown as complementary to that of creative fantasy. *Collages* closes with the reluctant emergence of a woman writer from a bitter, self-imposed isolation. Elderly Judith Sands allows herself to be "courted" by Renate and an Israeli admirer, Dr. Mann. Made more trusting by their friendship, Sands actually shows the visitors one of her manuscripts. Its opening words are the same words with which *Collages* begins. This repetition helps endow *Collages* with its circular form and also underscores Nin's conviction that there is an unbroken connection from one person to another, one imaginative writer to another, and that life is redeemed through the alchemical transformation of art. *Collages* is an assured and accomplished example of Nin's skill at adapting techniques from the nonverbal arts to literature; it is also the most imaginatively conceived of display of her convictions about the mutually nourishing exchange between art and life.

Sharon Spencer

Other major works

SHORT FICTION: *Under a Glass Bell and Other Stories*, 1944; *Delta of Venus: Erotica*, 1977; *Waste of Timelessness and Other Early Stories*, 1977; *Little Birds: Erotica*, 1979.

NONFICTION: *D. H. Lawrence: An Unprofessional Study*, 1932; *Realism and Reality*, 1946; *On Writing*, 1947; *The Diary of Anaïs Nin: 1931-1934*, 1966; *The Diary of Anaïs Nin: 1934-1939*, 1967; *The Novel of the Future*, 1968; *The Diary of Anaïs Nin: 1939-1944*, 1969; *The Diary of Anaïs Nin: 1944-1947*, 1971; *Paris Revisited*, 1972; *The Diary of Anaïs Nin: 1947-1955*, 1974; *A Photographic Supplement to the Diary of Anaïs Nin*, 1974; *A Woman Speaks: The Lectures, Seminars, and Interviews of Anaïs Nin*, 1975; *The Diary of Anaïs Nin: 1955-1966*, 1976; *In Favor of the Sensitive Man and Other Essays*, 1976; *Linotte: The Early Diary of Anaïs Nin, 1914-1920*, 1978; *The Diary of Anaïs Nin: 1966-1974*, 1980; *The Early Diary of Anaïs Nin: Volume Two, 1920-1923*, 1982.

Bibliography

Evans, Oliver. *Anaïs Nin*. Carbondale: Southern Illinois University Press, 1968. The result of a twenty-year study of the work and life of Nin. Through extensive research, reading, and lengthy personal interviews, Evans provides new and insightful interpretations of *House of Incest*, Nin's first two diaries, and other major fiction works, but omits Nin's nonfiction works. Nin is presented as a writer in the genre of her good friend Henry Miller. Also contains detailed end notes and an index.

Franklin, Benjamin, and Duane Schneider. *Anaïs Nin: An Introduction*. Athens: Ohio University Press, 1979. A complete study of the canon of Nin's works, encompassing all of her early fiction works (*Under a Glass Bell and Other Stories* through *Collages*) and devoted to much discussion of the first six volumes of her diary (written between 1931 and 1966). A third section briefly covers Nin's criticism and her nonfiction and presents Nin as a

feminist writer. Notes to every chapter are included, as well as an excellent
selected bibliography (with an annotated list of secondary sources) and an
index.

Hinz, Evelyn J. *The Mirror and the Garden: Realism and Reality in the
Writings of Anaïs Nin*. 2d ed. New York: Harcourt Brace Jovanovich, 1973.
Envisioned as a continuing study of a living writer, viewing Nin not only as
a feminist writer but also as an American one. Her understanding and
presentation of the psychological novel is examined at length in the context
of her major fiction works. Nin's self-examination in her first four diaries
and her critical methodology are also discussed. A bibliography of works
and secondary sources (including journal articles) is included with an
index.

Spencer, Sharon. *Collage of Dreams: The Writings of Anaïs Nin*. Chicago:
Swallow Press, 1981. Represents a definitive study of the diaries of Nin.
Spencer painstakingly compares the themes of important Nin works—
including a brief mention of the D. H. Lawrence study—to events in her
life as documented in the diaries. Augmented by an index, a selected
bibliography, and extensive notes.

Zaller, Robert, ed. *A Casebook on Anaïs Nin*. New York: New American
Library, 1974. This collection of essays is useful as a chronological study
of the emergence of Nin as a feminist and novelist. Focuses on her early
novels, including *House of Incest*, and moves on quickly to *Cities of the
Interior* and the first and fourth volumes of her diary.

FRANK NORRIS

Born: Chicago, Illinois; March 5, 1870
Died: San Francisco, California; October 25, 1902

Principal long fiction

Moran of the Lady Letty, 1898; *McTeague*, 1899; *Blix*, 1899; *A Man's Woman*, 1900; *The Octopus*, 1901; *The Pit*, 1903; *Vandover and the Brute*, 1914.

Other literary forms

Frank Norris' published work includes poems, short stories, essays, newspaper articles, novels, and literary criticism. Although he is best-known today for his novels, Norris is also remembered for his popular short-story contributions to the San Francisco *Wave*, and his insightful literary criticism, published in *The Responsibilities of the Novelist* (1903) and *The Literary Criticism of Frank Norris* (1964).

Norris' first published book, *Yvernelle: A Tale of Feudal France* (published in 1892 while Norris was still in college), was neither a short story nor a novel, but a medieval love poem written in the romantic-verse style of Sir Walter Scott. Had it not been subsidized by Gertrude Norris (the author's mother), the book would probably never have been published. Today it is notable only for the high price it brings in the rare book trade.

Norris' success as a reporter was also minimal. His reports on the Boer War were published in the San Francisco *Chronicle*, but his later writings on the Spanish-American War were not published for some time afterward, and never by *McClure's Magazine*, which originally sent him there.

Norris was successful, however, as a short-story writer. Much of his early work first appeared in the San Francisco *Wave*, a weekly newspaper featuring mostly local literary talent. The stories he wrote for the newspaper were later collected in three volumes: *A Deal in Wheat and Other Stories of the New and Old West* (1903), *The Third Circle* (1909), and *Frank Norris of "The Wave"* (1931).

The majority of Norris' writings were collected in a ten-volume *Complete Edition*, published by Doubleday, Doran and Company in 1928. That same year, Doubleday also issued the Argonaut manuscript edition of Norris' works. Identical in content with the *Complete Edition*, the Argonaut manuscript edition was finely bound and included a manuscript page from *McTeague*. In recent years, more Norris pieces have been unearthed, including his Harvard student theses. Today, the record of his brief literary career is almost complete. His major works are still in print in both hardcover and inexpensive paperbound editions.

Achievements

Called by many (including himself) "the boy Zola" because his style was so reminiscent of that French author's writings, Norris spearheaded the naturalistic movement in American literature. Although Norris' contemporaries were, by and large, critical of his portrayal of the savage, seamy side of life, it is that very quality in his work which has helped to keep his fiction alive and readable. Even more than his challenge to the Victorian code of the turn of the century, Norris' capacity to portray corruption and its evil effects upon man and his ability to make scenes and characters seem vibrant and real, will rank him high among twentieth century writers.

Norris never achieved the immense popularity of some of the other writers of his day, such as Jack London. He did not even live to see his most successful novel, *The Pit*, become a best-seller. Indeed, it was not until publication of *The Octopus* that he was able to enjoy even a modest financial success. His readers were simply not able to accept his preoccupation with sordid realities, including his treatment of sex, which by Victorian standards was quite shocking. Because of his unsavory choice of subject matter, Norris was ignored by reviewers who understood only the elegant prose and fine writing of an earlier era. Today, Norris' pioneering work in American naturalism is universally acknowledged.

Biography

Frank Norris was the son of Benjamin Franklin Norris, a successful businessman specializing in wholesale jewelry, and Gertrude Doggett. Born in 1870, Norris' early years were spent in Chicago. Except for a trip to Europe when he was eight, Norris' childhood was rather uneventful.

At fourteen, Norris moved with his family to California. They settled first in Oakland and then moved to a large house on Sacramento Street in San Francisco. Benjamin Norris began a real-estate-development business, building cheap houses for working-class people to rent, and enjoyed financial success. His son would later write about these houses in his first novel.

Frank Norris found San Francisco stimulating. The family home was located only a block from fashionable Van Ness Avenue with its ongoing series of parades and pageants, and only a few blocks from the business section of Polk Street with its rich variety of small shops—there was even a dental parlor with a grotesque golden tooth sign hanging from the building. The scenes and settings were memorable, and Norris captured many of them for later use as local color in his novels.

In 1885, Norris was enrolled in the Belmont Academy. This marked the beginning of a long, largely unsuccessful attempt at formal schooling. Norris had neither the temperament nor the talent in mathematics for scholarship, and, after breaking his arm playing football scarcely a year after enrolling, he quit the Academy for a convalescence at home. It was during this period that he made up his mind to pursue a career as an artist.

After a short stint at Boy's High School, Norris convinced his parents to send him to the San Francisco Art Association School. His success there persuaded Benjamin Norris to send him to the finest art schools in Paris. While Norris did not learn how to paint in Paris, he did learn the fundamentals and principles of art, and also the discipline which would later serve him well as a writer.

Convinced that his son was not spending his time painting, Norris' father called him home in 1889. Norris returned from France with a new interest in writing and, more important, a solid foundation upon which to build his writing career.

In the fall of 1890, Norris entered the University of California, determined to become a writer. Almost at once he found himself at odds with the English Department faculty over proper methods of composition. His academic progress in mathematics was abysmal. Norris turned to a more social life and joined Phi Gamma Delta fraternity. There he found a perfect outlet for his frustrations and a wealth of amusements to occupy his time. Although his academic career at Berkeley was undistinguished, Norris' fraternity pranks were memorable.

While Norris was gaining a reputation as a prankster, his family was quickly breaking apart, and Benjamin Norris left, alone, for Europe; while on the trip, he fell in love with another woman. Upon his return, he divorced Gertrude, married his new love, and moved to Chicago; Norris never saw his father again.

In 1894, Norris' marginal academic success caught up with him. Although he had done well in Joseph Le Conte's science classes, his failures in mathematics forced him to leave the university without a degree. Harvard appealed to him as the proper place to polish his writing talents, so he enrolled the following fall as a special student, taking courses in English and French. There he found success in the classes taught by Professor Lewis Gates. Under Gates's watchful eye, Norris began work on his first two novels: *Vandover and the Brute* and *McTeague*.

After a year at Harvard, Norris returned to San Francisco, taking a job with the *Chronicle* as a special correspondent. He convinced the paper to send him to South Africa, where he covered the beginnings of the Boer War. Norris' reports from the strife-torn land were not memorable, but the tropical fever he contracted would later contribute to his death.

Norris next joined the staff of the San Francisco *Wave*, then under the editorship of John O'Hara Cosgrave. As an assistant editor, Norris wrote short stories, reviewed books and art exhibits, and composed feature stories to fill the pages of the weekly newspaper. He found it impossible to work for extended periods of time, however, and interrupted his employment at least twice: once to journey to the Big Dipper Mine near Colfax, California, where he finished *McTeague*; another time to begin work on his third novel, *Moran of the Lady Letty*. He found no trouble selling the first installments of this new novel to the magazines, and as it was running, the story caught the eye of S. S. McClure, who invited Norris to join the staff of Doubleday as a reader. The position paid poorly and offered little status, but Norris took it anyway, perhaps because it allowed him time to finish *Moran of the Lady Letty* and begin other projects as well. After a time, however, Norris began to hate his self-imposed poverty and, at the outbreak of the Spanish-American War, begged McClure to send him to Cuba to cover the conflict as a correspondent for *McClure's Magazine*. McClure agreed; Norris went to Cuba, met Stephen Crane, suffered another attack of fever, and was forced to return to New York. *McClure's Magazine* did not publish any of Norris' war reports.

Never sure of his status with McClure, Norris left the firm in 1899 to join the newly founded firm of Doubleday, Page & Company, again as a part-time, poorly paid reader. He wrote *Blix* and *A Man's Woman*, and began *The Octopus* during this time, and also married Jeannette Black. His major contribution to the firm came when Theodore Dreiser's *Sister Carrie* was submitted; Norris read the novel in manuscript and insisted upon its publication. After a contract was signed, Doubleday raised objections to the novel and tried to cancel publication. Norris counseled Dreiser to stand firm and insist that his contract be upheld; whereupon Doubleday issued *Sister Carrie* in a limited edition and allowed it quickly to go out of print.

As Norris' royalities grew from the sale of his own novels, he found the financial independence to return to California, and he made plans to purchase a ranch in the southern range of the Santa Cruz mountains. He completed *The Pit*, the second book in his projected trilogy of wheat novels, and planned a journey to the tropics with his wife. That journey was interrupted, however, when Jeannette underwent surgery to remove an inflamed appendix. While she was recovering in the hospital, Norris, too, began suffering stomach pains. Thinking it only a minor ailment, he refused to go to a doctor until he became seriously ill. Suffering from peritonitis and weakened by fever, Norris entered Mt. Zion hospital in San Francisco and died there on October 25, 1902, at the age of thirty-two.

Analysis

Frank Norris was one of a handful of writers at the turn of the century who applied the literary naturalism of Émile Zola to American subjects and themes. As a writer in this tradition, Norris treated his subject matter brutally but sincerely. His characters are but pawns, driven by outside forces over which they have no control. Devoid of souls, they are helpless creatures determined by their heredity and environment. In Norris' most successful novels, these naturalistic ideas are employed with great faithfulness, and his depiction of human beings following a slow but inevitable course toward destruction has an enduring power.

Norris' fiction underwent various stages of development. In *McTeague* and *Vandover and the Brute*, Norris focused his attentions on the naturalistic novel of character, where both McTeague and Vandover proceed slowly toward their inevitable destruction. In Norris' next three novels, *Moran of the Lady Letty*, *Blix*, and *A Man's Woman*, he bowed to social pressure: moral values overwhelm deterministic forces in these inferior works. In Norris' last two novels, *The Octopus* and *The Pit*, he again returned to naturalistic themes, but in a broader, more worldly sense, showing greater compassion and involvement with his characters. The progression from *Vandover and the Brute*, a highly dispassionate view of one man's descent, to *The Pit*, which analyzes the social forces at work in the wheat industry, marks Norris' own maturation as both a writer and a man, and his increasingly complex world view.

Written while Norris was still in college, *Vandover and the Brute* is concerned with moral weakness. It is the story of a wealthy man who, unable to sustain his ambition to become an artist, descends to a bestial level. As a study of moral and physical disintegration, the novel follows a characteristically didactic naturalistic course. Vandover's descent is governed by a series of chance events and hastened by his own flawed heredity. Because his position in society allows it, Vandover leads a life of pointless leisure. Unable to focus his desire to become an artist, he starts gambling, drinking, and begins leading a loose sexual life. A chance cut on his lip, followed by an unwanted kiss from Flossie (who by chance has contracted syphilis), passes a venereal disease to Vandover and eventually causes lycanthropy.

With the aid of Professor Le Conte's classes in science, Norris was able to research the disease which plagued Vandover. His careful analysis led to Vandover's realistic progression toward lycanthropy, which begins with the suicide of Ida Wade, one of the girls whom Vandover has seduced. Soon after Ida's death, Vandover's father dies, an event which seems to give Vandover direction, but the beast within him soon triumphs, the disease is allowed to run its course, and Vandover becomes a wretched, broken man. The novel concludes with Vandover cleaning the cheap houses Norris' father built for the San Francisco working class, although in the novel, the houses belonged to Vandover.

McTeague was written soon after the completion of *Vandover and the Brute*; like Norris' first book, it emphasizes themes of chance, disintegration, and heredity. The novel is a study of the temperaments of two characters: McTeague, a scoundrel born in a California mining town, and Trina Sieppe, a working-class girl whose hoarding instincts eventually overcome her.

As the novel begins, McTeague is working with his father in the California mines. A traveling dentist arrives shortly after McTeague's father dies, and the young boy is apprenticed to the dentist so that he might learn a trade. McTeague is not bright enough to learn much—the result of his heredity—

but he eventually learns enough to survive, and when his mother dies, he sets up dental parlors in San Francisco. The rich descriptive detail with which Norris renders McTeague's surroundings greatly contributes to the success of the novel.

McTeague is well-satisfied with his existence: the earnings from his practice keep him supplied with a daily glass of steam beer, and allow him enough leisure time to practice his concertina and socialize infrequently with his friends, among them Marcus Schouler, who lives in the flat above McTeague. Chance, however, intervenes in McTeague's ordered existence when Marcus' girl friend, Trina, breaks a tooth, and Marcus brings her to McTeague for treatment. While they wait in the parlors, Trina buys a lottery ticket from the cleaning woman—a ticket which, later, will be worth five thousand dollars.

McTeague falls in love with Trina at first sight, and Marcus, rather than fighting for his girl, aids McTeague in courting her, even to the point of introducing him to Trina's parents. The path paved, McTeague asks Trina to marry him, and, on the day the announcement is made public, Trina wins the money through the lottery. It is this chance event which sparks Trina's inherited passion for hoarding, first evident on the day of the lottery payment when Trina, to McTeague's dismay, decides not to spend her winnings on a nice apartment, but rather to save the money. This first clash of temperaments leads to others as McTeague and Trina continue toward their eventual disintegration.

At first, Trina and McTeague are happy; they move into a flat across from the dental parlors and live comfortably. McTeague's ambitions to live in more spacious quarters, however, conflict with Trina's thrifty attitudes. Marcus reenters their lives; embittered by McTeague's good fortune, he attacks McTeague with a knife. This first conflict arouses physical violence in both men only briefly, but during their second encounter, which begins as a friendly wrestling match at the park, Marcus bites off McTeague's earlobe and McTeague retaliates by breaking Marcus' arm. After the incident, Marcus leaves the city, but not before first notifying the authorities that McTeague is practicing dentistry without proper credentials.

Stripped of his profession, McTeague loses his income, thus exacerbating his conflict with Trina over the management of their money. The animal within him brought to the surface, McTeague is no longer able to cope with his environment or with Trina's hoarding, which has become obsessive. He deserts Trina and then comes back and steals her money. After he has spent all the money, McTeague returns to Trina for more. This time, however, he beats her so mercilessly that she dies. Taking her entire lottery winnings, McTeague flees the city for the gold mines and his birthplace. He is followed, however, and forced to flee again, to Death Valley, where he again meets Marcus. This time, however, the struggle their encounter precipitates is fatal to both.

The parallels between *McTeague* and *Vandover and the Brute* are numerous. Both novels owe their genesis to the idea of human degeneracy: *Vandover and the Brute* is the story of one man's descent into the abyss; *McTeague* shows how the interaction of two characters hastens their descent. Chance also plays an important part in both novels. Vandover's cut lip becomes Trina's broken tooth; gambling for Vandover becomes the lottery for Trina. Life itself is a gigantic lottery; Norris is emphatic when he labels the agent of the lottery a "man of the world."

By separating himself from his characters in *McTeague*, Norris was able to deal objectively with the impact of instinct and chance upon them. McTeague becomes an animal—a brute from the mines. Trina, too, crippled by her hoarding instinct both physically (her fingers are amputated) and mentally, becomes little more than an animal, defending her gold as a wolf might defend its kill. *McTeague* is Norris' most powerful and successful novel; his rendering of the seamy, bestial side of human life is masterful.

Moran of the Lady Letty was Norris' third novel in manuscript, but his first in print. Unlike his first two books, *Moran of the Lady Letty* emphasizes the idyllic side of San Francisco: its festive life and colors and the invigorating wind from the Pacific. The story of a strong, primitive woman and an over-civilized man, the novel lacks the realistic intensity of *McTeague*; it is in many ways merely a popular romance.

Ross Wilbur is, like Vandover, a wealthy man. He spends every waking moment attending "functions": teas, cotillions, parties, and other festive gatherings of society. He also enjoys life at the docks and often spends time there gazing at the ships setting out to sea. One day, his shipwatching activities prove perilous, as Wilbur finds himself drugged and shanghaied aboard a filthy schooner piloted by a brutal captain and manned by an unsavory Chinese crew. Wilbur awakens to face the filth of the cabin and a new life aboard the *Bertha Milner*. Quickly, he shows his adaptive abilities as he adjusts to his new environment, hastened by a smashing blow to the chin by the half-civilized captain. As he adjusts to his new life, Wilbur also learns the intricacies of navigation (as Norris did when writing the novel) and the wonders of the sea, including the excitement of a sea-turtle chase. Life, it seems, is not so bad after all.

Soon after weighing anchor, the Chinese crew sights a ship at sea. The captain realizes that the bark they have sighted, the *Lady Letty*, is deserted save for its dead captain and his half-dead daughter, Moran. Consumed with greed, Captain Kitchell plots a salvage of the *Lady Letty* and her cargo, and Moran's murder, too, should she stand in his way. The greed which destroyed Trina in *McTeague* also kills Kitchell, however, when, while he is drunk aboard the *Lady Letty*, a sudden squall sinks the ship. Wilbur and Moran are suddenly left to fend for themselves aboard the *Bertha Milner* with her Chinese crew.

The strange adventures which follow serve to further Wilbur's advancement

Critical Survey of Long Fiction

to manhood. Encountering a Chinese junk, Wilbur and Moran become embroiled in a battle with its crew over a piece of ambergris. In the heat of the battle, Moran mistakes Wilbur for the enemy, and he is forced to subdue her physically. She melts at his physical prowess and surrenders to him. Ross Wilbur, at last, through the vigorous life of the sea, has become a man. In keeping with the theme of the novel—that civilization and social convention are corrupting—Wilbur's softness, brought on by society's overcivilization, is defeated. He has overcome Moran, who knows only the law of the strongest, and has vanquished her according to her own rules.

Except for the naturalistic details of sheer strength and primitive passions, and a few realistic descriptive passages, *Moran of the Lady Letty* is little more than "a corking good story," as Norris described it. He followed similar popular conventions in his next two novels, *Blix* and *A Man's Woman*, before returning in a more ambitious fashion to the naturalistic formulas he so ably employed in *McTeague*.

The third stage of Norris' development as a novelist came about with his projected trilogy on the wheat industry. In the first novel of the trilogy, *The Octopus*, Norris returned to naturalistic formulas. In *The Octopus*, the wheat is planted, grown, and harvested. In *The Pit*, the wheat is traded and taken to market. In *The Wolf*, the planned but never written conclusion to the trilogy, the wheat would be consumed by the hungry masses of Europe. Norris did not live to complete this third book. When he died in 1902, the second volume was only then being serialized.

The Octopus and *The Pit* both deal with the problems of society as a whole rather than with the individual. While Norris was successful in remaining true to his theme in *The Octopus*, the theme and naturalistic treatment is blurred somewhat in *The Pit* by a dual story: the trading of wheat in the Chicago Board of Trade, and the love story featuring the protagonists of the novel, Curtis Jadwin and Laura Dearborn.

Jadwin, a weak, irresolute man, is a famous capitalist speculator. A taker of chances, he manages for a time to corner the wheat market and enjoy financial prosperity. His fortunes are wiped out, however, when the wheat crops of the West are harvested. Helpless in the face of vast economic forces which he cannot control—and helpless too in the face of his own heredity, which has forced upon him an uncontrollable urge to gamble—Jadwin is destroyed.

There is another story in *The Pit*, however, which runs concurrent to the story of Jadwin's business: the story of the love between Jadwin and Laura, his wife. Laura feels alone and deserted when Jadwin occupies himself in the pit, completely absorbed in the business of trading wheat, and so has an affair with Sheldon Corthell, a superficial artist. The collapse of Jadwin's fortune in wheat breaks him completely and, with nowhere else to turn, he reasserts his love for Laura. The novel ends, anticlimactically, with Laura and Jadwin facing the west, ready to begin life anew. Thus, although powerful in its conception, Norris' last novel is not equal to his best work. He largely neglects his theme (the wheat is rarely physically present in the novel), abandoning naturalistic forces in favor of a love story with autobiographical overtones.

At his best when objectively and dispassionately analyzing his characters and allowing them to be subjected, like pawns, to the naturalistic forces of the universe, Norris faltered when he became too closely involved with his subject. When as in *Blix, Moran of the Lady Letty,* and *The Pit,* romantic themes are allowed to gain paramount importance, Norris' naturalistic intentions and power are subverted. Norris was more, however, than a didactic sociologist in the guise of a novelist. His best work is characterized by a faithful reproduction of setting, by creative exuberance. Thus, one does not merely read about Polk Street in *McTeague,* or the San Joaquin Valley in *The Octopus,* or the Board of Trade in *The Pit,* but one also breathes the air of these places, smells their pungent smells. It is this fundamental sense of reality which gives Norris' fiction a lasting appeal.

David Mike Hamilton

Other major works

SHORT FICTION: *A Deal in Wheat and Other Stories of the New and Old West,* 1903; *The Joyous Miracle,* 1906; *The Third Circle,* 1909; *Frank Norris of "The Wave,"* 1931 (Oscar Lewis, editor).

POETRY: *Yvernelle: A Tale of Feudal France,* 1892; *Two Poems and "Kim" Reviewed,* 1930.

NONFICTION: *The Responsibilities of the Novelist,* 1903; *The Surrender of Santiago,* 1917; *The Letters of Frank Norris,* 1956; *The Literary Criticism of Frank Norris,* 1964.

MISCELLANEOUS: *The Complete Edition of Frank Norris,* 1928.

Bibliography

Dillingham, William B. *Frank Norris: Instinct and Art.* Lincoln: University of Nebraska Press, 1969. This compact book provides useful information, outlining Norris' life, career, themes, forms, and style. Identifies the mystery instinct, the dark side of humanity, and masculinity as three important themes and addresses Norris' sense of fiction. Includes a bibliography, notes, and an index.

French, Warren. *Frank Norris.* Boston: Twayne, 1962. This book-length study supports John Berryman's comment that Norris was "a romantic moralist, with a style like a great wet dog." Argues that Norris is more closely linked to transcendentalism than to European naturalism. Contains a chronology, notes, a bibliography, and an index.

Graham, Don. *The Fiction of Frank Norris: The Aesthetic Context.* Columbia:

University of Missouri Press, 1978. Following an apologia for writing about an author who some readers may not enjoy greatly, Graham analyzes the aesthetic aspects of Norris' *Vandover and the Brute*, *McTeague*, *The Octopus*, and *The Pit*. An afterword highlights Norris' uniqueness. Supplemented by a good bibliography and an index.

Marchand, Ernest. *Frank Norris: A Study*. New York: Octagon Books, 1964. Studies Norris in the context of the wider social, intellectual, and literary background of his period. Addresses his view of the novel, social ideas, and style and ends with a critical evaluation, a bibliography, and an index.

Pizer, Donald, ed. *The Literary Criticism of Frank Norris*. Austin: University of Texas Press, 1964. Attempts to correct deficiencies in a posthumous 1903 collection of Norris criticism. The collection is organized into five parts, each of which treats a relevant facet of criticism. Contains an introductory essay, a note on authorship, a bibliographical note, a checklist of literary criticism, and an index.

_____. *The Novels of Frank Norris*. Bloomington: Indiana University Press, 1966. Studies Norris' mind and art by examining his novels and ideas. Approaches the novels as "all of a piece," maintaining that they "arise out of a coherent conception of man, nature, and God." In addition to a preface and an introduction, includes notes, a selected bibliography, and an index.

JOYCE CAROL OATES

Born: Lockport, New York; June 16, 1938

Principal long fiction

With Shuddering Fall, 1964; *A Garden of Earthly Delights*, 1967; *Expensive People*, 1968; *them*, 1969; *Wonderland*, 1971; *Do with Me What You Will*, 1973; *The Assassins: A Book of Hours*, 1975; *Childwold*, 1976; *The Triumph of the Spider Monkey*, 1976; *Son of the Morning*, 1978; *Unholy Loves*, 1979; *Cybele*, 1979; *Bellefleur*, 1980; *Angel of Light*, 1981; *A Bloodsmoor Romance*, 1982; *Mysteries of Winterthurn*, 1984; *Solstice*, 1985; *Marya: A Life*, 1986; *Lives of the Twins*, 1987 (as Rosamond Smith); *You Must Remember This*, 1987; *American Appetites*, 1989; *Soul/Mate*, 1989 (as Rosamond Smith); *Because It Is Bitter, and Because It Is My Heart*, 1990; *I Lock My Door Upon Myself*, 1990; *The Rise of Life on Earth*, 1991.

Other literary forms

Oates's first play, *Miracle Play*, appeared in 1974, and others have since opened to appreciative audiences. In addition her short-story anthologies have been published with regularity. They include *By the North Gate* (1963), which predated her first novel; *Upon the Sweeping Flood* (1966); *The Wheel of Love* (1970); *Marriages and Infidelities* (1972); *The Goddess and Other Women* (1974); *The Hungry Ghosts* (1974); *Where Are You Going, Where Have You Been?* (1974); *The Poisoned Kiss* (1975); *The Seduction* (1975); *Crossing the Border* (1976); *Night-Side* (1977); *All the Good People I've Left Behind* (1978); *A Sentimental Education* (1980); *Last Days* (1984); *Raven's Wing* (1986); *The Assignation* (1988); and many others. Oates is the editor of several anthologies, including *Night Walks* (1982) and *First Person Singular* (1983). Her poems have also been anthologized, and in 1974 Oates and her husband founded *The Ontario Review*.

Achievements

As a writer who avidly embraces the contingencies of this world and a teacher who maintains her classroom along with an amazing proliferation of writing, Joyce Carol Oates has been awarded numerous and varied prizes. Among them are the 1967, 1969, and 1973 O. Henry Prize Awards, the Richard and Hinda Rosenthal Award of the National Institute of Arts and Letters (1968), the National Book Award for 1970, and the Lotos Club Award of Merit (1975).

Biography

Joyce Carol Oates was born on June 16, 1938, in Lockport, New York. She received a modest education in a one-room schoolhouse and, as a child, had very little exposure to literature. This, however, did not quell her desire to write, and she spent much of her time as a child writing stories and short books. Even with all the writing and composing experience from her childhood, she would not publish her first story until 1959. While studying at Syracuse University, she won the *Mademoiselle* college fiction award for her short story "In the Old World." This would be her first in a series of public recognitions for her writing.

After receiving her B.A. from Syracuse in 1960, where she was valedictorian, she went on to receive her M.A. from the University of Wisconsin. During her term at Syracuse, she had met her future husband, Raymond J. Smith, and they married in 1961. The Smiths then moved to Beaumont, Texas, and Oates began to work on her Ph.D. at Rice University. She would never accomplish this task; she and her husband moved to Michigan in 1962. While in Michigan, she taught English at the University of Detroit. This would continue until 1967, when she and her husband began teaching at the University of Windsor in Ontario. During their tenure at the university, Smith and Oates cofounded *The Windsor Review*. After leaving the university in 1978, she went on to join the Princeton University Creative Writing Program. While a member of this program, she wrote not only fiction but also some brilliant essays on writers ranging from William Shakespeare to Norman Mailer.

Analysis

To say that Joyce Carol Oates is one of the most talented and prolific writers in America is to say that the ocean is salty. There have been few to match her for sheer numbers—her novels, plays, short stories, and poems appear to multiply by themselves on library shelves. Yet even though the curse of quantity is normally mediocrity, Oates consistently supplies a product of the highest quality, dense with meaning and filled with beautiful words and full-blown characters.

Oates's poor, unimaginative characters typically ply their swords through a fogged-in existence inflicted upon them by a fatalistic creator. They cannot escape from the miasma they must breathe, and so they are poisoned by it, confused by muddled thoughts in an unkind world. The characters finally become enraged by their situation and so do bloody battle to extricate themselves from it.

In her first novel, *With Shuddering Fall*, Oates introduces a theme that would pervade almost all the rest of her fiction works: the awful responsibility of freedom. Her characters struggle to divest themselves of their little lives in order to achieve personal freedom, but they are unable to cope with the consequences of their release from their former lives. They learn that they have abandoned not only their pasts but also their identities. Then they must struggle either to reclaim their selves or to forge new ones.

With Shuddering Fall is one character's reconciliation with her life, and this treaty gains for her a new appreciation of her history and that of her family. Karen must endure a sort of familiar ritual under the hands of her father, Hert, and her lover, Shar. At first Karen rejects her father's values. He is a legendary figure who wields great power and enjoys a close relationship with Karen; however, this is destroyed by the arrival of the violent, virile Shar who deposes Hert. Shar is not a new ruler, however, but an anarchist who wishes only to topple kings, not replace them. He leaves, and Karen follows, not because she believes in him but because she seeks to escape Hert and "a life dominated by fathers." Once free from her father, Karen begins to feel uprooted, aimless and nameless. Without Hert, she has "nothing of herself but a face, a body, a set of emotions." There is nothing of depth to her being. She discovers that she needs her familial history to add meaning to her identity and so finally refuses the history-less Shar and his attempts at nihilism.

One of these trials is Shar's proclivity for race-car driving in the lowland town of Cherry River. Cherry River is a town that seems to exist for the edification of the summer tourists and little else. It offers appreciation of self-gratification but not of history. The high point of the summer seems to be when Shar commits suicide on the race track. Oates seems to be saying that in a community with no shared history, the only communal ties that exist are with shared acts of violence.

The spokesperson for the novel is Max, a self-centered businessman, who is the only one intelligent enough to share Oates's philosophy with the reader. He appears in many other novels as the maniacal oracle who tries to make Fate subservient to his will. He tries to cheat Karen of her birthright by confounding her with questions, but she eludes him and is, thus, saved. She returns to herself, her family.

An unusual tale, *Expensive People* opens with the fictional narrator explaining to the reader that he is telling the truth. Richard Everett begins by setting up a paradox because nothing he "tells" can ever be the truth since everything in the book is imagined. Then he goes on to explain he is—or was—a child murderer in the sense that when he was young, he killed someone. *Expensive People* is written as a memoir, a memoir of someone who does not exist. In fact, Everett confesses that "it's possible that I'm lying without knowing it."

If *Expensive People* appears to be a parody of comic nihilism, of the nothingness of suburban life, it is. From Ernest Hemingway to John Barth, Oates pokes fun at those serious authors who proclaim the world to be formless and empty. Everett's mother, ironically nicknamed Nada, writes in her journal: "[I]n any first-person narration there can be a lot of freedom. Certain central events—what the hell can they be?—leading up to the death," certainly no less a self-criticism of the very novel she is in as well as those she despises for their negativism.

If Nada consoles herself with her own writing, poor Richard has little with which to comfort himself, unless it is the thought of his mother's death. He is convinced that she hates him, despite his near genius I.Q., and wishes to stave off his affections with a series of unwanted puppies. Finally, Richard's fantasies of matricide become confused with reality. In the end, the newspapers show nothing of Nada, only of their house. Richard fades into closure of the book.

It is not chance that Lewis Carroll's child adventure and Oates's novel *Wonderland* bear the same word in the title. Oates considers the work of this nineteenth century English mathematician to ask the pertinent questions of life: Can all of life be just a game, and am I the only one who is not cheating? Both protagonists in the novels—Alice and Jesse Harte—run and jump from square to square on a large, mostly unseen chessboard. Along the way they are both transmogrified into oddly sized versions of their original selves. Finally, in order to survive, Jesse and Alice regain their normal proportions and become resolved with their communities.

In the beginning of Oates's novel, the newly orphaned Jesse travels from his grandfather's farm to an orphanage and finally to the home of Dr. Pedersen, a brilliant but unbalanced surrogate father. He is the first of a triumvirate of adoptive fathers whom Jesse must survive. His biological father's initial attack has given Jesse the strength to deal with these surrogates. His father has slaughtered his wife and their unborn child and wounded Jesse before killing himself. Jesse escapes to his grandfather's farm where he recuperates until he must start his strange odyssey. In the Pedersen family, Jesse learns of things small and fantastic. He studies cell life and becomes involved in Dr. Pedersen's cancer research. The more he learns, the more he is confused by his father's view of life, which is overshadowed by death. At last, Pedersen grows impatient with Jesse and dismisses him from the family, saying, "You have no existence. You are nothing." Jesse must seek another, more receptive, life-style.

Jesse enters medical school, is graduated, marries, and tries to forge a new family, a home, for himself. He keeps returning, however, to the site of his father's tragic demise in his dreams. His own children gradually start to shrink away like the Cheshire Cat. Michelle becomes Shelley and ultimately Shell, until Jesse can no longer grasp her—or the rest of his family—with any degree of certitude. Even Jesse's two father-figures, Drs. Cady and Perrault, become in turn distant and disdainful. Dr. Cady will not acknowledge anything but the ethereal, and Dr. Perrault will not admit that the mind is anything but actual. These two opposing views further succeed in alienating Jesse from a "real" life. To offset these unrealistic real people, Jesse creates an unreal friend, or series of friends, but she only promises disharmony and death, so he eventually rejects her, too.

In the end of the novel, the action picks up speed, racing toward the now of the narrative, 1971. Jesse finally returns to his father's psyche and discovers the final, perfect answer: "A clean, pure, empty being, a void." It is only through the total destruction of the universe that a peaceful existence (or non-existence) can be enjoyed.

The setting of *Childwold* is again Eden Valley, scene of the action in *With Shuddering Fall* and *Wonderland*. The novel is peopled by a variety of characters and is narrated by several of them in turn, as each becomes the lover of the central figure's mother, Arlene Bartlett. Arlene's daughter, Laney Bartlett, is the unconscious catalyst for much of the violence in the novel.

The primary reaction between Laney and another character occurs between her and Fitz John Kasch, a fiftyish hermit who lives among the debris of his large but deceased family. In Laney, Kasch sees not only his failed marriage but also his repressed desires. She becomes for him both an icon and a Tantalus, love and passion. Unable to avail himself of her, Kasch woos and wins Arlene and becomes another in a lengthy retinue of lovers.

Arlene is a figure of the sex goddess, but, unlike so many untouchable figures, she is the small statue in the back of the church, worn down by the grasp of many hands. This, however, does not dismay her; indeed, it invigorates her. Where many single women would not welcome pregnancy, Arlene revels in it; her children reaffirm her existence in a world of many people. Kasch, on the other hand, is unable to enjoy the company of others. He secrets himself in a small part of what was once the family manse, now a museum. He blames his self-imposed isolation on his divorce, brought on by his former wife's infidelity. Retiring into his hermitage, however, only amplifies his feelings of detachment from life. Although he seeks to redefine himself in various ways (as a voyeur, among others), he remains at one, in harmony with only himself. When he finally becomes reconciled to the Bartletts' violent way of life, he remains unfulfilled. He can satiate himself neither with the daughter nor with the mother.

Instead of an object of violence, of rape or murder, Laney becomes an object of Kasch's creation. It is at this point that *Childwold* most neatly resembles Vladimir Nabakov's *Lolita*: the story of a middle-aged man's obsession with a nubile, young teen. As did Humbert Humbert, Kasch casts a spell about Laney, using art as a medium, but she eventually escapes, moving though the two-dimensional world of Kasch's photographs to the world of nature outside his museum/prison. She frees herself from the world he is doomed to inhabit.

It is a world that is of his own design. After Arlene has joined Kasch, her former lover, Earl Tuller, returns to threaten and bully her. In a rage, Kasch kills him and seals his fate as a prisoner. He has dreamed of being a murderer, but now that his fantasy has been accidentally granted, he is unable to bear the results. He has been defeated by his own desires mixed with the mindless tide of the universe. The novel ends with Arlene musing over the turn of events their lives have taken. Laney returns to Kasch's mansion, but he will not answer the door. Imagining that she sees him behind a curtained window, she calls out. She feels she is strong enough, has changed enough from the girl that she was, to save him, and so in a flush of anticipation she waits for "a sign, a sign," but it never comes. Oates demonstrates in *Childwold* the tragic consequences of the conflict between man's ambitions and the machinations of the world.

In *Bellefleur*, Oates combines the Gothic grotesque and a sense of realism to create a novel that, incredibly, has believable un-human creatures. If this type of book seems out of character for her, it may be she wishes to warn her audience that what seems extraordinary may, upon examination, be simply ordinary. In one episode, a huge rodent runs screaming into the house; the next morning, it is nothing but a cat. On the other hand, normality might suddenly become monstrous.

Bellefleur traces the history of the Bellefleur family through several generations and as many psychological aberrations. There are psychics in the family, the gnome who serves Leah Bellefleur, and several ghosts. Jedediah Bellefleur is the manifestation in this novel of the character who forces himself to exist against the will of nature. He is a recurring character in Oates's novels, and in *Bellefleur*, Jedediah is delightfully crazy. In the end, he is persuaded to continue the Bellefleur line despite his (and the reader's) misgivings.

The novel is difficult to read, because it jumps back and forth from past to present. Another difficulty stems from the fact that the main character of interest, the telepathic Germaine Bellefleur, ages only four years from her birth during the entire action of the novel, but her father ages two or three decades. The setting of the novel itself—the Adirondack mountain range—ages thousands of years. In addition, the mountains and the people shrink or grow spasmodically. The final chapters contain spiritual references that, at first, seem disjointed. After Gideon's transformation into the skeletal Angel of Death, however, a Native American appears to the ancestral Jedediah and tells him to embrace the world that he has abandoned. This is Oates's final message to the reader, that only in a full and relished life is there union with God's body. Thus, as in her first novel, Oates's characters do battle with their own existences, their own beings. They struggle, escape, and wander only to return to their initial resting places within themselves and within the confines of their destinies.

The characters in *Mysteries of Winterthurn*, however, appear to have relinquished their resting places for ghostly—and ghastly—forays among the living. This Gothic mystery novel has been hailed as a feminist dissertation, a charge that has not been denied by Oates. Although the main character is male and the action in the novel is seen through his eyes, most of the victims are women and children, and it is to their plight that the narrator and the reader grow sympathetic. In *Mysteries of Winterthurn*, Oates discusses the existence of women in a male-dominated society, and a pitiable existence it is.

Even though Oates owes much of her presentation of the situation of nineteenth century women and children to several other popular authors, her interpretation is uniquely her own. Her victims are disposable pawns in a society that is more than willing to sacrifice them for its own (male) devices. Oates inserts the supernatural into the novel to allow her women a modicum of revenge upon these perpetrators. If this seems to be impossible (the unreal attacking the real), Oates insists that once something is thought to be real, it becomes so whether it should be real or not. Thus, the view of women as passive, thoughtless beings is true for the males in her novel, even though it is a false concept. The women victims in the novel are freed by this misconception to react violently to those who misuse them because they (the women) cannot have acted in such a manner within the male scheme of things.

To drive this point home, Oates repeats it three times during the novel. The first story, "The Virgin in the Rose-Bower," deals with a sadistic husband and father, Erasmus Kilgarven, who has a hand in the brutal deaths of his two wives and commits incest for several years with his daughter, Georgina, causing her to become pregnant several times. Georgina kills her infants but claims that they have been destroyed by angels painted on the ceiling of her bedroom. The narrator, young Xavier Kilgarven, sees one painted angel bleed, and this leads to the discovery of several other infant corpses, silent witnesses to Erasmus Kilgarven's hideous habit. By claiming supernatural murder (and rape), Georgina is able to evade guilt and exact a small amount of revenge on her father.

In the persona of Iphigenia, her pen name, Georgina is also able to free her female family members by publishing her poetry. The money she receives from this enterprise, until her father forbids it as unseemly, is later used to finance even more unfeminine exploits by the young Perdita. Perdita needs no spectral avenger; she takes matters into her own hands, although she is never seen as a murderer by anyone but the reader. The only people who are capable of violent acts in *Mysteries of Winterthurn* are male; the females are those upon whom these acts are perpetrated. Thus, an invisible shield is created around Perdita, enabling her to murder several people in order to achieve her goal, union with young Xavier.

The third sister, Thérèse is able to profit from her sisters' cloaked deeds, and, indeed, there are indications that she may be involved in Perdita's violent crimes in a peripheral manner. But this is only hinted at; outwardly, Thérèse appears to be a happy, modern woman. It is here that Oates's use of paradox—the woman who is both angel and demon, visible and invisible—culminates. All the women in the novel have been so seduced by the theory of their own guilt that they must violently oppose it in order to free themselves.

Jennifer L. Wyatt

Other major works

SHORT FICTION: *By the North Gate*, 1963; *Upon the Sweeping Flood*, 1966; *The Wheel of Love*, 1970; *Marriages and Infidelities*, 1972; *The Goddess and Other Women*, 1974; *The Hungry Ghosts*, 1974; *Where Are You Going, Where Have You Been?*, 1974; *The Poisoned Kiss*, 1975; *The Seduction*, 1975; *Crossing the Border*, 1976; *Night-Side*, 1977; *All the Good People I've Left Behind*, 1978; *A Sentimental Education*, 1980; *Last Days*, 1984; *Raven's Wing*, 1986; *The Assignation*, 1988.

POETRY: *Women in Love*, 1968; *Anonymous Sins*, 1969; *Love and Its Derangements*, 1970; *Angel Fire*, 1973; *The Fabulous Beasts*, 1975; *Women Whose Lives Are Food, Men Whose Lives Are Money*, 1978; *Invisible Woman: New and Selected Poems, 1970-1982*, 1982.

PLAYS: *Miracle Play*, 1974; *Three Plays*, 1980.

NONFICTION: *The Edge of Impossibility: Tragic Forms in Literature*, 1972; *The Hostile Sun: The Poetry of D. H. Lawrence*, 1973; *New Heaven, New Earth: The Visionary Experience in Literature*, 1974; *Contraries: Essays*, 1981; *The Profane Art: Essays and Reviews*, 1983; *On Boxing*, 1987; *(Woman) Writer: Occasions and Opportunities*, 1988.

ANTHOLOGIES: *Scenes from American Life: Contemporary Short Fiction*, 1972; *The Best American Short Stories of 1979*, 1979 (with Shannon Ravenel); *Night Walks: A Bedside Companion*, 1982; *First Person Singular: Writers on Their Craft*, 1983.

Bibliography

Chell, Cara. "Un-tricking the Eye: Joyce Carol Oates and the Feminist Ghost Story." *Arizona Quarterly* 41 (Spring, 1985): 5-23. This lengthy article successfully defends *Mysteries of Winterthurn* as not only a Gothic mystery but also a modern criticism of the plight of women in a society that viewed them as invisible, voiceless beings—as ghosts.

Creighton, Joanne V. *Joyce Carol Oates*. Boston: Twayne, 1979. The Twayne series of books on authors always gives satisfactory coverage of a writer's life and works to date. This handy reference lists Oates's achievements in a chronology and includes notes, a selected bibliography with annotated secondary sources, and an index. The text itself examines Oates's life and the influences on her writing, including William Faulkner, and examines her early novels as well as her short stories grouped into patterns of theme of characterization.

Friedman, Ellen G. *Joyce Carol Oates*. New York: Frederick Ungar, 1980. This text gives very clear and concise criticisms of nine of Oates's novels, from *With Shuddering Fall* to *Son of the Morning*. After a first chapter that provides a biographical and environmental background for the longer works, each chapter is devoted solely to one novel. There are no comparisons that make researching one subject so annoying; these are included in the epilogue. Notes, a bibliography, and an index round off the book.

Grant, Mary Kathryn. *The Tragic Vision of Joyce Carol Oates*. Durham, N.C.: Duke University Press, 1978. As a study of the use of violence in Oates's fiction, this text delves into the early works (1963-1975) and examines the impact of inner-city danger on her themes and characters. The chapters are augmented by references to specific works, and the text itself includes a bibliography, notes, an appendix, and index.

Waller, G. F. *Dreaming America*. Baton Rouge: Louisiana State University Press, 1979. From *With Shuddering Fall* to *Crossing the Border*, this book is an extensive examination of Oates's works as delicate and accurate recordings of "the emotional dynamics of our time." Far from viewing her works as clever rehashings of earlier fiction (for example, some view Wonderland as a rewritten Lewis Carroll novel), Waller admires Oates for her ability to transcribe the pulse of the American people into her novels and short stories. Includes a selected bibliography.

EDNA O'BRIEN

Born: Tuamgraney, Ireland; December 15, 1930

Principal long fiction

The Country Girls, 1960; *The Lonely Girl*, 1962 (reprinted in 1964 as *Girl with Green Eyes*); *Girls in Their Married Bliss*, 1964; *August Is a Wicked Month*, 1965; *Casualties of Peace*, 1966; *A Pagan Place*, 1970; *Zee & Co.*, 1971; *Night*, 1972; *I Hardly Knew You*, 1977; *The Country Girls Trilogy and Epilogue*, 1986; *The High Road*, 1988.

Other literary forms

Edna O'Brien's short stories appear regularly in magazines such as *The New Yorker* and *The Atlantic*; some of them have been collected in *The Love Object* (1968), *A Scandalous Woman and Other Stories* (1974), and *Mrs. Reinhardt* (1978). O'Brien has also written plays including, *A Cheap Bunch of Nice Flowers* (1962) and *Virginia* (1981); screenplays, *Girl with Green Eyes* (1964), *Time Lost and Time Remembered* (1966), *Three into Two Won't Go* (1968), and *X, Y and Zee* (1971); television plays, *Mrs. Reinhardt* (1981); and nonfiction, including the autobiographical *Mother Ireland* (1976), a travel book, *Arabian Days* (1977), an anthology, *Some Irish Loving* (1979), and an essay on the Joyces, *James and Nora* (1981).

Achievements

After moving to London from Dublin in 1959, O'Brien published at a furious pace, mining her early experiences in Ireland and then as a single parent with two sons to rear in England. There was something of a lull in her long fiction, however, from 1977 to 1986. Nearly always from a female narrator's point of view, O'Brien has brilliantly transmuted her personal experiences into art. Her recall and selection of the tiny details that make up the texture of life, particularly in her Irish scenes (*The Country Girls*, *The Lonely Girl*, *A Pagan Place*) are most dazzling. Impressive, too, is her evident love and savoring of words, sometimes clearly in a James Joyce fashion, for their own sake, and often in good dialogue. Perhaps because of the speed with which she works, the vivacity and brilliance of her prolific output is frequently marred by awkward grammar, punctuation, and syntax. Apparently, her editors have felt these stylistic lapses are all part of her Irish use of the language and have accordingly let them stand.

O'Brien was a feminist before the term became fashionable, but her works also affirm a wider humanistic sympathy for all people. Early, she took up the topics of women's attitudes toward their bodies, their sexuality, and their roles as mothers and daughters. In Ireland her books are banned because of their often negative comments on the Roman Catholic Church, more common in her early work, and her frequent employment of graphic sexual terms and scenes. Outside Ireland, her reputation as a writer of fiction seems assured. Her acclaim will be even more certain when she can distance more effectively the bitterness she feels about her Irish upbringing, achieving the balance typical of the best of the many Irish writers in exile.

Biography

Edna O'Brien was born to Michael and Lena (Cleary) O'Brien in Tuamgraney, County Clare, Ireland, on December 15, 1930. She has one brother and two sisters. She first attended Scarriff National School in 1936, then boarded at the Convent of Mercy, Loughrea, County Galway, in 1941 before going off to the Pharmaceutical College of Ireland in Dublin in 1946. In 1951, O'Brien married novelist Ernest Gebler (the marriage ended in 1964). Two sons were born, in 1952 and 1954. In 1959, the family moved to London and O'Brien's career as a published writer was quickly launched: in three weeks, far from County Clare, she wrote *The Country Girls*, tracing the development of fourteen-year-old Caithleen Brady. The trilogy was continued in *The Lonely Girl* and *Girls in Their Married Bliss*, and appended with an *Epilogue* in 1986.

Since 1959, O'Brien has been based in London, frequently traveling abroad to Europe, the Middle East, and the Americas—for pleasure and profit, as a tourist and as a reader-lecturer.

Analysis

Edna O'Brien's concerns are most readily accessible in her very eccentric travel/autobiography *Mother Ireland*. Her Irishness is something of which O'Brien is proud: "It's a state of mind." She is not, however, blind to Ireland's faults, appreciating that there must be something "secretly catastrophic" about a country that so many people leave. After an iconoclastic opening chapter on Irish history, with its uncanonized patron saint and its paunchy Firbolgs, follow six chapters in which are sketched O'Brien's dominant themes: loneliness; the longing for adventure (often sexual); the repressive Irish Roman Catholic Church; family ties (the martyred mother and the rollicking father); the courageous hopelessness with which life at best must be lived.

It would be a melancholy picture if it were not for O'Brien's saving, ironic sense of humor and the skill with which she roots her observations in the sensual details of the actual world. Her readers share vividly with her a world of wet-batteries for radios, ink-powder, walls with fragments of bottles embedded in their tops, Fox's (Glacier) Mints, orange-boxes, and lice fine-combed from a child's head onto a newspaper. O'Brien's recurring themes, her experiments with form, and the feeling she succeeds in communicating that this Irish microcosm has its universal significance are all clearly present in *Mother Ireland*.

From its detailed, evocative opening page, redolent of genteel poverty, *The Country Girls*, O'Brien's first novel, serves notice of an unusual voice. The shy and sensitive Caithleen tells her first-person story and shares the action with her alter ego, the volatile and malicious Baba. It is a world divided into two warring camps, male and female, where Caithleen's aspirations toward romantic love are doomed to failure. Mr. Gentleman is the first in a long line of rotters (the drunken, brutal father; Eugene Gaillard; Herod; Dr. Flaggler), far outnumbering the few men with decent inclinations (Hickey, Auro); in such a world women stand little chance, single, married in the usual sense, or brides of Christ.

The repressive effects of poverty and a patriarchal society are hardly alleviated by the Church and its proscriptions. Her mother drowned, Caithleen spends her mid-teen years boarding in a strict convent-school from which Baba contrives their expulsion for writing a ribald note. In their late teens, joyously, they come up to Dublin, Baba to take a commerical course, Caithleen to work as a grocer's assistant until she can take the Civil Service examinations. Loneliness, however, follows them: Baba contracts tuberculosis; Caithleen's Mr. Gentleman lets her down; yet with the resilience of youth her last line in this novel is, "I was almost certain that I wouldn't sleep that night."

The Lonely Girl continues the saga two years later, Baba healthy again; it is, however, largely Caithleen's story; again she is the narrator. The repressive effects of her family, her village community, and her convent education are again in evidence. O'Brien has her heroine involved romatically with Eugene Gaillard, whose face reminds her of a saint, and who is about the same height as her father; he is a cultivated snob, and in an often cold fashion he begins the further education of his naïve, prudish, "student," both in bed and in the salon. (In *Edna O'Brien*, 1974, Grace Eckley points out that Caithleen's stiff tutor and O'Brien's former husband, Ernest Gebler, share the same initials.) At the novel's conclusion, Caithleen, wild and debased "because of some damned man," is learning, is changing; she is, as she says, finding her feet, "and when I'm able to talk I imagine that I won't be alone." Still seeking their connection, she and Baba sail on the *Hibernia*, from Dublin to Liverpool and London.

Girls in Their Married Bliss continues the story of the two in London, where, for the first time, Baba assumes the first-person narration, alternating with an omniscient voice distancing O'Brien and the reader from Caithleen's role—a process she will carry even further with her protagonist in *A Pagan Place*. The women, now about twenty-five years old, have not left their Irish baggage behind in Dublin; there is a splendid, blustery Celtic quality to the scapegrace Baba's style. Kate (as Caithleen is called), too, has her share of one-liners, word associations, epigrams, and zany metaphors: "Self-interest," she observes on one occasion, "was a common crime"; on another, at a party, she is amused by a girl wearing a strawberry punnet on her head to make herself taller.

In these early novels, O'Brien, like her leading characters, is learning and developing her skills. In *Girls in Their Married Bliss*, the topic is still the female search for love and connection: the novel is a precisely observed account of a marriage failing. People rub exquisitely on one another's nerves in the larger context of women's role in society; in the smaller context of bedroom politics, "Men are pure fools." Marriage, at least on the grounds on which the women enter it here, is evidently no end to the quest: Baba makes a calculated move for comfort; Kate sees that her interest in people is generated solely by her own needs. They have matured to the point where they no longer believe much in romantic plans. Kate's answer to the biological unfairness of God's scheme for women, as Baba sees it, is to have herself sterilized; she will not make the same mistake again: no other child of hers will be abducted by its father; no further child of hers will in its turn become a parent.

The complete trilogy was reissued in 1986 in one volume, with a brief *Epilogue* in the form of a monologue delivered by Baba. Here the ebullient Baba brings the reader up to date: the despairing Kate is dead; she drowned, perhaps deliberately.

In O'Brien's next, new, full-length novel, *August Is a Wicked Month*, an omniscient narrator describes the protagonist's abortive attempts at self-liberation, largely through sexual activity. Ellen is a Kate-like, superstitious, convent-bred, twenty-eight-year-old Irish magazine writer, formerly a nurse, living in London when the novel begins. She takes a trip to France when the husband from whom she is separated and their eight-year-old son, Mark, who lives with her, go on a camping holiday together. Her "pathetic struggles towards wickedness" involve rejecting the first sexual invitations she encounters. Eventually, however, when Ellen does become intimately involved with a high-living group, O'Brien subjects her to two catastrophic accidents: she receives a call from her husband, who tells her that her son has been killed by a car in a roadside accident, and she fears, wrongly as it turns out, that she has contracted a venereal disease. The guilt and the judgment are clear; perhaps they are too clear to make this novel an artistic success. Ellen finally finds an uneasy autumnal peace, unlike the women in O'Brien's next novel, who have a genuine joy ripped away from them.

In *Casualties of Peace*, Willa McCord, artist in glass, and her earthy domestic, Patsy Wiley, are the protagonists, exemplary victims of male violence. An omniscient narrator views the two unhappy women—Willa having escaped from a nightmarish marriage to the sadistic Herod, Patsy presently suffering her husband Tom's blows. Both have their dreams of happiness outside marriage shattered. There was a chance for peace for them, but accidents prevented them from knowing joy: Patsy blabs to Willa about leaving Tom rather than doing it immediately, as planned, and her lover, Ron, believes she has let him down; Willa, just when a loving connection with Auro seems possible, is murdered by Tom, who mistakes her for Patsy.

Casualties of Peace is, with the exception of *Night*, which it anticipates to some extent, O'Brien's most Joycean novel to date. Patsy's love letters to Ron are reminiscent of the earthiest of James Joyce and Nora Barnacle's correspondence; Patsy indeed is a kind of Molly Bloom figure (more clearly developed in *Night*). Willa's letters to Auro, delivered posthumously, share the same stream-of-consiousness qualities: words pile up into lists; associations trigger other more graphic associations; "memory is the bugger." At times lyrical, at times humorous, O'Brien develops here the Celtic flair with words that is associated with Joyce or Dylan Thomas. Her theme is loneliness and its myriad causes; her characters search to alleviate their pain, to make connections, to overcome their feelings of guilt for being themselves.

A Pagan Place is a very odd novel; it is largely a sophisticated rewrite of *The Country Girls*, as O'Brien perhaps would have written that work had she had ten years more reading, writing, and living behind her at the time. Baba is dropped in favor of one unnamed, preadolescent girl whose sexual arousal when her father beats her accomplishes her move toward adolescence. Getting away from her Irish family and Irish community with their hereditary guilt will, it is suggested, take her yet a stage further. At the end of the novel she leaves to the accompaniment of an eerie Hibernian howl.

Throughout the work an omniscient narrator, who sometimes uses dialect forms, sometimes very erudite words, and who is clearly unreliable in matters of fact (putting an English "general" on Nelson's pillar), places the reader at the center of the action by using the second-person narrative. No one but "you," then, is at the center of the action; the narrator and the writer are similarly distanced from the action. Perhaps in this novel O'Brien exorcised the worst of her Irishness; certainly, very violent feelings surface, all in the consciousness of a young girl. O'Brien, in contrast to her contemporaries among Irish writers of fiction, such as Brian Friel or Benedict Kiely, really seems to dislike her Celtic community. Here is a very bitter indictment of the Church, and perhaps its ultimate rejection in the priest's attempt to seduce "you," masturbating and ejaculating on "you." Here, too, is a savage, repressive, guilt-ridden world of so-called Christians, where unwed mothers receive no *caritas*, where legally wed mothers and fathers show no love either. It is a world where Holy Water is sprinkled on thoroughbred foals, where a black dog, chasing a frog that jumps out of the ashes at Della's wake, is seen as one and the same with the devil. All in all, it is, with few exceptions, a nightmarish community, especially for a child. For "you" as a child at the center of this world, deserted even by "your" mother at one period, a thing "you" thought would never happen, the only certainty is that "you" want to escape, whatever the burden of guilt "you" carry.

The theme of escape is continued in *Zee & Co.*, where O'Brien's heroines are back in London, and again, a pair. Zee moves increasingly aggressively and ruthlessly to hold her man, Robert, while dominating Stella, her rival. She succeeds in both endeavors. As the war of the sexes heats up, Zee refuses to be a victim: she is no patsy. O'Brien's long preoccupation with the defensive role of women in society appears to be shifting to the offensive in her later works as her heroines themselves become less fragmented. A person needs to be integrated psychically to withstand not only sexual partners and spouses, but also all manifestations of phantoms, prejudice, repression, guilt, and loneliness. This new positive attitude is well-illustrated in the rambunctious Mary Hooligan, whose nightlong monologue forms O'Brien's next work, *Night*.

In form and style, *Night* is O'Brien's most Joycean novel. In a harangue from her bed in England, Mary Hooligan—Irish, abused, divorced—delivers herself of an aggressive, courageous, independent, first-person autobiographical statement. Beginning with an Anglo-Saxon monosyllable in the opening paragraph, the nonconciliatory tone of her monologue is established. "I am a woman," Mary affirms, and proceeds to weave, in time and place, the story of her connection with her father and mother, her former husband—"the original Prince of Darkness"—and her son. It is an exuberant linguistic spree: from a "trepidation" of gelatinlike dessert to the welcome "tap o' the mornin'," metaphors and apt words are savored and invented. The pervasive humor is wry; the aggressive tone and confident technique perfectly match the content of a work whose burden is rebellion against loveless unions and ignorance.

Mary Hooligan is another in O'Brien's procession of outsiders, an Irish woman in England, merely house-sitting so even less important in the community. O'Brien, however, establishes Mary as a force on her own: Mary rejects her friend, Madge (Mary needs no Kate figure to complement her being); she is complete on her own. The theme under review remains the eternal search for love in its myriad manifestations; what is new here is the heroine's joyful attack as she continues her pilgrimage to "the higher shores of love." Family, community, and marriage settings are again explored. Many of the details are familiar: the vicious father, the ignoramuses who could not tell cheese from soap, the cold-fish husband. Constant and familiar in O'Brien is the warm regard for children, particularly the mothers' regard for their sons. This aspect of love leads her to flirt with incest in her most violent work, *I Hardly Knew You*, where the narrator has an affair with and then murders her son's friend.

Nora, the protagonist of *I Hardly Knew You*, tells her story in yet another night monologue, from her prison cell, as she awaits trial for the murder of Hart, her young lover. Again, O'Brien's narrator is an Irish exile in England, divorced from an overly frugal husband, with a son, and literally in prison, isolated from all society. Loneliness is at the core of her existence, as it is, she remarks, at the core of Celtic songs. Her monologue shuffles time and space more formally than Mary Hooligan's in *Night* and reveals a world of increasing violence. Details and incidents from O'Brien's previous works, as far back even as *The Country Girls*, show up: the drunken father taking the cure; the abducted-child threat; the child scraping the toilet-seat paint; the kicking-match engaged in by the brutish relatives. The world has become an increasingly violent place, and the response of O'Brien's narrator matches it. Like Mary's, Nora's personality is integrated, but toward the Kate side. She engages in an explicitly lesbian encounter, but she needs no other woman to complement her. Indeed, she acts increasingly like the worst stereotype of the sadistic male predator, who uses and abuses other people, particularly women and especially wives. This is a chilling picture of a person driven to violence, to kill without regret. Here is a woman who has lost her balance and whose sweeping indictment of men must surely be viewed as just as reprehensible as male chauvinism. "I am proud . . . to have killed one of the breed to whom I owe nothing but cruelty, deceit, and the asp's emission," she avers, ignoring absolutely O'Brien's often stated support for "human decency" and kindness among people of whatever sex.

The graph of O'Brien's fictional, split personalities is by no means a straight line. A clearly differentiated pair in the early trilogy, each "Kate" and "Baba" is subsequently given an alternating fictional forum. The *Epilogue* may have seemed to clear the way for Baba and zesty Baba types, but *The High Road*, which comes next, has readers once again seeing a sophisticated society through the moist eyes of a Kate type.

Anna, the narrator in *The High Road*, like many of the women in O'Brien's short stories as well, has come on Easter Sunday to a Mediterranean paradise to get over a London love doomed from its inception. In this exotic setting, she encounters eccentric members of the international set: the superannuated debutante, Portia; the grotesques who make up a German fashion-magazine staff, on location; the fading jet-setter, Iris; the itinerant Irish painter, D'Arcy, with the Joycean language flair; and Catalina, the hotel chambermaid, with whom she has an affair.

It all ends in murder; D'Arcy, to buy some time, paints "Lesbos" on a multitude of walls, not merely on Catalina's gable, where the word first appeared, but to no avail. Clutching a scarf full of Catalina's blood-soaked hair, in what in its accumulation of similes seems at times a parody of the Gothic romance, Anna sets out, she says, for the last time, for home. Whether she has left behind her the purgatory of motherhood, in its various manifestations, remains to be read.

O'Brien, then, is a writer from Ireland whose many years there have profoundly affected her view of the world, and particularly of women's relationships and their place in society. Being Irish, she says in *Mother Ireland*, gives one a unique view of pleasure and punishment, life and death. O'Brien's work is lyrical and lively. Her memory for people and places, for the minutiae of daily living, is prodigious; her zest for language is Joycean. She is often on the attack, but at her best, which is often, she transcends her immediate cause to encourage, with a grain of humor, those who still dream of love achieved through kindness and decency—common virtues still no more common than they ever were.

Archibald E. Irwin

Other major works

SHORT FICTION: *The Love Object*, 1968; *A Scandalous Woman and Other Stories*, 1974; *Mrs. Reinhardt*, 1978 (better known as *A Rose in the Heart*); *Returning*, 1982; *A Fanatic Heart*, 1984; *Lantern Slides*, 1990.

PLAYS: *A Cheap Bunch of Nice Flowers*, 1962; *A Pagan Place*, 1972; *Virginia*, 1980.

SCREENPLAYS: *Girl with Green Eyes*, 1964; *Time Lost and Time Remembered*, 1966 (with Desmond Davis); *Three into Two Won't Go*, 1969; *X, Y, and Zee*, 1971.

TELEPLAYS: *The Wedding Dress*, 1963; *Nothing's Ever Over*, 1968; *Mrs. Reinhardt*, 1981.

NONFICTION: *Mother Ireland*, 1976; *Arabian Days*, 1977; *Some Irish Loving*, 1969; *James and Nora*, 1981.

CHILDREN'S LITERATURE: *The Dazzle*, 1986.

Bibliography

Eckley, Grace. *Edna O'Brien*. Lewisburg, Pa.: Bucknell University Press, 1974. The first book-length study of O'Brien. Eckley discusses individually, in a very sympathetic and perceptive fashion, O'Brien's longer works of fiction through *Night* (1972). This excellent starting place for a study of O'Brien needs to be brought up to date, however, in its primary and secondary sources. O'Brien's work generally is reviewed in the major dailies and weeklies; she grants many interviews but is largely ignored by the Academy.

Guppy, Shusha. "The Art of Fiction, LXXXII: Edna O'Brien." *Paris Review* 26 (Summer, 1984): 22-50. Presents a comprehensive interview with O'Brien.

Haule, James M. "Tough Luck: The Unfortunate Birth of Edna O'Brien." *Colby Library Quarterly* 23 (December, 1987): 216-224. Examines, particularly in the short story, "A Scandalous Woman," the potential difficulties of mothering in Ireland.

Irwin, Archibald E. "Give Us Baba." *Irish Literary Supplement*, Spring, 1987, 19. A review of *The Country Girls Trilogy and Epilogue*, highlighting the split personality of O'Brien's heroines.

O'Brien, Peggy. "The Silly and the Serious: An Assessment of Edna O'Brien." *The Massachusetts Review* 18 (Autumn, 1987): 474-488. A provocative psychological appraisal to account for the mixed responses to O'Brien's work. O'Brien's blurring of the boundaries between herself and her protagonists, and the evaluative doubts that result, are seen as a product of the author's unresolved parental influences.

Roth, Philip. "A Conversation with Edna O'Brien." *The New York Times Book Review* (November 18, 1984): 38-40. A perceptive, supportive interview, in which the importance of place in O'Brien's fiction is examined.

Woodward, Richard B. "Edna O'Brien: Reveling in Heartbreak." *The New York Times Magazine* (March 12, 1989): 42, 50, 51. An essentially snide, though revealing, look at O'Brien's ambivalences.

FLANN O'BRIEN
Brian O'Nolan

Born: Strabane, Ireland; October 5, 1911
Died: Dublin, Ireland; April 1, 1966

Principal long fiction
At Swim-Two-Birds, 1939; *An Béal Bocht*, 1941 (published in the United States as *The Poor Mouth*, 1973); *The Hard Life*, 1961; *The Dalkey Archive*, 1964; *The Third Policeman*, 1967.

Other literary forms
Flann O'Brien was the pen name used by Brian O'Nolan for the four novels he wrote in English, and so it is used here, although his work in other forms appeared under other names. He was a talented and prolific journalist as well as a novelist. He began to write satirical essays for student publications at University College, Dublin; a sampling of this student work was reprinted in the "Flann O'Brien Number" published by the *Journal of Irish Studies* in 1974. Although a civil servant by profession, O'Brien also wrote a famous column for *The Irish Times* under the name Myles na Gopaleen. This column continued to be printed on a regular basis for twenty-five years; selections have been reprinted in *Cruiskeen Lawn* (1943), *The Best of Myles* (1968), and *The Various Lives of Keats and Chapman and the Brother* (1976). Throughout his career, O'Brien sporadically produced skits for theater, essays other than journalism, and short stories. These are most conveniently located in two posthumous collections. *Stories and Plays* (1973) reprints two dramatic skits, two short stories, an essay on James Joyce called "A Bash in the Tunnel," and the seven existing chapters of an unfinished novel called *Slattery's Sago Saga*. *A Flann O'Brien Reader* (1978) includes examples of his journalism, short fiction, and essays, along with excerpts from his five novels.

Achievements
O'Brien's contemporary reputation rests on the rediscovery of his first novel, *At Swim-Two-Birds*, an event that occurred about twenty years after the novel was published. The novel had received praise from James Joyce, Dylan Thomas, and Graham Greene, among others, but its possibilities for broad critical and popular success were thwarted by the onset of World War II. His next novel, *The Third Policeman*, could find no publisher until after his death, and his third novel, *The Poor Mouth*, was written in Gaelic and thus limited to an extremely small audience. These three novels are now considered to be O'Brien's most important works. About 1960, O'Brien's work was rediscovered by the American writers S. J. Perelman and William Saroyan. Their praise, principally of his journalism, led to a reissue of *At Swim-Two-*

Birds and critical recognition of it as an important novel. In response to this
renewal of interest in his fiction, O'Brien wrote *The Hard Life* and *The Dalkey
Archive*, but neither of these later novels is as interesting nor as important
as his three earlier novels. O'Brien's journalism, in posthumous collections,
is the source of most of his popular appeal today, particularly in Ireland. The
focus of almost all critical interest in his work, however, is on his novels,
especially *At Swim-Two-Birds* and *The Third Policeman*. O'Brien is now
universally recognized as the most important Irish novelist of his generation.

Biography

The novelist known as Flann O'Brien was born Brian O'Nolan on October
5, 1911, in Strabane, County Tyrone, Ireland. He was the third of twelve
children of Michael Victor O'Nolan, a customs officer, and Agnes Gormlet
O'Nolan. O'Brien's family was frequently relocated in the course of his father's profession, and this postponed his early formal education. His family was
extremely literate, however, and in the home O'Brien developed early fluency
in Irish Gaelic as well as English and also some familiarity with Latin and
Greek classics. It was only in 1923, when his father was transferred to Dublin,
that O'Brien was enrolled at the age of twelve in the Synge Street School run
by the Christian Brothers. In 1925, his father was appointed a revenue commissioner in Dublin Castle, and this advancement permitted the family to
settle permanently in Blackrock, a southern suburb of Dublin, in 1927. In
that year, O'Brien was enrolled in Blackrock College, a preparatory school.
In 1929, he matriculated at University College, Dublin.

At University College, O'Brien was a success in his studies and in extra-
curricular literary activities. In 1933, he earned his B.A. in English, Irish,
and German, won the school's gold medal for debate, and was awarded a
scholarship for study at the University of Cologne. After a year in Germany,
he returned to University College and earned his M.A. in 1935 with a thesis
on Irish poetry in Gaelic. The early intimations of his literary career, however,
were more apparent in his nonscholarly activities. In 1931, he invented the
persona "Brother Barnabas" for the student magazine *Comhthrom Féinne*.
A subsequent series of articles under this name was brought to a close in
1934 by a "posthumous" piece called "Scenes from a Novel" that anticipates
the metafictional premise of *At Swim-Two-Birds*. In 1934, O'Brien also invented
the persona "Count O'Blather" for his own short-lived magazine in English
called *Blather*.

Following the conclusion of his graduate work, O'Brien joined the Irish
Civil Service in 1935; he would continue in its employ until 1953. In 1935,
he also began work on *At Swim-Two-Birds*, which was published in 1939 but
commercially undone by the decimation of English book sales by World War
II. By 1940, he had completed *The Third Policeman*, which was not published
until after his death. In subsequent years, O'Brien told friends that he had

lost this manuscript, but he nevertheless reworked it into the much more superficial novel *The Dalkey Archive* two decades later.

These discouraging setbacks were offset to some extent by the success of an outrageous literary scam. Under a series of fictitious names, O'Brien and Niall Sheridan began an attack on Dublin's presiding literary deities in the pages of *The Irish Times*, and, during the exchange of heated letters to the newspaper that followed, they began to attack their own original position under new fictitious names. When the scheme came to light, *The Irish Times* editor R. M. Smyllie had the goodwill and foresight to hire O'Brien to write a regular column. First in Irish and then in English, these columns of Myles na Gopaleen appeared at a rate of approximately three per week from October 4, 1940, until his final illness in 1966. As an outgrowth of his first columns in Irish, O'Brien wrote *The Poor Mouth* in Irish under the name Myles na Gopaleen in 1941.

O'Brien had thus completed his three important novels by the age of thirty: one was generally ignored, one remained in manuscript, and one was published in a language inaccessible even to most Irish citizens. A combination of cynicism and absorption in journalism effectively ended his career as a novelist at that point. By the time of the rediscovery of *At Swim-Two-Birds*, O'Brien was already suffering from the effects of lifelong heavy drinking. He managed to respond to interest in his past work with *The Hard Life* and *The Dalkey Archive*, but these works lack the textual complexities of his earlier and more important novels. It is a final, appropriate irony that Flann O'Brien, inventor of fictional disguises and elaborate literary conceits, died of alcohol-related maladies on April Fools' Day of 1966.

Analysis

Flann O'Brien's first and most important novel, *At Swim-Two-Birds*, was published the year that W. B. Yeats died. The coincidence is notable because the novel was a parodistic melange of styles spawned by the Irish literary revival championed by Yeats and because all of O'Brien's important novels critique literary fabrications akin to those of the revival. The Irish literary revival was based on the rediscovery of the special identity of Ireland, especially as this was apparent in the literature of the Celtic legends. In popularizing these legends, the participants in the revival, many of whom—unlike O'Brien—had no fluency in the Gaelic language, were prone to literary extravagance and inflated notions of Celtic nobility. The literature of the revival was instrumental in arousing political energies that led to the creation of the Irish Free State, but after this goal of political independence had been realized, many of the revival's own literary excesses became apparent. Modern problems such as economic recession, entanglements of church and state, and the entrenched conservatism of an emerging middle class made the essential artifice of the inspiring revival literature especially visible for the first time.

O'Brien wrote none of the important fiction about the Irish Republic of his own day; instead, his major works look back to the earlier mythologizing of Celtic identity and modern Irish culture. *At Swim-Two-Birds*, *The Third Policeman*, and *The Poor Mouth* all ridicule the pretensions of literature by emphasizing its artificiality. O'Brien's work is satirical in effect because it implicitly corrects notions of literary authority, cultural privilege, and innate national aristocracy. Its primary mode is parody, adoption and exaggeration of a variety of recognizable literary styles to demonstrate their essential mandacity.

The salient quality of O'Brien's career is ambiguity concerning his name and identity. He took the pen name Flann O'Brien from Gerald Griffin's 1829 novel *The Collegians*, while the name Myles na Gopaleen came from Dion Boucicault's play *The Colleen Bawn* (1860), based on Griffin's novel. Both of these pseudonyms recall stage Irishmen, a stereotype of nineteenth century English fiction. In the revival, a new domestic stereotype of the Irish prevailed, one as falsely noble as the earlier English one was debased. Thus, these names attached to O'Brien's novels challenged the new literary identity of Ireland as a sheer fabrication.

O'Brien's first three novels are relentless in their scrutiny of fabricated literary identities; his later two novels are less successful because that scrutiny is limited, and because some assumptions about identity are allowed to stand unchallenged. Ultimately, his finest works have affinities with that strain of modern literature which asserts the reality of a metaphysical void, a senseless core of anonymity beneath the guises, literary and otherwise, protectively adopted to give life a semblance of meaning. This is especially true of *The Third Policeman*, which is freer of provincial references than O'Brien's other novels. The relish for parodying things Irish most apparent in *At Swim-Two-Birds* and *The Poor Mouth*, however, suggest that the primary frame of reference for O'Brien's novels will always be the cultural history of early twentieth century Ireland.

At Swim-Two-Birds, O'Brien's first and most important novel, which takes its name from the literal translation of a Gaelic Place-name, is the most complete critique in novel form of the excesses of the Irish literary revival. O'Brien was fluent in Gaelic and a talented parodist, and in this novel he exploits the essential artifice of revival literature by placing its various literary styles in collision with one another. Here Finn MacCool, evoked in all his epic splendor, meets the hack writer Dermot Trellis; the mad bard Sweeny, whose verses are included in hilarious literal translations into English, meets Jem Casey, poet of porter; the Good Fairy, taken from the most sentimental of Irish tourist literature, sits down to cards with urban characters taken from the bleak world of James Joyce's *Dubliners* (1914). The product is a novel about the unreality of various kinds of fictions, an exercise in style whose only subject is the extravagance of the styles it exploits by parody.

At Swim-Two-Birds is a collection of brief fragments organized only by the desire to express the multiple contrasts of their incompatible styles. The thread that links these fragments is situational rather than narrative: a university student is attempting to write a novel whose three possible openings and four possible conclusions frame *At Swim-Two-Birds*; among the characters in his novel is Dermot Trellis, himself a novelist with a work in progress; the characters in Trellis' novel are dissatisfied with their treatment and so wreak revenge by writing their own novel about Trellis, whose authorial control lapses when he sleeps. This conceit allows O'Brien to include in his novel a plethora of styles from imaginary authors, especially rich in ironies for readers knowledgeable about Irish literature from the Celtic legends to modern writers such as Yeats.

As many of its commentators have pointed out, *At Swim-Two-Birds* has far more appeal and significance than most metafictional novels about a novel in progress. It is, above all else, exuberantly comic rather than pretentious. It also carries the possibilities of metafiction to a new extreme because of the intricacy and multiplicity of its narrative levels. The novel has a special significance in the history of modern Irish fiction because its sources and frames of reference are entirely local, unlike the more exotic allusions that control Joyce's *Ulysses* (1922) and Samuel Beckett's early novels: *At Swim-Two-Birds* is a critique of Ireland and Irish fictions written from within the Republic rather than from cosmopolitan France. One effect of this circumstance is that *At Swim-Two-Birds*, while it lacks the international literary ambitions of the comparable works by expatriate Irish writers, is more thoroughly imbued with the literary climate of Dublin and more convincing in its criticisms of local literary preoccupations.

Although it was not published until after O'Brien's death, *The Third Policeman* was written immediately after *At Swim-Two-Birds*, and it should be considered beside that novel, despite its publication date. Like *At Swim-Two-Birds*, it is a very modernist exercise in the novel as a self-contained and self-generating literary text. In this case, however, O'Brien is less concerned with the identifiable styles of the Irish revival than with the ways any style creates an identity in narrative fiction, the ways style is a source of authority and control in fiction. It is crucial to this novel that the narrator be nameless; without the identity provided by a name, he must create a persona for himself by appropriating styles of expression.

The novel opens with the robbery and murder of a businessman named Mathers by the narrator and his accomplice, John Diviney. The fantastic events that ensue concern the narrator's attempts to recover the stolen money and to hide his complicity in the crime from an omniscient but apparently uninterested pair of policemen. The appearance of Fox, the third policeman, seems to promise the release of the narrator from his predicament, but in fact it presages the realization that the narrator has been dead since the opening pages, betrayed and himself murdered by Diviney.

Released from even the faintest restraints of realism by setting his novel in the afterlife, O'Brien is free in *The Third Policeman* to allow language and rhetoric, rather than cause and effect, to determine the direction of his tale. The most prominent style and source of authority in the novel is an academic one related to the narrator's interest in a fictional philosopher named de Selby, whose works are evoked for the sake of clarification, summarized, and cited in scholarly footnotes throughout the novel. Elsewhere, *The Third Policeman* sporadically adopts the style of the modern murder mystery, a pretentious opera review, scientific analysis, eastern myticism, and Gothic romance. These intrusive styles color the events of the novel for the reader, much as the alien laws of the afterlife color the experiences of the narrator: they are oblique, intriguing, and ultimately baffling.

The Third Policeman lacks the dimension of cultural commentary provided by evocation of local literary styles in *At Swim-Two-Birds*. This same generalized environment, however, makes O'Brien's second novel an even richer contemplation on the nature of identity than his first, one that is capable of generalizations about definitions of self that rise above provincial contexts. It is also fully self-contained by a cyclic conclusion that returns the narrator, now accompanied by Diviney, to the earliest situations in the novel. It is precisely this degree of absorption in the interior logic of its own conceits that distinguishes *The Third Policeman* from O'Brien's later, less interesting reworking of these ideas in *The Dalkey Archive*.

In a letter to Sean O'Casey quoted in *The Flann O'Brien Reader*, the author described *The Poor Mouth*, in its original Gaelic version, as "an honest attempt to get under the skin of a certain type of 'Gael,' which I find the most nauseating phenomena in Europe." This kind of Gael was in fact more a creation of the literary revival than a significant social group. *The Poor Mouth*, as translated by Patrick C. Power after O'Brien's death, is a parody of a literary genre rather than a parody of life in *Gaeltachts*, the remote Irish-speaking areas of Ireland that continue to erode in character despite well-intentioned government subsidies. The primary targets of the parody are the enormously popular autobiographies of *Gaeltacht* life such as *Twenty Years A-Growing* (1933) by Maurice O'Sullivan, but O'Brien's more general object of parody is all fictionalized versions of peasantry, from the folktales of Standish Hayes O'Grady to the plays of Lady Gregory and J. M. Synge.

The title of the novel evokes the idiom of "poormouthing," or inventing poverty for self-serving purposes, and *The Poor Mouth* is about the discovery by enthusiastic outsiders of a *Gaeltacht* in the midst of truly astonishing poverty. The wretched cohabitation of these peasants with their pigs in leaky shacks is a source of some tall-tale humor in the novel, although this poverty does have its darker side, as indicated by casual references to disease and death from starvation, alcoholism, and fighting. O'Brien's real focus here, however, is on the willful self-degradation of the peasants at the feet of their enlightened English-speaking visitors, who gauge the merit of Gaelic tales by the poverty of the teller and limit their own charity lest they spoil the purity of the peasants' profound misery.

The great irony of *The Poor Mouth*, and an essential component of its publication in Gaelic, is that these visitors are, rather than actual Englishmen, Anglicized Irishmen enamored of the peasantry. The pure bile of the novel, which is well-preserved in its English translation, derives from this image of Ireland foisting a factitious sterotype on itself, of romanticizing a peasantry in such rigid ways that all males in this *Gaeltacht* are called James O'Donnell. The use of this collective name is only the most obvious indication of the novel's relevance to O'Brien's governing interest in the theme of identity. Rather than a parody of multiple identities, however, *The Poor Mouth* is a portrait of surrender after limited resistance to a bleak and uniform identity. It has a special importance in O'Brien's work for this pessimism, for its publication in Gaelic, for his refusal to permit a translation, and for the fact that he would not write another novel until twenty years later.

The Hard Life lacks the literary frames of reference that give O'Brien's first three novels their focus and energy. Published in the wake of the rediscovery of *At Swim-Two-Birds*, it is a charming rather than derisory treatment of characteristically Irish forms of naïveté and provinciality, one that panders to audience expectations about Irish writing that were ridiculed by the ironies of O'Brien's earlier novels. It is harsh in its criticisms of the Jesuit Father Kurt Fahrt, the misguided Dubliner Mr. Collopy, and his slatternly daughter Annie. These satirical elements, however, are rendered benign by the time frame of the novel, written in 1961 but set in the years preceding 1910. The most attractive qualities of the novel—its digressive narration, bitter account of lower-class Dublin propriety, and the extravagantly misinformed conversations of Father Fahrt and Collopy—are facile if skillful entertainments never qualified by the shrewd ironies surrounding such mannerisms in O'Brien's earlier novels.

In all of O'Brien's novels, narrative structure is incidental to stylistic preoccupations, but in *The Hard Life* there is no literary focus to compensate for the lack of narrative structure. The comedy of the Fahrt-Collopy conversations and of several of the improbable events in the novel is brilliant, but the lack of an informing literary prespective renders them isolated exercises in caricature, resembling in tone and length the best of O'Brien's newspaper columns.

In reworking some of the central conceits, notably the de Selby material, from *The Third Policeman*, O'Brien made *The Dalkey Archive* his only novel narrated in the third person. This alteration eliminates many of the ambiguities and complications found in his earlier novels because of their limited narrators. In other respects, too, *The Dalkey Archive* turns away from the most imaginative conceits of O'Brien's earlier work. As such, it represents a distinctly regressive coda in the works of O'Brien.

The novel individually treats the imaginative constructions of three personages. St. Augustine appears and reveals that neither his youthful sins nor his religious conversion were as complete as have been supposed. Sergeant Fottrell reveals his theory that the molecules of men and bicycles mix during riding, with predictable results. Finally, James Joyce, discovered living in retirement in the seaside resort called the Skerries, denounces *Ulysses* as a scam perpetrated by Parisian intellectuals and reveals that his true vocation is writing pamphlets for the Catholic Truth Society. These three are joined by their shared intellectual pride, a characteristic that the novel condemns even as it luxuriates in the pleasures of intricate shams.

O'Brien's first three novels were entirely enclosed within their literary conceits. In *The Dalkey Archive*, however, the elaborate shams and crazed logic are dispersed and corrected by the omniscient narrator on surprisingly moralistic grounds. In O'Brien's first three novels, no assumptions about identity were exempt from scrutiny, but *The Dalkey Archive* ends with an extremely complacent announcement of betrothal by its lackluster central characters Mick and Mary. With this gesture, O'Brien's last novel relinquishes the imaginative explorations of self and the elaborate metafictional elements of his finest novels.

Brian O'Nolan adopted the pseudonyms Flann O'Brien and Myles na Gopaleen with a characteristically ironic purpose: he would, under the names of one literary fabrication about Ireland and the Irish, expose the fabulous nature of a later image of the country and the people. At the end of his life, he wrote two novels, *The Hard Life* and *The Dalkey Archive*, deficient in the ironic intent of his important novels. It was as if at this point in his career he actually became Flann O'Brien, the stage Irishman, content with the identity foisted upon him. In *At Swim-Two-Birds*, *The Third Policeman*, and *The Poor Mouth*, however, the ironies surrounding his choice of pseudonyms were in full operation. The complexities and opacities of those novels represent a break from the mainstream of modern Irish literature and the most probing examination of the new national literature's roots in the mythologies of the Irish literary revival.

John P. Harrington

Other major works

NONFICTION: *Cruiskeen Lawn*, 1943; *The Best of Myles*, 1968; *The Various Lives of Keats and Chapman and the Brother*, 1976.

MISCELLANEOUS: *Stories and Plays*, 1973; *A Flann O'Brien Reader*, 1978; *Myles Away from Dublin*, 1985.

Bibliography

Clissmann, Anne. *Flann O'Brien: A Critical Introduction to His Writings*. New York: Barnes & Noble Books, 1975. An exhaustive discussion of all the author's writings in English, with lengthy chapters on the major novels. Very useful for its discussion of O'Brien's student writings and for its review of the end of his career, including his attempts to write for television. Contains a bibliography.

Clissmann, Anne, and David Powell, eds. "A Flann O'Brien-Myles na Gopaleen Number." *Journal of Irish Studies* 3 (January, 1974). A special issue devoted to O'Brien's work. Contains juvenilia, stories, critical essays on O'Brien, and the texts of two of his short plays, including his version of Karel Capek's *The Insect Play*. Also includes a selection of O'Brien's letters and a valuable checklist of his publications.

Cronin, Anthony. *No Laughing Matter*. London: Grafton, 1989. As close as there is likely to be to a conventional biography of the complex and somewhat reclusive O'Brien. Written by a poet, novelist, and man of letters who was acquainted with O'Brien and his Dublin. The focus is on the man, rather than on the work, and some little-known personal details illustrate the narrative. A thorough treatment of a difficult subject.

Imhof, Rudiger, ed. *Alive, Alive O! Flann O'Brien's "At Swim-Two Birds."* Dublin: Wolfhound Press, 1985. A compilation of key contemporary reviews, critical articles and background readings on one of the author's masterpieces. Valuable as a research tool, containing a comprehensive bibliography.

O'Keeffe, Timothy, ed. *Myles: Portraits of Brian O'Nolan*. London: Martin Brian & O'Keeffe, 1973. An invaluable source of biographical information and critical commentary on O'Brien. Contains reminiscences by friends, colleagues, and one of the author's brothers. Among the critical commentaries must be singled out the essay by J. C. C. Mays, "Flann O'Brien: Literalist of the Imagination."

Ryan, John. *Remembering How We Stood: Bohemian Dublin at Mid-Century*. New York: Taplinger, 1975. An attractive and informative memoir of the social and cultural milieu to which O'Brien belonged, structured as an overview followed by a presentation of individual participants in the scene. Devotes a chapter to O'Brien called "The Incomparable Myles" and also contains a number of inimitable glimpses of him. Illustrated.

KATE O'BRIEN

Born: Limerick, Ireland; December 3, 1897
Died: Canterbury, Kent, England; August 13, 1974

Principal long fiction

Without My Cloak, 1931; *The Anteroom*, 1934; *Mary Lavelle*, 1936; *Pray for the Wanderer*, 1938; *The Land of Spices*, 1941; *The Last of Summer*, 1943; *That Lady*, 1946 (also known as *For One Sweet Grape*); *The Flower of May*, 1953; *As Music and Splendour*, 1958.

Other literary forms

Kate O'Brien's first success was a play, *Distinguished Villa*, which had a three-month run in London's West End in 1926. She successfully dramatized her novel *That Lady* for a Broadway production (1949) in which Katherine Cornell played the title role. O'Brien was also the author of two travel books, *Farewell Spain* (1937) and *My Ireland* (1962). Her *English Diaries and Journals* was published in 1943, and a biography, *Teresa of Avila*, in 1951. Her last major published work was a book of reminiscences, *Presentation Parlour* (1963).

Achievements

While her first novel, *Without My Cloak*, received two of the English literary establishment's most prestigious awards, the Hawthornden Prize and the James Tait Black Memorial Prize, Kate O'Brien's most notable achievement may best be assessed in the context of contemporary Irish literature. In this context, she remains—together with, though in a much more culturally significant manner than, her perhaps better-known contemporary Elizabeth Bowen—an exemplary representative not only of women's writing but also, through her works and career, of women's potential, broadly considered. Partial recognition of her achievement came in 1947 with her election to the Irish Academy of Letters.

Biography

Kate O'Brien was born in the city of Limerick, Ireland, on December 3, 1897, to a comfortable, middle-class family. Educated at a local convent, she went on to attend University College, Dublin, at a time when Ireland's capital was witnessing the consolidation of the Irish Literary Revival, though the cultural enthusiasm of the time left little or no mark either on O'Brien's student days or on her writing.

The years immediately following graduation seem to have been marked by a degree of uncertainty. She worked at first in England as a journalist for the (then) *Manchester Guardian* and as a teacher. A brief period in Washington,

D.C., as a diplomatic aide was followed by a sojourn in Bilbao, Spain, as a governess. Returning to London in 1924, she married Gustav Renier; the marriage was not a success. Spain soon became her second home, though for more than ten years after the completion of her World War II service at the Ministry of Information in London she was refused admission to the country, her depiction of King Philip II in *That Lady* having rendered her persona non grata. By this time, O'Brien was no stranger to controversy arising out of her fiction: her 1941 novel, *The Land of Spices*, was notoriously banned by the Irish Censorship Board for alleged sexual impropriety. In 1950 she took up residence again in Ireland and lived there until 1961, when she returned to England. She died on August 13, 1974.

Analysis

Kate O'Brien's career emerged and developed during a difficult time for Irish writing; indeed, models of Irish women novelists who might have provided her with beneficial influence and nurturing were virtually nonexistent. Despite these unpromising cultural origins, and despite the obvious struggle O'Brien experienced in order to express herself and command a responsive and sustaining audience, her career can be seen in historical retrospect to be marked with notable integrity, independence of mind and action, and devotion to her art. In a literary culture where women have not always received sufficient critical attention and have not had their works readily incorporated into the canon of a given generation's achievements, critical responses to O'Brien's life and work have belatedly been seen as manifestations of unwarranted narrowness. The belatedness of this view is perhaps a result of the author's long years of exile, along with the fact that her one major popular success, *That Lady*, published when a fresh audience was ready for her work, is a historical romance rather than another in her sequence of novels about Irish family life. Yet the republication of many of her works during the 1980's not only has facilitated a reappraisal of her literary achievements but has also had the effect of redrawing the map of Irish literary culture at a crucial period in its development.

The generation of Irish writers to which O'Brien belongs had the unenviable task of following in the path-breaking footsteps of the principal artists of the Irish Literary Revival—the novelist George Moore, the poet William Butler Yeats, and the playwright J. M. Synge. O'Brien's generation was as different in background and outlook from these three illustrious avatars as it is possible to be. Provincial in upbringing, nationalist in politics, unexperimental in art, and Catholic in cultural formation, this generation had at once a greater intimacy with the actual life of its fellow citizens and a more actively critical perception of the society in whose name it had elected to speak. It also had the not inconsiderable disadvantage of attempting to assert its cultural and artistic validity and viability while the star of the Revival had not yet entirely waned, and while Yeats, for example, was willing to coopt new voices to articulate the agenda of his cultural politics.

The most important writers of this generation—those who went on to establish a somewhat more populist orientation for Irish literature, or at least a more populist role for the Irish writer—have long been considered to be Sean O'Faoláin, Frank O'Connor, and Liam O'Flaherty. The different orientation that they represent may be initially discerned in the fact that they each espoused a form largely neglected by the Revival—namely prose fiction, in particular the short story—and implicitly rejected the formal and ideological explorations of their more modernist forbears. O'Brien is a member of this generation not merely by virtue of her provincial background and conventional education but also because her works reflect this generation's concerns, a reflection that receives added point and importance from the fact of its feminist—or, to be historically accurate, protofeminist—perspectives. The disillusion and disorientation that emerge as a resonant theme in Irish fiction during the 1930's, the problematized rendering of the independence that the country has lately secured in juridical and political terms, and the conflicts between tradition and individuality as the culture seeks not merely aesthetic but moral renewal, far from being neglected by O'Brien, are all the more authentically present in her work through being presented from the standpoint of already marginalized female protagonists. (With the exception of *Pray for the Wanderer*, with its protagonist Matt Costello, all O'Brien's works feature female protagonists.)

O'Brien's first novel, *Without My Cloak*, rehearses a number of the problems that arise from her heritage and anticipates the most important of her fiction's preoccupations. A family saga, it brings to awareness through the use of an essentially nineteenth century model the social and psychological forces that gave cultural and moral legitimacy to O'Brien's own class and ideological background. The novel traces the development of the Considine family through three generations from the late eighteenth century, plausibly detailing its establishment in an urban, mercantile setting, for which the author uses her native Limerick. A major motif in the work is the question of security. The Considine ethos consists of a sublimation of development in consolidation, and the emotional claustrophobia that results from this mode of behavior within the family circle is memorably detailed. The security motif is tensely related to its obverse, a quest for independence; the dynamics of the novel enact the struggle familiar from nineteenth century fiction between individual and society, between the assertion of selfhood and institutional constraints, with the emphasis in this instance falling on the power of institutions.

In particular, the social and moral function of the Catholic church receives special attention in *Without My Cloak* and retains a particularly important place throughout O'Brien's fiction. Because of its status in her first novel, it is possible to refer to the Considine family as embodying an ethos, since the church operates as a source of moral and social identity, and alternative sources of such security and self-awareness are nowhere to be found. The power of the Church to authorize selfhood as a tissue of constraints makes of it a second, larger, more absolute family, and the matter of the effect of its power on the individual conscience and consciousness, rather than being resolved in *Without My Cloak*, becomes an increasingly emphatic preoccupation in O'Brien's fiction prior to the publication of *That Lady*. (The fact that O'Brien herself seems to have considered the conflicts of her first novel unresolved may be inferred from their reenactment in condensed and more artistically disciplined form in her next work, *The Anteroom*.) The role and power of the church is so central to her work that O'Brien has frequently been thought of as a Catholic, more than as an Irish, novelist. Like most Irish writers, however, she is concerned with the culture of Catholicism, its social, personal, and interpersonal influence, and its significance as a generator of a politics of the spirit rather than as a spiritual convalescent home. Indeed, one of her most fundamental fictional preoccupations is with the difficulty of dealing with impersonal authority, whether conceived as institutional or, as in the portrait of Philip II in *That Lady*, monarchical.

The fact that O'Brien perceived her preoccupations as continuing difficulty rather than as eventual solution is suggested by the regularity with which her protagonists, for all the author's sympathetic dramatization of their intensity of their struggles, typically fail to attain the independence they desire. An exception to this general outcome is the eponymous heroine of *Mary Lavelle*. This novel, which draws more directly on immediate personal experience than *Without My Cloak* does, tells of a young Irish woman working as a governess for a bourgeois Spanish family. In some sense an account of an innocent abroad—Mary seems to be innocence itself—the novel is also a narrative of conflicting loyalties. The heroine is in many respects an ideal employee, fitting into the Areavaga family with the ease of somebody familiar with a culture in which people know their places. It is Mary's very compliance, however, that is responsible for the novel's central drama. She involuntarily falls for Juanito, the married son of the house, a state of affairs that brings her into conflict not only with the outlook in which she had been rigorously brought up in Ireland but also with its powerfully reinforced presence in Doña Consuelo, the commanding head of the household. The conflict between duty and freedom, between individual desire and ethical obligation, in addition to the novelist's welcome transposition of her concerns to a non-Irish locale and the development of a sexual dimension to Mary's struggle for authentic womanhood, contributes to an impressive sense of the novelist's development. Nevertheless, it is not clear what the overall effect of Mary's experiences has been, whether she accepts or rejects the conflict-laden nature of her experiences. "Anguish and anger for everyone and only one little, fantastic, impossible hope," read the closing lines of *Mary Lavelle*, "was the fruit of her journey to Spain." An unexpected fruit of the publication of *Mary Lavelle*, however, was its banning by the Irish Censorship of Publications Board, an act that may be read now as an unintended tribute to O'Brien's insightful presentation of her heroine's moral authenticity but that, at the time, deepened the alienation from her background that her works articulated with increasing conviction.

This alienation reached its highest level when her next novel, *The Land of Spices*, met with a similar fate to that of *Mary Lavelle* at the hands of the censors, as a result of which the novel achieved unjust notoriety—and subsequently, when censorship was relaxed in the early 1970's, a certain amount of popular success. The banning of *The Land of Spices* proved instrumental in calling the censorship board's procedures into question and led indirectly to a revision of its mode of operation. It might be argued that the board's very existence was in itself strongly illustrative of the cultural conflicts and repressions that, from a broader, nonbureaucratic, social perspective, form the core of O'Brien's fictional concerns. The pretext for banning *The Land of Spices* was so slender—consisting of a mere handful of words with potentially homosexual implications—that it came to be seen as a paradigm of the narrow-minded, prurient, and often-antifeminist orientation of the official guardians of Irish literary culture.

The Land of Spices can be read as a redeployment and intensification of the mother-and-governess relationship in *Mary Lavelle*, a relationship that is emblematic of relationships conceived throughout O'Brien's work as exercises in power. On this occasion, foreignness of setting and the enclosed nature of the immediate environment are combined to attain a new level of intensity: the action takes place within an Irish convent of a French order of nuns. In addition, this work's animating relationship now has the intimacy of teacher, Mère Marie-Hélène Archer, and pupil, Anna Murphy, with all of its reverberations of nurturing and mastery, the source of which is the overarching presence of Mother Church. The pressures Mary Lavelle felt with regard to her moral development and sense of autonomy are here articulated more dramatically, given how much more difficult it is to escape them, and the sexual component of *Mary Lavelle* is similarly intensified.

Yet the novel has a more meditative than critical tone. Taking its title from the English Metaphysical poet George Herbert's "Prayer (1)" ("Church bells beyond the stars heard, the soul's blood,/ The land of spices, something understood"), the emphasis falls on the ritualistic and selfless aspects of the vocational life, on the complexities of agape rather than the challenge of eros, on the willingness to serve rather than the urge to escape, while at the same time remaining crucially sensitive to the urgent presence of humanity and its needs. *The Land of Spices* will seem to many to be O'Brien's most satisfying production, in which she attains more objective possession of her psychological and spiritual preoccupations without running the risk of compromising them.

O'Brien's characterization of a woman's fate in the context of power relationships receives its most lavish treatment in her greatest popular success, *That Lady* (as well as being adapted for the stage, *That Lady* was filmed with Olivia de Havilland in the title role in 1955). Set in sixteenth century Spain, the novel tells the story of Ana de Mendoza y de la Cerda, Princess of Eboli and Duchess of Pastrana; clearly, despite O'Brien's strong Spanish interests, it is an entirely new departure for her as a novelist. Instead of concentrating on the various stages of Ana's life as a woman in an attempt to reconstruct a novel of historical verisimilitude, O'Brien concentrates instead on the years of Ana's unlikely liberation into an experience of womanhood that had hitherto been hidden from her. The reader is explicitly informed in a foreword that this "is not a historical novel"; instead, the imaginative treatment of the material dwells centrally on a dramatization of the psychological and emotional conflicts of the case. Thus, despite a certain amount of costumery, inevitable under the circumstances, *That Lady* achieves an internal consistency with O'Brien's other novels.

That Lady covers the years spent by Ana, now widowed, in state service. To some extent, her work for the Spanish Crown during this brief period recapitulates her early years, when by virtue of her noble birth and excellent marriage she became intimate with affairs of state. Together with the old intimacy, however, there now comes a new, and this development of an additional dimension in Ana's life is at once enhancing and destructive, enriching her personal existence while risking a scandal that would entail the king's serious displeasure. Because of the character of the prevailing power structure, the most significant experience in Ana's personal life—the affair with Don Antonio Pérez—becomes the occasion of her banishment and confinement. The novel's heightened courtly context accentuates rather than dilutes its emphasis on tensions familiar from O'Brien's earlier novels—between passion and form, between desire and responsibility, between a woman's external role and her internal needs. To these tensions and conflicts her work returns again and again, and it is in her identification and negotiation of them that O'Brien's fiction is worthy of the critical attention that, beginning in the late 1980's, it has at length come to receive.

O'Brien's work is noteworthy on two levels. In the first place, it represents significant additions to the history of Anglophone women's writing in the period between the two world wars. Her location of her female protagonists in conditions of moral difficulty, emotional complexity, cultural unfamiliarity, and even geographical estrangement provides a comprehensive method of dramatizing women's experience as problematic and unamenable to tidying away by the powers that be. O'Brien's own willingness to live a life as autonomous as that sought by her protagonists testifies to her steadfastness, courage, and integrity. The fact that so much of her writing life was spent in exile is a tribute to both her singularity and her perseverance.

In addition, however, her accomplishments become all the more significant when seen in an Irish context. While her novels do not articulate the concerns of her generation as explicitly as the critiques of nationalism and assumption of embattled cultural and ideological positions favored by many of her contemporaries, her work belongs with theirs as part of a concerted effort to render more authentically—that is, with greater respect for individuality and its internal realities—the life of her time. Kate O'Brien's original contributions to this effort make her the first important woman writer of independent Ireland.

George O'Brien

Other major works

PLAYS: *Distinguished Villa*, 1926; *That Lady*, 1949.

NONFICTION: *Farewell Spain*, 1937; *English Diaries and Journals*, 1943; *Teresa of Avila*, 1951; *My Ireland*, 1962; *Presentation Parlour*, 1963.

Bibliography

Boland, Eavan. "That Lady: A Profile of Kate O'Brien." *The Critic* 34 (Winter, 1975): 16-25. An insightful assessment of O'Brien's contribution to Irish women's writing by the best-known contemporary Irish woman poet.

Dalsimer, Adele. *Kate O'Brien: A Critical Study*. Dublin: Gill and Macmillan, 1990. The first comprehensive study of Kate O'Brien's entire literary output. The emphasis is on her works' feminist dimension, and a critical case is made for the significance of her generally neglected later works. O'Brien's attainment is set in its larger biographical, cultural, and political contexts. A useful bibliography is included.

O'Brien, Kate. "The Art of Writing." *University Review* 3 (1965): 6-14. An article that provides valuable insights into the author's thoughts about writing.

Reynolds, Lorna. *Kate O'Brien: A Literary Portrait*. Totowa, N.J.: Barnes & Noble Books, 1987. A succinct portrait by an academic who knew Kate O'Brien. The study is divided into two parts, the first dealing with the major fiction in chronological order and the second surveying O'Brien's treatment of various major themes. Also contains a valuable treatment of O'Brien's family background.

Stony Thursday Book 7 (1981). This Kate O'Brien issue of the periodical contains much important material, including an extract from a final, unfinished novel, "Constancy"; a review of *The Land of Spices* by O'Brien's noteworthy contemporary, the poet Austin Clarke; and critiques of O'Brien by such leading authorities on her achievement as Eavan Boland and Benedict Kiely.

FLANNERY O'CONNOR

Born: Savannah, Georgia; March 25, 1925
Died: Milledgeville, Georgia; August 3, 1964

Principal long fiction
Wise Blood, 1952; *The Violent Bear It Away*, 1960.

Other literary forms
Flannery O'Connor, most renowned as a writer of short fiction, published the short-story collection *A Good Man Is Hard to Find* in 1955; her canon also includes two posthumous collections, *Everything That Rises Must Converge* (1965) and *The Complete Stories of Flannery O'Connor* (1971). Three posthumous nonfiction works provide insight into her craft and thought: *Mystery and Manners* (1969), a collection of her occasional lectures and essays on literary art; *The Habit of Being: Selected Letters of Flannery O'Connor* (1979), which consists of letters compiled by her literary executor, Sally Fitzgerald; and *The Presence of Grace* (1983), a collection of her book reviews.

Achievements
O'Connor's art was best suited to the medium of the short story, where her sharp, shocking, and grotesque characterizations could have full impact on the reader. Nevertheless, her depiction of the Christ-haunted Hazel Motes in *Wise Blood* ranks as the most memorable and piercing postmodern delineation of Western society's anxiety over God's absence. O'Connor's ability to create supernatural tension, to provoke the potentially hostile reader into considering the possibility of divine invasion of the human sphere, is unparalleled by any postwar writer. Seeing "by the light of Christian orthodoxy," O'Connor refused to chisel away or compromise her convictions to make them more congenial to her readers. She knew that it is difficult to place the Christian faith in front of the contemporary reader with any credibility, but her resolve was firm. She understood, in the words of the late John Gardner (*On Moral Fiction*, 1978), that "art which tries to tell the truth unretouched is difficult and often offensive," since it "violates our canons of politeness and humane compromise." O'Connor succeeded not in making Christianity more palatable but in making its claims unavoidable.

O'Connor was committed not only to telling the "truth unretouched" but also to telling a good story. This meant rejecting predetermined morals— homilies tacked on to stories and processed uncritically by her readers: "When you can state the theme of a story, when you can separate it from the story itself, then you can be sure the story is not a very good one." Instead of literary proselytizing, she offered a literature of evangelism, of incarnation, a fusing of literary form with authorial vision. Her evangelistic mode was not proselytizing, but *proclaiming*, the ancient and more honorable practice of declaring news, of heralding its goodness to a usually indifferent, sometimes hostile audience. O'Connor had a keen perception of her audience's mindset and cultural milieu; her proclamation was calculated to subvert the habitualization of faith and to make such notions as redemption, resurrection, and eternal life seem new and strange to a Western society which had reduced them to commonplaces empty of significance. Readers and critics continue to respond to O'Connor's clear spiritual vision and piercing narrative style, a style uncluttered by a false pluralism or sectarian debate. O'Connor, the devout Catholic, neither preached nor compelled; she simply proclaimed.

Biography

Mary Flannery O'Connor was born in Savannah, Georgia, in 1925, and moved with her mother to Milledgeville, Georgia, in 1938. She took her B.A. degree from Women's College of Georgia in 1945 and received an M.F.A. degree from the State University of Iowa in 1947. She published her first short story, "The Geranium" (*Accent*, 1946), during her years in Iowa. In 1947, she won the Rinehart-Iowa fiction award for a first novel with a portion of *Wise Blood*.

On the strength of this award and her promise as a writer, O'Connor was offered a fellowship by the Yaddo Foundation. She accepted, and spent several months at Saratoga Springs, New York, but eventually returned to Milledgeville. A few months later, O'Connor moved in with the Robert Fitzgerald family in Connecticut to complete *Wise Blood*. A serious illness, lupus erythematosus, redirected her life in 1951 back to Milledgeville; there she would do the rest of her writing, and there she would die in 1964. From Milledgeville, she carried on a lively correspondence with friends, readers, critics, and her editors at Farrar and Giroux. When health permitted, she made trips to colleges and universities, many of them Catholic schools, to discuss her work and literary art.

O'Connor won a Kenyon Review fellowship in fiction in 1953, a National Institute of Arts and Letters grant in 1957, and an O. Henry first prize in short fiction for 1957. She also was granted honorary degrees from St. Mary's College (1962) and Smith College (1963). She spent the last months of her life completing the stories eventually published in her posthumous collection *Everything That Rises Must Converge. The Complete Stories of Flannery O'Connor* won the National Book Award for Fiction in 1971.

Analysis

Few postmodern writers have spoken as articulately and as compellingly about their craft and the relationship of their fiction to its perceived audience as did Flannery O'Connor. In her occasional prose, in her letters, and in her book reviews, O'Connor evinced an uncommonly perceptive grasp of her readers and the society in which they lived. Addressing the children of a demythologized and desacralized century, she confronted boldly the rancor and apathy with which modern culture meets the religious and the supernatural. To shake and sharpen the sensibilities of a culture made lethargic by the heritage of American civil religion, she turned to shock, to the literally awful and the grotesque, to proclaim her gospel: "To the hard of hearing you shout, and for the almost-blind you draw large and startling figures."

The underlying premise which informs all of O'Connor's fiction, and especially her two novels, *Wise Blood* and *The Violent Bear It Away*, is that man, as he is, is not *whole*. This "wholeness," lost in Eden, is now embodied and supplied to man freely in the person of the incarnate Son of God. In order to make this now familiar theme "seeable" and creditable to her readers, O'Connor was led to herald a Christ who bore little resemblance to the "gentle Jesus, meek and mild" of childhood hymnody. Her Christ is a Tiger who disturbs and terrorizes; "bleeding stinking mad," He "upsets the balance around her," winning men or driving them away. One thinks here especially of Hazel Motes, evangelist of the "Church of Christ without Christ" in *Wise Blood*, who fights ferociously to avoid that Jesus "in the back of his mind, a wild, ragged figure motioning to him to turn around and come off into the dark where he was not sure of his footing, where he might be walking on water and not know it and suddenly know it and drown."

Motes is a child of the fundamentalist South, but in O'Connor's economy, he is also Everyman; those who refuse Christ's offer to help them, force Him to haunt them. O'Connor used sudden death, disease, or trauma to depict the devastating encounter with Christ which must occur before one can be truly alive in this world. Worse things than mere death can befall a person made in God's image; her characters more often than not must be brought to the brink of crisis or death to see themselves as they are: in dire need of repentance and grace. In O'Connor's view, mankind did not accidentally stumble into rebellion against God; each man or woman deliberately chooses to do so. Consequently, she records with merciless precision the rationalizations of her protagonists, stripping them bare of their pretensions of goodness and innocence. She endeavored to confront her readers with the full scandal of Christianity. Those O'Connor characters who attempt to redeem themselves with arrant scientism or sheer intellectualism meet a savage Savior—manifested in a bull, a haunting prophecy, or a terrifying vision—who will not release them until they confess Him or utterly denounce Him.

For O'Connor, there was no middle ground, no neutral corner; all who are not with Him are against Him. Her narrative voice had little room for authorial compassion or tenderness. Relentlessly exposing human pride, avarice, and weakness, she agreed with C. S. Lewis that all things that are not eternal are eternally out of date. Western culture was already too sentimental, too complacent about Christ and Christianity; her mission was to pound on the table, to cast the moneychangers—sacred or secular—out of the literary temple.

One must ask how O'Connor avoided mere tractarianism, as her continuing popularity among critics and ubiquity in college literature anthologies attest she did. Part of the answer is that she frankly confronted the tenuous relationships which obtain among audience, medium, story, and craft. It was her genius to lead her readers through and from the seemingly mundane and ordinary to a vision of reality as sacramental, as always pointing to a divine presence in human activity. "When I write a novel in which the central action is baptism, I am aware that for a majority of my readers, baptism is a meaningless rite . . . so I have to see that this baptism carries enough awe and mystery to jar the reader into some kind of emotional recognition of its significance." Her fiction strips away the jaded images of the faith, forcing a dynamic confrontation with the gospel as it is played out in the lives of professed believers and as it is rejected by the worldly-wise. As the reader follows Hazel Motes or Francis Marion Tarwater on his journey to belief, he is confronted with grace—a grace which enlarges his perception of the world, enabling him to see both the natural and the supernatural anew, to both discover and retrieve deeper images of the *real*. As O'Connor states it, this journey frequently entails "an action in which the devil has been the unwilling instrument of grace. This is not a piece of knowledge that I consciously put into my stories; it is a discovery that I get out of them." It is this "awful rowing toward God" that is chronicled in O'Connor's two novels, *Wise Blood* and *The Violent Bear It Away*.

Hazel Motes, the protagonist of *Wise Blood*, is, O'Connor says, a "Christian *malgrè lui*," a believer in spite of himself, a harried wayfarer who has been displaced from Eastrod, Tennessee, and from the religious life of the South. That religious life is distinctively Protestant, the religion of a South of beleaguered prophets and street-corner preachers, a South haunted by Jesus and by a theological definition of man's identity and destiny. Motes is determined to escape salvation and anything which smacks of supernatural origin. Like Francis Marion Tarwater in *The Violent Bear It Away*, Motes's story is a reverse *Bildungsroman*, a novel of an antiquest in which the protagonist tries to *avoid*, rather than *seek*, his destiny.

O'Connor maintained that *Wise Blood* is a "comic novel," and nonetheless so because it deals with "matters of life and death." Though many readers try to locate the integrity of Motes in his vigorous struggle to escape that "ragged figure moving from tree to tree in the back of his mind," O'Connor avers: "His integrity lies in his not being able to [escape] it." His attempted flight from Jesus begins on the train to Taulkinham. Discharged from military service, Motes parries with a Mrs. Hitchcock, challenging her claim to redemption. "If you've been redeemed," Motes snaps, "I wouldn't want to be." Later, he exclaims to no one in particular, "Do you think I believe in Jesus? . . . Well, I wouldn't even if He existed. Even if He was on this train."

Motes has determined that the way to avoid Jesus is to avoid sin; one who is not a sinner needs no redemption—he is already "clean"—if he is free from transgression. This "freedom," however, does not mean that Motes can avoid becoming a preacher. When he first reaches the city and decides to look up Miss Leora Watts—who owns the "Friendliest Bed in Town"—both she and the cabdriver who brings him there accuse him of being a preacher; he simply looks the part.

Very soon, Motes encounters some potential disciples: Enoch Emery, who wants to help him find a "new jesus," and Sabbath Lily Hawks, the lustful daughter of a street preacher who feigns blindness. Following Sabbath and her father in order to ridicule their shallow evangelism, Motes declares that he will start a new church, a church *without* Christ. "I don't need Jesus," he tells the crowd gathering about him, "I got Leora Watts." Motes's obsession with the Hawks duo leads him to drive around the city in his beat-up Essex. His desperate flight from belief compels him to hound Asa Hawks, confronting him with the strange fact of his blindness—if Jesus is real, then why does He not heal His servants? Motes is tortured by his lack of a theodicy, a defense of God's absence; his only solace is to throw himself into his own "ministry": street-side preaching of the "Church of Christ without Christ" from the hood of his Essex.

His nightly forays into sermonizing yield only one "convert," a would-be Aaron to Motes's Moses, Onnie Jay Holy—a slick packager of religion and faith who knows a money-making scam when he sees it. Crediting Motes-the-Prophet with changing his life, Holy drowns out the frustrated anti-preacher, who learns to speak the truth in spite of himself: "Listen!" Motes screams. "It don't cost you any money to know the truth!" It is at this point that O'Connor's protagonist has begun his inexorable trek toward recognizing his true state and the call of God. When Enoch Emery answers Motes's call for a "new jesus" by stealing a mummified pygmy from a local museum and delivering it to the now domesticated Sabbath Lily Hawks, the reader is introduced to what Caroline Gordon called "the unholy family." Slinking into Motes's room, Sabbath introduces the mummy as their child. Sensing the blasphemy of the moment, Motes seizes the mummy and crushes it against the wall. The Prophet must now leave this desecrated place and search for a new city in which he can begin his ministry afresh. Before he can leave, however, he must confront a False Prophet—hired by Hoover Shoats, nee Onnie Jay Holy—who has supplanted him on the streets of Taulkinham. Following him out onto a lonely road, Motes first knocks his car into the ditch and then runs over his counterpart, killing him and thus carrying out the Old Testament vengeance against false prophets.

From here, Motes inevitably heads for his own Calvary, his own "death unto life": the words of Jesus in Matthew 5:29, "And if thy right eye offend thee, pluck it out," are taken literally. Motes blinds himself so that he can see with a spiritual vision which bogus believers such as Asa Hawks and Hoover Shoats can never attain. He is fully focused now; there is no intent to escape or flee. His landlady, Mrs. Flood, represents the kind of "Christian" O'Connor loved to contrast with her dramatic, utterly committed antisaints such as Hazel Motes, the Misfit in "A Good Man Is Hard to Find," and Manley Pointer in "Good Country People." She cannot fathom Motes's sudden devotion—which extended to the bearing of the marks of Christ on his body: "I'm as good, Mr. Motes, not believing in Jesus as many a one that does," she boastfully proclaims. When she sees the barbed wire wrapped around his chest, she exclaims, "There's no reason for it. People have quit doing it." His reply, anthem and testimony for all latter-day believers, seals his fate: "They ain't quit doing it as long as I'm doing it." Motes's death is as anticlimactic as Christ's; the policemen who discover him in the drainage ditch, like the soldiers at the foot of the cross who bargain for Christ's robe, mouth inanities and treat Motes as a troublesome derelict, quite worthy of being put out of his misery.

The story of Hazel Motes is the tale of one of God's creatures and his struggle with the fundamental choice to serve God or deny Him. O'Connor's avowed purpose was to "deepen the mystery of free will," which is not the war between one will and another but of "many wills conflicting in one man." In *Wise Blood*, whose title comes from Enoch Emery's claim to "know things" because of his ancestral blood, O'Connor has created a parable of twentieth century man's inner debate over God's existence and presence in the modern world. It is ironic, although not too surprising, that O'Connor's Christian readers sometimes responded less enthusiastically to her achievement than did her nonreligious readers. Such a response was simply a corroboration of O'Connor's perceptions regarding the state of belief in postwar America.

In her second novel, *The Violent Bear It Away*, written some ten years after she had originally begun *Wise Blood*, O'Connor once again returned to the theme of the antiquest, this time with a protagonist who tries to escape the daunting prophecy of his great-uncle. The title comes from an ambiguous passage found in Matthew 11:12: "From the days of John the Baptist until now, the kingdom of heaven suffereth violence and the violent bear it away." It is the dual message of this scripture which, in part, gives the novel its underlying power as still another O'Connor portrayal of the conflict of wills within man, a conflict of reason tempered with godly knowledge and an uncritical, gullible trust in the scientific method. The passage suggests, first, that with the coming of the promised Messiah, mankind can receive the kingdom of God; second, it suggests that there remain calloused and unprincipled unbelievers who will seek to bar the faithful from entering that hallowed ground. These two opposing forces are focused in the protagonist and antagonist of the novel: Francis Marion Tarwater and Rayber the schoolteacher.

Mason Tarwater had reared his nephew, Francis, to be "more than a Christian, a prophet." His prophetic task consisted of two matters: one, he was to make sure that the elder Tarwater had a proper burial, his gravesite marked by a cross; two, he was to baptize Bishop, the "dimwitted child" of Rayber. Mason had earlier tried to rear Rayber as a prophet, too, but he encountered a resistance which eventually turned into a vigorously antireligious posture. Mason Tarwater had finally broken off all relations with Rayber after the latter wrote a psychoanalysis of Tarwater for a "schoolteacher's magazine" which mocked his beliefs. Francis Tarwater, also, does not come easily to his prophetic office. At his great-uncle's death, he abandons the old man and burns down his house, balking at his obsession with Jesus; the choice is not between "Jesus and the devil," he resolves—"it's Jesus or me." Francis, like Hazel Motes, is nevertheless haunted by the presence of Jesus: "Jesus? He felt a terrible disappointment in that conclusion, a dread that it was true." He can no more escape his destiny than Motes could; it is "hidden in the blood."

Rayber is a familiar O'Connor character-type, the rationalist who attempts to explain away religion as illusion or delusion. He will have no part of the Tarwaters' prophetic ministry. Just as the sense of sight was a potent symbol in *Wise Blood*, O'Connor here uses the sense of hearing, Rayber's need for a hearing aid, to underscore his spiritual ignorance: "Do you think in the box," Francis Tarwater ridiculed, "or do you think in your head?" The religious people of Rayber's acquaintance—the Tarwaters, the Carmody family—have all been "exploited" people, bilked by the foolish rhetoric of insane cadgers and shysters. Yet Rayber's will is not powerful enough to withstand the force of a prophet of God. True to his call, Francis must drown Bishop in baptism, the enduring Christian symbol of new life from death.

O'Connor organized the events of this novel into three distinct parts. Part 1 reveals the eccentric life of the prophet; as Elijah the Old Testament prophet gave his mantle to the younger Elisha, so Mason Tarwater passes his own "burden" to his charge. Part 2 depicts Francis Tarwater's struggle to free himself, like a latter-day Jonah, from the burden laid upon him; here the city is emblematic of all the distractions and temptations which might deter him from his task. Part 3 relates the purification and cleansing of the prophet who encounters his burning bush and receives his commission to "warn the children of God of the terrible speed of mercy" in the "dark city" beyond him.

The Violent Bear It Away develops more fully themes O'Connor explored in such short stories as "The Enduring Chill," "The Artificial Nigger," "Good Country People," and "The Lame Shall Enter First." Her consistent focus is placed upon the human will tortured by indecision, clouded by technology, and rendered impotent by its flight from knowledge of God. The only remedy offered is the laying down of weapons and the complete surrender of the soul. Francis Tarwater and Hazel Motes both discover that their only rest from this ordeal is acquiesence to the will of God.

Throughout her fiction, O'Connor defamiliarized the all-too-familiar con-

2574 Critical Survey of Long Fiction

cepts of conversion and discipleship and articulated the shallow view of Christ lurking behind modern faith. She wanted her readers to escape the jaundiced vision of their own time. In *Mystery and Manners*, she paralleled her task with that of St. Cyril of Jerusalem, who, in instructing catechumens, warned them of passing by the dragon on their way to the Father of Souls:

> No matter what form the dragon may take, it is of this mysterious passage past him, or into his jaws, that stories of any depth will always be concerned to tell, and this being the case, it requires considerable courage at any time, in any country, not to turn away from the storyteller.

O'Connor refused to turn away from the dragon or the storyteller and she asked of her twentieth century readers the same courage.

Bruce L. Edwards, Jr.

Other major works
SHORT FICTION: *A Good Man Is Hard to Find*, 1955; *Everything That Rises Must Converge*, 1965; *The Complete Stories of Flannery O'Connor*, 1971.
NONFICTION: *Mystery and Manners*, 1969; *The Habit of Being: Selected Letters of Flannery O'Connor*, 1979; *The Presence of Grace*, 1983; *The Correspondence of Flannery O'Connor and Brainard Cheneys*, 1986.
MISCELLANEOUS: *The Complete Works of Flannery O'Connor*, 1988.

Bibliography
Asals, Frederick. *Flannery O'Connor: The Imagination of Extremity.* Athens: University of Georgia Press, 1982. Asals' stated intention in this volume is to point out thematic patterns which he believes are consistent throughout all of O'Connor's fiction. As a result, this study is comprehensive, dealing with lesser-known works as fully as with those usually treated. Includes an introduction containing a useful analysis of O'Connor criticism, a full bibliography, and an index.
Core, George, ed. *Southern Fiction Today: Renascence and Beyond.* Athens: University of Georgia Press, 1969. Essays in this volume by C. Hugh Holman and Louis D. Rubin, Jr., explain the importance of O'Connor's religious views in the context of the Southern literary tradition. Rubin also notes the relevance of her theology to her use of the grotesque. Stimulating comments by two major scholars.
Desmond, John F. *Risen Sons: Flannery O'Connor's Vision of History.* Athens: University of Georgia Press, 1987. Traces O'Connor's artistic development in the context of her spiritual development. Desmond's assumption is that O'Connor's Christianity, and particularly her growing understanding of the principle of redemption, dominates her fiction. A complete bibliography and an index are provided.

Lawson, Lewis A. *Another Generation: Southern Fiction Since World War II*. Jackson: University Press of Mississippi, 1984. The introduction to this volume discusses the importance of O'Connor to the other major writers of her generation. Also includes a significant essay dealing with O'Connor's use of the grotesque in *Wise Blood*.

O'Connor, Flannery. *Mystery and Manners: Occasional Prose*, selected and edited by Sally and Robert Fitzgerald. New York: Farrar, Straus & Giroux, 1969. This collection of O'Connor's own comments, some published, some from manuscript notes, ranges in subject matter from the importance of literature in schools to the importance of the church, from the Southern grotesque to writing as a craft. An ideal starting point for the student of O'Connor.

Paulson, Suzanne Morrow. *Flannery O'Connor: A Study of the Short Fiction*. Boston: Twayne, 1988. In addition to an excellent critical analysis of O'Connor's short stories, Paulson's volume contains relevant comments by O'Connor, her friends and acquaintances, and her editors. Concludes with a collection of excerpts from various critics, a bibliography, and an index.

Stephens, Martha. *The Question of Flannery O'Connor*. Baton Rouge: Louisiana State University Press, 1973. Stephens explores what she sees as an ambiguity in tone which is evident throughout O'Connor's fiction: on the one hand, the assertion of faith in Christianity, and on the other hand, a pervading pessimism, which suggests the improbability of redemption. Includes a useful annotated bibliography, a full list of sources, and an index.

JOHN O'HARA

Born: Pottsville, Pennsylvania; January 31, 1905
Died: Princeton, New Jersey; April 11, 1970

Principal long fiction

Appointment in Samarra, 1934; *Butterfield 8*, 1935; *A Rage to Live*, 1949; *The Farmer's Hotel*, 1951; *Ten North Frederick*, 1955; *A Family Party*, 1956; *From the Terrace*, 1958; *Ourselves to Know*, 1960; *Sermons and Soda Water*, 1960; *The Big Laugh*, 1962; *Elizabeth Appleton*, 1963; *The Lockwood Concern*, 1965; *The Instrument*, 1967; *Lovely Child: A Philadelphian's Story*, 1969; *The Ewings*, 1972.

Other literary forms

John O'Hara was a prolific writer of short stories, and eleven volumes of stories were published during his lifetime. After O'Hara's death, Random House, his publisher since 1947, brought out two additional collections: *The Time Element and Other Stories* (1972) and *Good Samaritan and Other Stories*, (1974). Scattered through the short-story collections are most of O'Hara's works in the novella form; the only novellas to be separately published are the three in *Sermons and Soda Water*. The play version of the story "Pal Joey" was published in 1952, and in 1961 it was reissued with four others in *Five Plays*. O'Hara's last complete play, *Far from Heaven* (1962), was first published posthumously in 1979 along with an unproduced original screenplay, *The Man Who Could Not Lose* (1959), under the title *Two by O'Hara*. Like many other writers of his period, O'Hara wrote and collaborated on film scripts from the 1930's through the 1950's, and several of his novels were made into films during his lifetime. O'Hara began his writing career as a journalist, and he was several times a newspaper columnist. Two collections of his columns were published: *Sweet and Sour*—columns written for the Trenton *Sunday Times-Advertiser*—and *My Turn*, a series of syndicated columns written for *Newsday*. A collection of O'Hara's speeches, essays, and interviews, entitled *An Artist Is His Own Fault*, was edited by Matthew J. Bruccoli in 1977.

Achievements

Often dismissed as a popular novelist with tendencies toward sensationalism, or as a "social historian," O'Hara has nevertheless secured a faithful following among many literary critics for his skill at storytelling and his evocation of times, places, and manners in American society in the first half of the twentieth century. O'Hara himself was equivocal about the label "social historian." In a speech in 1961, he said, "I deny that I am a social historian"; yet he went on to say that "before deciding to write a novel, I consider what opportunities a story offers for my comments on my times." Matthew J.

Bruccoli is probably most accurate in calling O'Hara a "novelist of manners," in the sense that he was primarily concerned with the accurate depiction of a social matrix and its effect on human behavior and potential. Like William Faulkner and other twentieth century American novelists, O'Hara turned the realities of his hometown experience into a fictional world; unlike Faulkner, he probed this milieu with a dedication to social realism rather than elevating it to mythic status. In addition to his native Eastern Pennsylvania, O'Hara used New York and Hollywood as frequent settings for his fiction. Although he lived and worked in both places, he is most clearly identified with the "Region" of Pennsylvania on which he could bring to bear an insider's perceptions.

The fact that O'Hara was a realistic storyteller rather than an "experimental" novelist was detrimental to his critical reputation during his lifetime. Ironically, the explicit sexuality in much of his work (though restrained by today's standards), which was partially responsible for creating wide popular interest in his novels and which caused *Ten North Frederick* to be suppressed in several cities, overshadowed the depth of his concern with societal mores and pressures. Although he emphasized the role of fate and chance, O'Hara is usually considered a realist rather than a naturalist, largely because he allowed the possibility of moral choice. His long, detailed novels characteristically show people of a privileged socioeconomic level struggling with the realities of social class, personal worth, and complex human relationships.

O'Hara's treatment of his women characters has been overlooked by most critics, yet it may help to account for his enormous contemporary popularity. Long before it was fashionable or even allowable to do so, O'Hara realistically portrayed women as sexual human beings, and even dealt openly with lesbianism in some of his novels and stories. Though several of his major female characters (such as Edith Chapin in *Ten North Frederick* and Elizabeth Appleton in the novel by the same name) are stereotypically manipulative, they are believable, complex people whose motivations are clearly the result of cultural pressures. It would be inaccurate to call O'Hara a "feminist" novelist, but he acknowledged women's power and their problems in ways which set him apart from most novelists of his period.

Whatever the eventual critical evaluation of O'Hara as a twentieth century American novelist, it is certain that his work will be used as a valuable resource for information about customs, manners, and attitudes in America from the 1920's through the 1950's, much as one consults the work of Theodore Dreiser, Sinclair Lewis, or John Updike. The ear for dialogue, the eye for detail, and the perception of human nature which made him a popular novelist will also ensure his continued importance.

Biography

John Henry O'Hara was born on January 31, 1905, in Pottsville, Pennsylvania. The town of Pottsville became the "Gibbsville" of his fiction, and the surrounding Eastern Pennsylvania anthracite coal-mining area, known to residents as the "Region," was the locale of his major novels and stories. The author's father, Patrick O'Hara, was a doctor whose father had settled in the area during the Civil War, and his mother, Katharine Delaney O'Hara, was the daughter of a prosperous businessman in nearby Lykens, which became O'Hara's fictional "Lyons." Dr. Patrick O'Hara was a respected surgeon, necessarily specializing in injuries resulting from mining accidents, and he was seriously disappointed at his first-born son's refusal to study medicine. Rather than inspiring a dedication to the medical profession, O'Hara's travels with his father to the scenes of medical emergencies provided him with regional lore which found its way into his writing.

Living on Pottsville's "best" street, Mahantongo ("Lantenengo" in the fictional Gibbsville), was a sign of the O'Hara family's relative affluence, and provided O'Hara with an awareness of the rigid economic and ethnic stratification of the town. Until his father's early death in 1925, O'Hara led a fairly privileged existence, and his dream of attending Yale was thwarted less by lack of funds than by O'Hara's dismissals from three preparatory schools for low grades and disregard of discipline. The alternative to college was a job as a reporter on the Pottsville *Journal* in 1924, which effectively launched O'Hara's career as a writer.

In 1928, O'Hara left Pottsville for New York, where he worked briefly for the *Herald-Tribune* and *Time*, and began to contribute stories to *The New Yorker*, which eventually published more than two hundred of his short stories; accordingly, some have attributed to O'Hara the creation of that subgenre, the "*New Yorker* story." During these early years in New York, O'Hara established friendships with Franklin P. Adams (F. P. A.)—to whose New York *World* column "The Conning Tower" he sometimes contributed—Robert Benchley, Dorothy Parker, and F. Scott Fitzgerald. In 1931, he married Helen Ritchie Petit ("Pet"), but his heavy drinking and frequent unemployment led to a divorce in 1933.

Appointment in Samarra, the first of O'Hara's fifteen novels, was published in 1934, and his first collection of short stories, *The Doctor's Son*, appeared the following year. Although he was not financially secure for some time, O'Hara's reputation as a fiction-writer grew steadily, and for the next twenty years, he lived alternately on the East Coast and in Hollywood, where he wrote film scripts. Although he intermittently aspired to be a playwright, O'Hara's only successful play was *Pal Joey*, based on a series of stories in *The New Yorker* which ran on Broadway between 1940 and 1941, and was made into a film in 1957. In 1956, O'Hara was given the National Book Award for *Ten North Frederick*, and in 1957 he was inducted into the National Institute of Arts and Letters, from which he resigned in 1961 because he had not been nominated for its Gold Medal for fiction.

In 1937, O'Hara was married for the second time, to Belle Mulford Wylie, the mother of his only child, Wylie Delaney O'Hara, born in 1945. The O'Haras moved to Princeton, New Jersey, in 1949, and in 1953, a serious ulcer condition prompted O'Hara to quit drinking permanently. Following Belle's death in 1954, O'Hara married Katharine Barnes Bryan ("Sister") in 1955, and the family moved two years later to "Linebrook," a home in Princeton which O'Hara and Sister had designed. O'Hara died at Linebrook in April 11, 1970, while working on a sequel to *The Ewings*, his last published novel.

Analysis

In the spring of 1960, John O'Hara wrote as part of his Preface to *Sermons and Soda Water*: "The Twenties, the Thirties, and the Forties are already history, but I cannot be content to leave their story in the hands of the historians and the editors of picture books. I want to record the way people talked and thought and felt." Despite his frequent rejection of the seemingly derogatory critical label of "social historian," which seemed to separate him in the minds of critics from more "serious" novelists, O'Hara was committed throughout his career to providing accurate records of the decades and places in which he lived. The novels and novellas which resulted from this commitment are uneven in quality as examples of the art of fiction, but they provide an unmatched portrait of segments of American society in the first half of the century. The central characters of much of his fiction are wealthy, prominent people, whether they are the leading citizens of "Gibbsville," Pennsylvania, or Hollywood film stars, yet O'Hara frequently illuminates their circumstances by juxtaposing them with members of other socioeconomic groups: servants, tradesmen, laborers. The result is a panoramic social canvas, consonant with O'Hara's conception of the traditional novel form. Occasionally, as in *From the Terrace*, the realist's attempt at panoramic vision overwhelms artistic control; as Sheldon Grebstein remarks in *John O'Hara* (1966), "*the tranche de vie . . .* has been cut too thick to be digestible." At his best, however, O'Hara's work reflects the rich diversity of American society, as in his counterpointing of the savvy political boss Mike Slattery and the wealthy, naïve, would-be politician Joe Chapin in *Ten North Frederick*.

As the example of politics suggests, one of O'Hara's major themes is power—not only the power of money, though that is a central metaphor, but also the power inherent in talent, morality, and sexuality. O'Hara shared with F. Scott Fitzgerald a fascination with wealth and social prestige, but his treatment of their influence is far more analytical. His novels typically trace the establishment of a family dynasty, as in *The Lockwood Concern*, or the progress of an individual's aspirations for himself or herself, as in *Ten North Frederick*, and *Elizabeth Appleton*—always within the constraints of a social web rendered palpable by realistic settings and dialogue. O'Hara is concerned particularly to show the limits of human power, not in the face of an overwhelming fate, but as the result of miscalculation, error, or simple human frailty. When Julian English throws a drink in the face of Harry Reilly in *Appointment in Samarra*, or when George Lockwood, in *The Lockwood Concern*, builds a wall around his mansion, neither can foresee the fatal conseqences, but both have made choices which dictate inevitable results.

As money is a metaphor for power in O'Hara's fiction, sexuality is an ambivalent metaphor for love. Though he was accused of sensationalism and bad taste in his relatively explicit depiction of sexual relationships, O'Hara was primarily interested in showing the potential for manipulation in the human sexual relationship. Women as well as men are portrayed as captive to sexual desire, and both sexes frequently mistake love for possession, or sex for love. From Grace Caldwell Tate's injudicious couplings in *A Rage to Live* to the tender relationship between Jim Malloy and Charlotte Sears in *The Girl on the Baggage Truck*, the possibility of true romantic love seems remote in O'Hara's fiction. His realistic approach assumes a basic human egotism and desire for power which renders such love rare.

The structures of O'Hara's novels and novellas reinforce the sense of inevitability of consequence. His novels frequently begin with an apparently small but significant event or action which spins out in mystery-story fashion to create the web which catches the characters and demonstrates their ultimate powerlessness. Yet, he avoids the predictability of formulaic fiction by using multiple points of view and a wealth of complex, believable characters to play out the drama. In the novellas, the structure is frequently circular, the story beginning at a moment of culmination and then tracing the events which have brought the characters to that point. Common too, especially in the novellas, is O'Hara's use of a narrator, usually Jim Malloy, a journalist whose background and attitudes resemble those of O'Hara. Although these structural devices were not original with O'Hara, he used them skillfully to suit his fictional purposes.

Character is of supreme importance in O'Hara's fiction, and the achievement of adequate characterization determined the form he used. As he said in one of his Rider College lectures, "before I have finished two pages of manuscript my author's instinct has told me how much I want to tell about this character, and thus the length of the story is dictated." The majority of O'Hara's characters inhabit the Pennsylvania "Region" in which he spent his youth, and the fictional canon provides a vivid picture of relationships among people of various social levels over time. The reappearance of certain characters in many works reinforces the sense of a coherent world within which the codes of morality and propriety dictate the shape of both society and individual human lives.

In its settings, characters, and incidents, O'Hara's fiction is strongly autobiographical, a circumstance which is a natural outgrowth of his desire to be a recorder of his times. Though he did not live in Pottsville, Pennsylvania, after 1930, the town and its people continued to serve as a microcosm of the American culture he dissected throughout his career. Like his autobiographical narrator Jim Malloy, O'Hara returned to Pottsville "only long enough to stand at a grave, to toast a bride, to spend a few minutes beside a sickbed," but the years he spent there left an indelible impression. From his vantage point as the doctor's son, O'Hara observed both the leading citizens and the transients, and later he explored, in his novels and novellas, the lives he imagined to exist behind the placid exterior of the American small town. Part of the autobiographical content of the fiction, however, comes from O'Hara's unfulfilled aspirations rather than from his actual experience. Although his dream of attending an Ivy League college was thwarted by his checkered prep school record and the death of his father, O'Hara's upper-class male characters typically attend prestigious universities and benefit from larger family fortunes than O'Hara's family ever enjoyed. His fiction, like that of Fitzgerald, thus conveys an ambivalent attitude toward the privileged: the wistfulness of the outsider and the realist's desire to reduce them to understandable human terms.

The span of O'Hara's career, from 1934 to 1970, coincided with a period of intense experimentation in literary forms. The fiction of James Joyce and William Faulkner, among others, tested the limits of the novel, and critical opinion during these years favored attempts to break the mold of traditional fiction, to push beyond the bounds of realistic documentation of recognizable human events. Thus, O'Hara's accurate rendition of dialogue lost place to stream of consciousness as an acclaimed technique, and the chronicling of successive generations was less favored than novels spanning a single day, controlled by a single consciousness. O'Hara's novels continue to be appreciated more for their documentary usefulness than for their creative force, yet within the limits of the traditional novel form, O'Hara was a master craftsman who captured and conveyed the human drama and social fabric of a complex period in American life.

In 1961, O'Hara referred to *Appointment in Samarra* as "a live novel twenty-five years after first publication." More than twenty years later, this novel, O'Hara's first, is still "live" in several senses. It is obviously the work of a professional writer; O'Hara's powers of observation and skill in plot construction are already highly developed in this short novel. Also, *Appointment in Samarra* is set in the "Region" of Eastern Pennsylvania, the setting of much of his long fiction throughout his career, and it has strong autobiographical elements. Finally, the novel deals starkly and dramatically with the themes of power and fate, and demonstrates O'Hara's understanding of individual human destiny as a delicate balance between necessity and accident. The novel's title derives from a quotation from W. Somerset Maugham; the "appointment in Samarra" is an inescapable appointment with death, yet Julian English, O'Hara's main character, is doomed by his own actions—his tragedy is of his own making.

The story of Julian English is set against a richly detailed social and geographical background. O'Hara takes pains to provide the reader with the flavor of the early Depression years: the names of popular songs, the intricacies of the bootlegger's profession, and the subdued desperation of both rich and poor. To tie even further the novel to an era, there are topical references; Julian English mentions having recently read Ernest Hemingway's *A Farewell to Arms* (1929), and Irma Fleigler counts on President Herbert Hoover's promise that next year will be better for everyone, so that she and her husband can join the country club to which the Englishes belong. The club, and the town and region of which it is the social pinnacle, are treated with the same careful detail. O'Hara devotes several pages to the peculiarities of the anthracite coal region and the social hierarchy of Gibbsville, making clear that no person or action is independent of the social context. Despite the anxieties of what was called in 1930 a "slump," Gibbsville and its inhabitants are filled with self-importance, and none more so than Julian English, the doctor's son.

English and O'Hara share several biographical similarities. Julian, like O'Hara, has refused to adopt his doctor-father's profession, and his refusal has caused a serious rift in the father-son relationship. Julian English admires Franklin P. Adams (F. P. A.), to whom O'Hara dedicated *Appointment in Samarra*, and when a priest asks him whether he is a "frustrated literary man," Julian answers, "I'm not anything. I guess I should have been a doctor." The most important similarity between English and his creator is the sense of insecurity betrayed by this remark, an insecurity which leads both men to heavy drinking and defensive belligerence. The significant difference is that Julian English does not survive his own nature.

To dramatize his perception that the individual is inextricably bound up in his social context, O'Hara deftly shifts the point of view in the novel from interior to exterior views of Julian English, emphasizing the extent to which one person becomes the object of others' scrutiny. The novel covers the last three days of Julian's life, from the moment he throws a drink in Harry Reilly's face at the country-club Christmas party until he commits suicide by carbon monoxide poisoning, yet the narrative begins and ends with the observations of Luther and Irma Fleigler, a middle-class couple whose solid respectability and loving relationship contrasts sharply with the weakness and manipulation of the far wealthier Julian and Caroline English. Julian's action is, in itself, insignificant—a social error from which all parties could have recovered in time—but it becomes symbolic of Julian's misperception of his own strength and power. With the inevitability of Greek tragedy, social ostracism follows Julian's throwing of the drink; he becomes an outsider to his own group, and he fails in all his efforts to pick up the pieces of his life.

O'Hara presents, one by one, the sources of comfort to which twentieth century men turn in times of personal trouble, and shows them all to be ineffective. Family, sex, work, drink, religion, even a simple apology—none provides solace to Julian, who is the isolated twentieth century man, left with nothing in which to believe. If Julian does not understand the motivation for his action, neither does anyone else around him, and neither his father, Dr. English, nor his wife can respond adequately to his anguish. Work fails as an escape because, as the president of a Cadillac dealership, Julian is dependent upon precisely the good will of potential customers which his action has temporarily denied him, and drink leads to either self-pity or further belligerence. Monsignor Creedon, to whom Julian, a Protestant, feels obscurely drawn, confesses that he has sometimes wished he had chosen a different life's work; lacking a true vocation, he cannot provide a spiritual solution to Julian's guilt and loneliness.

Although the major conflict in the novel is that between Julian's personal responsibility for his own actions and fate and the effect of his social surroundings on that fate, O'Hara introduces a third element: heredity. Conscious of his own family heritage, and especially of his forebears' struggle through generations for greater status and respectability in the "Region," O'Hara places great importance on a sense of heritage. His characters are typically aware of where they come from, who their ancestors are, and to what this background entitles them on the social scale. Julian English's grandfather had committed suicide after embezzling money from a bank, and after Julian's suicide, Dr. English consoles himself regarding his own reputation by assuming that people "would see how the suicide strain has skipped one generation to come out in the next."

Dr. English reappears in several of O'Hara's later works, as do several other characters introduced. Jim Malloy, mentioned previously, becomes the narrator of the novellas in *Sermons and Soda Water*, and the relationship between Whit Hofman, here a minor character, and Pat Collins is the basis of the novella *Pat Collins*. In short, *Appointment in Samarra* established O'Hara's major locale, characters, and themes, and much of his fictional canon enlarged upon what was set forth in this novel.

The critical reception of O'Hara's first novel was generally favorable, though some reviewers were disturbed by its relatively explicit sexuality. This reaction was intensified by his next two major novels, *Butterfield 8* and *A Rage to Live*, both of which sold well in part because of the furor, while his collections of short stories were consistently well-received. *Appointment in Samarra* had launched its author on a successful career.

Although many of the short stories O'Hara published in the five collections between 1935 and 1947 were set in the "Region," *Ten North Frederick* was the first novel after *Appointment in Samarra* to deal with that locale. *Ten North Frederick* marked the beginning of the major phase of O'Hara's work as well as a new stage in his life. Two years before its publication, he had

suffered the bleeding ulcer which convinced him to give up alcohol permanently, and a few months before, he had married Katharine Barnes Bryan,
whom he referred to as "Sister." For the next fifteen years until his death,
O'Hara would live a more settled, productive life than ever before. The timing
of the novel's publication also began a tradition that continued for the rest
of his career. Because O'Hara, always sensitive to reviews, wanted the task
of reviewing *Ten North Frederick* to fall to a particular writer for *The New
York Times*, the novel was issued on a Thursday in late November. The day
was Thanksgiving, and the publication of an O'Hara novel or collection became
an annual Thanksgiving event.

   Butterfield 8 had been a *roman à clef*, based on the sensational and tragic
story of Starr Faithfull, but despite certain resemblances between the lives
of Joe Chapin and Franklin Delano Roosevelt, *Ten North Frederick* is not.
Rather, as Matthew Bruccoli suggests, the novel is a "what-if study: what if
Roosevelt had been a Gibbsville Republican?" O'Hara undoubtedly had Roosevelt in mind as he created Joe Chapin, and used some elements of Roosevelt's life—the strong mother with ambitions for her son and a physical
crippling in mid-life—but his intention was not, as it was in *Butterfield 8*, to
write a fictional account of a well-known person. Indeed, whereas Roosevelt's
story is one of triumph over personal adversity, *Ten North Frederick* chronicles
the failure of Joe Chapin's ambitions.

   Those ambitions are far from modest. Joe Chapin wants nothing less than
to leave each of his children a million dollars upon his death and to become
president of the United States. That he achieves neither goal is in part the
result of circumstances (the Depression reduces his financial assets) and in
part of errors in judgment, such as his attempting to circumvent the local
political system managed by Mike Slattery. Despite the magnitude of his
hopes, Chapin is neither grasping nor overwhelmingly egotistical. Although
he makes some ill-considered decisions about the lives of others—notably his
daughter's abortion and the dissolution of her marriage to an Italian musician—he is not a power-hungry schemer. Instead, he is unaware that his own
power has limits. Reared to believe in the privileges of wealth and status and
trained in the proprieties of social forms, Chapin is merely inflexible. Rules
and forms have taken precedence over human responsiveness, and his one
extramarital affair, late in his life, seems to be the only spontaneous action
of which he is capable.

   Joe Chapin's life thus has an opaque surface which prevents even his closest
Gibbsville associates from knowing him well. At Chapin's funeral, one of his
cousins remarks, "I could never figure Joe out," to which Mike Slattery
replies, "We knew exactly what Joe wanted us to know. And believe me, that
wasn't much." Coming at the beginning of the novel, this exchange might
have foreshadowed the revelation of a secret life which Chapin had hidden
carefully from his friends, but O'Hara's intention instead is to show that the

reality of Chapin's life is one with its facade. Behind the mask of respectability is a life which is just as sterile as the mask would suggest. With the exception of minor scandals such as his daughter's elopement and pregnancy, Chapin's experience has been one of single-minded devotion to the accumulation of wealth and status.

Beginning *Ten North Frederick* with the funeral of his main character, O'Hara employed a structural device which attested to his development as a novelist. Both *Appointment in Samarra* and *Ten North Frederick* begin with a moment of crisis or transition, but whereas in *Appointment in Samarra* the rest of the novel traces the inevitable results of that moment, *Ten North Frederick* begins with the conclusion—the death of Joe Chapin—and then proceeds to explore the life which has ended. The fact that the major threads of that life are introduced in the conversations at Chapin's funeral and are later developed in all their complexity has caused Sheldon Grebstein to call this a "tapestry novel." Having revealed the significant facts about Joe Chapin's life early in the novel, O'Hara must compel the reader to continue by means other than suspense.

The major strength of *Ten North Frederick*, as of most of O'Hara's fiction, is its characterization. The novel deals with three generations of the Chapin family, beginning with Joe Chapin's parents, though instead of a straight chronological narrative O'Hara uses a flashback technique, weaving past and present together to emphasize the effect of family—especially women—on the formation of character and ambition. Both Joe's mother, Charlotte, and his wife, Edith, have plans for his life; both are women for whom love means power and ownership, and for whom sex is a form of manipulation. Edith Chapin articulates this persistent theme of O'Hara's novels as she thinks, on her wedding night, "It was not Love; Love might easily have very little to do with it; but it was as strong a desire as Love or Hate and it was going to be her life, the owning of this man." As clearly as anywhere in his fiction, O'Hara here portrays women who, because they are denied most masculine forms of power, participate vicariously by requiring their men to succeed in their stead.

Yet Joe Chapin is a failure. If there is a "secret" in his life it is the depth of his desire for high political office. On the surface a personable, respected pillar of Gibbsville, highly regarded by most of its leading citizens, Chapin nurses the ambition for which his mother has groomed him, but he is not willing to play the political games required to gain the backing of Mike Slattery's organization, nor can money buy him the office he seeks. After he is forced to withdraw from the political arena, only his brief affair with his daughter's friend Kate Drummond gives his life meaning, and when that ends he slowly begins to commit suicide by drinking heavily.

Many of O'Hara's own feelings about accomplishment and aging informed his creation of Joe Chapin. O'Hara was fifty when the novel was completed. Like Chapin, he had gained the respect of many of his contemporaries, but certain measures of "success" had eluded him: in particular, recognition as a first-rate novelist. Both O'Hara and his character had suffered frightening indications of poor health; Chapin ignored the warning that alcohol was killing him, but O'Hara did not. Time had become precious to him, and he reflects on this in the final paragraph of *Ten North Frederick*: "There is always enough to do while the heart keeps pumping. There is never, never enough time to do it all." O'Hara was rewarded for his persistence when *Ten North Frederick* received the National Book Award for 1955. The award citation read in part: "Tough-minded as usual, Mr. O'Hara has written a novel of emotional depth and moral conviction."

The swift passing of time to which O'Hara referred in *Ten North Frederick* was one of the reasons he turned to the novella form in the three pieces which comprise *Sermons and Soda Water*. The novella took, he said, "a minimum of research," as compared to the "big novel" he was working on simultaneously (probably *The Lockwood Concern*). He wrote these novellas to "get it all down on paper while I can"; "at fifty-five I have no right to waste time." The novella, in other words, could be written quickly, from memory, rather than requiring years of research and writing. This distinction between the novel and the novella suggests that the material for the latter was more likely to be autobiographical, and his use of Jim Malloy as narrator in these three novellas adds to the impression that these are personal narratives.

Although O'Hara never fully defined the terms "novella" and "novelette" as he used them, he suggested in 1968 that the important consideration was character. The form, he said, "tells all that you need to know about certain people in certain circumstances so that those people become figures in the reader's personal library." He had first experimented with a form midway in length between the short story and the novel in the title story of *The Doctor's Son and Other Stories*, his first collection of short stories, but during the last decade of his career, beginning with *Sermons and Soda Water*, he developed the novella form as a means of disentangling one thread from the usual complex tapestry of his novels. The novella as O'Hara conceived of it has an episodic structure. It follows one conflict, relationship, or problem through a lengthy time span, isolating for dramatic attention only the crucial periods, and briefly summarizing intervening months or years. There are no subplots, and minor characters are functional rather than centers of interest in their own right.

The use of a first-person narrator with a limited consciousness, rather than the omniscient point of view O'Hara employed in most of his novels, helps to ensure the sharp focus required for the novella. Jim Malloy, the narrator of *Sermons and Soda Water*, tells the reader about the people he has known in his hometown of Gibbsville or those he meets as a journalist in New York. He is a thin mask for O'Hara in the early days of the author's career: the young man from the coal region who begins his career in New York, encounters the wealthy and famous, and keeps up with a few of the people back home. Yet, Malloy has the mature vision of O'Hara at fifty-five, and his perspective on the characters' lives is that of a concerned friend rather than an impressionable young man. Malloy, like O'Hara, is a shrewd observer of human nature, one who finds patterns in life. In *We're Friends Again*, the third novella in *Sermons and Soda Water*, he comments on this ability: "The way things tie up, one with another, is likely to go unnoticed until a lawyer or a writer calls our attention to it." Malloy's function in these novellas is to demonstrate how "things tie up" while remaining more or less removed from the central stories.

In this ultimate detachment from the lives of the characters he describes, Malloy underscores the central theme of *Sermons and Soda Water*: human loneliness and isolation. At the end of *We're Friends Again*, Malloy calls loneliness "the final condition of us all," and O'Hara shows that it affects people at all levels of society, from Charlotte Sears, the film star in *The Girl on the Baggage Truck*, to Pete and Bobbie McCrea of Gibbsville in *Imagine Kissing Pete*. The solution to loneliness is love, but, as O'Hara so often suggests, love is elusive, and one often settles for approximations: attraction, sex, power. As Charlotte Sears says about her relationship with the wealthy, reclusive Thomas Hunterden, "There ought to be another word for love, for people like Hunterden and me." It is left to Malloy, as the controlling consciousness, to find meaning in the lives he relates, and that meaning resides ultimately in his capacity as a writer to discern patterns of inevitability in human life.

Of the novels written during O'Hara's last decade, *The Lockwood Concern* is particularly interesting as a culmination of many aspects of his career. During this period he used a variety of settings for his fiction—Hollywood in *The Big Laugh*, Philadelphia in *Lovely Child*—but in *The Lockwood Concern* he returned to the "Region," to the characters and situations that he handled with ease and familiarity. Throughout the early 1960's, O'Hara referred to a "big" novel on which he was working, and at one point he projected that it would be a two-volume work. *The Lockwood Concern* is in fact a one-volume work of average length, but its scope justifies O'Hara's adjective: it is a multigenerational novel, a "century-spanning saga," as the jacket blurb proclaimed.

The theme of *The Lockwood Concern* is consistent with much of O'Hara's other work, and reaches back to *Appointment in Samarra*: the ultimate powerlessness of the individual against the force of circumstance, particularly the folly of attempting to control the destinies of others. The attempts of Abraham and George Lockwood, the second and third generations of the Lockwood family of Swedish Haven (actually Schuylkill Haven, near Pottsville), to establish a family dynasty break down in the fourth generation when George Lockwood's son and daughter reject the town and the family and adopt ways of life antithetical to dynastic responsibilities. The "concern" of the title is a Quaker concept, denoting an overwhelming sense of mission. Abraham Lockwood, in the late nineteenth century, has secularized this religious concept and translated it into a vision of generations of Lockwoods enjoying increasing wealth and prestige, including entrée to the clubs and other bastions of gentility denied him by the uncouth background and behavior of his own father, Moses Lockwood.

The central figure of *The Lockwood Concern* is George Lockwood, who has adopted Abraham's dream and brought it to the point of realization. George Lockwood's children will be the first generation to enjoy full acceptance by elite society, and as an emblem of this progress he has built a family mansion near Swedish Haven. The high, spiked wall around the house testifies to George's sense of exclusivity; it is also the cause of the death of a neighboring farm boy, who becomes impaled while attempting to climb the fence before the house is completed. This tragedy, which George Lockwood hastens to keep quiet, opens the novel, a signal of the crumbling of the erstwhile dynasty. From this point, George struggles to maintain the "concern" against increasing evidence of its demise until he finally falls to his death down a secret staircase he has had built in the still-uninhabited mansion.

O'Hara here used the circular structure which he had perfected in both long and short fiction throughout his career. The novel begins and ends in the mid-1920's, but ranges back to the mid-nineteenth century as O'Hara details the history of the "Lockwood concern." It opens with the death of the unnamed farm boy and closes with the death of George Lockwood and, by implication, of the "concern." Simultaneously, the novel has the linear thrust of the historical novel. From the canny, vigorous survival of Moses Lockwood to the effete California existence of George's son Bing, the generations move through historical and cultural change, reflecting shifting values in American society. The novel argues that such change is inevitable, and that George Lockwood's attempt at consolidation and stasis is doomed from the start. Social flux is mirrored even in the names of the male Lockwoods over time, from the tradition and authority of "Moses" and "Abraham" to the frivolity of "Bing." Even with such change, however, basic human nature does not alter; George and Bing Lockwood are, in different ways, as conniving and self-interested as their ancestors, though protected by wealth and attorneys against open public disapproval.

The Lockwood Concern is a summation of much that O'Hara had tried and accomplished during thirty years of writing. Though not his best novel, it is one of his most ambitious in subject matter and scope. It provides a history of the "Region" from the time of O'Hara's ancestors until the time when he left it for New York, and shows the growth of the region from a backwoods settlement to a thriving coal-mining and farming area which sent its sons to Princeton and Harvard. Thematically, the novel shows that O'Hara had come to some conclusions about the interplay of destiny and choice. He had shown in *Appointment in Samarra* that an individual's power over his own life was limited by the influence of society and the intervention of chance. In *Ten North Frederick*, he added great wealth and ambition to the equation and demonstrated their ineffectuality. By the time he wrote *The Lockwood Concern*, O'Hara saw the limits to human power as determined not only by conflicting wills and accidents of fate, but also by the very sweep of time and change. Human aspiration pales before the only human certainty—death—which is described as a "secret" known only to those who have experienced it.

By entitling his biography of the author *The O'Hara Concern* (1975), Matthew J. Bruccoli suggests that O'Hara felt a sense of mission similar to that of the Lockwoods. If so, O'Hara's "concern" was not related to a family dynasty but instead to establishing himself among the first rank of American novelists. His lifelong war with literary critics and reviewers over the value of his contribution is evidence that he was never secure in his own reputation. Although he rejected the terms "social realist" and "social historian," these are appropriate characterizations of his best work. O'Hara's sense of history, his precise rendering of detail and dialogue, and his command of narrative technique make him one of the most significant chroniclers of American life in the first half of the twentieth century. The fact that he was a popular novelist during his career, in part because of the more sensational aspects of his work, has detracted from his critical reputation, but his position as an important novelist of manners seems secure.

Nancy Walker

Other major works

SHORT FICTION: *The Doctor's Son and Other Stories*, 1935; *Hope of Heaven*, 1938; *Files on Parade*, 1939; *Pal Joey*, 1940; *Pipe Night*, 1945; *Hellbox*, 1947; *Assembly*, 1961; *The Cape Cod Lighter*, 1962; *The Hat on the Bed*, 1963; *The Horse Knows the Way*, 1964; *Waiting for Winter*, 1966; *And Other Stories*, 1968; *The O'Hara Generation*, 1969; *The Time Element and Other Stories*, 1972; *Good Samaritan and Other Stories*, 1974.

PLAYS: *Five Plays*, 1961; *Two by O'Hara*, 1979.

NONFICTION: *Sweet and Sour*, 1954; *My Turn*, 1966; *A Cub Tells His Story*, 1974, *An Artist Is His Own Fault*, 1977.

Bibliography
Bruccoli, Matthew. *John O'Hara: A Descriptive Bibliography*. Pittsburgh: University of Pittsburgh Press, 1978. A thorough, scholarly bibliography on all aspects of O'Hara's work. A must for the serious student.
_____. *The O'Hara Concern: A Biography of John O'Hara*. New York: Random House, 1975. The expertise of Bruccoli is evident here in

this comprehensive biography of O'Hara. Contains valuable background, critical references to his works, and a useful bibliography.

Grebstein, Sheldon Norman. *John O'Hara*. New York: Twayne, 1966. This critical study both interprets and assesses O'Hara's work. Grebstein is mostly sympathetic toward O'Hara, but has some reservations about his writings. Also assesses other criticism on O'Hara.

MacShane, Frank. *The Life of John O'Hara*. New York: E. P. Dutton, 1980. Looks at O'Hara's life through his work. A thorough study well worth reading for its valuable insights.

Shannon, William V. *The American Irish*. New York: Macmillan, 1963. Deals with O'Hara's work from the point of view of his Irish ancestry and his desire to escape from it.

GEORGE ORWELL
Eric Arthur Blair

Born: Motihari, India; June 25, 1903
Died: London, England; January 21, 1950

Principal long fiction
Burmese Days, 1934; *A Clergyman's Daughter*, 1935; *Keep the Aspidistra Flying*, 1936; *Coming Up for Air*, 1939; *Animal Farm*, 1945; *Nineteen Eighty-Four*, 1949.

Other literary forms
Since the mid-1940's, George Orwell has been considered one of the world's premier essayists. Combining reportage, the polemical essay, fictional techniques, and refracted autobiographical detail, his works defy precise generic definition. Orwell's numerous nonfiction works have been compiled in *The Collected Essays, Journalism, and Letters of George Orwell* (1968), edited by Sonia Orwell and Ian Angus.

Achievements
Although Orwell is widely recognized as one of the best essayists of the twentieth century, his reputation as a novelist rests almost entirely on two works: the political allegory *Animal Farm* and the dystopian *Nineteen Eighty-Four*. Both have been translated into so many other languages and have been so widely read that the adjective "Orwellian" has international currency, synonymous with the "ghastly political future," as Bernard Crick has pointed out (*George Orwell: A Life*, 1980). Indeed, Jeffrey Meyers is convinced that Orwell, the writer of essays, political tracts, and fiction, "is more widely read than perhaps any other serious writer of the twentieth-century" (*A Reader's Guide to George Orwell*, 1975).

Biography
George Orwell was born Eric Arthur Blair, the son of Richard Walmesley Blair and Ida Limouzin (Blair). Orwell was born in India and lived there for four years, until his father moved the family back to England, to a small house named "Nutshell" in Henley-on-Thames. After a short leave, Orwell's father returned alone to India, leaving his wife and children in England, and rejoining them later, at his retirement. Upon his father's return, Orwell, like most male members of the upper middle class, was sent away to boarding school, St. Cyprian's, located at Eastbourne on the Sussex Coast. After several miserable years, as Orwell described them in his autobiographical *Such, Such Were the Joys*, he won a scholarship to Eton, the public school

that would forever set him apart from the working classes about which he was so concerned during most of his adult life.

Considered rather unacademic at Eton, Orwell was graduated in December, 1921, and, after a decision not to attend the university, he applied to the India Office for the position of Imperial Police Officer. Five years in Burma, from 1922 to 1927, shaped the impressionable young man so as to make him forever after sympathetic to individuals victimized by governmental bureaucracy and imperialistic power. Orwell left Burma in the summer of 1927, ostensibly on sick leave (he suffered from a lung condition most of his life). At some point early in his leave, Orwell wrote a letter of resignation to the India Office, explaining to his skeptical parents that all he really wanted was to write.

In 1928, Orwell commenced a long, five-year apprenticeship as a writer, time spent as a tramp in both Paris and London, and in the writing and rewriting of countless manuscripts. By 1933, he had assumed the name by which he is known and had produced, in addition to at least two destroyed novels, the nonfictional *Down and Out in Paris and London* and his first novel, *Burmese Days*, published one year later.

From 1933 to 1937, Orwell continued to develop his literary talents, producing two more novels, a book about his experiences with poverty-stricken coal miners in Wigan (*The Road to Wigan Pier*), and several essays, occasional pieces, and book reviews. By the end of this period, he had also married, for the first time, and, within a year or so of that, went to Spain. Perhaps the most singular experience of his life to date, the Spanish Civil War found Orwell on the front lines, a member of a *Partido Obrero de Unificación Marxista* (a Marxist worker's party) brigade; henceforth, Orwell passionately declared himself a fighter for "democratic Socialism" and, in that context, wrote his most famous nonfictional work, *Homage to Catalonia*. After being wounded (and nearly imprisoned), Orwell escaped Spain with the help of his wife, returned to England, and continued his literary career. Within another year, his lungs still causing problems, Orwell moved to the dry climate of Morocco, where he wrote much of *Coming Up for Air*.

His fourth novel was buried under mounting war concerns and preparations. Orwell, unable to join the military because of health, became a spokesman for the British Broadcasting Corporation. During the last years of the war, Orwell finished writing *Animal Farm*, only to see it rejected by almost every major publisher in England and America. Finally brought out in August, 1945, during the last days of the Pacific War, *Animal Farm* was a work of near perfection, making Orwell's name internationally known, so that when *Nineteen Eighty-Four* was published four years later, the world came to realize that both works would henceforth be considered literary classics, satires ranking with Thomas More's *Utopia* (1516) and Jonathan Swift's *A Tale of a Tub* (1704). Orwell's death in 1950 at the age of forty-six was a tragic loss to the world of letters and to the larger world with which he always kept in touch.

Analysis

Excepting *Animal Farm*, most critics view George Orwell's fictions as aesthetically flawed creations, the work of a political thinker whose artistry was subordinate to his intensely didactic, partisan passions. This reaction to Orwell's novels was generally promoted posthumously, since his fiction in the 1930's was often ignored by the larger reading public and panned by those reviewers who did pick up one of his books. The early academic critics—up to the late 1960's—were often Orwell's personal friends or acquaintances, who tended to see his early novels as conventionally realistic and strongly autobiographical. Even his masterpieces, *Animal Farm* and *Nineteen Eighty-Four*, were viewed as formally undistinguished, however powerful their message. It was not until the second generation of critics began looking at Orwell's fiction that a more balanced assessment was possible.

Orwell's first published novel, *Burmese Days*, concerns the life of John Flory, an English policeman in Burma during the early 1920's. The plot is fairly straightforward. After a lengthy introduction to Flory's personality and daily life, Orwell dramatizes him as a man blemished with a physical stigma, a birthmark, and puzzled by moral dilemma—how to deal with the increasingly rebellious natives, with whom he is secretly sympathetic but against whom he must wield the club of imperialistic authority. In the middle of this dilemma, Elizabeth arrives, a young English woman who is fresh-faced but decidedly a traditional "burra memsahib." Flory attempts to win both her heart and mind—much to the dismay of his Burmese mistress, Ma Hla May—and succeeds in doing neither, even though he manages to half-succeed in proposing marriage during an earthquake. With a mind too closed to anything not properly British, and a heart only to be won by someone very English, Elizabeth forgets Flory's attentions with the arrival of Verrall, an English military policeman, who will in turn reject her after his billet is completed. A humble Flory waits for Elizabeth, and after Verrall has left takes her to church services, confident that he has outlasted his rival. Unfortunately, Flory is humiliated by Ma Hla May, is repulsed yet again by Elizabeth, and, in a mood of despair, commits suicide, killing both his dog and himself.

Burmese Days is interesting for its accurate psychological portrayal of a man trapped between two worlds: Loving England, yet hating English imperialistic politics; loving and hating the subject people, the Burmese, yet fascinated by their culture and the beauty of their environment. Flory is strangely sympathetic to their struggle for independence while doing everything possible to keep it in check.

In such a world, Flory is emphatically not meant to be a sympathetic character, but rather a victim of the very political order he has sworn to uphold. In effect, Orwell has laid a trap for the unwary reader. Too close an identification with Flory, too intense a desire to have him succeed in marrying Elizabeth—an unholy alliance of imperialistic Englishwoman and revolutionary thinking pariah—will prevent the reader from recognizing the irreconcilable contradictions inherent in the British presence in Burma.

Orwell's fourth published novel, *Coming Up for Air*, was written in Marrakesh, Morocco, shortly after he had recovered from yet another bout with tubercular lesions of the lungs. Although the novel sold moderately well for the time (a first printing, according to Bernard Crick, of two thousand copies and a second printing of one thousand), many critics were vaguely condescending toward the hero, George Bowling, a middle-class insurance salesman who longs for the golden country of the past while simultaneously dreading the horrors of a second world war, then only months away. Many of the themes more fully developed in *Nineteen Eighty-Four* find their initial expression in Orwell's last conventional novel, set before the outbreak of the devastation that the next six years would bring.

Coming Up for Air is set in London during the late 1930's; Orwell employs a first-person narrative to describe the life of George Bowling, a middle-aged, middle-class salesman, whose first set of false teeth marks a major milestone in his life. Musing in front of a mirror while he prepares for work one morning, George's mind wanders back to the past, the golden England of thirty years earlier when he was growing up. As he goes about his day, disgusted with all the evidence of modern life in front of him—the casual brutalities, the tasteless food, the bombers overhead—George forms a plan to return to Lower Binfield, his childhood home, and, by extension, the simple life he had once led. Unfortunately, his return only confirms the all-pervasive slovenliness of the modern world: Lower Binfield has been swallowed by a sprawling suburb, his adolescent sweetheart has become a frowsy old married woman (she is all of two years older than he), and the fishing hole, once filled with huge finny dreams, has been emptied of water and filled with trash. Shocked and completely disenchanted, Bowling makes plans to get at least a relaxing few days from the trip when a bomber accidentally drops a bomb close by, killing and wounding several people. In thorough disgust, Bowling packs, leaves, and returns home to face his wife, who has somehow found out where he has gone, although his motives for going will be forever incomprehensible to her.

A plot summary of the novel fails to do justice to the subtle tonal shifts and complicated psychological changes Orwell employs in presenting his portrait of the average man waiting for the apocalypse. Orwell has used the ancient theme of the double (or *Doppelgänger*) to illustrate the self-fragmentation of European man prior to the outbreak of the war. George Bowling is divided into two "selves": Tubby is the outwardly fat, insensitive insurance tout who is able to function successfully in a fast-paced, competitive world that would eat up less hardened personalities, but his character can only survive at the cost of any sort of satisfying inner life. Georgie, on the other hand, would be lost in the modern rat-race and so is protected by Tubby; nevertheless, Georgie can give expression to the memories, the sensitivities, the love for natural pleasures that Tubby (and George Bowling) would have to forgo to remain functional. Thus, George Bowling devised a strategy for living both materially successful and psychologically well in the modern world, doing so by splitting his identity into Tubby and Georgie. *Coming Up for Air* details the ongoing dialogue between these two "selves"—a conversation which reflects the strains of modern living as well as any other novelist has done in recent times.

Furthermore, Orwell has modified the literary conventions of the *Doppelgänger* to suit his own needs. Whereas the death of one-half of the double usually means the destruction, ultimately, of both, Orwell has Tubby live on after Georgie is symbolically destroyed by the bombing plane. The tonal change at this point, rather like the tonal change in Joseph Heller's *Catch-22* (1961) with the death of Kid Sampson, shows the reader the world that Orwell envisioned between 1938 and 1939, one horrible enough to prevent total escape even by death. It is, however, typically Orwellian that however horrible human bondage can make the cultural world, nature, of which mankind is a part, has enough ebullient energy to wait out any social mess, a wait without immediate hope, without idols, but also without hopeless despair. George Bowling leaves Lower Binfield, returning to his scold of a wife, Hilda, to the everlasting round of bills, worries, war clouds on the horizon, and a death-in-life without Georgie, but, as the novel's epigraph states, "He's dead, but he won't lie down."

Animal Farm is one of those rare books before which the critic lays down his pen. As a self-contained "fairy story," the book can be read and understood by children not old enough to pronounce most of the words in an average junior high school history text. As a political satire, *Animal Farm* can be highly appreciated by those who actually lived through the terrible days of World War II. As an allegory concerned with the limitations and abuses of political power, the novel has been pored over eagerly by several generations of readers.

The novel is built around historical events in the Soviet Union, from before the October Revolution to the end of World War II; it does so by using the frame of reference of animals in a farmyard, the Manor Farm, owned by a Mr. Jones. Drunk most of the time and, like Czar Nicholas of Russia in the second decade of the twentieth century, out of touch with the governed, Jones neglects his farm (allegorically representing the Soviet Union, or by extension, almost any oppressed country), causing much discontent and resentment among his animals. One day, after Jones does his nightly rounds, Major, an imposing pig (V. I. Lenin), tells the other animals of a dream he has had concerning theories about the way they have been living. Animals have been exploited by Mr. Jones and mankind generally, but Major has dreamed of a time when they will throw over their yokes and live free, sharing equally both the profits and hazards of their work. Major teaches the animals the words

Critical Survey of Long Fiction

to a song, "Beasts of England" (The Internationale), and tells them to look to the future and the betterment of all animals; three days later he dies.

The smartest of the animals, the pigs, are aroused by his speech and by the song; they secretly learn to read and write, developing a philosophical system called animalism (Communism, Bolshevism) whose principles are taught to all the animals. When Jones forgets one day to feed them (as Russians starved near the end of their involvement in World War I), the animals revolt spontaneously, driving out Jones, his wife (Russian nobility), and Moses, the raven (the Russian Orthodox Church). The animals rejoice, feeling a sense of camaraderie and *esprit de corps*, and set about to build a new life.

The pigs, however, by taking on the responsibility of organization, also take over certain decision-making processes—as well as all the milk and apples; in fact, Orwell has himself stated that the first sign of corruption, the taking of the cow's milk, led to the inevitable destruction of everything else. Two pigs in particular, Snowball (Leon Trotsky) and Napoleon (Joseph Stalin), argue constantly, while a third, Squealer (*Pravda*, Tass) appears more than happy to endorse any course of action with his adroit use of language and his physical habit of skipping from side to side as he speaks. After changing the name from Manor Farm to Animal Farm, the pigs paint on the the side of the barn the seven commandments of animalism, the most important being: "All animals are equal." Meanwhile, Napoleon has been privately raising puppies born on the farm after the overthrow of Jones, puppies that develop into savage attack dogs (secret police, NKVD); with these, he will one day drive off the farm all of his personal enemies, especially the brilliant theoretician, Snowball. Also soon to be lost to Animal Farm is Mollie (the bourgeoisie), who shows up at Pilkingtons (the West, England).

At this point, the work becomes more difficult, the pigs assume practical control, and the arguments become more intense. Even though Benjamin, the donkey (Tolstoyan intellectuals), remains cynical about the supposed heaven on earth, Boxer, the horse (the peasantry), vows to work harder; nevertheless, the animals continue to lose their spirit and cohesiveness until attacked by Farmer Jones, who tries to regain the Farm. Because of Snowball's brilliant strategy, Jones is driven off in what is thereafter called the Battle of the Cowshed (the Civil War).

Following the victory celebration, Snowball and Napoleon move toward a decisive parting: the former wants to move full speed ahead with the building of the windmill (permanent revolution), while the latter thinks the most important task immediately ahead is the increase in food production (develop socialism in Russia first). After much debate and just before what could be an affirmative vote for Snowball's policies, Napoleon unleashes his secretly kept dogs on his rival, chasing him out of Animal Farm forever. Henceforth, the unchallenged leader abolishes Sunday meetings, increasingly changes rules at will, and even announces that the building of the windmill was his idea.

The animals continue to work hard, still believing that they are working for themselves. The changes Napoleon institutes, however, are so at variance with the initial rules of Animal Farm, and life gets to be so much drudgery, that no one has the memory to recall the ideals of the past, nor the energy to change the present—even if memories were sound.

Very soon, life at Animal Farm seems indistinguishable from the life the animals led at Manor Farm. Orwell is not so much ultimately pessimistic as he is realistically moral: institutionalized hierarchy begets privilege, which begets corruption of power. The first mistake of the animals was to give over their right to decide who got the the milk and apples. Lord Acton's famous statement could not be more appropriate: "Power tends to corrupt; absolute power corrupts absolutely."

Nineteen Eighty-Four is Orwell's most famous work. As a fantasy set in the future, the novel has terrified readers for more than thirty years—frightened them into facing the prospect of the ultimate tyranny: mind control. As a parody of conditions in postwar England, it is, as Anthony Burgess has argued in *1985* (1978), a droll, rather Swiftean exaggeration of then-current trends straining the social and political fabric of British culture. As a critique of the way in which human beings construct their social reality, the novel has so affected the modern world that much of its language (like that of its predecessor, *Animal Farm*) has entered into the everyday language of English-speaking peoples everywhere: *doublethink, newspeak, thoughtcrime,* and *Big Brother.* Bernard Crick argues that the novel is intimately related to *Animal Farm*—more so than most critics have hitherto acknowledged—and that both works convey Orwell's most important message: liberty means telling people what they do not want to hear. If the vehicle for the telling gets corrupted, then the message itself will always be corrupted, garbled; finally, the very thoughts which led to the utterances in the first place will be shackled, constrained not only from the outside but also from the inside. To think clearly, to speak openly and precisely, was a heritage Englishmen received from their glorious past; it was a legacy so easily lost that it needed to be guarded fiercely, lest those who promulgated ideologies of right or left took away what had been won with such difficulty. That was where the danger lay, with those who practiced the "smelly little orthodoxies" which are still "contending for our souls."

The story begins with a man named Winston Smith who is hurrying home on a cold, windy April day as the clocks are striking thirteen. With this ominous beginning, the reader is quickly plunged into a gritty, decaying world where the political order so dominates everyday life that independent thought is a crime, love is forbidden, and language seems to say the opposite of what one has normally come to expect. As Winston's daily life unfolds, the reader quickly learns that the whole world has been divided into three geographical areas: Oceania, Eurasia, and Eastasia. All are engaged in perpetual warfare with one or both of the others, not for territorial or religious reasons but primarily for social control. At some point, atomic warfare had made total war unthinkable, yet it suits the political leaders of Oceania (the same is also true of the other two political areas) to keep the population in a general state of anxiety about foreign attack. Under the guise of national concern, Oceania's leaders keep the population under their collective thumb by the use of propaganda (from the Ministry of Truth), by outright, brutally applied force (from the Ministry of Love), by eternally short rations (Ministry of Plenty), and by the waging of perpetual war (Ministry of Peace). The ruling elite, called the Inner Party, makes up only two percent of the population; the Outer Party, the next thirteen percent. The remainder, some eighty-five percent of the population, are called Proles, the oppressed masses.

Winston, a member of the Outer Party, has been disturbed by strange thoughts of late, and one day purchases a small, bound volume of blank paper, a diary where he can record his most private thoughts without being observed by the omnipresent telescreen, manned by members of the Thought Police. In his diary, he records his first thought: "Down with Big Brother!" To compound such a heinous thoughtcrime, he begins a liaison with a pretty young woman, a member of the antisex league, named Julia. After their affair has progressed for some time, they are contacted by a man named O'Brien, who enlists their aid in combating Big Brother by joining a group called the Brotherhood. O'Brien gives Winston a book, written by a man named Emannuel Goldstein, called *The Theory and Practice of Oligarchical Collectivism*. Having made love to Julia in a room rented from an old Prole (secretly a member of the Thought Police), Winston begins reading to her from Goldstein's book, actually an exposition of the theory which Orwell has used to construct *Nineteen Eighty-Four*.

Although Winston is fascinated, Julia, a rebel from the waist down only, falls asleep, and, after a while, so does Winston. They awake many hours later, are captured by the Thought Police, who apparently knew of their hideaway from the first, and are taken to rooms in the Ministry of Love. There, they find that O'Brien is in reality a member of the Thought Police; he alternately tortures and debates with Winston, trying to convince him that he must love Big Brother.

When torture fails, Winston is taken to Room 101, where he will be subjected to that which he fears most—in his case, rats. He gives in, begs them to "do it to Julia," and is ultimately convinced that he loves Big Brother. The novel ends as Winston, having exchanged mutual conversations of betrayal with Julia, sits at the Chestnut Café, drinking Victory Gin, completely brainwashed and committed to Big Brother.

Much has been said about the ultimate pessimism of *Nineteen Eighty-Four* being related to Orwell's fatal illness, which he fought unsuccessfully during the composition of the novel. If, however, one thinks of Orwell's fiction less in biographical terms and more in relation to artistic intention, then such a conclusion could be subject to argument. Although the novel ends with Winston in what Northrop Frye calls the sixth level of irony, unrelieved bondage, one should draw a distinction, as Orwell does in his other writings (most notably in the essay "A Good Word for the Vicar of Bray"), between man's actions as a cultural being and his activities as a creature of planet Earth, a natural being.

As a political creature, man and his purely cultural institutions could, Orwell believes, develop a world such as the one portrayed in *Nineteen Eighty-Four*. As a biological resident of the planet Earth, however, this would be impossible. Mankind never displays his hubris more graphically than does O'Brien in his speech about the party's supposed control of nature. In Orwell's view, man will never fully control nature, because man is only a part of that which he wishes to control. The great chestnut tree blossoming over Winston and his degeneration as a free being is Orwell's symbol indicating that the natural world can outlast man's cultural and political aberrations. "The planting of a tree," says Orwell, "if [it] takes root . . . will far outlive the visible effect of any of your other actions, good or evil." If there is hope for Oceania in the Proles, perhaps it is because they are instinctively closer to the natural world symbolized by the chestnut tree. Nevertheless, whether one thinks there is any hope for the people of that world or not, their existence has served as a warning to the larger world: the price of the right to tell people what they do not want to hear is never too high to pay.

John V. Knapp

Other major works

NONFICTION: *Down and Out in Paris and London*, 1933; *The Road to Wigan Pier*, 1937; *Homage to Catalonia*, 1938; *Inside the Whale and Other Essays*, 1940; *The Lion and the Unicorn*, 1941; *Critical Essays*, 1946 (published in the United States as *Dickens, Dali, and Others*); *Shooting an Elephant and Other Essays*, 1950; *Such, Such Were the Joys*, 1953; *The Collected Essays, Journalism, and Letters of George Orwell*, 1968 (Sonia Orwell and Ian Angus, editors, 4 volumes).

MISCELLANEOUS: *Orwell: The Lost Writings*, 1985; *Orwell: The War Commentaries*, 1986.

Bibliography

Bloom, Harold, ed. *George Orwell*. New York: Chelsea House, 1987. This compilation includes thirteen articles from leading critics and scholars which deal for the most part with major themes and well-known novels. A short bibliography and chronology are also included.

Crick, Bernard. *George Orwell: A Life*. Boston: Little, Brown, 1980. The most important full-scale effort so far, considering all phases of Orwell's career and pointing out some odd contrasts and anomalies that lay beneath what was outwardly very much a private life. The first biography to benefit from unlimited rights of quotation from Orwell's works held under copyright. Based upon extensive use of the writer's archives and other manuscript sources, as well as numerous publications.

Gardner, Averil. *George Orwell*. Boston: Twayne, 1987. This interesting and sensible summary treatment of Orwell's career and literary contributions takes note of areas where interpretive controversies have arisen. The chronology and the annotated selected bibliography are also useful.

Rai, Alok. *Orwell and the Politics of Despair: A Critical Study of the Writings of George Orwell*. Cambridge, England: Cambridge University Press, 1988. While acknowledging the genuinely incisive qualities of Orwell's work, the author considers the political views developed in his writings to be overwrought and one-sided. Some readers may be put off by the left-to-neutralist standpoint from which Rai's argument is mounted.

Reilly, Patrick. *"Nineteen Eighty-Four": Past, Present, and Future*. Boston: Twayne, 1989. This spirited defense of Orwell's last novel upholds his conceptions against the claims of modern detractors. Contains a detailed chronology and an annotated bibliography. Reilly also wrote an earlier critical study of Orwell's fiction, *George Orwell: The Age's Adversary* (New York: St. Martin's Press, 1986).

Rodden, John. *The Politics of Literary Reputation: The Making and Claiming of "St. George" Orwell*. New York: Oxford University Press, 1989. Essentially a study of publications about Orwell rather than of the writer himself. Points to the seemingly ubiquitous impact of phrases and concepts associated with his ideas, many of which have been used in recent contexts that Orwell himself scarcely could have foreseen. The breadth of Rodden's research, in more obscure newspapers and journals, is impressive.

Sandison, Alan. *George Orwell After "Nineteen Eighty-Four."* London: Macmillan, 1986. This interpretive effort, based on an earlier work, regards Orwell's writings as a reflection of a long intellectual tradition of religious and philosophical individualism. A lengthy postscript presents Sandison's views on other works about Orwell.

Slater, Ian. *Orwell: The Road to Airstrip One*. New York: W. W. Norton, 1985. This attempt to trace the events of Orwell's life by way of his major works becomes slightly awkward in places but also reaches some interesting conclusions on matters of politics and literature.

Stansky, Peter, and William Abrahams. *Orwell: The Transformation*. London: Constable, 1979. Deals with Orwell's work through his period of combat service in the Spanish Civil War, discussing the origins of five early works. Concludes that Orwell's political point of view had begun to take a definite shape by 1937 as a result of his own experiences.

—————————. *The Unknown Orwell*. London: Constable, 1972. Orwell's early years in India, at Eton, in Burma, in Paris, and in London are considered in the light of his decision to become a writer in the period leading up to the publication of his first book in 1933. Information provided by those who had known him personally has supplied details about Orwell's education and the beginning of his literary career.

WALTER PATER

Born: London, England; August 4, 1839
Died: Oxford, England; July 30, 1894

Principal long fiction
Marius the Epicurean, 1885; *Gaston de Latour*, 1896.

Other literary forms
Walter Pater is principally remembered as a critic. His most influential work, *Studies in the History of the Renaissance* (1873; generally known as *The Renaissance*), decisively changed the Victorian conception of art as a vehicle for the expression of uplifting sentiments or edifying ideals. Pater, whose unnamed antagonist was John Ruskin, argued that art is preeminently concerned with the dextrous elaboration of its own sensuous ingredients. Form, color, balance, and tone: these are the elements of which art is constituted. Hence, the imposition of a moral upon a painting, a poem, or a musical composition subverts the integrity of the work and distorts the function of criticism. The genuine critic begins with an analysis of the impression which a painting or a poem communicates and then endeavors to trace that impression to the structural elements of which the work is composed. Ultimately, as the notorious "Conclusion" to *The Renaissance* makes clear, art is chiefly to be cherished as a means of enhancing, expanding, and enlarging the faculties of sensuous apprehension and as a catalyst in the pursuit of more varied, exquisite, and complex sensations. In the last analysis, Pater was inclined to evaluate and judge life itself as an aesthetic phenomenon.

Pater qualified this position in his later works, however, and since *Marius the Epicurean*—his one completed novel—was expressly written to revise and reevaluate the conclusion of *The Renaissance*, it is necessary to acquire some preliminary understanding of Pater's earlier and less complex point of view.

By way of preparation for *Marius the Epicurean*, Pater composed a series of stories which foreshadow the mature techniques of his novel. The best of these stories, "The Child in the House," traces the influence of a child's environment upon the formation of his sensibility and character. Here, in a statement which may be regarded as a keynote to the author's subsequent utterances, Pater expresses through the character of Florian Deleal the distinguishing quality which informs not only his own sensibility but also the sensibility of Marius and, indeed, of all his protagonists: "For with the desire of physical beauty," observes Pater of Florian, "mingled itself early the fear of death—the fear of death intensified by the desire of beauty."

Before examining the implications of this sentiment in the context of *Marius the Epicurean*, it is interesting to note that virtually all of Pater's other works—in both criticism and fiction—are meditations on the propinquity of beauty and death and on the desire which this meditation engenders in Pater to conceive of an absolute which defines itself in and gives broader significance to the sensuous flux of existence. As Pater observes in his study of Plato, "to realize unity in variety, to discover *cosmos*—an order that shall satisfy one's reasonable soul—below and within apparent chaos: is from first to last the continuous purpose of what we call philosophy."

In addition to *The Renaissance*, then, Pater's other works are briefly these: *Imaginary Portraits* (1887), a collection of stories which prefigure *Marius the Epicurean* in their emphasis on the aesthetic quality and philosophical repercussions of experience upon a sensitive and circumspect temperament rather than with the dramatization of experience itself; *Appreciations* (1889), a heterogeneous collection of literary criticisms which apply the principals adduced in *The Renaissance* to the examination of English and French literary figures; *Plato and Platonism* (1893), the philosophical and theoretical counterpart to *Marius the Epicurean*, which examines the respective relations between the temporal and the eternal, the relative and the absolute, the ideal and the real in the works of Plato; *Greek Studies* (1895), an examination of the myths of Dionysus and Persephone and their symbolic relation to the spirit of art; *Miscellaneous Studies* (1895), a grouping of Pater's most important writings on figures of literary, religious, and artistic significance. Of special interest in the latter, is the short essay "Diaphaneite," wherein Pater delineates those attributes which go into the making of an ideal and yet realizable humanity. Finally, *Essays from The Guardian* (1901) is a collection of Pater's reviews on the writers of his day.

Achievements

Pater's achievement as a novelist and a critic is central to the modern vision of art. Though he was not always edified by the scandalous manner in which his disciples interpreted his message, nor gratified by the distortion of his ideas by an entire generation of aesthetes and decadents, Pater, when he is fully understood, emerges as a figure of incalculable importance in the evolution of twentieth century literature. In the first place, he did away with much of the fustian which obscured the appreciation of art in his own day and left a critical legacy which extended into the present century in the works of Bernard Berenson and Roger Fry. Moreover, as Harold Bloom observes of Pater's most memorable character, "Marius, more than any fictional character of our age, is the representative modern poet as well as the representative man of literary culture who remains the only audience for that poet." As a stylist, too, Pater was wonderfully suggestive and original. Adapting the rich and ornate cadences of Ruskin to his more subtle purpose, Pater evolved a style which is the last word in delicacy, refinement, and understated eloquence. His sentences are characterized by elaborate parentheses, delicately wrought rhythms, and mannered circumlocutions—annoying to some readers—and his malleable prose matches with minute accuracy the uncertainties, doubts, and deliberations of a mind in debate with itself: a mind, that is to say, fastidiously alive to the full complexity of human experience and scrupulously intent upon a verbal music which, in its hesitant rhythms, remains faithful to that experience. In this regard, he clearly anticipates Marcel Proust.

It is not, however, on the level of style alone that Pater's influence has been indelible. *Marius the Epicurean*, in the role which it assigns to memory, its tone of melancholy retrospect, its analysis of a highly developed sensibility enamored of perfection yet resigned to uncertainty, anticipates, to a remarkable degree, the structural, tonal, and thematic underpinnings of Proust's novels. When one adds to this Pater's lasting influence on Oscar Wilde, James Joyce, André Gide, and William Butler Yeats—(the last of whom claimed that *Marius the Epicurean* is "the only great prose in modern English"), one is compelled to admit that Pater was one of the first major sensibilities of the modern age.

Biography

For a writer who was to become the subject of numerous debates and controversies regarding the tendency of his works, the quality of his influence, and the dubiety of his doctrines, Walter Horatio Pater's life seems, at first glance, a singularly colorless affair. The youngest son of a dedicated physician who died prematurely, Pater was reared in a household dominated by his sisters, his mother, and his godmother. He remained, throughout childhood, indifferent to the activities or sports of his peers, preferring to imagine a world of ceremonious gallantry and hieratic ritual. He mainifested a deep attachment to the solemn devotions and sumptuous worship of the Anglican Church. A need to remain true to the irrepressible skepticism and intellectual scrupulousness of his own nature prevented him, at the last, from acting upon his early impulses and taking orders. With a temperament more than commonly inclined to self-analysis and introspection, Pater, following his matriculation at Queens College, Oxford, chose to pursue an academic career. He was elected a junior fellow at Brasenose College in 1864.

From the first, the young don was regarded with certain suspicions, "having acquired," as Humphrey Ward observed, "a new and daring philosophy of his own, and a wonderful gift of style." Benjamin Jowett, the famous translator of Plato, was acutely displeased with the seemingly subversive conclusion to *The Renaissance* and successfully hindered Pater's advancement at Oxford. In defiance, however, of Jowett's reprobations, Pater continued to enjoy a steady advance in influence and reputation. Ultimately, his increased fame warranted the taking of additional rooms in London, and there, in the company of sisters and friends, Pater enjoyed the sympathy and civility which were sometimes denied him at Oxford. Modest, retiring, elusive, and enigmatic: these are the epithets which most frequently occur in contemporary portraits of Pater. It was doubtless these qualities which won him the admiration of his most famous pupil: Gerard Manley Hopkins. It is interesting to note (and much to Pater's credit) that, in the surcharged evangelical atmosphere of Oxford, where professors more often strove to win converts than to foster independence of mind, Pater was the single instructor who continued to be loyal to Hopkins after his embrace of Catholicism. Indeed, Pater's elasticity and insouciance, his careful cultivation of what John Keats called "negative capability," was as characteristic of the man as it was of the artist. Pater died as a result of a heart attack in 1894.

Analysis

Walter Pater's *Marius the Epicurean* is the culminating expression of a fictional genre which began in the 1830's and continued until the turn of the century. This genre, a peculiar mixture of religious speculation and personal confession, developed almost synchronously with the assault of science against traditional Christianity, beginning with the publication, in 1832, of Sir Charles Lyell's *Principles of Geology*. Lyell's book, which exploded the biblical account of creation, was the first of several—the most famous being Charles Darwin's—which shook Western culture to its foundations. The passage of the Reform Bill, the theories of Darwin and Karl Marx, the development of the so-called "higher" criticism in the exegesis of biblical texts, the rise in population and the spread of revolution, were but a few events which challenged the inherited certainties of Victorian England. Men were forced to reevaluate old beliefs, to doubt discredited traditions, to revise social policies, to change moral valuations. It is not surprising that the confessional novel, the novel of doubt and faith, should acquire an unprecedented significance during such a period. The absence of reliable guideposts threw men back upon themselves and obliged them to search for unity, purpose, and direction in the kaleidoscopic sequence of their own lives.

Marius the Epicurean is one of the finest offshoots of a literary tradition inaugurated by Thomas Carlyle's *Sartor Resartus* (1835) and sustained in such works as John Henry Newman's *Loss and Gain* (1848), William Hale White's *The Autobiography of Mark Rutherford* (1885), and Mrs. Humphrey Ward's *Robert Elsemere* (1888). Pater chose to set his search for meaning and purpose amid the disintegrating spectacle of Antonine Rome, but its bearing on the condition of late Victorian England is emphatically underlined: "Let the reader pardon me if here and there I seem to be passing from Marius to his modern representatives—from Rome, to Paris or London," Pater interpolates at one point. Marius is clearly meant to be prototypical: he dramatizes a quest for religious values which satisfies the demands of modern consciousness and reflects the ambiguity of a shattered world.

This is not to say that his growth is haphazard or random; on the contrary, Pater implies an underlying teleology in Marius' development: however dim and faint the sense of a superintending providence, his life is oriented toward the climactic moment of self-sacrifice with which the novel ends. Marius does not, however, fully resolve the conflicting calls of conscience and sensation, beauty and duty, engagement and withdrawal, in the fulfillment of that end. Though Pater evidently sees Marius' entire existence as an elaborate preparation for the revelatory moment in which his moral and spiritual being are ultimately defined, critics have generally judged that this is accomplished, if at all, without dramatic conviction.

Marius' youth is characterized, as was Pater's, by a more than common susceptibility to sensuous impressions. His home, "White Nights," a villa with adjacent farm, contributes to these susceptibilities. The note of grave beauty, of life lived under the conditions of animal sacrifice and seasonal change, develops, in the boy, a wistful reverence and wonder which deepen with the passage of years. The Wordsworthian element in all this is not fortuitous, for Marius is destined to enact precisely that pattern of spiritual growth enunciated in "Lines Composed a Few Miles Above Tintern Abbey" and "Ode: Intimations of Immortality"—a pattern which involves a gradual conversion from the sensory to the spiritual planes of existence, a slow but steady ascension from the "aching joys" and "dizzy raptures" of his first impulsive response to beauty to the sober steadfastness of a mind which recognizes "a sense sublime of something far more deeply interfused." This conversion, if such it may be called, does not, for Marius, issue in the renunciation of his former pleasures, but rather in a deepening awareness of their ultimate origin and tendency. In brief, Marius comes to dwell consciously in the presence of a spirit which is implied in his first naïve responses to nature and beauty. Hence, the pagan ceremonies which solicit Marius' devotion and awe already foreshadow "certain heavy demands" which will not become apparent to the lad until he acquires the mature self-consciousness of adulthood. It is then, on the level of discursive thought that he will begin to recognize "some ampler vision, which should take up into itself and explain this world's delightful shows." "White Nights" is, therefore, as Pater suggests, not only a domestic dwelling-place, but also state of mind peculiar to youth and prior to self-dedication which maturity exacts.

In any event, it is not long before Marius is obliged to abandon the "world's delightful shows" in the pursuit of a more bracing conception of beauty. To cure a childhood illness, Marius is sent to the Temple of Aesculapius. The process of healing is complemented by meditations on Platonic texts. While these constitute a cherishable legacy for Marius, the boy reacts against a world of abstract essences. The impalpable ideas of Plato attract him only insofar as they fuse with the world of spatiotemporal objects, "green fields, for instance, or children's faces." Here, Pater is clearly attempting to revise the "impressionism" of his youth, itself a recrudescence of the Heraclitean theory of perpetual flux, with a symbolist theory of correspondences. Beauty will no longer be an end in itself but "an outward imagery identifying itself with unseen moralities." While Marius does not achieve such an identification at once or without great difficulty, Pater clearly intends that the boy's unthinking empiricism should be shaken and unsettled. In a word, the exhortation "to burn with a hard gem-like flame" which Pater formerly enunciated in *The Renaissance* is now being duly qualified by an obligation "to discriminate, ever more and more fastidiously, select form and colour in things from what was less select." Pater is avid to demonstrate, through his hero Marius, the correct application of the aesthetic theory to life, an application which requires a transvaluation of the concept "Beauty" to include "not pleasure, but fulness of life, and insight as conducting to that fulness . . . whatever form of human life, in short, might be heroic, impassioned, ideal." Marius' stay at the temple initiates an intellectual or moral awakening, a search for a hieratic order of conduct and beauty which is truly serviceable to that ideal. Dissatisfied with the abstractness of the Platonic method, Marius rejects the world of ideal forms in the pursuit of its equivalent in a living community, a veritable body of fellow aspirants. His search for this community determines the subsequent shape of the novel.

Immediately prior to his departure from the temple, Marius is vouchsafed a distant view of a city which appears to be an earthly incarnation of the Platonic archetype he is seeking. This first glimpse of Rome kindles in Marius the illusion that it, perhaps, is that "new city coming down 'like a bride out of heaven'" of which Plato discoursed so eloquently. Accordingly, Marius takes practical steps to bring him closer to "the most religious city in the world." He moves next to Pisa, preparing for his future obligations as secretary to the Emperor Aurelius. He is soon befriended by an aspiring youth of literary ambitions by the name of Flavian—a character who clearly represents one aspect of Marius' own divided consciousness.

Flavian's function in the novel is to bear involuntary witness to the limitations of aesthetic hedonism. Pater clearly intends through this subordinate character to disabuse his devotees of the notion that burning with a hard, gemlike flame is equivalent to self-indulgent dissipation. Beneath "the perfection of form" which Flavian achieves in his bearing and his poetry, Marius recognizes "a depth of corruption" which compels him to follow his friend only so far. Pater anticipates, here, to a remarkable degree the theme of Thomas Mann's *Death in Venice* (1913): the awareness that an exclusive preoccupation with artistic form may have the effect of neutralizing both good and evil by reducing them to complementary colors, lights, and shades, in a composition. Nevertheless, Flavian performs a vital role in the drama of Marius' development: it is he who introduces Marius to the "golden book" of Apuleius.

At this point, Pater reproduces in full Apuleius' tale of Cupid and Psyche. Through subtle and strategic modifications of the original, Pater conceives of the tale as a presentiment of Marius' spiritual development. Evoking the solemn harmonies of the King James version of the Bible and softening the racy idiom of Apuleius, Pater endows the story of Cupid and Psyche with a "gentle idealism" and facilities its interpretation as an allegory. Just as Psyche, symbol of the human soul, is redeemed from death by the intervention of Cupid, so Marius—bewildered, distracted, and divided by the contradictory sects and philosophical schools of decadent Rome—is presumably redeemed from despair by the appearance of a community which claims to satisfy the deepest needs of the human spirit. The road to that community is, however, difficult, uncertain, and devious.

Flavian's life is prematurely ended by an outbreak of plague. Marius, who remains, as ever, faithful to the evidence of his senses, is convinced of "nothing less than the soul's extinction." It may be parenthetically observed that despite his later sympathy with the Christian response to suffering, Marius never fully abandons those scruples "which can make no sincere claim to have apprehended anything beyond the veil of immediate experience." With his departure for Rome, he remains in a state of suspended judgment with regard to the ultimate destiny appointed for the human soul.

The actual journey to the capital of the ancient world includes a number of incidents which undermine the philosophic detachment of the young Marius. Notwithstanding the glory of the Roman *campagna*, the many idyllic details of which Marius, with his habitual eye for the concrete, discerns with "a fresh, primeval poetry," he is plunged, following a scarcely averted accident, into further uncomfortable wrestling with the eternal questions. This accident—a loosened boulder falls from a wall beside the path Marius is following—has the effect of shaking him into a recognition that "his elaborate philosophy had not put beneath his feet the terror of mere bodily evil." The force, however, which is destined to correct the deficiencies in Marius' scheme of existence is not far away. Stopping at an inn to revive his spirits, Marius orders a glass of wine and muses vacantly over the "ring of delicate foam" which sparkles in his cup. Presently, his attention is arrested by a voice—"a youthful voice, with a reassuring clearness of note, which completes his cure." As he will soon learn, it is the voice of Cornelius, a young Roman soldier whose influence is destined to supersede that of Flavian's. It is not, however, until much later in his pilgrimage that Marius discovers that the origin of Cornelius' gracious alacrity of spirit is traceable to "some new knighthood or chivalry, just then coming into the world."

Marius, however, is not yet in a position to be irresistibly won over to that knighthood. He must first extend his philosophical hypotheses beyond the immediate circle of his own sensations; the role of Marcus Aurelius in the novel is to facilitate this extension. Unlike Flavian and Cornelius, the philosophical emperor of Rome is more than merely a shadowy personification of Marius' fractured ego: Aurelius is a figure of vital warmth and sympathy who encourages Marius to enlarge his spiritual perspective and to discover that an exclusive preoccupation with the passing moment may actually narrow the range of experience, curtail the development of character, and inhibit the acquisition of wisdom. The upshot of Aurelius' teachings is to reinforce Marius' search for a "comely order . . . to which, as to all other beautiful phenomena in life, he must, for his own peace, adjust himself."

While his influence is certainly salutary, Aurelius remains, in the final analysis, incapable of reconciling his devotion to that "comely order" with the debased reality of Antonine Rome. It is not long before Marius discovers a number of serious shortcomings in Aurelius' view of existence. To be sure, Marius accepts the merits of a philosophical scheme which posits a universal reason or logos, a point of rest and a center of calm from which to withstand the vertiginous whirl of feelings and events, the traumatic blows of fate and destiny. Unfortunately, such a scheme, as Marius equally recognizes, may easily devolve into a pretext for neglecting one's fellowmen in the here and now, for averting one's eyes from the plenitude and plurality of the living world. While freely granting the efficacy of believing in a "universal commonwealth of mind"—the sense of expanded horizons, the freedom from petty vexations, the glimpse of imperishable ideals which it allows—Marius rejects the concomitant calm and serenity which Aurelius, for example, maintains in the midst of human misery.

Two episodes in particular underline the deficiencies of the stoical system. The first of these occurs during a performance at the Colosseum over which Aurelius, notwithstanding his own aversion to the gladitorial games, presides with an air of tolerance. This indifference to the unspeakable butchery of men and animals, a consequence of the stoic divorce of reason from reality, provokes Marius "to mark Aurelius as his inferior, now and for ever, on the question of righteousness." When it comes, however, to the suffering and death of his son, Lucius Verus, Aurelius is presented in a more sympathetic light. This episode, too, leaves an indelible mark in Marius' consciousness. The disparity between the imperturbable calm of the professed stoic and the irrepressible grief of the stricken parent is poignantly dramatized when the boy, after an operation of surpassing agony, lapses into a coma from which he never recovers.

The chapter which immediately follows this episode signals the direction which Marius henceforth will take. An epigraph from the Psalms—"My heart is ready, O God, a ready heart is mine"—clearly enunciates the imminence of that spiritual crisis toward which his whole life has been moving. It would be a mistake, however, to construe this crisis as a sudden shattering encounter with the divine. On the contrary, nothing in the sense of a clear dramatic conversion may be said to happen. The epiphany which Marius is vouchsafed has all the character of a Wordsworthian "spot of time." In one of his vagrant wanderings on the outskirts of Rome, Marius pauses at an outdoor inn to gaze at the extensive Roman *compagna*. His attention is divided among a number of apparently trivial and unrelated details—"a bird came and sang among the wattled hedge-roses: an animal feeding crept nearer: the child who kept it was gazing quietly"—when, suddenly, the entire scene presents itself as the outward and tangible emblem of "that . . . Ideal, to which the Old Testament gives the name of Creator, which for the philosophers of Greece is the Eternal Reason, and in the New Testament the Father of Men." The mundane world is transfigured and transvalued in a moment of privileged perception: no less and no more. The departure of this mood is as quiet and unobtrusive as its inception, but it leaves Marius with the firm conviction that the remainder of his life must be "a search for the equivalent of that Ideal . . . a gathering together of every trace and token of it, which his actual experience might present." The event is clearly something of a watershed.

At this juncture, Marius is given the opportunity to visit a pair of houses which represent two opposing visions of reality. The first house represents the finest flowering of classical antiquity. It is here that Marius meets his former idol, the poet Apulius; enjoys the refined pleasures and urbane conversation of the Roman intelligentsia; and delights in the delectations of a banquet replete with music, dance, and fine condiments. The whole proceedings, however, are tainted by a certain foppish connoisseurism, a pampered elegance, a "facility" and "self-complacency" in the exchange of ideas. Marius departs with a nagging sense of weariness and disillusion.

The second house, to which he is introduced by Cornelius, is that of the Christian saint, Cecilia. It is characteristic that Pater should choose the canonized patroness of music as the agent of Marius' contact with Christianity. Presumably, if art can obscure the moral being of man, as in the case of Flavian, it can also reveal that moral being. The grave, refined, and simple dignity of the Christian community—its air of domestic and filial piety, its comely rectitude of spirit, its solicitude for the departed, care for the living, and faith in things to come—stand in favorable contrast to the enervating amusements and facile wit of the Roman upper crust. Yet it is important to note that the early Church, as Pater presents it, has nothing of that apocalyptic fervor which looks forward to the end of the world and the last things. On the contrary, "the contrast between the church and the world" Pater tells us, "was becoming less pronounced." By far the largest part of Marius' attraction to this community derives from his contemplation of "the beautiful house of Cecilia, its lights and flowers, of Cecilia herself, moving among the lilies, with an enchanted grace."

The fact is that Marius remains ultimately indifferent to the dogmatic foundations of Christianity. To be sure, he returns to his childhood home and supervises the reburial of his ancestors according to the usages of the early Church. Furthermore, he willingly intercedes on Cornelius' behalf following an officially sanctioned purge of the growing Christian community. There is, however, a considerable degree of ambiguity involved in Marius' position vis-à-vis the Christian faith. Marius is arrested along with Cornelius for being present at a community act of worship. An outbreak of plague shatters the fragile tolerance extended to the Church and initiates widespread persecution of the Christians. On the strength of his relations with Aurelius, Marius contrives to have Cornelius released. He is compelled, however, to give a deposition on his friend's behalf and to join the other prisoners in the long and arduous journey to Rome. This generosity of spirit on the part of Marius is prompted by a mistaken notion that Cornelius is Cecilia's intended: the latter's vows of chastity entirely elude Marius' understanding. Traveling to Rome in company with the other captives, Marius is stricken with plague and abandoned at a neighboring farm which, as it turns out, is the dwelling of some recent converts. Lying in a state of semidelirium for several days, he finds consolation, during the lucid intervals allowed him, in "the scent of new-mown hay . . . and the sounds of cattle . . . from the green places around." The occupants, erroneously assuming that he is a Christian, minister to the dying Marius the last rites of their faith.

Is Marius, then, a Christian? This question has been the subject of critical debate since the novel's appearance. For Paul Elmer More, *Marius the Epicurean* is "only another manifestation of that aestheticism which Pater sucked from the Romantic school of his century and disguised in the phraseology of ancient faith." He further adds, "to write thus was to betray Christianity with a kiss." T. S. Eliot has no hesitations in asserting that "of the essence of the Christian Faith . . . Pater knew almost nothing." Arthur Benson is equally forthright in claiming that "the very peace which Marius discerns in Christianity is the old philosophical peace over again." The point is that Marius fails to grasp and remains largely indifferent to the theoretical foundations of Christianity. "Our creeds," as Pater observes, "are but the brief abstract of our prayer and song." Inasmuch as Christianity invests that song with a deeper pathos, frees the mind from its empirical trammels, and endows existence with a warmer hope, it is clearly a serviceable hypothesis for the questing human spirit. Its dogmatic underpinnings, however, are of secondary importance.

Some might claim that Pater's enterprise in *Marius the Epicurean* is fundamentally affiliated with the Christian existentialism of Søren Kierkegaard. There is, however, one signal and important difference. Unlike Kierkegaard, who posits a leap of faith in which reason is virtually annihilated, Pater viewed all such leaps as a source of potential fanaticism. Christianity, for Pater, is clearly a stage in the development of human potential, but he would jealously protect that potential from any claim that might threaten its autonomy. The Church of Cecilia is, at bottom, a fictive structure in which there is "no forced opposition between soul and body, the world and the spirit." It is even identified, at one point, with that "half-humorous placidity of soul, of a kind illustrated later very effectively by Montaigne." Just as modern-day theologians who attempt to gerrymander Christianity into the camps of Marx, Sigmund Freud, Friedrich Nietzsche, or Ludwig Feuerbach, Pater has created a church of his own making—distinctly unrecognizable to the average believer. From the perspective of Christ's statement, "He who is not with me is against me," Marius is most certainly not a Christian; on the other hand, if one considers the earlier phrasing of this statement in the gospel of Mark, "He who is not against us is for us," then the question of Marius' death as "a kind of sacrament with plenary grace" remains open.

Moreover, as Pater was to recognize in *Gaston de Latour*, institutional Christianity, insofar as it defines itself in what man professes rather than in what he is, is as prodigal of sectarian bigotry and bloodshed as the worst excesses of pagan Rome. Like *Marius the Epicurean*, *Gaston de Latour* examines the situation of faith in an "age of transition . . . when the problem of man's destiny and his relations to the unseen was undergoing a new solution." Though Pater never lived to complete the novel—it remains, at best, a series of discontinuous meditations on the religious and political ferment of the Reformation—its essential outlines are as follows. Born in the midst of growing strife between Huguenots and Catholics, Gaston comes of age in "the cornlands of France" in close proximity to the cathedral of Chartres and amid the luxuries of his rustic manor house. He becomes acquainted with King Charles the Ninth, joins the "episcopal household of Chartres as a page," and falls under the influence of the poetry of Pierre de Ronsard. Like Marius, in a different context, he becomes the votary of a great philosopher: in this instance, Michel de Montaigne. He eventually travels to Paris and takes up with a spirited Huguenot girl; under the pressure of her brothers, he marries her in a Protestant ceremony which exerts no real claim upon him: "The transaction seemed to have but that transitoriness as also the guilt of a vagrant love." Miscalculating the forces of destruction gathered on the eve of St. Bartholomew, Gaston returns to his homestead at Deux-manoirs, "his wife left behind there in Paris." He later learns of the death of his wife "while the stairways of the Louvre, the streets, the trap-doors of Paris, run blood." Following the banishment of King Charles, Gaston returns to Paris and falls under the influence of the heterodox monk, Giordano Bruno. Here the novel abruptly ends.

What is clearly significant about this work is its relation to *Marius the Epicurean*. Just as Marius qualifies the hedonism of *The Renaissance*, so *Gaston de Latour* qualifies the Christianity of *Marius the Epicurean*. Indeed, of Gaston himself the reader is told that "the very genius of qualification followed him through his keen, constant, changeful consideration of men and things."

Pater's attitude is obvious. He clearly distrusts the external machinery of a church which absorbs the individual conscience and resolves all doubts in cozy conformity, irresponsible anonymity, and superstitious fear. Pater rejects dogmatic formulations and ideologies of any kind, especially insofar as these inhibit the cultivation of human sympathy or the development of individual character. "The man who never alters his opinion is like standing water, and breeds reptiles of the mind," wrote William Blake, and Pater would have most certainly agreed. Indeed, the true saint of the Reformation, for Pater, is Montaigne, and the legitimate attitude in all matters speculative and religious is not the intransigence of the doctrinaire but the suspended judgment of a humanist. "It was something to have been," writes Pater of Montaigne, "in the matter of religious tolerance, as in so many other matters of justice and gentleness, the solitary conscience of the age."

In the final analysis, the question of whether Pater's protagonists are ultimately Christian pales before the question of whether they are comprehensively human. Thoughtful, but without energy; sensitive, but without resolve; scrupulous, but without conviction: both Marius and Gaston remain imprisoned, each in his own consciousness and incapable of genuine community with others. The essentially selfish conviction which informs these novels and which may be taken as a motto for Pater's life and work is perhaps stated most succinctly in one of the Pythian Odes of the Latin poet, Pindar: "O my soul, do not aspire to immortal life, but exhaust the limits of the possible." Pater once remarked of Marius that his was a philosophy which at least guaranteed its possessor of living a life without harm to others. The question remains, however, whether such a philosophy is adequate to the full range of human experience. In the absence of more solid and substantial convictions than those which Pater demonstrates in his writings, this question remains a point of legitimate concern in any final estimate of his achievement.

Stephen I. Gurney

Other major works
SHORT FICTION: *Imaginary Portraits*, 1887.
NONFICTION: *Studies in the History of the Renaissance*, 1873; *Appreciations*, 1889; *Plato and Platonism*, 1893; *The Child in the House*, 1894; *Greek Studies*, 1895; *Miscellaneous Studies*, 1895; *Essays from the Guardian*, 1901.

Bibliography
Bloom, Harold, ed. *Modern Critical Views: Walter Pater*. New York: Chelsea House, 1985. Bloom has compiled what he considers some of the best criticism available on Pater. The introduction by Bloom provides a useful overview of Pater's work and contains much insight. Also includes a reprint of an unabridged pamphlet on Pater by Ian Fletcher, a highly respected critic of Pater. A valuable and well-rounded study.
Buckler, William E. *Walter Pater: The Critic as Artist of Ideas*. New York:

New York University Press, 1987. This scholarly study examines the breadth and depth of Pater's prose and poetry, as well as his role as a critic, acknowledging him as a major but underrated writer. Focuses on Pater's aestheticism in his work, and chapter 8 examines Pater's *Plato and Platonism*, which has been generally ignored by critics.

Court, Franklin E. *Walter Pater: An Annotated Bibliography of Writings About Him*. De Kalb: Northern Illinois Press, 1980. This volume includes a checklist of a representative body of criticism on Pater from 1871 through 1973. Contains abstracts of critical articles, reminiscences, biographies, and letters to editors. A rich source of bibliographical information for the Pater scholar.

Levey, Michael. *The Case of Walter Pater*. London: Thames and Hudson, 1978. An appreciative study of Pater, largely biographical and executed with thoroughness. Levey promotes Pater's case but alludes to the difficulty in placing Pater's writing because he moved so fluidly from fiction to fact.

Monsman, Gerald. *Walter Pater*. Boston: Twayne, 1977. A chronological look at Pater's work and life. Examines the heroes in his works, in particular the hero in *Marius the Epicurean*. A useful study for the beginning reader of Pater. A selected bibliography is provided.

Ward, Anthony. *Walter Pater: The Idea in Nature*. London: MacGibbon & Kee, 1966. A full-length study on Pater that examines Pater's "temperament" as a writer, the influence of Johann Wolfgang von Goethe on his work, and his ideas in relation to Georg Wilhelm Friedrich Hegel. Also discusses *Marius and the Epicurean* and Pater's essays on Renaissance painters. Focuses on Pater's mind and thoughts and on the context of his writing.

THOMAS LOVE PEACOCK

Born: Weymouth, England; October 18, 1785
Died: Halliford, England; January 23, 1866

Principal long fiction

Headlong Hall, 1816; *Melincourt*, 1817; *Nightmare Abbey*, 1818; *Maid Marian*, 1822; *The Misfortunes of Elphin*, 1829; *Crotchet Castle*, 1831; *Gryll Grange*, 1860.

Other literary forms

Before turning his talents to the satirical novel, Thomas Love Peacock wrote poetry. His early works include *Palmyra and Other Poems* (1806), *The Genius of the Thames* (1810), *The Philosophy of Melancholy* (1812), and *Sir Proteus: A Satrical Ballad* (1814). When his principal efforts turned to prose, Peacock continued to produce the occasional elegant lyric or rousing song, many of them incorporated into his novels. His long narrative poem *Rhododaphne* (1818), "a nympholeptic tale," attracted considerable contemporary attention and has retained a measure of continued critical esteem; his satirical *Paper Money Lyrics* (1837), topical and crochety, is largely ignored. Early in his literary career Peacock also wrote two farces, *The Dilettanti* and *The Three Doctors*, both of which remain unpublished. Throughout his life, and particularly during the periods when his responsibilities at the East India Company precluded sustained literary projects, Peacock wrote essays and reviews, the most famous being his unfinished but incisive "Essay on Fashionable Literature," in *The Four Ages of Poetry* (1820), the satirical critique of contemporary poetry's debasement that provoked Percy Bysshe Shelley's *A Defense of Poetry* (1840) and Peacock's four-part *Memoirs of Shelley* (1852-1862), which the reserved and fastidious Peacock, who deplored the publication of private matters, wrote grudgingly, as a corrective to the muddled enthusiasms and posthumous scandal-retailing that admirers and acquaintances of Shelley were offering as literary biography.

Achievements

From the beginning of his career as a satirical novelist, Peacock has always had an attentive audience, but never a wide one. His career in several ways has invited comparison with that of his contemporary, Jane Austen. Each writer set out to please himself or herself, uninfluenced by desire for fame or gold. Each swam against the Romantic mainstream. Each produced a slim shelf of novels distinguished by elegance, irony, and—detractors might add—limited scope. Whereas Austen limited herself to matters suitable to the notice of a lady, Peacock restricted himself yet more narrowly. Except for *Maid Marian* and *The Misfortunes of Elphin*, respectively set in the picturesque past of Merrie England and Arthurian Wales, Peacock's novels take place in an idyllic country-house world where conversation, varied by singing, dining, drinking, flirtation, and sightseeing, is the chief activity. Even so, in this Pavonian realm, the reader who is able to read the signs aright can find, as critic Marilyn Butler reveals, serious and well-grounded discussion of moral, political, aesthetic, economic, and scientific concerns.

The dense if oblique topicality of these conversations is something of an obstacle for the twentieth century reader. Another hurdle for the general public in any age is Peacock's learning: only those who share Peacock's passion for the past, especially classical antiquity, can enjoy the novels' esoterica and allusions, and only readers nurtured in Greek and Latin (or possessing editions whose annotations compensate for such deficiency) can smile at the puns and scholarly jokes Peacock presents in the names and adventures of his characters. Writing for a few congenial spirits, Peacock attained in his own time the respect of Shelley, George Gordon, Lord Byron, and John Cam Hobhouse. He has retained the appreciative but limited audience Shelley's lines from *Letter to Maria Gisbourne* (1820) seem to prophesy: "his fine wit/ Makes such a wound, the knife is lost in it;/ A strain too learned for a shallow age,/ Too wise for selfish bigots."

Biography

Thomas Love Peacock was born at Weymouth in Dorset, England, in 1785. His father, Samuel, was a London merchant, his mother, Sarah, a woman of Devonshire. He attended a private school at Englefield Green until he was thirteen. After leaving school, he served for some time as a clerk at a mercantile house and as a private secretary. In his youth, Peacock found employment uncongenial, however, and his private resources, although insufficient to send him to a university, did preclude his having to work. Peacock used his leisure well. An apt and diligent student, he became a sound classicist through his independent reading. In 1812, Peacock met Percy Bysshe Shelley through the agency of a mutual friend, Thomas Hookham. For the next few years he was often a part of the Shelley circle. Closely involved in Shelley's tangled domestic affairs, Peacock attempted to be true to his friend, fair to the poet's wife Harriet, and civil to his new love, Mary Godwin. When Shelley went abroad, Peacock corresponded with him and transacted business for him. When Shelley died, Peacock, along with Byron, was named executor of the estate.

In 1819, Peacock was appointed Assistant to the Examiner in the East India Office. The salary he derived from his position enabled him to marry Jane Gryffydh, a rector's daughter whom he had last seen in 1811, when he had been on a walking tour of Wales. The Peacock marriage was not a particularly happy one; the professional appointment proved rather more auspicious. In 1837, on the retirement of James Mill, Peacock became Examiner at East

India House. He capably held this important administrative post until his retirement in 1856.

The pleasures of Peacock's maturity were those he ascribes to various characters (most of them urbane clergymen) in his novels: good wine, good dinners, hours in the garden or in his study with the classics, rural walks from his house at Halliford in the Thames valley. One of the few new friends Peacock made during the latter half of his life was John Cam Hobhouse, Lord Broughton. Peacock's peaceful old age was saddened by the unhappiness of his favorite daughter, the talented Mary Ellen, who had imprudently married the novelist George Meredith, and by her death in 1861. Peacock died at Halliford in 1865.

Analysis

A writer with strong intelligence but weak invention is not likely to become a novelist. His talents would seem to be most serviceable elsewhere in the literary realm. Even so, the example of Peacock suggests that such a deficiency need not be fatal to a writer of fiction. True, his plots are often insignificant or implausible, and his characters tend to be sketches rather than rounded likenesses or, if three-dimensional, to have more opinions than emotions. His novels are nevertheless readable and re-readable, for he excels in anatomizing the follies, philosophies, and fashions that the age presents to his satirical eye. It is not enough for Peacock to make clear the inconsistencies and absurdities of pre-Reform Toryism, Byronic misanthropy, or the modern educational system: his talent for phrase-making ensures that even the bores and half-wits he creates spout golden epigrams.

Clear thinking and stylish writing are not the rarest of Peacock's gifts, though. Perhaps his distinctive excellence is his ability to embrace limitation without accepting diminution. He revels in ideas and delights in the good things of the world. A thoroughgoing classicist in his own views, he accurately understands most of the contemporary opinions and ideas he attacks (Samuel Taylor Coleridge's transcendentalism is a notable exception). He is opinionated without being ill-humored. His erudition does not preclude strong practicality. The narrow range of emotions he articulates is the result of a positive rather than a negative quality, of brave stoicism rather than heartlessness. Although Peacock's novels are for the most part slender, they never seem the productions of a small mind.

Headlong Hall, Peacock's first novel, is far from being his finest piece, but it is a mature work in which the characteristic devices of Peacock's career are effectively, if not perfectly, deployed. One finds charming description of picturesque countryside, in this case Wales, where Peacock had happily traveled in 1809. One finds a rich rural lover of good conversation, Squire Headlong of the Hall, who to gratify his taste assembles a diverse set of wise and foolish talkers. Most important, one finds the talkers themselves.

In this novel, as in several of the later ones, Peacock's satire is general; his own perspective is not to be precisely identified with that of any one character. The principal way of grouping the speakers at Squire Headlong's symposium is to distinguish the philosphers, who genuinely seek to discover truth via Socratic dialogue, from the cranks, who find in conversation a chance to ride forth on their particular intellectual hobbyhorses, and who would rather lecture than learn. When Peacock wrote *Headlong Hall* in 1815, he was in daily contact with the Percy Bysshe Shelley circle, and the novel's three philosophers reason from stances Shelley, Peacock, and their friend Thomas Jefferson Hogg adopted in their intellectual discussions. Peacock's naming of the three characters indicates their respective positions. Foster the perfectabilian (φωστηρ, "one who guards a flame") articulates a position that Shelley sometimes took, that the human race is improving largely through technological advances. At the other pole is Escot the deteriorationist (ες σκοτor, "one looking on the dark side"), who takes the Rousseau-derived view that man has fallen from his pristine excellence, and largely because, as Shelley's friend J. F. Newton argued, he eats meat. Balancing these opposites is Jenkinson, the embracer of the status quo (αιer ες ιοωr, "one who from equal measures can produce arguments on both sides"), who gives voice to Hogg's skepticism.

To fan the flames of intellectual discourse, Peacock provides an assortment of windy enthusiasts and eccentrics, none so finely drawn as later incarnations were to be, but none failing to amuse. The Reverend Mr. Gaster begins Peacock's series of gourmandizing clergymen; Panscope is his first and thinnest burlesque of Coleridge's transcendentalism. Marmaduke Milestone speaks for the Reptonian school of picturesque gardening, a taste Peacock deplored. The phrenologist Mr. Cranium leads off the series of freakish scientists that continues down to *Gryll Grange*. Representing literary enterprises, if not strictly speaking literature, are the poets Nightshade and Maclaurel, the reviewers Gall and Treacle, and Miss Philomela Poppyseed, a writer of feminine novels and one of the few stupid women in Peacock's gallery. Lest the fine arts be neglected, Peacock supplies Sir Patrick O'Prism, a painting dilettante, and Cornelius Chromatic, an amateur violinist.

The characters feast, drink, talk, sing. Having served their host's (and their author's) purposes, they are paired in the ordering dance of marriage, an inevitable conclusion according to the systems of both Foster and Escot, and an empirical state in which one suspects the two philosophers' theories will prove of precisely equal value.

Peacock's second and longest novel, *Melincourt*, is generally considered his weakest. At the time of its composition, Peacock's principal association was with Shelley, and in this novel Peacock drops the objectivity of the "laughing philosopher" and presents political views he shared with the poet, who was even then giving them poetic form in what was to be Shelley's *The Revolt of Islam* (1818). Melincourt sincerely satirizes the Tory government and, as Lord

Byron's *The Vision of Judgment* (1822) would later do, former liberals such as the Lake Poets, Robert Southey, William Wordsworth, and Coleridge (Feathernest, Paperstamp, and Mystic in the novel) who had grown less critical of the establishment as their places in that order grew more comfortable. Certain episodes in *Melincourt* are memorable. The election at Onevote presents a marvelous empirical case for parliamentary reform, and the Anti-Saccharine Fête celebrates Peacock's belief that sugar, because its production permitted the West Indian slave trade to prosper, was a morally and politically abominable commodity to be abjured by all true philanthropists "till it were sent them by freemen." For the most part, though, this sort of candor makes *Melincourt* shrill rather than forceful.

The romantic thread on which the beads of satiric incident are strung is likewise not among Peacock's strongest. The heroine of the piece and owner of its principal location is Anthelia Melincourt, "at the age of 21, mistress of herself and of ten thousand a year, and of a very ancient and venerable castle in one of the wildest valleys of Westmoreland." More than one critic has noticed that the assets mentioned and the rhetoric employed in this, *Melincourt's* opening passage, call to mind the famous first sentence of Jane Austen's *Emma*, published two years earlier in 1815. Unlike Austen's charming and self-deluded Miss Woodhouse, Miss Melincourt is an earnest and judicious lady, a fit match for Mr. Sylvan Forester, the second Peacock hero to embody Shelley's intellectual idealism.

These two young people so obviously suited for each other lose no time in discovering their mutual regard. The novel's complications and the lovers' tribulations must come from without: Anthelia is abducted to Alga Castle by the enamoured Lord Anophel Achthar. Having lost his bride-to-be, Forester, ostensibly seeking her, wanders about England's Lake District and calls on poets and reviewers at Mainchance Villa and Cimmerian Lodge. His dilatory pursuit gives Lord Anophel time to tire of waiting for Anthelia to yield to his repeated proposals. He threatens to compromise her, and, even though the lady is too strong-minded to think that his wickedness will be her disgrace, she is nevertheless grateful enough to be rescued from a test of her theory by Forester and his companion Sir Oran Haut-ton, who is barely prevented from administering "natural justice" by throwing Lord Anophel out the window.

The fierce, faithful, mute Sir Oran is, most readers agree, the book's chief delight, curious though it might seem for a speechless character to be the chief excellence in a book by a writer noted largely for his characters' conversations. In Sir Oran, who plays the flute, goes out in society, and gains a parliamentary seat, Peacock presents with only slight exaggerations a theory of the Scottish jurist Lord Monboddo that the orangutan is a "noble savage" distinguished from the rest of the human race only by its inability to speak. In the world of literature at least, Monboddo's argument may have more validity than readers might expect: a literary Darwin examining popular fiction might well be tempted to see in the still thriving breed of strong, silent, active heroes Sir Oran's not-too-distant descendants.

Peacock began writing his third novel, *Nightmare Abbey*, after Shelley and Mary Godwin departed England for Italy in March of 1818. The book is arguably his finest, certainly his best-focused and plotted, and easily his most controversial. In this novel, Peacock, one of the great English admirers of Aristophanes, lays himself open to the same sort of unfair criticisms that have been heaped on the Greek dramatist for his comedy *The Clouds* (423 B.C.). Just as Aristophanes was censured by various critics, from Plato on, for inaccurately and irresponsibly portraying Socrates, so Peacock has been condemned for faithlessness and poor taste by readers who consider *Nightmare Abbey* an unseemly depiction of one of the less commendable interludes in Shelley's life—his period of wanting to have Mary Godwin without giving up his wife Harriet.

There are indeed resemblances between Shelley and the novelist's protagonist Scythrop—part romantic idealist, part misanthrope, part would-be reformer. Marionetta O'Carroll, the sprightly coquette of a cousin Scythrop professes to love, is like Harriet Shelley in spirit and appearance. Scythrop's other love, the heiress Celinda Toobad (known to him as Stella) is tall and raven-haired, the physical opposite of Mary Godwin, but very like Peacock's impression of that grave lady in her passion for philosophical speculation, political discussion, and transcendental romantic literature. Invention of detail was at no time Peacock's strong suit; he was obliged to borrow from real life.

Yet, despite having drawn certain details of his novel from Shelley's situation in 1814, Peacock was neither so tasteless nor so unkind as to write a book centering on his friend's romantic and domestic difficulties. The surest sign of Peacock's goodwill is Shelley's own admiration of the novel: "I am delighted with *Nightmare Abbey*," he wrote from Italy. "I think Scythrop a character admirably conceived and executed; and I know not how to praise sufficiently the lightness, chastity, and strength of the language of the whole." Rather than personalities, Peacock's targets were the dark gloom of modern literature, Byron's *Childe Harold's Pilgrimage* (1812), and such other determinedly dismal works, and the black bile and blue devils introduced by this literature into the lives of its readers.

Nightmare Abbey is the only Peacock novel to take place at one scene only, namely the dreary and semidilapidated seat of Christopher Glowry, a gentleman "naturally of an atrabilarious temperament, and much troubled with those phantoms of indigestion which are commonly called *blue devils*." Disappointed in love and marriage, the gloomy squire of the Abbey surrounds himself with owls, ivy, water weeds, and servants with the most dismal names: Raven, Crow, Graves, Deathshead. His son Scythrop, a reader of Gothic novels and transcendental philosophies, stalks the Abbey like a grand inquisitor. The young man is ruled by two passions: reforming the word by repairing the "crazy fabric of human nature" and drinking Madeira. These preoccupations alter materially when Mr. Glowry's sister and brother-in-law, their niece and ward Marionetta, and a host of other guests arrive for an extended taste of what hospitality the Abbey can afford. Among the houseguests are a particularly fine array of representative embodiments of morbid romanticism. The Honorable Mr. Listless, who spends whole days on a sofa, has perfected ennui. Mr. Flosky, who "plunged into the central opacity of Kantian metaphysics, and lay *perdu* several years in transcendental darkness, till the common daylight of common sense became intolerable to his eyes," is one of Peacock's more successful sketches of Coleridge. Mr. Toobad is a Manichaean Millenarian, the Byronic Mr. Cypress, a poet who having quarreled with his wife feels absolved from all duty and is about to set off on his travels.

Finely drawn though the gentlemen may be, as Marilyn Butler has noted in her treatment of *Nightmare Abbey*, Scythrop's two ladies divide the book between themselves. Scythrop's attraction to the volatile Marionetta, who playfully spurns him when he seems devoted and charms him when he seems distant, dominates the first half of the book, while his fascination for the mysterious and brilliant "Stella," a creature of veils and conspiracies, overshadows lesser matters in the second half of the story. Scythrop can bring himself to dispense with neither lady: "I am doomed to be the victim of eternal disappointment," he laments in the tone of German high tragedy, "and I have no resource but a pistol." The two unrenounceable ladies, however, find it possible to renounce their suitor. Wishing Scythrop joy of Miss O'Carroll, Celinda/Stella turns to the metaphysical Mr. Flosky. Wishing him all happiness with Miss Toobad, Marionetta engages herself to Mr. Listless. His disappointment validated, his misanthropy doubly confirmed, Scythrop thinks himself likely to make a figure in the world. His story ends not with a gunshot but with a sound more familiar in the Peacock world: "Bring some Madeira."

Peacock's next two novels, *Maid Marian* and *The Misfortunes of Elphin*, depart from the prevailing "country house conversation" pattern. Both works are generally labeled "satirical romances," being set in the picturesque past but laying out oblique observations on present-day situations.

The first of these romances is perhaps Peacock's most widely known story, primarily because it forms the basis for a popular operetta by J. R. Planché, *Maid Marian: Or, The Huntress of Arlingford* (1822). Peacock was sometimes considered to have borrowed portions of his novel from Sir Walter Scott's *Ivanhoe* (1820), but actually Scott and Peacock, who wrote most of his novel in 1818, shared their primary source: Joseph Ritson's *Robin Hood*, a collection of ancient poems, songs, and ballads about that hero. Like Scott's work, Peacock's novel is no plausible portrait of medieval life. Robin Hood is not a responsible steward of the wealth he commandeers; his superiority lies in being less hypocritical than his adversaries, the sheriff and Prince John. Friar

Tuck is one in Peacock's long gallery of wine-loving clergymen; Maid Marian, whose swordsmanship and archery are commendable and who decides in liberated fashion at the novel's end to retain her virginal title "though the appellation was then as much a misnomer as that of Little John," is one of Peacock's admirably independent heroines. The satiric object of the forest idyll? To mock the repressive and reactionary Holy Alliance, on which Byron, too, was then turning his sights in his *Don Juan* (1819-1824).

As a perennial wandering woodsman, particularly in Windsor Forest, which had recently been enclosed, Peacock might have grown up with an interest in the Robin Hood material. His interest in the legendary past presented in *The Misfortunes of Elphin* dates to a more specific series of events. In 1820, Peacock married Jane Gryffydh, a young woman he had met on his travels in Wales ten years before, and her fluency in Welsh reawakened his interest in the Celtic legends of Elphin, Taliesin, and Arthur on which his story is based. Peacock's pastiche of Welsh myths is notable for its rousing songs and its depiction of the splendidly amoral inebriate Seithenyn. Its political satire is particularly effective. The crumbling of the ruinous seawall and castle administered by the drunken Seithenyn could be an apt allegory for any self-indulgent, backward-looking ruling class blind to imminent revolution and indifferent to public responsibility. The situation and the speeches of Seithenyn, however, superbly transmuted from those of the nineteenth century politican George Canning, are particularly relevant to an England on the brink of parliamentary reform.

Crotchet Castle, written two years after *The Misfortunes of Elphin*, returns to the Pavonian mainstream. Here the mansion is glorified villa; the owner, a rich and recently retired Scottish stockbroker; the target, progressive hypocrisy, represented in real life by Henry Brougham and in the novel by the "March of Mind." The novel divides into three parts. A houseparty at Crotchet Castle, carefully designed by its host to pit "the sentimental against the rational, the intuitive against the inductive, the ornamental against the useful, the intense against the tranquil, the romantic against the classical," is followed by a floating caravan proceeding up the Thames to the rural depths of Wales; and the novel concludes with a Christmas gathering, more than a little Pickwickian, at the quasimedieval residence of Mr. Chainmail, a sturdy but sensitive anachronist patterned, as critic David Garnett has observed, after Sir Edward Strachey.

This tale of past and present—that is, the past as it should have been and the future that the present shows all too much promise of becoming—sets Mr. Chainmail and the Reverend Dr. Folliot, one of Peacock's fiercer Tory clergymen, against the liberal utilitarians of the "march of mind" school, preeminent among them one Mr. MacQuedy (*"Mac Q.E.D."*, son of a demonstration," as Peacock annotates his own pun). Two pairs of lovers require proper pairing as well. Mr. Chainmail, by story's end, overcomes his excessive regard for old names and blood and marries Susannah Touchandgo, a financier's daughter once engaged to the prospering speculator Crochet, Jr. Having lost her fiancé when her father lost his fortune and decamped for America, Miss Touchandgo has withdrawn to a salubrious Welsh seclusion of music, country cream, fresh air, and exercise, in which charming situation Mr. Chainmail comes upon her.

If old names must be foresworn, so must new money; in the romance dovetailed with the Chainmail-Touchandgo one, Lady Clarinda Bossnowl, generally acclaimed as the most delectable of Peacock's exceptionally pleasing heroines, breaks her engagement to young Crotchet and commits herself to the poor, pedigreed, and talented Captain Fitzchrome. Perhaps the best philosopher in the Crotchet Castle party, Lady Clarinda begins by playing at utilitarianism, intent not to give her heart away when she can sell it. The journey from the stockbroker's villa to romantic Wales, however, gives her judgment time to concur with what her feelings long have suggested: that love in a cottage—and not even a *cottage ornée*—with the Captain is better than comfort at the Castle. Lady Clarinda's raillery, Folliot's prejudices, and Chainmail's enthusiasms make the novel's conversation particularly fine, and the climax, a spirited defense of Chainmail Hall against "Captain Swing" and that "coming race," the mob, is perhaps Peacock's most active.

Peacock, preoccupied with official duties and family concerns, did not write another novel for thirty years, but *Gryll Grange*, his last one, is of a vintage worth waiting for. Few readers would suspect that the author of this suave and mellow production was well acquainted with sorrow and disappointment. The satire here is less incisive and the development of character richer than in the earlier books—in part because the people portrayed have feelings as well as opinions, in part because Peacock's wit plays not on the characters but on the world outside Gryll Grange, the modern England of scientific advance, technological development, competitive examinations, and spiritualism—a society mocked by the Gryll Grange houseparty in their own satirical comedy "Aristophanes in London."

For the plot of *Gryll Grange*, Peacock harks back to the situation of *Melincourt*. Morgana, the niece and heiress of Gregory Gryll (the family, we learn, is descended from that Gryllus who alone among Ulysses' crewmen declined being released from the spell by which Circe has turned him into a pig), needs a fit husband who will take her name. Squire Gryll's friend the Reverend Dr. Opimian, a hearty man much like Peacock in his relish for "a good library, a good dinner, a pleasant garden, and rural walks," finds just such a suitor in Mr. Falconer, the new resident of a nearby tower significantly called the "Duke's Folly" by the neighborhood. Falconer, the last of Peacock's fictional projections of the young Shelley, is an idealistic recluse who lives a comfortable, scholarly life with seven beautiful sisters who manage his household and make his music. Once juxtaposed by the well-tried divine machine of a thunderstorm, Miss Gryll and Falconer are mutually attracted: the subsequent story in large measure centers on the hero's vacillations. Should he renounce his monastic retreat and the seven maidens who have been his companions since childhood, or should he forswear the social world so fetchingly represented by Gryll Grange and the one lady he loves?

Also staying at the Grange are Lord Curryfin, a lively, inventive, and engagingly ridiculous fellow, and the serenely beautiful Miss Niphet. Their presences further complicate the romantic dilemma. Lord Curryfin, at first drawn to Miss Gryll, finds himself increasingly enamoured of the other charmer and knows not where to offer his heart and title. Miss Niphet, a good friend to Morgana, loves the young lord but hesitates to bag a bird on whom she believes her friend's sights to be trained. Miss Gryll, who knows she loves Falconer but doubts whether she can get him, believes she can get Lord Curryfin but wonders whether she could truly love him. This tangled web of love, honor, and jealousy so mild that it never becomes a vice is straightened out by an event yet more providential than the convenient thunderstorm: the appearance and acceptance of seven stalwart rustics who want to marry the maidens of the tower and who thereby free Falconer from his reservations. The novel ends with all the lovers properly betrothed, a multiple wedding, and, as is fitting in the Peacock world, a vinuous salute. Addressing the wedding party, Dr. Opimian concludes, "Let all the corks, when I give the signal, be discharged simultaneously; and we will receive it as a peal of Bacchic ordnance, in honor of the Power of the Joyful Event, whom we may assume to be presiding on this auspicious occasion."

Peter W. Graham

Other major works

POETRY: *The Monks of St. Mark*, 1804; *Palmyra and Other Poems*, 1806; *The Genius of the Thames*, 1810; *The Philosophy of Melancholy*, 1812; *Sir Proteus: A Satirical Ballad*, 1814; *Rhododaphne*, 1818; *Paper Money Lyrics*, 1837.

NONFICTION: *The Four Ages of Poetry*, 1820; *Memoirs of Percy Bysshe Shelley*, 1858-1862.

Bibliography

Burns, Bryan. *The Novels of Thomas Love Peacock*. London: Croom Helm, 1985. Focuses on Peacock's novels, providing a close reading and analysis for each. The introduction traces his intellectual debts, especially to classical authors. The novels are read with a primarily textual approach, discussing language, characterization, syntax, and irony and suggesting that they are "dialectical" in nature. Burns does not offer much interpretation of Peacock's novels, but does a good job of looking at their style, emphasizing their similarities but also insisting on their diversity. The bibliography is selective but includes important works, and the index is thorough.

Butler, Marilyn. *Peacock Displayed: A Satirist in His Context*. London: Routledge & Kegan Paul, 1979. A first-rate study of Peacock which focuses not only on him as an individual but also on the society in which he lived and worked. Discusses the relationship between Peacock and Percy Bysshe Shelley, contending that they derived mutual intellectual benefit from their friendship which is revealed in their work. Butler emphasizes Peacock's satiric abilities, attempting to explain that he does not debunk everything— a common charge against him—but instead is highly skeptical of systems. Includes a detailed reading of each of his major novels, plus an examination of Peacock as a critic. The introduction sets him in his literary, social, and biographical context.

Dawson, Carl. *His Fine Wit: A Study of Thomas Love Peacock*. Berkeley: University of California Press, 1970. Discusses most of Peacock's work in detail, including his poetry, essays, and music criticism. Does a very good job with his works and provides an alternative view, but is somewhat outdated. The chapter on Peacock's *The Four Ages of Poetry* provides illuminating background on the book and also on Percy Bysshe Shelley's response to it, which culminated in his famous *A Defense of Poetry*. Even so, Dawson does not treat Peacock as a minor writer or as a disciple of Shelley, as many critics do; in fact, he paints Shelley as something of a hypocrite. The index and chronology are not strong, and there is no bibliography. Does include notes which could serve as a substitute.

Mills, Howard. *Peacock: His Circle and His Age*. Cambridge, England: Cambridge University Press, 1969. Mills asserts that his book "is equally about [Percy Bysshe] Shelley, [Samuel Taylor] Coleridge and [Lord] Byron" because Peacock is important primarily in relation to them, and he therefore includes chapters on these poets and other contemporaries. One purpose of this approach is to demonstrate Peacock's intellectual debt to these writers. Attempts to chronicle his reactions to the intellectual currents around him, especially the fading eighteenth century classicism and the growing trend of Romanticism, competing forces during the Regency.

Mulvihill, James. *Thomas Love Peacock*. Boston: Twayne, 1987. An excellent short sourcebook on Peacock, providing biographical background and sound context for each of his major works from his poetry to his novels (*Headlong Hall*, *Melincourt*, *Nightmare Abbey*, *Crotchet Castle*, *Gryll Grange*, *Maid Marian*, *The Misfortunes of Elphin*), as well as his essays and reviews. Attempts to place each work into its appropriate literary and historical background and provide a detailed, interesting, although fairly standard reading. A good starting place for work on Peacock because of its brevity. The bibliography and good chronology are helpful, as Peacock is such a little noticed author.

WALKER PERCY

Born: Birmingham, Alabama; May 28, 1916
Died: Covington, Louisiana; May 10, 1990

Principal long fiction
The Moviegoer, 1961; *The Last Gentleman*, 1966; *Love in the Ruins: The Adventures of a Bad Catholic at a Time Near the End of the World*, 1971; *Lancelot*, 1977; *The Second Coming*, 1980; *The Thanatos Syndrome*, 1987.

Other literary forms
As a writer of imaginative literature, Walker Percy has devoted himself exclusively to the novel. He has, however, also written more than fifty reviews and essays on many of the same topics that inform his novels: existential philosophy, language theory, modern scientific method, contemporary American culture, the South, and literature. With one or two exceptions, the most important of these essays are collected in *The Message in the Bottle* (1975), which has as its peculiarly Percyean subtitle, *How Queer Man Is, How Queer Language Is, and What One Has to Do with the Other*. An indispensable book, *The Message in the Bottle* not only clarifies the author's major concerns as well as his commitment to that most basic philosophical question, "What is man?," but also details the formidable intellectual foundation upon which his fiction so unpretentiously rests. That unpretentiousness is especially evident in *Lost in the Cosmos* (1983), ironically subtitled *The Last Self-Help Book*, in which Percy employs satire and semiotics in an effort to clarify the human being's social and more especially spiritual predicament as a uniquely "lost" creature needing the good news of the gospels but all too often willing to settle for the insights of scientist Carl Sagan and talk-show host Phil Donahue.

Achievements
Percy is perhaps most easily described as a Catholic-Existentialist-American-Southern novelist, a baggy phrase that at least has the virtue of identifying the various currents which are blended together in his distinctive works. In Percy's fiction, Mark Twain's Huck Finn from the novel *The Adventures of Huckleberry Finn* (1884) and Jean-Paul Sartre's Antoine Roquentin from *Nausea* (1938) meet in a single character adrift in a world where, despite the formless sprawl of mass society, the possibility of grace still exists. Percy's fiction is readily identifiable by its distinctive narrative voice. That voice—laconic yet disarmingly honest and filled with wonder—has gained for Percy both critical respect and a dedicated readership. Percy received the National Book Award for *The Moviegoer*, the *Los Angeles Times* Book Award for *The*

Second Coming, and the St. Louis Literary Award for *Lost in the Cosmos*. Among his other literary honors are memberships in the National Institute of Arts and Letters and the American Academy of Arts and Sciences.

Biography

Walker Percy was born in Birmingham, Alabama, on May 28, 1916. When his father, lawyer Leroy Percy, committed suicide in 1929, the widow and her three sons moved to Greenville, Mississippi, where they lived with Leroy's bachelor cousin, William Alexander Percy, who adopted the boys in 1931, following their mother's death in an automobile accident. The Greenville home served as something of a local cultural center; the uncle, the author of several works, including an autobiographical memoir of the South entitled *Lanterns on the Levee* (1941), entertained such houseguests as William Faulkner, Carl Sandburg, Langston Hughes, David Cohn, and Harry Stack Sullivan. In the early 1930's, Percy attended Greenville High School, where he wrote a gossip column and became the close friend of Shelby Foote, who was by then already committed to a literary career. At the University of North Carolina, which was noted for its school of behaviorism, Percy majored in chemistry and received a B.S. in 1937. He then enrolled in Columbia's College of Physicians and Surgeons (M.D., 1941), where, in addition to his studies, Percy underwent psychoanalysis and became a frequent moviegoer. The turning point in his life came in early 1942 when, as a resident at Bellevue Hospital in New York, Percy contracted tuberculosis. During his two-year convalescence at Saranac Lake, he began reading extensively in philosophy and literature (Sartre, Albert Camus, Søren Kierkegaard, Gabriel Marcel, Fyodor Dostoevski, Nikolai Gogol, Leo Tolstoy, Franz Kafka). What he discovered was that as a medical doctor he knew much about man but had no idea what a man really is.

Following a relapse and further convalescence in 1944, Percy seemed sure of only two things: he was a doctor who did not wish to practice medicine; he was literally as well as existentially homeless (his uncle having died in 1942). In 1945, he traveled with Shelby Foote to New Mexico and then stayed on alone for a time. On November 7, 1946, he married Mary Bernice Townsend, and less than a year later they both converted to Catholicism. (The decision to convert was, Percy said, in large measure the result of their reading of Kierkegaard's essay, "The Difference Between a Genius and an Apostle.") Soon after, the Percys moved from Sewanee, Tennessee, to New Orleans, Louisiana, where Percy continued his contemplative life, financially secure—thanks to his uncle's estate—and intellectually rich—his landlord, Julius Friend, a professor of philosophy, introduced him to the writings of Charles Saunders Peirce, whose triadic theory of language formed the basis of Percy's own linguistic speculations. (Percy's interest in language had another and more personal source: the younger of his two daughters was born deaf.) In 1950, the Percys moved to Covington, Louisiana, "a pleasant non-place," Percy said, where it is possible to live as a stranger in one's own land; it is neither the "anyplace" that characterizes mass society nor the "some-place" of the New Orleans or a Richmond, where the past haunts the present.

In the 1950's, Percy began publishing essays in such journals as *Thought*, *Commonweal*, and *Philosophy and Phenomenological Research*. After discarding two early novels, he began writing *The Moviegoer* in 1959, revising it four times before its publication two years later. Until his death on May 10, 1990, Percy lived quietly in Covington, Louisiana, a serious and meditative novelist, who was also a Catholic, an existentialist, and a Southerner, pondering the world in thought, fiction, and an occasional essay.

Analysis

Walker Percy acknowledged that Soren Kierkegaard's writings provided him with "a theoretical frame of reference," and one of the most important ideas which he adapted from this frame is Kierkegaard's rejection of Hegelian rationalism in favor of a subjective and intensely passionate commitment on the part of the individual. In Percy's view, modern science in general and the social sciences in particular have mistakenly and indiscriminately adopted the behaviorist, or biological, method and have consequently defined man reductively and abstractly. Existentialism, including the existential novel, on the other hand, presents an alternative to behaviorism: a "concrete" phenomenological approach whose aim is the recovery of man's uniqueness. Percy admits that the behaviorist method is valid to a point; ultimately, however, it must fail, because, in classifying man as a biological organism acting in accordance with rules applicable to all biological organisms, it fails to deal with what is distinctly human in man, man's nonbiological goals. Concerned solely with sameness, the scientific method cannot account for Fyodor Dostoevski's underground man except as a deviation from the norm. Existentialism, Percy believes, does account for him, as does Christianity, which acknowledges the Fall of Man, his distance from God, and defines his existence as "the journey of a wayfarer along life's way." Denying the Fall, modern science makes the Gnostic mistake; it attempts to build Eden, the secular city, where man's guilt and anxiety are conditioned away, where all of man's biological needs are met, and where his existence is certified for him by experts.

Percy rejects this "brave new world" and calls instead for a "radical anthropology" that can account for the ontological as well as the biological aspects of human existence. Guilt and anxiety, he points out, are not symptoms of maladjustment to be gotten rid of so that the individual (as human organism) can live the life of the satisfied consumer; rather, these signs of estrangement serve to summon him not to self-fulfillment but to authentic existence. Man is on earth not to have his needs met, Percy says, not to surrender his sovereignty to the theories of experts (a view raised more recently by Christopher Lasch in his controversial book, *The Culture of Narcissism*, 1979) but to be saved, and that necessitates consciousness of his situation as a castaway.

It is important to realize that Percy's sovereign wayfarer, or castaway, is not entirely identifiable with Kierkegaard's knight of faith. In place of Kierkegaard's extreme subjectivity, Percy posits the intersubjectivity of Gabriel Marcel, a Christian existentialist whose *we are* stands in stark contrast with both Kierkegaard's *I choose* and René Descartes' *I think*. We know we exist, Marcel says, by participating in the world. He does not think of being as experience, however, but as a presence within experience which is to be understood as simultaneously transcendent *and* immanent. To separate the two components of being is to pervert them and to transmogrify man as sovereign wayfarer into either angel—the abstract knower, the objective consciousness—or beast—a culture organism satisfying its needs. (The terms are Percy's, borrowed from Blaise Pascal.)

Marcel's quest for being, which is the quest for salvation as well, manifests itself in Percy's theory of language as intersubjective communication, where *we name* implies the same religious affirmation as Marcel's *we are* and Martin Buber's *I-Thou*. Percy originally turned to language theory in order to answer the question "What is man?" because the answer provided by the behaviorist method was reductive and because the old theological view, along with the words in which it was couched, has been rendered ineffective by the general acceptance of the scientific method, which predisposed modern man to view himself as the behaviorists had defined him. Percy then set himself the task of finding "the delta factor": that which makes man what he is and not something else. According to the old theological view, man's singularity is his "soul," a meaningless word in a scientific age that demands empirical proof. For soul, Percy substitutes language, which he defines not as a sign system (the behaviorist position) but as the uniquely human process of symbolization. At the heart of language (and therefore at the heart of man as well) is something mysterious (compare Marcel's "mystery of being"). The mystery is explained by what Percy calls the "coupling process," the intersubjective human context by which man names, or symbolizes, the world and in this way comes both to know it and to share it. Language is, therefore, an attempt to bridge the gap between self and other, or, considered in the religious context of the Fall of Man, between self and God. What complicates the situation is the fact that today, Percy believes, language has become as meaningless, as clichéd, as the old theology. Before there can be intersubjective communication, man must again learn how to speak.

To learn to name and therefore to know and share that knowledge with another is the basic plot of a Percy novel. As Robert Coles has pointed out, Percy's novels trace the protagonist's movement from lofty observation to active participation in the openness of life—its possibilities and the necessity of making choices. Each of his major characters feels estranged "from being, from his own being, from the being of other creatures in the world, from the transcendent being. He has lost something, but what he does not know; he only knows that he is sick to death with the loss of it." Since this quest for being is a quest for God, it involves the hero's progress through Kierkegaard's three stages: the aesthetic (the pursuit of pleasure; the self becomes an uncommitted ironic spectator detached from himself and from others); the ethical (living within a general human code, such as marriage); the religious (requiring an entirely personal and—Kierkegaard would say—absurd leap of faith). The hero's search for being begins only when he becomes conscious of his despair and tries either to understand it or to alleviate it in one of two ways: rotation or repetition. Rotation—the quest for new experiences to offset "everydayness"—makes up the comic substance of Percy's novels. Repetition—the return to the past—may be rendered comically, but more often it serves a darker purpose, for Percy's heroes are, like William Faulkner's, haunted by the past; as a result, they do not live fully in the present. Only when they confront the past directly and become conscious of it can they break its spell and become sovereign wayfarers.

Frequently, Percy equates the past with the Southern stoicism his uncle espoused, which, in Percy's judgment, leads only to pessimism, obsession with death, and "the wintry kingdom of self"; in short, it is the very antithesis of Percy's Christian existentialism. Rotation and repetition provide only temporary relief from the malaise that prevails within the aesthetic stage. The only escape from "aesthetic damnation" is through ordeal, especially the death of a loved one. Ordeal brings the hero face to face with mortality and enables him to see his world and himself as if for the first time. The search he then begins is in effect a rejection of the absurdist position of aesthetic existentialists such as Albert Camus and Jean-Paul Sartre. The world is not absurd; it is a world to be named, known, and shared by the authentic self and the other in a mode of existence that is not so much religious *or* ethical as a synthesis of the two.

There are analogues for Percy's religious-phenomenological conception of man's search for being in his method of composition and in his prose style. The author's search for narrative form parallels the hero's search for being. Beginning with a situation rather than a plot or set of characters, Percy wrote with no fixed purpose or end in mind. As he explained, the writing, while not "haphazard," involved "many false starts, many blind detours, many blind passages, many goings ahead and backing up. . . ." Stylistically, his elegantly and precisely written novels suggest wonder, humor, and forbearance rather than the ponderous solemnity of other existential novelists such as Sartre. Moreover, his prose is richly and sensuously detailed; like two other converts to Catholicism, Marcel and even more particularly Gerard Manley Hopkins, he took pleasure in a natural and human world that is, although marred by evil, essentially sacramental.

John Bickerson Bolling—"Binx"—is the narrator and main character of *The Moviegoer* and the first of Percy's spiritually "sick" protagonists. At age twenty-nine, he is a successful broker in a modern world where the church has been replaced by the brokerage house. Although financially secure, Binx feels uneasy; although adept at planning his client's futures, he has trouble living his own life from day to day, fearful that he may at any moment succumb to that worst of all plagues, the malaise of "everydayness." To counter its effects, Binx becomes a moviegoer, partly because movies project a "heightened . . . . resplendent reality," albeit temporary, and partly because movies provide Binx with accepted role-models; thus his impersonations of such canonized figures as Gregory Peck, Clark Gable, Dana Andrews, and Rory Calhoun (who also serves as his confidant). The impersonation can never fully satisfy the moviegoer, however, who must eventually face the fact that the reality of his own life can never attain the heightened illusion of the star's gestural perfection. Moviegoing serves Binx in two additional ways: it enables him to view his world through the perspective of the films he has seen and, more important, to observe the world as if it were itself a movie and he the passive audience.

Binx's detachment is both a virtue and a vice. As the detached spectator, he observes those around him closely and accurately, thus exposing the roles they have unknowingly adopted. Appropriately, the novel's temporal setting is the week before Mardi Gras, the period of rehearsals for New Orleans' city-wide impersonation. Instead of recognizing their situation as castaways, these others feel serenely at home in the world, whereas in fact they are, as Binx understands, "dead." Neither virtuous nor sinful, they are merely "nice"; they speak, but in clichés; they ask questions, but neither expect nor desire answers. Binx, who fears becoming invisible—losing his identity—is right to keep his distance from these shadowy others. At the same time, however, he longs to be like them, to have his identity certified for him by such spurious means as movies, identity cards, *Consumer Reports*, newspaper advice columns, and radio shows such as "This I Believe," which broadcasts the meaningless affirmations of abstracted religionists to a half-believing, half-skeptical Binx.

If it is his ironic detachment that saves Binx from the unreflective life of mass man, then it is his "search" that most clearly characterizes his longing for authenticity and being. "To become aware of the possibility of the search is to be onto something," Binx says. "Not to be onto something is to be in despair." Binx distinguishes two kinds of search. The "vertical" leads to abstraction: theories that explain the world but fail to explain what man is. (One alternative to such abstraction is the romanticism that killed Binx's father and that the son wisely rejects.) The other is the "horizontal" or phenomenological search that Percy himself counsels in *The Message in the Bottle*. While Binx is indeed "onto something," his search is different from Percy's; it constitutes a "debased" form of the religious search because, as Percy explained, Binx, like Sartre, "has already ruled God out." His search takes a purely aesthetic form. To ease "the pain of loss," he pursues money and women, but the pursuit leads only to boredom and depression because the novelty of his possessions quickly wears off and everydayness inevitably returns to remind him of his inauthenticity and his position as a castaway. Fortunately, Binx's yearning has a deeper current. As a college student, he found himself "lost in the mystery of being alive at such a time and place"; upon his return from the Korean War, he began his eight-year "exile" in the New Orleans suburb of Gentilly, which, like Covington, is a "nonplace"; and as a broker he has taken to reading *Arabia Deserta*, by the self-styled "God's pilgrim," Charles Montagu Doughty, concealed inside a Standard & Poor binder.

Binx's search begins with the fact of his own "invincible apathy" and eventually leads, after many wrong turns, to authenticity and intersubjective relationships with his fourteen-year-old half-brother, Lonnie Smith, and his twenty-five-year-old cousin Kate Cutrer. There exists a "complicity" between Binx and the dying Lonnie, who faces life with true serenity because he understands it religiously. Like the other dying children in Percy's novels, Lonnie represents the paradox of unmerited suffering in a world ruled by a supposedly benevolent God, a paradox Percy resolves by depicting their spiritual victory in a "world full of God's grace where sorrow and death do not have the final word." Binx attends to the "good news" that Lonnie embodies because, in part, Lonnie's monotonous way of talking makes his words fresh and therefore meaningful, "like a code tapped through a wall."

Kate, unlike Lonnie, lives in pure anxiety, swinging wildly between various extremes, especially the longing to be free and the desire "to be an anyone who is anywhere." Although she lacks Binx's degree of awareness as well as his ironic detachment and is more prone to impersonation than he, Kate, like Binx, is aware of her dis-ease, which others can only understand in psychological terms. (Thus, the novel's epigraph, taken from Kierkegaard: "the specific character of despair is precisely this: it is unaware of being despair.") Binx and Kate neatly complement each other: his childlike "simplemindedness" allows her to feel secure enough to speak honestly, while she correctly points out that in his search Binx may be overlooking something "obvious." Her request that Binx be her God—by which she means he is to tell her what to do—is not at all absurd given Marcel's brand of Christian existentialism. Significantly, her other suitors play the part of intersubjective God rather badly: one wants to send her to a high-priced psychoanalyst; the other promises an interminable vista of "niceness" and everydayness.

Binx's leap from nominal Catholic existing in despair to sovereign wayfarer and authentic being occurs very late in the novel and is effected by what, in a parallel context, Percy calls "some dim dazzling trick of grace." In fact, only a few pages from the end Binx laments that, having but one gift, "a good nose for merde," the only course for him to follow is "to fall prey to desire." There is even some justice to his Aunt Emily's judgment of him: in crucial situations, Binx invariably chooses to "default," to "exit." Yet, in the final pages, it is clear that Binx will do so no longer. Neither, however, will he play the part his aunt has chosen for him: Southern stoic. He will go to medical school, not because she wants him to but because now he knows what to do: to observe *and* to serve others. Binx's leap is reflected in the very texture of Percy's prose. Until the epilogue, which takes place one year later, Binx has narrated his tale chiefly in what may be termed his detached, matter-of-fact, moviegoer style, against which the very few lyrical passages, used to underscore Binx's wonder and the gracefulness of his world, stand in vivid contrast. In the epilogue, Binx drops the moviegoer style (and the references to movies) entirely; instead, he speaks easily, authentically, authoritatively. The man who earlier had been cousin, half-brother, and ironic impersonator, now is husband, brother, and sovereign wayfarer.

The protagonist of Percy's second novel, "Williston Bibb Barrett or Billy Barrett," is a modern-day version of Dostoevski's Prince Myshkin in *The Idiot* (1868). Although far less ironic than Binx Bolling, Barrett is far more disturbed, as his periodic fugue states and bouts of amnesia and *déjà vu* attest. Existing in a state of pure possibility, he is incapable of making any one decisive act or choice. He has tried and failed both to live the therapeutic life and to "engineer" his own destiny. Knowing something is missing in his life, Barrett seeks to recover reality and find his being in the "gap" between self and other. Specifically, these others are the members of the Vaught family, and his search is a spiritual odyssey, modeled on Mark Twain's *The Adventures of Huckleberry Finn* (1884), that takes him from New York to his native Ithaca, then on to Mississippi, and finally to Santa Fe, New Mexico, and the Sangre de Cristo mountains (Holy Faith and the Blood of Christ).

The search begins when Barrett accidentally discovers Kitty Vaught and her sister-in-law, Rita, in Central Park. Rita, a secular humanist and advocate of self-fulfillment, quickly realizes she will not be able either to control or to convert Barrett and tries unsuccessfully to get rid of him. Barrett, however, has already fallen in love with Kitty, a rather pale version of Kate Cutrer— less anxiety-ridden, more successful in her impersonations. Barrett's love affair is both furthered and complicated by Kitty's younger brother, Jamie, whose traveling companion he becomes. The fact that Jamie is dying establishes definite limits to the pure possibility of his and Barrett's lives and causes Barrett to consider his search more profoundly when he meets Jamie's sister, Val, and brother, Sutter, the two "absentee experts" (as Barrett calls them) who force him to make his existential choice. Val, a convert to Catholicism and a nun, has dedicated herself to teaching mute children to speak and to believe the Catholic religion. (All people are like her children, she claims;

they are waiting to be told what to do.) Whereas she is hopeful and apostolic, Sutter, a diagnostician and pathologist, is suicidal and ironically quixotic. He rejects her belief in man as wayfarer, claiming "We are doomed to the transcendence of abstraction and I choose the only reentry into the world which remains to us": "lewdness," cynicism, and detachment.

Sutter's mistake, as Barrett well understands, is the positing of extreme alternatives such as God or no God, transcendence or immanence. Moreover, Sutter's concern for Jamie betrays his basically religious nature, and it is this, more than his medical expertise, that has led Barrett to look to him for answers. At Jamie's baptism, it is Sutter who comprehends what is happening. Barrett, although he acts as interpreter between Jamie and the priest, misses the religious significance. He does understand that something has happened, however, and to discover what that something is he tracks down Sutter, who has decided to commit suicide. Barrett's search for an answer is, as Percy has noted, a search for a father, ultimately for the Father, God; his own father, Barrett finally realizes, had looked for his answer in all the wrong places— solitude, "old sad poetry," and the music of Johannes Brahms. The son's "wait" did not keep the father from killing himself, but it does save Sutter, who appears in the final tableau less as an oracle than as Barrett's self-chosen—and therefore sovereign—responsibility.

Subtitled *The Adventures of a Bad Catholic at a Time Near the End of the World*, *Love in the Ruins* is a broad satire on the state of the modern world— in particular, its behaviorist assumptions and political absurdities. The novel may be flawed, as some reviewers have contended, by the author's insistent and at times rather heavy-handed social criticism; there is, however, a comic vitality in this novel that seems to offset such reservations about it as literary art. This comic vitality, quite unlike the irony and understatement that characterize Percy's earlier novels, is appropriate to a work that has the topics of community and reconciliation as two of its major concerns. As Percy explained in an essay entitled "Notes for a Novel about the End of the World," the apocalyptic novelist serves two purposes: as prophet, or canary in the coal mine, he cries out in order to avert disaster, and as coupling agent, he connects man with reality. It is by means of the coupling process that disaster is averted, as Percy quietly suggests in the novel's closing image of a couple "twined about each other as the ivy twineth," in which what has been a sign of ruin (the ivy) is transformed into a symbol of intersubjective love.

The story, which is spoken into a pocket tape recorder by the hero, Tom More, as he keeps watch for snipers, follows a five-part structure (July Fourth, First, Second, Third, Fourth) that progressively becomes more chaotic until, in the epilogue ("Five Years Later"), peace and order are restored. The time of the novel is a not too distant future that bears a clear, if comically exaggerated, resemblance to the American 1960's: the fifteen-year war in Ecuador continues, racial tensions and Bantu uprisings are increasing, and the Catholic

Church has split into three factions. In short, "the center did not hold." The physical setting is just as perverse as the social-political: Paradise Estates, home of the well-to-do and the spiritually impoverished; Fedville, a sprawling compound which includes a Masters and Johnson Love Clinic, where ex-priest Kev Kevin reads *Commonweal* and presides over the vaginal console; Honey Island Swamp, a counterculture retreat; and the golf course, where a banner proclaims "Jesus Christ, the Greatest Pro of Them All."

Percy's hero is as troubled as his society but in a different way. Forty-five years old and a collateral descendent of Sir/Saint Thomas, he is at once a doctor and a mental patient, a diagnostician but also a metaphysician in a world of behaviorists ready and willing to condition away any remaining feelings of guilt he may have. Loving, in descending order of importance, women, music, science, God, and, "hardly at all," his fellow man, he is the type of what Kierkegaard termed aesthetic damnation. He has lost that thread in the world-labyrinth which, until the death of his daughter Samantha, made the world seem sensible and holy. His faith gone, More has his own messianic ambition, a plan to "save" America with More's Qualitative Quantitative Onotological Lapsometer. His invention—"the stethoscope of the spirit . . . the first caliper of the soul"—is designed to measure the "gap" between the outer, social self and true, inner being; he hopes to modify the lapsometer so that it can cure as well as diagnose man's "fall" from being, to put together what Descartes tore apart. Like Percy and, to a degree, like Sutter Vaught, More is troubled by modern man's indifference to being and his willingness to define himself in half-measures: the angel that, falling prey to abstraction, is unable to "reenter the lovely ordinary world," or the beast that adapts to its environment and so becomes the organism behaviorists say man is.

Art Immelmann—Mephistopheles to More's Faust—tempts him with spurious "good news": a multimillion dollar development grant and the Nobel Prize. The price is, of course, More's soul—his being, his sense of personal responsibility. More resists the devil and so escapes aesthetic damnation; by not committing the unpardonable sin (refusing God's grace), he puts an end to the "feasting on death" that has preoccupied him since the onset of his daughter's illness and begins to live in the "lovely ordinary world" once again. Instead of an apocalypse, the novel ends with a new beginning, a Christmas morning. Reborn, Tom More no longer loves abstractly or bestially; he has married his former nurse, Ellen Oglethorpe, a Georgia Presbyterian, whose belief takes the form of charity. Equally important, More now knows what it is he wants: not prizes or women, but "just to figure out what I've hit on. Some day a man will walk into my office as ghost or beast or ghost-beast and walk out as a man, which is to say sovereign wayfarer, lordly exile, worker and waiter and watcher."

Percy's fourth novel, *Lancelot*, is by far his most troubling. Structurally, it follows the odd dialogue form of Camus' *The Fall* (1956); until the last two pages, only the voice of the protagonist is heard, addressing a "you" whose responses are not given. More disturbing is the fact that, as Joyce Carol Oates has pointed out, the views of the main character, a self-righteous and unrepentant murderer, are strikingly similar to those of the author. Readers must recognize, as Percy surely does, the nature of the protagonist's grotesque mistake—the sources from which it derives and the ends to which it leads.

Lancelot Andrewes Lamar speaks his Poe-like tale from the Center for Aberrant Behavior in New Orleans, where he has been confined for one year. Although in the course of his apologia/confession Lance identifies his wife Margot's infidelity as the immediate cause of his murdering her and the members of the film company with whom she was involved, the actual causes go much further back and have less to do with Margot than with his own wasted life and his position as the last in a fallen line of Southern aristocrats. As a Lamar, Lance has inherited not only the family homestead, Belle Isle, but also a way of judging mankind in absolute terms. His first wife, Lucy, was (or so Lance remembers her) an angel, whereas Margot, who for a time he turned into a goddess, became beast or devil. Dividing his life into two parts— before he discovered his wife's adultery and after—he proclaims that the past is "absolutely dead" and the future will be "absolutely new." This penchant for absolutes suggests Lance's inability or unwillingness to confront the ambiguity and mystery of human existence and is related to the way the Lamars view a man's life in terms of individual, historically significant events. Thus, Lance's life is reduced to his 110-yard touchdown run against Alabama and his destruction of Belle Isle and everyone in it. Lance does understand that performing such feats are actually less difficult than living an ordinary life, but when he turns Margot's infidelity into a quest for the "unholy grail," he in effect sidesteps the ordinary life which is far "more complicated and ambiguous" than either the historical events venerated by the Lamars or the clichéd movies of Margot and her friends.

Like their movie, Lance's quest is superficial and derivative (it is cast in the mold of the Raymond Chandler detective novels he has been reading). Moreover, it leads Lance, as Cleanth Brooks has demonstrated, to commit a modern version of the Gnostic heresy. Claiming that the original sin was something God did to man and judging Christianity as much a failure as Southern stoicism, Lance determines to destroy the present age, which he cannot tolerate, and start over in a new Eden with his new Eve, Anna, a fellow patient who, he believes, as the victim of a brutal gang rape, has been restored to innocence. Lance is wrong about Anna, however; she never lost her innocence. He is also wrong about Christianity, if one distinguishes as Kierkegaard did, between Christianity (as embodied in Percival, Lance's listener to whom the novel is spoken) and Christendom, which Lance is right to reject as a viable alternative to his intolerable age.

Lance's confession as well as his predicament bring his friend Percival's spiritual ambivalence into sharp focus; Percival, the "Prince Hal" of their early manhood who has since been ordained Father John, is torn between two roles—priest and psychiatrist—and two approaches to human existence—the religious and the behavioral. It is Percival's fellow psychiatrists who certify Lance as sane, even though both Lance and Percival know there is still something wrong, something missing. As a psychiatrist, Percival cannot help Lance, whose problem is ontological and spiritual rather than psychological and whose self-righteous ranting masks his deeper uncertainty and longing. When, at the very end of the novel, Lance asks, "Is there anything I can do for you before I leave?," Percival's "*Yes*" identifies him as the apostolic Father John, the bearer of the good news for which Lance has been waiting. Against such grand gestures as blowing up Belle Isle, Percy offers the power of a small, ordinary word freshly heard.

The Second Coming was, as Percy noted, his "first unalienated novel." Instead of the ambiguity that characterizes the endings of his earlier novels, here the author celebrates the unequivocal victory of love over death. While such a conclusion did not please all reviewers, many of whom found it unconvincing or even sentimental, it is consistent with Percy's religious vision and his flexible aesthetic with its various tones and broad range of narrative structures: the novelist's version of God's plenty.

The novel picks up the life of Will Barrett some twenty years after *The Last Gentleman*. At age forty-three, Will is a retired lawyer, a wealthy widower living in Linwood, North Carolina, and recent recipient of the Rotary's man-of-the year award; yet, he is still a sick man, subject to dizzy spells and tricks of memory. What troubles Will is not the loss of his wife Marion but the sudden realization that he has wasted his life and been "only technically alive." At the brink of the abyss, he sees himself as a total stranger; only two percent of himself, he sets out to find the missing ninety-eight percent. His search takes him in a number of directions. One is back to his father, or more specifically to the only "event" in his life. This is a hunting accident that he comes to realize was no accident at all but instead the father's attempt to kill his son and then himself and so free them both from lives not worth living.

Like his father, Will rejects the "death in life" that characterizes modern believers as well as unbelievers; Will also rejects his father's solution, suicide, because it proves nothing. Instead, he devises the "ultimate scientific experiment" which will, he believes, provide conclusive proof of either God's existence or His nonexistence/noninvolvement. As the narrator points out, Will is mad; moreover, his plan (to starve himself and so force God either to save or abandon him) is badly flawed in two important ways. The language Will uses to define his experiment (actually more a "covenant") betrays his egotism as well as his legalistic frame of reference; to his "huge" bequest (his life), he attaches a "huge" condition (God's appearing to him). Not until much later in the novel does he learn "the economy of giving and getting" and the superiority of ordinary existence to his own ultimate experiments or his father's extraordinary "events." In addition, Will is looking for God in the wrong place. While waiting in the cave for "a clear yes [or] no," he misses the unambiguous beauty of Indian summer; and while he assails God's "unavailability," his own "fade outs," such as the cave experiment, preclude the very intersubjective relationships through which God manifests Himself to man. The sign he does receive, a toothache, is "a muddy maybe" that cuts short the experiment and sends Will howling in pain out of the wilderness of self and into a world that, while not physically new, can be seen in an original way.

The person who changes Will's angle of vision is Allison Huger (Kitty Vaught's daughter), who has just escaped her own cave, a mental hospital, and begun a new life in an abandoned greenhouse. She resembles Will in that she feels uncomfortable around other people, as well she should, for the Allison they see is the mentally disturbed organism for whom they can imagine nothing better than "the best-structured environment money can buy." Although she wants to live an entirely self-reliant life, each afternoon about four o'clock she experiences a sense of loss or emptiness. What she feels is identical to one of the symptoms of Will's disease (Hausmann's syndrome), which the doctors call "inappropriate longing." There is a pill to control Will's disease, but there is only one way to satisfy the longing, and that is by loving Allison, by finding his being in her just as she finds hers in him. As Allison explains in her characteristically melodic way, "Our lapses are not due to synapses." Percy's love story is not, therefore, simply romantic; rather, it is religious in the Christian existential sense. Their love is, to quote Allison again, "be-all" but not "end-all." When, in the novel's concluding scene, Will Barrett confronts Father Weatherbee, an old priest,

> his heart leapt with joy. What is it I want from her and him, he wondered, not only want but must have? Is she a gift and therefore a sign of the giver? Could it be that the Lord is here, masquerading behind this simple holy face? Am I crazy to want both, her and Him? No, not want, must have. And will have.

Here, as in the four earlier novels, one finds what Sartre called man's "useless passion," but for Percy this passionate longing is not useless at all because the world is not absurd. Percy's search is not one of Sartre's purely arbitrary "projects"; rather it is a thoroughly modern and, for many readers, an entirely convincing rendition of John Bunyan's *The Pilgrim's Progress* (1678, 1684) in an age mired in the slough of behaviorism and unbelief.

The Thanatos Syndrome, Percy's sixth and last novel, ends a bit differently, which is to say less insistently. Narrator-protagonist Dr. Tom More's "well well well" befits the "smaller scale" of his latter-day desires, yet this fit proves ironic, given the novel's overgrand, at times messianic ambitions (of the kind More himself had in *Love in the Ruins*). Similarities between the two novels are obvious (they share a number of the same characters and the same futurist-fantasy approach), but both the strengths and the weaknesses of *The Thanatos Syndrome* owe far more to *Lost in the Cosmos* than to *Love in the Ruins*: the satirizing of contemporary absurdities (inauthenticity in some of its craziest manifestations) and, unfortunately, the hardening of that spiritual need, which characterizes Will Barrett and Binx Bolling, into religious dogma. What was a translation of Christian belief into psychological, cultural, and semiotic terms in the earlier novels has begun to sound here like a propounding of conservative Catholic teachings, which undermines a novel that otherwise effectively mixes Sir Thomas More's *Utopia*, medieval romance, Fyodor Dostoevski, and Robin Cook.

The novel picks up the life and times of Tom More in the mid-1990's, a short while after his release from federal prison, where he has served a two-year term for illegally selling drugs. A brilliant diagnostician, More describes himself as "a psyche-iatrist, an old-fashioned physician of the soul" who believes that it is better, psychologically and spiritually speaking, to be sick (anxious, even terrified) than well, for dis-ease is prolapsarian man's natural state. Many of the people around him are, he realizes, anything but anxious. They are, instead, content: without inhibitions, without anxiety, without anything more than rudimentary language skills, and, most important, without a sense of self. With the help of his epidemiologist cousin Lucy Lipscomb, More discovers "Blue Boy," a clandestinely funded pilot project which involves introducing heavy sodium into the local water supply in order to stem the tide of social deterioration (crime, teenage pregnancy, even Autoimmune Deficiency Syndrome).

Director of Blue Boy and indeed of the entire "Fedville" complex (including an "Equalitarian Center" with facilities for "pedeuthanasia" and "gereuthanasia" and a propensity for obfuscating acronyms) is the ironically "graceful" Bob Comeaux (née Robert D'Angelo Como), who calls Blue Boy "our Manhattan Project." He tries to cajole, seduce, bribe, and threaten More into complicity, all to no avail. Although he remains a lapsed Catholic throughout, the doctor nevertheless sides with the enigmatic, certainly depressed, previously alcoholic, perhaps mad Father Simon (as in Simeon Stylites and Simon Peter) Smith, who spends all of his time up in a fire tower silently triangulating the positions of forest fires, atoning for his sins, and on one notable occasion claiming that all tenderness inevitably leads to the gas chamber (or to the Equalitarian Center, which may be the same thing in a different, more socially acceptable, guise). Comeaux would make everyone happy, at the cost of his or her freedom as well as awareness of himself or herself as a distinctly human being: a creature caught in the malaise, lost in the cosmos, in need of something other than heavy sodium, self-help, or Phil Donahue. Like Saul Bellow's *The Dean's December* (1982), *The Thanatos Syndrome* expresses More's faith (in there being "more" than Comeaux allows) in the form of a doubt concerning the modern belief that the causes and cures of man's problems are invariably physical. To the extent that *The Thanatos Syndrome* articulates this doubt, it, like Percy's other novels, succeeds extraordinarily well. To the extent that it propounds Catholic dogma in response to a host of topical issues (abortion, "quality of life," sexual "freedom," child abuse, bio- and behavioral engineering, among others), it fails according to the very terms that Percy himself adopted at the time of his conversion, turning the triadic mystery of Soren Kierkegaard's apostle into dyadic pronouncement, sign into signal, spiritual "predicament" into position paper.

Robert A. Morace

Other major works

NONFICTION: *The Message in the Bottle*, 1975; *Lost in the Cosmos: The Last Self-Help Book*, 1983; *Conversations with Walker Percy*, 1985.

Bibliography
Allen, William Rodney. *Walker Percy: A Southern Wayfarer*. Jackson: University Press of Mississippi, 1986. Allen reads Percy as a distinctly American, particularly Southern writer, claiming that the formative event in Percy's life was his father's suicide, not his reading of existentialist writers or conversion to Roman Catholicism. Allen's readings of individual novels emphasize the presence of weak fathers and rejection of the Southern stoic heritage on the part of Percy's protagonists.
Baker, Lewis. *The Percys of Mississippi*. Baton Rouge: Louisiana State University Press, 1983. Although the single chapter devoted to Walker Percy is Baker's weakest, the book is nevertheless valuable for its detailing of family background and, in the aforementioned chapter, Percy's use of family material in his fiction.
Broughton, Panthea Reid, ed. *The Art of Walker Percy: Strategies for Being*. Baton Rouge: Louisiana State University Press, 1979. Comprises Reid's introduction and fourteen solid essays on *The Moviegoer*, *The Last Gentleman*, *Love in the Ruins*, *Lancelot*, Percy's theory of language, and use of Gnostic beliefs and of archetypes.
Coles, Robert. *Walker Percy: An American Search*. Boston: Little, Brown, 1978. An early but always intelligent and certainly sensitive reading of Percy's essays and novels by a leading psychiatrist whose main contention is that Percy's work speaks directly to modern man. In Coles's words, Percy "has balanced a contemporary Christian existentialism with the pragmatism and empiricism of an American physician."
Hardy, John Edward. *The Fiction of Walker Percy*. Urbana: University of Illinois Press, 1987. The originality of this book, comprising an introduc-

tion and six chapters (one for each of the novels, including *The Thanatos Syndrome*), derives from Hardy's choosing to read the novels in terms of internal formal matters rather than (as is usually the case) Percy's essays, existentialism, Catholicism, or Southern background. Hardy sees Percy as a novelist, not a prophet.

Lawson, Lewis A. *Following Percy: Essays on Walker Percy's Work.* Troy, N.Y.: Whitson, 1988. Collects essays originally published between 1969 and 1984 by one of Percy's most dedicated, prolific, and knowledgeable commentators. Discussions of *The Moviegoer* and *Lancelot* predominate.

Percy, Walker. *Conversations with Walker Percy*, edited by Lewis A. Lawson, and Victor A. Kramer. Jackson: University Press of Mississippi, 1985. This indispensable volume collects all the most important interviews with Percy, including one (with the editors) previously unpublished. The volume is especially important for biographical background, influences, discussion of writing habits, and the author's comments on individual works through *Lost in the Cosmos*.

Tharpe, Jac, ed. *Walker Percy: Art and Ethics.* Jackson: University Press of Mississippi, 1980. Ten essays by diverse hands, plus a bibliography. The essays focus on settings, existential sources, Martin Heidegger, Percy's theory of language, the semiotician Charles Saunders Peirce, Percy's politics, and *Lancelot* (in terms of his essays, Roman Catholicism, medieval sources, and semiotics).

_____. *Walker Percy.* Boston: Twayne, 1983. Reading Percy as a Roman Catholic novelist concerned chiefly with eschatological matters, Tharpe divides his study into ten chapters: "Biography, Background, and Influences," "Theory of Art," "Christendom," "Techniques," one chapter on each of the five novels through *The Second Coming*, and conclusion. The annotated secondary bibliography is especially good.

DAVID PLANTE

Born: Providence, Rhode Island; March 4, 1940

Principal long fiction

The Ghost of Henry James, 1970; *Slides*, 1971; *Relatives*, 1972; *The Darkness of the Body*, 1974; *Figures in Bright Air*, 1976; *The Family*, 1978; *The Country*, 1981; *The Woods*, 1982; *The Francoeur Novels*, 1983 (includes the preceding three novels); *The Foreigner*, 1984; *The Catholic*, 1985; *The Native*, 1987.

Other literary forms

David Plante is a frequent contributor of short fiction to *The New Yorker* magazine, including stories such as "Mr. Bonito" (July 7, 1980), "Work" (September 21, 1981), "The Accident" (August 9, 1982), and "A House of Women" (April 28, 1986). Plante has also published one book of nonfiction, *Difficult Women: A Memoir of Three* (1983), an account of his relationships with Sonia Orwell, George Orwell's widow, and writers Jean Rhys and Germaine Greer.

Achievements

While Plante has never enjoyed a large readership, he has achieved considerable recognition among his peers, winning the acclaim of Philip Roth and other prominent contemporaries. Plante began his career with several self-consciously artistic novels, but in his later works he has fashioned a spare, radically simplified style with a deceptive look of artlessness. In contrast to the minimalist writers to whose works his fiction bears a superficial resemblance, Plante uses this pared-down style as a vehicle to explore the consciousness of his protagonists, which he presents in a manner that differs sharply from the involuted style of most novels of consciousness. This is Plante's distinctive achievement in contemporary American fiction.

Plante's sixth novel, *The Family*, was nominated for the National Book Award in 1979. In 1983, while teaching writing at the University of Tulsa, in Tulsa, Oklahoma, Plante received a Guggenheim grant, and in the same year he won the Prize for Artistic Merit from the American Academy and Institute of Arts and Letters.

Biography

David Plante was born in Providence, Rhode Island, on March 4, 1940, the son of Anaclet Joseph Adolph and Albina (Bison) Plante. From 1959 to 1960, he attended the University of Louvain in Belgium, and in 1961 he was graduated with a B.A. from Boston College. After graduation, Plante taught at the English School in Rome, Italy, at the Boston School of Modern Languages, and at St. John's Preparatory School. He also worked for two years (1962-1964) as a researcher for *Hart's Guide to New York* in New York City. Plante has been a writer-in-residence at the University of Tulsa (1979-1983) and at King's College, Cambridge (1984-1985). He has lived in England since 1966.

Analysis

The dominant themes in the novels of David Plante concern the nature of relationships and the efforts of the individual to break out of his own self-consciousness in order to participate in these relationships. He explores the forces which unite people, whether family members, friends, or lovers, and the ability of these forces to bind as well as alienate, create as well as destroy. His method of narration in his early works reveals unconventional techniques which he would later incorporate into his more traditional novels. In his earliest works, such as *The Ghost of Henry James*, *Slides*, *Relatives*, *The Darkness of the Body*, and *Figures in Bright Air*, Plante experiments with an almost plotless structure with an emphasis on language and the expression of consciousness, echoing Henry James, Nathaniel Hawthorne, James Joyce, and Gertrude Stein. Instead of a narrative of progression and movement within a defined space and time, these novels present random associations from constantly changing perspectives. Plante often creates snapshots of consciousness in the form of numerous brief narrative sections which flash in front of the reader, revealing not concrete images but glimpses of various characters' impressions, perceptions, and emotions. Through this technique, Plante attempts to use a character's consciousness to define and describe meaning, leading many critics to observe that these early novels are not novels at all but rather collections of psychological fragments which, though often powerful, ultimately confuse and disappoint the reader.

With the publication of his largely autobiographical trilogy, *The Francoeur Novels*, in 1983 (which includes *The Family*, *The Country*, and *The Woods*), Plante continued to develop his theme of relationships between family members through the perspective of subjective consciousness and fragmented images, but he integrated these experimental techniques into a more traditionally defined narrative. The first book of the trilogy, *The Family*, introduces Daniel Francoeur, Plante's autobiographical counterpart in the trilogy, and his six brothers born to a Catholic, working-class, French-Canadian couple, Jim and Reena Francoeur. The novel is set primarily in Providence, Rhode Island, at the Francoeurs' newly acquired lake home. Plante traces the emotional struggle of the nine family members to remain unified, communicative, and productive in the face of internal tension and external threat. Because of their ethnic background and unsophisticated social orientation, the family members feel alienated from the Providence community, and when the father loses his job through union pressure, the internal problems within the family are magnified at the same time that the bonds of love and dependency between individual members are tested. Though most of the narrative is seen and evaluated through Daniel's consciousness, the focus of the novel is not on him or any one character but rather on the Francoeur family as a single living organism trying to support and nurture all of its parts for the survival of the whole. The dependency of each family member on the others' well-being is exemplified by the hysterical disintegration of the family unit when the mother experiences a recurrence of an emotional illness.

Plante develops Reena's character more fully than he does the others in *The Family*, and he examines her closely through Daniel's eyes, making her the touchstone for the novel's major theme: the fragility of the seemingly indestructible. Reena possesses the objectivity to see quite clearly the flaws in each son's character while simultaneously loving each totally; she is unable, however, to acknowledge her husband's inability to cope with his unemployment. Her failure to deal with her husband as a fallible human being forces her sons to take sides against their father and ultimately to question their familial duties. Despite her strength and authority as the Francoeur matriarch, Reena remains a child-wife, puzzled and victimized by an uncommunicative, brooding husband. She confides frequently in Daniel, who comes to see his mother's position in the family as isolated and vulnerable. The only woman in a world full of men, an interloper in a fraternity house environment, Reena has tried to remain as unobtrusive as possible in her husband's and sons' world, from avoiding flowers and lacy decorations which might intrude upon their male starkness to suppressing her fears and anger. She has created, literally, seven times over, a world which she can never enter. When her emotional breakdown occurs and Jim resists medical help for her, afraid she would come back from the sanatorium as something other than his submissive wife, the family organism suffers a shock and responds with violence: sons against father, mother against sons, brothers against brothers. The novel concludes with a semblance of unity, but the organism has been damaged.

The damage is subtly revealed in the second (though last written) book of the trilogy, *The Woods*. Peace has returned to the Francoeur home, but only because Jim and Reena have surrendered to a self-imposed isolation and stagnant existence. They appear only peripherally in the novel, and the focus remains on Daniel, who visits his parents' home during a vacation from college. An extremely self-conscious adolescent, Daniel finds himself facing terrifying indecision and overwhelming freedom. Though little action takes place in the novel's three brief chapters, Plante conveys in simple yet intense language Daniel's need to belong, to anchor himself somewhere, to overcome his apathy and lack of ambition. Daniel's first sexual experience brings him no closer to what he wants as he becomes increasingly obsessed with the maleness of his own body. His decision to file with the draft board as a conscientious objector, despite the influence of his older brother Albert, a life-long military man, role model, and major source of financial support for the Francoeurs, does give Daniel a sense of definition, though mixed with shame. In *The Woods*, Plante creates in Daniel a representation of the time in adolescence when passivity is the safest action, when any other action seems too great a risk, and when even one's own body appears strange and threatening.

This period in Daniel's life has long passed when *The Country* opens. Once again Daniel, now a writer living in London, returns to his parents' home in Providence, where he joins his six brothers, not for any holiday or family celebration but as a response to the final assault on the family unit: the slow, degrading physical and mental deterioration of Reena and Jim Francoeur. Now in their eighties, they are weakened to the point of partial immobility and senility. The sons, some with wives and children, gather to take care of their parents' basic needs as well as attempt, in quiet desperation, to restore the bonds of familial understanding and love. Reena's mental problems have intensified with age, and Daniel listens, as always, to her frightened and of-ten bitter ramblings about her sacrifices to her husband and family. In more tender moments, however, Reena shows her devotion to her dying husband, frequently enveloping his withered body in her arms, grasping his hands in silence, and kissing his cheek. Reena is also still able to express love toward her sons, sharing their secrets and laughing at the jokes whispered to her in French.

The Country does not, however, use Reena as a symbol for the state of the Francoeur family as the first novel did. Except for a brief flashback to twenty years earlier at a tense family gathering at the lake house, the last book of the Francoeur trilogy explores the character of Jim, who, in the earlier works, received uneven and ambiguous treatment. Through a first-person narrative, Daniel attempts to understand the complexities of a man who once seemed so simple. In moments of lucidity, Jim expresses to Daniel his doubts about having been a good father, husband, and worker, and Daniel realizes that, despite his father's domination over his mother and the unrelenting sense of social and familial duties imposed on his sons, Jim loved his family in every way that his old-world cultural background permitted, limited greatly by an inability to express his emotions. As Daniel witnesses the pathetic deterioration of his once hearty and active father, he frantically tries to re-establish communication and a sense of tradition. In response, his father awkwardly attempts to understand his son's life as a writer in a foreign coun-try. Ultimately, the father, drifting in and out of the present in a cloudy mind, leaves his son the only wisdom he knows: "Work hard. . . . And be a good boy" When his father dies, Daniel is able to grieve honestly for a man who, he now realizes, "could not think of himself, but had to think of his duty to the outside world." Reena, after an initial feeling of emancipation from her husband's authority, reacts to his death by retreating into incessant speech and fearful imaginings, once again alone among the men she created.

In *The Country*, the strongest work in the trilogy, Plante achieved what he had been working toward since his first novels: the subordination of plot with an emphasis on emotion and perception. The only significant action in *The Country* is the observation of time and death, but the helplessness of every member of the Francoeur family is a haunting and consistent echo throughout the novel. This echo gives *The Country* a power never realized in the earlier works.

In the two novels succeeding the Francoeur trilogy, Plante's protagonist continues to narrate in the first person, though he is never mentioned by name in the earlier work, *The Foreigner*; only through allusions to the hero's family background does the author identify him as a member of the Francoeur family, probably Daniel once again. Adam Mars-Jones suggests in his review of *The Foreigner* in the *The Times Literary Supplement* that the narrator may be Daniel's older brother Andre, noting that at the end of *The Family* the Francoeurs receive a postcard from Andre, who is in Europe, the same postcard which is mentioned in *The Foreigner*. This connection does exist, but the narrator of *The Foreigner* undeniably possesses the same history, voice, and sensibility as the protagonist of *The Francoeur Novels*, whatever name the reader gives him.

The Foreigner does not relate to the trilogy in any other way, nor does it follow the previous work chronologically. In this novel, the hero is twenty and leaving his Rhode Island home in 1959 to travel to Europe, hoping to shed his "Americanisms" and experience the expatriate life-style in the fashion of Ernest Hemingway, whose epigraph, "In Spain you could not tell anything," introduces the book. Instead of the romance and rebirth he expected, the narrator discovers loneliness and alienation from the environment and the people, even his American college friends who meet him in France. Wanting to get as far away as possible from what these friends represent, he is grateful to find in Spain a mysterious black woman he met previously on his crossing from America. From the moment he links himself with Angela Johnson and her emotionally disturbed lover Vincent, the strangeness and danger he craved are never far from him, though never fully defined. Angela and Vincent demand all of their new friend's money, leaving him totally dependent upon them by the time he realizes that they are possibly involved in illegal activities. The narrator's odd relationship with Angela and Vincent is revealed in the Hemingway style of terse dialogue and matter-of-fact description blended with Plante's characteristically fragmented narrative and vivid images of consciousness. *The Foreigner* is a unique work for Plante, however, in that it does make some attempt, though sporadic and uneven, toward a climactic scene, the street-dance suicide of Vincent. No other Plante novel uses this traditional narrative element. Yet the circumstances which lead up to the story's climax remain subordinate to Plante's interest in the objective correlatives of his protagonist's consciousness, the means of representing his thoughts and emotions as concrete objects or communicable expressions. Many of these thoughts reflect the narrator's voyeuristic, homosexual obsession with Vincent and the total sense of alienation brought about by this attraction.

Daniel's homosexuality, only obscurely implied in *The Francoeur Novels*, is made explicit in *The Foreigner* and becomes the major focus of *The Catholic*. Early in the Francoeur trilogy, Daniel became obsessed with the figure of the nude, crucified Christ, a ubiquitous presence in his Catholic home. As he grew older, Daniel developed strange correlations between the body of Christ and the power of male sexuality. In *The Catholic*, Daniel decides that the only way for him to overcome his intense self-consciousness and escape from his body's prison is to surrender himself physically and spiritually to another man. Women, in Daniel's perception, have no spirituality: They are fixed, concrete, earthbound objects and therefore can only give him back to himself as a mirror does, thus increasing his awareness of himself. Although Daniel turns to women as confidantes and advisers, sexually they cannot provide the transcendental experience he seeks. When Daniel falls in love with Henry, he mistakes sexual obsession with heightened consciousness. They spend only one night together, and Daniel immediately realizes that Henry wants to maintain his autonomy and selfhood as desperately as Daniel wants to lose his. The novel becomes little more than an explication of Daniel's frightening sexual compulsions and the aftermath of grief and guilt. *The Catholic* does not develop the narrative structures attempted in *The Francoeur Novels* and *The Foreigner* and resembles more closely the earlier novels in its extremely obscure language and disturbing images.

Plante's work is significant mostly for its contribution to the genre of the modernist novel of consciousness. His early experimental novels, though static and highly derivative, adumbrate the techniques Plante would later refine in novels which artfully explore the self-consciousness of the individual as he strives to understand his relationship with the external world. Especially in *The Francoeur Novels*, Plante succeeds in creating, through an often masterful command of language, a powerful synesthesia, blending paintings of the mind with the art of storytelling.

Penelope A. LeFew

Other major work
NONFICTION: *Difficult Women: A Memoir of Three*, 1983.

Bibliography
Batchelor, John Calvin. "Good Bye, Ennui—Hello, Mom." *The Village Voice*

(April 23, 1979): 85. Reviews Plante's works from his first novel, *The Ghost of Henry James*, up to and including *The Family*. Points out flaws in Plante's earlier works, stating that they either lack energy or substance. Acknowledges *The Family*, however, as Plante's first, full-fledged novel in which he has mastered storytelling. Batchelor calls this work "an affirmation of the family."

Gunton, Sharon R., and Jean C. Stine, eds. *Contemporary Literary Criticism*. Vol. 23. Detroit: Gale Research, 1983. Contains excerpts of reviews of Plante's work from 1970 to 1982, including reviews from *The Times Literary Supplement*, *The New York Times Book Review*, and *The Village Voice*. Most reviewers acknowledge that Plante finds his voice only with the trilogy *The Family*, *The Country*, and *The Woods*. Despite concerns that his first few novels, in particular *The Ghost of Henry James*, are derivative, Plante receives recognition—both favorable and unfavorable—for his experimental, minimalist writing.

Kaiser, John R. "David Plante." In *Dictionary of Literary Biography: Yearbook 1983*, edited by Mary Bruccoli and Jean W. Ross. Detroit: Gale Research, 1983. Discusses Plante's writings in Britain between 1970 and 1974 and places him in the context of experimental writing in vogue at the time. There is substantial commentary on *The Ghost of Henry James*, which makes reference to Plante's identification with James. Kaiser also examines Plante's other novels, in particular the trilogy with its "subtle expression of Catholicism by means of thought and action rather than ritual."

Phyllis, Carmel, and Dedria Bryfonski Mendelson, eds. *Contemporary Literary Criticism*. Vol. 7. Detroit: Gale Research, 1977. Contains excerpts from criticism of Plante's earlier works, such as extracts from a review in *The Listener* in which Plante is rebuked for being a "harbinger of important change in English writing and it sickens me." In contrast is the *New Statesman* review which hails Plante as a "thoughtful writer, capable of producing fine flashes of prose." Presents conflicting views on Plante's work.

Plante, David. Interview by John F. Baker. *Publishers Weekly* 222 (December 24, 1982): 12-13. This interview was conducted just prior to the publication of *Difficult Women*, a study of Germaine Greer, Jean Rhys, and Sonia Orwell, which has been dubbed a "deadpan literary memoir." Plante gives an overview of his development as a writer.

KATHERINE ANNE PORTER

Born: Indian Creek, Texas; May 15, 1890
Died: Silver Spring, Maryland; September 18, 1980

Principal long fiction
Pale Horse, Pale Rider: Three Short Novels, 1939; *Ship of Fools*, 1962.

Other literary forms
Katherine Anne Porter is best known for her short fiction. Her stories appear in *Flowering Judas and Other Stories* (1930), *The Leaning Tower and Other Stories* (1944), and *The Old Order* (1944) and were gathered in *The Collected Stories of Katherine Anne Porter* (1965). Criticism, essays, and poems were collected in *The Days Before* (1952) and *The Collected Essays and Occasional Writings* (1970).

Achievements
Porter's solid and lasting reputation as a writer is based on a very small output of published work: one novel, a handful of novellas, and less than two dozen stories. This slender output, however, represents only a small portion of the fiction she wrote during her lifetime. Exacting and self-critical, she discarded many more stories than she published. By the time her first story appeared in print, she had already developed her fictional techniques to near perfection, and the maturity and craft of her style in *Flowering Judas and Other Stories*, her first published collection, never was surpassed by her later fiction.

Porter early established her reputation with literary critics and only later became widely known and read. In 1931, one year after the publication of her first volume, she was granted a Guggenheim Fellowship, an award she received again in 1938. The Society of Libraries of New York University awarded her its first annual gold medal for literature in 1940 upon the publication of *Pale Horse, Pale Rider*. A Modern Library edition of *Flowering Judas and Other Stories* appeared that same year. In 1943, she was elected a member of the National Institute of Arts and Letters, and in 1949, she accepted her first appointment as writer-in-residence and guest lecturer at Stanford University. In later years, she was to hold similar positions in many other colleges and universities, including the University of Chicago, the University of Michigan, Washington and Lee University, the University of Liège, and the University of Virginia.

By the time she published *Ship of Fools* in 1962, Porter had received three more honors: a Ford Foundation grant in 1959, and in 1962, the O. Henry Memorial Award for her story "Holiday," and the Emerson-Thoreau Bronze medal of the American Academy of Arts and Sciences. *Ship of Fools* became a Book-of-the-Month Club selection and an immediate best-seller. In the face of its overwhelming popular success, some critics charged that Porter had forsaken her artistic standards in favor of writing a book that would appeal to a large audience. *Ship of Fools* also was criticized for its pessimism and for its failure to conform neatly to the structure of a novel, a supposed flaw especially irksome to those who had admired the formal perfection of Porter's earlier works. Porter herself was surprised by the book's popularity. She had abandoned the form of her earlier work—with its tight plots centered on the fate of a single character—but she had moved deliberately on to something else. She was still writing "honest," she claimed, a quality that characterized all her fiction. First and last, she was still an artist, a label she applied to herself unhesitatingly.

Although Porter published no new fiction after *Ship of Fools*, her critical and public acclaim grew. It reached its peak when she received both the Pulitzer Prize and the National Book Award for Fiction in 1966.

Biography

Katherine Anne Porter was born Collie Russell Porter in Indian Creek, Texas, on May 15, 1890. She was the third of five children born to Harrison and Mary Alice Jones Porter. When her mother died in 1892, she and her brothers and sisters moved to Kyle, Texas, where they were cared for by their paternal grandmother, Catherine Anne Porter. When Mrs. Porter senior died in 1901, Harrison Porter sold the farm in Kyle and moved with his family to San Antonio.

Facts about Porter's early life and education have been difficult to substantiate, partly because Porter's own accounts were evasive or inconsistent. Although her family apparently was Methodist, Porter attended convent schools, possibly for a time in New Orleans, which may be why later researchers have reported that she was a Catholic from birth. Porter denied this allegation when it appeared in a biographical sketch published by the University of Minnesota series on American writers. Precocious as a child and rebellious as a teenager, she ran away from school at age sixteen to marry. The name of her first husband is not known, although the marriage lasted three years.

After the divorce, Porter moved to Chicago, already cherishing the ambition of becoming a professional writer. She worked as a reporter on a Chicago newspaper for a time and signed on as an extra with a motion-picture company for a few months. Passing up the opportunity to travel to Hollywood with the film company, she returned to Texas, where she reported that she made a living as a traveling entertainer, singing Scottish ballads, dressed in a costume she made herself. Thereafter, she wrote drama criticism and society gossip for a Fort Worth weekly, *The Critic*. One year later, she moved to Denver, Colorado, and became a reporter for the *Rocky Mountain News*. In Denver, during the influenza epidemic of 1918, she became severely ill and almost died. This experience, which she fictionalized in *Pale Horse, Pale Rider*, affected her profoundly. "I really had participated in death," she said years later in an interview with Barbara Thompson of the *Paris Review*. She had had "what the Christians call the 'beatific vision'"; she was no longer "like other people."

In 1919 she moved to New York City, where for a brief time she worked as a hack and ghostwriter. The following year she went to study in Mexico. Again she stayed only a short time, but for the next ten years Mexico was to be the center of her intellectual and imaginative life. Returning to Fort Worth, she began to write the stories based on her experiences there. During the next decade she traveled extensively, reviewed books for leading national magazines and newspapers, and worked and reworked the stories that were published in 1930 in *Flowering Judas and Other Stories*.

Supported by a Guggenheim Fellowship granted that year, she returned to Mexico. In 1931, she sailed aboard a German ship from Veracruz to Bremerhaven. This voyage gave her the setting for *Ship of Fools*, which was not to be published for another thirty years. She lived until the mid-1930's in Paris, marrying and later divorcing Eugene Pressly, a member of the American Foreign Service, and working on her fiction. After her divorce from Pressly, she married Albert Erskine, Jr., of the Louisiana State University faculty. Until her divorce from Erskine in 1942, she lived in Baton Rouge. During this time, she continued to work on her short fiction, but not until the late 1950's did she begin sustained effort on her only full-length novel, *Ship of Fools*. Although by that time many of her acquaintances believed she never would finish it, fragments of the novel appeared in magazines, and, in 1962, *Ship of Fools* was published. Porter wrote no more new fiction after that, although *The Collected Essays and Occasional Writings of Katherine Anne Porter* appeared in 1970. On September 18, 1980, at the age of ninety, Katherine Anne Porter died in Silver Spring, Maryland.

Analysis

Katherine Anne Porter once suggested that when she sat down to write about her life as accurately as possible, it turned into fiction; indeed, she knew no other way to write fiction. Whether this anecdote is true, it is certain that capturing the past with great detail was an important ingredient in her writing. In a number of the short stories, and in two of the best short novels, Miranda, the central character, is very close to being Porter herself. These stories follow Miranda's life from infanthood in her grandmother's house in South Texas, to her scrape with death from influenza in Colorado at the age of twenty-four—her first major step toward maturity.

Concerning the time of her illness, Porter has said that it was as though a line were drawn through her life, separating everything that came before from everything that came after. She had been given up and then had survived, and in some ways all her time after that was borrowed. Perhaps that is why her overtly autobiographical stories deal with the time before that line, the time when she was "alive" and therefore had a life to record. The stories which take place after that incident present her, if at all, as an observer, as someone slightly distant and alienated from life. (It is a question of degree: Miranda is also, of course, an acute observer in the stories in which she takes part. Her name, in fact, means "observer" in Spanish.) Porter was in real life a passenger on the ship about which her novel *Ship of Fools* was written, but she speaks of herself as purely an observer, who scarcely spoke a word on the entire voyage. She does not appear directly as a character in the novel.

The girl, Miranda, in the short novel *Old Mortality*, runs away from school to get married, in part to escape from her family, so suffocatingly steeped in its own past. At the conclusion of the novella, she is determined to free herself once and for all from that past, so that she can begin to consider her own future; but she determines this, the reader is told in the ironic concluding lines, "in her hopefulness, her ignorance." The irony is that Miranda-Porter herself became so obsessed with that past that much of her best work is devoted to it. The explanation for Porter's obsession with the past can perhaps be guessed from the conclusion of "Pale Horse, Pale Rider." Everything of importance to Miranda has died; only her ravaged body, her spark of a soul somehow survives. She finds that she has no future, only the slow progression to death once again. The past, then, is all she has, yet the past is finally intangible, as the girl in *Old Mortality* discovers as she sifts through all the evidence. At last no truth can be discovered, no objectivity, only the combined and contradictory subjectives: the only truth, once again, is the truth of fiction.

Porter has said that in her fiction she is not interested in actions so much as she is interested in the various and subtle results of actions. Certainly, of all her works, *Old Mortality* deals directly with the ramifications of past actions. This short novel spans ten years in the life of the protagonist, Miranda, from the age of eight to the age of eighteen. In that time, the reader learns little of Miranda's life, except that she is bad-tempered and that, unlike many of the young women in her widely extended family, she is not going to be a "beauty." She is, rather, the recording center of the novel: the events are brought to her and have their effect on the person she is becoming.

The crucial actions have occurred in the preceding generation. Miranda's family is obsessed by a past event. Miranda's aunt Amy was a great beauty, the measure, in fact, against which all the current crop of beauties are found wanting. She was glamorous, racy, even though tubercular, and for a long time spurned Gabriel's devoted courtship. Gabriel was himself wild, ran a string of racehorses, and was heir to the fortune. Only when he was disinherited and Amy found herself in the terminal stage of her illness, did she consent to marry him. The couple went to New Orleans on their honeymoon, and almost immediately Amy died. Miranda tries to sift out the truth of the story. She looks at the photograph of Amy and does not find her so impossibly beautiful, and indeed thinks she looks silly in her out-of-fashion dress. Later, she is introduced to Gabriel, and instead of the dashing young man who had once challenged a rival to a duel over Amy, she finds him fat and drunken, down on his luck; the woman whom he married after Amy is bitter and depressed from living with a ne'er-do-well who has spent their whole married life talking about Amy. Later still, Miranda meets Eva, a homely spinster cousin from Gabriel's generation, and Eva says the real truth is that Amy was a lewd woman, who married only because someone else got her pregnant, and took her own life with an overdose of drugs.

After a moment of shock, Miranda realizes that Eva's version, in its negative way, is just as romantic as the others. Miranda does not want to know where the truth lies. By this time, she has left school and has run off to get married. Her father is cool with her, thinking she has deserted the family; indeed she has, and deliberately. She refuses to be trapped in the past, represented by this unknowable woman whose brief life still haunts the family. She wants instead to discover who she—Miranda—is; she wants her own life to exist in the present and future. This is what she determines—in the novel's ironic final line—"in her hopefulness, her ignorance."

In her ignorance, Miranda-Porter learns that her past is what she is, the result of those past actions. She has been touched by Amy even more than the others, for she has become Amy, the Amy who refused to live by the others' rules, and at last ran off, married, and never returned—just as Miranda has done. In so doing, Amy and Miranda become separated from the rest of the family, freezing its members in their moment of history just as Porter herself became separated from her family so that she could re-create them forever in her stories.

Noon Wine is set in the rural turn-of-the-century South Texas of Porter's childhood but does not deal with her family. The characters in this short novel are poor and uneducated farmers, but this does not stop the story from being an intricate and subtle moral allegory. The lingering effect of past actions is not the central theme, as it was in *Old Mortality*, but a sense of the cumulative force of a man's actions gives the story a tragic inevitability. Mr. Thompson is a proud man, and as a result he marries above himself. Instead of a strong woman to help him in the strenuous operation of his farm, he marries a delicate and genteel woman who quickly becomes a near invalid. Further, she insists that they have a dairy, a bit higher class than an ordinary row-crop farm. In the end, Thompson is left with a wife who cannot help him and a kind of farmwork that he does not feel is masculine, and which he therefore shirks. The farm is deteriorating, and the couple are about to go under entirely, when a strange taciturn Swede from North Dakota arrives, asking for work. Instantly there is a revolution. The Swede fixes, paints, repairs everything, and shortly the failing farm becomes productive. As the years go by, the couple are able to buy such luxuries as an ice box, and Mr. Thompson is able to sit on the porch while the work is being done. One day Hatch arrives, a thoroughly evil man. He is a bounty hunter; the Swede, it is revealed, is an escaped homicidal maniac who in a berserk fury stabbed his own brother to death. Thompson refuses to give up the Swede. There is a scuffle; the Swede suddenly appears and steps between them; Thompson believing he sees Hatch stabbing the Swede in the stomach, smashes Hatch's skull with an ax.

The confrontation is remarkably complex. Hatch, as he is presented in the story, seems a pure manifestation of evil, and so perhaps he should be killed, but ironically he has in fact done nothing. The Swede is a primal murderer, a brother-killer like Cain, and is a threat to murder again. Thompson believes Hatch has stabbed the Swede, and acts to defend him, but after he has killed Hatch, the Swede does not have a mark on him, not even, perhaps, the mark of Cain, which has been transferred to Thompson.

Thompson is easily acquitted of the crime in court, but his fundamentalist neighbors in the close-knit community look on him as a murderer. Most important, he must examine his own motives. Was he defending the Swede, or was he defending the success of his farm, which, he must have guiltily realized, was not the result of his work, but of the work of another, a sinner, a primal murderer? With his mark of Cain, Thompson goes the rounds of his neighbors, trying to tell his side of the story, believing it less each time himself, until he kills himself, the final consequence of his original pride.

Porter has called sleep "that little truce of God between living and dying." If dreams, therefore, take place in a landscape somewhere between life and death, it is appropriate that *Pale Horse, Pale Rider* begins with one of Miranda's many dreams to be recorded. Although the story is set during World War I in a small town in Colorado where Miranda is working for a newspaper, symbolically the story takes place in the dreamlike zone between life and death. In that initial dream, Death rides alongside Miranda, but she tells him to ride on ahead; she is not quite ready to go with him. She wakes up only to be reminded of the war, which is poisoning the lives of many people, who are full of despair because of their inability to control their destinies. The streets are filled with funerals, as the influenza epidemic kills people like a medieval plague. Miranda's work on the paper is hateful, and her only release is when, after work, she meets Adam. Adam, as his name suggests, is the man who should be her companion, her mate in life. He is a soldier, however, on his way to war and committed wholly to death, and so Miranda struggles to withhold her love from him.

The war and the plague, as presented in the novel, are symbols of the struggle of life and its vulnerability. Miranda and Adam differ from others in being existentially aware; all that exists for them is the present tense of their lives. They dance together in a cheap café, knowing that it is all they will ever have. Because they have so little—a brief moment of troubled life, and then death—the integrity of their actions becomes their only value. Miranda tells Adam that he is stupid to fight in a war in which old men send young men to die. He agrees, saying, however, that if he does not go, he can no longer face himself. Miranda has her own costly sense of integrity: as a reporter for the paper, she witnesses a pathetic scandal, and when the victims beg her not to write the story, she does not. The rival papers do, however, and her editor is furious; her colleagues think she is senseless. She is demoted to writing entertainment reviews. Even there, when she writes an unfavorable review of a vaudeville act, she is confronted by the old, broken, has-been actor, her subsequent compassion struggles against her dedication to her job. Her colleagues counsel her to fake the reviews and make everyone happy, but writing honest reviews is an important value to her.

Miranda gets the flu, and in a long delirious dream comes to the point of death and has a beatific vision. The doctor and nurse fighting to preserve her, working with their own existential integrity, bring her back, but it is so painful being taken away from her vision and back to life, that when life-giving drugs are injected into her, she feels them like "a current of agony."

Miranda had fought, with her tiny spark of consciousness, to survive, to survive for Adam. Then she learns that Adam, perhaps having caught flu from her, has himself died. Her dream of Heaven had been so brilliant that the real world seems to her a monochrome, a bleak field in which, with Adam gone, she has nothing. The reader, however, can see beyond this point. Earlier, Miranda and Adam had sung an old spiritual together, of a pale horse with a pale rider, who takes a girl's lover away, leaving her behind to mourn. Miranda is the singer who is left behind to mourn, and to record the story for the rest of the world.

Porter has described her fiction as an investigation of the "terrible failure of the life of man in the Western World." Her one full-length novel, *Ship of Fools*, is a bleak cross section of modern civilization. It follows the lives of literally dozens of characters, from all levels of the particular society it is observing. More than forty characters of various nationalities are presented in some detail: American, Spanish, Mexican, Cuban, German, Swiss, Swedish. The time is 1931 and chaos is spreading. Soon Adolf Hitler will be in charge, the extermination camps will be in operation, and another world war will be under way. The title *Ship of Fools* is a translation of Sebastian Brant's medieval moral allegory, *Das Narrenschiff* (1494). The ship is the world; the time of the journey is the lifetime of the characters. They, of course, do not see it that way. They think of it as a temporary voyage. The lies they tell, the treacheries they enact, the hopeless relationships they form, are only temporary, have nothing to do with the course of their real lives, with the objectives they mean to obtain, the moral codes by which they mean to live.

The ship, the *Vera* (truth), leaves Veracruz, Mexico, for the nearly month-long journey to Bremerhaven. It is a German ship, and the German passengers sit at the captain's table. From the pompous and second-rate captain on down, they are comic grotesques, guzzling their food swinishly and looking suspiciously at everyone who does not eat pork, or who has a slightly large nose, as potentially Jewish. The only seemingly human Germans are Wilhelm Freytag, concealing as long as he can the fact that he has a Jewish wife, and Dr. Schumann, the ship's doctor, the novel's most sympathetic character, urbane, gentle, wise—who, to his own horror, commits perhaps the basest act of anyone on board. The American characters are only slightly less grotesque. William Denny the Texan is pure caricature: to him everyone but a white Texan is a nigger, spick, wop, or damyankee. He devotes all his time pursuing sexual pleasure, but is fearful that he will be cheated into paying too much for it. The comic result is that he pays out everything, and gets nothing in return but a severe drubbing. Mrs. Treadwell, a forty-five-year-old divorcee, is utterly selfish, yet she wonders why she gets nothing from life. David Scott and Jenny Brown, living together, fighting constantly, are, with Dr. Schumann and Wilhelm Freytag, the novel's main characters. David Scott is tied up within himself, and will give up nothing to another. Jenny Brown sporadically gives up everything to mere acquaintances, yet seems to have nothing of her own within.

One character after another debates man's nature: Are all men basically good; are all men naturally depraved; are the pure races good and the mongrel races evil? The characters seem intent on acting out all these possibilities. The most disciplined of them regularly lapse into helpless sentimentality. Freytag thinks that each woman he meets is the beautiful love of his life. One of these women is a Jewess, whom he married during a period of extreme romanticism and now he is déclassé among his German compatriots and cannot admit to himself how full of regret he is. David and Jenny, needing everything from each other, have only got so far as learning each other's weaknesses, of which they take full advantage to lacerate each other. They continue to cling together, always saying they will separate at some later time. Most painful is the folly of the sympathetic Dr. Schumann. He convinces himself that he is in love with a neurotic Spanish countess (he has a wife at home), and under pretense of caring for her as her doctor, he turns her into a hopeless and helpless drug addict in order to keep his power over her.

The most purely evil characters on the ship are the shoddy Spanish dance troupe. Through herculean efforts they almost take control of the ship, and certainly take control of the lives of the characters, bringing out their deepest and worst traits, but at the end they sit listless and exhausted, as though the effort were immensely greater than any return they have had from it. This troupe of carnival performers cheats, steals, blackmails, and even kills right before the others, who remark on it, but do nothing to stop them, each character feeling it is not his place to do anything. At length, the troupe is sitting confidently at the captain's table, having rearranged everyone's position on the ship. In a kind of Walpurgis Night, they bring the many characters to some sort of climax in an eruption of drunken violence. It is Porter's vision of how World War II began: low thugs and gangsters taking power with the casual, half-intentional connivance of the world.

In the midst of this bleak and pessimistic picture of the Western world, there is one possibility of redemption. The rare positive moments in the novel are when the characters suddenly, often to their own surprise, come together in the act of sex—Porter emphasizing the sensuality of the contact rather than any spiritual qualities. Perhaps Porter is saying that in their fallen state human beings must start at the bottom, with earthly sensuality, in order to slowly acquire a knowledge of spiritual beauty.

Norman Lavers

Other major works

SHORT FICTION: *Flowering Judas and Other Stories*, 1930; *The Leaning Tower and Other Stories*, 1944; *The Old Order*, 1944; *The Collected Stories of Katherine Anne Porter*, 1965.

NONFICTION: *My Chinese Marriage*, 1921; *Outline of Mexican Popular Arts and Crafts*, 1922; *What Price Marriage*, 1927; *The Days Before*, 1952; *A Defence of Circe*, 1954; *The Collected Essays and Occasional Writings*, 1970; *The Never-Ending Wrong*, 1977.

Bibliography

Givner, Joan. *Katherine Anne Porter: A Life*. New York: Simon & Schuster, 1982. A thorough biography that was begun with Porter's blessing before she died. Contains an overabundance of information: for example, it is difficult to locate the dates of publications of her books. Nevertheless, a complete and intriguing picture of a complex life.

Hardy, John Edward. *Katherine Anne Porter*. New York: Frederick Ungar, 1973. An introduction to Porter's life and fiction that is well organized and gracefully written. Includes a bibliography and would be useful to any student.

Hendrick, George, and Willene Hendrick. *Katherine Anne Porter*. Rev. ed. Boston: Twayne, 1988. This efficient book covers Porter's life and offers criticism of most of her work. Examines her short fiction and her only novel, *Ship of Fools*. Includes an annotated bibliography.

Langer, Elinor. *Josephine Herbst: The Story She Could Never Tell*. Boston: Little, Brown, 1984. Contains a complete account of the close relationship between Herbst and Porter. Herbst blames their break-up on Porter's betrayal. Highly readable, if not entirely academic or essential to the study of Porter's work.

Unrue, Darlene Harbour. *Truth and Vision in Katherine Anne Porter's Fiction*. Athens: University of Georgia Press, 1985. Porter believed that people want to understand the truth of their existence, Unrue maintains, but they get distracted by the things of this world, such as romanticized love and ideology. Provides criticism of Porter's fiction based on this thesis.

CHAIM POTOK

Born: New York, New York; February 17, 1929

Principal long fiction
The Chosen, 1967; *The Promise*, 1969; *My Name Is Asher Lev*, 1972; *In the Beginning*, 1975; *The Book of Lights*, 1981; *Davita's Harp*, 1985; *The Gift of Asher Lev*, 1990.

Other literary forms
Wanderings: Chaim Potok's History of the Jews (1978) is a personal reconstruction of four thousand years of Jewish history. Potok has also written essays and book reviews for Jewish and popular periodicals and newspapers. In January, 1988, his stage adaptation of *The Chosen* opened as a short-lived Broadway musical, with music by Philip Springer and lyrics by Mitchell Bernard.

Achievements
Critical acceptance and public acclaim have greeted Potok's novelistic explorations of the conflict between Orthodox Judaism and secular American culture. Potok received the Edward Lewis Wallant Award and a National Book Award nomination for *The Chosen*, his first novel. He received the Athenaeum Award for its sequel, *The Promise*. His sympathetic (critics would say sentimental) portrayal of Jewish fundamentalism and those who choose to leave it highlights the poignancy of an individual's break with tradition. Indeed, Potok's novels test the ability of traditional communities to contribute to the modern world without themselves being assimilated. His evocation of Jewish life in New York in the latter two-thirds of the twentieth century has universal appeal and disturbing implications.

Biography
Born of Orthodox Jewish parents in the Bronx in 1929, Chaim Potok was reared in a fundamentalist culture. Potok's father, Benjamin Potok, was a Polish émigré and no stranger to the pogroms of Eastern Europe. The young Potok was taught that the profound suffering of the Jews would one day transform the world. Yet, as Potok suggests in *Wanderings*, his service as a Jewish chaplain with the United States Army in Korea (1956-1957) confronted him with a world of good and evil that had never heard of Judaism. His attempt to come to terms with this larger world led Potok to a critical investigation of his own Jewish heritage and the limitations of the fundamentalist perspective. Though he had been ordained a Conservative rabbi in 1954, attracted by doctrines more liberal than those of strict Jewish Ortho-

doxy, Potok has continued his struggle to reconcile fundamental Judaism with the findings of science (as historiography and textual criticism shed new light on ancient traditions). *The Chosen* inaugurated his public search for a voice with which to speak to his heritage as well as to the larger world.

In the early 1960's, Potok taught at the Jewish Theological Seminary in New York, edited *Conservative Judaism*, and in 1965 became an editor with the Jewish Publication Society of Philadelphia. He was married to Adena Mosevitzky in 1958, with whom he would reside in Merion, Pennsylvania. The Potoks would have three children: Rena, Naama, and Akiva.

Analysis

In his novels, Chaim Potok returns again and again to the story of a young protagonist coming of age in a culture (usually Jewish) at once mysterious, beautiful, sad, and somehow inadequate. Usually told in the first person, Potok's stories surround the reader with forebodings of the larger, evil world (news of pogroms in Europe, the Holocaust, the first atom bomb) into which his characters are plunged. Potok creates a microcosm of feeling and reaction to events that shake the world. His sentences are simple and reportorial, at times almost a parody of the staccato style of Ernest Hemingway. The stories develop chronologically, though they are frequently invaded by dreams, visions, or voices from the "Other Side."

In each of his stories, Potok sets for himself a question to be answered and reworks his own experiences until he is satisfied with at least a provisional resolution. Controlling metaphors help shape the questions. In *The Chosen*, the baseball game symbolizes the competition between two Jewish cultures, the very strict Hasidic and the more openly assimilationist. What happens to those caught in between those two traditions? The vision of pups being born in *The Book of Lights* represents the entrance of fertile Cabala mysticism into a world of strict Jewish law. How can Jewish mysticism enrich Orthodoxy? Asher Lev's dreams of his mythical ancestor foreshadow the young artist's confrontation with his own culture. What happens when art brings great hurt? The sound of a little door harp symbolizes the transforming power of the imagination for Ilana Davita Chandal of *Davita's Harp*. What is the place of the imagination in Jewish Orthodoxy? What is the place of women? (Davita is Potok's first female protagonist.)

The Chosen recounts the story of Danny Saunders, brilliant son of a Hasidic rabbi, chosen by tradition to one day succeed his father as leader of the fundamentalist community in Brooklyn, New York. Yet Danny is less interested in studying the Talmud (Jewish law) than in probing the works of Sigmund Freud and other secular psychologists. The story closes with the inevitable confrontation between Danny and his father, which is mediated by Danny's friend Reuvan Malter. In the climactic scene in Reb Saunders' office, the old rabbi turns to his son and addresses him as a father for the first time. (For years, Danny had been reared in silence, except for times of Talmud study.) With fatherly tears, Reb Saunders explains that the years of silence created a soul of compassion within his brilliant son. Though he may well leave the Hasidic community for secular studies, Danny will always carry with him the legacy of Jewish suffering. That legacy will provide the moral force to change the world.

Reuvan, son of a Talmud scholar of the new school of textual criticism, chooses to become a rabbi. The choices, for Reuvan and for Danny, do not, however, come easily. Reuvan faces ostracism by the Hasidic community for suggesting that some Talmudic texts were of inferior quality and subject to misinterpretation. Danny must seemingly turn against his father if he is to pursue secular studies and abandon his leadership obligations.

The novel is structured almost as a diary, with pages of detailed descriptions of schoolwork in the Jewish high school, visits to the local synagogue, and the ebb and flow of Reuvan's life. Though at times tedious, the very innocence of the language contributes to a certain dramatic intensity. The conflict in the novel is mirrored in the frequent news reports of World War II and in the ensuing controversy over the creation of a Jewish state, Israel, in 1949. The Hasidic community is content to wait for the Messiah to create such a state; Reuvan's father calls for an immediate political settlement. Political questions are present in each of Potok's novels and are of central interest in *Davita's Harp*.

Silence is again present in Potok's second novel, *The Promise*, which continues the story of Danny Saunders and Reuvan Malter as they enter their professional lives. The novel begins with shouts of rage from young Michael Gordon, the son of Professor Abraham Gordon, a controversial Jewish philosopher. Michael has been cheated at a carnival booth by an old Jewish man, and both Reuvan and his date, Rachel Gordon, Michael's cousin, stare in horror as Michael angrily denounces Orthodoxy. Michael's father had questioned the supernatural accounts in the Hebrew Bible and, as a result, was excommunicated from the Orthodox community, now Michael is releasing his hate on those who persecuted Professor Gordon. Subsequently, Michael is taken to Danny Saunders, now a psychologist at a residential treatment center. When the boy refuses to speak, Danny isolates him. The agonizing silence breaks Michael's will and he reveals the hate he feels for his father and his writings, writings that have brought condemnation to them both. Eventually, Michael is finally able to accept his own feelings and reconcile with his parents, and Danny and Rachel are married, the powerful coupling of the brilliant Hasid with the cosmopolitan daughter of a secularist philosopher.

The Promise continues the exploration of Reuvan's choice to receive his rabbinate from an Orthodox seminary and his refusal to become a secular Jew, as Professor Gordon has done. Yet Reuvan is uneasy with the traditional method of Talmud study advanced by Rav Kalman, one of his teachers. If the Talmud is the sacred oral tradition of the Jews in written form, contradictory commentaries from rabbis down through the centuries must always be reconciled by newer interpretations, so as not to call God's Word into question. For Reuvan, there is another possibility; a corrupt text could be the source of confusion. Any correction, however, would mean violence to sacred scripture. Reuvan will become a rabbi so that he might debate Rav Kalman and the others from within a common tradition.

Reuvan's father, David Malter, is the voice of quiet wisdom throughout both books. Though a proponent of the new Talmud studies, he is sympathetic toward those whose tightly knit culture is being threatened. As he tells Reuvan in *The Promise*, "We cannot ignore the truth. At the same time, we cannot quite sing and dance as they do. . . . That is the dilemma of our time, Reuvan. I do not know what the answer is." Earlier, Reuvan's father had challenged his son to make his own meaning in the world. Those who had committed themselves to the Hasidic traditions had kept the faith alive through incomprehensible persecution. Now Reuvan must also choose with the greatest seriousness and fervency, for he, too, must make a mark on the world and endure hardship of his own.

Potok picks up this theme in his third novel, *My Name Is Asher Lev*. Covering the period of the late 1940's through the late 1960's, the book is an apologia for the artist. The Orthodox Jewish surroundings are familiar, but this time the controversy is not over textual criticism but rather representational art. Painting is not strictly forbidden to the Orthodox Jew, but it is regarded as useless, as foolishness, as a waste of time better devoted to the study of the Torah, the five books of Moses. Moreover, certain pictures could come close to violating the Commandment forbidding graven images. Asher Lev is a born painter, however, and throughout the novel, as he develops his talent, he is increasingly isolated from his family and culture. Asher is born in Crown Heights in Brooklyn in 1943. His father travels extensively for the local Rebbe in an effort to establish Ladover Hasid communities throughout Europe and to aid families emigrating to the United States. Asher's mother must stay with her son in New York because Asher refuses to leave his familiar streets to join his father in Europe. There are long nights of loneliness, waiting for Asher's father to return from some mission or other. Asher's mother suffers a breakdown when her brother, also on a mission for the Rebbe, is killed. She begins to find herself again by plunging into her Russian studies, picking up the work her brother left unfinished. Metaphors of things unfinished and things completed permeate the novel. Asher's father is continually on the move because of the great unfinished work of the Ladover. Asher himself finds that he must bring some kind of completeness to the world by painting not only what he sees with his eyes but also what his inner vision reveals to him. Those visions are not always beautiful; his paintings can be like knives, plunging the reality of evil into the soul of the onlooker. The wise Rebbe, sensing Asher's vast talent, entrusts him to Jacob Kahn, himself an artistic genius and a nonobservant Jew. Kahn forces Asher to absorb the work of Pablo Picasso, especially *Guernica* (1937), a painting inspired by the German bombing of the Basque capital during the Spanish Civil War. In time, Asher begins to surpass his teacher.

Asher becomes virtually a stranger to his father. At the end of the novel, Asher's parents stare with mixed rage and amazement at the two crucifixions he has painted. Both are of his mother, looking in abstract fashion at Asher the stranger on one side and the always-traveling husband on the other. The image of the cross for Asher has become the supreme symbol of suffering, devoid of any Christian preoccupation. The image is too much, however, for his parents, Orthodox Jews. As the Rebbe tells him, "You have crossed a boundary. I cannot help you. You are alone now. I give you my blessings."

There is a marked contrast between Asher's sensitive paintings (an effort to say what must be said about the evil in the world) and his selfish behavior toward his parents. He is one of the least sympathetic of Potok's protagonists because he struggles less with his own anguish than with his need to express his artistic gift at whatever cost. Jacob Kahn's advice, "Be a great painter, Asher Lev. . . . That will be the only justification for all the pain your art will cause," seems too facile. Asher is determined to remain an observant Jew, but he will do so on his own terms. The Commandment about honoring one's parents must be radically reinterpreted. The book suffers from the technical difficulty that Asher Lev must be identified as a genius early in the story in order for Potok to create the kind of tension he needs to interest a reader. A mediocre artist who causes pain is merely self-indulgent.

Yet the book reveals something of Potok's larger purpose. Art must be true to itself even if that means surprise or hurt. The artist, painter, or writer must speak from the heart; anything else is mere propaganda. Potok is seeking to provide a rationale for his novelistic critiques of fundamentalist communities.

Potok introduces something else into Asher's story: Asher often dreams of his "mythic ancestor," a Jew who served a nobleman only to have the nobleman unleash evil upon the world. Just as Asher envisioned that ancient Jew traveling the world, seeking to redress the wrong he had a part in, so must the artist reshape evil into art and so bring a kind of balance to the world. Asher's visions are forerunners of Potok's use of mysticism or imaginative visions themselves as ways of coming to terms with a world gone crazy.

In the Beginning is the story of young David Lurie and his childhood in an Orthodox family in the Bronx in the 1920's. The novel is patterned after the Book of Genesis: David falls from his mother's arms, develops a keen interest in the accounts of the Flood, and learns through the study of the Torah the power of words to shape a world. Potok's fourth novel was his most complex to date, departing from the forthright exposition found in *The Chosen* in favor of a more subtle panoply of impressions of growing up. Like all Potok's protagonists, David is precocious, constantly questioning the world around him, trying to have it make sense. He is sickly, bullied by other boys, and plagued with recurring nightmares. David functions in the novel as an idealized figure to focus the reader's attention on how Orthodoxy confronts anti-Semitism and growing secularization. David imagines the Golem of Prague crushing those who would harm the Jews like some powerful living robot; as David grows, though, he learns that words can be more powerful than the Golem. Eventually, helped by those who practice textual critique of the Torah, David heads for graduate study at the University of Chicago. Yet, as in Potok's other works, there must also be some kind of reconciliation of the demands of Jewish Orthodoxy with those of secular learning. It is achieved through a vision David has years later as he tours the site of the Bergen-Belsen death camp. David's vision of his dead father, and of his father's brother, David's namesake, is a moving conclusion to the book. David's father despairs that he has lost his son to the evil world, to the very world that took the lives of millions of Jews. He is reassured by David's uncle, however, that the son must journey into that world in order to bring something back to enrich Orthodoxy, which has become moribund. The son must venture out but must never forget his own roots. No anger of man can strike evil from the world. Only the patient use of words, with faith in their power to transform creation, can accomplish the task. That will be a new beginning for the world, and for Orthodoxy.

Potok's earlier novels tell the story of those in conflict with their Orthodox heritage. For the first time, *In the Beginning* pictures a reconciliation as a vision or story within the context of the novel. It is a kind of blessing from the beyond; here is the artist at work, crafting the resolution to the story.

The Book of Lights, narrated in the third person, uses the technique of mystical reconciliation for a more universal purpose. If the Master of the Universe truly exists, how is a believer to accept the death light of the twentieth century, the atomic bomb? Potok's answer is that through the imaginative use of Jewish mysticism, the spark of God can be found in an evil world.

The story departs from Potok's previous novels, which traced the childhood of the protagonist. Only a few pages are devoted to Gershon Loran's early life before his seminary days and subsequent chaplaincy in Korea. Those first pages, however, are significant. Gershon witnesses the birth of some pups on a rooftop in the midst of his rundown neighborhood; he is awed by the presence of life even amid wreckage.

In seminary, Gershon is introduced to the study of the Cabala and its *Zohar*, a Jewish mystical work from the thirteenth century. The *Zohar* is the book of lights of the novel's title, describing the creation of the world through the emanations of God. There are places where God has withdrawn his light;

that has enabled humankind to come on the scene but it has also ushered in great evil. Now the mystic is called to ascend through those emanations to find God.

Such mystical tradition is complex and even contradictory. For Gershon, however, it is the pounding heart of a living faith. Gershon's quiet moments of reverie serve him well during his chaplaincy. Though Potok paints a detailed picture of Gershon's activities in Korea, the crucial story is elsewhere. Gershon's seminary friend, Arthur Leiden, travels with him to Kyoto and Hiroshima. At the Hiroshima monument, Arthur reads from the Psalms and pleads to God in vain for some kind of atonement. Arthur's father had worked with other scientists in developing the atom bomb, and Arthur is haunted by the memory. Later, Arthur is killed in a plane crash; Gershon, visiting Arthur's parents, hears a portion of one of Arthur's letters: "All the world, it seems, is a grayish sea of ambiguity, and we must learn to navigate in it or be drowned." That is Potok's message in the novel; "Loran" is itself a navigational acronym. If Judaism were merely the law, the faith would break on the shoals of the gritty world. Its mystical tradition infuses the faith with the ambiguity of real life. It does not explain but rather affirms the nature of God's creation. The *Zohar* is an imaginative understanding of the nature of God; in it, God enfolds both good and evil. It is a light by which to view a decaying civilization, a light that will survive the death light. In his final mystical vision of his old cabala teacher, Gershon learns that the mystical light will help mend the world so that it can be broken again in yet new acts of creation.

It is the "mending power" of imagination that is at the heart of *Davita's Harp*. The harp referred to is a small instrument that fits on a door, with little balls that strike piano wires when the door is opened or closed. Here Potok returns to the first-person narrative, tracing the childhood of Ilana Davita Chandal, his first female lead character. She is the daughter of a nonbelieving Jewish mother and a nonbelieving Christian father. Spanning the years from the mid-1930's to 1942, the novel speaks with a new voice yet recapitulates some familiar themes. Davita grows up in the New York area; she remembers frequent moves, strange people coming and going, and the constant singing of the door harp. Her parents are involved in the Communist Party, attempting to fight Fascism in Spain and in the United States. Davita is precocious and inquisitive and her mother intelligent and cool, forever supplying Davita with the meaning of new words: proletariat, strike, idea, magic, war. Davita is spurred in her imaginative development by Aunt Sarah, a devout Episcopalian nurse, who tells her Bible stories, and by Jakob Daw, an Austrian writer, now suffering from having been gassed in World War I, who had loved Davita's mother when they were both in Vienna. Daw is sheltered for a time by Davita's parents and spins odd stories for her. There is the story of the little bird, flying to find the source of a beautiful music that soothes the world of the horrors of war. Only if the bird could stop the deceitful music would the world wake to its pain.

Davita's father, Michael Chandal, a journalist with *New Masses*, is killed during the bombing of Guernica during the Spanish Civil War. Soon after, both Jakob Daw and Davita's mother, Channah, become disillusioned with the Stalinists because the Communists, too, have committed atrocities. Davita has taken to attending a Jewish high school and becomes an outstanding student. Jakob Daw returns to Europe, where he dies, though his stories live in Davita's heart. Not long afterward, Ezra Dinn, an Orthodox Jew who had loved Davita's mother years ago, marries Channah. Slowly, Davita's mother regains her sense of place.

Davita's time of innocence is over. Before Jakob Daw left for Europe, he finished his strange story of the bird. The bird, he said, gave up searching for the music of the world and became very small to fit inside the door harp. There, said Daw, the music was not deceitful but full of innocence. Now, however, Davita encounters something sinister in her adopted tradition. She is the most brilliant student at her yeshiva but she is passed over for the Akiva Award because, she is told, she is a woman. It is 1942. Another student is selected for the award but learns the truth and refuses it. He is Reuvan Malter, first introduced in *The Chosen*.

Ilana Davita had wanted the prize because it would have given her the opportunity to tell her Jewish community a few words of farewell. "I had made this community my home, and now I felt betrayed by it. . . . I felt suddenly alone. And for the first time I began to understand how a single event could change a person's life." Later, in a vision, Jakob Daw and Davita's father appear, as well as Aunt Sarah. They want to hear her words, and so Davita speaks. She does not understand a world that kills its very best. She had wanted to speak public words of goodbye to her father and Jakob Daw the storyteller. The harp appears in her vision as well, singing in memorial to all the Davitas who would never have an opportunity to "speak their few words to this century."

In the end, Davita will go on to public school, angry with "sacred discontent." In an interview, Potok explained that Davita's experience was based on that of his wife, who was passed over as valedictory speaker because of her sex. *Davita's Harp* is a new exploration for Potok, that of Orthodoxy and feminism. Yet the novel also draws from Gershon Loran, David Lurie, and Asher Lev in recognizing the power of the artist's imagination to transform pain and ambiguity into some kind of meaning. A writer is a kind of harp, playing new music that mends the world.

The Gift of Asher Lev is framed by death. It begins with the funeral of Yitzchok Lev, Asher's uncle, and the ending of Asher's exile in France to attend the services in Brooklyn. Asher Lev is forty-five; he is joined by his wife Devorah, their daughter Rocheleh, eleven, and five-year-old son Avrumel. Though his family adapts well to the life of the Brooklyn Hasidim, Asher is haunted by the memory of a strange telephone call he received eighteen years earlier, the last time he had visited his parents in New York. It was a voice from the "Other Side," threatening death.

Asher is unable to paint (though he is given to sketching) and he seems to wander aimlessly through the local shops and galleries, as if waiting for a renewal of his gift. In the last year, critics had detected Asher's repetition of old themes, and he feels in danger of losing his gift should he become acclimated to his parents' community. Morose and determined to flee to France again, Asher is asked by the Rebbe to stay, at least for a while. Eventually it becomes clear to Asher that he and the aging Rebbe are woven inextricably together, as darkness and light. The Rebbe has no heir, and it is apparent that the leadership of the Ladover must pass soon to Asher's father; but there can be stability in the community only if there is assurance of the line of succession. If not Asher, then the next heir must be Avrumel, Asher's only son.

By the end of the novel, which takes Asher's story to the late 1980's, the artist has exiled himself again to France, but not without sacrifice. He has left his wife and children in New York, promising to return to them several months hence; yet in his isolation he has begun to paint again. "What kind of God creates such situations?" Asher asks himself as he walks with Devorah. "He gives me a gift and a son, and forces me to choose between them." Later, in France, Asher is visited by the image of the far-away Rebbe: "Slowly you begin to unravel the riddle," the vision says. "Your answer may save us and return you to your work. . . . It is sometimes possible for a man to acquire all of the world to come by means of a single act in this world. . . . You will redeem all that you have done and all that you are yet to do." Paradoxically, the sacrifice of Avrumel for the good of the community is a kind of death that redeems that artist himself; a gift on behalf of the world to come in exchange for the gift of the world as it is, in all its ambiguity and horror, and the ability to capture it on canvas.

These novels of Chaim Potok are offered as a gift of imagination to the Orthodox world and to all who are children of a restrictive past. The gift is risky, but it may well infuse new life into old ways or serve as a beacon for those who must plunge into the world in their search for meaning.

Dan Barnett

Other major works

NONFICTON: *Wanderings: Chaim Potok's History of the Jews*, 1978; *Tobiasse: Artist in Exile*, 1986.

Bibliography

Abramson, Edward A. *Chaim Potok*. Boston: Twayne, 1986. The first book-length study of Potok, this volume is the fullest available introduction to his life and works. After a biographical sketch, Abramson discusses each of Potok's novels through *Davita's Harp* and also devotes a chapter to *Wanderings*. Supplemented by a chronology, notes, a good selected bibliography (including a list of secondary sources with brief annotations), and an index.

Guttman, Allen. *The Jewish Writer in America: Assimilation and the Crisis of Identity*. New York: Oxford University Press, 1971. While this study includes a brief, insightful discussion of *The Chosen* and *The Promise*, it is valuable primarily as an account of the context from which Potok's work emerged.

Potok, Chaim. "An Interview with Chaim Potok." Interview by Elaine M. Kauvar. *Contemporary Literature* 27 (Fall, 1986): 290-317. In this lengthy and wide-ranging interview, Potok discusses his work through *Davita's Harp*. He is revealed as a novelist who, more than most, writes with a clearly formed plan in mind. Of particular interest is his intention to take up the stories of the protagonists of his first six novels and interweave them in subsequent works.

_____. "Judaism Under the Secular Umbrella." Interview by Cheryl Forbes. *Christianity Today* 22 (September 8, 1978): 14-21. In this excellent interview, Potok defines his concept of "core to core culture confrontation" and explains how each of his novels through *In the Beginning* deals with such a confrontation. In *The Chosen*, for example, the confrontation is between Orthodox Judaism and Freudian psychoanalysis (which Potok identifies with "the core of Western secular humanism"); in *My Name Is Asher Lev*, there is a conflict between Judaism and art's claim to autonomy.

Studies in American Jewish Literature 4 (1985). This special issue devoted to Potok includes several valuable critical essays, an interview with Potok conducted in 1981 by S. Lillian Kremer, and an autobiographical essay by Potok, "The First Eighteen Years." An indispensable source.

ANTHONY POWELL

Born: London, England; December 21, 1905

Principal long fiction

Afternoon Men, 1931; *Venusberg*, 1932; *From a View to a Death*, 1933; *Agents and Patients*, 1936; *What's Become of Waring*, 1939; *A Dance to the Music of Time* series (includes *A Question of Upbringing*, 1951; *A Buyer's Market*, 1952; *The Acceptance World*, 1955; *At Lady Molly's*, 1957; *Casanova's Chinese Restaurant*, 1960; *The Kindly Ones*, 1962; *The Valley of Bones*, 1964; *The Soldier's Art*, 1966; *The Military Philosophers*, 1968; *Books Do Furnish a Room*, 1971; *Temporary Kings*, 1973; *Hearing Secret Harmonies*, 1975); *O, How the Wheel Becomes It!*, 1983; *The Fisher King*, 1986.

Other literary forms

Although Anthony Powell has produced much writing other than his long fiction, he remains primarily a novelist. Powell has been an editor, an author of prefaces, a prolific book reviewer, and a screenwriter. While his miscellaneous writing includes light verse and fictional sketches, the stories, such as the ironic sequels to Charles Dickens' *A Christmas Carol* (1843) and D. H. Lawrence's *Lady Chatterley's Lover* (1928), are facile parodies, amusing but of limited interest. His skill in characterization and the fine art of gossip, basic to his major work, *A Dance to the Music of Time*, helps explain Powell's empathy with a seventeenth century expert in these matters, John Aubrey, author of *Brief Lives* (1813). Powell edited Aubrey's works and wrote a biographical study, *John Aubrey and His Friends* (1948, 1963). Powell also wrote two plays, *The Garden God* and *The Rest I'll Whistle* (published together in 1971). These comedies of manners, while containing crisp dialogue and entertaining dramatic scenes, do not suggest that Powell is a dramatist *manqué*. Finally, he has written his memoirs, in four volumes under the general title *To Keep the Ball Rolling* (1976, 1978, 1980, 1982). These books provide a valuable account of experiences which Powell transmuted into fiction; they also present vivid characterizations of many of Powell's contemporaries, including Constant Lambert, the Sitwells, Evelyn Waugh, Cyril Connolly, and George Orwell. In 1990, Powell published a substantial selection of his essays and reviews, *Miscellaneous Verdicts: Writings on Writers, 1946-1989*.

Achievements

Powell's career as a novelist started with five novels published in the 1930's. These books had generally favorable reviews and reasonable sales; they established Powell's reputation as a skilled and successful, if perhaps minor, novelist. His reputation grew steadily with his twelve-volume sequence *A Dance to the Music of Time*, begun after World War II and completed in 1975, and he is now generally recognized as one of the major English writers of the century. He is frequently compared to Marcel Proust, although, as Evelyn Waugh pointed out, Powell's *roman-fleuve* is more realistic and much funnier.

A Dance to the Music of Time is indeed funny. Becoming more somber in tone as it proceeds, incorporating numerous tragic events, never lacking a certain fundamental seriousness, the series nevertheless remains comic, a comedy in more aspects than Honoré de Balzac's meaning of a broad social portrait. The series does present a picture of various segments of English society—essentially the privileged segments—during the empire's decline since World War I. It has, thus, a certain limited value as sociological documentation—as what W. D. Quesenbery termed an "anatomy of decay"—but this is at best a secondary aspect. Primarily as excellent entertainment, the novels are appreciated by a wide range of readers. One may enjoy, in each of the individual novels, the wit, especially in dialogue, the characterization, and incident. In the series as a whole, there is the additional pleasure of observing the complex interactions of the characters as they appear, disappear, and reappear, forming unexpected patterns in the "dance," the whole bound together, if somewhat loosely, by theme.

From the first volume of the sequence, *A Question of Upbringing*, the work was well-received, although it was, of course, only as subsequent volumes appeared that readers, in increasing numbers, came to appreciate the complex interconnections of the separate books. Powell's wit and style were commended, as was his characterization, expecially the creation, in Kenneth Widmerpool, one of the great comic villains in all of English literature. It was the narrative structure, however, that eventually produced the most critical interest.

Although the series moves chronologically forward, through the half century from 1921 to 1971, it is presented through the memory of the narrator, Nicholas Jenkins, who employs flashback and foreshadowing in a complex manner, recalling, for example, in the sixth book, his childhood in 1914. Such a structure suggest Proust's *A la recherche du temps perdu* (1913-1927, *Remembrance of Things Past*). The comparison is relevant, and both Powell and his protagonist Nick Jenkins admire the French writer. Powell's narrator is not similar to Proust's however, Nick's mind operates differently. In addition, Henri Bergson's theory of time, so important to Proust, has limited relevance to Powell's work.

If Powell is not an English Proust, comparisons with other novel-sequences make even more clear the unique quality of *A Dance to the Music of Time*. In its focus upon the individuality of character, it is diametrically opposed, for example, to "unanimism," the ideology of collective experience which informs Jules Romains' *roman-fleuve*, *Les Hommes de bonne volonté* (1932-1947). One of the few English novel-sequences of comparable length, C. P.

Snow's *Strangers and Brothers* (1940-1970), employs a structure quite different from Powell's. The eleven volumes of Snow's work shift between those that focus on the life of the central figure, Lewis Eliot, and those that do not, whereas Nick Jenkins remains in each book simultaneously a participant in, and an observer of, the "dance" that the series chronicles.

Powell's achievement, springing from an interest in character, expressed through matchless style, and distinctly structured, has then, as does any great work of art, a *sui generis* excellence. It has won Powell a devoted and varied audience; the British Broadcasting Corporation has produced the series; *A Dance to the Music of Time*'s translations include a Bulgarian version. A share of worldly honors, such as an honorary fellowship in the Modern Language Association of America and an honorary D.Litt. from Oxford, have come to Powell. Perhaps more significantly, he has earned the respect of fellow writers, those his own age and those younger, those who share his conservative beliefs and those who do not. In sincere flattery, at least one other writer, the major Canadian novelist Hugh Hood, is writing his own series of novels in admiring emulation of Powell's work.

Biography

Anthony Dymoke Powell (pronounced "Antony Diemoke Pole") was born December 21, 1905, in London, England. His mother was the daughter of a barrister; his father, himself the son of a colonel, was a lieutenant in the army who was to win decoration in World War I and retire as a lieutenant colonel. Powell, his parents' only child, spent his early years in a military environment. He was to have a continuing respect for the service; General Conyers, in *A Dance to the Music of Time*, is only one of a number of sympathetically portrayed army officers in Powell's fiction.

As a member of a well-to-do family, Powell had an upper-class education and acquired the values of his class. He entered Eton in 1918, where he made friends, such as Hubert Duggan, a source for Stringham, who were to contribute to his subsequent characterizations. When, in 1923, Powell matriculated at Balliol College, Oxford, he continued to collect the friends and the personal impressions that were to serve him well when he later described Nick Jenkins' experiences. Powell's memoirs, *To Keep the Ball Rolling*, written after *A Dance to the Music of Time*, are invaluable in dealing with the complex issue of the relation between fiction and "real life," but it may be said that Powell is not always entirely forthcoming, and that many of his fictional characters are based, often rather closely, upon particular prototypes.

While at Oxford, Powell made various vacation trips to the Continent; in 1924, he traveled to Finland, where his father was stationed. Later, he drew upon this travel in his early novel *Venusberg*.

Powell was graduated from Oxford in 1926, and went to work for the publishing firm of Duckworth, in London. There, Powell lived the quasibohemian life that is described in *A Buyer's Market* and subsequent volumes in *A Dance to the Music of Time*, and which is also reflected in his five prewar novels. He spent much time in the company of painters and musicians, meeting, among them, the composer Constant Lambert, who was to become a lifelong friend and the prototype for Hugh Moreland in Powell's series.

On December 3, 1934, Powell married Lady Violet Pakenham; they were to have two sons, Tristam and John. With his marriage, Powell acquired a large set of interesting in-laws; collectively, they were to contribute something to his fictional portrait of the Tollands; his brother-in-law Frank Pakenham, the seventh Earl of Longford, was to serve as a major source for the character Kenneth Widmerpool.

After his wedding, Powell left Duckworth's, and, in 1936, worked as a scriptwriter for Warner Bros. in London. There he met Thomas Phipps, the original of Chips Lovell. In 1937, he went, via the Panama Canal to Hollywood, California, in search of a scriptwriting job. Although the job did not work out, before returning, the Powells enjoyed an interesting interlude that included a meeting with F. Scott Fitzgerald. Upon his return to London, Powell engaged in journalism and wrote his fifth novel, *What's Become of Waring*. As World War II began, Powell, in 1939, became commissioned a lieutenant in the Welsh Regiment.

His war experiences are fairly accurately portrayed in the military trilogy, the third "movement" of the four in *A Dance to the Music of Time*. Powell, like Nick Jenkins, served first in a line regiment in Northern Ireland; he was transferred, in 1941, to Army Intelligence, worked as a liaison officer with Allied forces, served in France and Belgium, and gained the rank of major.

Just as Nick, after leaving the army at the end of the war, worked on a study of Robert Burton, so did Powell engage in historical research on John Aubrey, publishing his study in 1948, and an edited collection of Aubrey's work the next year. With Aubrey "finally out of the way," as Powell writes, he turned again to novel-writing, and began with *A Question of Upbringing*, his *roman-fleuve*. The novels in the series appeared at fairly regular intervals, averaging one every two years from 1951 until 1975. During these years, Powell continued his career in journalism, contributing sketches, articles, and reviews to *Punch*, the London *Daily Telegraph*, and other periodicals. In 1956, he was made a C.B.E; in 1961 he lectured in America at Dartmouth College, Amherst College, and Cornell University. He was appointed a trustee of the National Portrait Gallery in 1962. His plays, *The Garden God* and *The Rest I'll Whistle*, were published in 1971, the same year in which the University of Sussex awarded him the D.Litt.

During his outwardly quiet postwar years, Powell continued to enjoy and expand his circle of friends, thereby finding some additional prototypes for the characters introduced in the later volumes of his series. The writer Julian Maclaren-Ross, the prototype of X. Trapnel, is a notable example.

Upon completing *A Dance to the Music of Time*, Powell began his memoirs, publishing *Infants of the Spring* in 1976, followed, at two-year intervals, by *Messengers of Day*, *Faces in My Time*, and *The Strangers All Are Gone*.

In 1983, a year after the appearance of the final volume of his memoirs, Powell published a short novel or novella, *O, How the Wheel Becomes It!*, a satirical *jeu d'esprit*, his first work of fiction since the completion of *A Dance to the Music of Time*. This was followed in 1986 by *The Fisher King*, a full-length novel published to excellent reviews. During most of the period of his major work, Powell and his wife lived at Somerset, where they still reside. Powell continues to receive honors—including a D.Litt. from Oxford in 1980—to write, and, it may be assumed, to enjoy his unique perception of the patterns formed by the secret harmonies of time.

Analysis

Of the many pleasures and rewards offered by Anthony Powell's novels, none surpasses that to be found in coming to know, and continually being surprised by what happens to, a variety of fascinating characters. For Powell, an interest in character is primary. This can be seen in his absorption in the biographies sketched by John Aubrey, in the series of verbal portraits which dominate *To Keep the Ball Rolling*, and in his statement that a concern for character was central in his beginning *A Dance to the Music of Time*.

Successful fiction, though, involves more than the presentation of a series of characters, however intriguing. When characterization is conveyed with wit, both in dialogue and description, when the style becomes a pleasure in itself, as it does in Powell's work, one has enough ingredients to produce writing worth reading, but not enough for a novel, certainly not for a novel of the scope and stature of *A Dance to the Music of Time*. Such a novel, like any successful work of art, must satisfy the aesthetic requirement of unity— a sense of structure and order must be conveyed.

Although not the sole ingredient upon which a unified structure depends, character does help provide this sense of balance. For example, a degree of unity is achieved by having a single narrator, Nicholas Jenkins. Yet, *A Dance to the Music of Time* is not really the story of Nick Jenkins, just as it is not essentially the story of Kenneth Widmerpool, important as both these characters are. Although himself a participant in the "dance," Nick basically observes and reports; he does not give structure to the events that he relates: no persona, only Powell himself, can do this.

Many writers, certainly, achieve structure through plot, which may be the soul of fiction as Aristotle thought it was of drama. For Powell, however, the demands normally implied by "plot" run counter to his fundamental sense of time's complex mutability; to give his work a definite beginning, middle, and end, with action rising to and falling from a specific climax, would be justified neither by his sense of reality nor his artistic intentions.

This is not to say that conscious arrangement of incident is not present in *A Dance to the Music of Time*. On the contrary, because the author has exercised intelligent concern for such arrangement, continual surprises are enjoyed in a first reading, and anticipation of the irony of coming events gives a special pleasure to rereading the series. It would be yielding too readily to the seductive appeal of paradox, however, to claim that it is a crafted sense of the random which gives basic structure to *A Dance to the Music of Time*—that its order lies in its apparent lack of order.

If not to be found primarily in character or plot, what is the key to the structure of the dance? Unwilling, with reason, to accept the idea that it *has* no clear structure, that it is, even if cut from a loaf made of remarkably milled flour, essentially "a slice of life," critics have proposed a variety of answers.

The title of the series, as Powell has explained, derives from an allegorical painting in the Wallace Collection in London, Nicholas Poussin's *A Dance to the Music of Time*. Comparisons between the painting and the novel may be ingeniously extended, but it seems improbable that they were extensively worked out by Powell as he began a series which, he writes in *Faces in My Time*, would consist of a number of volumes, "just how many could not be decided at the outset." It would appear more probable that the Poussin painting, expressing the French artist's sense of the permutations time produces in human life, while an important analogue to Powell's intention in the series, was only one of a number of sources of the work's pattern. Another source might have been Thomas Nashe's *Summer's Last Will and Testament* (1592), a masque organized around the four seasons, contrasting the arts and the utilitarian spirit, and involving a sophisticated, semidetached "presenter"; it was the basis of a musical composition by Powell's close friend Constant Lambert.

Other structural keys have been proposed, including the importance of mysticism (the Dr. Trelawney, Mrs. Erdleigh aspect) and the signs of the zodiac. There would seem to be some validity in most of these interpretations, but the attempt to see any one as a single key to the series appears reductionist, in the sense that a strict Freudian or Marxist reading of William Shakespeare is too limiting. Insofar as the pattern of the dance can be extrapolated from the work itself, most critics have agreed that it must be seen as a reflection of theme.

Of the many thematic strands, that which is central appears to be the conflict between power and art, or imagination and will. Jenkins himself suggests this at more than one point in the series. From the perspective of this conflict, in which Widmerpool, the extreme example of the self-centered power-seeker, is thematically contrasted to Hugh Moreland the musician, and later to X. Trapnel the writer, the characters and their actions fall into a meaningful, if somewhat shadowy, pattern. The pattern is hardly simple, though; few characters are purely villainous or heroic; some artists seek power; some professional soldiers and businessmen are artistic and imaginative; both victories and defeats tend to be temporary.

Furthermore, the sexual designs woven in the "dance" complicate a bipolar view of theme. Sexual attraction, or love, in the novel usually involves both an imaginative appreciation of a perceived beauty in the desired partner, and some attempt to impose one's will upon another. Thus, with vagaries of desire, thematic antitheses and syntheses may fluctuate within individual characters. It is clear, however, that when Matilda Wilson goes from the artist Moreland to the industrialist Sir Magnus Donners, or Pamela Flitton leaves Widmerpool for the novelist X. Trapnel, a thematic point is made. (Indeed, the women in the series, generally less convincingly presented than the men, often seem to serve as scoring markers in the thematic game.)

That this thematic conflict, while it should not be simplistically defined, was essential to Powell's concept of the work's structure is shown additionally by the way prototypes were transmuted into fictional characters. Frank Pakenham, for example, unlike his fictional "counterpart" Widmerpool, not only would seem to have a number of virtues, but also has enjoyed a long and happy marriage, blessed by eight children. Clearly, the structure of the series requires that such satisfaction be denied its thematic villain.

A suggestion, then, may be made as to the probable way Powell proceeded in constructing his series. He apparently started with a novelist's interest in certain people that he knew, those he felt would be worth portraying. Then, to create order in his work, he fitted these people's fictional representatives into thematic patterns, changing reality as needed to accomplish this patterning. Using the thematically identified characters, he then, at a lower order of priority, considered and manipulated the plot, using plot itself to demonstrate another major theme, that of "mutability." The result was a uniquely constructed work of art.

Before beginning his major work, Powell wrote five novels; a case can be made for their being excellent works in their own right. Had Powell not gone on to write his *roman-fleuve*, they may have gained him a certain lasting recognition. As it is, inevitably they are regarded primarily as preparation for his masterpiece. The use of the "detached" narrator, coincidence in plot, ironic style, clipped dialogue, the theme of power, art, and love—all of these attributes of *A Dance to the Music of Time* are anticipated in the early novels. *Afternoon Men*, picturing a London social scene the young Powell knew well, is the first of the five early novels. Powell has described it as "something of an urban pastoral . . . depicting the theme of unavailing love," with not much plot in the conventional sense. He sees the design of this first novel to be "not without resemblance to the initial framework" of the sequence. Although the protagonist, William Atwater, is not the story's narrator—it is told mainly from his point of view, with the author occasionally intruding in his own voice—he may be compared, in his wit and detached forbearance, to Nicholas

Jenkins. It is essentially in its ironic style, however, especially in the dialogue, that *Afternoon Men* anticipates the later series.

Venusberg, Powell's second novel, also has a protagonist, Lushington, who is comparable to Nick Jenkins. Flashback, a technique later significant to the series, is employed in this novel's construction, and the theme of love is extended to include adultery, while power and clairvoyance, topics prominent in *A Dance to the Music of Time*, are introduced. Powell's next novel, *From a View to a Death*, dealing with the interrelated themes of art, love, and power, emphasizes the latter. Arthur Zouch, a painter and womanizer, uses art and love in his search for the power he believes is his by right of his being an *Übermensch*. Fittingly, for one who not only debases the gift of imagination but is also a would-be social climber, he is defeated by a member of the country gentry. Technically, the book is interesting in that Powell experiments with a shifting point of view.

Art, sex, and power—specifically money—are the subjects that provide structure in *Agents and Patients*. In this novel, two confidence men, Maltravers and Chipchase, each attempt to fleece a naïve young man, Blore Smith, Maltravers by playing upon Smith's sexual innocence, Chipchase by playing upon his artistic innocence. As the title, drawn from John Wesley, suggests, the issue of free will and determinism, significant in a less direct way in *A Dance to the Music of Time*, is an underlying theme. Excellent as it is as satiric comedy, *Agents and Patients* puts such an emphasis upon plot and theme that the characterization, usually Powell's strongest suit, tends somewhat toward caricature.

What's Become of Waring, Powell's last novel before the war, is perhaps a less impressive achievement than the four that preceded it. It is, however, close to *A Dance to the Music of Time* in more than chronology. Although it has a carefully worked-out, conventional plot, Powell still manages, as James Tucker observes, to "slip out of it and pursue his concern for people." In this work, a first-person narrator is employed. He is a publisher's reader; the work draws upon Powell's experience at Duckworth's. Never named, the narrator, in his overall attitude and as a partial alter ego for Powell, resembles Nicholas Jenkins. Again, the mystical element, later present in the series, is introduced through seances. Significantly, given the thematic center of *A Dance to the Music of Time*, *What's Become of Waring* ends with the narrator, as he drifts off to sleep, free-associating on the idea of power.

That Powell, after his lengthy hiatus from novel-writing, returned to the idea of the quest for power is clear even from the first of the three volumes that constitute "Spring," the initial movement of his sequence. *A Question of Upbringing* introduces, at the very start, the series' most important character, Widmerpool, and it is clear that even as a schoolboy he is determined to dominate.

The early introduction of the major themes is an important aid to unity, for the start of a long series poses particular problems for its author. As Powell suggests in *Faces in My Time*, early volumes, in preparation for future ones, must introduce undeveloped characters and potential situations; additionally, some characters and situations, in view of their subsequent importance, must be overemphasized. These requirements may tend to confuse the reader, unless patterns are perceived.

A Question of Upbringing, which covers Nick's youth at public school and university, introduces an important pattern of repetition of related incidents by having Nick meet his Uncle Giles at both the beginning and the end of the volume. Another recurring structural device, the alternation of scenes described in dramatic detail with linking sections provided by Nick's subjective impressions, is present, as are the patterning devices of allusion and symbolism. The series begins with a scene of workmen gathered around a fire, repeated at the conclusion of the sequence, twelve volumes later, and mentions the Poussin painting which provides the title for the whole sequence. References to paintings are important throughout the series, including the Tiepolo ceiling in *Temporary Kings* and the oft-mentioned Modigliani drawing which is rescued in the final volume.

Although the themes of love and art which, along with the interrelated theme of power, dominate the series are present in the first volume, they are more prominent in the second, *A Buyer's Market*. In this book, dominated by the social life of parties and dances which Nick, down from the university, enjoys, not only do sexual activities become important to Nick (a late bloomer as compared to his friends Templer and Stringham), but also the theme of the quest for power is extended to include politics. The radical young woman, Gypsy Jones (with whom Nick apparently loses his virginity), is utilized in one of Powell's recurring attacks upon the political Left, as well as to serve as an object of frustrated lust for Widmerpool, whose sex life is to be, throughout the series, eccentric and unsatisfactory.

The Acceptance World, the third volume in this movement, begins with another meeting between Nick and his Uncle Giles, who is now associated with Mrs. Erdleigh, a clairvoyant. She plays a major role in the dramatization of the subtheme of mysticism. Mysticism in the series, as seen later in Dr. Trelawney, and finally in Scorpio Murtlock, is related to an attempt to escape from what Mrs. Erdleigh calls the "puny fingers of Time," and gain power. Power in *The Acceptance World*, though, is considered more in political terms; there is an extension of the political satire against the Left, especially through Quiggin (whose character owes something to Cyril Connolly's), a university friend of Jenkins who moves in left-wing intellectual circles.

The volume's love interest involves Nick in a serious affair with Jean Templer, a school friend's sister. Much later in the series, in *The Military Philosophers*, Nick realizes that Jean, who breaks off the affair, really is attracted to money and power; she ultimately marries a Colonel Flores, who becomes a Latin American dictator. As Nick reflects in the first volume, "being in love is a complicated matter"; staying in love is even more so. The balance of thematic opposites, necessary to love, is seldom maintained. Nick is to be virtually unique in the series by virtue of his lasting, successful marriage, but the reader is given little direct insight into the secret of his success.

Nick's courtship and engagement are described in the first volume of the second movement, "Summer." This volume is entitled *At Lady Molly's*; Lady Molly Jeavons is a fictional amalgam of actual people including Rosa Lewis, the famous proprietor of the Cavendish Hotel, and Lady Astor, celebrated mistress of the magnificent country mansion, Cliveden, the prototype of the novel's Dogdene. Lady Molly, whose easygoing hospitality attracts a variety of guests, is the aunt of Chips Lovell (a character based on Thomas Phipps), who works with Nick as a scriptwriter for films. Powell here, as throughout the series, introduces new characters, thereby continually revivifying his novel, personifying its themes with variety, and causing the reader to wonder who, as well as what, is coming next. The actions of the two most permanent characters, Nick and Widmerpool, form the core of the volume; Nick's developing and successful love for Isobel Tolland is contrasted with the debacle that occurs when Widmerpool attempts a premarital seduction of his fiancée, Mildred Haycock.

Love and marriage are even more central to the next book, *Casanova's Chinese Restaurant*, which introduces and focuses upon one of the series' most important and attractively realized characters, the composer Hugh Moreland, who becomes one of Nick's closest friends, just as Moreland's real-life prototype, Constant Lambert, became very important to Powell. Moreland is, thematically, *the* artist. As such, he is Widmerpool's antithesis, even though the two have too little in common to be antagonists other than thematically— the few occasions when they encounter each other are singularly, but not surprisingly, undramatic. One critic has suggested that even their names, Widmerpool's suggesting wetness, and Moreland's the opposite, indicate their antithesis. (Powell's names, as most readers will have noticed, are frequently suggestive and apt, as well as sometimes amusing—consider, for example, the name of the sexually experienced woman whom Widmerpool so decidedly fails to satisfy, Mrs. Haycock.)

A more significant difference between Moreland and Widmerpool is in their talk. Moreland produces very witty and pleasurable conversation; Widmerpool is given to pompous pronouncements that often entertain the reader by their unconscious self-satire. Like Widmerpool, however, although quite differently and for different reasons, Moreland has trouble with his love life; interconnections of art and love form much of the subject matter of the volumes in this movement.

Other perspectives on love are introduced in *The Kindly Ones*, the last volume of "Summer," in which Widmerpool temporarily fades into the background, until the last chapter. The work begins with a flashback to Nick's childhood in 1914, thereby relating World War I to the approach of World War II in 1938, the time to which the book returns. The chronology is particularly complicated in this volume, and coincidence, always a feature of the series' plotting, is pushed to its limits when Nick, having gone to the seaside hotel where his Uncle Giles has died, meets, along with others from his past, Bob Duport, the former husband of Nick's past lover, Jean. The fact that for many readers, the complex structure of *The Kindly Ones* is unobtrusively successful, provides some measure of Powell's legerdemain.

At the end of *The Kindly Ones*, Nick has arranged for his commission in the army; the third movement, "Autumn," carries him though World War II. The reader learns from the autobiographical *Faces in My Time* that Nick's army experiences closely parallel Powell's own. Nick's service is distinguished, but the focus is more upon the tedium of war than its heroism.

In treating this often tedious, but different world of the service, Powell faced technical problems. He had to maintain the structure of his series within an entirely new environment. New characters, some from a social background that the novel had previously ignored, had to be used in a manner in accordance with the controlling themes. Furthermore, the style had to make some adaptation to the grim subject matter. Powell was not going to emphasize the comic elements of war, even though they are not ignored. The basic solution to these problems was to alternate the army scenes with those occurring when Nick is on leave. Thereby, the reader is able to experience the new, while still maintaining an interest in the old characters and themes.

The first volume of the movement, *The Valley of Bones*, introduces, among many new characters, a particularly significant one, Captain Gwatkin. Gwatkin, while no artist—he had worked in a local Welsh bank—is a man of imagination, a sort of Miniver Cheevy actually in armor. He has romantic ambitions to be a perfect soldier, ambitions doomed to failure in his encounters with the men of power who are his superiors. Although he is eventually relieved of his command, Gwatkin finds some consolation in love, only to lose it when he learns of the unfaithfulness of his beloved barmaid Maureen. Between these army scenes, Nick, while on leave, observes the continued amatory maneuvers of his friends and relations. The book ends with the dramatic appearance of Widmerpool as an influential major.

In the next volume, *The Soldier's Art*, Nick is working as Widmerpool's junior assistant, in a position to observe his superior's continuing struggle for power, transferred from civilian to military life. Widmerpool hovers upon the verge of disaster, but at the end of the book his career is saved. Previously, he had failed to assist an old school fellow of his and Nick's, Stringham, now reduced to being an enlisted man working in the officers' mess, subsequently to die in a Japanese prisoner-of-war camp. Meanwhile, personal entanglements continue to form new patterns, while some of the characters, including

Chips Lovell and Lady Molly, are killed in a bombing raid.

The final volume of the movement, *The Military Philosophers*, finds Nick in the war office, working on liaison with allied troops. This book, stylistically notable for its increased use of allusion, presents a number of the real personnel with whom Powell worked, little changed in their fictional guises. It is, however, an imagined character, or at least one for whom no prototype has been established, who reappears at this point, having been briefly introduced earlier as a young girl, subsequently to be a major figure. Pamela Flitton is, like Widmerpool, Stringham, Moreland, and Trapnel, one of the series' most memorable creations. She is a kind of ubiquitous nemesis, capable of bringing down both the men of art and of power. Outstanding even in a cast of remarkably unusual and individual characters, she is made by Powell both larger than life and yet believable, beautiful and yet repulsive, contemptible and yet capable of arousing the reader's sympathies. Although not all readers find her entirely convincing, she is certainly one of Powell's most fascinating characters. As the war ends, she is engaged to Widmerpool. No one could deserve her less, or more. With Pamela's entrance into the series, the tone, previously not essentially grim, even with the many deaths occurring during the war, changes.

In the final movement of the series, "Winter," the style also changes as Powell moves toward a concluding "wintery silence." While a sense of the comic is never abandoned, the mood becomes more somber, the action more direct. The first novel in this movement, *Books Do Furnish a Room*, is primarily the story of X. Trapnel, a novelist heavily based on Powell's friend, Julian Maclaren Ross. Trapnel, the artist, is juxtaposed with Widmerpool, the man of power, through the agency of Pamela Flitton, who leaves Widmerpool to live with Trapnel. The triumph of the artist is temporary, however, for not only is Pamela discovered to be both sexually insatiable and frigid, but she also destroys a manuscript of Trapnel's most recent novel by dumping it in the Maida Vale Canal, and returns to Widmerpool.

In the next volume, *Temporary Kings*, which begins at an international literary conference in Venice, where the first half of the novel is set, Pamela is a dominant character. Her sexual debauchery continues, unsettling Widmerpool, but she encounters a man upon whom her charms fail, Professor Russell Gwinnett. Continuing his ability to rejuvenate the series by introducing new characters, Powell brings in this American scholar with necrophilic tastes, who is writing a book on Trapnel. Nick finds him "an altogether unfamiliar type," with "nothing simple" about his personality.

Thematically, Gwinnett, a curious variant of the *deus ex machina*, may embody a kind of resolution of the conflict between art and power. Having both an involvement with art and an exceptionally strong will, Gwinnett, whose superior psychic strength provokes Pamela's suicide, perhaps in a necrophilic ritual, may be thought to have avenged Trapnel, if not Widmerpool.

Any resolution with Gwinnett is, however, a dark one, incorporating the cult rites with which he becomes involved before returning to America, and necessarily suggesting that to which he is most strongly related, death.

The final volume of the sequence, *Hearing Secret Harmonies*, is focused on Widmerpool, who, with the exception of Nick himself, is the series' most enduring character. After becoming a kind of hero to rebellious youth, he joins a pagan religious cult and struggles with its leader, Scorpio Murtlock, for dominance. Finally, running at the end, just as he was in his first appearance in the sequence, he falls dead, exhausted by his effort to take the lead in a ritual run.

The ending of such a long work poses a particular problem. After twelve books, certainly some feeling of conclusion must be produced, yet the whole structure, the whole sense of the continually evolving dance of time, renders any strong sense of climax inappropriate. Powell, by having Nick learn at secondhand of Widmerpool's death, and then returning to the initial image of the workmen's fire, quoting Robert Burton, and providing a carefully worded final image, skillfully solves this problem. The ending is a final reminder of the quality of literary skill and talent that is sustained through all the volumes of singularly satisfactory achievement.

William B. Stone

Other major works

PLAYS: *The Garden God and The Rest I'll Whistle: The Text of Two Plays*, 1971.

POETRY: *Caledonia: A Fragment*, 1934.

NONFICTION: *John Aubrey and His Friends*, 1948, 1963; *To Keep the Ball Rolling*, 1976-1982 (includes *Infants of the Spring*, 1976; *Messengers of Day*, 1978; *Faces in My Time*, 1980; *The Strangers All Are Gone*, 1982); *Miscellaneous Verdicts: Writings on Writers, 1946-1989*, 1990.

Bibliography

Brennan, Neil. *Anthony Powell*. Boston: Twayne, 1974. Covers Powell's work up to 1973, when the eleventh volume of *A Dance to the Music of Time* was published. One-third of this study is devoted to *A Dance to the Music of Time*, Powell's tour de force; the rest is an analysis of his other works, including early novels such as *Afternoon Men* and *From a View to a Death*. Contains a chronology of Powell which includes his family ancestry.

Morris, Robert K. *The Novels of Anthony Powell*. Pittsburgh: University of Pittsburgh Press, 1968. The first book-length study of Powell's writing. Morris discusses all Powell's novels up to 1968 and focuses on what he discerns as Powell's central theme: the struggle between the power hungry and sensualists. The second part of this study analyzes the first eight volumes of *A Dance to the Music of Time*.

Russell, John. *Anthony Powell: A Quintet, Sextet, and War*. Indianapolis: Indiana University Press, 1970. This thorough study, which compares his early novels with later works, is a must for Powell scholars. Russell argues for Powell's linguistic strengths and the uniformity of his writing, but also for his unpredictability. Discusses the first nine volumes of *A Dance to the Music of Time*.

Spurling, Hilary. *Invitation to the Dance: A Guide to Anthony Powell's "Dance to the Music of Time."* Boston: Little, Brown, 1977. Spurling intends this as a reference cum "bedside companion for readers who want to refresh their memories." Whether or not it makes for bedside reading, this volume certainly is a useful guide to the complexities of Powell's opus. Contains a synopsis of each volume, by chapter and time sequence, and includes an extensive character index.

Tucker, James. *The Novels of Anthony Powell*. New York: Columbia University Press, 1976. An extensive appraisal of the twelve volumes of *A Dance to the Music of Time*. Includes a "Who's Who" of characters, themes, style, narrative, and method. A scholarly work, but quite readable. Also contains a bibliography.

DAWN POWELL

Born: Mount Gilead, Ohio; November 28, 1897
Died: New York, New York; November 14, 1965

Principal long fiction

Whither, 1925; *She Walks in Beauty*, 1928; *The Bride's House*, 1929; *Dance Night*, 1930; *The Tenth Moon*, 1932; *Jig Saw: A Comedy*, 1934; *The Story of a Country Boy*, 1934; *Turn, Magic Wheel*, 1936; *The Happy Island*, 1938; *Angels on Toast*, 1940 (later as *A Man's Affair*, 1956); *A Time to Be Born*, 1942; *My Home Is Far Away*, 1944; *The Locusts Have No King*, 1948; *The Wicked Pavilion*, 1954; *The Golden Spur*, 1962.

Other literary forms

Though Dawn Powell is known primarily as a novelist, she had originally intended to write for the theater. Her play *Big Night* was produced by the Group Theatre in 1933, and *Jig Saw*, based on her novel *Jig Saw: A Comedy* (1934), had a short run in 1934. Powell also wrote a musical comedy and scripts for radio, television, and film and published essays, reviews, and short stories in distinguished national magazines. A number of her short stories were collected in *Sunday, Monday and Always* (1952).

Achievements

While such contemporaries as Ernest Hemingway and John Dos Passos considered Dawn Powell one of the finest writers of their time, she never attained their popularity. Shortly before her death in 1965, Powell was honored with an honorary doctorate and an award from the National Institute of Arts and Letters, but despite occasional attempts by her admirers, such as Edmund Wilson, to call attention to her achievements, she remained relatively obscure, and her sixteen novels, all out of print, were difficult to find. Fortunately, in the next two decades, there was a revolution in the American sensibility. One of the results of the feminist movement was that the critics and publishers had to admit sins of omission; they had minimized the talent of many fine women writers simply because they were women. Dawn Powell, who has been called an American equivalent to English satiric novelists such as Evelyn Waugh and Anthony Powell, is an obvious example. In 1987, author and critic Gore Vidal launched the campaign to obtain proper recognition for Powell. In a lengthy essay published in *The New York Review of Books*, he traced her life and her literary career and concluded by bemoaning the fact that the novels of the person he considered America's best comic novelist were all out of print. As a result of his article, several of her later books were reprinted, all with Vidal's essay as an introduction, and the reviews that followed suggest that Powell may at last receive the recognition denied her during her lifetime.

Biography

Dawn Powell was born in Mount Gilead, Ohio, on November 28, 1897, the daughter of Roy K. Powell, a traveling salesman, and Hattie B. Sherman Powell. After the death of her mother when Dawn was six, for six years she and her two sisters lived with various relatives on farms and in small towns. After her father's remarriage, the girls went to live with him and their step-mother on a farm. Dawn was already a dedicated writer; indeed, after her stepmother punished her by burning her stories, Dawn fled to the home of an aunt. After graduating from high school, Powell went to Lake Erie College, where she received her B.A. in 1918. That year she entered military service and moved to New York, where she remained, working in public relations and in advertising. In 1920, she married Joseph Roebuck Gousha, an executive with an advertising agency, by whom she had one son, Joseph Roebuck Gousha, Jr. Failing in her attempts to break into the theatrical world as a playwright, Powell began writing novels, publishing the first, *Whither*, in 1925. Over the next four decades, fifteen more were to appear, the early ones set in her native Ohio, most of the later ones in Greenwich Village, in what became her world, the small circle of writers, publishers, actors, producers, artists, and critics who were at the intellectual center of the nation. Still without being widely recognized, Dawn Powell died of cancer at St. Luke's Hospital in New York City on November 14, 1965.

Analysis

The primary purpose of a Powell novel is to describe a society. To do so, she brings a number of characters together, perhaps in an Ohio boarding-house, perhaps at a New York party or a bar. Then the characters seem to take over, as if they are determined to dramatize their own world. They act and interact, they talk, they boast, they scheme, they lie, and they confess to one another. To this extent, Powell's novels could be called realistic. They also, however, include an element of satire. It is primarily noticeable in the characters' inner deliberations, which Powell reveals to her readers in illuminating detail. The characters' confusion about facts, their muddled reasoning, and above all their clearly selfish motivations, reported with such painstaking care, leave the reader no doubt as to Powell's satiric intentions, which are further stressed in her occasional wry and witty comments.

Although Powell's first book, *Whither*, was set in New York City, all but one of the six novels published during the next six years were placed in the rural Midwest. These works introduce the themes that would dominate Powell's later work: the alienation of an individual from society, the frustration of the failing artist, the random nature of love, the limits of friendship, and above all the rule of money. Beginning with *Turn, Magic Wheel*, Powell wrote a series of seven novels to which Vidal refers as her "New York cycle." Most critics consider these novels to represent Powell's highest artistic achievement and, indeed, a unique contribution to American literature.

The third of these novels, *Angels on Toast,* illustrates Powell's approach. The world that she both summarizes and satirizes is defined in the first chapter of the book. The story begins with two businessmen, Jay Oliver and Lou Donovan, on the train from Chicago to New York. The self-absorption that marks most of Powell's characters is evident from the first. Their world is neither abstract nor cosmopolitan. At its simplest it is made up of their own bodies and their own clothes. Jay admires his own shoes, which he thinks reflect his polished personality, and his socks, which are so dazzling that he must mention how expensive they were. Lou contemplates and assesses his weight, his shoulders, then is delighted to tell Jay how much his shirt cost and to invite him to feel the material. For men so fascinated with the most trivial details about themselves, it is not surprising that both friendship and love are limited in depth. From the facile comment that Jay is his best friend, Lou soon has moved to the notion that Jay may know too much about him; indeed, it is Jay's company that is his best friend, not Jay himself, Lou muses. If Jay were replaced, the new man would become Lou's best friend. Lou's capacity for love is similarly limited by circumstances. For example, when he married above himself, he found it convenient to forget having been married before, and he is now worried because that ex-wife has turned up in Chicago. In a typical Powell passage, however, Lou congratulates himself because he has been faithful to his wife except for casual encounters in places where she would never go. Jay, on the other hand, is shockingly unfaithful, picking up his regular mistress on the train and taking her to New York with him. It is not adultery, but taking such chances, that Lou considers immoral.

Thus by re-creating conversations and by reporting her characters' thoughts, Dawn Powell reveals their attitudes and their values. Her satirical intention is clear, when she lets Lou congratulate himself for what are in fact very low moral standards; it is obvious that for him and his society, love and friendship will never stand in the way of making money.

In Powell's later novels, New York City itself might as well be listed as one of the characters. It is symbolic that the first chapter takes place on the way to New York, instead of on the way back to Chicago. In New York, the businessmen think, they can get away with anything. It is, of course, ironic that the city proves to be much smaller than the out-of-town visitors think it is; unfortunately, paths do cross, and wives do find out what is occurring.

In *Angels on Toast*, the compelling attraction of New York City is also dramatized in the attitude of an eccentric old lady who lives in a seedy hotel. When her daughter suggests that they both move to Connecticut, the idea is greeted with horror. Obviously, even a dingy hotel in New York is better than a mansion anywhere else. Actually, the old lady's real home is the hotel bar; its inhabitants are the only people she needs or wishes to know.

Except for the fact that Ebie Vane is a commercial artist, the conflict between the creator and his crass, indifferent world is not as important in *Angels on Toast* as it is in Powell's last three novels, in which the alienation of the artist from society is a major theme. The cohesiveness of New York's literary and theatrical world is suggested by the title of the first of these books, *The Locusts Have No King*. The quotation, which comes from the biblical Proverbs, emphasizes the idea that although there is no single leader among locusts, they seem to have a mysterious single direction. They move in hordes, and, it should be added, destructive hordes. It is such mindless human groups which can destroy the will and the hopes of an artist or, perhaps worse, turn an artist into a commercial success at the cost of creative integrity and personal relationships.

At the beginning of *The Locusts Have No King*, there seems to be no possibility that the protagonist, Frederick Olliver, a writer of scholarly books, will ever become successful enough to find his soul endangered. In contrast, his mistress Lyle Gaynor, a successful playwright, is a celebrity who knows every other celebrity in the literary world. Lyle is completely devoted to Frederick. Indeed, she would marry him except for the fact that she feels a duty to remain with her ill-tempered husband because he is an invalid. In order to help Frederick, Lyle includes him in every party she gives and arranges for him to be invited to every party she attends. Nevertheless, Frederick always feels that he is an alien in Lyle's world. In response, he voices his scorn of the successful, including his generous mistress. The fact that one lover is inside the magic circle and the other, outside, clearly imperils their relationship.

Powell's theme of alienation appears in three different typical situations. The first involves characters such as Frederick, who, though they are not new to New York, have simply not had enough success to be accepted. The second involves a young person who, like Jonathan Jaimison in *The Golden Spur* and like the young Dawn Powell herself in 1918, has recently arrived in New York City, usually from the Midwest, and must be initiated into its ways. Although the misunderstandings and mistakes of the innocent can be highly comic, they do not provide the occasions of satire that Powell sees in the third kind of alienation. Like all the great satirists, she delights in exposing the pretensions of characters who attempt to be accepted in a complex, cultivated society but who are too foolish to master its mannerisms or even its idiom.

An example of this kind of alienated character, who unlike the other types has no hope of being accepted as a result of eventual success or deliberate adaptation, is Dodo Brennan in *The Locusts Have No King*. Dodo has chosen to think of herself as a Southern belle, and she has come from Baltimore to conquer New York with cuteness. Unfortunately, her poses and her baby talk make her ludicrous. Although Frederick becomes involved with Dodo and introduces her into Lyle's circle, Dodo's vulgarity, her stupidity, and her inability to realize that her idiotic speeches have no resemblance to wit ensure her status as a permanent alien in the literary world.

In *The Locusts Have No King*, however, the theme of alienation is most important as it relates to the central love story. When by chance Frederick and Lyle reverse their places in society, when Lyle's fortunes decline and Frederick becomes a commercial success, ironically the psychological barriers to their union disappear. Unlike most of Powell's lovers, whose short-term entanglements are motivated by chance, lust, and ambition, Frederick and Lyle prove to be capable of profound attachment, which only grows stronger in the face of change.

Even though sexual liaisons are important in Powell's novels, the real action takes place not in bedrooms but in the living rooms and bars where her characters gather. Although the title of her next novel, *The Wicked Pavilion*, is taken from a reference to the Brighton Pavilion in England, Powell's pavilion is simply a New York café, where many of the characters from her preceding books reappear, now older but hardly wiser. The book is carefully crafted, with two plots that are intertwined, both of which depend upon frequent appearances in the Café Julien. One of them involves an incomplete love story. Haunted by the memory of his passion for a young woman whom he met at the café during the war, Rick Prescott has returned to search for her and for the happiness he believes that he somehow lost. In developing this plot, Powell again emphasizes the transitory nature of most human relationships, especially love, which despite lovers' illusions depends heavily on chance and on the imagination.

The second plot exposes the phoniness of the artistic world. When a painter dies, two of his unsuccessful fellow artists discover that they can make a large amount of money by forging works supposedly painted by him; their scheme is complicated, however, when they find that he is not dead but has pretended to die and is now profiting by the greatly increased value of his old paintings, as well as of the new ones he is producing, which he can market as lost masterpieces. It is evident that Powell is in sympathy with the artists, who on at least one occasion have thus triumphed over the commerciality of art dealers and the arrogant stupidity of art critics.

In Dawn Powell's final novel, *The Golden Spur*, it is not the artist but the innocent who triumphs over the glittering and corrupt world that Powell knew, loved, and satirized. Again, the title refers to a bar, but in this case the reference is not oblique. The Golden Spur is indeed the name of a bar that has a special significance to a young man from the Midwest, Jonathan Jaimison. In her youth, his mother, then Constance Birch, had come to New York as a real innocent, had fallen in love with the city and with one of its residents, and then, pregnant, had returned to Ohio to marry an unsuspecting flour salesman named John Jaimison. Now another innocent, Connie's son, has come to New York City. In his response to the city, he is like his mother. Within eighteen hours he is hopelessly in love with it. Unlike her, however, he is not destined to become a victim. As he seeks out the various men mentioned in the diaries, any of whom might possibly be his father, he finds that instead of being horrified at the prospect of scandal, they are all pleased. Even those who cannot remember Connie would like to talk themselves into the memory of an affair with her, which could have produced this appealing son. Yet the prospective son is less than enthusiastic about the various candidates, who, though they may be rich and famous, do not live up to the dream father who has appeared in his imagination.

Certainly, Powell is pointing out that reality rarely equals illusion. In this final book, however, there is a special significance in Jonathan's disenchantment. Like Dawn Powell herself, in her sixties at the time that *The Golden Spur* appeared, the people of the magic circle have aged, and the old New York is dead. At the end of *The Wicked Pavilion*, the Café Julien was torn down; at the end of *The Golden Spur*, an artist insists that the real money of the twenty-first century will be not in creation but in demolition. His ambition does not stop with seedy hotels and run-down cafés; he yearns to take the big ball to the Metropolitan Museum. Thus Powell's final book does not mark merely the end of a young man's dream; it commemorates the end of the world she knew.

In Robert van Gelder's book of interviews, *Writers and Writing* (1946), Dawn Powell answered the repeated criticism of her work, that she did not deal with significant people, by pointing out that most people have no real goals in life. The answer was that of a realist. Still, she might better have appealed to the standards of her genre. The satirist causes readers to laugh at people, not to revere them. In her latest and best novels, Dawn Powell points out the follies and the vices of New Yorkers like those she knew: the vulnerable or vulgar innocence of newcomers, the desperate need of the alien to become accepted, the misuse of reason to justify lust and ambition, the betrayal of love and friendship, and above all, the enslavement to greed. It is appropriate that Dawn Powell has had a revival. Certainly she has immortalized a society forever gone, but more important, she has created characters whose weaknesses are all too universally human.

Rosemary M. Canfield Reisman

Other major works
SHORT FICTION: *Sunday, Monday and Always*, 1952.
PLAYS: *Big Night*, 1933; *Jig Saw*, 1934.

Bibliography
Trilling, Diana. "Fiction in Review." *The Nation* 166 (May 29, 1948): 611-612. Trilling expresses the standard criticism of Powell: that she dealt with less than serious themes and that her characters were too unimportant to be

worthy of consideration. Her viewpoint is rebutted in Gore Vidal's essay, cited below.

Van Gelder, Robert. *Writers and Writing*. New York: Charles Scribner's Sons, 1946. This interview, dated November 3, 1940, focuses on the reason for Powell's small readership, which she believes has to do with the fact her work is satirical in nature. Powell comments in particular on her most recent work at the time, *Angels on Toast*.

Vidal, Gore. "Dawn Powell, the American Writer." *The New York Review of Books* 34 (November 5, 1987): 52-60. This essay, which also serves as the introduction to the Vintage Press editions of *Angels on Toast, The Golden Spur*, and *The Wicked Pavilion*, is perhaps the most important work of Powell criticism to date. In it, Vidal summarizes her life, suggests reasons for her obscurity, presents a chronological summary of her novels, and discusses her importance in American literature.

Wilson, Edmund. "Greenwich Village in the 50's." *The New Yorker* 38 (November 17, 1962): 233-236. A review of *The Golden Spur* by one of the literary giants who shared Powell's world. Wilson compares her genius to that of Anthony Powell, Evelyn Waugh, and Muriel Spark.

_____. *The Thirties: From Notebooks and Diaries of the Period*, edited by Leon Edel. New York: Farrar, Straus & Giroux, 1980. An excellent source, not only because of the references to Dawn Powell but also because it provides a full picture of her period. Edel's introduction is also illuminating. Illustrated.

J. F. POWERS

Born: Jacksonville, Illinois; July 8, 1917

Principal long fiction

Morte d'Urban, 1962; *Wheat That Springeth Green*, 1988.

Other literary forms

J. F. Powers is highly regarded for his prowess as a short-story writer. "Lions, Harts, Leaping Does" (1943), only his second story to be published, appeared in the O. Henry and Martha Foley anthologies in 1944. His first short-story collection, *Prince of Darkness and Other Stories*, was published by Doubleday & Company in 1947. (Random House issued this collection in 1979.) Doubleday & Company published his second collection of stories, *The Presence of Grace*, in 1956. In 1963, Time, Inc. published *Lions, Harts, Leaping Does and Other Stories*, a collection culled from Powers' first two books. His third collection, *Look How the Fish Live*, was published by Alfred A. Knopf in 1975. Powers' stories appeared first in magazines such as *Accent*, *Colliers*, *Commonweal*, *The Nation*, *Kenyon Review*, *Partisan Review*, and *The New Yorker*. Powers has also written reviews of poetry and fiction, autobiographical pieces, and articles dealing with social issues. His nonfiction, like most of his fiction, is often satirical in tone.

Achievements

Powers is to be numbered among those American writers—others include Katherine Anne Porter and J. D. Salinger—who have produced a relatively small body of work distinguished by meticulous craftsmanship. Powers has been praised by critics and fellow writers such as Alfred Kazin, William Gass, Thomas Merton, and Stanley Edgar Hyman; the Irish master of the short story, Frank O'Conner, judged Powers to be "among the greatest of living story tellers." When he has drawn negative critical response, it has often been for what is deemed to be his overly parochial concerns, his narrow focus on the world of the Catholic Church in America, and especially the clergy. In fact, Powers' narrow focus is a source of strength; he writes about what he knows best, and, like excellent writers everywhere, he discovers the universal in the particular. He has a permanent place in American literature as one of the most accomplished short-story writers of the twentieth century.

Biography

James Farl Powers was born in Jacksonville, Illinois, on July 8, 1917, to James Ansbury and Zella Routzong Powers. He is one of three children. His father was a manager for Swift and Company, and the family lived in comfortable circumstances. Jacksonville was a predominantly Protestant community, and that made the Catholic Powers family part of a minority.

In 1924, the Powerses moved to Rockford, Illinois, where they lived for seven years and where James attended public schools. After another move, to Quincy, Illinois, in 1931, Powers became a student at the Franciscan-run Quincy Academy, from which he was graduated in 1935. He then moved to Chicago, where, over the next eight years, he held various jobs: insurance salesman, clerk at Marshall Field, chauffeur, editor with Chicago Historical Records Survey, and clerk at Brentano's bookstore. From 1938 to 1940, he was taking night courses at Northwestern University. It was while he was working at Brentano's, in 1942, that he wrote his first story, "He Don't Plant Cotton," published the following year in *Accent* magazine. He was fired from Brentano's for refusing to buy war bonds.

In 1943, Powers experienced what J. V. Hagopian (*J. F. Powers*, 1968) describes as a religious crisis. Since moving to Chicago, he had become increasingly sensitive to social issues; the status of black Americans and war were two issues with which he was particularly concerned. His moral revulsion at the injustices to which blacks were subjected was tellingly expressed in such stories as "He Don't Plant Cotton" and "The Trouble." Powers became a pacifist in 1943. Arrested two weeks after he failed to report for induction, he was, after pleading not guilty and waiving trial by jury, sentenced to serve three years in Sandstone Federal Prison in Minnesota. He was paroled in late 1944, after serving thirteen months of his sentence. He then went to St. Paul and worked as a hospital orderly. In 1945, he met Elizabeth Alice Wahl at St. Benedict's College, St. Joseph's, Minnesota, and the following year they were married. She, like Powers, is a writer, and a good one. Powers was a resident at the Yaddo community in 1947, the year in which *Prince of Darkness and Other Stories*, his first collection of stories, was published. The book met with very favorable critical response. In 1948, Powers received grants from the Guggenheim Foundation and the National Institute of Arts and Letters, and taught at St. John's University of Collegeville, Minnesota. He continued teaching for several years, this time at Marquette University, and had another residency at Yaddo. Throughout the 1950's, Powers and his growing family (he has five children—Katherine, Mary, James, Hugh, and Jane) lived either in Minnesota or Ireland. In 1956, during which his second collection of stories, *The Presence of Grace*, was published, he taught at the University of Michigan. He has said that teaching was something he turned to out of need, when he ran out of money.

Powers' first novel, *Morte d'Urban*, was published by Doubleday & Company in 1962. It won the 1963 National Book Award and the Thermod Monsen Award, given by the Chicago critics for the best book written by a Midwesterner. Powers was writer-in-residence at Smith College between 1965 and 1966. His third collection of stories, *Look How the Fish Live*, appeared in 1975. His second novel, *Wheat That Springeth Green*, was published in

1988. Besides receiving grants from the National Institute of Arts and Letters, of which he is a member, and the Guggenheim Foundation, Powers has received Rockefeller Fellowships on three occasions. He now lives in his adopted state of Minnesota.

Analysis

J. F. Powers is an idealist; he is also a moralist. The two attitudes need not necessarily be incorporated in a single person, but they naturally combine when, as is the case with Powers, the ideal is perceived to be something which is not only to be admired but is also to be sought. The vision of the pure idealist tends to be illuminated chiefly by aesthetic considerations; a discrepancy between the ideal and the real is seen primarily as an artistic failure. For the idealist-moralist, on the other hand, the discrepancy between the ideal and the real, while it can profitably be seen in aesthetic terms, is essentially a matter of morality. To call Powers an idealist is not to say that he is a perfectionist. Falling short of the ideal is, for fallen human beings, to be expected; but to abandon the ideal, to give up the pursuit of perfection, is to fail morally. As a moralist, Powers has quite distinct notions of what constitutes good and evil, and the difference between them is sharp. His morality is based on Catholic theology.

Powers' "world," his equivalent of William Faulkner's Yoknapatawpha County, is the American Catholic Church, more particularly that Church as it manifests itself in the Midwest, more particularly still, the clergy of that Church. Unquestionably, Powers' best fiction is that written about Catholic priests. Choosing to write about priests was in itself an ingenious artistic ploy. The priest is by vocation, if not by disposition, an idealist, and therefore presents for an idealist-moralist an excellent focal point for examining the discrepancy between the ideal and the real. His characters are not drawn from the common people but from a kind of scaled-down aristocracy, people from whom readers would be justified in expecting more because more has been given them.

Some of the critical reaction that followed immediately upon the publication of *Morte d'Urban* was adverse. Perhaps because of the fact that certain chapters had previously been published individually as short stories, the judgment was made that the work lacked the unity of structure necessary for a novel and was only a gathering of loosely associated tales. Only the most superficial reading of the work could sustain a judgment of this sort, for the novel is possessed of remarkable unity of theme and structure. The chief unifying element in the novel is its main character, Father Urban Roche. Father Urban is presented as a very attractive character, but what is at work here is a peculiar kind of deceptive satire at which Powers excels. So attractive is Father Urban that the unwary reader might be led erroneously to conclude that the novel demonstrates the insensitivity of the powers-that-be within the Catholic

Church, treating in shabby fashion a man of Father Urban's talent and charm.

Morte d'Urban is essentially a comic novel, not only in the sense that it is funny, which it certainly is, but also, and more important, in the sense that it is the obverse of tragic. It is the story of a priest who, though by no means a bad man, is not manifesting in his life the type of goodness of which he is capable and, more pointedly, to which he is dedicated by vows. Father Urban is a Roman Catholic priest, but on the basis of the attitudes that dominate his consciousness and the behavior in which he engages, he is more appropriately identifiable as the all-American boy. He is George F. Babbitt with a Roman collar, always on the lookout for the ecclesiastical main chance. He is intelligent, imaginative, witty, well spoken, and possessed of a seemingly inexhaustible fund of energy. He is doubtless sincere in his conviction that the various projects to which he dedicates his talents are eminently worthwhile—that is, for the good of the Church and, ultimately, for the greater glory of God. Father Urban is an activist, and there is something almost intrinsically admirable in the activist, but he is a man for whom activity has become altogether too much. His "can do" attitude toward his vocation, which puts a premium on tangible results, has been nurtured over the years at the expense of his interior life. While ostensibly a man oriented toward the spiritual, he is in fact a materialist.

Father Urban is a member of the Order of St. Clement, the Clementines, of whom it has been said that their uniqueness consists in their being noted for nothing at all. He concurs in this cruel judgment, but if he belongs to a third-rate order, he takes consolation in the fact that he is its star, the scintillating exception in an organization composed, for the most part, of bland mediocrities. He behaves toward his confreres with *pro forma* charitableness, a disguise for condescension. He is in fact an accomplished preacher, and in much demand as a conductor of parish missions. When he is assigned to the Order's latest white elephant, then, a retreat house in rural Minnesota, his paranoid conviction that he is persecuted by his foolish superiors because they are jealous of his talents is only more firmly established. After a depressing first few months in his new assignment, and thanks to the reinvigorating experiences associated with his filling-in as pastor at a nearby parish, he regains his old gusto. His term as acting pastor of St. Monica's allows him to display with verve all his talents as a get-up-and-go priest, a cleric with zip who knows the right people to befriend and is always building for the future—a brisk optimist and a "bricks and mortar man" *par excellence*. When the priest for whom he is substituting dies suddenly (of a heart attack while vacationing in the Bahamas), Father Urban entertains the possibility that the bishop might appoint him as the permanent pastor of St. Monica's. He cleverly attempts to further his cause with the bishop, but to no avail. The appointment is given to another priest.

Father Urban, though disappointed, is not floored by this turn of events, for by this time, he has begun to see possibilities for the retreat house, St. Clement's Hill. With the financial backing of Billy Cosgrove, a wealthy Chicago layman and friend, he secures the permission of the Clementine Provincial Superior and the local bishop to build a nine-hole golf course at St. Clement's Hill. The idea behind the venture is to make the facility more attractive for the better sort of Catholic laymen, those who will not only come there to make a retreat but also leave behind them a generous donation. It would seem that Father Urban's characteristic *modus operandi* has stood him in good stead even in the backlands of Minnesota, but his streak of successes is put in jeopardy by the rumor that the bishop may take the retreat house away from the Clementine Order and turn it into a seminary for his diocese. The bishop visits St. Clement's Hill with a young priest of the diocese who is an expert golfer. They all take to the links together, and as the game progresses, it becomes evident to Father Urban that in his match with the young priest, the bishop's man, he has symbolically entered the lists and is involved in a trial of strength. Whatever might be the eventual fate of St. Clement's Hill, it becomes a point of honor for him that he win the golf match. Having made a nice approach shot to the final green, he is apparently on the verge of doing so when events are suddenly reversed: Father Urban is struck on the head and knocked unconscious by a golf ball hit by the bishop. This seemingly absurd incident marks the turning point of the novel.

After the accident on the golf course, as a result of which the bishop drops his plans to take over the retreat house, Father Urban's attitude toward life and toward his vocation slowly changes. His being felled by a golf ball, while not comparable to St. Paul's being knocked off his horse on the road to Damascus, precipitates a period of reassessment. During this period, Father Urban undergoes three trials, which are consonant with the Arthurian theme which is one of the informing elements of the novel. In one trial, he tries and fails to persuade Mrs. Thwaites, an elderly benefactress, with whom previously he had attempted to ingratiate himself, to restore to an innocent employee money which she had effectively stolen from her. His eyes are thus opened to the unpretty realities of Mrs. Thwaites's hypocrisy and stark avariciousness, which in the past he was inclined to overlook as supportable eccentricities. In the second trial, he goes on a fishing trip with his friend Billy Cosgrove, which results in the dissolution of the friendship. The experience proves to be painful but educative. He is made fully aware that Billy Cosgrove is not a noble human being. He is rich, yes, but he is also egotistical, childish, and pathologically cruel. In the third trial, Father Urban is put upon by Mrs. Thwaites's daughter, Sally Hopwood, rich, sophisticated, bored, and bereft of principles, who attempts to seduce him. She fails, but out of the ordeal, Father Urban comes to a new, and disturbing, consciousness of himself; he realizes that had he chosen to follow a vocation other than the priesthood, his outlook on life would not have been appreciably different from the one he entertains as a priest. He is brought to see that there is something fundamentally lacking in the quality of his priestly life.

The novel is brought to an abrupt and significant close after Father Urban is elected as the Provincial Superior of the Chicago Province of the Clementines. It is a position for which, when he was possessed of the consciousness of the "old man," he had often longed, as it would provide him with the power base to implement the kind of progressive reforms about which he had always dreamed. Here would be his chance to get the Clementines off dead-center, to shake them up, to move them toward becoming a first-rate order that had a reputation for gumption. Those who elect Father Urban to the post have in mind the type of man who can make the right kind of friends for the order, people such as Billy Cosgrove, people who have the money to make things happen. The Father Urban who moves back to Chicago from Minnesota to become Father Provincial, however, is a radically changed man. He has undergone a conversion.

Father Urban does not die physically, but as the title *Morte d'Urban* suggests, a death does take place. Father Urban dies to the kind of life, superficial and meretricious, to which he had devoted the better part of his days, and turns to a life which, though less flamboyant, is decidedly more promising.

J. F. Powers' long-awaited second novel, *Wheat That Springeth Green*, was published in 1988. Although it was nominated for a National Book Award shortly after its publication, that honor was to elude Powers this time around. Like its predecessor, *Morte d'Urban*, this second novel is primarily the story of a priest. In this case, the protagonist is one Father Joe Hackett, who is a member of the presbyterate of an unnamed diocese in Minnesota. The world of the novel is essentially the world of the Catholic Church. The novel might be described as a portrait of a modern priest, set against the background of a Church, as well as a larger society, which finds itself in a state of disorientation and turmoil.

The narrative covers the whole of Father Hackett's life, but equal time is not given to every stage. Most of the action of the novel takes place in the late 1960's, when the protagonist is in his forties. The reader is introduced to Joe Hackett when he is little more than a toddler, but even at so tender an age he comes across as someone with a penchant for easy egocentrism. One's next glimpse of him is as a boy of grade-school age, revealing two incongruous personality traits that seem to be permanent by the time he reaches adulthood—a scrappy competitiveness and a tendency to run and hide when the world is not going the way he wants it to go. Next Powers provides a brief look at Joe's adolescent years, the centerpiece of which is a set of rather fantastical sexual escapades with the girls next door. One suspects that this chapter is to be read as a parody of the adolescent imagination. In the following chapter, Joe is a young man in his early twenties; he has put his sinful ways behind him and is now a seminary student, preparing for the Catholic priesthood. He is an earnest seminarian, possessed of a considerable capacity to take himself with the utmost seriousness. This displays itself in odd behavior at times. For one who is an advanced student in theology, and apparently doing quite well in his studies, he nurtures comically crude and naïve notions concerning the nature and requirements of the spiritual life.

The reader next encounters Joe as a young priest. One watches, and is not terribly surprised, as his tenuously founded idealism begins to give way to a spiritless pragmatism. Discovering that the daily life of a priest is often composed of prosaic and undramatic demands, he loses his initial fervor. He makes accommodations. Slowly and subtly, he becomes worldly, although his worldliness is not something of which he himself is fully aware. In fact, he tends to interpret this worldliness as something positive: his own peculiar, and canny, brand of antiestablishmentarianism. An ominous accompaniment of this downward slide is a steady increase in his drinking. Joe is, indeed, in the incipient stages of alcoholism, which typically, he does not admit to himself.

The latter two-thirds of the novel takes place in the present, relative to the narrative. The year is 1968; Father Joe, now forty-four years old, is the comfortably established pastor of a well-to-do suburban parish. He fulfills his rather tightly circumscribed duties in a conscientious fashion and shows a lively alertness to the particulars of his situation. Significantly, he is guided by what has now become a conviction that his is the right way of doing things. He has developed a strong, although low-key, propensity to regard himself as somewhat the ecclesiastical "genuine article." On occasion, he seems to view himself as a lonely warrior for the right, engaged in constant battle on several fronts with several varieties of benighted bumblers and pretenders, both inside and outside the Church, by whom he is surrounded. By this time, he has become a habitual drinker, dependent upon alcohol to see him through the day. The novel ends abruptly, as if *in medias res*, after Father Joe seemingly undergoes a sort of conversion experience, which is as sudden as it is difficult to understand. In his final state, which is simply announced to the reader, Father Joe has given up drinking, as well as his suburban pastorate; he now ministers among the poor in the inner city. Somehow, the authenticity of this latest transformation is less than fully convincing. Has Father Joe finally found himself and his proper place in the Church and in the world, or is it but the stage to a further impetuous move?

It is possible to read *Wheat That Springeth Green* as an extended exercise in irony, the kind of thing one would expect from Powers. Clues to such a reading can be found, for example, in the parallels one can make between the objects of Father Joe's constant criticism and the patterns of his own behavior. He is an acute and relentless critic, in general, of the ways of the world, and, in particular, of certain ways and personality types to be found within the Church. Specifically, he has what comes close to being an obsessive concern for what he regards as the Church's preoccupation with money. He strives to present himself as the refreshing antithesis of the type of pastor who is absorbed with money, but it is debatable whether his own way of handling the finances of his parish does not in the end succeed in giving more, or at least as much, attention to money matters. Father Joe appears to have convinced himself that he is virtuously antimaterialistic because he is not concerned with "big bucks," but what the reader witnesses is a man whose daily concerns are taken up primarily with things material. Materialism is no less materialism for being low-budget. The point is that the demands of a genuine poverty of spirit do not seem to be key factors in Father Joe's life. In addition, Father Joe has a low tolerance for those among his fellow clerics whom he sees as mindless and unimaginative—not to say cowardly—functionaries, people with little or no understanding of the Church's mission and how a priest should be leading his life.

This attitude of Father Joe is in many respects commendable. Yet it loses much of its moral force when one considers that Father Joe himself scarcely comes across as a paragon of priestly virtue. He is not what would be identified as "pastoral" in his inclinations; he is anything but outgoing, and any thought to the continuing spiritual needs of his parishioners that he may have fails to manifest itself in his day-to-day activities. Moreover, he has a habit of confining himself to the immediate precincts of the rectory.

Father Joe's idea of a good pastor is all too easily reducible to the role of the faithful middle manager, someone who keeps regular office hours, makes sure the parish books are kept in the black, and maintains an eccentrically rigid control over the population of the parish school. In sum, it is difficult to see how Father Joe's interpretation of the proper duties of the conscientious priest stands as a marked improvement over the behavior he vigorously criticizes. Hence the irony.

Father Joe Hackett, then, is an intensely ordinary priest, a priest who is running on the outside of the track, and perhaps a bit behind the pack, but who has long since persuaded himself that all the while he has been sticking to the inside rail. He is certainly not a bad man. For that matter, neither is he mediocre. Nevertheless, he is possessed of a kind of ordinariness which can prove dangerous because of its penchant for mistaking moral limitations for real moral advantages. Be that as it may, Father Joe falls far short of qualifying as the great Midwestern hope of a confused and blundering Church.

Dennis Q. McInerny

Other major works

SHORT FICTION: *Prince of Darkness and Other Stories*, 1947; *The Presence of Grace*, 1956; *Lions, Harts, Leaping Does and Other Stories*, 1963; *Look How the Fish Live*, 1975.

Bibliography

Hagopian, John V. *J. F. Powers*. New York: Twayne, 1968. Apart from a collection of essays edited by Fallon Evans (1968) and a thesis accepted at the University of Minnesota in 1980, this book-length study of Powers is to date the only one available. Following the general plan of the American Authors series, the volume provides a useful, comprehensive account of Powers and his work. The critical analysis is thoughtful and reliable.

Henault, Marie. "The Saving of Father Urban." *America* 108 (March 2, 1963): 290-292. Within the space of merely a few pages, this article offers a crisp summation of salient features of *Morte D'Urban*, as well as some pointed interpretation. Henault argues for the success of the book precisely as a novel and shows how Powers uses satire and Arthurian material to effect his artistic purposes. Father Urban is to be seen as neither a Babbitt nor a pathetic antihero, but as a man who has seen the light and has changed his ways.

McInerny, Ralph. "The Darkness of J. F. Powers." *Crisis* 7 (March, 1989): 44-46. Novelist Ralph McInerny first discusses Powers' place and importance in modern fiction. He then provides a careful and revealing critique of *Wheat That Springeth Green*. He finds that though the novel is structurally weak, it nevertheless carries considerable force because of Powers' sheer verve as a writer.

Merton, Thomas. "*Morte D'Urban*: Two Celebrations." *Worship* 36 (November, 1962): 645-650. This article contains some astute insights into Powers' first novel, especially with respect to how it makes use of satire. Merton, himself a Catholic priest, has some particularly pertinent things to say about the protagonist of the novel, Father Urban. In all, Merton regards Powers' character as artistically successful.

Schmitz, Anthony. "The Alphabet God Uses." *Minnesota Monthly* (December, 1988): 35-39. In this lively and informative interview, Powers talks about his writing, as well as larger philosophical and religious issues. Especially revealing are his attitudes toward the Catholic Church. The article offers some interesting details concerning his biography.

REYNOLDS PRICE

Born: Macon, North Carolina; February 1, 1933

Principal long fiction

A Long and Happy Life, 1962; *A Generous Man*, 1966; *Love and Work*, 1968; *The Surface of Earth*, 1975; *The Source of Light*, 1981; *Kate Vaiden*, 1986; *Good Hearts*, 1988; *The Tongues of Angels*, 1990; *The Foreseeable Future: Three Long Stories*, 1991.

Other literary forms

Late Warning: Four Poems (1968), *Lessons Learned: Seven Poems* (1977), *Vital Provisions* (1982), and *The Laws of Ice* (1986) are collections of Reynolds Price's poetry. *The Names and Faces of Heroes* (1963) is an early collection of his short stories; it was followed by *Permanent Errors* (1970). *Things Themselves: Essays and Scenes* (1972) and *A Common Room: Essays 1954-1987* (1987) contain his most salient essays on writing. Among Price's retellings of biblical stories are *Presence and Absence: Versions from the Bible* (1973), *Oracles: Six Versions from the Bible* (1977), and *A Palpable God: Thirty Stories Translated from the Bible with an Essay on the Origins and Life of Narrative* (1978). His dramas include *Early Dark* (1977), *Private Contentment* (1984), and the teleplay *House Snake* (1986). Price's autobiography is *Clear Pictures: First Loves, First Guides* (1989).

Achievements

Focusing on a single region of North Carolina just south of the Virginia border, Reynolds Price has moved beyond the limitations one sometimes finds in regional writers and in his work has dealt with universal themes, particularly with those that concern original sin and free choice; biological determinism, particularly as it is reflected in heredity; and the meanings of and relationships between life and death. In Price's novels, children inherit the burden of sin passed on by their parents, and, try as they will, they cannot escape this burden. They have free will, they can make choices, but the choices they make are almost identical to the choices their progenitors have made before them, so they grow up to be like those who have spawned them, no matter how much they struggle to avoid such a resemblance.

Biography

Born on February 1, 1933, in the rural North Carolina town of Macon, the son of William Solomon and Elizabeth Rodwell Price, Edward Reynolds Price was a child of the Depression. Although because of the closeness of his family structure his welfare was not seriously threatened by it, the boy was aware of the social dislocations around him and had what his biographer, Constance Rooke, calls Dickensian terrors of abandonment and destitution. His parents, hard pressed economically, lost their house when the father could not raise a fifty-dollar mortgage payment.

Upon graduation from Needham-Broughten High School in Raleigh, Price became an English major at Duke University in 1951, where he came under the influence of William Blackburn, who taught creative writing. Through Blackburn, he met Eudora Welty, who respected his work and ten years later was instrumental in helping to get Price's first book, *A Long and Happy Life*, published.

Upon receiving the bachelor's degree from Duke, Price attended Merton College, University of Oxford, as a Rhodes Scholar; there he received the bachelor of letters degree in 1958. He returned to Duke University in that year as an assistant professor of English and, except for brief intervals, has taught there ever since. Since 1977, he has been James B. Duke Professor of English at that institution, where he regularly teaches courses in creative writing and on the poetry of John Milton.

Price, who has never been married, burst on the literary scene auspiciously when *Harper's Magazine* devoted the whole of its April, 1962, issue to printing *A Long and Happy Life*, which was being released in hardcover at about the same time. The critical reception of this first novel was enthusiastic and brought Price the prestigious Faulkner Foundation Award for a first novel.

In 1963, he visited England, and in the same year a collection of his short stories, *The Names and Faces of Heroes*, was released. This collection included "Michael Egerton," the short story that had first impressed Eudora Welty when she gave a reading at Duke in the early 1950's. The title story, told from the perspective of a young boy, is an especially sensitive study in point of view.

Price's second novel, *A Generous Man*, appeared in 1966 and focused on the Mustian family, as had his first book. The second book is a warm, rollicking story based on a hunt for a python named Death that has escaped from a snake show after being bitten by a dog diagnosed as rabid. The concept is openly allegorical, and Price drives home the allegory well while also presenting an extremely amusing story, with the hydrophobic python constituting the most outrageous phallic symbol in American literature. In 1977, Price produced a play, *Early Dark*, based on the Mustian cycle, and, in 1984, *Mustian: Two Novels and a Story* was issued, consisting of the first two novels and "The Chain of Love," a short story.

Love and Work and the loosely woven collection *Permanent Errors* both explore matters of heredity and its effect upon people. Neither received overwhelming praise, although they had support among some critics. Price, however, was busy with a much larger project, an ambitious saga of the Kendal-

Mayfield family through four generations. The first novel of this story, *The Surface of Earth*, was received with skepticism by some critics when it appeared in 1975, but few could deny the creative zeal it reflected. The second volume of the Kendal-Mayfield story was published in 1981 under the title *The Source of Light*, and it, too, received mixed reviews.

A turning point in Price's life came in 1984, when he was in the middle of writing *Kate Vaiden*. He was stricken with spinal cancer, and the surgery that saved his life also left him a paraplegic. Pain drove Price to seek the help of a psychiatrist who specialized in hypnosis, in the hope that hypnosis might be a key to controlling his pain. Little did he suspect that through hypnosis he would be put in touch with a distant past that he had not realized existed. Suddenly details of his earliest childhood and of his family surfaced. When *Kate Vaiden* was published in 1987, it was, because of these unexpected insights, a quite different novel from what Price had originally projected.

Price's hypnosis unlocked the memories from which his autobiography, *Clear Pictures: First Loves, First Guides*, published in 1989, evolved. *The Tongues of Angels*, a novel published in 1990, is also a product of Price's hypnotic communication with his past.

Although he is best known as a novelist, Price's short fiction is sensitively written and helps to give readers a balanced picture of his writing. His poetry, his retelling of biblical stories, and his dramas, while they are not consistently of the quality of his best novels, are all clearly the work of an author with a strong sense of what he is doing. His collections of essays include some extremely interesting insights into what Price is trying to accomplish philosophically and stylistically in his long fiction.

Analysis

Any reading of all Reynolds Price's novels quickly demonstrates that Price has, throughout his career as a novelist, been grappling with puzzling questions. Preeminent among these questions is the effect that families have on communities and on the broader societies outside the isolated communities that provide Price with his microcosms.

Price also harbored from his earliest memories questions about his mother and about his parents' relationship to each other. He seldom forgot that his mother almost died in bearing him and that she was left mutilated by his difficult birth. His later relationships with her were always colored by that recollection and by the feeling of guilt he had over it. The guilt of the child is reflected most clearly in *Kate Vaiden*, where Kate blames herself for an act that was as much out of her control as was Elizabeth's difficult confinement out of Reynolds' control.

Despite Kate's innocence of any blame, she continues to blame herself after her father murders her mother and then turns the gun on himself, and her entire adult life—indeed, her life from age eleven onward—is so profoundly impacted by that single event, which brought an end to her childhood innocence, that it takes her forty-five years to begin to come to grips with her problems in any effective way. *Kate Vaiden* does not end on any realistic note of hope or promise; rather, it ends with a large question mark. Through writing the novel, however, Price presumably enhanced his understanding of his mother, who, like Kate, was orphaned at an early age.

Price was working toward the solution of problems like those that *Kate Vaiden* poses in his earlier *Love and Work*, in which Thomas Eborn, like Price himself a novelist and a professor, is forced to examine his relationship to his mother and his parents' relationship to each other and to society when his mother dies unexpectedly. Tom has been a dutiful son; he has helped provide for his mother financially. Yet he is also a compulsive writer who husbands his time and guards it jealously, organizing his life in such a way that he will always be able to write.

Because of this dedication, he misses his mother's last telephone call; he is busy writing and will not talk with her. Shortly thereafter, she is dead. Price has created in this novel a story that uses place most effectively. Tom Eborn teaches in a Southern town not unlike Durham, North Carolina, where Price has spent his professional career. Tom has arranged his life to eliminate from it any unnecessary distractions, and in doing this he has excluded from it as well much human contact.

Tom's turf—completely his own—is his study, his inviolable space where he can be alone, where he can create. No one dare intrude upon it. His mother's unanticipated death, however, makes Tom realize the wrongness of isolating himself as fully as he has from humankind.

It is clear that one can find much of Reynolds Price in Tom Eborn. To make a simple equation between the two, however, would be fatuous and misleading. *Love and Work* is a novel, and although Price has said that a writer's experience and background have as much to do with writing fiction as has imagination, he also warns that writers slip in and out of autobiography, so that their novels cannot be read as accurate autobiographical statements.

One can profitably read *Love and Work* against Price's consciously constructed autobiography, *Clear Pictures: First Loves, First Guides*, and can find the correspondence between his life and Tom Eborn's. Such a comparison will show Price's departures from autobiographical revelation in this novel. The same caveat must be made for *Kate Vaiden*, which strongly reflects Price's background but which is far from an authentic autobiographical representation.

Price's consuming interest in the family as the fundamental unit of society is found in his first novel, *A Long and Happy Life*, and pervades his future writing. *A Long and Happy Life* and *A Generous Man*, along with several of Price's short stories and his novel, *Good Hearts*, have to do with the Mustian family, who live in Macon, North Carolina, the town on the Virginia border in which Price was born and reared. *A Long and Happy Life* revolves around the romance between twenty-year-old Rosacoke Mustian and her boyfriend of six years, Wesley Beavers, two years her senior.

Wesley motorcycles to his native Macon to visit Rosacoke whenever he can take a weekend away from the naval base in Norfolk, 130 miles to the northeast. Wesley is sexually experienced but Rosacoke is a virgin when the story opens in July. On a scorching day, Rosacoke rides on the back of Wesley's motorcycle to the black church from which her friend Mildred Sutton is to be buried. Mildred has died while giving birth to her child Sledge.

Wesley roars up to the church, deposits Rosacoke, and stays outside polishing his bike. The church moans in ecstasies of religious transport. One woman cries, "Sweet Jesus," and Wesley, hearing her cry, is transported to a sweaty bed in Norfolk, where one of his many women uttered an identical cry at a crucial point in their lovemaking.

Reminded of this, Wesley zooms off in a cloud of red dust so dry and thick that reading about it almost makes one want to wash it off. Wesley has to get ready for the afternoon, for the church picnic that he and Rosacoke will attend. Price's descriptions in this portion of the book are masterful and memorably comic, although the import of what is being communicated is deadly serious and universally significant.

At the church picnic, Wesley tries to seduce Rosacoke, but she resists him, as she always has in the past. The picnic itself is a jolly affair. As the picnickers are about to sit down to their meals, Uncle Simon discovers that his false teeth are missing. Those who have not already begun to consume their barbecued pork and Brunswick stew help Simon look for his teeth. Someone asks him when he last remembers having them.

Simon, after due deliberation, proclaims that he took them out while he was stirring the large kettle of Brunswick stew. With this revelation, all eating comes to an abrupt halt. Simon eventually finds his teeth—they were in his back pocket all along. Still, the eating never quite gets back to normal, because of the general uncertainty about where the lost denture was. It is vignettes like this that help Price to convey a deeply philosophical message to readers without immersing them in specialized terminology or in abstruse and abstract thinking.

In *A Generous Man*, published four years after *A Long and Happy Life*, Price goes back several years in time and writes about the Mustian family before Wesley Beavers was known to them. Rosacoke is only eleven years old during the action of the later novel. The basic concept of the book is so outrageous that it would have seemed completely ridiculous if not handled delicately and well.

This novel essentially takes up a young boy's coming of age. Milo, Rosacoke's fifteen-year-old brother, has just lost his virginity to Lois Provo, the girl who runs the snake show at the Warren County Fair. Years ago, Lois' mother was impregnated by a bounder, who proves to be Milo's cousin. Once the truth was known, he abandoned the woman, leaving her only her memories and his eighteen-foot python, Death, which still thrives.

Milo, the morning after his maiden voyage with Lois, wakens to find that his dog, Phillip, is ill. The family gathers for a trip to the alcoholic veterinarian, who promptly diagnoses the dog's illness as rabies. For reasons unrevealed, he neither confines the dog nor destroys it. Instead, he provides a muzzle, and the Mustians leave with their muzzled mutt to go to the fair.

Rato, the retarded son, takes the dog's muzzle off. Despite his retardation, Rato has known all along that the dog does not have rabies but is merely suffering from worms, a bit of information he keeps to himself, not wanting to put his knowledge of dogs and their maladies up against the vet's.

As it turns out, Phillip has a prejudice against snakes, and when he encounters Death, he attacks it. By the time the dust has settled, the dog, the snake, and the retarded Rato have disappeared into the woods. Sheriff Rooster Pomeroy, citing the dangers of having a hydrophobic snake abroad among the loblolly and kudzu, collects a posse, a group of men keen for excitement and camaraderie, to hunt down the missing boy, the dog, and, most urgently, the snake. Spirits are high, and liquor flows freely.

In the course of the hunt, Milo, unaccustomed to alcohol, gets drunk enough to wander out of the woods, straight to Pomeroy's house, where Mrs. Pomeroy has been left alone. Because the sheriff is impotent, Mrs. Pomeroy finds her sexual satisfaction wherever she can, and Milo looks very good to her. They end up in her bed, where, during their pillow talk, Milo learns that Mrs. Pomeroy's first sexual encounter was with his cousin, the same bounder who sired Lois and gave Death to her mother.

Despite his prurient intentions, Milo cannot complete his act because the doorbell rings, prompting him to bolt through the open window, carrying his clothing with him. He rejoins the unlikely search, and it is he who finds Death. The snake wraps itself around Milo, almost choking the life out of him, but ironically Sheriff Pomeroy comes to the rescue and defeats Death with a well-placed gunshot.

Soon Milo wants to resume his lovemaking with Lois, but she is unwilling, because their first encounter left her quite unsatisfied. She classifies Milo among those men who are takers rather than givers in love encounters, and she lets him know it. He promises to reform; in his second encounter with her, his performance is indeed altered. Thus the book's title: Milo has become a man, but, having learned that he must give as well as take, he must mature further to become a generous man.

Price's difficulties with the critics when he produced the first volume of the Kendal-Mayfield saga, *The Surface of Earth*, stemmed largely from an inability of many Northeastern critics to respond with understanding to a convoluted familial saga that had heavy biblical overtones, that had to do fundamentally with original sin, guilt, conflicted race relations, incestuous feelings, incredibly frequent suicides, and much that is a more common part of rural Southern experience than of urban Northern experience. Southern families like the two Price writes about in the Kendal-Mayfield novels are smothering families. Their members sometimes try to escape, but the magnetic pull back into the decaying bosom of the family is too strong for them to resist. In that respect, this saga is not unlike William Faulkner's *The Sound and the Fury* (1929), in which the Compsons can never escape their heredity and all that it has predestined for them.

It is significant that the family members in the Kendal-Mayfield saga (including those in *The Source of Light*, the sequel to *The Surface of Earth*) resemble one another so closely. Not only do they sound alike but, more tellingly, they also think alike and act alike from generation to generation. Readers become particularly aware of this because of the compression of the novels: a large time span is telescoped into a few hundred pages.

On a literal level, the events of the saga might seem unlikely; taken symbolically, they assume a broader and deeper meaning and a greater artistic plausibility. Perhaps reflection on the outrageous unreality of parts of *A Generous Man* can help readers to understand some of the quintessential symbolic elements of the two Kendal-Mayfield sagas. Such comparable sagas as the five novels that make up John Galsworthy's *The Forsyte Saga* (1922) or the three novels of Sigrid Undset's *Kristin Lavransdatter* (1920-1922) suffer from a similar sense of unreality if they are read without conscious consideration of their symbolic contexts.

A considerable amount of the symbolic content of Price's two Kendal-Mayfield novels can be found in the dream sequences that are integral to the books. There are more than twenty of them in the first novel, and these sequences serve many purposes beyond suggesting the subconscious state of the characters who have the dreams.

The beginning of the Kendal family history as Price reveals it in *The Surface of Earth* is Bedford Kendal's rendition to his children of their grandparents' tragedy. Their grandmother died in giving birth to their mother. Their grandfather, considering himself responsible for his wife's death, killed himself, leaving his newborn daughter (like Price's own mother) an orphan. Bedford, having married this orphan when she grew to adulthood, soon realized that she was consumed by guilt and that she had a strong aversion to sex, all tied up with the guilt she suffered at the thought of having, through her birth, killed her own mother and driven her father to suicide.

Bedford's children, hearing this story, build up their own guilt feelings and their own aversions to sex. His daughter Eva, the strongest student of thirty-two-year-old Latin teacher Forrest Mayfield, elopes with him. Forrest is looking for family ties and thinks that he has found them among the Kendals, who, on the surface, seem to be an enviable family. Yet his marrying Eva disrupts the family's delicate balance, so all that Forrest hopes for in the marriage is not available to him.

The title of book 1 in the novel, "Absolute Pleasures," seems to be both an irony and a warning. Eva has her absolute pleasure, her unremitting sexual release on her wedding night, but then guilt possesses her. She dreams an Electra dream of her father stretched out over her body, and she is never able to enjoy sex again. She passes on her sexual aversion to her children, suggesting to her son Rob that he masturbate rather than become ensnared in love relationships with women.

Forrest, meanwhile, has his own hereditary baggage to carry. Forrest and Eva, whose names, as Rooke notes, suggest something primal and essentially sexual, ironically are trapped by their pasts. Price emphasizes another theme on which he has dwelt before: marriage disrupts the family balance, but guilt over that disruption—at least among the Kendals and the Mayfields—in turn disrupts the marriage. The family and heredity are exacting taskmasters, and they are inescapable.

Eva, like many of Price's women, barely survives the birth of her son Rob, and in this difficult birth, which also severely threatens the life of the infant, one sees an entire cycle recurring. The mother, with her cargo of guilt about sex and about her mother's death in childbirth, has a difficult delivery that will increase her aversion to sex and that will impose upon her newborn child the same guilt with which she has lived. So has it always been with the Kendals; so presumably will it always be.

Eva and Forrest both settle for lives of frequent masturbation, and their masturbation fantasies are tied to their respective father and mother. Forrest, having abjured further sexual encounters with Eva, meditates on a poem by Gaius Valerius Catullus that has to do with ritual castration. He ultimately leaves Eva and makes a ritualized journey back to Bracey, his hometown, to live with his sister Hatt, a widow.

Book 2 of *The Surface of Earth*, the real heart of the novel, is the story of Eva and Forrest's son, Rob Mayfield, named for his paternal grandfather. Rob, now seventeen, is leaving the family nest, but the family surges within him. He has no more hope of leaving it than did any of the Kendals before him. There is no escape from either the biological heredity or the strong pull of memory and custom that families impose.

Rob, obsessed with Oedipal feelings since the onset of puberty, hopes that contact with other women will help him to overcome the shameful feelings that disturb his equilibrium. He tries to seduce his date for the senior prom, but she denies him, whereupon he sheds her. Like Milo in *A Generous Man*, his sexual thoughts are only of his own gratification, and his masturbation gives him an independence when he is rebuffed.

Rob contemplates suicide several times in his period of flight from the nest. He comes closest to it when he sees a clutch of boys shooting at a turtle, trying to kill it. The turtle comes to represent for Rob all the isolation and insensitivity that have plagued his recent life, that have brought him closer to suicide than ever in the past.

Rob seeks to overcome his problems by marrying Rachel, whose father manages a hotel, Panacea Springs, in Goshen. Not in love with Rachel, Rob wavers in his commitment to marry her, and he goes—as his father before him had gone to the first Rob—to his father for counsel. Forrest is now living in a heterodox arrangement with Polly, a woman with whom he makes love only ten times a year, fearing that more frequent contact would jeopardize what they have struggled to achieve. Having seen his father's relationship, Rob can now return to Rachel and marry her.

The dinner on the night before the wedding brings together all the elements of the family that Price needs to show to make his story work. In this evening of premarital celebration, the family history and all that it implies is made clear. That being done, the only task remaining to Price artistically is to kill Rachel off in childbirth, which he promptly does. Rachel dies giving birth to Hutch, whose story becomes the next portion of the saga.

The sequel to *The Surface of Earth* is a more optimistic book than its predecessor. It focuses on Hutch and on the aging and death of his father. In *The Source of Light*, both Hutch and Rob seem to have reached an accord in their lives, to have matured into acceptance of what seems for them inevitable. The pull of the family and the inevitability of their heredity are both still operative, but they are less oppressive than they were in the earlier book.

Throughout his writing, Price is concerned with showing that people cannot outrun their past. Price's characters are dots on a long, seemingly infinite continuum, and the continuum assumes a life of its own. It is like a steadily flowing river that moves unrelentingly toward the sea. Anything in it that tries to swim upstream is destined to defeat. Even the strongest of swimmers, the ones who make a little progress against the inevitable flow, will be caught ultimately by the flow and swept along with it.

Underlying this theme of the strength of the family and the inability of people to resist their heredities is a pervasive theme of guilt, all of it tied up with pleasure, as manifested by sex, versus death or mutilation, as represented by the childbirth catastrophes of many of Price's characters.

Price's intimate and sensitive knowledge of Southern rural life enables him to write some of the most accurate and memorable descriptions in print of the locale in which most of his stories are set. He has grasped the speech rhythms, vocabulary, and syntax of northern North Carolina with an authenticity that remains consistent throughout his novels and stories, as do the unshakably consistent points of view of his characters.

R. Baird Shuman

Other major works

SHORT FICTION: *The Names and Faces of Heroes*, 1963; *Permanent Errors*, 1970.

PLAYS: *Early Dark*, 1977; *Private Contentment*, 1984; *House Snake*, 1986 (teleplay).

POETRY: *Late Warning: Four Poems*, 1968; *Lessons Learned: Seven Poems*, 1977; *Nine Mysteries (Four Joyful, Four Sorrowful, One Glorious)*, 1979; *Vital Provisions*, 1982; *The Laws of Ice*, 1986.

NONFICTION: *Things Themselves: Essays and Scenes*, 1972; *A Common Room: Essays 1954-1987*, 1987; *Clear Pictures: First Loves, First Guides*, 1989.

TRANSLATIONS: *Presence and Absence: Versions from the Bible*, 1973; *Oracles: Six Versions from the Bible*, 1977; *A Palpable God: Thirty Stories Translated from the Bible with an Essay on the Origins and Life of Narrative*, 1978.

Bibliography

Brown, Rosellen. "Travels with a Dangerous Woman." *The New York Times Book Review*, June 29, 1981, 40-41. Brown's review of *The Source of Light* gives a good overview of Price's thinking and writing, successfully relating this novel to the corpus of his work. Patterns relating to the family are shown to recur in Price's writing. *The Source of Light* can be seen as an early step in the direction of *Kate Vaiden*.

Kreyling, Michael. "Reynolds Price." In *The History of Southern Literature*, edited by Louis D. Rubin et al. Baton Rouge: Louisiana State University Press, 1985. Although this article is brief, it is easily accessible and does much to update the earlier sources about Price. It appeared too early to deal with his post-hypnotic years and with such books as *Kate Vaiden* and *Good Hearts*, but it is a fresh point of view clearly expressed.

Oates, Joyce Carol. "Portrait of the Artist as Son, Lover, and Elegist." *The New York Times Book Review*, April 26, 1981, 3, 30. Despite this article's brevity, it does a fine job of placing Price's work in perspective as that of a regional writer whose interests far exceed the region about which he is writing. Oates understands the central role family plays in Price's entire view of life.

Price, Reynolds. "A Conversation with Reynolds Price." Interview by Wallace Kaufman. *Shenandoah* 17 (Summer, 1966): 3-25. The most important early interview with Price, and one of the most extensive. It is reproduced in its entirety under the title "Notice, I'm Still Smiling," in *Kite Flying and Other Irrational Acts*, edited by John Carr (Baton Rouge: Louisiana State University Press, 1972). Kaufman has excellent insights into Price's Southernness but realizes that his writing goes far beyond regionalism.

_____. "Reynolds Price on Writing." Interview by Ashby Bland Crowder. *Southern Review* 22 (Spring, 1986): 329-341. Anyone interested in

Price as a stylist must read this interview, for it is the best brief treatment in print of how Price approaches his writing, both physically and philosophically. Crowder is an excellent interviewer. The piece is easily accessible to the reader not overly familiar with Price's work.

Rooke, Constance. *Reynolds Price*. Boston: Twayne, 1983. The only full-length treatment of Price. Despite its excellent coverage and intelligent analysis, it is badly dated because some of Price's most interesting work came after his hypnosis in 1984. One hopes that Rooke will bring out a revised edition or that some other scholar will do a solid analytical study of this author whose versatility continues to amaze and whose command of his major medium has not waned.

Sadler, Lynn Veach. "Reynolds Price and Religion: The 'Almost Blindingly Lucid' Palpable World." *Southern Quarterly* 26 (Winter, 1988): 1-11. Religion, both traditional and nontraditional, plays a fundamental part in Price's novels, and this article intelligently assesses some of his central religious beliefs, partly as shown through his translated biblical stories but also as they are revealed in some of his other work.

J. B. PRIESTLEY

Born: Bradford, England; September 13, 1894
Died: Stratford-Upon-Avon, England; August 14, 1984

Principal long fiction

Adam in Moonshine, 1927; *Benighted*, 1927; *The Good Companions*, 1929; *Farthing Hall*, 1929 (with Hugh Walpole); *Angel Pavement*, 1930; *Faraway*, 1932; *I'll Tell You Everything*, 1933 (with George Bullett); *Wonder Hero*, 1933; *They Walk in the City: The Lovers in the Stone Forest*, 1936; *The Doomsday Men: An Adventure*, 1938; *Let the People Sing*, 1939; *Blackout in Gretley: A Story of—and for—Wartime*, 1942; *Daylight on Saturday: A Novel About an Aircraft Factory*, 1943; *Three Men in New Suits*, 1945; *Bright Day*, 1946; *Jenny Villiers: A Story of the Theatre*, 1947; *Festival at Farbridge*, 1951 (published in the United States as *Festival*); *Low Notes on a High Level: A Frolic*, 1954; *The Magicians*, 1954; *Saturn over the Water: An Account of His Adventures in London, South America, and Australia by Tim Bedford, Painter; Edited with Some Preliminary and Concluding Remarks by Henry Sulgrave and Here Presented to the Reading Public*, 1961; *The Thirty-first of June: A Tale of True Love, Enterprise, and Progress in the Arthurian and ad-Atomic Ages*, 1961; *The Shape of Sleep: A Topical Tale*, 1962; *Sir Michael and Sir George: A Tale of COMSA and DISCUS and the New Elizabethans*, 1964 (also known as *Sir Michael and Sir George: A Comedy of New Elizabethans*); *Lost Empires: Being Richard Herncastle's Account of His Life on the Variety Stage from November, 1913, to August, 1914, Together with a Prologue and Epilogue*, 1965; *Salt Is Leaving*, 1966; *It's an Old Country*, 1967; *The Image Men: Out of Town and London End*, 1968; *The Carfitt Crisis*, 1975; *Found, Lost, Found: Or, The English Way of Life*, 1976; *My Three Favorite Novels*, 1978.

Other literary forms

In addition to the nearly thirty novels that he published after *Adam in Moonshine* in 1927, J. B. Priestley wrote approximately fifty plays, upon which his future reputation will largely depend. These include such memorable works as *Dangerous Corner* (1932), *Eden End* (1934), *Time and the Conways* (1937), *An Inspector Calls* (1945), *The Linden Tree* (1948), and *The Scandalous Affair of Mr. Kettle and Mrs. Moon* (1956). He also collaborated with Iris Murdoch on the successful stage adaptation of her novel *A Severed Head* (1964).

There is, besides, a long list of impressive works which characterize Priestley as the twentieth century equivalent of an eighteenth century man of letters, a term he professed to despise. This list includes accounts of his travels both in England and abroad, the best of these being *English Journey* (1934), an account of English life during the Depression; *Russian Journey* (1946); and *Journey down a Rainbow* (1955), written in collaboration with Jacquetta Hawkes. Priestley produced several books of reminiscence and recollection, which include *Rain upon Godshill* (1939), *Margin Released* (1962), and *Instead of the Trees* (1977). His literary criticism includes studies of George Meredith, Charles Dickens, and Anton Chekhov; and his familiar essays, thought by many to be among his finest works, are represented in the volume entitled *Essays of Five Decades* (1969), and by *Postscripts* (1940), his broadcasts in support of England at war. Priestley created several picture books of social criticism such as *The Prince of Pleasure and His Regency, 1811-1820* (1969), *The Edwardians* (1970), and *Victoria's Heyday* (1972), and his far-reaching historical surveys detail an idiosyncratic view of man in time: *Literature and Western Man* (1960) and *Man and Time* (1964). Priestley's short-story collections include *Going Up* (1950) and *The Other Place and Other Stories of the Same Sort* (1953).

As this list indicates, no aspect of modern life escaped Priestley's scrutiny, and no genre was left untried. In a long and prestigious career, he earned for himself a secure place in the annals of literature.

Achievements

Although Priestley's accomplishments in the theater may prove more significant than his work in the novel, perhaps because of his experimentation within the dramatic genre, his fiction has nevertheless secured for him a high place in contemporary literature; it has been read and cherished by a large and very appreciative audience. *The Good Companions*, a runaway best-seller in 1929, allowed Priestley to turn his attention from journalism and the novel to the theater in the 1930's, but he kept returning to the novel form throughout his career.

Priestley produced no novel that equals James Joyce's *Ulysses* (1922) in scope or intellectual subtlety, no novel as prophetic as D. H. Lawrence's *The Rainbow* (1915), no novel illustrative of the intuitive faculty equal to Virginia Woolf's *To the Lighthouse* (1927), or of ethical concern equal to Joseph Conrad's *The Secret Agent* (1907) or William Faulkner's *Light in August* (1932). His place on the scale of literary achievement may be lower than theirs, but his audience has been, by and large, greater. Priestley aimed for and caught a popular audience that remained loyal to him through five decades of writing. His novels and plays have been widely translated and acted, most notably in the Soviet Union. His craft in the novel genre shows the influence of Charles Dickens, of the English Romantics, especially of William Wordsworth and William Hazlitt, and of the English music hall and its traditions. Priestley himself made no great claims for his fiction, beyond good-naturedly protesting once or twice that there is more to it than meets the top-speed reviewer's eye. His finest novel, *Bright Day*, however, earned general

critical approval when it was published in 1946, and merited the praise of
Carl Jung, who found its theme consonant with his notion of the oneness of
all men.

Biography

John Boynton Priestley was born in Bradford, Yorkshire, on September 13,
1894. His mother died soon after his birth, and he was reared by a kind and
loving stepmother. His father Jonathan was a schoolmaster whom Priestley
has characterized in the autobiographical *Margin Released* as the man Socialists have in mind when they write about Socialists.

Bradford, in Priestley's early years, offered much to feed a romantic boy's
imagination: theater, the music halls, a playgoer's society, an arts club, the
concert stage, a busy market street, and a grand-scale arcade called the Swan.
A tram ride away were the Yorkshire Dales and moors. As a young man,
Priestley worked in a wool office, writing poetry and short stories into handmade notebooks. An important early influence was Richard Pendlebury, his
English master. Priestley later observed that Bradford and its environs did
more for his education than did Cambridge University, which he attended
years later.

In 1915, Priestley enlisted in the army. He was sent to France, invalided
back to England after being wounded, and then sent back to France. Significantly, his experience of war does not figure explicitly in any fictional piece,
with the single exception of a haunting short story entitled *The Town Major of
Miraucourt* (1930). Priestley's entire creative output may, however, have been
an attempt to put war and its ravages into a long-range context, a notion that
pervades his *Postscripts* broadcasts for the British Broadcasting Corporation
(BBC) during World War II. At the end of his army service, Priestley went to
Cambridge, where he studied, between 1919 and 1922, literature, history,
and political theory. His first book, *Brief Diversions* (1922), received good reviews but did not sell.

Leaving Cambridge for London and the precarious life of a journalist,
Priestley worked for J. C. Squire and the *London Mercury*, for the *Daily
News*, and for the Bodley Head Press. Meanwhile, he published critical books
on George Meredith, Thomas Love Peacock, and modern literature. His first
novel, *Adam in Moonshine*, appeared in 1927. Shortly thereafter, Hugh Walpole offered to collaborate with Priestley on a novel called *Farthing Hall* in
order to give the younger writer a much-needed publisher's advance so that
he could continue his work. In 1929, *The Good Companions* appeared, and
Priestley was fully embarked on a long and distinguished career.

Priestley was married three times; his first marriage, to Pat Tempest, came
in 1919. A year after her death, in 1925, he married Mary Holland Wyndham
Lewis, from whom he was divorced in 1952. The two marriages produced
four daughters and a son. In 1953, he married the distinguished anthropolo-

gist Jacquetta Hawkes. During his adult life, Priestley resided in London, on the Isle of Wight, and in Alveston, just outside Stratford-upon-Avon. He traveled widely, frequently using his journeys as background for his novels and plays. During World War II, he and his wife ran a hostel for evacuated children; after the war he campaigned vigorously for nuclear disarmament. He served as a UNESCO delegate and on the board of the National Theatre. He refused a knighthood and a life-peerage but did, in 1977, accept membership in the Order of Merit. In 1973, he happily accepted conferment of the Freedom of the City from his native Bradford.

Priestley did not retire from his writing work until well after he turned eighty. He died in 1984, one month shy of his ninetieth birthday.

Analysis

In his novels J. B. Priestley largely portrays a romantic view of life. His focus is primarily England and the English national character, and on those aspects of man that ennoble and spiritualize him. Yet, there is a no-nonsense view of life portrayed in his fiction; hard work, dedication to ideals, willingness to risk all in a good cause are themes which figure prominently. At times, the darker aspects of humanity becloud this gruff but kindly Yorkshireman's generally sunny attitudes. Ultimately, life in Priestley's fictional universe is good, provided the individual is permitted to discover his potential. In politics, this attitude reduces to what Priestley has called "Liberal Socialism." For Priestley, too much government is not good for the individual.

Romanticism largely dictated characterization in Priestley's novels, and his most valid psychological portraits are of individuals who are aware of themselves as enchanted and enchanting. These characters are usually portrayed as questers. It is Priestley's symbolic characters, however, who are the most forcefully portrayed, occasionally as god-figures, occasionally as devil-figures, but mostly as organizers—as stage-managers, impresarios, factory owners, butlers. Priestley's female characters fall generally into roles as ingenues or anima-figures. There are, however, noteworthy exceptions, specifically Freda Pinnel in *Daylight on Saturday*.

It is primarily through the presentation of his organizers that Priestley's chief plot device emerges: the common cause. A group of disparate characters are assembled and organized into a common endeavor; democratic action follows as a consequence. "Liberal democracy. Expensive and elaborate, but best in the end," says a choric figure in *Festival at Farbridge*, echoing one of his author's deepest convictions.

A romantic view of man in space and time also dictated the kind of novels that Priestley wrote. His fiction falls easily into three main categories. The first is the seriously conceived and carefully structured novel, in which symbolism and consistent imagery figure as aspects of craft. The best of this group are *Angel Pavement, Bright Day*, and *It's an Old Country*. The second category can be termed the frolic or escapade. This group includes *The Good Companions, Festival at Farbridge*, and the delightful *Sir Michael and Sir George*. The third category is the thriller or entertainment, which includes such science-fiction works as *The Doomsday Men* and *Saturn over the Water* as well as the detective story *Salt Is Leaving*. Priestley's favorite novel, and his longest, *The Image Men*, published in two volumes in 1968 and as one in 1969, incorporates these three categories within a controlled and incisive satirical mode.

In many of his works, but more so in his plays than in his fiction, Priestley dramatized a theory concerning the nature of time and experience which derived from his understanding of J. W. Dunne's *An Experiment with Time* (1927) and *The Serial Universe* (1931) and P. D. Ouspensky's *A New Model of the Universe* (1931). Briefly stated, this time theory, most explicit in *The Magicians*, a gothic tale which presents Priestley's characterizations of the Wandering Jew, and *Jenny Villiers*, originally written as a play for the Bristol Old Vic, proposes a means of transcendence. Priestley believed that Dunne's Serialism— "we observe something, and we are conscious of our observation . . . and we are conscious of the observation of the observation, and so forth"—permitted him to deal with character "creatively." For the ordinary individual, to "Observer One," the fourth dimension appears as time. The self within dreams becomes "Observer Two," to whom the fifth dimension appears as time. Unlike the three-dimensional outlook of Observer One, Observer Two's four-dimensional outlook enables him to receive images from coexisting past and future times. From Ouspensky, Priestley refined the notion that time, like space, has three dimensions; these three dimensions, however, can be regarded as a continuation of the dimensions of space. Wavelike and spiral, time provides for eternal recurrence, but a recurrence not to be confused with Friedrich Nietzsche's "eternal retour," with reincarnation, or with the Bergsonian *durée*. Ouspensky provided Priestley with the possibility of re-creation—that is, of intervention in space and time through an inner development of self. In other words, self-conscious awareness of self in past time can re-create the past in the present; sympathetic re-creation of self and others in what Priestley terms "time alive" can give new meaning to the present and shape the future. For Priestley, the seer—whether he be a painter or a musician, or the organizer of a festival or of a traveling group of entertainers, or even a butler in a country house—by looking creatively into the past, ameliorates the present and shapes a brighter future. Consequently, the organizer is Priestley's most forceful and symbolic character, and the thematic purpose of his novels depends upon an understanding of this character's motives.

Priestley's first successful novel, *The Good Companions*, presents a cozy fairy tale against an essentially realistic background, the English music halls of the 1920's. A determined spinster, Elizabeth Trant, organizes a down-and-out group of entertainers who have called themselves the Dinky Doos into a successful group renamed the Good Companions. The adventures of these troupers on the road and on the boards provide the novel with its zest and comedy.

Angel Pavement is in some ways a departure from this earlier work inasmuch as its tone appears dark and ominous. In *Angel Pavement*, the organizer is not a cheerful woman of thirty-seven giving herself a holiday on the roads as an impresario, but a balding, middle-aged adventurer named Golspie. "A thick figure of a man but now slow and heavy," Golspie enters the London firm of Twigg and Dersingham, dealers in wood veneers, and breathes new life into the business in a period of economic depression. With his only commitment being his daughter Lena, Golspie seems at first the firm's savior, for he provides a supply of veneer from the Baltic at half the domestic price. Perhaps because he and his daughter are rejected by the more polite segments of London society, Golspie feels it unnecessary to play fair with his employers. Eventually, he ruins Twigg and Dersingham, putting the employees out of work. At the novel's end, he and Lena leave London for South America and new adventure.

What most distinguishes *Angel Pavement* is its portrayal of the city, London, in the midst of the Depression, and of those who people it. Lilian Matfield, the head secretary, is fascinated by Golspie but refuses to accept the life of adventure he offers her, and Henry Smeeth, the bookkeeper, accepts a raise in salary, only to discover that once Golspie has abandoned Twigg and Dersingham, the company is bankrupt and he is out of work. The streets, the offices, the pubs, the tobacco stands, the amusements, all combine to present a view of human enervation and despair. A confidence man but not exactly a charlatan, Golspie locks the novel to a seemingly pessimistic view. Despite the enervation and apathy portrayed, Golspie offers freedom. Through his sinister organizer, Priestley portrays the life of romance that lies beneath the ordinary. What *Angel Pavement* finally achieves is a startling view of the modern metropolis as a prison from which only the romantic can escape.

One of his own favorite works, Priestley's *Bright Day* has been justly admired by critics and readers alike. Its uniqueness lies not so much in its dexterous use of such novelistic techniques as the time-shift and memory digression as in the way it looks behind and beyond its immediate focus into that sense of race and identity all men share. Although the novel deals with time, Priestley here shows a greater indebtedness to Henri Bergson and Marcel Proust than he does to Ouspensky and Dunne.

Music, specifically a Franz Schubert trio, returns a middle-aged screenwriter, Gregory Dawson, the narrator, who has taken refuge from his unhappy life in a genteel hotel in Cornwall, to a memory of youth and joy. An old couple reminds him of the boy of eighteen he was when he fell in love with a family called Alington in Bruddersford, a wool-producing northern town. The

Alingtons, charming and gracious, had sentimentally attached the young Gregory to themselves and had introduced the would-be writer to their world, which he had seen as one of grace and beauty. Ironically, the old couple who trigger the middle-aged Dawson's memories are in fact the Eleanor and Malcolm Nixey who had opportunistically intruded on his youthful idyll and brought an end to the prosperous wool business on which the Alingtons and their gracious world depended, and to Gregory's idealism as well.

In *Bright Day*, Priestley, concerned with a rite of passage, presents Gregory's initiation into a world of greed and suspicion, of appearance and falsehood; his is in fact an initiation into the modern world, and the novel symbolically spans the period of the two world wars. In the course of reconstructing the past, Gregory comes to terms with himself in the present, and it is his recognition of self in time that makes a commitment to the future possible for him. This liberation is confirmed by the stunning revelation made to him by Laura Bradshaw, who had also known the Alingtons, that Joan Alington in a jealous rage had pushed her sister Eva to her death from a cliff. The cancer of destruction had been in the Alingtons themselves; the Nixeys had merely served as catalysts.

Although Gregory Dawson is a quester for truth through self-knowledge, he is much more than a symbolic character. His psychological validity makes his growth in the course of the novel persuasive and compelling. The rediscovery of his romantic self in the present time of the novel is the rediscovery of a moment of beauty that had lain dormant in the rich soil of his memory. Many of Priestley's novels largely describe romance; *Bright Day* recreates its essence, as does Evelyn Waugh's *Brideshead Revisited* (1945), with which it has much in common.

Published in 1965 and representative of the novels Priestley produced in the later stages of his career, *Lost Empires* is in some ways a return to the world of *The Good Companions*, employing as it does the music hall as background. Unlike *The Good Companions*, however, whose chief interest was the high jinks of the troupers on the road, the theater serves here as a metaphor for the theme of appearance and reality and allows Priestley to allegorize loosely the politics of a world destined for war.

The protagonist, Dick Herncastle, one of Priestley's romantic questers here presented as an artist, is contrasted to his uncle, Nick Ollanton, the organizer, who is portrayed as a magician or mesmerizer. Ollanton and his "turn" allegorize the political activist and his propaganda techniques as he bends men to his will, much as does Thomas Mann's Cipolla in "Mario and the Magician." A time-perspective on Ollanton's influence on young Dick, who works as his assistant, is presented by means of a deftly presented prologue and epilogue, which encompass the action proper of the novel, set in the period of World War I. The main action ends with Dick succumbing to the illusion of a better world after the end of the war, and with Ollanton himself leaving the Old World for the United States, revealing his bag of tricks as a private escape from the "bloody mincing machine" of global war. There, he will manufacture machine-gun sights for warplanes. The novel proper, however, ends with the account in the prologue of Dick's return from the war and his successful career as a watercolorist, an illusionist of another sort.

The charm of *Lost Empires* goes well beyond its symbolic dimension; it lies chiefly in the presentations of the performers and the turns they perform on the boards. The juggler Ricardo, the comedian Beamish, the ballad singer Lily Farrish, and many others add to the plot and charm of the novel. That they are logically placed within the melodramatic and symbolic structure of the novel is simply another testimony to the skill of their author.

A. A. DeVitis

Other major works

SHORT FICTION: *The Town Major of Miraucourt*, 1930; *Going Up: Stories and Sketches*, 1950; *The Other Place and Other Stories of the Same Sort*, 1953; *The Carfitt Crisis and Two Other Stories*, 197*f*

PLAYS: *The Good Companions*, 1931 (adaptation of his novel, with Edward Knoblock); *Dangerous Corner*, 1932; *The Roundabout*, 1932; *Laburnum Grove*, 1933; *Eden End*, 1934; *Cornelius*, 1935; *Duet in Floodlight*, 1935; *Bees on the Boat Deck*, 1936; *Spring Tide*, 1936 (with George Billam); *People at Sea*, 1937; *Time and the Conways*, 1937; *I Have Been Here Before*, 1937; *Music at Night*, 1938; *Mystery at Greenfingers*, 1938; *When We Are Married*, 1938; *Johnson over Jordan*, 1939; *The Long Mirror*, 1940; *Goodnight, Children*, 1942; *They Came to a City*, 1943; *Desert Highway*, 1944; *The Golden Fleece*, 1944; *How Are They at Home?*, 1944; *An Inspector Calls*, 1946; *Ever Since Paradise*, 1946; *The Linden Tree*, 1947; *The Rose and Crown*, 1947 (one act); *The High Toby*, 1948 (for puppet theater); *Home Is Tomorrow*, 1948; *The Plays of J. B. Priestley*, 1948-1950 (3 volumes); *Summer Day's Dream*, 1949; *Bright Shadow*, 1950; *Seven Plays of J. B. Priestley*, 1950; *Dragon's Mouth*, 1952 (with Jacquetta Hawkes); *Treasure on Pelican*, 1952; *Mother's Day*, 1953 (one act); *Private Rooms*, 1953 (one act); *Try It Again*, 1953 (one act); *A Glass of Bitter*, 1954 (one act); *The White Countess*, 1954 (with Hawkes); *The Scandalous Affair of Mr. Kettle and Mrs. Moon*, 1955; *These Our Actors*, 1956; *The Glass Cage*, 1957; *The Pavilion of Masks*, 1963; *A Severed Head*, 1963 (with Iris Murdoch; adaptation of Murdoch's novel).

SCREENPLAY: *Last Holiday*, 1950.

POETRY: *The Chapman of Rhymes*, 1918.

NONFICTION: *Brief Diversions: Being Tales, Travesties, and Epigrams*, 1922; *Papers from Lilliput*, 1922; *I for One*, 1923; *Figures in Modern Literature*, 1924; *Essayist Past and Present: A Selection of English Essays*, 1925 (edited); *Fools and Philosophers: A Gallery of Comic Figures from English Literature*, 1925 (published in the United States as *The English Comic Characters*); *Tom Moore's Diary: A Selection*, 1925 (edited); *The Book of Bodley Head Verse*, 1926 (edited); *George Meredith*, 1926; *Talking: An Essay*, 1926; *The English Novel*, 1927, 1935, 1974; *Open House: A Book of Essays*, 1927; *Thomas Love Peacock*, 1927; *Too Many People and Other Reflections*, 1928; *Apes and Angels: A Book of Essays*, 1928; *The Balconinny and Other Essays*, 1929 (published in the United States as *The Balconinny*, 1931); *English Humour*, 1929, 1976; *The Female Spectator: Selections from Mrs. Eliza Heywood's Periodical, 1744-1746*, 1929 (edited); *The Lost Generation: An Armistice Day Article*, 1932; *Self-Selected Essays*, 1932; *Albert Goes Through*, 1933; *English Journey: Being a Rambling but Truthful Account of What One Man Saw and Heard and Felt and Thought During a Journey Through England During the Autumn of the Year 1933*, 1934; *Four-in-Hand*, 1934; *Midnight on the Desert: A Chapter of Autobiography*, 1937 (published in the United States as *Midnight on the Desert: Being an Excursion into Autobiography During a Winter in America, 1935-1936*); *Rain upon Godshill: A Further Chapter of Autobiography*, 1939; *Our Nation's Heritage*, 1939 (edited); *Britain Speaks*, 1940; *Postscripts*, 1940; *Out of the People*, 1941; *Britain at War*, 1942; *British Women Go to War*, 1943; *The Man-Power Story*, 1943; *Here Are Your Answers*, 1944; *The New Citizen*, 1944; *Letter to a Returning Serviceman*, 1945; *Russian Journey*, 1946; *The Secret Dream: An Essay on Britain, America, and Russia*, 1946; *The Arts Under Socialism: Being a Lecture Given to the Fabian Society, with a Postscript on What Government Should Do for the Arts Here and Now*, 1947; *Scenes of London Life, from "Sketches by Boz" by Charles Dickens*, 1947 (edited); *Theatre Outlook*, 1947; *Delight*, 1949; *Journey down a Rainbow*, 1955 (with Jacquetta Hawkes); *All About Ourselves and Other Essays*, 1956; *The Writer in a Changing Society*, 1956; *The Art of the Dramatist: A Lecture Together with Appendices and Discursive Notes*, 1957; *The Best of Leacock*, 1957 (edited); *The Bodley Head Leacock*, 1957; *Thoughts in the Wilderness*, 1957; *Topside: Or, The Future of England, a Dialogue*, 1958; *The Story of Theatre*, 1959; *Four English Novels*, 1960 (edited); *Literature and Western Man*, 1960; *William Hazlitt*, 1960; *Four English Biographies*, 1961 (edited); *Charles Dickens: A Pictorial Biography*, 1962; *Margin Released: A Writer's Reminiscences and Reflections*, 1962; *Adventures in English Literature*, 1963 (edited); *The English Comic Characters*, 1963; *Man and Time*, 1964; *An Everyman Anthology*, 1966 (edited); *The Moments and Other Pieces*, 1966; *All England Listened: J. B. Priestley's Wartime Broadcasts*, 1968; *Essays of Five Decades*, 1968 (Susan Cooper, editor); *Trumpets over the Sea: Being a Rambling and Egotistical Account of the London Symphony Orchestra's Engagement at Daytona Beach, Florida, in July-August, 1967*, 1968; *The Prince of Pleasure and His Regency, 1811-1820*, 1969; *Anton Chekhov*, 1970; *The Edwardians*, 1970; *Over the Long High Wall:*

Some Reflections and Speculations on Life, Death, and Time, 1972; *Victoria's Heyday*, 1972; *The English*, 1973; *Outcries and Asides*, 1974; *A Visit to New Zealand, Particular Pleasures: Being a Personal Record of Some Varied Arts and Many Different Artists*, 1974; *The Happy Dream: An Essay*, 1976; *Instead of the Trees*, 1977.

CHILDREN'S LITERATURE: *Snoggle*, 1972.

Bibliography

Atkins, John. *J. B. Priestley: The Last of the Sages*. London: John Calder, 1981. Cites Priestley as a major but neglected writer. A comprehensive look at his novels and plays as well as his career as a critic which contains much valuable information.

Braine, John. *J. B. Priestley*. London: Weidenfeld & Nicolson, 1978. Not a critical analysis of Priestley's work, by Braine's admission, but a look at a selection of his writings. Braine, a fellow Bradfordian, offers a knowledgeable view of Priestley.

Cooper, Susan. *J. B. Priestley: Portrait of an Author*. London: Redwood Press, 1970. A sympathetic account of Priestley written in an informal style. Cooper gives both criticism of his work and looks at the man himself: "warm hearted, generous."

DeVitis, A. A., and Albert E. Kalson. *J. B. Priestley*. Boston: Twayne, 1980. A good introduction to Priestley which focuses on some eighty novels and plays, from the late 1920's to the 1960's. The authors note that Priestley's work has an "unerring ability to deal incisively with the idiosyncrasies of the English national character."

Evans, Gareth Lloyd. *J. B. Priestley: The Dramatist*. London: Heinemann, 1964. Analyzes the three collected volumes of Priestley's plays, which Evans has divided into "Time-plays," "Comedies," and "Sociological plays." An authoritative study that is primarily concerned with the dominant themes in Priestley's plays.

V. S. PRITCHETT

Born: Ipswich, England; December 16, 1900

Principal long fiction
Claire Drummer, 1929; *Shirley Sanz*, 1932 (also known as *Elopement into Exile*); *Nothing Like Leather*, 1935; *Dead Man Leading*, 1937; *Mr. Beluncle*, 1951.

Other literary forms
V. S. Pritchett is recognized above all as a master of the short story. His stories rely less on plot than on character—character revealed principally through dialogue. Many of Pritchett's stories were first published in magazines; they have been collected, however, in more than a dozen volumes.

Pritchett is also widely known as a travel writer and a literary critic and biographer. As the former, he produced several works, among which *The Spanish Temper* (1954) was perhaps most highly praised. *The Offensive Traveller* (1964; also published as *Foreign Faces*) collected numerous previously published travel essays. Pritchett's literary biographies include *Balzac: A Biography* (1973), *The Gentle Barbarian: The Life and Work of Turgenev* (1977), and *Chekhov: A Spirit Set Free* (1988). His criticism ranges across more than four decades, from *In My Good Books* (1942) to *A Man of Letters* (1985).

Two autobiographical works by Pritchett, *A Cab at the Door* (1968) and *Midnight Oil* (1971) are regarded as classics of the genre.

Achievements
During the second half of the century, Pritchett's readership and influence in America have grown considerably. Since the 1950's, his stories have appeared frequently in *The New Yorker*, and a selection of his reviews appear each year in *The New York Review of Books*. He has been the Christian Gauss Lecturer at Princeton University (1953), writer-in-residence at Smith College (1966), Beckman Professor at the University of California at Berkeley (1962), and visiting professor at Brandeis University (1968). His fiction and criticism alike are enjoyed and praised by American critics; his fiction for its social comedy, acute characterization, and subtle manner, his criticism for its focus, lucidity, and balance. As a "literary journalist," he has been compared to Edmund Wilson, and his sentences, whether in fiction or nonfiction, are thought to be among the best written in English in the twentieth century. In England, he is an elder statesman of letters, many times honored. He has been the Clark Lecturer at Cambridge University (1969) and was awarded a D.Litt. by Leeds University (1972). He served as president of the British

Association of Poets, Playwrights, Editors, Essayists, and Novelists (PEN) in 1970 and of the International PEN Club in 1974. He is the recipient of two awards for nonfiction, the Heinemann in 1969 and the International PEN Club in 1974. He is a Fellow of the Royal Society of Literature and an honorary member of the American Academy of Arts and Letters. In 1969, he was made a Commander of the British Empire, and in 1975, he was knighted.

Biography

In December of 1900, in lodgings over a toy shop in Ipswich, England, Victor Sawdon Pritchett was born, the first child of Beatrice Martin and Walter Pritchett, who had met in the milliner's shop where they both worked. The marriage apparently began passionately, three children following quickly after Victor, but because of Walter's many business misadventures and his conversion to Christian Science, the marriage was soon unsettled and its passion converted to quarrelsomeness. Although the Pritchetts were not shiftless, their household was often shifted about: by the time Pritchett was twelve, the family had moved around London at least fourteen times, usually so that Walter Pritchett could escape creditors, twice to hide his bankruptcy. Beatrice Pritchett lived in constant fear of creditors—once denying her identity on opening the door to an officer attempting to serve a writ—and in outspoken jealousy of the "other women" in her husband's life—his mother, his business partner ("Miss H"), and Mary Baker Eddy.

Because the family never stayed in one place for long, Pritchett felt that he belonged nowhere, that he was an outsider everywhere but in his own, rather strange, family. Besides moving with his parents, he was sent at intervals to his grandparents in Yorkshire, an arrangement contrived, apparently, to ease the burden on Walter Pritchett's purse. New problems complicated their home life from 1910, when in Camberwell, Walter was converted to Christian Science. His conversion brought on quarrels with Beatrice about "that woman" which lasted well into the night, and later his business failed. After a year's separation, during which time Pritchett formed a vague idea that he would become a painter, Beatrice and the children rejoined Walter in Dulwich, where he had established an art needlework trade with his former bookkeeper, Miss H.

Until he moved to Dulwich, Pritchett had received only sporadic schooling, and then only in rough Methodist and penny-a-day schools, because his father did not trouble himself about the children's education. Finally, Beatrice grew impatient with Walter's ruminations over the prospectuses from Eton and Harrow, for which Pritchett would never have qualified because, among other things, he knew no Latin, and she enrolled him in Rosendale Road School. There he was awarded John Ruskin's *Modern Painters* for one of his paintings, and there too, under a man named Bartlett, he read his first literature. He promptly began to read whatever he could find, having decided to become a writer. He became known in the family as "Dirty Poet" and "Professor." Two years later, to impress Miss H, his father allowed him to sit for an examination for a scholarship to the Strand School (Streatham), which he failed. Pritchett identifies this failure in *A Cab at the Door* as a turning point in his life, for he believes that had he won the scholarship, he surely would have continued at a university and died as a writer. Instead, at Miss H's expense, he entered Alleyn's School, a London grammar school founded to educate the lower-middle classes. There he learned that he was good at languages, and he also enjoyed a few classroom successes with his writing. Around this time, he sprained his ankle, and this accident was the occasion of his first hearing the Christian Science argument from his father. Not long afterward, Pritchett professed his belief in it, probably out of a need to please his father, but his faith seems never to have been very strong. Church provided a social outlet for him, the children otherwise not being allowed to go out.

In 1916, at the instigation of his grandfather, Pritchett was taken from school and put to work as a clerk in a London leather-manufacturing firm. After fighting with another clerk on the office floor, he was promoted out of the office to learn the other phases of the trade. For four years he commuted into London, so happy with the idea of thoroughly learning a trade that for a while he abandoned his literary ambitions. At the end of 1920, however, he fell ill, and when he recovered, he did not go back to the leather business but instead went to Paris, which he had dreamed of doing for several years.

With two hundred pounds saved from his earnings and a typewriter from his father, Pritchett arrived in Paris in the spring of 1921. He found a job as a photographer's assistant and settled joyfully into Parisian life. Christian Science had taught him that sex should be avoided as the chief avenue of Animal Magnetism, the force that created the illusion of Evil, but by this time, it is fair to say, he was tormented by his virginity. Finally, he managed a brief affair with a Danish girl, who soon after returned to Denmark and married another man. Pritchett had a few other friends, mostly from the church, but he knew no writers, least of all the American expatriates. He spent most of his time alone, continuing the autodidacticism which for the most part had been his education; it was in his room, remembering J. M. Barrie's advice to write about small things, that he began his career as a writer. His first three sketches were taken almost immediately by *The Saturday Westminster*, *Time and Tide*, and *The Christian Science Monitor*. Soon he was emboldened to quit the photographer's shop for a job as a shellac salesman. He was happy to be part of the workaday city, to walk the streets with his samples, but he sold nothing and was fired. Once again, he began to write and to place articles, but then his luck changed, he ran out of money, and *The Christian Science Monitor* did not pay him for a series of articles he had written. When he was on the verge of starvation, he was fed by his landlady and given money by friends. Storing his belongings in Paris, he returned to

England, two years after leaving, to see the London editor of *The Christian Science Monitor.*

In Paris, Pritchett had proven to himself and to his father that he could lead an independent and manly life as a writer, so once back in London, he looked for regular work writing. At *The Christian Science Monitor,* the new editor was not immediately forthcoming, but eventually he paid Pritchett and gave him a trial assignment in Ireland, where Pritchett met Æ, James Stephens, Sean O'Casey, and William Butler Yeats himself, with whom he argued about George Bernard Shaw. In Ireland, too, he fell in love with another journalist and rashly married her after agreeing to go to Spain for *The Christian Science Monitor.* He did not much like his role as foreign correspondent because he disliked politics, preferring instead to write about places, people, customs, and manners. Tiring of journalism, he began to write short stories, none of which was published for several years. Over a period of three years of writing from Ireland, Spain, and the United States, his writing (by his own account) had grown self-conscious and contorted. At long last, *The Christian Science Monitor* tired of it and fired him.

In London again, Pritchett sustained himself by translating business letters for a foreign language school, serving as the librarian to the Bath Club for one pound a week, and selling a few stories and sketches. Unable to find a publisher for a collection of sketches, poor, and inspired by D. H. Lawrence's *Sea and Sardinia* (1921), he decided to walk across Spain and write a book about it upon his return to England. *Marching Spain* (1928) sold only six hundred copies before it was remaindered, but it won Pritchett two contracts, one for a book of stories and another for a novel. In the meantime, he was hired again by *The Christian Science Monitor,* this time as a reviewer, a job he kept until he published "The Saint" in the 1930's and was fired for the last time. Also in 1928, he began what proved to be a long association with *New Statesman* (he eventually became the director), published a few stories in *The Fortnightly Review,* and became the novel reviewer for *The Spectator.* In 1929, his first book of stories, *The Spanish Virgin and Other Stories,* was published as well as his first novel, *Claire Drummer.* The book of stories surprised everyone by selling three thousand copies; the novel sold fewer than a thousand.

Throughout the 1920's, Pritchett and his wife had been separated much of the time, partly because she was pursuing an acting career. By the 1930's, Pritchett had earned some measure of peace and security from his writing, but it was not until 1934 that the transiency and emotional tension which had characterized his entire life were relieved. In this year, he met Dorothy Rudge Roberts, who, after his divorce in 1936, became his second wife. It was not merely to fulfill a tedious convention that he dedicated all of his subsequent books to her, for—believing that love released the tension responsible for his bad writing—it was to her and their marriage that he attributed the great burst of creativity that overtook him. Through the 1930's he published three more novels, but, as portended by the response to *The Spanish Virgin*, it was in the short story that he excelled. During the war years, he gardened and reviewed books; in the 1950's, he published his only truly successful novel, *Mr. Beluncle*, and *The Spanish Temper*, which is generally thought to be one of the best books ever written on Spain; throughout the 1960's, 1970's, and 1980's he continued to write stories and reviews. He also completed two volumes of memoirs in 1968 and 1971.

In his later years, Pritchett continued to live in London with his wife. The critical praise he received for his 1988 biography, *Chekhov*, was testimony to the fact that even as he approached ninety he remained a masterful scholar and wordsmith.

Analysis

Two central forces shaped V. S. Pritchett's artistry: his family and his urge to break away from it. The picture that Pritchett gives of his home life in *A Cab at the Door* is of a fantastic edifice of dreams, resounding with the words of Walter Pritchett—self-complacent, moralizing, and sometimes angry words. The family life Walter tried to create was a fantasy that Beatrice chipped away at. She wailed jealous complaints and remonstrated; she told stories about dead relatives, dead pets, and dead royalty; above all, she told jokes which ended with her bursting into hysterical laughter, rocking on her chair, and peering out at her audience from behind spread fingers, her skirts hoisted above her knees and her bloomers showing. If his father's words imprisoned the young Pritchett, his mother's opened a chink into the world where people voiced their feelings and cried, and where, most important, they laughed.

When Pritchett began to read widely, he discovered fictions other than his father's and was led to a consideration of the worlds which prompted them. (That he thought there was some literal place where life was better is demonstrated by his early desire to travel.) It is characteristic of his imagination that as a young man going to work in London he was reminded of Charles Dickens, rather than of London when reading Dickens, and that as a septuagenarian he described himself as two people—the writer, "the prosing man at the desk," and the other self, "the valet who dogs him and does the living" (*Midnight Oil*). For Pritchett, in short, life followed art, and this order of things is important for understanding the writer.

Probably because his interest in literature arose suddenly from his recognition that print is like paint, that it can create pictures which open onto other perspectives, his writing is predominantly descriptive, his narrative perhaps more lyric than dramatic. Added to his visual acuity is a good ear for dialect, developed from adjusting his own language to whatever new neighborhood he found himself in as a boy and from speaking French and Spanish as a young man. The mundane world, consequently, is richly evoked in his works. He is not primarily concerned with recording the details of the external world, however, for he is too much of an essentialist in purpose and too richly comic in manner to be preoccupied with strict representationalism. Like the Victorians, he studies characters in a social setting; like Dickens and Thomas Hardy, his first-loved novelists, he concerns himself with the social environment as a condition of character. Place and class are important as limiters— of experience, language, and the stuff of fantasy. He evokes them with selected, exaggerated, and often symbolic images, usually visual, and by the words the characters speak. There is perhaps no living writer as adept as Pritchett at representing society through these brilliant half-strokes. Yet, in the sense of upholding the value—whether mythical, political, or moral—of one class above another, he is ultimately one of the least class-conscious of English writers. His authorial position is class-free, his attitude independent.

His real divergence from social realism is most obvious in his characters, who ring true, but not because they are singly imitative of individuals with whom one might rub shoulders in the real world. The eccentrics who populate his books are instead caricatures through which are enacted certain emotional, intellectual, and aesthetic problems. The conflicting versions of the world created by the various characters produce a collision at the climax which is often understated and ironic, and perhaps it is the frequency of this "silent" climax that has led to the charge by critics that Pritchett's plotting is weak. Then, too, character and situation above all capture his attention. In a relatively static fashion, one resembling portraiture more than dramatic literature, he touches and retouches his central point.

The unifying theme of Pritchett's fiction concerns dreaming as an ambiguous mechanism of the imagination, for it can lead either to freedom or to imprisonment. According to their way of dreaming, his characters fall loosely into two categories. The first is the egotist. He has many faces, but essentially he is the one who, as is said of Mr. Beluncle, never dreams at all—except when he is awake. Usually he is treated humorously, under a Dickensian light, and when there is an objective narrator, in the Meredithian manner: incisively, ironically, and epigramatically. The egotist, by placing himself at the center of things and acting out his dreams, tries to negate the three-dimensional world. His dreams are for the most part unrealizable and his version of the world untenable, and he appears comically two-dimensional as a result. The second character type, the artist, recognizes and belongs to the world where perspectives shift. Like the egotist, he dreams, but, unlike the egotist's desires, his longings and aspirations are curbed by an awareness of actual conditions. He is, moreover, capable of holding contradictory dreams, or accounts of the world, in his mind at the same time.

Pritchett's first three novels draw upon his experiences in Ireland, Spain, and London. They were not successful, and in *Midnight Oil* he writes that they were "machines for conveying [his] characters into a trap." In *Dead Man Leading*, he tried something new. Instead of looking for essences in the stuff of his own experience, he concocted a material world to convey the essence of masochism. His idea, that explorers are motivated by masochism, he inferred from reading biographies; his setting, Brazil, was known to him only through literature. To pick up mundane details he read missionaries' diaries and talked about Manaos with a drunk businessman on leave, and to fix the setting clearly in mind, he made a small model of the river in his garden. This method of writing the book is partly responsible for both its strengths and weaknesses. It is overloaded with the pop-Freudianism that infects the literature of the 1930's and is too imitative in its symbolism, whether consciously or not, of Joseph Conrad. Still, it shows an uncommon force of imagination in other respects and a strong narrative power, and—being a symbolic tale approaching psychological allegory—it sheds light on his other works.

The story concerns an expedition by three men, each of whom is an egotist of sorts. The first is Charles Wright, a famous explorer, now middle-aged, who is making the expedition to complete a former, aborted one. The second is Harry Johnson, the chosen companion of Wright, a young Englishman who works in the Brazilian timber industry and uses his leaves to explore the far reaches of the world. He and Wright are "camp companions," initiates into the thoroughly masculine world where women are "bad luck." The third is Gilbert Phillips, who stands outside their circle, a stranger to their code. He envied Harry when they were boys together, and now, as a journalist, he is trying to acquire courage by following bold men. These characters—especially Wright and Johnson—are less persuasive as people than as Freudian symbols.

Despite Wright's nominal leadership, Johnson is at the head of the group. The expedition, which occurs in three stages (not counting the long expository flashback), is a primal regression into the interior of Johnson's being, a gradual peeling-back of his adult self. The flashback, in which we learn that Johnson has had an affair with Wright's stepdaughter, Lucy, and is now burdened with guilt and a desire for self-punishment, lays the foundation for the analysis of his puritanical, masochistic psychology, according to which Wright and Lucy (to whom Wright had been attracted before marrying her mother) serve as father and mother surrogates. Through the first stage of the expedition, the journey upriver with Phillips to meet Wright, Johnson grows feverish and, in an irrational effort to avoid Wright, tries to persuade Phillips to disembark and strike out overland. When they do rendezvous with Wright, Johnson is put to bed in the house of a whiskey-besotted Cockney named Calcott, who entertains him while Wright and Phillips are off hunting turtle eggs. He encourages Johnson in his misogyny ("all women are dagoes") and insists that Johnson is there to look for his father, a missionary who slept in the same room before disappearing into the jungle years earlier. Calcott's Portuguese confidant, Jose Silva, lends support to Calcott by pretending to be the voice of the dead man in a seance arranged for Johnson's benefit. When Phillips and Wright are detained for several days by a storm and Johnson grows impatient to try his luck, Silva, thinking there might be gold in it for him, encourages Johnson to set out and to take him along. When Phillips and Wright return, then, Johnson is gone—now leading the expedition.

The second stage consists of Johnson's trip with Silva. Johnson, making a conscious decision neither to flee his friends nor to follow his father, simply goes on without turning back. Loosened from the "net" the minds of others cast over him, he drifts into a world where the birds whistle "like boys" and Silva chatters and frolics in the sand. Silva is like a boy-genie (an "artist," the narrator calls him) released by Harry's subconscious to grant his deepest wishes. After several days, however, Johnson is overtaken and, in a strained reunion with Wright, breaks down, regressing to an angry child wishing for the death of his father. Wright, attempting to restore harmony, invites him to go out hunting. While they are spearing fish in a mudhole, a jaguar surprises them and, in the panic of the moment, Wright shoots himself. By the time Johnson is able to bring him in, Wright is dead. Characteristically, Johnson thinks this accident has been caused by his own weakness and that his weakness has been brought upon him by Lucy. He now feels "that he had no longer a self, that he was scattered, disintegrated—nothing."

So begins the third and final stage of the expedition. Johnson's idea, if he has one, is to walk until he encounters the Indians who are presumed to have killed his father. Although Phillips has lost his interest in the expedition with the death of Wright, he has promised Lucy, with whom he also has had an affair, that he will take care of Johnson. Consequently, when Silva and the crew turn back, Phillips follows him overland, hoping to save him from the ultimate solitude of the grave. At first, Johnson tolerates his company, but after a few days, Phillips conceives the idea that he intends to leave him behind. When Phillips is nearly dead of thirst, Johnson decides to search for water, leaving a note and his gun behind. Roused from delirium before Johnson is out of sight, Phillips believes he is being abandoned and fires at him. Johnson is last seen looking back at Phillips before turning and automatically marking a trail he will not follow back. Without Phillips, representative perhaps of the social aspect of the ego, Johnson is finally alone, free to rejoin his father, death.

The setting, seemingly so important to the action, is largely created by images drawn from the characters' private states of mind. When England to Gilbert is a fresh memory, for example, the wake of the boat is "like an old mat" and the "slow clapping" of vultures' wings is "like dusty and ragged rugs being shaken." Later, when he is obsessed with keeping the fire low, the vultures wheeling overhead are "like two bits of charred paper tossed up by the draught of a fire." As it is imagined by the characters, the setting helps to describe and explain their motivations. As a stage for playing out a psychological drama, it is nowhere better adapted to the purpose than in the chapter presenting Wright's death. In the topography, the mudhole, and the appearance of the jaguar, the imagery binds character to setting and the action expresses subconscious desires.

The role of language in shaping the world surfaces as an explicit theme in each stage of the expedition. In the first, Silva speaks in the "voice" of Johnson's father and in the second in the voice of the child within. By a Freudian model, Silva can be understood as the voice of Johnson's ego, at one time speaking out of the super-ego and at another out of the id. In the third stage of the expedition, when Johnson feels disintegrated, Silva is absent. In this last stage, Johnson and Phillips develop a special camaraderie, complete with its own vocabulary, which the narrator explains at some length. First they coin new words for the essentials of their life—"water" becoming "mud," for example—then they abbreviate them, and then they lapse into nearly total silence. This loss of society, of language, of the vocabulary necessary for cultivating the physical world, parallels Johnson's regression.

As analyzed in *Dead Man Leading*, the desire to explore is masochistic, and masochism arises from the sexual guilt produced by puritanism. Puritanism, Walter Allen has noted, is Pritchett's main study, and in no other book is his recurring theme more evident. Yet Pritchett's attitude toward Johnson's puritanism and toward Johnson himself is not clear. Although Johnson behaves ridiculously, he is not treated as a comic character. Indeed, Pritchett creates a good deal of sympathy for him, portraying him as a troubled, possibly even tragic, hero. Certainly, by doing what others cannot do, he is great: he cuts through the world of social convention and conscious activity directly into the world of unadulterated egotism, into the dream world where accidents really do make wishes come true. In this sense, Johnson is like Beluncle, an artist of egotism. The general ambivalence of the authorial attitude toward Johnson, however, is probably caused by the thorny subject matter: the relationship between father, mother, and son, which Pritchett eventually mastered in late middle-age.

It was not until 1951, after a decade of book-reviewing and short-story writing, that Pritchett published his next novel. *Mr. Beluncle* is concerned with what he calls in *Midnight Oil* his "obsessive subject": his father. *Dead Man Leading* was concerned with this obsessive subject, too, but the father in question was not drawn directly from Pritchett's own, and it was the son's, not the father's, story. In *Mr. Beluncle*, however, there is an unmistakable portrait of Walter Pritchett. Pritchett's manner in this book is not, as it had been in *Dead Man Leading*, to approach his subject and character earnestly but to create an attitude, which can be termed "objective sympathy," out of a barbed, epigrammatic wit reminiscent of George Meredith. Both books concern the quality of the individual's imagination and the power of dreaming, but *Mr. Beluncle* is far superior, its subject and manner being natural to Pritchett's genius and fully under control. Indeed, all of Pritchett's strengths are united in *Mr. Beluncle* to produce what is surely his finest novel.

Compared to *Dead Man Leading*, so like a boy's adventure story, *Mr. Beluncle* is a quiet book. Both books are, in a sense, character studies, but in *Dead Man Leading*, to the extent that it is psychological allegory, the primary means of characterization is action, while in *Mr. Beluncle*, it is portraiture. *Mr. Beluncle* works largely through long gazes at Beluncle penetrated by a quick narrative omniscience, through set presentations of monologues and incremental repetition of ritualized behavior, and through a panorama of supporting characters. Many of the minor characters are eccentrics in their own right, but in the narrative, they serve Mr. Beluncle in his fantastic egotism.

Mr. Beluncle occupies two domains, in each of which he possesses a helpmate and a family. At home, it is his wife, Ethel, and his sons, Henry, George, and Leslie. At work, it is his business partner, Mrs. Linda Truslove, his junior partner, Mr. Everard Chilly, and his typist. At home, he is a tyrant, self-complacently moralizing to his family, filling his drawers with expensive clothing while neglecting to give Ethel housekeeping money, and refusing to allow the family members to go out alone or to have friends. A fleshy man himself, he does not want them to leave him because he feels diminished; they are "like vultures pulling his flesh off him." At work, he is a fake, busying himself with writing aphorisms on slips of paper, daydreaming about a new house, issuing commands, and driving the company car over to the showroom. It is in fact Mrs. Truslove who runs the company, who has bought the car, and who has tried to save the business from Beluncle's extravagances.

Mrs. Truslove has been in love with Beluncle for years and subject to his persuasions, but it is not she who basically enables him to live in his house of delusion. That role is reserved for his other "mistress," the Church of the Last Purification. With its easy transcendentalism and its central doctrine that evil is illusion, the religion has enabled him to dismiss as illusory anything unpleasant and to achieve such a degree of self-importance that God, like his family and associates, serves him. "God is a radio station," he asserts in an expansive moment; "God is Supply" in a moment of financial need. His most immediate need, he thinks, is another new house; having heard that in the Father's house are many mansions, he is certain that "one has been prepared" for him. Especially congenial to his sensibility is the church's equating evil and sex. A very clean man married to a somewhat slovenly woman, Beluncle finds it "hard to realize that woman is a Divine Idea." Because his "sexual instinct interfered with the acquisitive," he is gratified by church doctrine, since, as Lady Roads, head of the local church, says, "it takes sex out of love." His way is thus clear to express it more naturally, by using his attractiveness to women (his sister, his mother, Lady Roads, Mrs. Truslove, and Mrs. Robinson, a tearoom manageress) to seduce them out of their money. He manages everything with charm and righteousness, always depending on God, who is (as Mrs. Truslove thinks of it) the "joker in his pack." The story is about the collapse of his house of cards.

Beluncle's huge capacity for dreaming has produced his success to date, but it is the very thing which destroys him in the end. Encouraged to daydream by the transcendental aspect of Purification theology, he ignores factual circumstances. Accountants, for example, amaze him because they actually believe the figures on paper. "You can add it up this way, you can add it up that way and every time you get a different answer," he opines and adds, "As Shakespeare says, it's all in your mind." Mrs. Truslove, though, is one who believes the figures on paper, and because she is finished loving him, signals her intention of withdrawing from the business. At home, he has disappointments too. Chief among them is his son Henry, who without Beluncle's knowledge has fallen in love with the stationmaster's daughter, Mary Phibbs. When Beluncle confronts Henry with the "idea" of Mary, the boy is unable to stand up to him, but, in defeat and humiliation, he flings the more cutting decision at him: he has no intention of entering the business. Thus, Beluncle's dream for his son, who would have belonged to him forever and brought him a girl with money for the business, collapses. Yet, the more the world submits evidence that his dreams are ashes, the harder he clings to them. All that is needed, he thinks, is a miracle to vindicate and save him, so when Judy Dykes, the crippled sister of Mrs. Truslove, is brought to her feet by the verbal assault of a fanatical newspaper vendor, he launches into a new round of expenditures. Instead of saving him, this miracle completes his ruin. It calls into question the soundness of the Purification, for Judy's recovery is the prelude to her death, and once she is gone, Mrs. Truslove is free to pursue a new life. When Mr. Beluncle receives word of Judy's death, he is prompted to make his first and last speech in his new board room, to an imaginary board of directors. He begins by denying the death. "It's a mistake, a dream and—by the way, I'll give you a thought there, where is the dream when you wake up?"

Everyone in *Mr. Beluncle* dreams: Judy Dykes that she will walk, Mrs. Truslove that someday something will come of her love for Beluncle, Henry that he will free himself from his father. Each character attempts to force reality to conform to the dream: Judy Dykes by accumulating fashionable shoes; Mrs. Truslove by using the business as a marriage; Henry by loading the slender figure of Mary Phibbs with his many nameless desires. Judy dies, however, and Mrs. Truslove parts with her desire for Beluncle, which has been "exhausted by the imagination." Henry, who has imitated his father in many respects, observes Mary's reaction to his declaration that he has lost his faith and realizes for the first time that she is "not an extension of himself, but another human being." Everyone wakes up to find the dream gone, except for Mr. Beluncle, who uses language to keep it alive.

If the quality of the individual's dream is the moral topic of the book, then the manner by which language serves the imagination is its aesthetic corollary. Mr. Beluncle's extraordinary force of personality expresses itself by his physical substance and demeanor but also, and more important, by his words. He is a man who likes to roll words in his mouth like fine chocolates and bestow his thoughts on those around him like a king. Never mind that what he says is absurd, his manner convinces. To Mr. Chilly, one of Beluncle's admirable traits is his ability to "make a statement and then appear to lean physically upon it." One thought uttered, he is hoisted to another, word by word exchanging fact for fancy, as if to speak were to make the world anew. To Beluncle, the narrator explains, talking is "a way of turning realities into unrealities," and placing written messages, such as "Eternity = Now," next to letters from creditors is typical of his way of doing business. In various other ways, too, the fundamental connection between dreaming and speaking, image and word, is emphasized. One major way is by the character of Henry, who imitates his father in his love of the creative power of language, especially when he is with Mary Phibbs. To her, he tells stories about his family, improved by an artistic juggling of detail, without noticing that she hates them because of "their importance to him and his pride in them"—because, basically, of their self-centeredness. Other characters, too, spin their wishful accounts of the world.

A second, more symbolic way in which the role of language in projecting the dream world surfaces is in two characters who exist primarily as "voices"— a technique Pritchett had practiced in *Dead Man Leading*. One is the youngest Beluncle boy, Leslie, who emerges in the middle of the book to utter the blunt, innermost thoughts of the family which are ordinarily blurred by Beluncle's rich discourse, and the other is Mary's sister. Leslie attaches himself to Henry in one key scene in the garden, and Mary's sister sleeps with her and teases her with the things that Mary is afraid to think directly. Henry and Mary do not, however, give in entirely to this dream voice, as does Harry Johnson. Rather, they hear it along with another one, that of the waking world, and out of the two they harmonize a public voice. Mr. Beluncle, unlike them, is afraid of hearing two voices. He is afraid of the inner voice, because it whispers to him of his own mortality, but he is also afraid of the outer voice, because it denies the complete gratification of his infantile desires. A puritan who has adopted a transcendental explanation of human nature in order to live with himself, he has succeeded, it would seem, in killing one of the voices—exactly which one is moot. It is enough to say that his inner voice has been made public, that his dream is his life. Thus, he is one-dimensional, hollow, his ego merely an expanding shell.

That Henry hears two voices makes possible a doubling of perspective which will eventually lead him out of egotistic confinement into artistic freedom.

Henry is the foil to Beluncle's charlatanry, the nascent artist of the book, and clearly the autobiographical character; what is especially remarkable about the book is that he never nudges Beluncle out of the limelight. For being an autobiographical novel of sorts, and one incorporating elements of comedy, *Mr Beluncle* is surprisingly unconcerned in any overt way with the triumph of son over father, youth over age. In this, his major study of egotism, Pritchett never forgets that the archetypal egotist in his private imagination is his father. If his earliest desire was to surmount him, then he succeeds in this novel, not by assuming center-stage himself, not by painting himself large, but by reducing himself, by exercising the artist's negative capability to create one of the most memorable eccentrics in English literature.

Linda F. Tunick

Other major works

SHORT FICTION: *The Spanish Virgin and Other Stories*, 1930; *You Make Your Own Life*, 1938; *It May Never Happen and Other Stories*, 1945; *Collected Stories*, 1956; *The Sailor, The Sense of Humour and Other Stories*, 1956; *When My Girl Comes Home*, 1961; *The Key to My Heart: A Comedy in Three Parts*, 1963; *Blind Love and Other Stories*, 1969; *The Camberwell Beauty and Other Stories*, 1974; *Selected Stories*, 1978; *On the Edge of the Cliff*, 1979; *Collected Stories*, 1982; *More Collected Stories*, 1983.

NONFICTION: *Marching Spain*, 1928; *In My Good Books*, 1942; *The Living Novel and Later Appreciations*, 1946; *Why Do I Write? An Exchange of Views Between Elizabeth Bowen, Graham Greene, and V. S. Pritchett*, 1948; *Books in General*, 1953; *The Spanish Temper*, 1954; *London Perceived*, 1962; *The Offensive Traveller*, 1964 (also known as *Foreign Faces*); *New York Proclaimed*, 1965; *The Working Novelist*, 1965; *Dublin: A Portrait*, 1967; *A Cab at the Door*, 1968; *George Meredith and English Comedy*, 1970; *Midnight Oil*, 1971; *Balzac: A Biography*, 1973; *The Gentle Barbarian: The Life and Work of Turgenev*, 1977; *The Myth Makers: Literary Essays*, 1979; *The Tale Bearers: Literary Essays*, 1980; *A Man of Letters*, 1985; *Chekhov: A Spirit Set Free*, 1988.

Bibliography

Baldwin, Dean R. *V. S. Pritchett*. Boston: Twayne, 1987. A useful introduction for the beginning reader of Pritchett. Acknowledges him as a master of the short story, but also examines his novels and nonfiction works. A sympathetic study, noting that Pritchett deserves more attention than he has received.
Lanc, Denis, and Rita Stein, eds. *Modern British Literature*. Vol. 5. New York: Frederick Ungar, 1985. The chapter on Pritchett gives a concise, appreciative overview of his work, naming his strengths as a creative and

intelligent writer. Discusses a review by Douglas A. Hughes of Pritchett's collection of short stories, *On the Edge of the Cliff.* According to Lane and Stein, these short stories earn for Pritchett credit as "finest short story writer of our time."

Lucas, John. "V. S. Pritchett." In *Great Writers of the English Language: Novelists and Prose Writers*, edited by James Vinson. New York: St. Martin's Press, 1979. Lucas acknowledges Pritchett as a "distinguished man of letters" and cites as an example *The Tale Bearers*, considered by many to be the standard in its field. Rates *Dead Man Leading* as Pritchett's finest novel, but considers his short stories more impressive. Also discusses Pritchett's two autobiographical novels, *A Cab at the Door* and *Midnight Oil*.

Peden, William. "V. S. Pritchett." In *The English Short Story, 1880-1945: A Critical History*, edited by Joseph M. Flora. Boston: Twayne, 1985. Traces Pritchett's development through his short stories with incisive comments on the best ones. Includes comments by Pritchett on his own work from an interview with Peden. An excellent analysis and critique.

Vannatta, Dennis P., ed. *The English Short Story, 1945-1980: A Critical History*. Boston: Twayne, 1985. Discusses Pritchett's short stories in the context of his contemporaries. Contains some thoughtful analyses of individual stories with appreciation for Pritchett's singular characters and the comedy in his writing.

FREDERIC PROKOSCH

Born: Madison, Wisconsin; May 17, 1908
Died: Plan de Grasse, France; June 2, 1989

Principal long fiction

The Asiatics, 1935; *The Seven Who Fled*, 1937; *Night of the Poor*, 1939; *The Skies of Europe*, 1941; *The Conspirators*, 1943; *Age of Thunder*, 1945; *The Idols of the Cave*, 1946; *Storm and Echo*, 1948; *Nine Days to Mukalla*, 1953; *A Tale for Midnight*, 1955; *A Ballad of Love*, 1960; *The Seven Sisters*, 1962; *The Dark Dancer*, 1964; *The Wreck of the "Cassandra,"* 1966; *The Missolonghi Manuscript*, 1968; *America, My Wilderness*, 1972.

Other literary forms

Frederic Prokosch published five books of poetry. Some of his poems enjoyed a transitory popularity and appeared in anthologies, notably those of Oscar Williams. In addition, he translated the love sonnets of Louise Labé, some of the poetry of Friedrich Hölderlin, and the *Medea* of Euripides.

Many of the poems in his first collection, *The Assassins* (1936), celebrate places and journeys and aspire to create an exotic mood. The collection also contains one of his most anthologized poems, "The Dolls," where Prokosch writes at his musical best of the sweet, crescent-eyed shapes, which, reaching into the poet's "secret night," become the "furies" of his sleep. Dylan Thomas later parodied this poem, giving to his own poem the title "The Molls."

Prokosch's second volume of poems, *The Carnival* (1938), depends less on the dazzling imagery of geography and more on the ordinary things of life and was an attempt, according to the author, to convey the darkness of the prewar decade, as in "Fable," where the "rippled snow is tracked with blood,/ And my love lies cold in the burning wood." The volume contains a long, autobiographical "Ode" that describes the phases of Prokosch's first thirty years of life and his various discoveries (of fairy tales, his body, the past, Asia). His "Nocturne," beginning "Close my darling both your eyes,/ Let your arm lie still at last," shares similarities with W. H. Auden's well-known poem "Lay your sleeping head, my love,/ Human on my faithless arm."

The poems contained in *Death at Sea* (1940) concern the plight of the individual in a chaotic world. In "The Festival," for example, a pair of lovers who are apparently homosexual note the "coming tempest" and follow "Silent the paths of longing and regret/ Which all our learning taught us to despise"; the poem is set against a backdrop of earrings trembling in the dark and fairies huddling by a bridge.

Reviewers were not kind to Prokosch the poet, and time itself has been still less kind. Although he assembled an anthology, *Chosen Poems*, in 1944, it was not until 1983 that he published his next volume of verse, *The Sea*, a collection of sonnets that once again reflects Prokosch's fascination with geography.

Finally, in 1983, Prokosch published his memoirs, *Voices*, a series of vignettes in which many of the literary giants of the twentieth century appear in a decidedly unheroic light.

Achievements

Prokosch is said to have created the novel of geography, a distillate of the reflective travelogue. More than half of his sixteen novels fall into this category, and even those that do not are dominated in some way by the theme of geography and involve cosmopolitan, travel-loving characters. With the publication of his first novel, *The Asiatics*, in 1935, a book highlighted by Asian scenes and attitudes when other American novelists were writing realistic novels set in their own country, Prokosch achieved instant fame and maintained a high reputation for approximately the next ten years. William Butler Yeats was deeply struck by Prokosch's poetic gifts, and André Gide, Thomas Mann, and Albert Camus all praised his works during his stellar decade. Even his later works were praised by Somerset Maugham, Thornton Wilder, and Marianne Moore. *The Asiatics*, which was translated into seventeen foreign languages and was even more popular in Europe than in the United States, has been in print for more than fifty years. *The Seven Who Fled* won the Harper Novel Prize, awarded by a panel of judges consisting of Thornton Wilder, Sinclair Lewis, and Louis Bromfield. In 1944, Warner Brothers made *The Conspirators* into a motion picture starring Hedy Lamarr and Paul Henreid.

Radcliffe Squires has observed that Prokosch's recurring theme—the death-defying search-for-truth in travel—began to seem irrelevant to a postwar generation looking for stability in suburbia. Subsequently, his novels were not so much condemned by the critics as they were ignored. Nevertheless, no complete discussion of twentieth century literature can afford to gloss over the fictional subgenre pioneered by the wunderkind Prokosch, the novel of geography.

Biography

Frederic Prokosch was born in Madison, Wisconsin, on May 17, 1908, the middle child of three children born to Eduard and Mathilde Dapprich Prokosch. His father, who had left Austria to escape a duel, was professor of Germanic philology at the University of Wisconsin, and his mother was an accomplished pianist. In 1913, Eduard Prokosch assumed a position at the University of Texas at Austin, which he lost six years later as a result of the anti-German hysteria that followed World War I.

Prokosch was sent in 1914 to spend a year in Europe, visiting his grandfather in Austria and attending private schools there and in Munich. His Austrian-

Slavic-Germanic ancestry and his early acquaintance with European culture encouraged Prokosch's cosmopolitan spirit and love for geography. As a child, he developed an interest in fairy tales, and this he credits for his fascination as a novelist with picaresque and allegorical characters who strive inexorably for fulfillment.

In 1920, the family moved to Bryn Mawr, where Prokosch attended high school; in 1922, he entered Haverford College. In college, he became an athlete, particularly in tennis and squash, which, indeed, he did not abandon for years to come; he won the national squash championship of France in 1939 and that of Sweden in 1944. An avid lepidopterist, in later years he became as dexterous wielding his butterfly net as he had been with a racket.

After receiving his first master's degree from Haverford in 1928, Prokosch proceeded to earn a second one from King's College, Cambridge, in 1930. Two years later, he earned his doctorate at Yale. While a doctoral student, Prokosch taught English (from 1931 to 1933), continuing as a research fellow in 1934. The following year, *The Asiatics* appeared, and he returned to England, later visiting Africa and Asia. In 1936 and 1937, he was teaching at New York University, but when in 1937 he received both a Guggenheim Fellowship and the Harper Novel Prize of $7,500, he abandoned teaching altogether. He was then at the apogee of his renown as a writer, and he could write from Prague in 1937 that one of his main interests was "trying to avoid the vulgarizations of money and publicity." Ironically, the vagaries of the reading public would facilitate this goal considerably in coming years.

After the fall of France, Prokosch spent two years in Lisbon, which served as the setting for *The Conspirators*. When the United States entered the war, Prokosch returned home to enter government service in the Office of War Information and then spent two years (1943 to 1944) as an attache in the American Legation in Stockholm. After the war, he went to Rome (1947 to 1953), where, on a Fulbright Scholarship (1951 to 1952), he researched in the Vatican Library the material for his first attempt at a historical novel, *A Tale for Midnight*, about the Renaissance Cenci family.

The 1960's found Prokosch living in Paris; he finally settled in Grasse in the south of France. He continued his writing—now largely ignored by critics—and indulged his interest in rare books. Between 1968 and 1970, he printed and bound a series of elegant gift books, each containing a single poem by a well-known modern writer; these books' imprints dated the printing between 1933 and 1940, making them collectors' items. Eventually Nicolas Barker exposed these "self-forgeries" and Prokosch admitted to the books' late date.

Prokosch died in June, 1989, in Plan de Grasse, France.

Analysis

The creator of the novel of geography, Frederic Prokosch was a lover of travel and even of maps themselves. In *America, My Wilderness*, he defines the place-name as a "talisman that guides us through the terror of anonymity," and his novelist's fascination with place-names is, at its best, lyrical and evocative, at its worst, pedantic and tedious. It follows that such a lover of the places of this world would be a proponent of internationalism, and in most of his novels written after 1940, Prokosch urged his American readers to abandon their isolationism and to nurture links and bonds with the other peoples of the world.

All of Prokosch's fiction is an attempt in some way to probe the spiritual malaise characteristic of the twentieth century. In his novels of the 1930's, there is an abiding, non-Western fatalism. A sense of impending doom for the world saturates *The Asiatics* as the natives philosophize to the young American traveler about the resignation implicit in the Asian personality. This doom is counterbalanced by the lyrical nature of the writing and by the luxuriance of detail, however, and the beguiling, unutterable beauty of life strains to prevail even in these prewar novels. When the fear and foreboding of the 1930's was eventually replaced by worldwide optimism after the war, the tenor of Prokosch's novels changed in tune with the times. In *Storm and Echo*, the emphasis is on Africa as a new continent rather than on Asia as a dying one, and the hint of a positive note in the destiny of man is unmistakable.

In the picaresque narrative of *The Asiatics*, the nameless young American hero crosses the entire Asian continent from Lebanon to China. The character of the hero is elusive and vague, and many of the secondary characters with whom he forms friendships—friendships that are sometimes intense but always temporary—seem to take on more life than he. The hero is jailed in Turkey and suffers a plane crash in Iran, but always keeps his mind open and unbiased in order to soak up all the aphorisms proffered him both by the Asians and by the Western travelers whom he encounters. There is a chillingly prophetic mood to the novel; Asia is old and tired and waiting for death. When the hero enters a snowy-domed dagoba in Kandy and begins to converse with an old monk, it is of the coming of the twenty-fifth Buddha and of the accompanying dissolution of the world into Nirvana that they speak. The novel never ceases to analyze and emphasize the decadence and resignation of the enigma that is Asia.

In *The Seven Who Fled*, Prokosch weaves an allegory around a group of seven travelers, each representing a country in Europe (England, France, Spain, Germany, Austria, Belgium, and Russia), set adrift in the hostile vastness of Chinese Turkestan. After their caravan reaches Aqsu from Kashgar, the two German-speaking geologists are put into prison by local authorities; two others are kept as hostages; and the Frenchman de la Scaze falls prey to a fever. Only the Englishman Layeville and de la Scaze's beautiful Spanish wife are free to proceed; the former joins a caravan to Tibet, and the latter continues eastward on a caravan in the company of Dr. Liu, a wealthy Chinese merchant. Much of the first half of the book details the disintegration and eventual death of Layeville in the icy summits of Tibet. In his relationship with the barbaric and tantalizing Tansang, his Turgot guide whose powerful face combines the strengths of "a young man, a woman and a child," Layeville feels the possibility of a renewal of his spirit, but he loses his last chance when Tansang dies.

Like Layeville and Tansang, the hostages back in Aqsu, the Russian Serafimov (an inarticulate bear of a man) and the Belgian thief Goupilliere, form an uneasy pair. When Serafimov is rejected by the Russian prostitute Madame Tastin while his companion Goupilliere is accepted, Serafimov consummates his hatred for the Belgian by murdering him. The two geologists, the German Wildenbruch (who worships heroism and ambition) and the blond, angelic Austrian Von Wald, escape from prison together and travel to Shanghai, where the tubercular Wildenbruch departs for home and Von Wald decides to remain. The last pair, the most mismatched of all, are Paul and Olivia de la Scaze. Olivia, who abandons her husband in Aqsu, comes under the complete control of Dr. Liu and ends up joining a house of prostitution in Shanghai. Paul recovers from his fever, eventually catches cholera from a dancing girl, and dies.

Although the seven characters do not correspond exactly to the seven cardinal sins of medieval theology, each sin is very much in evidence. Certainly sloth is implied in the flight of the seven from the responsibilities of their European lives to the distractions of adventure abroad. Lust is evident in Layeville's reminiscences of homosexuality, in Olivia's eventual choice of occupation, and in Serafimov's obsession with Madame Tastin. Wildenbruch feels envy for the innocence of Von Wald, and only Von Wald seems relatively immune to the ravages of the deadly sins.

Nine Days to Mukalla is the story of four plane-crash survivors who make their way from an island in the Indian Ocean to Mukalla in Arabia, where they will be able to get a boat for Aden and return to civilization. The novel employs the rich, evocative style that characterizes Prokosch's best work and allegorizes the contrasting sensibilities of the four victims lost in a mysterious Arabia, which, in its capacity to distill good and evil, "reveals the human skeleton." The group is composed of two Englishwomen, Miss Todd and Sylvia Howard, and two Americans, an archaeologist, Dr. Moss, and David Gilbert, who is the only survivor by the end of the novel. David, described by Miss Todd as not quite a typical American, seems symbolic of a new, postwar, cosmopolitan America. Miss Todd, although she dies early in the narrative, possesses such great vitality that her spirit persists throughout the novel. It is the gift of her jewelry to David that enables him to reach Mukalla successfully. Dr. Moss is Miss Todd's foil, and just as the party's Bedouin guide thinks of Miss Todd as their good spirit, Moss is viewed by him as their bad spirit. He steals some of Miss Todd's jewels, abandons the party in his own interest, and is finally murdered in the desert. The primness of Sylvia Howard, the sketchiest of the four characters, is broken down in the Arabian desert, and before she dies of exhaustion when she actually reaches Mukalla, she asks David to make love to her.

The Seven Sisters is Prokosch's first novel in which an American setting (Bishop's Neck, Maryland) is handled as powerfully as the foreign settings are in his earlier works. Each of the seven Nightingale sisters has a story, and the story of each sheds light on the character of Peter, an orphan who lives with the family. Peter is another of Prokosch's searching artists, but this time, untypically for Prokosch, his search ends in a kind of maturity. Five of the seven sisters, after frantic struggles, gradually achieve a kind of maturity as well.

The death of one of the sisters, young Elizabeth, who succumbs to a snake bite while still innocent, signals the real start of the action of the novel, suggesting a world divested of its innocence. The oldest sister, the repressed Augusta, marries a neighboring aristocrat, recognizes that the marriage is a mistake, and returns to her parents' home. Daphne leaves home dressed as a boy, falls in with a lesbian, meets a runaway New Yorker named Pancho, loses him to another man and to death, rejects the lesbian, and returns home. The elfin and visionary Grace never leaves home, but follows the advice of a ouija board, becomes pregnant, and goes to a cave, where she dies in the act of childbirth.

Consuelo, Barbara, and Freya, in the company of Peter and their mother, go to Europe. Consuelo links up with a Hungarian refugee. Blonde, beautiful Barbara marries a wealthy, aging Italian prince, falls in love with his handsome nephew, and ends up, after losing both, praying for forgiveness for her vanity and pride. Freya gives up her career as a painter and goes to Brazil as a social worker, where she perishes in the jungle. It is the character of Peter that acts as the cohesive force in the novel; it is with him that the novel begins and ends.

The Skies of Europe is Prokosch's first realistic novel and covers the events that led up to World War II. Philip, a young American journalist, loves Saskia, a failed artist who does not love him. The novel abounds in characters who are unsuccessful artists and neglected poets; one such unnamed character seems intended to represent Hitler. *The Skies of Europe* has affinities with a later novel, *A Ballad of Love*, Prokosch's most nearly autobiographical novel, his "portrait of the artist as a young man." It is, moreover, a portrait of a *defeated* artist. The hero, Henry, is a poet who grows up in Austria, Texas, and Wisconsin and becomes involved in a disastrous love affair similar to those in *The Skies of Europe* and *The Idols of the Cave*.

Three of Prokosch's novels are set against the backdrop of World War II. *The Conspirators*, which takes place in a wartime Lisbon filled with refugees and reeking of espionage, relates the detection and murder of a Nazi agent. Its atmosphere of historical change is haunting, and the degree of conventional suspense is rare in Prokosch's work. *Age of Thunder*, dedicated to the memory of Antoine de Saint-Exupéry, is not as realistic or as successful as *The Conspirators* and suffers from a preponderance of sketchily drawn characters, whereas the latter concentrates on a select few. As in all of Prokosch's novels, many of the scenes are brilliant, and they faithfully evoke the hypnotic atmosphere of war, but the dreamlike mission of the hero, Jean-Nicholas, through the Haute-Savoie seems to lack significance in the overall picture of the war. *The Idols of the Cave* makes use of the wartime atmosphere of New York as *The Conspirators* did with Lisbon. The city's brooding and sinister air is such that it almost overpowers the reader, and the unsuccessful love-story plot is little more than a duplication of that of *The Skies of Europe*.

Night of the Poor, the title of which was taken from a painting by Diego Rivera, is perhaps the author's weakest novel and amounts to little more than a conventional travelogue. It is the first of Prokosch's novels that has an American setting, and American place-names are savored and enumerated to such an extent that they tax the reader's patience. The plot chronicles the travels of Tom on his way to Texas after the death of an uncle in Wisconsin, and the gamut of depravity and inhumanity that he encounters on the way. Thirty-three years later, Prokosch would rework the same idea in *America, My Wilderness*, dressing it up with generous amounts of surrealism and modernistic bizarrerie. After the murder of his uncle in the Middle West, a half-black outcast named Pancho Krauss wanders from the Atlantic to the Pacific, savoring the "slow transition of one landscape into another."

Storm and Echo follows the pattern of Prokosch's first two novels, and the landscape of Africa is even more brilliantly painted than that of Asia in his earlier novels. There is a Conradian power in this tale of an American's search for a mysterious friend who has gone off to Mount Nagala. Central Africa is typically fraught with dangers of all kinds, but the friend is found (albeit as a corpse impaled upon a rock), and the protagonist emerges victorious over his own death wish.

Prokosch's historical novels include *A Tale for Midnight*, *The Dark Dancer*, and *The Missolonghi Manuscript*. The first, characterized by its author as "dedicated to storytelling per se and above all," seems to be just that, chronicling the murder of Count Francesco Cenci in 1599 by his wife and children and stressing the effect of the crime on the main conspirator, his daughter Beatrice. Its portrayal of sixteenth century Rome as plague-ridden, flood-ridden, and sin-ridden is graphic and effective. *The Dark Dancer* is laid in seventeenth century India at the zenith of the Mogul Golden Age, when Emperor Shah Jahan built the Taj Mahal for his wife Arjumand. The Emperor, however, is dispossessed of his empire by his sons, even as he himself had murdered to secure it, and gets to see the monumental building only when, as a prisoner, he is too weary even to admire it. *The Missolonghi Manuscript*, which purports to be the long-lost memoirs of Lord Byron unearthed by an American professor, is the strongest of Prokosch's postwar novels. Praiseworthy for its sensitive probing of Byron's personality and for its historical accuracy, the book is perhaps flawed by its overemphasis on the homosexual side of Byron's undeniably bisexual life-style.

The Wreck of the "Cassandra" is similar to *Nine Days to Mukalla*, but lacks the latter's allegorical sweep. Here, nine survivors of a shipwreck somewhere between Hong Kong and Australia reach a large island and settle down idyllically for a short time before the spirit of the island distills their person-alities into various shades of good and evil. The presence of hostile natives adds to the tensions in the group; they confront one another violently; and some of their number are lost before their inevitable rescue.

Prokosch is destined to be remembered, if not as a great novelist, as a pioneer of the novel of geography and as an internationalist, one who focused on the exotica of faraway lands but always called his fellow Americans to abandon their parochialism and recognize the underlying unity of human-kind.

Jack Shreve

Other major works

POETRY: *The Assassins*, 1936; *The Carnival: Poems*, 1938; *Death at Sea: Poems*, 1940; *Chosen Poems*, 1944; *The Sea*, 1983.

NONFICTION: *Some Poems of Friedrich Hölderlin*, 1943 (translation); *Love Sonnets of Louise Labé*, 1947 (translation); *Medea* in *Greek Plays in Modern Translation*, 1947 (translation, Dudley Fitts, editor); *Voices*, 1983.

Bibliography

Bishop, John Peale. *The Collected Essays of John Peale Bishop*. Edited by Edmund Wilson. New York: Charles Scribner's Sons, 1948. "Final Dread-ing," is a favorable poetry review by Bishop of Prokosch's *The Assassins*, his first book of poems. Refers to Prokosch's extensive travels and its influence on these poems and concludes with a brief commentary on Pro-kosch's technique and his relationship to Oswald Spengler and Saint-John Perse.

Carpenter, Richard C. "The Novels of Frederic Prokosch." *College English* 18 (1957): 261-267. Provides much insight into the development of Pro-kosch's novelistic style. An appreciative essay by a sympathetic critic of Prokosch.

Marowski, Daniel G., and Roger Matuz, eds. *Contemporary Literary Crit-icism*. Vol. 48. Detroit: Gale Research, 1988. The entry on Prokosch presents an overview of his works, citing him as a "highly regarded novel-

ist" who gained prominence in the 1930's. Included is a sampling of
reviews, mostly favorable, of his earlier works (*The Asiatics*, *The Assassins*, *The Seven Who Fled*), as well as later works, such as *The Missolonghi Manuscript* and his memoir, *Voices*, in which he addresses his
literary displacement.

Quartermain, Peter, ed. *Dictionary of Literary Biography*. Vol. 48. Detroit:
Gale Research, 1986. Provides a selected checklist of Prokosch's works,
giving more emphasis to his poetry, although he is better known as a
novelist. Discusses his poems between 1920 and the mid-1940's. Also
includes background information on Prokosch, including his numerous
travels, and some brief commentary on his novels.

Squires, Radcliffe. *Frederic Prokosch*. New York: Twayne, 1964. Presents
Prokosch's works in a chronological format and is useful as a critical
introduction. Squires focuses on the timeless qualities of "interplay of
emotion and intellect" in Prokosch's work but acknowledges that his writing was a "casualty" of World War II, which changed the values of the
reading public. A selected bibliography is provided.

JAMES PURDY

Born: Near Fremont, Ohio; July 14, 1923

Principal long fiction

Malcolm, 1959; *The Nephew*, 1960; *Cabot Wright Begins*, 1964; *Eustace Chisholm and the Works*, 1967; *Jeremy's Version*, 1970; *I Am Elijah Thrush*, 1972; *The House of the Solitary Maggot*, 1974; *In a Shallow Grave*, 1976; *Narrow Rooms*, 1977; *Mourners Below*, 1981; *On Glory's Course*, 1984; *In the Hollow of His Hand*, 1986.

Other literary forms

In addition to his novels, James Purdy has written in a variety of genres, including poetry, the short story, and drama. The most important of these other works are *63: Dream Palace* (1956); *Color of Darkness: Eleven Stories and a Novella* (1957); *Children Is All* (1961), ten stories and two plays; and a volume of poetry, *The Running Sun* (1971).

Achievements

Purdy is considered to be one of the most important of the postmodern American writers. Along with Thomas Pynchon, John Barth, and John Hawkes, Purdy is acknowledged as one of the best of the generation of post-Joycean experimental writers. He is a unique and powerful writer whose vision remains etched in the reader's mind. Like other postmodern writers, Purdy takes delight in experimenting with the texts and subtexts of a narrative and treats his themes with humor and irony. In essence, Purdy's characters are motivated by irrationality, his style is ornate and complex, and his themes are surreal; however, he is a writer whose works must be examined if the texture and ideas of the postmodern novel are to be appreciated.

Biography

James Purdy was born on July 14, 1923, near Fremont, Ohio. He attended the University of Chicago and the University of Puebla in Mexico. Later, he worked as an interpreter in Spain, Latin America, and France. From 1949 until 1953, he taught at Lawrence College in Appleton, Wisconsin. In 1953, he decided to devote himself to writing full-time. Purdy received Guggenheim Fellowships in 1958 and 1962 and a Ford Fellowship in Drama in 1961. He teaches at New York University and resides in Brooklyn, New York.

Analysis

Since James Purdy is so hesitant to make public the details of his private life, it is impossible to correlate any of his works with his personal experiences.

His works are hermetically sealed from his life, and must be examined as entities in themselves. Purdy's themes, style, and ideas change, develop, and expand from novel to novel, so it is not possible to delineate any one particular aspect of his work that is found consistently throughout. There are certain preoccupations, however, that are found, in varying degrees, in most of his works, and certain characteristics that are typical of postmodern fiction.

The characters in Purdy's novels are bizarre, grotesque, and governed by abnormal impulses and desires. Purdy uses his characters for purposes of symbolic manipulation, rather than for the purpose of character development in the traditional sense. Many of his characters are physically and/or mentally mutilated: they are tattooed, wounded, stabbed, raped, and, in one case, crucified. One of the major characteristics of all of his novels is his use of "unreal" characters whose thinking processes are "nonrealistic."

A primary concern of Purdy is the relationship of children to their parents; most of his novels include a domineering phallic woman, the search for a father, and the interrelationships within a family matrix. Many of his characters are orphans, illegitimate children, or children who have been abandoned by their parents. Along with these motifs, Purdy is preoccupied with the idea of being "grown-up" or mature. Within the quest for a father-figure, the idea of becoming mature is interwoven into the text, and within this framework Purdy usually parodies the search for identity and its resultant ambivalence.

The interplay of sex, love, and violence occurs frequently throughout his writing. Virtually no love between man and woman appears in Purdy's novels— the male/female relationships are either those of a prostitute and a man, or a man who rapes women. Purdy does include a number of homosexual affairs between men in his works, but these usually end in obsession and violence. In addition, many of the novels involve incest. Also interwoven in the stories are themes of tyranny, freedom, dominance, and obsessive love. Frequently, the female characters are aggressive and domineering, and often the male characters are passive and dominated. Many of the characters are attempting to find their "freedom" from dominance, but the nature of obsessive love does not permit this. Finally, in some manner or another, Purdy's novels all involve a writer within the narrative. In some books, this figure takes on more importance than in others; this device, typical of self-conscious "metafiction," serves to emphasize the autonomous reality of the fictive world.

Many of the themes, motifs, and preoccupations of his subsequent novels are found in Purdy's first novel, *Malcolm*. The orphan motif that occurs so frequently in Purdy's works plays a vital part in *Malcolm*. Malcolm (no last name given), the reader is told, belongs nowhere and to nobody. His father has disappeared, and Malcolm's search for him forms the central psychological structure of the book. The fifteen-year-old Malcolm is sitting on a park bench outside of the hotel where he is staying when Mr. Cox, an astrologer, takes an interest in him. He gives Malcolm a series of addresses in order to interest him in "things," and the ensuing visits to the people who live at the respective addresses form the core of the action in the novel. Malcolm becomes a parody of the picaro, for instead of acting he is acted upon. His main concern is to find his father, but his actions are governed by the tyrannical Mr. Cox and his circle of friends.

Within Mr. Cox's circle are Madame Girard and Girard Girard, an eccentric billionaire. At one point in the novel, Malcolm is offered a chance to be Girard Girard's son, but Malcolm tells him he has only one father and Girard Girard cannot take his place. Later, after Malcolm marries Melba, a famous black singer, he believes that he sees his father at a restaurant. Malcolm follows this man into the restroom. The man, however, disclaims that he is Malcolm's father and throws Malcolm down, causing Malcolm to hit his head. After this incident, Malcolm, who has deteriorated physically since his marriage, becomes too weak to get out of bed and eventually dies.

Thus, in this first novel, Purdy reveals many of his recurring preoccupations. In addition to the orphan's search for the father (paralleling the search for identity), Purdy also explores the topic of tyranny and the theme of the fatality of a loveless marriage. A concern with the maturation process is also found in *Malcolm*. Gus, one of Melba's ex-husbands, is chosen to help Malcolm mature before his marriage. Gus's solution to "maturing" Malcolm is to have Malcolm tattooed and to have him visit a prostitute.

In *Malcolm*, the characters are constantly questioning the substantiality of their existence; they are two-dimensional, almost comic-book figures. Malcolm is given addresses, not names, and consequently, places and events take primacy over the development of the personality. Malcolm himself has no last name, and when he dies there is no corpse in his coffin. All that is left of Malcolm are three hundred pages of manuscript that he had written, which Madame Girard attempts to organize.

In *The Nephew*, Purdy turns to the small town of Rainbow Center for his setting and tells a story which superficially resembles a slice of small-town life. Yet, underneath the seemingly placid exterior of Rainbow Center, as beneath the surface of the novel, much is happening. The text is surcharged with meanings, and the experience of reading this novel is similar to that of watching a movie with the sound track slightly off.

The plot is simple and straightforward. Alma Mason and her brother Boyd receive news that their nephew, Cliff, is missing in action during the Korean War. Cliff, another of Purdy's orphans, had lived with the Masons. In order to alleviate some of the grief of his death, Alma decides to write a memorial honoring Cliff. The novel focuses on Alma's attempts to gather material for the writing of Cliff's memorial. During this process, she discovers many facets of Cliff's existence of which she had been unaware—particularly that Cliff had hated the town and that he had had a homosexual affair with Vernon—

which lead her to some revelations about herself and her relationship to Boyd and others in the community.

One of Purdy's concerns that can be noted throughout the novel is the inadequacy of judging people by their actions and by what they say. Communication is always inadequate and misinterpreted. Alma never does finish her memorial to Cliff, another indication that one can never fully understand another person. By the end of the story, though, Alma does become much more tolerant in her attitude toward what she considers the foibles of others.

Like *The Nephew, Cabot Wright Begins* concerns the attempt to write about another person—in this case, a businessman-rapist named Cabot Wright. Instead of one narrative voice, as in *The Nephew*, many emerge in *Cabot Wright Begins*, and this blending and confusion of narrative voices further demonstrate the impossibility of learning the true story about another person.

Purdy's third novel is an extremely pessimistic indictment and extended meditation upon modern American culture. In *Cabot Wright Begins*, people are controlled by media-think, big business, and popular culture, and by all the superficial aspects of modern existence. Feelings, emotions, and actions are all superficial, and even the rape scenes involving Cabot Wright are narrated in a dispassionate manner—much like secondhand violence seen on television or in the cinema. People exist on the screen of the text, and their ability to function in normal human terms is questioned.

Cabot Wright, another orphan, is twenty-six years old during the time of the novel. He is a stockbroker turned rapist. Bernie Gladhart, a used-car salesman, has been cajoled by his wife into writing the great American novel and has decided that a life history of Cabot Wright would be the perfect subject matter. In fact, the tentative title of Bernie's novel is "Indelible Smudge," which indicates Purdy's judgment about American culture at this time. Princeton Keith, the owner of a large publishing house, however, has commissioned Zoe Bickle to write the story in terms of popular fiction. Through a skylight, Zoe literally falls upon Cabot Wright himself, and Cabot offers to help her ghostwrite his biography. In the process of turning his life into popular fiction, however, he becomes alienated from himself. To him, the story does not portray his real self.

Cabot Wright seems to symbolize the attempt of modern man to assert his identity through violence. Only through the act of rape can Cabot penetrate the surface of another, but even then he becomes increasingly alienated and less alive. For Cabot, there are no answers.

In *Eustace Chisholm and the Works*, Purdy presents his concept of the sacrificial, violent, and grotesque aspects of love. In many horrific scenes he shows the results of obsessional love. The story revolves around the homosexual love Daniel Hawes has for seventeen-year-old Amos Ratcliff. Amos, an illegitimate son, has been rejected by his father and has had incestuous relationships with his cousin (later revealed to be his mother). Daniel attempts to repress his feelings for Amos, but they finally become so overwhelming that he reenlists in the army to escape. Instead of escaping, however, he permits his homosexual love for Amos to be brought to the surface and projected upon his commanding officer, Captain Stadger. During the affair between these two, Captain Stadger becomes increasingly more sadistic until finally he kills Daniel by disemboweling him, and then commits suicide. This incident is the first in a series of homosexual blood-sacrifices found in Purdy's novels.

Once again, as in all the previous works, there is an author involved in an attempt to write the story. In this case, Eustace Chisholm is the writer who is attempting to incorporate the story of Amos and Daniel within the context of a larger epic poem that he is writing.

Purdy's next novel, *Jeremy's Version*, was written as Part I of a projected trilogy called *Sleepers in the Moon-Crowned Valleys*. Although Purdy had dealt with orphans, the search for a father-figure, and interrelationships among families in his previous works, this was his first novel in which the family matrix formed the basis for the entire work.

Again, there is a writer—in this case, Jeremy Cready—narrating the story being told to him by Uncle Matt. The basic story (that actually occurred more than fifty years before) involves the battle of wills between two strong women, Elvira Summerlad and Winifred Fergus, a divorce case, and the interrelationships of the three sons with one another and with their mother and father. Elvira Summerlad and Wilders Fergus were married, much against the wishes of his sister, Winifred, who thought the marriage was doomed. In a sense, Winifred was right, because Wilders abandoned Elvira and their sons. Winifred, however, goes to Wilders and tells him that since his sons are almost grown, he is needed at home. When he arrives, Elvira starts divorce proceedings against him.

The basic conflict is between Elvira and Winifred for custody of the children. Wilders is indifferent to the whole affair. One of Purdy's major themes—that of the son confronting the father—occurs during the divorce proceedings, when the homosexual oldest son, Rick, confronts Wilders. Rick demands that Wilders tell him the reason for his existence since his father has never been around before to teach him—he has only had his mother, who, he claims, has emasculated him. After Elvira wins the divorce case, her second son, Jethro, attempts to shoot her, but Matt saves her and is wounded. A similar shooting scene, between mother and son, occurs again in *The House of the Solitary Maggot*.

I Am Elijah Thrush is a dreamlike, ornate, and highly stylized book, populated with strange characters and filled with unusual events. More than any of Purdy's other novels, this book exists in the realm of allegory and symbols. Among the major characters are a famous mime, Elijah Thrush; his great-grandson, a mute, called the Bird of Heaven; Millicent De Frayne, a tyrannical old dowager who retains her youth by drinking the seminal fluid of young men; and Albert Peggs, the black memoirist who tells the story and who, himself, has a bizarre "habit." In addition, the novel incorporates many elements of mythology in a comic manner, suggesting the debasement of culture in modern America.

As in many of Purdy's previous novels, the plot in *I Am Elijah Thrush* involves a person (in this case, Albert Peggs) being hired by someone to write the story. Millicent De Frayne hires Albert to recount the story of Elijah Thrush. Once again, this story involves a clash of wills between two strong people—Millicent and Elijah. For more than fifty years, she has been trying to gain control of Elijah and marry him. Eventually, she succeeds by manipulating Albert, the Bird of Heaven, and Elijah onto her boat, where she finally marries him. Late in the novel, Albert's "habit" is discovered: he sustains the life of a golden eagle by permitting the eagle to feed upon him. At the wedding feast of Millicent and Elijah, the eagle is served as the entrée. After this incident, Albert "becomes" Elijah Thrush.

One of Purdy's major themes is that of confirming, or finding, an identity. In his novels, there is a plethora of name-changes, mistaken identities, disguises, masquerades, and other such motifs. The dreamlike structure of the narrative suggests that Albert Peggs is attempting to discover his identity by telling this story.

The House of the Solitary Maggot is Part II of the series called *Sleepers in Moon-Crowned Valleys*. The story is reconstructed—this time on a tape-recorder—by one of the characters, and, as in Part I of the series, *Jeremy's Version*, the family matrix is the psychological focus in the novel. The story involves Mr. Skegg, the magnate (the "solitary maggot"); Lady Bythewaite; and their three illegitimate sons: Clarence, who is legally "acknowledged" by the father; Owen, who is "acknowledged" by the mother; and Aiken, who is not "acknowledged" by either parent until later in the book.

The novel takes place in a dying community called Prince's Crossing. Owen, the youngest son, hero-worships his brother Clarence, who goes to New York to become a famous silent-film star. After Clarence leaves, Owen turns to the other older brother, Aiken, whom he also worships. The two become inseparable. Aiken, who himself has no acknowledged father or mother, serves as a father-figure to Owen, "maturing" him by giving him his first shave and taking him to visit a prostitute. After visiting the whore, Owen loses his sight. Aiken, who has finally been acknowledged by Lady Bythewaite as her long-lost son, buys the Acres, the showplace of the community. When Clarence returns and refuses to accept Aiken as his brother, Aiken, whose pride is hurt, burns down the house and marries the prostitute. This marriage is a failure, and Aiken decides to leave.

Although Aiken has been estranged from Owen, he loves him obsessively. When Aiken goes to say good-bye to Owen and their mother, Owen shoots him. Lady Bythewaite, one of Purdy's typical strong-willed, castrating women, then shoots Owen. In another of Purdy's characteristically grotesque scenes, Owen's eyeballs fall out and Aiken swallows them. While Aiken remains unconscious in the hospital, Clarence returns and wants to be acknowledged as Aiken's brother. When the unconscious Aiken cannot comply, Clarence slits his own throat. Eventually, Aiken comes to live with his mother. Mr. Skegg acknowledges him as his son and takes care of him in his illness. The story concludes with the death of Aiken, who, in a dreamlike sequence, tries to ride off on a horse with the dead Owen.

The protagonist of Purdy's next novel, *In a Shallow Grave*, is Garnet Montrose, a war hero who has been so badly wounded that he is turned almost inside-out and is the color of mulberry juice. Garnet seeks "applicants" to take messages from him to the Widow Rance, whom he wishes to court, but the applicants are so appalled by Garnet's appearance that they cannot accept the job. Finally, Quintus, a black adolescent, shows up by accident at Garnet's house and accepts the position. Quintus' responsibilities are to read to Garnet and to rub his feet. Later, one Daventry shows up. Even though he is not an applicant, he takes the position of messenger to the Widow Rance. Within this narrative structure, Purdy pursues many of his recurring themes.

One of the primary scenes involves a communion among Garnet, Quintus, and Daventry. Garnet is about to have his property taken away, but Daventry says that he will save Garnet's land and property if Garnet will commune with him. Daventry takes his knife, slits open his chest, and the three of them drink his blood. Later, they discover that Garnet's property has been saved by the Veteran's Administration, who heard of his plight and paid the mortgage. The wounding and shedding of blood, along with the religious connotations of the scene, seem to indicate that language is inadequate for portraying emotions, and that the only way to "love" another person is to shed blood for him.

Again, homosexual love appears in the novel, for Daventry and Garnet fall in love. They consummate their love in the dance hall where Garnet goes to dance by himself and relive the moments in the past when he was "normal." With Garnet's permission, Daventry marries the Widow Rance, but on his wedding night, he is swept up by a strong wind, smashed against a tree, and is killed.

Narrow Rooms is a story about the love-hate relationship between Roy Sturtevant (the renderer) and Sidney De Lakes. Roy Sturtevant had been in love with Sidney since the eighth grade, until Sidney slapped him publicly and humiliated him; from that time, Roy has been planning his revenge. The story opens after Sidney has returned from prison, where he has served time for killing Brian McFee. He finds a job as keeper of Gareth Vaisey, who has been injured in a fall from a horse. Sidney and Gareth fall in love and have an affair, but Roy Sturtevant still exercises a strange power over them. In the central scene in the novel, after Roy and Sidney have had a sexual encounter, Roy commands Sidney to crucify him on the barn door and then bring the body of Brian McFee to view the crucifixion. Roy, still alive, is taken down from the barn door and carried into the house. Sidney and Roy then pledge their love for each other, and Gareth, jealous, shoots them both. Subsequently, Gareth also dies. Though the subject matter of *Narrow Rooms* is largely sensational, the novel continues Purdy's exploration of the destructive nature of obsessive love.

In *Mourners Below*, Purdy returns to the theme of hero-worship. Seventeen-year-old Duane Bledsoe is mourning the death of his two half-brothers, Justin and Douglas, who have been killed in the war. Eugene Bledsoe, the father, with whom Duane lives, is aloof and psychologically distant. The central episode in the novel occurs when Duane goes to a fancy-dress ball at the mansion of Estelle Dumont (who had been Justin's lover), and Estelle seduces him. After the ball, another of Purdy's rape scenes occurs when Duane is homosexually assaulted by two men along the roadside. During the brief affair between Duane and Estelle, Estelle conceives a child, also named Justin. At the end of the story, Duane is given the child to rear, and Eugene states that it is Duane's destiny to rear a son.

Although this novel incorporates many of Purdy's familiar conceptions, it appears to be much more optimistic about the human condition than his previous novels. For example, Eugene and Duane do become reconciled in many ways, and there are many indications that Duane will make a good parent for the child. Furthermore, many of the grotesque and sadistic aspects of love are absent in this book. The men and the women in the story are not the tyrannical types found in previous works; they exhibit much more normal motivation. *Mourners Below* seems to indicate a new phase in Purdy's development, for in this novel he emphasizes the hopeful qualities of love and human existence.

The search for a lost son plays a crucial role in *On Glory's Course*. Adele Bevington, the main character in the novel, has had an illegitimate son taken away from her and placed for adoption. The rest of the novel revolves around her quest for her lost son. One of the wounded veterans living in Fonthill, the location of the novel, believes that he knows the identity of Adele's son—he is a soldier who has been gravely wounded in the war and is now residing at the Soldiers' Home, barely alive and unable to respond to any communication. Adele attempts to prove that this soldier, Moorbrook, is her son, but by the end of the novel, neither Adele nor the reader is certain about Moorbrook's identity. Once again, Purdy's recurring motif of the search for a father-figure is woven into the text of the novel.

In the Hollow of His Hand relates the kidnapping of a boy, Chad Coultas, by Decatur, a full-blooded Objiwa Indian. Decatur is actually the father of the boy and wishes to rear him as an Indian; however, Lew Coultas, the man who has brought up Chad, wishes to recapture him and take him "home." The mother of Chad, Eva Lewis, had not even realized that Decatur was the father until he returned home from the military and began taking Chad on rides after school. She then remembered that she had, indeed, had a one-day affair with Decatur years before the action in the novel begins. During the attempt to find Chad, the town of Yellow Brook is awakened to its small-town foibles and provincial attitudes, and once again Purdy reveals the darker side of small-town life and values. This novel is darkly satiric and deals with Purdy's attempts to create an almost mythological construct of his obsession with the search for an identity within the context of the family. Yet *In the Hollow of His Hand* is also an extremely humorous novel, delving into the souls of small-town America and American culture.

Earl Paulus Murphy

Other major works

SHORT FICTION: *Don't Call Me by My Right Name and Other Stories*, 1956; *63: Dream Palace*, 1956; *Color of Darkness: Eleven Stories and a Novella*, 1957; *The Candles of Your Eyes*, 1985.

PLAYS: *Mr. Cough Syrup and the Phantom Sex*, 1960; *Wedding Finger*, 1974; *Scrap of Paper, and the Berry-Picker*, 1981.

POETRY: *The Running Sun*, 1971; *Sunshine Is an Only Child*, 1973.

MISCELLANEOUS: *Children Is All*, 1961; *An Oyster Is a Wealthy Beast*, 1967; *My Evening: A Story and Nine Poems*, 1968; *On the Rebound: A Story and Nine Poems*, 1970; *A Day After the Fair: A Collection of Plays and Stories*, 1977.

Bibliography

Baldanza, Frank. "James Purdy on the Corruption of Innocents." *Contemporary Literature* 15 (Summer, 1974): 315-330. The recurring theme of "corruption" of an innocent, found throughout Purdy's works, receives critical discussion. The idea that the innocent enters into a corrupt and perhaps meaningless world is examined. A good introduction to the recurring motif of "innocence-corruption" found in Purdy.

Chudpack, Henry. *James Purdy*. Boston: Twayne, 1975. A good overview of Purdy's early works. Each of the early novels and short fictions is discussed in relationship to characters, plots, and themes. Contains a select bibliography and some additional notes.

Klein, Julia. Review of *Mourners Below*, by James Purdy. *The New Republic* 185 (July 18, 1981): 39-41. Klein discusses the recurring motifs in Purdy's works and how these motifs are extended and developed in *Mourners Below*.

Smith, Lee. Review of *In the Hollow of His Hand*, by James Purdy. *The New*

York Times Book Review (October 19, 1986): 15-16. Discusses Purdy as an important contemporary novelist, along with the basic themes of *In the Hollow of His Hand*.

Tanner, Tony. "Frames Without Pictures." In *City of Words: American Fiction, 1950-1970*. New York: Harper & Row, 1971. An excellent discussion of Purdy's early novels. The themes and concerns of these novels are examined and placed within the framework of postmodern American fiction. In particular, the paradoxical treatment of identity and meaning found in these novels is evaluated and analyzed.

BARBARA PYM
Mary Crampton

Born: Oswestry, England; June 2, 1913
Died: Oxford, England; January 11, 1980

Principal long fiction
Some Tame Gazelle, 1950; *Excellent Women*, 1952; *Jane and Prudence*, 1953; *Less Than Angels*, 1955; *A Glass of Blessings*, 1958; *No Fond Return of Love*, 1961; *Quartet in Autumn*, 1977; *The Sweet Dove Died*, 1978; *A Few Green Leaves*, 1980; *An Unsuitable Attachment*, 1982; *Crampton Hodnet*, 1985; *An Academic Question*, 1986.

Other literary forms
In 1984, Hazel Holt and Hilary Pym published a one-volume edition of Barbara Pym's diaries and letters, entitled *A Very Private Eye: An Autobiography in Diaries and Letters*. In 1987, Holt edited a miscellany, *Civil to Strangers and Other Writings*, which contained mostly fiction but some nonfiction.

Achievements
Pym was a writer of distinctive qualities who, having suffered discouragement and neglect for fifteen years, was rediscovered toward the end of her life, to take her rightful place as a novelist of considerable originality and force. Often compared favorably with Jane Austen's novels, Pym's are essentially those of a private, solitary individual, employing precise social observation, understatement, and gentle irony in an oblique approach to such universal themes as the underlying loneliness and frustrations of life, culture as a force for corruption, love thwarted or satisfied, and the power of the ordinary to sustain and protect the men and women who shelter themselves under it. Also like Austen, she has no illusions about herself and very few about other people: "I like to think that what I write gives pleasure and makes my readers smile, even laugh. But my novels are by no means only comedies as I try to reflect life as I see it."

The story of Pym's early achievements, her long enforced silence, and her remarkable rediscovery perhaps says more about the publishing world than about either her books or her readers. Between 1949 and 1961, while working as an editorial assistant at the International African Institute, Pym wrote a novel every two years. As each manuscript was finished, she sent it off to Jonathan Cape. Her first six novels established her style, were well-received by reviewers, and enjoyed a following among library borrowers. *Excellent Women*, her most popular novel, sold a little more than six thousand copies. Then, in 1963, Pym put her seventh novel, *An Unsuitable Attachment*, in the mail. A short time later, it was returned: times, she was told, had changed. The "swinging sixties" had no place for her gently ironic comedies about unconventional middle-class people leading outwardly uneventful lives. "Novels like *An Unsuitable Attachment*, despite their qualities, are getting increasingly difficult to sell," wrote another publisher, while a third regretted that the novel was unsuitable for their list.

Being a woman of determination and a certain modest confidence in herself, Pym went to work on an eighth novel, *The Sweet Dove Died*, and she sent it off to Cape; it too came back. She adopted a pseudonym—"Tom Crampton"—because "it had a swinging air to it," but twenty publishers turned down the novel. Humiliated and frustrated, she began to feel not only that her new books were no good, but also that nothing she had ever written had been good. *No Fond Return of Love* was serialized by the British Broadcasting Corporation (BBC) and Portway Reprints reissued five others; her books retained their popularity among library borrowers; and Robert Smith published an appreciation of her work in the October, 1971, issue of *Ariel*—but despite these signs of the continuing appeal of her work, Pym could not find a publisher, and by the mid-1970's, her name appeared to have been forgotten.

A renaissance in Pym's fortunes came with startling suddenness in 1977, when, to celebrate three-quarters of a century of existence, *The Times Literary Supplement* invited a number of well-known writers to name the most over- and underrated novelists of the century. Both Philip Larkin and Lord David Cecil—for years staunch admirers of hers—selected Pym as having been too long neglected, the only living writer to be so distinguished in the poll. Larkin praised her "unique eye and ear for the small poignancies and comedies of everyday life." Cecil called her early books "the finest example of high comedy to have appeared in England" in this century.

The publicity surrounding the article, not surprisingly, had positive effects on Pym's reputation. Macmillan published her new novel, *Quartet in Autumn*, near the end of 1977; later it was shortlisted for the Booker Prize. Cape began to reissue her earlier books; Penguin and Granada planned a series of paperbacks; she was widely interviewed; and she appeared on "Desert Island Discs" as well as in a television film called "Tea with Miss Pym." *The Sweet Dove Died* was published in 1978, followed by her last novel, the posthumously published *A Few Green Leaves* (1980). The manuscript of *An Unsuitable Attachment* was found among her papers after her death and published in 1982 with an introduction written by Philip Larkin. A book was prepared from her diaries and short stories.

Pym's novels are distinguished by an unobtrusive but perfectly controlled style, a concern with ordinary people and ordinary events, and a constant aim to be readable, to entertain in a world that is uniquely her own. They are also distinguished by a low-key but nevertheless cutting treatment of assumptions of masculine superiority and other sexist notions—all this well in advance of the women's movement, and without the rhetoric which mars so much feminist fiction. Although hers is a closed world—what Robert Smith called "an enchanted world of small felicities and small mishaps"—it is also real and varied in theme and setting, with its own laws of human conduct and values, its peculiar humor and pathos. Middle-aged or elderly ladies, middle-aged or elderly gentlemen, civil servants, clergymen, anthropologists and other academics—these are the people about whom Pym develops her stories.

The world in which Pym's characters live, whether urban or provincial, is also a quiet world—evoked in such detail as to make the reader feel that the action could not possibly take place anywhere else. Taken together, her novels constitute that rare achievement: an independent fictional world, rooted in quotidian reality yet very much the creation of Barbara Pym. Central characters from one novel appear in passing or are briefly mentioned in another; delightful minor characters turn up in unexpected places. This pleasure of cross-references is characteristic of Pym's art, in which formal dexterity and a marvelous sense of humor harmonize with a modest but unembarrassed moral vision. "I prefer to write about the kind of things I have experienced," Pym said, "and to put into my novels the kind of details that amuse me in the hope that others will share in this."

Biography

Barbara Mary Crampton Pym was born on June 2, 1913, in Oswestry, Shropshire, a small English town on the border of Wales. Like many of her characters, she led a quiet but enjoyable life among middle-class people with an Anglican background. Her father, Frederick Crampton Pym, was a solicitor and sang in the choir; her mother, Irena (Thomas), was of half Welsh descent and played the organ. Pym was given a good education (Huyton College, a boarding school near Liverpool; and St. Hilda's College, Oxford, from which she received a B.A., 1934, in English language and literature); saw some wartime service (Postal and Telegraph Censorship in Bristol, 1939, and the Women's Royal Naval Service in England and Italy, 1943-1946); and lived in various sections of London: Pimlico, Barnes, and Kilburn. She wrote down everything she saw in a series of little notebooks, and later "bottled it all up and reduced it, like making chutney."

In 1948, Pym began working at the International African Institute, first as a research assistant and later as an assistant editor of the journal *Africa*. She was given the job of preparing the research for publication, and regretted that more of the anthropologists did not turn their talents to the writing of fiction. In their work, she found many of the qualities that make a novelist: "accurate observation, detachment, even sympathy." Needed was a little more imagination, as well as "the leavening of irony and humour." Several of her novels draw on her years at the Institute to study the behavior patterns and rituals of a group of anthropologists. In *Less Than Angels*, for example, she portrays an anthropologist and his female co-workers, gently mocking the high seriousness with which they pursue their research among primitive African tribes and the shameless jargon in which they converse. No doubt the narrator is speaking for Pym herself when she concludes: "And how much more comfortable it sometimes was to observe [life] from a distance, to look down from an upper window, as it were, as the anthropologists did."

Although her first novel did not appear until 1950, Pym began writing when she was a schoolgirl, and even completed a novel when she was sixteen. After leaving Oxford, she started to write seriously and finished two more novels, but did not succeed in getting them published. By then, however, her literary tastes were well-set. Above all, she was addicted to novels. Anthony Trollope and Jane Austen were her favorite novelists, and she knew their works intimately; but she read all the fiction she could, and listed among her favorites Ivy Compton-Burnett, Anthony Powell, and Iris Murdoch. She was less tolerant of contemporary novels, and viewed popular and sentimental fiction with the critical eye of the satirist. Nowhere in her own fiction does the reader find the sentimental excesses and sensational unrealities of current popular fiction.

In 1971, Pym had a serious operation, and in 1974, she retired to live with her sister near Oxford. She died on January 11, 1980, at the age of sixty-six.

Analysis

Like most novelists, Barbara Pym was interested above all in human nature, and for most of her life she trained both eye and ear upon the exploration of that subject in its many fascinating dimensions. Her first published novel, *Some Tame Gazelle*, sets the tone and subject for what is to come as she casts her specialist's eye on British lower-class and lower-middle-class life and focuses on the quiet domestic lives of a few people. At the center are two unmarried women who have decided that they will be happier living alone together. An all-pervasive influence of the Anglican church, numerous references to anthropology and English literature, the weakness of men, realism, and a sometimes devastatingly comic tone are among the many distinctive features of not only this early novel but the later ones as well. Much the same judgment may be made for two posthumously published novels: *Crampton Hodnet*, which she had written in the 1930's but never intended to publish, and *An Academic Question*, for which she had written two drafts (one in first person, another in third person) but abandoned to write *Quartet in Autumn*. In 1986, Hazel Holt published an amalgamation of the two drafts. In spite of their thin plots and shallow characterization, both novels contain Pym's characteristically sharp observations and lively dialogue among the minor characters, as well as her concern with the elderly. Considered together, in all twelve of her novels Pym communicates her vision in an engaging, entertaining, and readable way. Her wit, her sense of style, her devotion to language and its revelation of character, and the richness of her invention all compel respect and critical attention.

"In all of her writing," Philip Larkin has written of Pym, "I find a continual perceptive attention to detail which is a joy, and a steady background of rueful yet courageous acceptance of things." In this statement, Larkin points to perhaps the single most important technique—and theme—in Pym's work. *Excellent Women, A Glass of Blessings,* and *Quartet in Autumn* develop their effects, as indeed do all of Pym's twelve novels, by exploiting the comedy of contemporary manners. Like her anthropologists, whom she quietly mocks for their esoteric detachment, Pym scrupulously notes and records the frustrations, unfulfilled desires, boredom, and loneliness of "ordinary people, people who have no claim to fame whatsoever." The usual pattern for the heroine is either retrenchment into her own world or, as a result of interaction with others, self-realization. By representing intensively the small world most individuals inhabit, it is Pym's method to suggest the world as a whole as well.

Usually Pym appoints a heroine to comment on the intimate details of social behavior. In *Excellent Women,* the assignment falls to Mildred Lathbury, who, as an observer of life, expects "very little—nothing, almost." Typical of Pym's "excellent women," Mildred is preoccupied with order, stability, and routine, but her special interest centers on the lives and crises of those around her—including her new neighbors, Rockingham and Helena Napier; the vicar, Julian Malory; and the anthropologist, Everard Bone. Faced with Mildred's honesty, diffidence, and unpretentiousness, the crises are resolved happily.

In Pym's fifth novel, *A Glass of Blessings,* the heroine is Wilmet Forsyth, a young and leisured woman bored with her excessively sober civil-servant husband. Her near-romances with a priest, her best friend's husband, and Piers Longridge (in whose friend Keith she discovers a rival) are only some of the pairings in this intricate drama of romantic errors. When the possibility of a love affair fails to materialize, Wilmet finds a different kind of consolation in religion.

Finally, Pym's anti-heroic view of life is particularly obvious in her most somber work, *Quartet in Autumn,* the first of her novels to be published after fifteen years of silence. Whereas her earlier work was a small protest against everyday life, *Quartet in Autumn* offered a formal protest against the conditions both of life itself and of certain sad civilities. The comedy is cold and the outlook is austere in this story of four people in late middle age who suffer from the same problem: loneliness. In its manipulation of the narrative among Edwin, Norman, Letty, and Marcia, the novel also represents Pym's greatest technical achievement.

Excellent Women, described by one critic as the most "felicitous" of all of

Pym's novels, explores the complications of being a spinster (and a religious one, at that) in the England of the 1950's. The setting is a run-down part of London near Victoria Station, but the very high Anglican Church of St. Mary's also provides the background for some of the events described. In the quiet comfort of this world, where everything is within walking distance and a new face is an occasion for speculation, the pleasantness and security of everyday life dominate. Only small crises—such as an argument between Winifred and Alegra over how to decorate the church altar—form the counterpoint to comfort. As the narrator says, "life was like that for most of us—the small unpleasantnesses rather than the great tragedies; the little useless longings rather than the great renunciations and dramatic love affairs of history or fiction."

Mildred Lathbury, the narrator, is representative of one of Pym's favorite character-types: the "excellent woman." She lives very much as she did growing up in a country rectory, working part-time for the aid of impoverished gentlewomen and devoting herself to the work of the parish. As one who tends to get involved in other people's lives, she knows herself, she says, "capable of dealing with most of the stock situations or even the great moments of life—birth, marriage, death, the successful jumble sale, the garden fête spoilt by bad weather."

In all of Pym's novels, says Philip Larkin, "a small incident serves to set off a chain of modest happenings among interrelated groups of characters." In this instance, it is the entry into Mildred's life of Rockingham Napier. A flag lieutenant to an admiral, Rockingham has just returned from Italy, where he served his country by being charming to dull Wren officers. His wife Helena, an anthropologist, does not welcome his return. Scornful of his easy charm and lack of serious purpose, she has become infatuated with another anthropologist, Everard Bone, her co-worker in Africa. As Helena pursues, however, Everard flees.

The reader depends upon Mildred for ironic commentary. Helena leaves her husband, who then departs for a cottage in the country. Excellent woman that she is, Mildred is invited by Rockingham to send him the Napier furniture; by Helena to get it back; by both to effect their reconciliation; and by Everard to read proof and make the index for his forthcoming book. Because the vicar, Julian Malory, needs to be protected from designing women and Everard needs her help with the book, it seems to Mildred that she may look forward to a "full life." Then she remembers Rockingham's smile and reads from Christina Rossetti: "Better by far you should forget and smile,/ Than that you should remember and be sad." "It was easy enough to read those lines and be glad at his smiling," she acknowledges, "but harder to tell myself there would never be any question of anything else." Still, Everard's affection is genuine, if undemonstrative—and not unmixed with a pragmatic desire to find a suitable typist, indexer, and all-around "helpmate"—and the reader is happy to learn, in a subsequent novel, that Mildred and Everard do indeed go on to wed.

Again set in the 1950's, town and country are contrasted in *A Glass of Blessings*, which Larkin regards as the "subtlest" of Pym's books. The novel opens in St. Luke's Church on the feast of its patron, the "beloved physician," as St. Paul called him. Celebrating the feast and her thirty-third birthday, Wilmet Forsyth, the narrator and heroine, is the well-to-do but aimless wife (subject to "useless little longings") of a typical Pym husband—hopelessly imperceptive, though well-intentioned and reliable. Like Jane Austen's Emma, whom Pym has in mind throughout the novel, Wilmet is unused and spoiled. A beautiful woman, always exquisitely dressed, Wilmet is childless, idle, and snobbish. She is also utterly unknown to herself, unable to imagine another life, and afraid to risk herself, even on the London buses, certain that any disturbance will be disillusioning. Bored, without training for a career, despising routine, she plans "to take more part in the life of St. Luke's, to try to befriend Piers Longridge and perhaps even go to his classes."

Piers Longridge is a sour, moody homosexual, a fact Wilmet never quite seems to grasp until well into the novel. He has taken a seemingly useless degree and now teaches Portuguese in adult education classes. Believing that she might relieve his unhappiness, she forces herself on him, hoping for the grand passion of her life, another fact that she never really admits. Finally, in a scene of high comedy and bitter pain, exasperated by Wilmet's attentions and her naïveté, Piers confronts her with his secret lover, Keith, a male model, and accuses Wilmet of being incapable of affection. It is the first time anyone has told her anything near the truth, and in response, she says to Mary Beamish, "sometimes you discover that you aren't as nice as you thought you were—that you're in fact rather a horrid person, and that's humiliating somehow."

When she witnesses the courtship and marriage of Mary Beamish, an orphan and ex-Anglican nun, and Father Marius Lovejoy Ransome, Wilmet begins to perceive the possibilities of being useful in the parish and even of passion. After she finds out that Rodney has had an innocent flirtation with his secretary, Wilmet sees him differently, thinking, "I had always regarded Rodney as the kind of man who would never look at another woman. The fact that he could—and indeed had done so—ought to teach me something about myself, even if I was not quite sure what it was." The truth of it is that Wilmet has failed to recognize her society, including the parish of St. Luke's, for what it is—an erotic conclave of beauty and variety, both dangerous and enlivening. It is like George Herbert's "glass of blessings," full of the "world's riches"—"beautie . . . wisdome, honour, pleasure."

In her first six novels, Pym treats her characters with warm compassion and gentle irony. With *Quartet in Autumn*, however, her tone becomes harsher, more bitter, as she examines with bleak detachment the lonely rejec-

Critical Survey of Long Fiction

tion of the retired. Letty Crowe, another of Pym's excellent women, is sixty-five and faces retirement from the unspecified office job she has shared for many years with her colleagues, Marcia, Norman, and Edwin. For Letty, life in a rooming house is "a little sterile, perhaps even deprived." Retirement gives her a feeling of nothingness, as if she had never existed. During sleepless nights, her life unrolls before her, like that of a drowning man: forty years wasted looking for love. Images of dead leaves drifting to the pavement in autumn and being swept away recur throughout the novel. Indeed, Letty tries not to dwell on the image of herself lying among the autumnal leaves "to prepare for death when life became too much to be endured."

Her former colleagues are of no help to Letty. Norman is a scrawny, sardonic bachelor. Edwin is a widower preoccupied with "the soothing rhythms of the church's year." Marcia is gravely ill and at least slightly mad—collecting tins of food she never opens and milk bottles which she hoards in a shed. The only pleasures she knows are visits to the clinic for check-ups and bus trips to look at the mansion of her adored surgeon. Incapable of thought, she is far more pathetic than Letty.

Unlike her colleagues, Letty does try to act bravely, reading books on sociology, participating in church activities, still caring for her hair and her dress. "She told herself, dutifully assuming the suggested attitude toward retirement, that life was still full of possibilities." At the close of the novel, she is, like Mildred and Wilmet, where she was at the beginning. Yet, at the slightest change in the routine of her eventless days, she courageously assures herself, "at least it made one realize that life still held infinite possibilities for change."

In *Excellent Women*, *A Glass of Blessings*, and *Quartet in Autumn*, Pym relies neither on violence nor on the bizarre. Nothing outwardly momentous happens, but the frustrations of a half dozen or more characters emerge clearly and poignantly. Some critics have felt that the narrowness of her life inevitably imposed limitations on her work. Beneath the calm surface of her novels, however, the events of the day do make an imprint—to a degree appropriate to the lives of ordinary middle-class people. Each novel is a miniature work of art, distinguished by an air of assurance, an easy but firm control of the material, and the economy of means to achieve it.

Dale Salwak

Other major works

NONFICTION: *A Very Private Eye: An Autobiography in Diaries and Letters*, 1984.

MISCELLANEOUS: *Civil to Strangers and Other Writings*, 1987.

Bibliography

Benet, Diana. *Something to Love: Barbara Pym's Novels*. Columbia: University of Missouri Press, 1986. Benet's fresh and insightful study examines Pym as "a chronicler of universal problems" whose focus—the many guises of love—moves, shapes, or disfigures all of her major characters. Includes an index.

Burkhart, Charles. *The Pleasure of Miss Pym*. Austin: University of Texas Press, 1987. A very readable discussion of Pym's life and autobiographical writings, as well as her fiction through *An Academic Question*. Focuses on her world view, the unique nature of her comedy, her religion, her place within the history of the novel, and her insights into male-female relationships. Includes photographs and an index.

Cotsell, Michael. *Barbara Pym*. New York: Macmillan, 1989. A cogent examination of all Pym's novels, paying particular attention to her characters' thoughts and feelings. Cotsell judges the novels to be "unabashedly romantic" and also considers Pym's sense of language, her unpublished writings, and her creative process. Includes an index.

Larkin, Philip. "The World of Barbara Pym." *The Times Literary Supplement*. (March 11, 1977): 260. An important essay that contributed to the resurgence of interest in Pym's novels. Offers an overview of her career and reputation and celebrates her distinctive qualities as a writer in her first six novels.

Liddell, Robert. *A Mind at Ease: Barbara Pym and Her Novels*. London: Peter Owen, 1989. In this invaluable study, Liddell draws upon his fifty years of friendship with Pym to write a critical survey through *Crampton Hodnet*. Considers the attention she gave to her characters' domestic and emotional lives, examines the reasons for her revival in popularity, and guides the reader through her novels, explaining which ones are or are not successful and why. Also corrects errors by critics and dilutes the common misconception that Pym is a modern-day Jane Austen.

Long, Robert Emmet. *Barbara Pym*. New York: Frederick Ungar, 1986. A helpful treatment of Pym's first eleven novels, paying particular attention to her recurring themes and character types, her modes of social comedy and satire, and her pervasive concern with "unrealized" love and solitude. Finds that Jane Austen's dynamic English provincial world has reached a point of breakdown in Pym. Includes a chronology, notes, and an index.

Nardin, Jane. *Barbara Pym*. Boston: Twayne, 1985. An excellent introductory study of Pym's life and career, noting the origins and development of her themes, character types, and style. Contains a chronology, notes, a bibliography (listing primary and secondary sources), and an index.

Rossen, Janice, ed. *Independent Women: The Function of Gender in the Novels of Barbara Pym*. New York: St. Martin's Press, 1988. This collection of ten original essays seeks to test Pym's reputation by considering her craftsmanship, the literary influences on her work, and her special use of language. Includes biographical, historical, and feminist approaches to explore her unique creative process as it relates to events in her life. Notes and an index are provided.

_____. *The World of Barbara Pym*. New York: Macmillan, 1987. Focuses on twentieth century England as Pym saw, lived, satirized, and enjoyed it. Defines her significance within the framework of the modern British novel, traces her artistic development, explores interrelations between her life and her fiction, and addresses broader themes regarding British culture in her work, such as spinsterhood, anthropology, English literature, the Anglican Church, and Oxford University. Notes and an index are provided.

Salwak, Dale, ed. *The Life and Work of Barbara Pym*. New York: Macmillan, 1987. Nineteen essays consider Pym's life and her novels, as well as her human and artistic achievements, from a variety of fresh perspectives. Includes notes and an index.

Smith, Robert. "How Pleasant to Know Miss Pym." *Ariel* 2 (October, 1971): 63-68. In this first important appreciation of Pym, Smith assesses her publishing career between 1960 and 1961. Considers her similarities to Jane Austen and comments on Pym's closed, enchanted world, her exact delineation of character, her form and style, her wit and sense of the ridiculous, and her treatment of religion and academe.

Snow, Lotus. *One Little Room an Everywhere: Barbara Pym's Novels*. Edited by Constance Hunting. Orono, Maine: Puckerbrush Press, 1987. In seven well-researched, clearly written chapters, Snow discusses Pym's interest in ordinary people and their mundane lives, her selection of character names, and her presentation of men and married women. Includes notes.

THOMAS PYNCHON

Born: Glen Cove, New York; May 8, 1937

Principal long fiction

V., 1963; *The Crying of Lot 49,* 1966; *Gravity's Rainbow*, 1973; *Vineland*, 1989.

Other literary forms

Before his novels began to come out, Thomas Pynchon published a handful of short stories. They include "The Small Rain" (1959), "Mortality and Mercy in Vienna" (1959), "Low-Lands" (1960), "Entropy" (1960), "Under the Rose" (1961—an early version of chapter 3 of *V.*), and "The Secret Integration" (1964). All except "Mortality and Mercy" appear in the 1984 collection *Slow Learner*. In addition to the odd review or introduction, Pynchon has published two articles: "A Journey Into the Mind of Watts" (1966) in *The New York Times Magazine* and "Is It O.K. to Be a Luddite?" (1984) in *The New York Times Book Review*. Two other magazine publications, "The World (This One), the Flesh (Mrs. Oedipa Maas), and the Testament of Pierce Inverarity" (1965) and "The Shrink Flips" (1966), are excerpts from *The Crying of Lot 49*.

Achievements

Among those contemporary novelists who enjoy both a popular and an academic following, Pynchon stands out as a virtual cult figure. His novels and stories stand up to the most rigorous critical analysis; they prove, like all great works of art, to be the product of a gifted sensibility and careful craftsmanship. At the same time, Dr. Samuel Johnson's "common reader" cheerfully wades through much abstruse matter because this author never fails to entertain—with bizarre plots, incandescent language, anarchic humor, and memorable characters.

With only four major works of fiction to his credit, Pynchon has an enormous, diverse, and fanatically loyal following. There are now approximately thirty books on his work, not to mention a triquarterly journal (*Pynchon Notes*, published at Wesleyan University) and special issues of other scholarly journals. Much of the fascination he holds for readers derives from his reclusive habits. He refuses to be interviewed, photographed, or otherwise made into a darling of the media. His residence, which probably changes frequently, is not a matter of public record.

Pynchon has been honored with a number of literary awards. He received the William Faulkner Foundation Award for *V.*, the 1967 Rosenthal Foundation Award of the National Institute of Arts and Letters for *The Crying of*

Lot 49, and the National Book Award for *Gravity's Rainbow* in 1974. Though the judging committee unanimously voted to award the Pulitzer Prize for fiction to Pynchon for *Gravity's Rainbow*, the committee was overruled by an advisory board which found the novel immoral and "turgid." The Howells Medal, awarded once every five years, was offered to Pynchon in 1975, but he declined it.

Though Pynchon has published, over the past quarter of a century, only four novels and a collection of stories, he remains, in the eyes of most followers of the current fiction scene, in the front rank. More than one distinguished critic has declared him America's finest novelist, and few would deny him a place among the best novelists now writing in the United States.

Biography

Because of Thomas Pynchon's passion for privacy, little is known about his life. His father was an industrial surveyor, and the family lived in Glen Cove, East Norwich, and Oyster Bay—all on Long Island in New York. His father, a Republican, eventually served as town supervisor of Oyster Bay. Pynchon was sixteen when he was graduated from Oyster Bay High School in 1953. He was class salutatorian and winner of an award for the senior attaining the highest average in English. With a scholarship at Cornell University, he first majored in engineering physics but, though he was doing well academically, abandoned that curriculum after the first year. A year later, he decided to do a hitch in the Navy before completing his baccalaureate degree. He attended boot camp at Bainbridge, Maryland, and did advanced training as an electrician at Norfolk, Virginia. The two years in the Navy, partly spent in the Mediterranean, provided Pynchon with a number of comic situations and characters, which he has exploited in "Low-Lands," *V.*, and *Gravity's Rainbow*. Pynchon finished at Cornell as an English major and was graduated in 1959. While at Cornell, Pynchon took a class taught by Vladimir Nabokov; Nabokov's wife, Vera, who did her husband's grading, remembers Pynchon for his distinctive handwriting.

Pynchon lived briefly in Greenwich Village and in uptown Manhattan before taking a job with the Boeing Company and moving to Seattle. With Boeing for two and a half years (until September, 1962), he worked in the Minuteman Logistics Support Program and wrote for such intramural publications as "The Minuteman Field Service News" and *Aerospace Safety*. After leaving Boeing, he lived in California and Mexico and completed *V.*, which was published in 1963 and hailed as a major first novel.

Rumors of Pynchon's whereabouts circulate often, some indicating that he has been seen in California, Mexico, and Oregon; in the late 1970's, he made a trip to England that mysteriously got noted in the national newsmagazines. Otherwise, there are only apocryphal stories of Pynchon which accompany the novels that have followed *V.* Would-be biographers have been frustrated, and some have simply written articles about their search for Pynchon, a search as beguiling and as ultimately inconclusive as the quests that figure in each of Pynchon's novels.

Pynchon has supplied a few tantalizing autobiographical facts in the introduction to *Slow Learner* and in the introduction he wrote for the 1983 Penguin reprint of Richard Fariña's 1966 novel, *Been Down So Long It Looks Like Up to Me*.

Analysis

The quest would seem to be the one indispensable element in the fictions of Thomas Pynchon, for each of his novels proves to be a modern-dress version of the search for some grail to revive the wasteland. Pynchon's characters seek knowledge that will make sense of their unanchored lives and their fragmented times; Pynchon hints that questing has a value irrespective of the authenticity of that for which one quests. The quest lends purpose to life, enabling one to function, to see life as worthwhile. At the same time, however, Pynchon invites his more privileged reader to recognize that the ordering principle thus projected is factitious. What is real is the gathering dissolution, the passing of human beings and whole civilizations. All attempts to discover or create order and system are doomed.

Even so, as Pynchon's career has developed, one notes what may be a tendency to define some grail of his own, an inclination to search for a way out of the cul-de-sac of a metaphysics perhaps unduly in thrall to the principle of entropy (broadly defined as the gradual deterioration of the universe caused by irreversible thermodynamic equalization). Pynchon's critics disagree sharply on this point. Some maintain that the intimation of counter-entropic orders in *The Crying of Lot 49* and *Gravity's Rainbow* is merely a hook by which to catch the unwary reader, a means of seducing him into system-making as delusive as that of any of Pynchon's characters. Other critics, unwilling to believe that Pynchon's frequently noted affinity with modern science has been frozen at a point attained some time in the 1950's, suspect that Pynchon means to hint at transcendental alternatives implicit in the vast mysteries of contemporary astronomy and particle physics.

Whether Pynchon is on a grail quest of his own (with all the propensity for mysticism that seems indispensable to such a quester), he continues to create intricate labyrinths in which readers experience the paranoia that also figures as a prominent theme in his work. Paranoia is the conviction that mighty conspiracies exist, that all things are connected "in spheres joyful or threatening about the central pulse of [one]self." Pynchon's protagonists come to believe in this infinite reticulation of conspiracy because it is preferable to the possibility that "nothing is connected to anything." Pynchon's readers, by the same token, encounter fictive structures that formally imitate the paranoid premise: all is connected in great, seamless webs of interdependent detail.

The dialectic between order and disorder is the dialectic between art and life, and it is with reference to this neglected commonplace that one should analyze Pynchon's artifice. In art, traditionally, humanity lays claim— sometimes piously, sometimes impiously—to the divine prerogative of creation, the establishment of order where all before was without form and void. Pynchon gives evidence, since the almost nihilistic *V.*, of a fascination with the religious belief that there are "orders behind the visible," orders analogous to those found beneath the surface in works of art ostensibly reflecting life in all its chaotic aspects. *Gravity's Rainbow*, for example, strikes one at first as a complete mishmash, a welter of all-too-lifelike confusion, but one subsequently discovers it to be as finely crafted as James Joyce's *Ulysses* (1922) or *Finnegans Wake* (1939). Perhaps Pynchon can best be imagined like William Blake, William Butler Yeats, and D. H. Lawrence, as countering the smugness and complacency of a scientific age with a calculated antirationalism.

These remarks adumbrate the last major topos in Pynchon's work—science and art. More than any other great writer, Pynchon knows and makes artistic use of science. He has, if nothing else, dispatched legions of humanists in search of information about modern physics, chemistry, and engineering— disciplines to which they had previously been indifferent. As suggested above, however, science serves vision, not the other way around. Pynchon has done more than any other writer—scientific or literary—to reverse the widening "dissociation of sensibility" that T. S. Eliot noted as part of the intellectual landscape since the seventeenth century. In Pynchon, and in his readers to a remarkable extent, C. P. Snow's "two cultures" become one again.

In his first novel, *V.*, Pynchon brilliantly interweaves two narratives, one in the present (mid-1950's), the other in the period 1880 to 1943. The historical narrative, presented obliquely, concerns an extraordinary woman who appears originally as Victoria Wren and subsequently under *noms de guerre* in which the letter *V* of the alphabet figures prominently: Veronica Manganese, Vera Meroving. This is V., who turns up whenever there is bloodshed in the course of the twentieth century. In 1898, for example, she appears at the periphery of the Fashoda crisis in Egypt, and the following year she gravitates to Florence, where the spies of several nations are jockeying for position, engaging in what Pynchon calls "premilitary" activity. In 1913, she is in Paris, involved in a bloody theater riot which, like the crises in Egypt and Florence earlier, proves an earnest of World War I—a kind of fulfillment for V. in her early phase. When World War I ends with Western civilization intact, though permanently altered, V. begins to be involved with those elements that will figure in the more satisfying carnage of the century's real climacteric, World War II. In 1922, she is in German South-West Africa, where the massacre of the native Hereros reenacts the even greater massacre of two decades earlier and anticipates the really accomplished genocide in

Europe between 1933 and 1945. On and off after 1918, she is on Malta, consorting with a group sympathetic to Mussolini and his Fascists. V. dies in an air raid on Malta in 1943—just as the tide turns against the Fascist cause with which she has become increasingly identified.

V.'s affinity with Fascism complements a decadent religiosity, and she comes to personify the drift to extinction of Western culture and of life itself. She gradually loses parts of her body and becomes more and more the sum of inanimate parts: false eye, false hair, false foot, false navel. She is a brilliant metaphor for entropy and the decline of civilization, and her baleful influence is projected in the novel's present in the decadence of the contemporary characters, most of whom are part of a group called the Whole Sick Crew. The Crew is exemplified by its newest member, the winsome schlemiel Benny Profane. Profane is incapable of love and emotional involvement; he is also perennially at war with inanimate objects. His dread of the inanimate suggests that he intuits the cultural situation as the century wanes. Though he is no thinker, he realizes that he and his fellows are Eliot's hollow men, on the way to their whimpering end. His inability to love is presented in comic terms—though fat, he is doted on by various desirable women, including the Maltese Paola Maijstral and the beautiful Rachel Owlglass. The failure is that of his entire circle, for though there is much sex among the Whole Sick Crew, there is no commitment, no love, no hope. The one baby generated by all the sexual freedom is aborted.

The Whole Sick Crew is what Western civilization has become as a result of entropic processes that are utterly random and mindless. The meaninglessness of entropy is something difficult for the human mind to accept, however, and in Herbert Stencil, a marginal member of the Crew, Pynchon presents what becomes his standard character, a person who must discover conspiracy to deal with the fragmentation of life and culture. It is Stencil who does the mythmaking, the elevating of Victoria Wren from mere perverted adventuress to something awesome and as multifaceted as Robert Graves's White Goddess. Nor is Stencil alone, for the undeniable desire for connectedness is quintessentially human. It is also shared by the sophisticated reader, who flings himself into the literary puzzle and becomes himself a Stencil, a quester for meaning in the convoluted plot of *V.* and in the identity of the mysterious personage who gives the novel its name. Pynchon's genius manifests itself in his ability to keep his readers suspended between his two mutually exclusive alternatives: that the clues to V.'s identity are the key to meaning and that V. is nothing more than a paranoid fantasy, the product of a mind that cannot deal with very much reality.

The fascination with which readers have responded to *V.* indicates that Pynchon is himself a brilliant mythmaker. Even after one has "solved" the mystery of V. and arrived at an enlightenment that Stencil explicitly rejects as a threat to his emotional and mental stability, one still finds the myth trenchant, moving, even terrifying. The decline of the West is a theme that one has encountered before, but never has one encountered it so cogently as in this woman who loves death and the inanimate. The real conspiracy, then, is an artistic one; the connectedness is that of the novel, the cabal between author and reader.

Pynchon's second novel, *The Crying of Lot 49*, seems slight between *V.* and *Gravity's Rainbow*, and Pynchon himself seems to consider it something of a potboiler. Some readers, however, believe it to be his most perfect work of art. It is the story of Oedipa Maas, who is named "executor, or she supposed executrix" of the estate of an ex-lover, the millionaire Pierce Inverarity. In carrying out her duties, she stumbles upon evidence of a conspiracy to circumvent the United States Postal Service. She discovers Tristero, a *sub rosa* postal system at war for centuries with all officially sanctioned postal services, first in the old world, then in the new. Tristero subsumes an extraordinary number of revolutionary or simply alienated groups. In its new-world phase, it seems to bring together all those within the American system who are disenfranchised, disaffected, or disinherited—all those defrauded of the American Dream.

Oedipa, like Herbert Stencil, finds that the harder she looks, the more connections to Tristero she discovers, until the connections start revealing themselves in such number and variety that she begins to doubt her sanity. Oedipa's mental condition, in fact, becomes the book's central conundrum. She first confronts the question in a flashback early in the story. She recalls visiting a Mexico City art gallery with Pierce Inverarity and seeing a disturbing painting by Remedios Varo. In the painting, a group of girls are imprisoned at the top of a circular tower and made to embroider *"el Manto Terrestre"*— the earth mantle. The tapestry they create, extruded through the tower's windows, contains "all the other buildings and creatures, all the waves, ships and forests of the earth," for "the tapestry was the world." Oedipa recognizes in the painting a representation of the fact that she—like any other human being—is imprisoned mentally and perceptually in the tower of her individual consciousness. External reality, in other words, may be nothing more than what one weaves or embroiders in one's cranial tower. Oedipa weeps at human isolation. Later, tracking down the clues to Tristero (which seems coextensive with Inverarity's estate and enterprises), she cannot free herself from the suspicion that the proliferating connections she is discovering all have their throbbing ganglion in her own mind. She realizes that she is becoming a classic paranoid.

Though Pynchon does not resolve the question of Oedipa's sanity, he hints that becoming sensitized to the problems of twentieth century American culture (and to the horrors of the spiritual void contingent on certain twentieth century habits of mind) involves a necessary sacrifice of sanity or at least serenity. At the end, Oedipa is faced with a harrowing choice: either she is insane, or Tristero—with its stupendous reticulation—really exists. When Oedipa attempts to rephrase the dilemma, she finds that the paranoia is somehow inescapable:

> There was either some Tristero beyond the appearance of the legacy America, or there was just America and if there was just America then it seemed the only way she could continue, and manage to be at all relevant to it, was as an alien, unfurrowed, assumed full circle into some paranoia.

Pynchon implies that Tristero, whatever its status as literal reality, is in effect a necessary fiction, a metaphor for the idea of an alternative to a closed system.

Oedipa's experiences are almost certainly an imaginative version of Pynchon's own. At the time of the novel, 1964, Oedipa is twenty-eight years old—the same age as Pynchon was in that year. Like Pynchon, she has attended Cornell and then gravitated to the West Coast. Like Pynchon, too, she comes to view herself as an "alien," unable to fit into the furrow of American success, prosperity, and complacency. Thus, one can read the novel as Pynchon's account of why he has gone underground. He has made common cause with America's disadvantaged; in all of his fiction, not to mention his article "A Journey into the Mind of Watts," one notes an obvious sympathy with minorities and something like loathing for the mechanisms of corporate greed responsible for the spoilage of the American landscape, both literal and psychic. *The Crying of Lot 49*, then, is a fictional hybrid of the spiritual autobiography—in the same tradition as St. Augustine's *Confessions* (397-401) and William Wordsworth's *The Prelude* (1850).

These speculations—the need for an alternative to a closed system, the hints of spiritual autobiography—are supported by Edward Mendelson's brilliant essay "The Sacred, the Profane, and *The Crying of Lot 49*" (the single most satisfying reading of the novel, this essay has been reprinted in Mendelson's *Pynchon: A Collection of Critical Essays*, 1978). Mendelson points out the novel's high density of language with religious connotations; he argues that what Oedipa really searches for—and behind her twentieth century man—is a new species of revelation, a way out of the agnostic, positivistic cul-de-sac of contemporary rationalism. He also provides an explanation of the novel's odd title. "Lot 49" is a group of stamps—Tristero forgeries—to be sold as part of the settlement of Pierce Inverarity's estate. The novel ends as lot 49 is about to be "cried" or auctioned. Oedipa, present at the auction, expects to confront some representative of the mysterious Tristero, who will attempt to acquire the evidence of the secret organization's existence. Mendelson suggests that the number "49" refers obliquely to the forty-nine-day period between Easter and the descent of the Holy Spirit at Pentecost; the revelation that awaits Oedipa at the crying of lot 49 is symbolically the revelation awaited by modern man, whose existence so tragically lacks a numinous dimension. Thus, Pynchon ends his novel on a note of expectation, a yearning for some restoration of mystery, some answer to what the narrator calls "the exitlessness, the absence of surprise to life" in the modern age.

All of Pynchon's books are filled with bizarre characters and incidents, but *Gravity's Rainbow* is especially dense and demanding. The hero is Tyrone Slothrop, an American army lieutenant attached to an allied intelligence unit in World War II. Slothrop's superiors become aware that the map of his sexual conquests (or his sexual fantasies; this is kept ambiguous) coincides with the distribution of German V-2 rockets falling on London. Significantly, the erection *precedes* the arrival of the rocket. This fact, which calls into question the usual mechanism of cause and effect (it complements the fact that the rocket, traveling faster than the speed of sound, is heard falling *after* it has exploded) is of central importance to the novel, for Pynchon means to pit two scientific models against each other. The older model, which few laymen question, posits a mechanistic universe that operates according to the laws of cause and effect.

The character associated with this world view is the sinister Dr. Pointsman, a diehard Pavlovian threatened by the new model, which posits a universe in which physical phenomena can be plotted and predicted only in terms of uncertainty and probability (Pynchon is on sound theoretical ground here; he is presenting the physics of Werner Heisenberg and Max Planck). The character who embraces the more up-to-date world view is the sympathetic Roger Mexico, a statistician. Between these two, poor Slothrop—a kind of Everyman—tries to stay alive and if possible free. Pointsman and his minions concoct an experiment with Slothrop; they will provide him with the best information they have on the German rocket and then observe him closely for further revelations. Slothrop, aware that he is being used, goes AWOL to embark on a private quest to discover the truth of his personal destiny—and perhaps the destiny of his age as well.

Pynchon picks his historical moment carefully, for World War II was the moment when technological man came of age. Technology offers man complete control of his environment and his destiny; it offers him something very like transcendence—or it offers him annihilation. Pynchon's novel is a meditation on the choice, which is seen nowhere more clearly than in the new rocket technology. Will man use the rocket transcendentally, to go to the stars, or will he use it to destroy himself? The answer has been taking shape since the German rocket scientists were sent east and west after World War II, and Pynchon concludes his great narrative with the split second before the ultimate cataclysm: the apocalyptic rocket plunges toward the "theatre" in which the film *Gravity's Rainbow* has unreeled before the reader. Critical opinion is split on the degree of bleakness in this ending. Figuratively, says Pynchon, the world is separated from its end only by "the last delta-t," the last infinitesimal unit of time and space between the rocket and its target. The delta-t, however, is a relative unit of measure. Modern man's folly has indeed set in motion the process of his own destruction, but the process might still be arrested by a reordering of priorities, human and technological.

As for Slothrop, he simply fades away. Pynchon says he becomes "scattered," and the world reveals a characteristic aspect of Pynchon's genius. Just as Joyce forced religious and liturgical language to serve his aesthetic ends, Pynchon forces technological language to serve humanistic and spiritual ends. "Scattering," a trope from particle physics, refers to the dispersal of a beam of radiation, but it also evokes *sparagmos*, the ritual dismemberment and dispersal of the divine scapegoat. Slothrop has been associated all along with Orpheus, whose dismemberment became the basis of one of the many fertility cults in the Mediterranean and Near East. In a sense, Slothrop dies for the sins of modern man, and his scattering coincides with the founding of the Counterforce, a group of enlightened, anarchic men and women devoted to reversing the technology of violence and death. The Counterforce, which has affinities with various countercultural movements waxing at the moment of this novel's composition, is not particularly powerful or effective, but it offers hope for a planet hurtling toward destruction.

After *Gravity's Rainbow*, Pynchon published no new fiction for seventeen years. During this period, the counterculture retreated as the forces of reaction, complacency, and materialism took over, and perhaps it was this frightening and disheartening development that was behind Pynchon's long silence. He may have abandoned a book or books that came to seem unattuned to the post-1960's *Zeitgeist*. Yet when the novelistic silence was at last broken, it was with a meditation on the historical polarization of the 1960's and the 1980's.

In his long-awaited fourth novel, *Vineland*, Pynchon returns to the California setting of *The Crying of Lot 49*. As in *V.*, Pynchon sets up a dual historical focus. He imagines characters in the present—the portentous year 1984—trying to come to terms with the period, twenty years earlier, when they and the whole country underwent a searing passage. Broadly, then, Pynchon here reflects on the direction the country's recent history has taken— from anarchic but healthy self-indulgence to neo-Puritan repression. These poles are visible in the People's Republic of Rock and Roll, with its ethic of freedom, pleasure, dope, music, and self-expression, and in the Nixonian and Reaganite reaction that put an end to the polymorphous perversity of the 1960's and ushered in the return to materialism and political conservatism.

The novel is structured—somewhat more loosely than is usual with Pynchon—around the quest of a girl named Prairie for the mother, Frenesi Gates, who abandoned her shortly after her birth. Prairie's father, Zoyd Wheeler, still loves Frenesi, as does the man with whom she was involved before him— the sinister Brock Vond, a federal agent who had used her to infiltrate and subvert PR[3] and other radical causes. Zoyd accepts his misery, but Vond will stop at nothing to get Frenesi back in his clutches—not even kidnapping Prairie, who could be made into an instrument of renewed control. Also involved in the action are female Ninja Darryl Louise—DL—Chastain, an old friend of Frenesi, and DL's companion, the "karmic adjuster" Takeshi Fumimota, a kind of Zen private eye.

The centrality of Prairie, Frenesi, and DL, not to mention the narrational attention to Frenesi's mother and grandmother (Sasha Gates and Eula Traverse), make this essay Pynchon's first in feminist fiction. (Though a woman, V., was central to his first novel, it was really a parody of the kind of matriarchal vision associated with Robert Graves and the White Goddess.) It is in terms of this feminism that he is able in *Vineland* to move beyond the apocalyptic obsession that characterizes all three of his previous novels, as well as the stories "Mortality and Mercy in Vienna" and "Entropy." *Vineland* ends with a vision of familial harmony that is nothing less than mythic—an augury of what an America-wide family might be. Here the reader sees Prairie reunited with her mother and half-brother, as Zoyd and others are also integrated. Vond alone is excluded (his surname is an apocope of the Dutch word *vondeling*, a foundling—as if to hint at his inability to be integrated into family wholeness). The reunion of the Traverse-Becker clans, which seem to center in their women, is Pynchon's Vonnegut-like imagining of the millennium, the era of peace and harmony that ironically succeeds the apocalyptic disruptions everywhere expected in the novel. Beyond apocalypse is millennium, and *Vineland* announces what will be a trend in fiction as the year 2000 approaches: it is a *fin-de-millénaire* novel.

Herein, too, is the meaning of Pynchon's setting, the imaginary community of Vineland that provides the novel with its title. Vineland, of course, is the name given to the American continent by the Vikings, its first European visitors, at the end of the first millennium. Pynchon's novel reminds American readers that their land has been known to history for a thousand years.

David Cowart

Other major work
SHORT FICTION: *Slow Learner: Early Stories*, 1984.

Bibliography
Cowart, David. *Thomas Pynchon: The Art of Allusion*. Carbondale: Southern Illinois University Press, 1980. This book contains some early biographical scourings, as well as an examination of Pynchon's use of art, cinema, music, and literature—especially as they define the pull in Pynchon between an "entropic" and a transcendental vision. Useful to beginning and advanced readers of Pynchon. Dust jacket has picture of Pynchon in the Navy.

Hume, Kathryn. *Pynchon's Mythography: An Approach to Gravity's Rainbow.* Carbondale: Southern Illinois University Press, 1987. A highly readable and important challenge to the critical argument that Pynchon, as postmodernist, relentlessly deconstructs myth.

Levine, George, and David Leverenz, eds. *Mindful Pleasures: Essays on Thomas Pynchon.* Boston: Little, Brown, 1976. Twelve important essays, by such critics as Richard Poirier, Tony Tanner, Edward Mendelson, and the editors themselves. Mathew Winston's biographical essay is especially useful for genealogical information.

Mead, Clifford. *Thomas Pynchon: A Bibliography of Primary and Secondary Materials.* Elmwood Park, Ill.: Dalkey Archive Press, 1989. Invaluable. Cites all of Pynchon's own writings, along with those of critics. Also reprints his endorsements of other writers, as well as his contributions to Oyster Bay High's newspaper, *The Purple and Gold.* Reproduces several pictures from the high school yearbook.

Mendelson, Edward. *Pynchon: A Collection of Critical Essays.* Englewood Cliffs, N.J.: Prentice-Hall, 1978. Part of the reliable Twentieth-Century Views series, this collection contains fourteen essays and reviews, by such important critics as Tony Tanner, Frank Kermode, Richard Poirier, Paul Fussell, and Mendelson himself.

Newman, Robert D. *Understanding Thomas Pynchon.* Columbia: University of South Carolina Press, 1986. From a series aimed at readers seeking basic introductions, this book is a good starting place for the beginner.

Schaub, Thomas. *Pynchon: The Voice of Ambiguity.* Urbana: University of Illinois Press, 1981. A reliable account of how entropy and uncertainty figure in Pynchon. Includes discussion of Marshall McLuhan's influence on *Lot 49* and the ironies attendant on Ivan Pavlov's role in *Gravity's Rainbow.* Places Pynchon in American literary tradition.

Slade, Joseph. *Thomas Pynchon.* New York: Warner Paperback Library, 1974. The first book on Pynchon and still one of the best, despite nearly thirty volumes of competition. A balanced and readable discussion, but especially strong on Pynchon's uses of science. Lack of an index reduces usefulness to the browser.

Tanner, Tony. *Thomas Pynchon.* London: Methuen, 1982. Tanner is one of Pynchon's most incisive—and earliest—critics. A short and readable introduction.

MRS. ANN RADCLIFFE

Born: London, England; July 9, 1764
Died: London, England; February 7, 1823

Principal long fiction

The Castles of Athlin and Dunbayne, 1789; *A Sicilian Romance*, 1790; *The Romance of the Forest*, 1791; *The Mysteries of Udolpho*, 1794; *The Italian: Or, The Confessional of the Black Penitents*, 1797; *Gaston de Blondeville*, 1826.

Other literary forms

In addition to her novels, Ann Radcliffe published *A Journey Made in the Summer of 1794 Through Holland and the Western Frontier of Germany* (1795). It recounts a continental journey made with her husband and includes copious observations of other tours to the English Lake District. The work became immediately popular, prompting a second edition that same year retitled *The Journeys of Mrs. Radcliffe*. Following a common practice of romance-writers, Radcliffe interspersed the lengthy prose passages of her novels with her own verses or with those from famous poets. An anonymous compiler took the liberty of collecting and publishing her verses in an unauthorized edition entitled *The Poems of Ann Radcliffe* (1816). This slim volume was reissued in 1834 and 1845. Radcliffe's interest in versifying was increasingly evident when her husband, in arranging for the posthumous publication of *Gaston de Blondeville*, included with it a long metrical romance, *St. Alban's Abbey* (1826). Radcliffe also wrote an essay, "On the Supernatural in Poetry," which was published in *The New Monthly Magazine* (1826). The record of her literary achievement remains available today as all of her novels and the poems are in print.

Achievements

Mrs. Radcliffe's fame as a novelist today in no way compares to the popularity she enjoyed in the 1790's. With the publication of her third novel, *The Romance of the Forest*, this relatively unknown woman established herself as the best-selling writer of the period, receiving rave reviews from the critics and increasing demand for her works from circulating libraries.

Radcliffe's five Gothic romances, published between 1789 and 1797, owed a portion of their motivation to Horace Walpole's *The Castle of Otranto* (1765) and two earlier Gothic writers, Sophia Lee and Clara Reeve. The Gothic tale reached its full development with Radcliffe's ability to manipulate the emotions of love and fear in such a manner as to provoke terror in both her characters and readers alike. Though managing an effective use of the little understood complexities of the imagination, she offered her readers stereotyped plots, characters, and settings. Her disguises of foreign characters and lands were as thin as the supernatural illusions which often seemed anticlimactic in their emotional appeal. These weaknesses did not deter Radcliffe's public, who remained fascinated by her distinctive brand of romanticism, which combined the gloomy darkening vale of the more somber poets of the graveyard school, the extremes of imaginative sensibility (as in Henry Mackenzie's *The Man of Feeling*, 1771), and the medieval extravagance of the Ossianic poems of James Macpherson, as well as the pseudoarchaic fabrications of Thomas Chatterton's Rowley poems (1777).

Radcliffe nurtured this cult of melancholy, primitivism, sentimentalism, exoticism, and medievalism in her novels, becoming the epitome of the Gothic genre to her contemporaries. *The Mysteries of Udolpho*, her best-known work, was satirized by Jane Austen in *Northanger Abbey* (1818) as representative of the entire mode. Her later importance was seen in a number of major Romantic writers who read her romances in their childhood. Percy Bysshe Shelley's *Zastrozzi* (1810), an extravagant romance, was a youthful answer to the genre. Lord Byron's *Manfred* (1817) appears as a Gothic villain committing spiritual murder in a landscape of "sublime solitudes." Matthew G. Lewis and Mary Wollstonecraft Shelley clearly benefited from Radcliffe's strengths as a novelist of suspense, mystery, and the picturesque. In America, Washington Irving's, Edgar Allan Poe's, and Nathaniel Hawthorne's tales of terror, along with Charles Brockden Brown's *Edgar Huntley* (1799), were suggested by Radcliffe's work.

As the most popular and perhaps most important novelist between the eighteenth century masters and Austen and Sir Walter Scott, Radcliffe continues to claim the attention of academicians. Psychological, feminist, folklorist, and the more traditional thematic studies have proved the strengths of her art. In 1980, Devendra P. Varma (*The Gothic Flame*, 1957) began serving as advisory editor for the Arno Press collection, *Gothic Studies and Dissertations*, which has published at least thirty-four texts dealing with Radcliffe's literary output; of those, fifteen discuss Radcliffe's novels at length. It is clear that there is at present a remarkable revival of interest in the Gothic and in Radcliffe's work.

Biography

Mrs. Ann Radcliffe, *née* Ward, was born on July 9, 1764, in Holborn, a borough of central London, the only child of William Ward and Ann Oates Ward. Her father was a successful haberdasher who provided the family with a comfortable life, allowing Radcliffe access to a well-stocked library and the time to read the works of every important English author, as well as numerous popular romances.

This quiet, sheltered existence was enlivened by the visits of her wealthy and learned uncle, Thomas Bentley, who was the partner of Josiah Wedgwood, the potter. Bentley's London home was a center for the literati; there, among others, the pretty but shy girl met Mrs. Hester L. Thrale Piozzi, the friend and biographer of Samuel Johnson; Mrs. Elizabeth Montagu, "Queen of the Blue-Stocking Club"; and "Athenian" Stuart.

In 1772, Radcliffe joined her parents at Bath, where her father had opened a shop for the firm of Wedgwood and Bentley. She remained sequestered in this resort until her marriage to the young Oxford graduate, William Radcliffe, in 1788. William Radcliffe had first decided to become a law student at one of the Inns of Court but abandoned this for a career in journalism. The couple moved to London soon thereafter, where William subsequently became proprietor and editor of the *English Chronicle*. The marriage was happy but childless, and the couple's circle of friends were primarily literary, which added encouragement to William Radcliffe's argument that his wife should begin to write.

With her husband away on editorial business, Radcliffe spent the evenings writing without interruption. Her first book, *The Castles of Athlin and Dunbayne*, was unremarkable, but her next two novels established her reputation as a master of suspense and the supernatural. *A Sicilian Romance* and *The Romance of the Forest* attracted the public's voracious appetite for romances. Both works were translated into French and Italian and numerous editions were published, as well as a dramatization of *The Romance of the Forest*, performed in 1794. Radcliffe's success culminated in the appearance of *The Mysteries of Udolpho*; her decision to rely less on external action and more on psychological conflict produced ecstatic reviews. The excitement created by the book threatened the relative solitude of the Radcliffes, but the publisher's unusually high offer of five hundred pounds freed them to travel extensively on the Continent.

In the summer of 1794, the Radcliffes journeyed through Holland and along the Rhine to the Swiss frontier. On returning to England, they proceeded north to the Lake District. While traveling, Radcliffe took complete notes concerning the picturesque landscape and included detailed political and economic accounts of the Low Countries and the Rhineland. These latter observations were probably contributed by her husband, though both Radcliffes found the devastation of the Napoleonic Wars appalling. In 1795, there appeared *A Journey Made in the Summer of 1794 Through Holland and the Western Frontier of Germany.*

Radcliffe's interest in the human misery of these regions and the legends and superstitions of the great fortresses and Catholic churches of the Rhineland suggested her next work, *The Italian: Or, The Confessional of the Black Penitents.* As a romance of the Inquisition, it explored character motivation in great detail, while action became a method of dramatizing personalities and not a simple vehicle for movement from one adventure to another. *The Italian*, though not as popular as *The Mysteries of Udolpho*, was translated immediately into French and even badly dramatized at the Haymarket on August 15, 1797.

At the age of thirty-three, Radcliffe was at the height of her popularity; though she had never decided on writing as a potential source of income, her means by this time had become quite ample. With the deaths of her parents between 1798 and 1799, she found herself independently wealthy. Whether it was because of her secure financial condition or her displeasure with the cheap imitations of her novels, Radcliffe withdrew from the public domain and refrained from publishing any more works in her lifetime. Innumerable reports surfaced that she was suffering from a terminal illness, that the terrors of which she had written in her novels had driven her mad, or that she had mysteriously died. These reports were without substance; in fact, she wrote another novel, a metrical romance, and an extensive diary.

After her death, Radcliffe's husband found among her papers a novel, *Gaston de Blondeville*, which he arranged to have published. Written after Radcliffe's visit to the ruins of Kenilworth Castle in 1802, it came near to comparing with the historical romances of Scott but lost itself in a preoccupation with historical precision, leaving action and character to suffer from a lack of emphasis. The narrative poem, *St. Alban's Abbey*, appeared posthumously with this last novel; though Radcliffe had been offered an early opportunity for publication, she broke off negotiations with the publisher.

Content with retirement and relative obscurity, she wrote in her last years only diary entries concerning the places she and her husband had visited on their long journeys through the English countryside. From 1813 to 1816, she lived near Windsor and probably at this time began suffering from bouts of spasmodic asthma. From all reports, she enjoyed the company of friends, maintained a ready wit and a sly humor, but insisted on delicacy and decorum in all things. Shortly before her final illness, she returned to London; she died there on February 7, 1823, in her sixtieth year. The "Udolpho woman" or "the Shakespeare of Romance Writers," as one contemporary reviewer called her, has achieved a secure place in the history of English literature.

Analysis

The novels of Ann Radcliffe serve as a transition between the major English novelists of the eighteenth century and the first accomplished novelists of the nineteenth century. In the years between 1789 and 1797, her five novels established a style which profoundly affected English fiction for the next twenty-five years and had a considerable impact in translation as well. From the negligible first novel, *The Castles of Athlin and Dunbayne*, to the sophisticated romances, *The Mysteries of Udolpho* and *The Italian*, Mrs. Radcliffe demonstrated an ability to enrich the motives, methods, and machineries of each succeeding work. Manipulating the conventions of the Gothic while introducing new thematic concerns and experiments with narrative techniques, Radcliffe became a master of her craft.

Improved control over the complex atmosphere of the Gothic romance proved an early factor in her success. Radcliffe went beyond the traditional Gothic devices of lurking ghosts and malevolent noblemen torturing innocent girls to an interest in natural description. This delight with nature's sublime scenery gave tone and color to her settings while emphasizing the heightened emotions and imagination that were produced in reaction to the landscape. A skillful use of numerous atmospherical factors such as sunsets, storms, winds, thunderclaps, and moonlight, intensified the romantic tendencies of her time.

A scene typifying the Radcliffe concept of landscape portraiture has a ruined castle in silhouette, arranged on a stern but majestic plain at nightfall. This view does not depend on precision of outline for effect but instead on an ominous vagueness, creating in the reader a queer mixture of pleasure and fear. Her delight in the architecture of massive proportions and in the picturesque derived in part from her reading of the nature poets and her study of the paintings of Claude Lorrain, Nicolas Poussin, and Salvator Rosa. She reflected a mid-eighteenth century English passion in cultivating an acute sensibility for discovering beauty where before it had not been perceived. While she made landscape in fiction a convention, it was her combining of beauty in horror and the horrible in the beautiful that reflected the romantic shift away from order and reason toward emotion and imagination.

Radcliffe's novels rely not only on strategies of terror, but also on the psychology of feelings. The novels of sensibility of the past generation offered her alternatives to the Gothic trappings made familiar in Horace Walpole's *The Castle of Otranto*; those Gothic aspects now became linked to various emotional elements in a total effect. By drawing on the poetry of Thomas Gray and Edward Young or the fiction of Oliver Goldsmith and Henry Mackenzie, Radcliffe created a minority of characters with complex natures who not only exhibited melancholy and doubt, love and joy, but also hate and evil intentions. She was one of the first English novelists to subject her characters to psychological analysis.

Of particular psychological interest are Radcliffe's villains. Cruel, calculating, domineering, relentless, and selfish, they are more compelling than her virtuous characters. Since their passions are alien to the ordinary man, she dramatically explores the mysteries of their sinister attitudes. Radcliffe's villains resemble those created by the Elizabethan dramatists, and their descendants can be found in the works of the great Romantics, Byron and Shelley.

At her best, Radcliffe manifested strengths not seen in her first two novels nor in her last. Her first novel, *The Castles of Athlin and Dunbayne*, exhibits the most obvious borrowings, from sources as well known as *The Castle of Otranto* to numerous other Gothic-historical and sentimental novels. Though immature, the work offers her characteristic sense of atmosphere with the marvelous dangers and mysteries of feudal Scotland depicted to full advantage. Its weaknesses become evident all too soon, however, as stock characters populate strained, often confused incidents while mouthing rather obvious parables about morality. Didacticism seems the motivating principle of the work; as David Durant observes in *Ann Radcliffe's Novels* (1980), "The characters are so controlled by didactic interests as to be faceless and without personality." The rigid obligations of *The Castles of Athlin and Dunbayne* to the morality of sentimental novels, the uniformity of a neoclassical prose style, and the repetitious, predictable action of the romance plot, trap Radcliffe into a mechanical performance.

Mrs. Radcliffe's second novel, *A Sicilian Romance*, has a new strategy, an emphasis on action and adventure while subordinating moral concerns. This approach, however, was not effective because of the obvious imbalance between the two methods, and characterization suffered before a mass of incident. The interest in fear was expanded throughout the tale as a long-suffering wife, imprisoned in the remote sections of a huge castle by a villainous nobleman (who has an attachment to a beautiful paramour), struggles helplessly until rescued, after much suspense, by her gentle daughter and the young girl's lover. The characters' shallowness is hidden by a chase sequence of overwhelming speed which prevents one from noticing their deficiencies. To dramatize the movement of plot, Radcliffe introduced numerous settings, offering the reader a complete vision of the romantic landscape.

Though *A Sicilian Romance* lacks the sureness of technique of the later novels and remains a lesser product, it did establish Radcliffe's ingenuity and perseverance. It was followed by the three novels on which her reputation rests: *The Romance of the Forest*, *The Mysteries of Udolpho*, and *The Italian*. Radcliffe's last novel, the posthumous *Gaston de Blondeville*, which was probably never meant for publication, exhibits the worst faults of the two earliest romances. Lifeless characters abound in a narrative overloaded with tedious historical facts and devoid of any action. In reconstructing history, Radcliffe was influenced by Sir Walter Scott but clearly was out of her element in attempting to make history conform to her own preconseptions. The primary innovation was the introduction of a real ghost to the love story. This specter, the apparition of a murdered knight demanding justice, stalks the grounds of Kenilworth Castle at the time of the reign of Henry III. Radcliffe detracts from this imposing supernatural figure when she resorts to explanations of incidents better left mysterious.

With the publication of her third novel, *The Romance of the Forest*, Mrs. Radcliffe moved from apprenticeship to mastery. Her technique had advanced in at least two important elements: the chase with its multitude of settings is scaled down to an exacting series of dramas set among a few extended scenes, and characterization of the heroine is improved with the reduction of external action. Though suspense is extended rather illegitimately in order to produce a glorious final surprise, the novel is a genuine exploration of the realm of the unconscious. This remarkable advance into modern psychology gave life to the standard situations of Radcliffe's stories, allowing the reader to create his own private horrors.

Radcliffe's new emphasis on internal action makes her protagonist, Adeline, more credible than the stock romantic heroines whom she in many ways resembles. Adeline suffers from a nervous illness after mysteriously being thrust upon the LaMotte family, who themselves have only recently escaped, under curious circumstances, from Paris. Soon the group discovers a Gothic ruin, which contains the requisite underground room, rotten tapestries, blood stains, and a general aura of mystery.

Instead of the familiar chase scenes, a series of unified set-pieces portray the exploration of the ruin, the seduction of the heroine, and the execution of the hero. The entire plot depends upon the actions of a vicious but dominating sadist, the Marquis Phillipe de Montalt, and his conspiratorial agent, Pierre de LaMotte, against the unprotected Adeline. Because of the uncertainty of her birth, the sexual implications of this situation involve the risk of incest. Among contemporary readers, *The Romance of the Forest* became an immediate success, owing to its well-constructed narrative, the charm of its description of romantic landscape, and a consummate handling of the principle of suspense.

Mrs. Radcliffe's next novel, *The Mysteries of Udolpho*, remains her best-known work. The sublimity of her landscapes and the control which she demonstrates in this novel mark an important change from her earlier novels; Radcliffe's handling of action and character also reached new levels of subtlety and success, moving the novel a step beyond the rather strict conventions of the sentimental mode to one of psychological inquiry.

The period of the novel is the end of the sixteenth century. The principal scenes are laid in the gloomy enclave of the Castle of Udolpho, in the Italian Apennines, but many glances are directed toward the south of France— Gascony, Provence, and Languedoc—and the brightness of Venice is contrasted with the dark horrors of the Apennines. Emily St. Aubert, the beautiful daughter of a Gascon family, is the heroine; she is intelligent and extraordinarily accomplished in the fine arts. Though revealing all the tender sensibilities of the characters associated with a hundred sentimental tales, Emily emerges as a credible figure who seems aware of the connections between the scenery around her and the characters who inhabit it. As a painter, she sees and thinks of life as a series of pictures. As David Durant explains in *Ann Radcliffe's Novels* (1980), "She does not merely feel fright, but conjures up imaginary scenes which elicit it . . . scenery inhabits the inner life of the heroine, as well as locating her actions." A further element of Emily's characterization that adds to her credibility is her internalizing of the suspense produced by the action in the narrative. Her heightened sensibility reacts to fear and terror in an all-inclusive way; this acuteness of sensibility makes her an easy prey for the villain, Signor Montoni. This sinister figure marries Emily's aunt for her money, and then conveys Emily and her unhappy aunt to the "vast and dreary" confines of the castle.

This impossible castle becomes a superbly appointed stage for the playing of the melodrama. As the melodrama has hopes of communicating a real sense of mystery, its action and characters remain subordinate to the environment which pervades the entire texture of the work. Description of landscape is a major part of the book's concept, and Radcliffe pays homage to Salvator Rosa and Claude Lorrain in emphasizing pictorial detail. The somber exterior of the castle prepares the reader for the ineffable horrors that lie within the walls and adumbrates the importance of landscape and massive architecture in the novel.

There are certain shortcomings in Radcliffe's method: landscape description strangles action; the visual aspects of the novel have been internalized; and the device of the chase over great stretches of land has been subordinated by mental recapitulation of past scenes—action becomes tableaux. This internal action is slow-moving, tortuously so in a novel of 300,000 words. Critics have also objected to Radcliffe's penchant for a rational explanation of every apparent supernatural phenomenon she has introduced; others, however, point out that Radcliffe's readers enjoyed terror only if they were never forced into surrendering themselves.

The Mysteries of Udolpho brought new energy to the picturesque, the sentimental, and the Gothic novel. Radcliffe alternated effectively between the picturesque vagueness of the landscape and the castle's hall of terrors. Her deft handling of sexual feeling, shown as antagonism between Montoni and Emily, is characteristic of her refusal to acknowledge sex overtly except as a frightening nameless power. The artificial terror, heightened sensibility, and the pervading air of mystery produced a powerful effect on her readers, yet many felt cheated by her failure to satisfy fully the intense imaginative visions awakened by the book. These readers would have to wait for *The Italian*, probably Radcliffe's finest work and the high-water mark of Gothic fiction.

The unity, control, and concentration of *The Italian* display a superb talent. Mrs. Radcliffe's narrative technique is more sophisticated than at any previous time, particularly in the subtle revelation of the unreliability of feelings based on first impressions rather than on rational judgment. The dramatic pacing remains rigorous throughout and relatively free from digressions. The story's impulse depends upon the Marchesa di Vivaldi's refusal to allow her young son, Vincentio, to marry the heroine, Ellena di Rosalba, whose origins are in doubt. The Marchesa relies on the sinister machinations of her monk-confessor, Schedoni, who decides to murder Ellena. Radcliffe's antipathy to

Roman Catholicism is evident in her account of the horrors of the Carmelite abbey and its order, including the labyrinthine vaults and gloomy corridors. A strange blend of fascination and disgust is evoked here and in the scenes of the trial in the halls of the Inquisition, the ruins of the Paluzzi, and in the prison of the Inquisition. Clearly, the Gothic aspects of *The Italian* function as representations of a disordered and morally evil past.

The vividness continues through to the climax of the story, when Schedoni, dagger in hand, prepares to murder Ellena but hesitates when he recognizes the portrait miniature she wears. Believing the girl is his lost daughter, he tries to make amends for his crimes. Though the solution involves more complex developments, the excitement of the confrontation between these two figures remains exceptional. Ellena has been a paragon of virtue, displaying piety, sensibility, benevolence, constancy, and a love of nature. To this catalog, Radcliffe adds intelligence, courage, and ingenuity. As an idealized character, Ellena represents the strengths necessary to prevail in the romantic conflict against external malign forces.

Schedoni, the devil/priest, is a figure of strong and dangerous sexual desire, associated, as is often the case in Radcliffe's work, with incest. Radcliffe counters the passivity and weakness of Ellena's virtues with this masculine version of desire—the lust of unregulated ambition. She describes him thus: "There was something terrible in his air, something almost superhuman. . . . His physiognomy . . . bore traces of many passions . . . his eyes were so piercing that they seemed to penetrate at a single glance into the hearts of men, and to read their most secret thoughts." His pride, greed, and loneliness combine to form a demonic figure vaguely suggesting John Milton's Satan.

Eino Railo, in *The Haunted Castle* (1964), believes *The Italian* and the central character, Father Schedoni, were created under the revivified romantic impulse supplied by the tragic monastic figure in Matthew G. Lewis' *The Monk* (1796). According to Railo, the difference between Ambrosio and Schedoni is that the latter "is no longer a young and inexperienced saint preserved from temptations, but a person long hardened in the ways of crime and vice, alarmingly gifted and strenuous, hypocritical, unfeeling and merciless." Radcliffe was inspired by "Monk Lewis" to write a more impressive book than earlier conceived; her bias against sexual and sadistic impulses and toward heightened romantic effect win out in *The Italian*. While Ambrosio's passions remain tangled and confused by his need for immediate satisfaction and his lack of any lasting goal, Schedoni has well-defined goals for power, wealth, and status. His Machiavellian inclinations blend with pride, melancholy, mystery, and dignity, making him Radcliffe's most fully realized character. Her protest against *The Monk* created a story of tragic quality that goes beyond the conventional Gothic paraphernalia and toward the psychological novel.

Mrs. Radcliffe remains the undisputed mistress of the Gothic novel and a central figure in the Gothic revival, beginning in the late 1950's, which has seen the resurrection of hordes of forgotten Gothic novelists and their tales. The generous volume of Radcliffe criticism in recent decades has redefined her place in literary history, acknowledging the prodigious sweep of her influence. On first reading her works, one must remember to search behind the genteel exterior of the artistry to discover the special recesses of terror, subconscious conflict, and the psychology of feelings which played a major role in the evolution of dark romanticism.

Paul J. deGategno

Other major works

NONFICTION: *A Journey Made in the Summer of 1794 Through Holland and the Western Frontier of Germany*, 1795.

POETRY: *The Poems of Ann Radcliffe*, 1816; *St. Alban's Abbey*, 1826.

Bibliography

Durant, David S. *Ann Radcliffe's Novels: Experiments in Setting*. Rev. ed. New York: Arno Press, 1980. Discovers a pattern of evolution in Radcliffe's novels from the sentimental *The Castles of Athlin and Dunbayne* to the historical *Gaston de Blondeville* that reflects the movement of eighteenth century British fiction and completes the transition between Fanny Burney's fiction and Sir Walter Scott's romances. This book still shows the shape of its original dissertation format, including footnotes: nevertheless, it is one of the few easily accessible books on Radcliffe. Devotes six chapters to detailed analyses of her six novels, putting them in the context of their time and genre and illustrating their experimental styles.

Kiely, Robert. *The Romantic Novel in England*. Cambridge, Mass.: Harvard University Press, 1972. An important book on Romantic fiction, including Radcliffe's Gothic romances, which analyzes in depth twelve Romantic novels to define the intellectual context of the era. Notes that concepts of reality were tested and changed by Romantic novels and that Edmund Burke's ideas of the sublime modified aesthetic forms. Radcliffe is given a prominent place in this general thesis and *The Mysteries of Udolpho* is analyzed in detail as the focus of her chapter. Her novel is shown as a progressive revelation that nature weakens beneath the power of human imagination to project itself upon nature, as her heroine is deprived of consolation from natural order. Finds a common drift toward death in most novels of this genre. Includes a set of notes and an index.

McIntyre, Clara Frances. *Ann Radcliffe in Relation to Her Time*. New Haven, Conn.: Yale University Press, 1920. Reprint. New York: Archon Books, 1970. A dated, but still useful, 104-page study of Radcliffe which reviews the facts of her life and surveys her work. Presents contemporary estimates of her novels, considers their sources, and lists translations and dramatizations of them. Argues that Radcliffe's main contribution is in her improvement of Horace Walpole's method of dramatic structure, demonstrated by an analysis of her structures and their influences on the structures of Sir Walter Scott, Mary Shelley, and others. Contains a bibliography which includes a list of references to magazines.

Murray, E. B. *Ann Radcliffe*. New York: Twayne, 1972. Surveys Radcliffe's life, drawing from her *A Journey Made in the Summer of 1794 Through Holland and the Western Frontier of Germany* to illustrate her novels' geography. Examines the background of the Gothic, with its supernatural elements, sentiment and sensibility, and sense of the sublime and the picturesque. Looks at Radcliffe's modern romance of medieval experience, *The Castles of Athlin and Dunbayne*; concentrates on the heroine's sufferings in *A Sicilian Romance*; examines the strengths in plot and atmosphere of *The Romance of the Forest*; views *The Mysteries of Udolpho* as her first successful synthesis of modern and medieval; and argues that *The Italian* is Radcliffe's best novel because it sustains the reader's interest. Provides an overview of Radcliffe's literary accomplishments and influence. Includes notes, a selected annotated bibliography, and an index.

Sherman, Leona F. *Ann Radcliffe and the Gothic Romance: A Psychoanalytic Approach*. New York: Arno Press, 1980. The most interesting of the Arno Gothic Studies publications on Radcliffe, concentrating on an analysis on *The Mysteries of Udolpho* as the most useful epitome of Radcliffe's work. Applying feminist methods and concepts of psychoanalysis borrowed from Freud and post-Freudian theorists, Sherman examines Radcliffe's novel as an important contribution to the origin of women's fiction. The Introduction surveys previous studies of Radcliffe and critiques the Gothic romance as cultural expression. Analyzes castle imagery, with its mother-child symbolism, and house imagery, with its symbolic expression of female sexuality. Discusses the underlying sexual fantasies contained in the novel and Radcliffe's means of personal expression through the narrative. Includes a section of notes, an appendix of definitions for psychoanalytic terms, and a list of cited works.

Smith, Nelson C. *The Art of the Gothic: Ann Radcliffe's Major Novels*. New York: Arno Press, 1980. Contains a valuable introduction which reviews the scholarship on Radcliffe between 1967 and 1980. Analyzes the ways Radcliffe developed the sophistication of her fiction from *The Castles of Athlin and Dunbayne* to *The Mysteries of Udolpho* and *The Italian* in a six-year period. Examines the nature of the Gothic in order to focus on Radcliffe's heroines of sensibility. Notes a decline of didacticism in Radcliffe's fiction by isolating her heroes and villains for study. Analyzes the narrative techniques used to craft the Gothic tale, and surveys the Gothic writers who followed Radcliffe. Includes end notes for each chapter and a bibliography.

RAJA RAO

Born: Hassan, India; November 5, 1908

Principal long fiction

Kanthapura, 1938; *The Serpent and the Rope*, 1960; *The Cat and Shakespeare: A Tale of India*, 1965; *Comrade Kirillov*, 1976; *The Chessmaster and His Moves*, 1988.

Other literary forms

Raja Rao's first efforts as a writer were in Kannada, his mother tongue. Between 1931 and 1933, he published three essays and a poem in Kannada in a journal called *Jaya Karnataka*. Around that time, he began to publish his earliest stories in English. These and others were collected and published as *The Cow of the Barricades and Other Stories* in 1947. A later collection, *The Policeman and the Rose* (1978), includes seven stories published in the earlier volume and three new ones written chiefly during the 1960's. In addition to novels and short stories, Rao has published essays, travelogues, and biographical sketches in various journals and popular magazines; these have not been collected as yet. Rao has also edited three books: the first two, anthologies of essays on India, are *Changing India* (1939) and *Whither India* (1948), coedited with Iqbal Singh; the third is *Soviet Russia: Some Random Sketches and Impressions* (1949) by Jawaharlal Nehru.

Achievements

Rao, with Mulk Raj Anand and R. K. Narayan, is generally regarded as one of the most important modern Indian English novelists. The reasons for his preeminence are both historical and artistic. Rao is important historically because his first novel, *Kanthapura*, was published during the decade of the 1930's, when Indian English fiction first began to gain recognition. Although the Indian English novel is considered to begin with Toru Dutt's incomplete romance, *Bianca: Or, The Young Spanish Maiden* (1878), it was in the 1930's that Indian English fiction began to demonstrate maturity and accomplishment with the publication of Anand's *Untouchable* (1935), Narayan's *Swami and Friends* (1935), and Rao's *Kanthapura*.

Artistically, Rao is important because of his unique formal and thematic accomplishments. Although his four novels seem meager in comparison to Anand's or Narayan's more prolific output, Rao's achievement is considerable. Formally and stylistically, he is the most adventurous of the three. As M. K. Naik has elaborated in his monograph *Raja Rao* (1972), Rao has consistently tried to adapt the Western form of the novel to suit his Indian subject matter. He uses traditional Indian genres such as Purana, *sthalakatha*, and the Indian beast fable to structure his works. Thus, formally, his novels are based on Indian models. Furthermore, they are written in an English that is uniquely Indian in style, tone, mood, and rhythm. This Indianness of style is achieved by relying heavily on translation, quotation, and the use of Indian proverbs, idioms, and colloquial patterns. Rao adroitly manipulates vocabulary and syntax to enhance the Indian flavoring of his English. The result is a style which, although distinctly Indian, is evocative and perfectly intelligible to Western readers as well.

Thematically, too, Rao is somewhat different from the other two major Indian English novelists, Anand and Narayan. Rao is a metaphysical novelist whose concerns are primarily religious and philosophical. *Kanthapura*, for example, shows a strong Gandhian influence as it documents the progress of a nonviolent agitation against the British in a remote South Indian village. *The Serpent and the Rope* and its sequel *The Cat and Shakespeare* are expositions of the ancient Indian philosophical outlook, Vedanta. *Comrade Kirillov* is an evaluation of the efficacy of Communism. Thus, in Rao's works there is an ongoing discussion of major philosophical systems, chiefly of India but also of the West.

Both stylistically and thematically, then, Rao succeeds in capturing the spirit of India in his works. His formal and stylistic innovations have expanded the expressive range of English and have influenced other writers who share Rao's predicament: the task of writing about a culture in a language that is not native to it. Although Rao's oeuvre is small, his reputation appears to be secure.

Rao was awarded the Sahitya Akademi Prize for 1964 by the Academy of Indian Literature. In 1969, he received the Padma Bhushan from the Indian government. In 1988, at the age of seventy-nine, Rao was awarded the tenth International Prize for Literature by Oklahoma University's international literary quarterly, *World Literature Today*.

Biography

Raja Rao was born into a respected Brahmin family in Hassan, South India, the eldest son in a family of two brothers and seven sisters. His father taught Kannada at Nizam's College in the neighboring Hyderabad state. The earliest influence on young Rao was his grandfather, with whom he stayed both in Hassan and in Harihalli, while his father was in Hyderabad. Rao seems to have inherited a spiritual orientation from his grandfather; his preoccupation has stayed with Rao throughout his life and is evident in all his work.

Rao joined his father in Hyderabad, going there to attend high school. He was then sent to Aligarh Muslim University in North India. These Aligarh days proved to be crucial in shaping Rao's intellectual growth. Under the influence of Eric Dickinson, a minor poet and a visiting professor from Oxford, Rao's literary sensibility was awakened. He met other interesting students such as Ahmed Ali, who became a famous novelist, and Chetan

Anand, who became an influential film producer. Rao also began learning French at Aligarh, which contributed to his decision to go to France a few years later. After matriculating in 1927, he returned to Hyderabad to enroll as a student for the B.A. at Nizam's College. Two years later, he was graduated, having majored in English and History.

In 1929, two other important events occurred in Rao's life: first, he won the Asiatic Scholarship of the Government of Hyderabad for study abroad. This marked the beginning of a new phase in his life; he left India for the first time to study at the University of Montpellier in France. Second, in that same year, Rao married Camille Mouly, who taught French at Montpellier. Camille was undoubtedly the most important influence on Rao's life during the next ten years. She not only encouraged him to write, but supported him financially for several years. In 1931, his early Kannada writing began to appear in the journal *Jaya Karnataka*. For the next two years, Rao researched the influence of India on Irish literature at the Sorbonne. His short stories were published in journals such as *Asia* (New York) and *Cahiers du Sud* (Paris). In 1933, Rao abandoned research to devote himself completely to writing.

Although he never settled permanently in India, Rao's awareness of Indian culture grew during his stay abroad. He became a compulsive visitor, returning to India again and again for spiritual and cultural nourishment; indeed, in a sense, Rao never completely left India. In 1933, he visited Pandit Taranth's ashram in his quest for self-realization. In 1938, his small masterpiece, *Kanthapura*, although written earlier, was published from London. One year later, Rao's marriage disintegrated; he found himself back in India, his spiritual search renewed. In the next few years, Rao visited a number of ashrams and religious teachers, notably Ramana Maharshi of Tiruvannamalai, Narayana Maharaj of Kedgaon, and Mahatma Gandhi at Sevagram. Around this time, Rao also became active in several social and political causes. He edited, with Singh, *Changing India* (1939), an anthology of modern Indian thought from Ram Mohan Roy to Nehru. He participated in the underground "Quit India" movement of 1942, boldly associating with a group of radical Socialists. In 1943-1944, he coedited with Ali a journal from Bombay called *Tomorrow*. He was the prime mover in the formation of a cultural organization, Sri Vidya Samiti, devoted to reviving the values of ancient Indian civilization; this organization failed shortly after inception. In Bombay, he was also associated with Chetana, a cultural society for the propagation of Indian culture and values. Finally, in 1943, Rao's quest appears to have been fulfilled when he met his spiritual preceptor in Atmananda Guru of Trivandrum. Rao even thought of settling down there, but returned to France following the death of his guru.

In 1960, twenty-two years after *Kanthapura*, Rao's masterpiece *The Serpent and the Rope* was published. Its sequel, *The Cat and Shakespeare*, came relatively soon, in 1965. About ten years later, *Comrade Kirillov* was published in English, although it had appeared in a French translation, *Le Comrade Kirillov* (1965) much earlier. From 1965 until his recent retirement, Rao was Professor of Philosophy at the University of Texas at Austin. In that same year, 1965, he married Katherine Jones, an American stage actress. They would have one son, Christopher Rama.

Analysis

An understanding of Raja Rao's art is enhanced by contextualizing his novels. Although Rao admits to several Western influences, his work is best understood as a part of the Indian tradition. Rao regards literature as *Sadhana* or spiritual discipline; for him, writing is a consequence of his metaphysical life. His novels, hence, essentially represent a quest for the Absolute. From *Kanthapura* to *Comrade Kirillov*, Rao's protagonists grapple with the same concerns: What is Truth? How is one to find it? Their methods vary, as do their results, but they share the same preoccupation. The novels, thus, become chronicles of this archetypal search. Formally, too, all four novels share certain features. Plot is deemphasized; the narrative is generally subjective—even idiosyncratic—and episodic. The progression of the narrative is not linear, but circular; in the *puranic* manner of storytelling which Rao adapts to the form of the Western novel, there are digressions, stories within stories, songs, philosophical disquisitions, debates, and essays. Characters, too, are frequently symbolic figures; often, the motivations for their actions might seem puzzling or insufficient. Finally, because the narration is subjective, the language of the narrator, too, tends to be unique, reflecting the narrator's peculiarities—his or her social, regional, and philosophical makeup.

Rao's first novel, *Kanthapura*, is the story of how a small, sleepy, South Indian village is caught in the whirlpool of the Indian freedom struggle and comes to be completely destroyed. In the Foreword, Rao himself indicates that the novel is a kind of *sthala-purana* or legendary history, which every village in India seems to have. These local *sthala-puranas* are modeled on the ancient Indian Puranas—those compendia of story, fable, myth, religion, philosophy, and politics—among which are the Upa Puranas, which describe holy places and the legends associated with them. Hence, several features of *Kanthapura* are in keeping with the tradition of *sthala-puranas*. The detailed description of the village at the opening of the novel is written in the manner of a *sthala-purana*, wherein the divine origin or association of a place is established. The village is presided over by Goddess Kenchamma, the *Grama-deveta* (village-deity) and the novel provides a legend explaining her presence there, recalling several similar legends found in the Puranas. Like the "place-Gods" of the Puranas, Kenchamma operates within her jurisdiction, where she is responsible for rains, harvests, and the well-being of the villagers. She cannot extend her protection to other villages or to outsiders. Thus, the village-deity symbolizes local concerns such as famine, cholera, cattle-diseases, and poor harvests, which may have little to do with the world outside the village. Like Kenchamma, the river Himavathy, too, has a special significance in the novel and recalls passages describing famous rivers in the Puranas, such as the description of the river Narmada in *Matsyapurana* and *Agnipurana*.

Similarly, *Kanthapura* shares certain narrative techniques with the Puranas. The story is told rapidly, all in one breath, it would seem, and the style reflects the oral heritage also evident in the Puranas. Like the Puranas, which are digressive and episodic, *Kanthapura* contains digressions such as Pariah Siddiah's exposition on serpent lore. The Puranas contain detailed, poetic descriptions of nature; similarly, *Kanthapura* has several descriptive passages which are so evocative and unified as to be prose-poems in themselves. Examples are the coming of Kartik (autumn), daybreak over the Ghats, and the advent of the rains. Finally, the narration of *Kanthapura* has a simplicity and lack of self-consciousness reminiscent of the Puranas and quite different from the narrative sophistication of contemporary Western novelists such as Virginia Woolf or James Joyce.

Kanthapura is also imbued with a religious spirit akin to that of the Puranas. The epigraph of the novel, taken from the *Bhaghavad Gītā* (c. fifth to second century B.C.), is the famous explanation of the Hindu notion of incarnation: "Whensoever there is misery and ignorance, I come." The doctrine of incarnation is central to the Puranas, too, most of which are descriptive accounts of the avatars of Vishnu. The avatar in *Kanthapura* is Gandhi, whose shadow looms over the whole book, although he is himself not a character. Incarnation, however, is not restricted to one Great Soul, Gandhi, but extends into Kanthapura itself, where Moorthy, who leads the revolt, is the local manifestation of Gandhi, and by implication, of Truth.

Although the form of *Kanthapura* is closely modeled on that of the *sthalapurana*, its style is uniquely experimental. Rao's effort is to capture the flavor and nuance of South Indian rural dialogue in English. He succeeds in this by a variety of stylistic devices. The story is told by Achakka, an old Brahmin widow, a garrulous, gossipy, storyteller. The sentences are long, frequently running into paragraphs. Such long sentences consist of several short sentences joined by conjunctions (usually "and") and commas; the effect is of breathless, rapid talking. The sentence structure is manipulated for syntactic and rhythmic effect, as in the first sentence of the novel: "Our village—I don't think you have ever heard about it—Kanthapura is its name, and it is in the province of Kara." Repetition is another favorite device used to enhance the colloquial flavor of the narrative. In addition to these techniques, translation from Kannada is repeatedly used. Nicknames such as "Waterfall Venkamma," "Nose-scratching Nanjamma," "Cornerhouse Moorthy" are translated; more important, Kannada idioms and expressions are rendered into English: "You are a traitor to your salt-givers," "The Don't-touch-the-Government Campaign," "Nobody will believe such a crow and sparrow story," and so on. The total effect is the transmutation into English of the total ethos of another culture. *Kanthapura* with its *Kannadized* English anticipates the lofty *Sanskritized* style of *The Serpent and the Rope*, which, stylistically, is Rao's highest achievement.

Kanthapura is really a novel about a village rather than about a single individual; nevertheless, Moorthy, the Brahmin protagonist of the villagers' struggle against the government, is a prototypal Rao hero. Moorthy is the leader of a political uprising, but for him, as for Gandhi, whom he follows, politics provide a way of life, indistinguishable from a spiritual quest. In fact, for Moorthy, Action is the way to the Absolute. In Gandhi, he finds what is Right Action. Thus, for him, becoming a Gandhi man is a deep spiritual experience which is appropriately characterized by the narrator as a "conversion." At the culmination of this "conversion" is Sankaracharaya's ecstatic chant "Sivoham, Sivoham. I am Siva. I am Siva. Siva am I," meaning that Moorthy experiences blissful union with the Absolute. Indeed, the chant, which epitomizes the ancient Indian philosophical school of Advaita or unqualified nondualism, is found in all Rao's novels as a symbol of the spiritual goal of his protagonists. Moorthy, the man of action, thus practices *Karma Yoga* (the Path of Action), one of the ways of reaching the Absolute as enunciated in the *Bhaghavad Gītā*. In the novels after *Kanthapura*, Rao's protagonists, like Moorthy, continue to seek the Absolute, although their methods change.

Published twenty-two years after *Kanthapura*, *The Serpent and the Rope* is Rao's most ambitious work. If the former is modeled on an Upa Purana (minor Purana), the latter is a kind of Maha Purana (major Purana) or epic: geographically, historically, philosophically, and formally, its sweep is truly epical. The novel includes a variety of settings, ranging from Paris to Ramaswamy's ancestral home in a South Indian village, from European locales such as Aix, Montpalais, Pau, Montpellier, Provence, Cambridge, and London to Indian locales such as Hyderabad, Delhi, Lucknow, Bombay, Bangalore, and Beneras. Rao delves into almost the whole of Indian history, from the invasion of the Aryans to the advent of British rule; European history, chiefly the Albigensian heresy; Chinese history—all of these come under discussion as the protagonist, Rama, a historian by training, expounds his theories in conversations with the leading characters. Philosophically, too, the novel's sweep is formidable: Rao discusses Hinduism, Buddhism, Catholicism, Islam, Taoism, Marxism, Darwinism, and Nazism. Hence, it is not surprising to find *The Serpent and the Rope* extremely diverse in form as well. Rao quotes from an array of languages, including Sanskrit, Hindi, French, Italian, Latin, and Provençal; only the Sanskrit quotations are translated. There are long interludes and stories, such as Grandmother Lakshamma's story of a princess who became a pumpkin and Ishwara Bhatta's "Story of Rama." In addition, the novel contains songs, myths, legends, and philosophical discussions in the manner of the Puranas. The main narrative, the gradual disintegration of Rama's marriage with his French wife, Madeleine, is thus only a single strand holding a voluminous and diverse book together.

The Serpent and the Rope is an extremely challenging work thematically as well; Savithri's words in the novel sum it up well: it is "a sacred text, a cryptogram, with different meanings at different hierarchies of awareness." It may be approached on at least two different levels, the literal and the symbolic, although the two usually operate simultaneously. On the literal level of plot, the novel may appear puzzling and unsatisfying. The crux is: Why does the marriage of Rama and Madeleine disintegrate? Critics have attempted various answers, ranging from incompatibility between the Indian Rama and the French Madeleine, to Rama's infidelity. Although such answers are plausible, they do not satisfy completely because these reasons are not perceived by the characters themselves. Rama and Madeleine are both aware of the growing rift between them, but they do not attempt to bridge it on a practical level. Instead, both watch the dissolution of the union with an almost fatalistic helplessness. Similarly, it is hard to understand why Rama seeks fulfillment in other women while averring his love for Madeleine at the same time, or why he never tells her of his affairs in spite of his claim that he keeps no secrets from her. Rama, the narrator, does not answer such questions; he only chronicles the breakdown of the relationship, almost impersonally, as if there were little *he* could do to save it. He also does not feel himself responsible for having affairs with other women, one of which involves a ritual second marriage, while being married to Madeleine at the same time. What is lacking, then, is an adequate motivation for the actions of the characters, something that most readers are conditioned to expect from the novel. Perhaps a better approach, however, instead of asking of the novel something that it did not intend to give, is to consider what it does clearly provide; indeed, questions which appear unresolved on the literal level are resolved more satisfactorily on the symbolic level.

Rama, the Brahmin hero, is a seeker of Truth both by birth and by vocation (a Brahmin is one who seeks Brahma, or the Absolute). As an Indian scholar in France, Rama is seeking Truth in the form of the missing link in the puzzle of India's influence on the West. According to Rama, this missing link is the Albigensian heresy: he thinks that the Cathers were driven to heresy by the influence of Buddhism, which had left India. Rama's quest for Truth is also manifested in his search for the ideal Woman because in the Hindu tradition, the union of man and wife is symbolic of the union of man and God. The marriage of Siva and Parvathi is one such paradigmatic union in which Siva, the Absolute, the abstract, the ascetic, is wedded to Parvthi, the human, the concrete, the possessor of the Earth. Another such union is that between the mythical Savithri and her husband Satyavan ("Satya" means "Truth"); Savithri, through her devotion, restores her dead husband to life.

In keeping with these paradigms, Rama—the thinker, the meditator, the seeker of Truth—can only find fulfillment in a Parvathi or a Savithri who can bring him back to Earth by her devotion. Madeleine, however, who has given up her Catholicism for Buddhism, becomes an ascetic, renouncing the Earth, denying her body through abstinence and penance. Significantly, her union with Rama is barren: both their children are stillborn. Madeleine also regards Truth as something outside herself, something that has to be striven for, in order to be realized. Her dualism is the philosophical opposite of Rama's nondualism; Rama believes, following the Advaita Vedanta, that the self is a part of Truth, as the wave is a part of the sea, and that all separateness is illusion, like the illusion in which a rope is mistaken for a serpent. Rama's true mate is an Indian undergraduate at Cambridge named, interestingly, Savithri. Savithri, despite her modishness—she dances to jazz music, smokes, wears Western clothes, and so on—is essentially an Indian. Unlike Madeleine, Savithri does not seek Truth, but instinctively and unselfconsciously *is* Truth. Her union with Rama is thus a natural and fulfilling one. Savithri, however, like Rama's sister Saroja, opts for an arranged marriage in the traditional Indian manner with someone else; hence, her relationship with Rama is never consummated. At the end of the book, Rama, divorced from Madeleine, sees a vision of his guru in Travancore and plans to leave France for India.

Rama's path to Truth, unlike Moorthy's *Karma Yoga*, is *Jnana Yoga* (the Path of Knowledge), also enunciated in the *Bhaghavad Gītā*. Rama is not a man of action but an intellectual. Although he has accumulated knowledge, he still does not apprehend Truth clearly; like the deluded seeker in the fable, he mistakes the rope for the serpent, failing to see himself already united with Truth as Savithri is. Traditionally, a guru is necessary for the *Jnana Yogi* because only a guru can cure his delusion by *showing* him that what appears to be a serpent is really a rope. Thus, in the end, Rama resolves to seek his guru to be cured of his delusion.

The Cat and Shakespeare, described by Rao as "a metaphysical comedy," clearly shows a strong formal *Upanishadic* influence. The spiritual experiences of its narrator, Ramakrishna Pai, are reminiscent of the illuminative passages in the *Chandogya Upanishad*, which describe the experience of the Infinite. The dialogues in the novel are also *Upanishadic* in their question-and-answer patterns; the best example is the conversation between Govindan Nair and Lakshmi in the brothel. Nair's metaphysical speculations, such as "Is there seeing first or the object first?," seem to be modeled on philosophical queries in the Upanishads. The cat links the novel to the Indian beast fable, and Nair's comic roguery shows similarities to the rogue fable in the *Pancha Tantra*. The major Western debt is to William Shakespeare, who is acknowledged in the title. Shakespeare is a symbol for the universal; according to

Rao, Shakespeare's vision transcends duality and arrives at a unified view of the universe. There are numerous allusions to *Hamlet* (1600-1601) in the novel, culminating in the "rat-trap episode" in which a cat is trapped in a large rat-trap; this prompts Nair to deliver a parody of *Hamlet* which begins: "A kitten sans cat, that is the question."

The Cat and Shakespeare is Rao's sequel to *The Serpent and the Rope* in that it shows what happens after a seeker's veil of illusion has been removed by the guru. Its theme may be summed up in Hamlet's words to Horatio toward the end of the play: "There's a divinity that shapes our ends,/ Rough-hew them how we will." A similar view of grace is embodied in the novel in what Nair, the man who is united to Truth, calls "the way of the Cat." The "way of the Cat," simply, is the notion that just as the kitten is carried by the scruff of its neck by the mother cat, man is completely at the mercy of the divine; consequently, the only way to live is to surrender oneself totally to divine grace, as the helpless kitten surrenders itself to the mother cat. Nair lives this philosophy and is responsible for teaching it to his ignorant neighbor, the narrator Pai. Pai is like the innocent hunter in the story who unknowingly heaped leaves on Siva and was rewarded with a vision.

Between Pai's house and Nair's is a wall over which Nair leaps everytime he visits Pai. The wall is an important symbol because it represents the division between illusion and Truth. Nair crosses it easily, but Pai has never gone across. Toward the end of the novel, following Nair's cat, Pai accidentally crosses the wall. Like the lucky hunter, he, too, is vouchsafed a divine vision: for the first time, Pai sees the whole universe as a unity. The novel ends with Pai's spiritual as well as material fulfillment, having partially realized his lifelong ambition of owning a three-story house. *The Cat and Shakespeare*, although not as ambitious as *The Serpent and the Rope*, is as successful on its own terms. The novel is an elaborate puzzle which the author challenges the reader to solve; a solution is not only possible at all levels, but is completely satisfying as well. The way to the Absolute here is not *Karma Yoga* or *Jnana Yoga* of the two previous novels, but *Bhakti Yoga*, or the path of devotion. The seeker recognizes himself as completely dependent on divine grace for his salvation and surrenders himself to the Benevolent Mother like a trusting kitten.

Comrade Kirillov, published in English in 1976, is generally recognized as Rao's least ambitious novel; it is clearly a minor work compared to its three illustrious predecessors. Formally, it is an extended *Vyakti-Chitra*, or character sketch, a popular genre in Indian regional literature. The main story, narrated by one "R.," is a mere ninety-three pages in large type, to which are appended twenty-seven pages of the diary of Kirillov's wife, Irene, and a concluding seven pages by the narrator; the effect is of a slight, sketchy novella. Kirillov, alias Padmanabha Iyer, leaves India for California to propagate Theosophy but, after a period of disillusionment, becomes a Communist. From California, he moves to London, where, marrying a Czech immigrant, Irene, he settles down to the life of an expatriate intellectual. Like Rao's other protagonists, Kirillov starts as a seeker of Truth, but after becoming a Communist, he is increasingly revealed by the narrator to be caught in a system which curtails his access to Truth. Thus, Kirillov continuously rationalizes the major events in the world to suit his perspective. Nevertheless, following a visit to India several years after he has left, he realizes that his Communism is only a thin upper layer in an essentially Indian psyche. Irene also recognizes in her diary that he is almost biologically an Indian Brahmin, and only intellectually a Marxist. By the end of the book, Kirillov is shown to be a man of contradictions: attacking and worshiping Gandhi simultaneously, deeply loving traditional India but campaigning for a Communist revolution, reciting Sanskrit *shlokas* but professing Communism.

The narrator is Kirillov's intellectual opposite, an adherent of Advaita Vedanta. There are numerous interesting discussions on Communism in the book, which has great value as a social document, capturing the life of an Indian expatriate intellectual between 1920 and 1950. Also of interest is Kirillov's relationship with Irene, which recalls Rama's relationship with Madeleine. Numerous similarities aside, this relationship is more successful: this marriage lasts, and the couple have a child, Kamal. Soon after Kirillov's return from India, however, Irene dies in childbirth, followed by her newly born daugher. Kirillov leaves for Moscow and is last heard of in Peking. The novel ends with the narrator taking Kamal, now in India, to Kanyakumari. Despite its humor, pathos, and realism, *Comrade Kirillov* falls short of Rao's three previous novels.

It is interesting to note that *Comrade Kirillov*, first published in a French translation in 1965, was written earlier. Thematically, it represents the stage of negation before the spiritual fulfillment of *The Cat and Shakespeare*. Kirillov, as a Communist and atheist, has negated the *Karma Yoga* of *Kanthapura* and the *Jnana Yoga* of *The Serpent and the Rope* by denying the existence of the Absolute; thus, his quest results in failure. The *Bhakti Yoga* of *The Cat and Shakespeare*, especially in the character of Nair, is the culmination of the various stages of spiritual realization in the earlier novels. Nair is the first character in Rao's novels who does not merely seek Truth, but who has found it, who actually practices it.

In the gargantuan *The Chessmaster and His Moves*, the translations, glossary and list of characters supplied by the author are much needed. This sprawling compilation is more like three novels (they are too long to be called novellas) in one. In it, Rao's desire for anonymity (he has said in interviews that "I am sorry I have a name") is echoed by his main characters, Sivarama (Siva) Sastri, a mathematician who is the son of an assistant commissioner (or "pro-pro-consul," as his son calls him), himself a failed mathematician.

Like his creator, Siva is from a respected Brahmin family; his father works for the last of the British Raj. Also like Rao, Siva goes from India to France, where he meets and marries a young Frenchwoman, Suzanne Chantereux, who has cured herself of tuberculosis through meditation. There is also Siva's sister, Uma Ramachandra, unable to have children and desperately unhappy about it. Suzanne has had a child, but he was a mongoloid who died young.

A long and complex (to say the least) tale, *The Chessmaster and His Moves* follows Siva's search for what Rao calls "the unknown guide": the force sought by humans in their spiritual quests. The underlying philosophy of Rao's writing is that a novel can play a more important role than mere entertainment; it can be used to help people in their search for a guide in their lives. His medieval conception of writing as an impersonal act is what he believes can supply the spiritual fulfillment he hopes to provide. He has said that he does not "think a person is creative—[rather, it is] the impersonal [that] is creative." Rao's talent in creating a map for modern humans to find their Holy Grail is what brings his work such high acclaim and what elevates his place among Indian English novelists to such a high level.

Makarand Paranjape

Other major works

SHORT FICTION: *The Cow of the Barricades and Other Stories*, 1947; *The Policeman and the Rose*, 1978.

Bibliography

Bhattacharya, P. C. *Indo-Anglian Literature and the Works of Raja Rao*. Delhi: Atma Ram, 1983. This work concentrates on Rao's work in the context of Indian literature written in English. Includes primary and secondary bibliographies.

Nasimi, Reza Ahmad. *The Language of Mulk Raj Anand, Raja Rao, and R. K. Narayan*. Delhi: Capital Publishing House, 1989. Here, Rao's writing is placed in context with the work of other Indian English novelists. Includes references and an index.

Niven, Alastair. *Truth Within Fiction: A Study of Raja Rao's "The Serpent and the Rope."* Calcutta: Writers' Workshop, 1987. This text is an in-depth analysis of Rao's *The Serpent and the Rope*. Niven provides references, bibliographies, and an index.

Ray, R. J. "The Novels of Raja Rao." *World Literature Today* 63 (Spring, 1989): 197-199. This article covers all Rao's novels, including *The Chessmaster and His Moves*. References and bibliographies are included.

Sharrad, Paul. *Raja Rao and Cultural Tradition*. New Delhi: Sterling Publishers, 1987. The decline of the Empire and the end of the British Raj have had an enormous influence on the Indian English novelists. Sharrad discusses these and other influences on Rao's work. Includes references, bibliographies, and an index.

World Literature Today 66 (Autumn, 1988). This issue, devoted to Rao, was published after Rao won *World Literature Today*'s Tenth International Prize for Literature in June, 1988. Includes references and bibliographies.

ISHMAEL REED

Born: Chattanooga, Tennessee; February 22, 1938

Principal long fiction
The Free-Lance Pallbearers, 1967; *Yellow Back Radio Broke-Down*, 1969; *Mumbo Jumbo*, 1972; *The Last Days of Louisiana Red*, 1974; *Flight to Canada*, 1976; *The Terrible Twos*, 1982; *Reckless Eyeballing*, 1986; *The Terrible Threes*, 1989.

Other literary forms
Ishmael Reed may be best known as a satirical novelist, but he is also a respected poet, essayist, and editor. His poetry collections, which include *Catechism of D Neoamerican Hoodoo Church* (1970), *Conjure: Selected Poems 1963-1970* (1972), *Chattanooga* (1973), *A Secretary to the Spirits* (1977), and *New and Collected Poems* (1988), have established him as a major Afro-American poet, and his poetry has been included in several important anthologies. In well-received collections of essays, including *Shrovetide in Old New Orleans* (1978), *God Made Alaska for the Indians* (1982), and *Writin' Is Fightin'* (1988), Reed has forcefully presented his aesthetic and political theories. He has also proved to be an important editor and publisher. *19 Necromancers from Now* (1970) was a breakthrough anthology for several unknown black writers. *Yardbird Lives!* (1978), which Reed edited with Al Young, includes essays, fiction, and graphics from the pages of the *Yardbird Reader*, an innovative periodical that published the work of minority writers and artists. Reed's most ambitious editing project resulted in *Calafia: The California Poetry* (1979), an effort to gather together the forgotten minority poetry of California's past.

Achievements
Reed has earned a place in the first rank of contemporary Afro-American authors, but such recognition did not come immediately. Most established reviewers ignored Reed's first novel, *The Free-Lance Pallbearers*, and many of the reviews that were written dismissed the novel as offensive, childish, or self-absorbed. Although *Yellow Back Radio Broke-Down* was even less traditional than its predecessor, it received much more critical attention and became the center of considerable critical debate. Some reviewers attacked the novel as overly clever, bitter, or obscure, but many praised its imaginative satire and technical innovation. Moreover, the controversy over *Yellow Back Radio Broke-Down* stirred new interest in *The Free-Lance Pallbearers*. Reed's increasing acceptance as a major Afro-American author was demonstrated when his third novel, *Mumbo Jumbo*, was reviewed on the front page of *The*

New York Review of Books. Both *Mumbo Jumbo* and *Conjure*, a poetry collection published in the same year, were nominated for the National Book Award.

Subsequent novels have maintained Reed's position in American letters. In 1975, Reed's *The Last Days of Louisiana Red* received the Rosenthal Foundation Award, and some reviewers viewed *Flight to Canada* as Reed's best novel. Yet his work has consistently been controversial. His novels have, for example, been called sexist, a critical accusation that is fueled by comparison of Reed's novels with the recent, powerful fiction written by Afro-American women such as Alice Walker and Toni Morrison. The charge of sexism is further encouraged by Reed's satirical attack on feminists in *Reckless Eyeballing*. Reed has also been called a reactionary by some critics because of his uncomplimentary portrayals of black revolutionaries. His fiction has been translated into three languages, and his poetry has been included in *Poetry of the Negro*, *New Black Poetry*, *The Norton Anthology of Poetry*, and other anthologies.

Biography

The jacket notes to *Chattanooga* glibly recount Ishmael Scott Reed's life: "born in Chattanooga, Tennessee, grew up in Buffalo, New York, learned to write in New York City and wised up in Berkeley, California." Each residence played a crucial role in Reed's development.

Reed was born the son of Henry Lenoir and Thelma Coleman, but before he was two years old, his mother remarried autoworker Bennie Reed. When he was four years old, his mother moved the family to Buffalo, New York, where she found factory work. Reed was graduated from Buffalo's East High School in 1956 and began to attend Millard Fillmore College, the night division of the University of Buffalo, supporting himself by working in the Buffalo public library. A satirical short story, "Something Pure," which portrayed Christ's return as an advertising man, brought Reed the praise of an English professor and encouraged him to enroll in day classes. Reed attended the University of Buffalo until 1960, when he withdrew because of money problems and the social pressures that his financial situation created. He moved into the notorious Talbert Mall Projects, and the two years he spent there provided him with a painful but valuable experience of urban poverty and dependency. During these last years in Buffalo, Reed wrote for the *Empire Star Weekly*, moderated a controversial radio program for station WVFO, and acted in several local stage productions.

From 1962 to 1967, Reed lived in New York City. As well as being involved with the Civil Rights movement and the black power movement, Reed served as editor of *Advance*, a weekly published in Newark, New Jersey. His work on the *Advance* was admired by Walter Bowart, and together they founded the *East Village Other*, one of the first and most successful "underground" newspapers. An early indication of Reed's commitment to encouraging the work of minority artists was his organization in 1965 of the American Festival of Negro Art.

In 1967, Reed moved to Berkeley, California, and began teaching at the University of California at Berkeley. Although he was turned down for tenure in 1977, he continued to teach there and at other universities: the University of Washington, the State University of New York at Buffalo, Yale University, and Dartmouth College. In 1971, with Al Young, Reed founded the Yardbird Publishing Company, which from 1971 to 1976 produced the *Yardbird Reader*, an innovative journal of ethnic writing and graphics. The Reed, Cannon, and Johnson Communications Company, which later became Ishmael Reed Books, was founded in 1973 and has published the work of William Demby, Bill Gunn, Mei Mei Bressenburge, and other ethnic writers. In 1976, Reed and Victor Cruz began the Before Columbus Foundation. In all of his publishing ventures, Reed has tried to expose readers to the work of Asian Americans, Afro-Americans, Chicanos, and Native Americans in an effort to help build a truly representative and pluralistic national literature.

Analysis

Ishmael Reed is consciously a part of the Afro-American literary tradition that extends back to the first-person slave narratives, and the central purpose of his novels is to define a means of expressing the complexity of the Afro-American experience in a manner distinct from the dominant literary tradition. Until the middle of the twentieth century, Afro-American fiction, although enriched by the lyricism of Jean Toomer and Zora Neale Hurston, concentrated on realistic portrayals of black life and employed familiar narrative structures. This tendency toward social realism peaked with Richard Wright's *Native Son* (1940) and *Black Boy* (1945), but it continued into the late twentieth century by authors such as James Baldwin. Reed belongs to a divergent tradition, inspired by Ralph Ellison's *Invisible Man* (1952), a countertradition that includes the work of Leon Forrest, Ernest Gaines, James Alan McPherson, Toni Morrison, and Alice Walker.

Because he believes that the means of expression is as important as the matter, Reed argues that the special qualities of the Afro-American experience cannot be adequately communicated through traditional literary forms. Like Amiri Baraka, Reed believes that Afro-American authors must "be estranged from the dominant culture," but Reed also wants to avoid being stifled by a similarly restrictive countertradition. In *Shrovetide in Old New Orleans*, Reed says that his art and criticism try to combat "the consciousness barrier erected by an alliance of Eastern-backed black pseudo-nationalists and white mundanists." Thus, Reed works against the stylistic limitations of the Afro-American literary tradition as much as he works with them. Henry Louis Gates, Jr., has compared Reed's fictional modifications of Afro-

American literary traditions to the Afro-American folk custom of "signifying," maintaining that Reed's novels present an ongoing process of "rhetori-
cal self-definition."

Although Reed's novels are primarily efforts to define an appropriate
Afro-American aesthetic, his fiction vividly portrays the particular social
condition of black Americans. In his foreword to Elizabeth and Thomas Settle's *Ishmael Reed: A Primary and Secondary Bibliography* (1982), Reed expresses his bitterness over persistent racism and argues that the personal
experience of racism that informs his art makes his work inaccessible and
threatening to many readers: "I am a member of a class which has been cast
to the bottom of the American caste system, and from those depths I write a
vision which is still strange, often frightening, 'peculiar' and 'odd' to some,
'ill-considered' and unwelcome to many." Indeed, Ishmael seems to be an
ironically appropriate name for this author of violent and darkly humorous
attacks on American institutions and attitudes, for the sharpness and breadth
of his satire sometimes make him appear to be a man whose hand is turned
against all other men. His novels portray corrupt power brokers and their
black and white sycophants operating in a dehumanized and materialistic
society characterized by its prefabricated and ethnocentric culture. Yet
Reed's novels are not hopeless explications of injustice, for against the forces
of repression and conformity he sets gifted individuals who escape the limitations of their sterile culture by courageously penetrating the illusions that
bind them. Moreover, in contrast to many white authors who are engaged in
parallel metafictive experiments, Reed voices a confident belief that "print
and words are not dead at all."

Reed's narrative technique combines the improvisational qualities of jazz
with a documentary impulse to accumulate references and allusions. In his
composite narratives, historical and fictional characters coexist in a fluid,
anachronistic time. In an effort to translate the vitality and spontaneity of the
oral, folk tradition into a literature that can form the basis for an alternative
culture, Reed mixes colloquialisms and erudition in novels which are syncre-
tized from a series of subtexts. The literary equivalent of scat singing, his
stories-within-stories parody literary formulas and challenge the traditional
limits of fiction.

Reed claims that his novels constitute "an art form with its own laws," but
he does not mean to imply that his work is private, for these "laws" are
founded on a careful but imaginative reinterpretation of the historical and
mythological past. The lengthy bibliography appended to *Mumbo Jumbo*
satirizes the documentary impulse of social realist authors, but it also underscores Reed's belief that his mature work demands scholarly research in
order to be decoded. This artistic process of reinterpretation often requires
the services of an interlocutor, a character who explicitly explains the events
of the narrative in terms of the mythological past. Reed's novels describe a

vision of an Osirian/Dionysian consciousness, a sensuous humanism that he presents as an appropriate cultural alternative for nonwhite Americans. His imaginative reconstructions of the American West, the Harlem Renaissance, the American Civil War, and contemporary American politics, interwoven with ancient myths, non-European folk customs, and the formulas of popular culture, are liberating heresies meant to free readers from the intellectual domination of the Judeo-Christian tradition.

Reed's first novel, *The Free-Lance Pallbearers*, takes place in a futuristic America called HARRY SAM: "A big not-to-be-believed out-of-sight, sometimes referred to as O-BOP-SHE-BANG or KLANG-A-LANG-A-DING-DONG." This crumbling and corrupt world is tyrannized by Sam himself, a vulgar fat man who lives in Sam's Motel on Sam's Island in the middle of the lethally polluted Black Bay that borders HARRY SAM. Sam, doomed by some terrifying gastrointestinal disorder, spends all of his time on the toilet, his filth pouring into the bay from several large statues of Rutherford B. Hayes.

The bulk of the novel, although framed and periodically informed by a jiving narrative voice, is narrated by Bukka Doopeyduk in a restrained, proper English that identifies his passive faith in the establishment. Doopeyduk is a dedicated adherent to the Nazarene Code, an orderly in a psychiatric hospital, a student at Harry Sam College, and a hapless victim. His comically futile efforts to play by the rules are defeated by the cynics, who manipulate the unjust system to their own advantage. In the end, Doopeyduk is disillusioned: He leads a successful attack on Sam's Island, uncovers the conspiracy that protects Sam's cannibalism, briefly dreams of becoming the black Sam, and is finally crucified.

The Free-Lance Pallbearers is a parody of the Afro-American tradition of first-person, confessional narratives, a book the narrator describes as "growing up in soulsville first of three installments—or what it means to be a backstage darky." Reed's novel challenges the viability of this Afro-American version of the *Bildungsroman*, in which a young protagonist undergoes a painful initiation into the darkness of the white world, a formula exemplified by Wright's *Black Boy* and James Baldwin's *Go Tell It on the Mountain* (1953). In fact, the novel suggests that Afro-American authors' use of this European form is as disabling as Doopeyduk's adherence to the dictates of the Nazarene Code.

The novel is an unrestrained attack on American politics. HARRY SAM, alternately referred to as "Nowhere" or "Now Here," is a dualistic vision of an America that celebrates vacuous contemporaneity. The novel, an inversion of the Horatio Alger myth in the manner of Nathanael West, mercilessly displays American racism, but its focus is the corruptive potential of power. Sam is a grotesque version of Lyndon B. Johnson, famous for his bathroom interviews, and Sam's cannibalistic taste for children is an attack on Johnson's Vietnam policy. With *The Free-Lance Pallbearers*, Reed destroys the presumptions of his society, but it is not until his later novels that he attempts to construct an alternative.

Yellow Back Radio Broke-Down is set in a fantastic version of the Wild West of popular literature. Reed's protagonist, the Loop Garoo Kid, is a proponent of artistic freedom and an accomplished voodoo *houngan* who is in marked contrast to the continually victimized Doopeyduk. Armed with supernatural "connaissance" and aided by a white python and the hip, helicopter-flying Chief Showcase, the Kid battles the forces of realistic mimesis and political corruption. His villainous opponent is Drag Gibson, a degenerate cattle baron given to murdering his wives, who is called upon by the citizens of Yellow Back Radio to crush their rebellious children's effort "to create [their] own fictions."

Although *Yellow Back Radio Broke-Down* satirizes Americans' eagerness to suspend civil rights in response to student protests against the Vietnam War, its focus is literature, specifically the dialogue between realism and modernism. The Loop Garoo Kid matches Reed's description of the Afro-American artist in *19 Necromancers from Now*: "a conjurer who works JuJu upon his oppressors; a witch doctor who frees his fellow victims from the psychic attack launched by demons." Through the Loop Garoo Kid, Reed takes a stand for imagination, intelligence, and fantasy against rhetoric, violence, and sentimentality. This theme is made explicit in a debate with Bo Shmo, a "neo-social realist" who maintains that "all art must be for the end of liberating the masses," for the Kid says that a novel "can be anything it wants to be, a vaudeville show, the six o'clock news, the mumblings of wild men saddled by demons."

Reed exhibits his antirealist theory of fiction in *Yellow Back Radio Broke-Down* through his free use of time, characters, and language. The novel ranges from the eighteenth century to the present, combining historical events and cowboy myths with modern technology and cultural detritus. His primary characters are comically exaggerated racial types: Drag Gibson represents the white's depraved materialism, Chief Showcase represents the Indian's spirituality, and the Loop Garoo Kid represents the Afro-American's artistic soul. Reed explains the novel's title by suggesting that his book is the "dismantling of a genre done in an oral way like radio." "Yellow back" refers to the popular dime novels; "radio" refers to the novel's oral, discontinuous form; and a "broke-down" is a dismantling. Thus, Reed's first two novels assault America in an attempt to "dismantle" its cultural structure.

In *Mumbo Jumbo*, Reed expands on the neo-hoodooism of the Loop Garoo Kid in order to create and define an Afro-American aesthetic based on voodoo, Egyptian mythology, and improvisational musical forms, an aesthetic to challenge the Judeo-Christian tradition, rationalism, and technology. Set in Harlem during the 1920's, *Mumbo Jumbo* is a tragicomical analysis of the Harlem Renaissance's failure to sustain its artistic promise. Reed's protagonist is PaPa LaBas, an aging hoodoo detective and cultural diagnostician, and LaBas' name, meaning "over there" in French, reveals that his purpose is to reconnect Afro-Americans with their cultural heritage by reunifying the Text of Jes Grew, literally the Egyptian Book of Thoth. Reed takes the phrase Jes Grew from Harriet Beecher Stowe's Topsy and James Weldon Johnson's description of Afro-American music's unascribed development, but in the novel, Jes Grew is a contagion, connected with the improvisational spirit of ragtime and jazz, that begins to spread across America in the 1920's. Jes Grew is an irrational force that threatens to overwhelm the dominant, repressive traditions of established culture. LaBas' efforts to unify and direct this unpredictable force are opposed by the Wallflower Order of the Knights Templar, an organization dedicated to neutralizing the power of Jes Grew in order to protect their privileged status. LaBas fails to reunify the text, a parallel to the dissipation of the Harlem Renaissance's artistic potential, but the failure is seen as temporary; the novel's indeterminate conclusion looks forward hopefully to a time when these artistic energies can be reignited.

The novel's title is double-edged. "Mumbo jumbo" is a racist, colonialist phrase used to describe the misunderstood customs and language of dark-skinned people, an approximation of some critics' description of Reed's unorthodox fictional method. Yet "mumbo jumbo" also refers to the power of imagination, the cultural alternative that can free Afro-Americans. A text of and about texts, *Mumbo Jumbo* combines the formulas of detective fiction with the documentary paraphernalia of scholarship: footnotes, illustrations, and a bibliography. Thus, in the disclosure scene required of any good detective story, LaBas, acting the part of interlocutor, provides a lengthy and erudite explication of the development of Jes Grew that begins with a reinterpretation of the myth of Osiris. The parodic scholarship of *Mumbo Jumbo* undercuts the assumed primacy of the European tradition and implicitly argues that Afro-American artists should attempt to discover their distinct cultural heritage.

In *The Last Days of Louisiana Red*, LaBas returns as Reed's protagonist, but the novel abandons the parodic scholarship and high stylization of *Mumbo Jumbo*. Although LaBas again functions as a connection with a non-European tradition of history and myth, *The Last Days of Louisiana Red* is more traditionally structured than its predecessor. In the novel, LaBas solves the murder of Ed Yellings, the founder of the Solid Gumbo Works. Yellings' business is dedicated to combating the effects of Louisiana Red, literally a popular hot sauce but figuratively an evil state of mind that divides Afro-Americans. Yelling's gumbo, like Reed's fiction, is a mixture of disparate elements, and it has a powerful curative effect. In fact, LaBas discovers that Yellings is murdered when he gets close to developing a gumbo that will cure heroin addiction.

In *The Last Days of Louisiana Red*, Reed is examining the self-destructive forces that divide the Afro-American community so that its members fight one another "while above their heads . . . billionaires flew in custom-made jet planes." Reed shows how individuals' avarice leads them to conspire with the establishment, and he suggests that some of the most vocal and militant leaders are motivated by their egotistical need for power rather than by true concern for oppressed people. Set in Berkeley, California, *The Last Days of Louisiana Red* attacks the credibility of the black revolutionary movements that sprang up in the late 1960's and early 1970's.

Flight to Canada, Reed's fifth novel, is set in an imaginatively redrawn Civil War South, and it describes the relationship between Arthur Swille, a tremendously wealthy Virginia planter who practices necrophilia, and an assortment of sociologically stereotyped slaves. The novel is presented as the slave narrative of Uncle Robin, the most loyal of Swille's possessions. Uncle Robin repeatedly tells Swille that the plantation is his idea of heaven, and he assures his master that he does not believe that Canada exists. Raven Quickskill, "the first one of Swille's slaves to read, the first to write, and the first to run away," is the author of Uncle Robin's story.

Like much of Reed's work, *Flight to Canada* is about the liberating power of art, but in *Flight to Canada*, Reed concentrates on the question of authorial control. All the characters struggle to maintain control of their stories. After escaping from the plantation, Quickskill writes a poem, "Flight to Canada," and his comical verse denunciation of Swille completes his liberation. In complaining of Quickskill's betrayal to Abraham Lincoln, Swille complains that his former bookkeeper uses literacy "like that old Voodoo." In a final assertion of authorial control and the power of the pen, Uncle Robin refuses to sell his story to Harriet Beecher Stowe, gives the rights to Quickskill, rewrites Swille's will, and inherits the plantation.

In *The Terrible Twos*, Reed uses a contemporary setting to attack Ronald Reagan's administration and the exploitative nature of the American economic system. In the novel, President Dean Clift, a former model, is a mindless figurehead manipulated by an oil cartel that has supplanted the real Santa Claus. Nance Saturday, another of Reed's Afro-American detectives, sets out to discover Saint Nicholas' place of exile. The novel's title suggests that, in its second century, the United States is acting as selfishly and irrationally as the proverbial two-year-old. The central theme is the manner in which a few avaricious people seek vast wealth at the expense of the majority of Americans.

Reckless Eyeballing takes place in the 1980's, and Reed employs a string of comically distorted characters to present the idea that the American literary environment is dominated by New York women and Jews. Although *Reckless Eyeballing* has been called sexist and anti-Semitic by some, Reed's target is a cultural establishment that creates and strengthens racial stereotypes, in particular the view of Afro-American men as savage rapists. To make his point, however, he lampoons feminists, using the character Tremonisha Smarts, a female Afro-American author who has written a novel of violence against women. Reed's satire is probably intended to remind readers of Alice Walker's *The Color Purple* (1982).

Because the novel's central subject is art and the limitations that society places on an artist, it is appropriate that Reed once again employs the technique of a story-within-a-story. Ian Ball, an unsuccessful Afro-American playwright, is the novel's protagonist. In the novel, Ball tries to succeed by shamelessly placating the feminists in power. He writes "Reckless Eyeballing," a play in which a lynched man is posthumously tried for "raping" a woman with lecherous stares, but Ball, who often seems to speak for Reed, maintains his private, chauvinistic views throughout.

Ishmael Reed's substantial body of fiction has established him as an important satirist. His innovative narrative techniques have stretched the limits of the American novel and dramatically broadened the scope of Afro-American literature.

Carl Brucker

Other major works

POETRY: *Catechism of D Neoamerican Hoodoo Church*, 1970; *Conjure: Selected Poems, 1963-1970*, 1972; *Chattanooga*, 1973; *A Secretary to the Spirits*, 1977; *Cab Calloway Stands In for the Moon*, 1986; *New and Collected Poems*, 1988.

NONFICTION: *Shrovetide in Old New Orleans*, 1978; *God Made Alaska for the Indians*, 1982; *Writin' Is Fightin'*, 1988.

ANTHOLOGIES: *19 Necromancers from Now*, 1970; *Yardbird Lives!*, 1978 (with Al Young); *Calafia: The California Poetry*, 1979.

Bibliography

Fabre, Michel. "Postmodern Rhetoric in Ishmael Reed's *Yellow Back Radio Broke-Down*." In *The Afro-American Novel Since 1960*, edited by Peter Bruck and Wolfgang Karrer. Amsterdam: Gruener, 1982. A valuable addition to the study of Reed regarding his postmodernism.

Fox, Robert Elliot. *Conscientious Sorcerers: The Black Post-Modern Fiction of LeRoi Jones/Amiri Baraka, Ishmael Reed, and Samuel R. Delaney*. New York: Greenwood Press, 1987. Situates Reed within both the tradition of black fiction and the self-conscious style of contemporary postmodernist fiction.

Gates, Henry Louis, Jr. *The Signifying Monkey: A Theory of Afro-American Literary Criticism*. New York: Oxford University Press, 1988. The section on Reed examines his fiction, especially the novel *Mumbo Jumbo*, as an extension of the tendency of black English to play deliberately with language.

Lee, A. Robert, ed. *Black Fiction: New Studies in the Afro-American Novel Since 1945*. New York: Barnes & Noble Books, 1980. Frank McConnell's essay on Reed uses a quotation about him from Thomas Pynchon's novel, *Gravity's Rainbow*, in order to speak broadly about parody in Reed's novels.

Martin, Reginald. *Ishmael Reed and the New Black Aesthetic Critics*. New York: St. Martin's Press, 1988. A comprehensive and important look at Reed's work and theories in relation to the evolution of the black aesthetics movement.

The Review of Contemporary Fiction 4 (Summer, 1984). A special issue devoted to Reed. Especially important is an essay by James Lindroth, "From Krazy Kat to Hoodoo: Aesthetic Discourse in the Fiction of Ishmael Reed," and an interview with Reed by Reginald Martin.

Settle, Elizabeth A., and Thomas A. Settle, eds. *Ishmael Reed: A Primary and Secondary Bibliography*. Boston: G. K. Hall, 1982. A helpful resource.

MARY RENAULT
Mary Challans

Born: London, England; September 4, 1905
Died: Cape Town, South Africa; December 13, 1983

Principal long fiction

Purposes of Love, 1939 (published in the United States as *Promise of Love*, 1940); *Kind Are Her Answers*, 1940; *The Friendly Young Ladies*, 1944 (published in the United States as *The Middle Mist*, 1945); *Return to Night*, 1947; *North Face*, 1948; *The Charioteer*, 1953; *The Last of the Wine*, 1956; *The King Must Die*, 1958; *The Bull from the Sea*, 1962; *The Mask of Apollo*, 1966; *Fire from Heaven*, 1969; *The Persian Boy*, 1972; *The Praise Singer*, 1978; *Funeral Games*, 1981; *The Alexander Trilogy*, 1984 (includes *Fire from Heaven*, *The Persian Boy*, and *Funeral Games*).

Other literary forms

All but two of Mary Renault's published works are novels. *The Lion in the Gateway: Heroic Battles of the Greeks and Persians at Marathon, Salamis, and Thermopylae* (1964) is a children's history of ancient Greek battles. *The Nature of Alexander* (1975) is a heavily documented biography placing the charismatic leader in the context of his time and customs, a book that also defines the two abiding preoccupations of Alexander's life and Renault's art. "Outward striving for honor," the Greek *to philotimo*, balances *arete*, the profound inward thirst for achievement knowingly made beautiful. Together, as Alexander himself wrote, they win immortality: "It is a lovely thing to live with courage,/ and die leaving an everlasting fame."

Achievements

Critics praised Renault's first five novels, written and set around World War II, for their realism, psychological depth, and literary technique. In 1946, one year prior to its publication, *Return to Night* won the MGM Award, $150,000, then the world's largest literary prize. Although this novel was never made into a motion picture, the award brought Renault American acclaim, augmented later by the success of her Greek novels, but her work has never gained the academic attention it deserves. She received the National Association of Independent Schools Award in 1963 and the Silver Pen Award in 1971, and she was a Fellow of the Royal Society of Literature.

Biography

Mary Renault (the pen name of Mary Challans), a physician's daughter, was born on September 4, 1905, in London. At eight, she decided to become a writer, and she read English at St. Hugh's College, Oxford, from 1924 to

1927, where she preferred to study the Middle Ages, the setting of an attempted historical novel she destroyed after several rejections. She had once thought of teaching, but after graduation she entered nurses' training at Radcliffe Infirmary, Oxford, where she received her nursing degree in 1937. She dated her literary career from 1939, though she continued as a neurosurgical nurse at Radcliffe Infirmary throughout the war, writing in her off-duty hours. Her first novels were widely popular, but she claimed that "if her early novels were destroyed irrevocably, she would feel absolutely no loss" (Bernard F. Dick, *The Hellenism of Mary Renault*, 1972).

Renault's postwar travels in the eastern Mediterranean provided the impetus for a new literary phase marked by her emigration to South Africa in 1948. After this move, her exhaustive self-taught knowledge of ancient Greek history and philosophy made her a mesmerizing novelist able to re-create a lost world. In the estimation of Dick, Renault was "the only bona fide Hellenist in twentieth century fiction."

Renault remained a resident of South Africa until her death on December 13, 1983.

Analysis

Mary Renault's novels celebrate and eulogize man's potential but transitory glory, a combination difficult for a world that has relinquished its acquaintance with the classics. Peter Wolfe regards Renault's first five novels as her literary apprenticeship, "1930's novels" marked by then-fashionable themes of political engagement and sexual liberation. Bernard F. Dick, her only other major commentator, believes her early fiction was influenced by the restrictive, pain-filled atmosphere of a World War II surgical hospital. Both are partly correct; Renault's early work deals with the individual's freedom from contemporary power structures and stifling social conventions.

Such topical concerns, however appealing to modern readers, are nevertheless peripheral to the core of Renault's art, the Platonism which she followed to the mythic depths of her later novels. When she began to write, Renault was already familiar with the Theory of Ideas developed in Plato's dialogues, wherein everything perceptible by human senses is imitative of changeless perfect Ideas beyond time and space. Each Idea corresponds to a class of earthly objects, all of which must inevitably change, leaving the Ideas the only objects of true knowledge in the universe. A transitory earthly object, however, may remind men of the Idea it represents. Plato theorized that before entering the body, the soul had encountered the infinite Ideas, and that once embodied, the soul might vaguely remember them. Renault often convincingly incorporates Plato's anamnesis, the doctrine that "learning is recollection," in her fiction. Plato also believed that human recognition of such natural truths as the mathematically perfect circle could lead men stepwise to the contemplation of Absolute Truth, which he equated with Absolute

Goodness and Absolute Beauty. He taught that the immortal human soul may be reborn through metempsychosis, or transmigration, another concept found throughout Renault's work.

Renault's novels are also informed by Plato's theory of love as defined by Socrates in *The Symposium*: love is the desire for immortality through possession of or union with the Beautiful. Love manifests itself on its lowest levels by human sexuality, proceeds upward through intellectual achievement, and culminates in a mystical union of the soul with the Idea of Beauty. That Renault's heroes aspire to such union is their glory; that being mortal they must fail is the fate she eulogizes.

Plato, like most classical Greeks, allowed heterosexual love only the lowest rung on his ladder of love, as the necessary element for reproduction. Only the homosexual relationship was considered capable of inspiring the lifelong friendships which offered each partner the ideal of *arete*. All of Renault's novels illustrate some aspect of Platonic love; in the first, *Promise of Love*, she shows Vivian, a nurse, and Mic, who loves her because she resembles her brother Jan, achieving self knowledge not through sexual passion but by affection, the ultimate stage of Platonic love, which at the close of the novel "recalls the true lover of [Plato's dialogue] the *Phaedrus* who is willing to sleep like a servant at the side of his beloved."

Renault's other early novels also have strong Platonic elements. *Kind Are Her Answers* foreshadows her interest in theater as mimetic form, Plato's first literary love, which she realized more fully in *The Mask of Apollo*. Her third novel, *The Middle Mist*, concludes with references to Plato's *Lysis*, his dialogue on friendship which claims that erotic satisfaction destroys *philia*, the more permanent nonphysical union promised by Platonic love, a theme to which Renault returned more successfully in *The Last of the Wine*. Renault attempted unconvincingly in *Return to Night* and *North Face* to state the *amor vincit omnia* tradition of "women's fiction" in mythological metaphors, and found that she had to develop a new fictional mode capable of expressing her archetypal themes with Platonic concepts.

Not published in the United States until 1959 because of its forthright treatment of homosexuality, *The Charioteer* (1953) is the only Renault novel to incorporate a systematic development of Platonic philosophy as the vehicle for commentary on contemporary life. In the *Phaedrus*, Plato depicted reason as a charioteer who must balance the thrust of the white horse of honor against the unruly black horse of passion. The image unifies Renault's tale of Laurie Odell, wounded at Dunkirk, who must come to terms with his homosexuality. After his friendship with the sexually naïve conscientious objector Andrew Raines dissolves, Laurie finds a lifelong partner in Ralph Lanyon, who brought him back wounded after they had fought at Dunkirk. Laurie attains an equilibrium between the two conflicting halves of his nature in a Platonic denial of sexual excess. As Renault comments in the epilogue, a Greek device she favors, "Now their [the horses'] heads droop side by side till their long manes mingle; and when the charioteer falls silent they are reconciled for a night in sleep."

In the ideal Platonic pattern, the older man assumes a compassionate responsibility for the honor of the younger, altogether transcending physical attraction and cemented by shared courage in battle. Renault is hindered in *The Charioteer* from an entirely convincing presentation of such friendship by the intolerance with which homosexual relationships are usually viewed in modern society and the often pathetic insecurity it forces upon them. Despite these handicaps, Renault sympathetically portrays Laurie as "a modern Hephaestus, or maimed artist," as Wolfe notes, a character who wins admiration through striving to heal his injured life and nature and make of them something lasting and beautiful.

From roots far deeper than Plato's philosophy, Renault developed the vital impulse of her eight Greek novels, her major literary achievement. Central is the duality of Apollo and Dionysus, names the Greeks gave to the forces of the mind and of the heart, gods whose realms the mythologist Walter Otto described in *Dionysus, Myth and Cult* (1965) as "sharply opposed" yet "in reality joined together by an eternal bond." In Greek myth, Zeus's archer son Apollo, wielder of the two-sided weapon of Truth, endowed men with the heavenly light called Art, by which he admonished mankind to self-knowledge and moderation through his oracle at Delphi. Paradoxically, Apollo shared his temple and the festival year at Delphi with his mysterious brother Dionysus, god of overwhelming ecstasy, born of mortal woman and all-powerful Zeus, torn apart each year to rise again, offering both wine's solace and its madness to mankind. Thought and emotion were the two faces of the Greek coin of life—in Otto's words, "the eternal contrast between a restless, whirling life and a still, far-seeing spirit."

Each of Renault's Greek novels focuses on a crucial nexus of physical and spiritual existence in Greek history. The age of legendary heroes such as Theseus of Athens, subject of *The King Must Die* and *The Bull from the Sea*, was followed by the Trojan War, 1200 B.C., the stuff of classical epic and tragedy and the harbinger of Greece's Dark Age, when only Athens stood against the Dorian invasion. By the sixth century B.C., the setting of *The Praise Singer*, Athens, under the benevolent tyrant Pisistratus, had become the model polis of the Greek peninsula, building a democracy that repelled imperial Persia and fostered the world's greatest tragedies in their Dionysian festivals. *The Last of the Wine* treats Athens' fall to Sparta in the Peloponnesian Wars, 404 B.C., torn by internal strife and bled by foreign expansion. The restored Athenian democracy of a half-century later is the milieu of *The Mask of Apollo*. Shortly after Plato's death, his pupil Aristotle taught a prince in Macedon who dreams of Homeric deeds in *Fire from Heaven*, accomplishes them in *The Persian Boy*, and leaves an empire to be shattered by lesser men in *Funeral Games*—Alexander the Great.

The Last of the Wine, like most of Renault's Greek fiction, is ostensibly a memoir, a form favored by classical authors. Its fictional narrator, a young and "beautiful" Athenian knight named Alexias, endures the agonizing aftermath of Athens' ill-fated Sicilian venture under Alkibiades, the magnetic but flawed former student of Sokrates. With Lysis, the historical figure on whom Plato modeled his dialogue on ideal friendship, Alexias begins the idealistic attachment they learned together from Sokrates, but physical passion, handled with sensitivity by Renault, overcomes them, and they ruefully must compromise their ideal. Sacrificing his honor for Lysis during the famine caused by the Spartan siege of Athens, Alexias models for sculptors, at least one lascivious, to feed his wounded friend, and in the battle to restore Athenian democracy, Lysis falls gloriously with Alexias' name upon his lips.

The novel's title, an allusion to the Greek custom in which the wine remaining in a cup is tossed to form the initial of a lover's name, metaphorically represents Athens' abandonment of the ideals of its Golden Age. Renault poignantly shows Lysis, a gentleman athlete in pursuit of *philotimo*, the hero's struggle for outward glory to emulate his ideal, beaten sadistically in the Isthmian Games by a monstrous professional wrestler, just as Athenian democracy is becoming warped by politicians such as the vicious Kritias and the cold-blooded Anytos, who will help condemn Sokrates. Alkibiades' personal disaster, abandoning Athens for its Spartan enemies, is an exemplary case of a leader who cannot resist abusing his charismatic gifts.

The Greek ideal of democracy learned at Sokrates' side and based on individual *arete*, inward pursuit of honor, still allows Lysis a moral victory often overlooked in this splendidly elegiac novel of the death of an era. "Men are not born equal in themselves," Lysis tells Alexias over wine one evening in Samos; "a man who thinks himself as good as everyone else will be at no pains to grow better." Lysis fights and dies for "a City where I can find my equals and respect my betters   and where no one can tell me to swallow a lie because it is expedient." At the end of the novel, as he listens to the distorted minds of bureaucrats, Alexias remembers the lamps of Samos, the wine-cup on a table of polished wood, and Lysis' voice: "Must we forsake the love of excellence, then, till every citizen feels it alike?"

Renault analyzes the ideal of kingship in *The King Must Die* and *The Bull from the Sea*. In the earlier novel, she traces Theseus' early life from Troezen and Eleusis, where with the bard Orpheus he establishes the Sacred Mysteries, to the labyrinthine palace of Crete, where he destroys the brutal son of King Minos, who oppresses Athens. In the second, she pursues Theseus' progressive rule in Athens through his abandonment of Ariadne to Dionysus' bloody cult and his capture of the Amazon Hippolyta to the great tragedy of his life, his fatal curse on their son Hippolytus. Stylistically more evocative of Homer's mighty simplicity than the Attic cadences of *The Last of the Wine*, Renault's

Theseus novels treat kingship as a manifestation of the divine inner voice that chooses the moment of willing consent when the monarch sacrifices himself for his people.

Both novels discuss a past so dim that its events have become the raw material of myth. Theseus' birth meshes the earthly with the supernatural, since it results from the divinely inspired compassion of the Athenian King Aigios for the stricken land of Troezen; the reader is left, as is customary in Renault's fiction, to decide where history ends and metaphysics begins. Until his son's death, Theseus practices the lesson learned from his grandfather's ritual sacrifice of the King Horse, one of the shocking joys hidden in pain that opens much of Renault's fiction: "The consenting . . . the readiness is all. It washes heart and mind . . . and leaves them open to the god."

By closing himself to the speaking god, however, obeying not his reason but his emotional reaction to his wife Phaedra's false accusations of Hippolytus, Theseus is lost. Only two bright moments remain to him, an anamnetic dream of Marathon where he fights beside the Athenians defending their City, his name their stirring war cry; and a glimpse before he dies of the boy Achilles, "as springy and as brisk as noonday, his arm round a dark-haired friend." Prescient, Theseus watches tragedy in the making: "The god who sent him that blazing pride should not have added love to be burned upon it," but—consoled that his own reputation has become Achilles' "touchstone for a man"—Theseus for the last time consents to the god of the sea.

By the mid-fourth century B.C., late in Plato's life, sophisticated Athenians had accepted the gods as metaphysical forces within the human personality. In *The Mask of Apollo*, Renault poses the primal duality of Apollo and Dionysus in Greek culture, the calm, farseeing force of reason and art balanced against the irresistible force of ecstasy. An old mask of Apollo, reputedly from the workshop of the Parthenon's architect Phidias, accompanies Renault's narrator Nikeratos through his successful acting career, the fascinating backdrop to the political career of Dion of Syracuse, Plato's noble friend, who might have become the ideal philosopher-king Plato postulated in *The Republic*.

Though Dion is a model soldier and a principled statesman, circumstances force him to abandon his philosophical ideals to save Syracuse from devastation. Renault parallels his fall with Nikeratos' performance in Euripides' *The Bacchae* (405 B.C.), the enigmatic masterpiece named for the followers of Dionysus. As he meditates before Apollo's mask, Nikeratos hears his own voice: "With *The Bacchae* he [Euripides] digs down far below, to some deep rift in the soul where our griefs begin. Take that play anywhere, even to men unborn who worship other gods or none, and it will teach them to know themselves."

Plato's tragedy, acted out by Dion, was the "deep rift" that made men unable to follow him with united minds and hearts: "No one would fight for

Dion, when he gave, as his own soul saw it, his very life for justice." By serving Apollo and Dionysus equally, however, Nikeratos the artist earns his gifts, one a Platonic dream of acting in a strange revenge drama, speaking lines beside an open grave to a clean skull in his hand. Through his love for his protégé Thettalos, whom he frees for achievements he knows will be greater than his own, Nikeratos plays Achilles in Aeschylus' *The Myrmidons* in a performance viewed by Alexander, a boy for whom men will fight and die, "whether he is right or wrong," a prince who "will wander through the world . . . never knowing . . . that while he was still a child the thing he seeks slipped from the world, worn out and spent." Had he encountered Plato's Ideals, which he instinctively sought, Renault proposes as the curtain falls on *The Mask of Apollo*, the Alexander of history might have made the philosopher-king Plato's Dion never could have been; but Nikeratos observes that "no one will ever make a tragedy—and that is well, for one could not bear it—whose grief is that the principals never met."

Renault's Alexander grows from boy to king in *Fire from Heaven*, in which she abandons the memoir form for more objective narration, as though no single point of view could encompass Alexander's youthful ideals, fired by the blazing Homeric *philotimo* in Achilles' honor he learned at the epic-conscious Macedonian court. Modern archaeology supports Renault's conviction that Alexander deliberately patterned his actions, even his father Philip's funerary rites, upon the *Iliad* (c. 800 B.C.), which he read as though returning home, recognizing in his mutual love with Hephaistion the tragic bond of Achilles and Patroclus, the basis of the Western world's first, perhaps greatest, poem.

Arete, which cloaks the heavenly Idea of excellence in earthly beauty, came to Alexander less from Aristotle than through his instinctive attraction to Sokrates through Plato's works, which he read as a boy in Macedon. After defeating Thebes' Sacred Band at Cheironeia, where Philip's Macedonians secured the domination of all of Greece, Alexander stands "with surmise and regret" at Plato's tomb in Athens, listening to his disciple Xenokrates: "What he [Plato] had to teach could only be learned as fire is kindled, by the touch of the flame itself."

The novel in which Renault most precariously treats the question of homosexuality, *The Persian Boy*, is narrated by Bagoas, the handsome eunuch once King Darius' favorite and now the lover of Alexander. Renault's choice of Bagoas' point of view reflects her belief that Alexander was not corrupted by Persian luxury and imperial power, as many historians from classical times to the present have asserted, but that he sought to assimilate Eastern ways as a means of uniting his realm in spirit as well as military fact. Just as Alexander's "passionate capacity for affection" could allow him to accept affection wherever it was sincerely offered from the heart and yet remain wholly true to Bagoas' "victor now, forever," Hephaistion, who Renault feels is the most underrated man in history, Alexander felt "Macedon was my father's country. This is mine"—meaning the empire he had won for himself.

Renault believes that Alexander's eventual tragedy was that he was humanly unable to achieve equilibrium between his followers' personal devotion to him and their pragmatic selfish desires. Through Alexander's complex relationship with his dangerous mother Olympias, herself a devotee of Dionysus, Renault exemplifies the peril of neglecting the god of ecstasy basic to *The Bacchae*, in which Olympias herself had acted during Alexander's youth as a shocking challenge to Philip's authority. Toward the end of his own life, Dionysus' cruelty touches even Alexander. Renault shows his purported deterioration as less his own fault than his men's when he must hold them by force as well as by love, even violating Macedon's dearest law, killing before their Assembly had condemned a man to death. The powerful god leads Alexander to excess; Bagoas sees that "his hunger grew by feeding." The Roman historian Arrian, following the memoir of Alexander's only faithful general Ptolemy, commented, "If there had been no other competition, he would have competed against himself."

Bagoas better than any also sees that "great anguish lies in wait for those who long too greatly." Alexander loses Hephaistion and with him nearly abandons his own senses, emerging only after his friend's funeral, in which he watches Thettalos, without Nikeratos for the first time, perform *The Myrmidons* one last time; "'perhaps,' Bagoas thought, 'the last of the madness had been seared out of him by so much burning.'"

At the close of *The Persian Boy*, Renault notes in her Afterword, "When his [Alexander's] faults (those his own times did not account as virtues) have been considered . . . no other human being has attracted in his lifetime, from so many men, so fervent a devotion. Their reasons are worth examining." In her two novels of Alexander's life, Renault not only has examined the reasons, but also has brilliantly probed to the heart of one of the greatest human mysteries: how one man can ask, as did Homer's Achilles, "now as things are, when the ministers of death stand by us/ In their thousands, which no man born to die can escape or even evade,/ Let us go."—and how other men, with all their hearts, can answer.

Such "true songs are still in the minds of men," according to the aged bard Simonides, narrator of *The Praise Singer*, recalling the "lyric years" when tragedy was being born of song and Athens was becoming the center of the earth. "We die twice when men forget," the ghosts of heroes seemed to tell him as a boy, and he has spent his life in "the bright and perilous gift of making others shine." In this novel, where Renault's heroic epitaph for *to philotimo* and her noble elegy for man's hope of *arete* have given place to a gentler, less exalted nostalgia, she recognizes that "praising excellence, one serves the god within it." Renault also notes in her Afterword that "the blanket generalization 'absolute power corrupts absolutely' is a historical absurdity," and she demonstrates that the respected rule of Pisistratus, nominally a "tyrant," formed the solid foundation on which Pericles erected Athenian democracy, even presaging through a discredited seer "a lightning flash from Macedon."

In Alexander's time, Renault has remarked, "the issue was not whether, but how one made [war]." At his death, brought about at least in part by his self-destructive grief for Hephaistion, Alexander's generals embarked on a cannibalistic power struggle—only Ptolemy, his half-brother, emerging with any of the dignity Alexander had worn so easily in conquering his empire. Renault's *Funeral Games* is "the ancestral pattern of Macedonian tribal and familial struggles for his throne; except that Alexander had given them a world stage on which to do it."

The most violent of Renault's Greek novels, *Funeral Games* contains a darkness that is alleviated only by flashes of Alexander reflected through the decency of the few who knew him best—Ptolemy; Bagoas; Queen Sisygambis, who looked upon Alexander, not Darius, as her son. In them, something of Alexander's flame lingers a little while, a heavenly light extinguished at last in the wreckage of his empire of human depravity which Alexander could not prevent nor Renault fail to record.

In her eight novels of ancient Greece, Renault far surpasses conventional historical fiction. She achieves a mythic dimension in her balance of Apollonian and Dionysian psychological forces and philosophical precision in her treatment of Platonic doctrines. Her style is adapted to the Greek literature of each period she delineates, Attic elegance for *The Last of the Wine* and *The Mask of Apollo*, Hellenic involution counterpoised against Alexander's Homeric simplicity of speech. Renault links all eight novels with a chain of works of art, a finely crafted touch the classical Greeks would have applauded: the great tragedies, *The Myrmidons* and *The Bacchae*, Polykleitos' sculpture of Hermes modeled on Alexias, and the bronze of the liberator Harmodios in Pisistratos' day all serve as shaping factors in the portrait of her ultimate hero, Alexander. Mastering time, space, and modern ignorance of the classical world, Renault captures the "sadness at the back of life" Virginia Woolf so aptly cited as the essence of Greek literature, the inevitable grieving awareness of man at the impassable gulf between his aspirations and his achievement. In the face of the eternal questions of existence, Renault's novels offer a direction in which to turn when, in Woolf's words, "we are sick of the vagueness, of the confusion, of the Christianity and its consolations, of our own age."

Mitzi M. Brunsdale

Other major works
NONFICTION: *The Nature of Alexander*, 1975.

CHILDREN'S LITERATURE: *The Lion in the Gateway: Heroic Battles of the Greeks and Persians at Marathon, Salamis, and Thermopylae*, 1964.

Bibliography
Burns, Landon C., Jr. "Men Are Only Men: The Novels of Mary Renault." *Critique: Studies in Modern Fiction* 4 (Winter, 1963): 102-121. A good, but limited, look at Renault's historical fiction. Burns examines character, theme, and use of classical myth in *The Last of the Wine*, *The King Must Die*, and *The Bull from the Sea*. Burns's careful study repeatedly stresses the high order of Renault's fiction.
Dick, Bernard F. *The Hellenism of Mary Renault*. Carbondale: Southern Illinois Press, 1972. An excellent introduction to Renault's work, examining her entire literary output through *Fire from Heaven*. Places Renault in the mainstream of fiction and applauds her as one of the most creative historical novelists of the century.
Wolfe, Peter. *Mary Renault*. New York: Twayne, 1969. The first full-length examination of the writer, but limited through *The Mask of Apollo*. Wolfe's study is both a plea for Renault's recognition by the critics as an important twentieth century writer and a critical analysis of her work. He has high praise for most of her novels but dislikes *North Face* and *The Bull from the Sea*.

JEAN RHYS
Ella Gwendolen Rees Williams

Born: Roseau, Dominica Island, West Indies; August 24, 1894
Died: Exeter, England; May 14, 1979

Principal long fiction

Postures, 1928 (published in the United States as *Quartet*, 1929); *After Leaving Mr. Mackenzie*, 1930; *Voyage in the Dark*, 1934; *Good Morning, Midnight*, 1939; *Wide Sargasso Sea*, 1966.

Other literary forms

Though Jean Rhys is now primarily remembered for her novels, her first published book was a collection of short stories, *The Left Bank and Other Stories* (1927). As Ford Madox Ford pointed out in the preface to the collection, Rhys's heroines are geographically, psychologically, and emotionally of "the Left Bank," not only of Paris—though Rhys captured the Paris of the 1920's as well as anyone—but also of all of the cities of the world. They are underdogs, alone, betrayed, on the edge of poverty; they are women in a man's world.

Besides *The Left Bank*, Rhys published two other collections of stories: *Tigers Are Better-Looking* (1968) and *Sleep It Off, Lady* (1976). In 1987, *The Collected Short Stories* brought together her work in this genre. At her death, she left an essentially completed first section of an autobiography with Diana Athill, who had edited *Wide Sargasso Sea* and *Sleep It Off, Lady*. Athill published this section and a less completed second section as *Smile, Please: An Unfinished Autobiography* in 1979. A collection of letters was published in 1984.

Achievements

When *Wide Sargasso Sea*, her last novel, was published, Jean Rhys was described in *The New York Times* as the greatest living novelist. Such praise is overstated, but Rhys's fiction, long overlooked by academic critics, is undergoing a revival spurred by feminist studies. Rhys played a noteworthy role in the French Left Bank literary scene in the 1920's, and between 1927 and 1939, she published four substantial novels and a number of jewellike short stories. Although she owes her current reputation in large measure to the rising interest in female writers and feminist themes, her work belongs more properly with the masters of literary impressionism: Joseph Conrad, Ford Madox Ford, Marcel Proust, and James Joyce. She began to publish her writing under the encouragement of her intimate friend Ford Madox Ford, and continued to write in spite of falling out of favor with his circle. As prizes and honors came to her in her old age after the publication of *Wide*

Sargasso Sea, it must have given her grim satisfaction to realize that she had attained entirely by her own efforts a position as a writer at least equal to that of her erstwhile friends.

Biography

Jean Rhys was born Ella Gwen Rees Williams in the West Indies on the island of Dominica in 1894, the daughter of a Welsh father and a part-Creole mother. English society classified her as "colored." Her child associates were often Creole, and she was surrounded by ideas peculiar to their culture, such as voodoo and witchcraft. At the same time, she attended a convent school and seriously considered the life of a nun. The colonial mentality was strong in Dominica, and the "proper" role for a well-bred young woman was sharply defined: passive, obedient, submissive.

In 1910, Rhys left Dominica and went to live in Cambridge, England, with her aunt, Clarice Rhys Williams. After a short term in a local school, she enrolled in the Royal Academy of Dramatic Art in London. Her father died soon after she arrived in England, and she found herself short of money. The transition from the West Indies to England must have been extremely painful for the sixteen-year-old girl: the climate harsh, the people cold, the social and economic situation threatening. Those who knew her as a young woman testified that she was strikingly beautiful. After a term at the Royal Academy of Dramatic Art, she toured as a minor actress or chorus girl with provincial theater troupes and did modeling. A young woman alone under these circumstances would have seen at first hand how male dominance and financial control in British society combined to exploit the female. Many of her stories and novels reflect scenes from her career on the stage, and most of them hinge on the theme of male exploitation of women through financial domination.

Near the end of World War I, Rhys married Jean Lenglet (alias Edouard de Neve), an adventurer who had served in the French Foreign Legion and who was probably employed by the French secret service during the war. The newlywed couple lived in Paris, constantly moving from one cheap hotel to another, although de Neve secured temporarily a position with the international mission administering Vienna. A son was born to them in 1919, but lived only three weeks. A daughter born in 1922 lived, but required special medical care. Rhys tried to earn a living in Paris by modeling and writing. Pearl Adam, the wife of a correspondent for *The Times* of Paris, took an interest in some of her sketches and introduced her to Ford Madox Ford, then editor of *The Transatlantic Review*. Through him, she entered into the expatriate community of the early 1920's, meeting James Joyce, Ernest Hemingway, and other prominent writers. Shortly after Rhys met Ford in the autumn of 1924, her husband was sent to prison for illegal dealing in antiques. Ford was living at the time with the artist Stella Bowen. Rhys, penniless, moved in with them and soon formed an intimate relationship with Ford. A casual episode in Ford's generally messy life was something much more serious for the young woman; Rhys treats this affair in her first novel, *Quartet*. De Neve never forgave her for her involvement with Ford. After her divorce from de Neve, Rhys became closely involved with a literary agent, Leslie Tilden Smith. They were eventually married and lived together until his death in 1945. Subsequently, she married his cousin, Max Hamer, who later served time in prison for mismanagement of his firm's funds. Throughout the 1940's and 1950's, Rhys suffered greatly from poverty, poor health, and family problems. Her books were all out of print.

She was not, however, entirely forgotten. The actress Selma Vaz Diaz adapted a dramatic monologue from *Good Morning, Midnight* for stage use in 1949. Eight years later, the BBC's third program presented Selma Vaz Diaz's monologue, which received excellent notices. The publication of *Wide Sargasso Sea* in 1966 and the rapid growth of feminist studies led to a Rhys revival, and the reprinting of all her works followed.

Analysis

Jean Rhys's first novel, *Quartet*, reflects closely her misadventures with Ford Madox Ford. The heroine, Marya Zelli, whose husband is in prison, moves in with the rich and respectable Hugh and Lois Heidler. Hugh becomes Marya's lover, while Lois punishes her with petty cruelties. The central figure is a woman alone, penniless, exploited, and an outsider. In her next novel, *After Leaving Mr. Mackenzie*, the central figure, Julia Martin, breaks off with her rich lover, Mr. Mackenzie, and finds herself financially desperate. *Voyage in the Dark* tells the story of Anna Morgan, who arrives from the West Indies as an innocent young girl in England, has her first affair as a chorus girl, and descends through a series of shorter and shorter affairs to working for a masseuse. In *Good Morning, Midnight*, the alcoholic Sasha Jensen, penniless in Paris, remembers episodes from her past which have brought her to this sorry pass. All four of these novels show a female character subject to financial, sexual, and social domination by men and "respectable" society. In all cases, the heroine is passive, but "sentimental." The reader is interested in her feelings, rather than in her ideas and accomplishments. She is alienated economically from any opportunity to do meaningful and justly rewarding work. She is an alien socially, either from a foreign and despised colonial culture or from a marginally respectable social background. She is literally an alien or foreigner in Paris and London, which are cities of dreadful night for her. What the characters fear most is the final crushing alienation from their true identities, the reduction to some model or type imagined by a foreign man. They all face the choice of becoming someone's gamine, garçonne, or femme fatale, or of starving to death, and they all struggle against this loss of personal identity. After a silence of more than twenty years, Rhys returned to these same concerns in her masterpiece, *Wide Sargasso Sea*. While the four early novels are to a large degree autobiographical, *Wide Sargasso Sea* has a more literary origin, although it, too, reflects details from the author's personal life.

Wide Sargasso Sea requires a familiarity with Charlotte Brontë's *Jane Eyre* (1847). In Charlotte Brontë's novel, Jane is prevented from marrying Rochester by the presence of his madwoman in the attic, an insane West Indian wife who finally perishes in the fire which she sets, burning Rochester's house and blinding him, but clearing the way for Jane to wed him. The madwoman in *Jane Eyre* is depicted entirely from the exterior. It is natural that the mad West Indian wife, when seen only through the eyes of her English rival and of Rochester, appears completely hideous and depraved. Indeed, when Jane first sees the madwoman in Chapter XVI of the novel, she cannot tell whether it is a beast or a human being groveling on all fours. Like a hyena with bloated features, the madwoman attacks Rochester in this episode.

Wide Sargasso Sea is a sympathetic account of the life of Rochester's mad wife, ranging from her childhood in the West Indies, her Creole and Catholic background, and her courtship and married years with the deceitful Rochester, to her final descent into madness and captivity in England. Clearly, the predicament of the West Indian wife resembles that of Rhys herself in many ways. In order to present the alien wife's case, she has written a "counter-text," an extension of Brontë's novel filling in the "missing" testimony, the issues over which Brontë glosses.

Wide Sargasso Sea consists of two parts. Part I is narrated by the girl growing up in Jamaica who is destined to become Rochester's wife. The Emancipation Act has just been passed (the year of that Imperial Edict was 1833) and the blacks on the island are passing through a period of so-called apprenticeship which should lead to their complete freedom in 1837. This is a period of racial tension and anxiety for the privileged colonial community. Fear of black violence runs high, and no one knows exactly what will happen to the landholders once the blacks are emancipated. The girlish narrator lives in the interface between the privileged white colonists and the blacks. Although a child of landowners, she is impoverished, clinging to European notions of respectability, and in constant fear. She lives on the crumbling estate of her widowed mother. Her closest associate is Christophine, a Martinique obeah woman, or voodoo witch. When her mother marries Mr. Mason, the family's lot improves temporarily, until the blacks revolt, burning their country home, Coulibri, and killing her half-witted brother. She then attends a repressive Catholic school in town, and her kindly colored "cousin" Sandi protects her from more hostile blacks.

Part II is narrated by the young Rochester on his honeymoon with his bride to her country home. Wherever appropriate, Rhys follows the details of Brontë's story. Rochester reveals that his marriage was merely a financial arrangement. After an uneasy period of passion, Rochester's feelings for his bride begin to cool. He receives a letter of denunciation accusing her of misbehavior with Sandi and revealing that madness runs in the family. To counter Rochester's growing hostility, the young bride goes to her former companion, the obeah woman Christophine, for a love potion. The nature of the potion is that it can work for one night only. Nevertheless, she administers it to her husband. His love now dead, she is torn from her native land, transported to a cruel and loveless England, and maddeningly confined. Finally, she takes candle in hand to fire Rochester's house in suicidal destruction.

In Brontë's novel, the character of the mad wife is strangely blank, a vacant slot in the story. Her presence is essential, and she must be fearfully hateful, so that Jane Eyre has no qualms about taking her place in Rochester's arms, but the novel tells the reader almost nothing else about her. Rhys fills in this blank, fleshing out the character, making her live on a par with Jane herself. After all, Brontë tells the reader a great deal about Jane's painful childhood and education; why should Rhys not supply the equivalent information about her dark rival?

It is not unprecedented for a writer to develop a fiction from another writer's work. For example, T. H. White's *Mistress Masham's Repose* (1946) imagines that some of Jonathan Swift's Lilliputians were transported to England, escaped captivity, and established a thriving colony in an abandoned English garden, where they are discovered by an English schoolgirl. Her intrusion into their world is a paradigm of British colonial paternalism, finally overcome by the intelligence and good feeling of the girl. This charming story depends on Swift's fiction, but the relationship of White's work to Swift's is completely different from the relationship of Rhys's work to Brontë's. Rhys's fiction permanently alters one's understanding of *Jane Eyre*. Approaching Brontë's work after Rhys's, one is compelled to ask such questions as, "Why is Jane so uncritical of Rochester?" and, "How is Jane herself like the madwoman in the attic?" Rhys's fiction reaches into the past and alters Brontë's novel.

Rhys's approach in *Wide Sargasso Sea* was also influenced by Ford Madox Ford and, through Ford, Joseph Conrad. In the autumn of 1924, when Rhys first met Ford, he was writing *Joseph Conrad: A Memoir*. Some thirty years earlier, when Joseph Conrad was just beginning his career as a writer, his agent had introduced him to Ford in hopes that they could work in collaboration, since Conrad wrote English (a language he had adopted only as an adult) with great labor. Ford and Conrad produced *The Inheritors* (1901) and *Romance* (1903) as coauthors. During their years of association, Ford had some hand in the production of several works usually considered Conrad's sole effort, although it has never been clear to what degree Ford participated in the creation of the fiction of Conrad's middle period. About 1909, after Ford's disreputable ways had become increasingly offensive to Conrad's wife, the two men parted ways. Immediately after Conrad's death in 1924, however,

Ford rushed into print his memoir of the famous author. His memoir of Conrad is fictionalized and hardly to be trusted as an account of their association in the 1890's, but it sheds a great deal of light on what Ford thought about writing fiction in 1924, when he was beginning his powerful Tietjens tetralogy and working for the first time with Rhys. Ford claimed that he and Conrad invented literary impressionism in English. Impressionist fiction characteristically employs limited and unreliable narration, follows a flow of associated ideas leaping freely in time and space, aims to render the impression of a scene vividly so as to make the reader see it as if it were before his eyes, and artfully selects and juxtaposes seemingly unrelated scenes and episodes so that the reader must construct the connections and relationships that make the story intelligible. These are the stylistic features of Rhys's fiction, as well as of Ford's *The Good Soldier* (1915), Conrad's *Heart of Darkness* (1899), Henry James's *The Turn of the Screw* (1898), and Joyce's *Ulysses* (1922).

An "affair"—the mainspring of the plot in an impressionist novel—is some shocking or puzzling event which has already occurred when the story begins. The reader knows what has happened, but he does not understand fully why and how it happened. The story proceeds in concentric rings of growing complication as the reader finds something he thought clear-cut becoming more and more intricate. In Conrad's *Lord Jim*, the affair is the scandalous abandonment of the pilgrim ship by the English sailor. In *The Good Soldier*, it is the breakup of the central foursome, whose full infidelity and betrayal are revealed only gradually. Brontë's *Jane Eyre* provided Rhys with an impressionist "affair" in the scene in which the mad West Indian wife burns Rochester's house, blinding him and killing herself. Like Conrad's Marlow, the storyteller who sits on the veranda mulling over Jim's curious behavior, or *The Good Soldier*'s narrator Dowell musing about the strange behavior of Edward Ashburnham, Rhys takes up the affair of Rochester and reworks it into ever richer complications, making the initial judgments in *Jane Eyre* seem childishly oversimplified. "How can Jane simply register relief that the madwoman is burned out of her way? There must be more to the affair than that," the secondary fiction suggests.

One of the most important features of literary impressionism is the highly constructive activity which it demands of the reader. In a pointillist painting, small dots of primary colors are set side by side. At a certain distance from the canvas, these merge on the retina of the eye of the viewer into colors and shapes which are not, in fact, drawn on the canvas at all. The painting is constructed in the eyes of each viewer with greater luminosity than it would have were it drawn explicitly. In order to create such a shimmering haze in fiction, Ford advises the use of a limited point of view which gives the reader dislocated fragments of remembered experience. The reader must struggle constantly to fit these fragments into a coherent pattern. The tools for creating such a verbal collage are limited, "unreliable" narration, psychological time-shifts, and juxtaposition. Ford observes that two apparently unrelated events can be set side by side so that the reader will perceive their connection with far greater impact than if the author had stated such a connection openly. Ford advises the impressionist author to create a verbal collage by unexpected selection and juxtaposition, and *Wide Sargasso Sea* makes such juxtapositions on several levels. On the largest scale, *Wide Sargasso Sea* is juxtaposed with *Jane Eyre*, so that the two novels read together mean much more than when they are read independently. This increase of significance is what Ford called the "unearned increment" in impressionist art. Within *Wide Sargasso Sea*, Part I (narrated by the West Indian bride) and Part II (narrated by Rochester) likewise mean more in juxtaposition than when considered separately. Throughout the text, the flow of consciousness of the storytellers cunningly shifts in time to juxtapose details which mean more together than they would in isolation.

Because *Wide Sargasso Sea* demands a highly constructive reader, it is, like *The Good Soldier* or *Heart of Darkness*, an open fiction. When the reader completes *Jane Eyre*, the mystery of Rochester's house has been revealed and purged, the madwoman in the attic has been burned out, and Jane will live, the reader imagines, happily ever after. *Jane Eyre* taken in isolation is a closed fiction. Reading *Wide Sargasso Sea* in juxtaposition to *Jane Eyre*, however, opens the latter and poses questions which are more difficult to resolve: Is Jane likely to be the next woman in the attic? Why is a cripple a gratifying mate for Jane? At what price is her felicity purchased?

The *Doppelgänger*, twin, or shadow-character runs throughout Rhys's fiction. All of her characters seem to be split personalities. There is a public role, that of the approved "good girl," which each is expected to play, and there is the repressed, rebellious "bad girl" lurking inside. If the bad girl can be hidden, the character is rewarded with money, love, and social position. Yet the bad girl will sometimes put in an appearance, when the character drinks too much or gets excited or angry. When the dark girl appears, punishment follows, swift and sure. This is the case with Marya Zelli in *Quartet*, Julia Martin in *After Leaving Mr. Mackenzie*, Anna Morgan in *Voyage in the Dark*, and Sasha Jensen in *Good Morning, Midnight*. It is also the case in Brontë's *Jane Eyre*. The education of Jane Eyre consists of repressing those dark, selfish impulses that Victorian society maintained "good little girls" should never feel. Jane succeeds in stamping out her "bad" self through a stiff British education, discipline, and self-control. She kills her repressed identity, conforms to society's expectations, and gets her reward—a crippled husband and a burned-out house. Rhys revives the dark twin, shut up in the attic, the naughty, wild, dark, selfish, bestial female. She suggests that the struggle between repressed politeness and unrepressed self-interest is an ongoing process in which total repression means the death of a woman's identity.

Todd K. Bender

Other major works

SHORT FICTION: *The Left Bank and Other Stories*, 1927; *Tigers Are Better-Looking*, 1968; *Sleep It Off, Lady*, 1976; *The Collected Short Stories*, 1987.

NONFICTION: *Smile Please: An Unfinished Autobiography*, 1979; *The Letters of Jean Rhys*, 1984 (also known as *Jean Rhys: Letters, 1931-1966*).

Bibliography

Angier, Carole. *Jean Rhys*. New York: Penguin Books, 1985. A brief account of Rhys's life and works. Organized chronologically, with the events of Rhys's life and her fiction discussed together, carefully bringing out the way in which the two exerted a mutual influence. The straightforward presentation and brevity of the book make it the best introduction to Rhys.

Benstock, Shari. *Women of the Left Bank: Paris, 1900-1940*. Austin: University of Texas Press, 1986. Discusses Rhys's work in the context of the Left Bank literary community. Rhys knew the members of the community but stood outside it, and Benstock demonstrates that Rhys's position as an outsider in life influenced her fiction.

Harrison, Nancy R. *Jean Rhys and the Novel as Women's Text*. Chapel Hill: University of North Carolina Press, 1988. Harrison is a feminist critic who argues that women tend to write, and respond to writing, in a different fashion from men. Women write in a way that invites the reader to join in the creation of the work; the author's activity of writing is stressed and the work is not offered as a finished product. Analyzes *Voyage in the Dark* and *Wide Sargasso Sea* along these lines.

James, Selma. *The Ladies and the Mammies: Jane Austen and Jean Rhys*. Bristol, England: Falling Wall Press, 1983. In addition to the unusual comparison of Austen and Rhys, James emphasizes Rhys's identity as an alien in her own society. Claims that Rhys's identity as a white West Indian woman exerted particular influence on *Wide Sargasso Sea*.

Rhys, Jean. *Smile Please: An Unfinished Autobiography*. New York: Harper & Row, 1980. This unfinished work is only 151 pages long and consists of a memoir of the author's childhood, along with fragmentary recollections of later life and excerpts from a diary. Offers many interesting glimpses into Rhys's personal life.

Staley, Thomas. *Jean Rhys: A Critical Study*. London: Macmillan, 1979. Probably most important for its first chapter, which gives an account of Rhys's life. Rhys has not been the subject of a full-length biography, and Staley's presentation of her life is the best available. Should be supplemented with Rhys's *Smile Please: An Unfinished Autobiography*, on which she was working at the time of her death in 1979.

DOROTHY RICHARDSON

Born: Berkshire, England; May 17, 1873
Died: Beckenham, England; June 17, 1957

Principal long fiction

Pilgrimage 1938, 1967 (includes *Pointed Roofs*, 1915; *Backwater*, 1916; *Honeycomb*, 1917; *The Tunnel*, 1919; *Interim*, 1919; *Deadlock*, 1921; *Revolving Lights*, 1923; *The Trap*, 1925; *Oberland*, 1927; *Dawn's Left Hand*, 1931; *Clear Horizon*, 1935; *Dimple Hill*, 1938; *March Moonlight*, 1967).

Other literary forms

Dorothy Richardson's literary reputation rests on the single long novel, *Pilgrimage*. She referred to the parts published under separate titles as "chapters," and they were the primary focus of her energy throughout her creative life. The first appeared in 1915; the last—unfinished and unrevised—was printed ten years after her death. Before 1915, she wrote some essays and reviews for obscure periodicals edited by friends and also two books growing out of her interest in the Quakers. She contributed descriptive sketches on Sussex life to the *Saturday Review* between 1908 and 1914. During the years writing *Pilgrimage*, Richardson did an enormous amount of miscellaneous writing to earn money—columns and essays in the *Dental Record* (1912-1922), film criticism, translations, articles on various subjects for periodicals including *Vanity Fair*, *Adelphi*, *Little Review*, and *Fortnightly Review*. She also wrote a few short stories, chiefly during the 1940's. None of this material has been collected. A detailed bibliography is included in *Dorothy Richardson: A Biography* by Gloria G. Fromm (1977).

Achievements

The term "stream of consciousness," adapted from psychology, was first applied to literature in a 1918 review of Richardson's *Pointed Roofs*, *Backwater*, and *Honeycomb*. In the twentieth century, novels moved from outward experience to inner reality. The experiments that marked the change were made almost simultaneously by three writers unaware of one another's work: the first two volumes of Marcel Proust's *Remembrance of Things Past* appeared in 1913; James Joyce's *Portrait of the Artist as a Young Man* began serial publication in 1914; the manuscript of *Pointed Roofs* was finished in 1913.

Richardson was the first novelist in England to restrict the point of view entirely to the protagonist's consciousness, to take for content the experience of life at the moment of perception, and to record the development of a single character's mind and emotions without imposing any plot or structural pattern. Her place in literature (as opposed to literary history) has been less certain; some critics feel that her work is interesting only because it dates the emergence of a new technique. The absence of story and explanation make heavy demands on the reader. Since the protagonist's own limited understanding controls every word of the narrative, readers must also do the work of evaluating the experience in order to create meaning.

Richardson wrote what Virginia Woolf called "the psychological sentence of the feminine gender"; a sentence that expanded its limits and tampered with punctuation to convey the multiple nuances of a single moment. She deliberately rejected the description of events, which she thought was typical of male literature, in order to convey the subjective understanding that she believed was the reality of experience. The autobiographical basis of *Pilgrimage* was not known until 1963. Richardson, like her protagonist and like other women of her period, broke with the conventions of the past, sought to create her own being through self-awareness, and struggled to invent a form that would communicate a woman's expanding conscious life.

Biography

Dorothy Miller Richardson, born on May 17, 1873, was the third of four daughters. Her father, Charles Richardson, worked in the prosperous grocery business that his father had established, but he wanted to be a gentleman. He abandoned Nonconformity for the Church of England and, in 1874, sold the family business to live on investments. During Dorothy's childhood, periods of upper-middle-class luxury (a large house, servants, gardens, membership in a tennis club) alternated with moves arising from temporarily reduced circumstances.

Charles Richardson had hoped for a son, and he took Dorothy with him to lectures in Oxford and meetings of scientific associations. She was sent at age eleven to a private day school for the daughters of gentlemen. It was late enough in the century for the curriculum to emphasize academic subjects; her studies included logic and psychology. In 1890, realizing that her family's financial condition had become seriously straitened, Dorothy looked to the example of Charlotte Brontë and *Villette* (1853) and applied for a post as pupil-teacher in a German school. Six months in Hanover were followed by two years teaching in a North London private school and a brief spell as governess for a wealthy suburban family.

By the end of 1893, Charles Richardson was declared bankrupt; in 1895, two of Dorothy's sisters married. Her mother, Mary Richardson, was troubled by an unusually severe bout of the depression that had gripped her for several years. Dorothy took her mother to stay in lodgings near the sea and found that she required almost constant companionship and supervision. On November 30, 1895, while her daughter was out for a short walk in the fresh air, Mary Richardson committed suicide.

At the age of twenty-two, responsible for her own support and severely shaken by the past two years' events, Richardson moved to an attic room in a London lodging house and took a job as secretary and assistant to three Harley Street dentists. For young women at that time, such a step was unusual, by taking it Richardson evaded the restraint, protection, and religious supervision that made teaching an acceptable profession for young women of good family. The nineteenth century was drawing to a close and London was alive with new ideas. Richardson explored the city, made friends with women who worked in business offices, and lived on eggs and toast so that she could afford concert tickets.

Soon after moving to London, she was invited for a Saturday in the country by an old school friend, Amy Catherine Robbins, who had married her science instructor at London University—a man named H. G. Wells. He had just published *The Time Machine* (1895). Richardson was fascinated by Wells and by the people and ideas she encountered at his house but angered by his way of telling her what to do. She was aware that she stood outside the class system and between the Victorian and modern worlds. She was drawn both to picnics with cousins at Cambridge and to Anarchist and Fabian meetings. She sampled various churches (including Unitarian and Quaker) but refrained from committing herself to any group or cause.

In 1902, Richardson began contributing occasional articles and reviews to *Crank* and other magazines edited by a vegetarian friend. She refused a proposal from a respectable physician and broke her engagement to a Russian Jew, Benjamin Grad. Her friendship with Wells passed at some point into physical intimacy, but she continued to struggle against being overwhelmed by his ideas and personality. In 1906, finding herself pregnant, she brought the affair to an end; she looked forward to rearing the child on her own and was distressed when she suffered a miscarriage.

Exhausted physically and mentally, Richardson left her dental job and went to Sussex to recover and think. In 1908, she began writing sketches for the *Saturday Review*. Then, as her fortieth year approached, she began deliberately searching for the form that would allow her to create what she called "a feminine equivalent of the current masculine realism."

Pointed Roofs was at first rejected by publishers; when it was published in 1915 it puzzled readers, distressed some reviewers, and failed to make money. Richardson persisted, however, on the course she had set, even while living an unsettled life in YWCA hostels and borrowed rooms and earning a minimal income by proofreading and by writing a monthly column for the *Dental Record*. In 1917, she married the artist Alan Odle, who was fifteen years younger than she and had been rejected for military service by a doctor who told him he had six months to live.

Richardson's books attracted some critical recognition in the years after World War I, but they never earned money; she was usually in debt to her publishers. She supported herself and Odle (who lived until 1948) and also coped with all the practical details of their life—housekeeping, paying taxes, writing checks, doing his business with publishers and exhibitors. The couple moved frequently, spending the off-season (when lodgings were less expensive) in Cornwall and going to rooms in London for the summer. During the early 1930's, Richardson took on the burden of five full-length translations from French and German. Returning to *Pilgrimage* and the state of mind in which it was begun became increasingly difficult for Richardson; the later volumes were weakened by extraliterary distractions and also by the psychological difficulty for the author in concluding the work that was based on her own life. The final segment, *March Moonlight*, was found unfinished among her papers after she died on June 17, 1957, at the age of eighty-four.

Analysis

Pilgrimage is a quest; the protagonist, Miriam Henderson, seeks her self and, rejecting the old guideposts, makes her own path through life. The book remains a problem for many readers, although since 1915 most of Dorothy Richardson's technical devices have become familiar: unannounced transitions from third-person narration to the first person for interior monologue, shifts between present and past as experience evokes memory, disconnected phrases and images and fragmentary impressions representing the continuous non-verbal operations of the mind. Looking back on the period when she was trying to find a way to embody Miriam Henderson's experience, Richardson described her breakthrough as the realization that no one was "*there* to *describe* her." Impressed by Henry James's control of viewpoint, she went one step further. The narrator and the protagonist merge; the narrator knows, perceives, and expresses only what comes to Miriam's consciousness. Furthermore, the narrator does not speak to any imagined reader and therefore does not provide helpful explanations. The scenes and people are presented as they impinge on Miriam's awareness—thus the most familiar circumstances are likely to be undescribed and the most important people identified only by name, without the phrases that would place them or reveal their relationship to Miriam. Many readers are discouraged by the attempt to follow the book and make meaning of it; some are tempted to use Richardson's biography as a pony to find out what "really" happened and others prefer to read isolated sections without regard to sequence, responding to the feeling and imagery as if it were poetry. Because there is no narrative guidance, meaning is continually modified by the reader's own consciousness and by the extent of identification.

The first three titles show Miriam Henderson in the last stages of her girlhood and form the prelude to her London life. *Pointed Roofs* covers her experience in Hanover; in *Backwater*, she is resident teacher in a North London school and still drawn to the possibility of romance with a young man from her suburban circle; in *Honeycomb*, she briefly holds a post as governess before her sisters' weddings and her mother's death complete the disintegration of her girlhood family. *The Tunnel* begins Miriam's years in London and introduces situations and characters that reappear in the next several volumes: the dental job, the room at Mrs. Bailey's lodging house, the new women Mag and Jan and the dependent woman Eleanor Dear, a visit to her school friend Alma who has married the writer Hypo Wilson. In *Interim*, Miriam perceives the difficulty of communicating her current thoughts and experiences to her sister and other old friends. *Deadlock* treats her acquaintance—growing into an engagement—with Michael Shatov. In *Revolving Lights*, she has decided not to marry Shatov and becomes increasingly involved with Hypo Wilson. *The Trap* shows her sharing a cramped flat with a spinster social worker and growing despondent about the isolation which, she realizes, she imposes on herself to avoid emotional entanglements. *Oberland* is a lyrical interlude about a holiday in Switzerland. In *Dawn's Left Hand*, Miriam has an affair with Hypo Wilson and an intense friendship with a young woman (Amabel) who becomes a radical suffragist. *Clear Horizon* concludes much of the practical and emotional business that has occupied Miriam for several years; she disentangles herself from Wilson, Shatov, and Amabel and prepares to leave London. In *Dimple Hill*, she lives on a farm owned by a Quaker family, absorbs their calm, and works at writing. *March Moonlight* rather hastily takes Miriam up to the point of meeting the artist who would become her husband and to the beginning of her work on a novel.

This summary of events is the barest framework. Life, for Miriam Henderson, exists not in events but in the responses that create her sense of awareness. The books are made up of relatively independent sections, each treating a single segment of experience or reflection. Because of the depth with which single moments are recorded, the overall narrative line is fragmentary. Despite *Pilgrimage*'s length, it embodies isolated spots of time. Frequently, neither narration nor the memories evoked by subsequent experience indicate what events may have taken place in the gaps between. Furthermore, the book concentrates on those moments important to Miriam's interior experience, and it leaves out the times when she acts without self-awareness—which may include significant actions that take place when Miriam is so engrossed by events that she does not engage in thought or reflection.

Richardson disliked the phrase "stream of consciousness" because it implies constant movement and change. She preferred the image of a pool—new impressions are added, and sometimes create ripples that spread over the previously accumulated consciousness. Thus, Miriam's interior monologue becomes steadily more complex as she grows older. Her consciousness widens and deepens; fragmentary phrases show her making connections with her earlier experiences and perceptions; her understanding of past events alters with later awareness. The earlier volumes have more sensory impression and direct emotion; later, as Miriam grows more self-aware, she has greater verbal skill and is more likely to analyze her responses. Because of her more sophisticated self-awareness, however, she also grows adept, in the later volumes, at suppressing impressions or fragments of self-knowledge that she does not want to admit to consciousness.

In many ways, Miriam is not likable—readers are sometimes put off by the need to share her mind for two thousand pages. In the early books, she is a self-preoccupied, narrow-minded adolescent, oppressively conscious of people's appearance and social class, annoyingly absorbed in wondering what they think about her, defensively judgmental. The wild swings in mood and the ebb and flow of her energies during the day appear to have little cause and to be unworthy of the attention she gives them. Most people, however, would appear unpleasantly selfish if their minds were open for inspection. Miriam creates her self by deliberate consciousness. The danger is that she tends to withdraw from experience in order to contemplate feeling.

The events of *Pilgrimage* span the decades at the turn of the century but, because of the interior focus, there is relatively little physical detail or explicit social history to create an objective picture of the era. Women's developing self-awareness, however, must be seen as one of the period's significant events. Miriam reflects the mental life of her times in her range of responses to religion, the books she reads, and the people, ideas, and movements she encounters.

A good deal of life's texture and even its choices take place at levels that are not verbalized. Richardson's first publisher described her work as "female imagism." Miriam responds particularly and constantly to the quality of light. Readers are also aware of her reaction to places, objects, and physical surroundings; ultimately, it is through mastering the emotional content of this response that she is able to discover what she needs to have in her life.

Another continuing thread is created by Miriam's thoughts about men, about men and women together, and about the roles of women in society. Her basic animosity toward men gives shape to a series of statements on their personal, emotional, social, and intellectual peculiarities that falls just short of a formal feminist analysis. Each possible romance, each rejected or fore-stalled proposal amounts to a choice of a way of life. The matter is, however, complicated by Miriam's sexual reticence. Even though she can talk about free love, she is not conscious—or perhaps will not permit herself to become conscious—of overt sexual urges or of physical attraction to men or to women. She struggles not to let her feeling for certain women lead her to be absorbed by their lives or roles. In *Backwater*, Miss Perne's religion is dangerously comfortable; Eleanor Dear's passive feminine helplessness forces Miriam to become her protector; Amabel's possessiveness is as stifling as Hypo Wilson's. At the end—in *March Moonlight*—there is a hint of emotional involvement with the unidentified "Jane." Struggling to know herself, Miriam is constantly faced with the problem of knowing other women.

Pointed Roofs comes close to being a structural whole—it begins with

Miriam Henderson's journey to Hanover and ends with her return home six months later. She is on her first trip away from home, looking at new scenes, anxious about her ability to do her job and earn her wages, having her first taste of independence. Since Miriam is seventeen—and, as a Victorian daughter, a relatively innocent and sheltered seventeen—the reader often understands more than Miriam does and can interpret the incidents that develop her sense of who she is and where she fits in the world. Some of Miriam's reactions are cast in the form of mental letters home or imaginary conversations with her sisters, which provide a structured way to verbalize mental processes. Miriam pays attention to the sights and sounds and smells of Hanover because they are new, giving readers a sense of the physical setting absent in many of the later books.

Miriam's moods are typically adolescent. An incident or object can set off a homesick reverie or a bout of self-recrimination; the sound of music or the sight of rain on paving stones can create an inexpressible transport of joy. She is alternately rebellious and anxious for approval; she is glad to learn that her French roommate is Protestant (because she could not bear living with a Catholic), proud of the skill in logic that allows her to criticize the premises of a sermon, moved by the sound of hymns in German. She worries about her plainness, her intellectual deficiencies, her inability to get close to people. Observing class and cultural differences lets her begin to understand that she has unthinkingly absorbed many of her tastes and ideas; she starts to grow more deliberate. This portrait of Miriam at seventeen—which forms the essential background for the rest of *Pilgrimage*—is also interesting for its own sake.

Because the narrative is limited to Miriam's consciousness, the reader is able to supply interpretation. In one key scene, the middle-aged Pastor Lahmann, chaplain to the school, quotes a verse describing his ambition for "A little land, well-tilled,/ A little wife, well-willed" and then asks Miriam to take off her glasses so that he can see how nearsighted her eyes really are. Miriam, who is both furious at being "regarded as one of a world of little tame things to be summoned by little man to be well-willed wives" and warmed by the personal attention that makes her forget, for a moment, that she is a governess, is oblivious to the sexual implications of Pastor Lahmann's behavior, and cannot understand why the headmistress is angry when she walks in upon the scene. Although Miriam's consciousness will develop in subsequent volumes, her combination of receptivity to male attention, anger at male assumptions, and blindness to sexual nuance will remain.

Deadlock contains a greater proportion of direct internal monologue than the earlier books. Miriam has grown more articulate; she interprets her emotional states and examines the premises underlying her conflicts. During her first years in London, she had cherished the city for the independence it gave her. By such acts as smoking, eating alone in restaurants, and dressing without regard to fashion, she deliberately rejected Victorian womanhood. In *Honeycomb*, she refused a marriage that would have satisfied her craving for luxuries because she could not accept a subordinate role. In *Deadlock*, Miriam is faced by the loneliness that seems inextricably linked to independence. Her work has become drudgery because she no longer has the sense of a social relationship with her employer. A Christmas visit to her married sister reveals the distance that has grown betwen them; Miriam had not even realized that Harriet's marriage was unhappy.

Deadlock is shaped by the course of Miriam's relationship with Michael Shatov. The romance forces her conflicts to the surface. Shatov is a young Jew recently arrived from Russia; a lodger at Mrs. Bailey's arranges for Miriam to tutor him in English. As she shows Shatov London, tired scenes recapture their original freshness. Miriam is excited by her ability to formulate ideas when she argues about philosophy or works on a translation. Yet, although Miriam is buoyed by the joy of sharing her thoughts with another person, Shatov's continual presence comes between her and the life that was her own. Her love has a maternal quality: though Shatov is only three years younger than Miriam, he is a foreigner and also, Miriam finds, rather impractical; she feels protective. She is also sexually reticent: because she has despised traditional femininity she does not know how to behave as the object of a courtship. The romance ends when Miriam deliberately engages Shatov in an argument that reveals his views of woman's limited nature. (The final scene restates the problem more concretely when Miriam visits an Englishwoman married to a Jewish man.) Beneath these specific difficulties lies the friction between Miriam's individualism and Shatov's tendency to see problems in the abstract—she talks about herself, he dwells on the future of the race. For Richardson, the conflict reflects the irreconcilable difference between masculine objectivity (or materialism) and feminine subjectivity. The images of darkness accumulate as Miriam realizes the extent of her deadlock; unable to be a woman in the sense that men see women, she seems to have no path out of loneliness and alienation.

Dawn's Left Hand is a prelude to the deliberate detachment and observation that would turn Miriam into a writer. *Oberland* (the preceding book) vibrates with the sensory detail of a two-week holiday in Switzerland that makes London complications seem far·away; returning, Miriam sees people objectively even when she is with them. The transitions between third-person narrative and internal monologue are less noticeable; Miriam and the narrator have virtually merged. The visual content of scenes reveals their meaning. Miriam looks at pictorial relationships and examines gesture and tone for the nonverbal communications that, to women, are often more meaningful than words. (During the years that she worked on *Dawn's Left Hand*, Richardson wrote regularly about films—which were still silent—for the magazine *Close Up*.)

Images of light carry emotional and symbolic content throughout *Pilgrimage*. When Miriam visits Densley's medical office early in *Dawn's Left Hand*, the drawn shades are keeping out the light; she refuses his proposal—one last offer of conventional marriage—with a momentary wistfulness that is immediately replaced by a great sense of relief. She is increasingly aware of herself as an actor in the scenes of her life. Self-observation allows physical compositions to reveal power relationships: when Hypo Wilson comes into Miriam's room she notices that he stands over her like a doctor, and when he embarks on a program of seduction to the music of Richard Wagner, she disputes his control by rearranging the chairs. On another occasion, in a hotel room, Miriam looks in the mirror to observe herself and Wilson. Her own position blocks the light and thus the scene is chilled even before she begins to see him as a pathetic naked male.

During the final stages of the Wilson affair, Miriam is increasingly preoccupied by a beautiful young woman—soon to be a radical suffragist—who pursues her ardently and pays homage to her as a woman in ways that bring home to Miriam the impossibility of real communion with men. Yet the deep commitment demanded by Amabel is frightening; her intense adoration forces Miriam into a role that threatens her independence more crucially than Hypo Wilson's overt attempts at domination. The advantage of being with people who interact only on superficial levels, Miriam realizes, is that she can retain her freedom.

Although Richardson struggled to bring the events in *March Moonlight* up to 1912, the year that she began writing *Pilgrimage*, her form and subject virtually required the book to remain unconcluded. The narrative techniques of *March Moonlight* grow more deliberate; when Miriam begins to write, she thinks and sees differently and is aware of selecting and arranging details. Thus, the book's ending is only a middle: Miriam's sense of self would inevitably change as she reexamined and re-created her experiences in order to write novels. Once traditional formulas are rejected and *being* itself becomes the subject, there can be no ending; there is no epiphany, no coming of age, no final truth but rather a continuous process of self-making through self-awareness.

Sally Mitchell

Other major works
NONFICTION: *The Quakers Past and Present*, 1914; *Gleanings from the Works of George Fox*, 1914; *John Austen and the Inseparables*, 1930.

Bibliography
Fromm, Gloria G. *Dorothy Richardson: A Biography.* Champaign: University of Illinois Press, 1977. An objective biography, including previously inac-

cessible details, which could provide invaluable data to the literary analyst. Carefully draws distinctions between the events of Richardson's life and those of her fictional characters, but also identifies clear correlations between the two. Extensively researched and well written and supplemented by illustrations, chapter endnotes, a comprehensive bibliography, and an index.

Gregory, Horace. *Dorothy Richardson: An Adventure in Self-Discovery.* New York: Holt, Rinehart and Winston, 1967. Gregory equates Richardson with her character Miriam of *Pilgrimage* so completely that he refers to Richardson with unsettling frequency as "Dorothy-Miriam." Richardson is undoubtedly important to the development of the genre of fictional autobiography, but Gregory's limited notes and lack of bibliographic documentation detract from this critical text's credibility.

Labovitz, Esther Kleinbord. "Dorothy Richardson: *Pilgrimage*: Four Volumes." In *The Myth of the Heroine: The Female "Bildungsroman" in the Twentieth Century.* American University Series 19, 2d ed. Vol. 4. New York: Peter Lang Publishing, 1986. This sixty-page text is limited almost exclusively to a discussion of well-documented phases in personality development as exemplified by Miriam in *Pilgrimage*; nevertheless, its potential impact upon the study of fictional characters from early adolescence to adulthood makes it well worth reading. An extensive bibliography, as well as chapter endnotes and an index, increases its value.

Marcus, Jane, ed. "Political Aesthetics: Virginia Woolf and Dorothy Richardson." In *Virginia Woolf: A Feminist Slant.* Lincoln: University of Nebraska Press, 1983. This brief comparison of the two authors provides interesting parallels between Woolf and Richardson from a feminist point of view. Additionally, critical comments by Woolf regarding Richardson help to supplement an intriguing and provocative analysis. Notes and an index are included.

Rosenberg, John. *Dorothy Richardson, the Genius They Forgot: A Critical Biography.* New York: Alfred A. Knopf, 1973. The strength of Rosenberg's biography lies in his scholarly credibility, as he aptly parallels events in *Pilgrimage* to Richardson's life. His concluding analysis of Richardson's pioneering impact upon the development of the novel, however, lacks the impact of his earlier writing. Contains both an index and an ample bibliography.

SAMUEL RICHARDSON

Born: Derbyshire, England; July 31 (?), 1689
Died: London, England; July 4, 1761

Principal long fiction

Pamela: Or, Virtue Rewarded, 1740-1741; *Clarissa: Or, The History of a Young Lady*, 1747-1748; *Sir Charles Grandison*, 1753-1754.

Other literary forms

In addition to the three novels on which his fame and reputation rest, Samuel Richardson's best-known work is a collection of fictitious letters which constitutes a kind of eighteenth century book of etiquette, social behavior, manners, and mores: *Letters Written to and for Particular Friends, on the Most Important Occasions* (1741), customarily referred to as *Familiar Letters*. It had been preceded, in 1733, by a handbook of instruction concerning the relationship between apprentices and master printers, which grew out of a letter Richardson had written to a nephew in 1731, *The Apprentice's Vade Mecum: Or, Young Man's Pocket Companion* (1733). Throughout his life, Richardson, like so many of his contemporaries, was a prolific letter-writer; notable selections of his correspondence include six volumes edited by his contemporary and early biographer, Anna L. Barbauld, the first of which was published in 1804; and his correspondence with Johannes Stinstra, the Dutch translator of his novels to whom Richardson had sent a considerably important amount of autobiographical material. A good recent representative collection is *Selected Letters of Samuel Richardson* (1964, John Carroll, editor). Of only minor interest is Richardson's *A Collection of the Moral and Instructive Sentiments, Maxims, Cautions, and Reflexions, Contained in the Histories of Pamela, Clarissa, and Sir Charles Grandison*, published anonymously in 1755, a series of excerpts emphasizing his conviction that "instruction was a more important obligation to the novelist than entertainment."

Achievements

Perhaps Richardson's most important contribution to the development of the novel was his concern for the nonexceptional problems of daily conduct, the relationships between men and women, and the specific class-and-caste distinctions of mid-eighteenth century England. He sought and found his material from life as he had observed and reflected upon it from childhood and youth as a member of the working class in a highly socially conscious society to his position as an increasingly successful and prosperous printer and publisher. He contemplated this material with passionate interest and recorded it with a kind of genius for verisimilitude that sets him apart from most of his predecessors. What one critic has called Richardson's "almost rabid concern for the details" of daily life and his continuing "enrichment and complication" of customary human relationship, account in large measure for his enormous contemporary popularity: In *Pamela*, for example, the relationships beteween Pamela and Squire B. are so persistently grounded in the minutiae of ordinary life as to create a sense of reality seldom achieved in prose fiction prior to Richardson; at the same time, the outcome of the emotional and physical tugs-of-war between the two main characters and the happy outcome of all the intrigue, sensationalism, and hugger-mugger have about them the quality of conventional romantic love.

Richardson learned to *know* his characters, so intimately, so thoroughly, as to triumph over his prolixity, repetetiveness, moralizing, and sentimentality. Equally important was his development of the epistolary novel. Other writers had used letters as a storytelling device, but few if any of Richardson's predecessors had approximated his skill in recording the external events and incidents of a narrative along with the intimate and instant revelation of a character's thought and emotions in the process of their taking place, a method so flowing, so fluid, so flexible, as almost to anticipate the modern technique of stream of consciousness. Richardson's works, along with those of his three great contemporaries—Henry Fielding, Tobias Smollett, and Laurence Sterne—prepared the way for the great achievements of the nineteenth century English novel.

Biography

The exact date of Samuel Richardson's birth is uncertain, but he was born in Derbyshire, probably on July 31, 1689. His father was a joiner and, according to Richardson, a "good draughtsman" who "understood architecture" and whose ancestors had included several generations of small farmers in Surrey; of his mother, the second wife of Richardson *père*, little is known. The family returned to London, where Richardson may have attended the Merchant Taylor's School in 1701 and 1702, at which time his formal education ended. In 1706, he was apprenticed to the Stationers' Company, and in 1715, he became a "freeman" of the Company. He married his former employer's daughter, Martha Wilde, in November 23, 1721, set up his own business as a printer, was admitted to the Stationers' Company in 1722, and soon became what his major biographers—T. C. Duncan Eaves and Ben D. Kimpel—term a "prosperous and respected" tradesman. Six children, none of whom survived infancy or early childhood, preceded their mother's death in January, 1731. Two years later (February 3, 1733), Richardson remarried, this time to Elizabeth Leake, also the daughter of a printer; four of their six children survived.

Richardson's career as an editor continued to prosper—among other distinctions, he was eventually awarded the lucrative contract to print the journals of the House of Commons—and by the mid-1730's, he had moved into a large house in Salisbury Court, where the family would live for the next two decades and where he would write the three novels on which his reputation rests.

For some time, two of Richardson's "particular friends," both of them London booksellers, had been urging him to compile a "little book . . . of familiar letters on the useful concerns of common life." An almost compulsive letter-writer since early childhood—before he was eleven he had written to an elderly widow, reprimanding her for her "uncharitable conduct"—Richardson began the undertaking, one letter of which was an actual account he had heard some years before, the story of a virtuous servant who eventually married her master. The recollection of the incident stimulated his imagination, and so, at the age of fifty, he temporarily abandoned the letters-project. In two months, writing as much as three thousand words a day, he completed the novel that, on November 6, 1739, without the author's name on the title page, was to explode upon the English scene:

> *Pamela: Or, Virtue Rewarded. In a Series of Familiar Letters from a beautiful Young Damsel, to her Parents. Now first published in order to cultivate the Principles of Virtue and Religion in the Minds of the Youth of both Sexes. A Narrative which has its Foundation in Truth and Nature; and at the same time that it agreeably entertains, by a Variety of Curious and affecting Incidents, is entirely divested of all those Images, which, in too many Pieces calculated for Amusement only, tend to inflame the Minds they should instruct.*

Pamela as an instant success, going through five editions in less than a year (in the interim, Richardson completed *Familiar Letters*, which was published January 23, 1741) and inspiring numerous burlesques, imitations, and parodies, including *An Apology for the Life of Mrs. Shamela Andrews* (1741, probably the work of Henry Fielding and the only parody of interest today) and serving as the impetus for Fielding's *The History of the Adventures of Joseph Andrews* (1742). *Pamela* was also dramatized in several forms and translated into German, French, and Dutch; its success, for the worse rather than the better, led Richardson to write a sequel, centering around his heroine's life after her marriage.

Meanwhile, Richardson continued to combine the roles of successful and prosperous businessman and author. Exactly when he began the novel which was to be his masterpiece is uncertain—one of his biographers thinks he was considering it as early as 1741—but he had the concept of *Clarissa* "well in mind" before 1744, began the actual writing in the spring or summer of that year, and by November was ready to send parts of the manuscript to his old friend Aaron Hill. Unlike *Pamela*, *Clarissa* did not have its origins in "real life"; Clarissa and Miss Howe, Richardson insisted, were "entirely creatures of his fantasy." The novel, almost a million words in length, was three years in the writing, including two "thorough" revisions, and published in seven volumes between December 1, 1747, and December 7, 1748; a subsequent eight-volume edition, "with Letters & passages restored from the original manuscript," was published between 1749 and 1751.

Though *Clarissa* was somewhat less controversial than *Pamela*, its reception was tumultuous; among other things, the author was accused of indecency because of the dramatic fire scene, and Richardson took the charges seriously enough to write an eleven-page pamphlet defending it. Sarah Fielding wrote what has been called an "ambitious defense" of the novel, and her brother Henry, whose masterpiece *The History of Tom Jones* was published soon after the last volumes of *Clarissa* in 1749, lavishly praised Richardson's work, although Richardson's dislike of what he considered Fielding's improprieties, along with the opening sections of *Joseph Andrews* and Fielding's possible authorship of *Shamela*, made any friendship between the two impossible (indeed, their relationship—or, more accurately, the lack of it—reflects little credit on Richardson).

One of Richardson's closest friends, Lady Bradshaigh, had written him soon after publication of the fourth volume of *Clarissa*, entreating him not to let his heroine die, and subsequently urged him to write a "novel about a Good Man." How much this influenced Richardson, if at all, is purely conjectural, but early in 1750, he had begun what was to be his last novel. Despite his stated intention not to publish this "new work," the first six volumes of *Sir Charles Grandison* were published late in 1753 (November 13 and December 11), and the concluding volume on March 14, 1754. As had been the case with *Pamela* and *Clarissa*, Dutch, German, and French translations soon followed.

In his Preface to *Sir Charles Grandison*, Richardson, in his guise as the "editor" of the manuscript, announced that after this third novel he would write no more. He had, however, been in the process of compiling a series of selections from his novels which was published in March, 1755, as *A Collection of the Moral and Instructive Sentiments, Maxims, Cautions, and Reflexions, Contained in the Histories of Pamela, Clarissa, and Sir Charles Grandison*. He continued to be active as a printer and to make minor revisions in his novels, particularly *Pamela*, but his "dislike to the pen" continued. During his last years, he devoted more and more time to his correspondence—since the early 1740's, he had kept copies of all or most of his letters—apparently with the idea of eventual publication. On June 28, 1761, he suffered a stroke that resulted in his death a few days later on July 4, 1761.

Analysis

"Why, Sir, if you were to read Richardson for the story, your impatience would be so much fretted that you would hang yourself. But you must read him for the sentiment, and consider the story as only giving occasion to the sentiment." Samuel Johnson's comment is only partly relevant. As James E. Evans states in his Introduction to Samuel Richardson's series of excerpts, the revival of Richardson's reputation in recent decades grows out of the assertion that he "remains a great writer in spite of his morality" and must be read "'for the story' (psychological realism and conscious artistry), because we no longer read 'for the sentiment.'"

Richardson himself stated quite clearly, in his Prefaces to *Pamela* and *Clarissa*, and in his letters, that his purpose as an author was to depict "real life" and "in a manner probable, natural, and lively." At the same time, however, he wanted his books to be thought of as instruments of manners and morals intended to "teach great virtues." Fiction, he insisted, should be "useful & instructive"; it should edify readers of all ages, but particularly should be relevant and appealing to youth. Richardson observed with passionate interest and recorded with a genius for infinite detail the relationships between men and women; the concerns of daily life; and the particular class and caste distinctions of mid-eighteenth century England. This intense interest in the *usual* sets him apart from such predecessors as Daniel Defoe or the seventeenth century writers of prose romances. In all of his novels, and particularly, perhaps, in *Pamela*, the relationship between his main characters has about it the quality of traditional romantic love; at the same time, the novels are so realistically grounded in the accumulation of a mass of day-to-day realistic details as to create a remarkable sense of authenticity. Characteristic of this creation of the illusion of real life is the account, possibly apocryphal, of *Pamela*'s being read aloud by the local blacksmith to a small group of the village's inhabitants on the village green; finally, when Pamela's triumph by her marriage to Squire B. was assured, the villagers indulged in a spree of thanksgiving and merrymaking; it was *their* Pamela who had conquered.

Richardson, then, was both a conscious, self-avowed realist, and also an equally conscious, self-avowed teacher and moralist. This dualism permeates all three of his novels and is perhaps most apparent—and transparent—in *Pamela*. It is, indeed, Richardson's hallmark, and is the source both of his strength and weakness as a novelist.

Reduced to its simplest terms, the "story" or "plot" of the first volume of *Pamela* is too well known to warrant more than the briefest summary. The heroine, a young servant girl, is pursued by her master, Squire B., but maintains her virginity in spite of his repeated and ingenious efforts, until the would-be seducer, driven to desperation, marries her. Thus is Pamela's virtue rewarded. The continuation of the novel in Volume Two, a decided letdown, is virtually plotless, highly repetitive, and highlighted only by Squire B.'s excursion into infidelity. Volumes Three and Four, written partly because of Richardson's indignation with the various parodies of the first volume of *Pamela*, have even less to recommend them. Labeled as "virtually unreadable" by one modern commentator, even Richardson's most understanding critic-biographers, T. C. Duncan Eaves and Ben D. Kimpel, have dismissed them as "Richardson at his worst, pompous, proper, proud of himself, and above all dull."

Despite his frequent excursions into bathos and sentimentality, when he is not indulging in sermonizings on ethics and morality, the Richardson of the first volume of *Pamela* writes vigorously, effectively, and with keen insight and intimate understanding of his characters. *Pamela* contains many powerful scenes that linger long in the reader's memory: the intended rape scene, the sequence in which Pamela considers suicide, even parts of the marriage scene (preceded by some prodigious feats of letter-writing to her parents on the day prior to the wedding, from six o'clock in the morning, half an hour past eight o'clock, near three o'clock [ten pages], eight o'clock at night, until eleven o'clock the same night and following the marriage) are the work of a powerful writer with a keen sense for the dramatic.

In the final analysis, however, the novel succeeds or fails because of its characters, particularly and inevitably that of Pamela herself. From the opening letter in which she informs her parents that her mistress has died and Squire B., her mistress' son, has appeared on the scene, to the long sequence of her journal entries, until her final victory when her would-be seducer, worn out and defeated in all his attempts to have her without marriage, capitulates and makes the "thrice-happy" Pamela his wife, she dominates the novel.

In effect, and seemingly quite beyond Richardson's conscious intent, Pamela is two quite different characters. On the one hand, she is the attractive and convincing young girl who informs her parents that her recently deceased mistress had left her three pairs of shoes that fit her perfectly, adding that "my lady had a very little foot"; or having been transferred to Squire B.'s Lincolnshire estate, laments that she lacks "the courage to stay, neither can I think to go." On the other hand, she is at times a rather unconvincing puppet who thinks and talks in pious platitudes and values her "honesty" as a very valuable commodity, a character—in Joseph Wood Krutch's words—"so devoid of any delicacy of feeling as to be inevitably indecent."

Squire B. is less interesting than Pamela, and his efforts to seduce Pamela tend to become either boring or amusing. Her father, the Old Gaffer, who would disown his daughter "were she not honest," similarly frequently verges upon caricature, although one distinguished historian of the English novel finds him extremely convincing; and Lady Davers, Squire B.'s arrogant sister, tends to be more unbelievable than convincing, as do Pamela's captors, the odious Mrs. Jewkes and the equally repulsive Colbrand.

In spite of its shortcomings, *Pamela* cannot be dismissed, as one critic has commented, as "only a record of a peculiarly loathsome aspect of bourgeois morality." *Pamela* has great moments, scenes, and characters that pass the ultimate test of a work of fiction, that of *memorableness*: scenes that remain in the reader's consciousness long after many of the events have become blurred or dimmed. It is equally important historically: among other things, its popularity helped prepare the way for better novelists and better novels, including what Arnold Bennett was to call the "greatest realistic novel in the world," Richardson's *Clarissa*.

Unlike *Pamela*, *Clarissa* did not have its origins in "real life"; his characters, Richardson insisted, were "entirely creatures of his fantasy." He commenced the novel in the spring or summer of 1744; it was three years in the making, two of which were primarily devoted to revision (it has been said that when his old friend Aaron Hill misread *Clarissa*, Richardson devoted a year to revising the text for publication). Almost a million words in length—the longest novel in English—the plot of *Clarissa* is relatively simple. Clarissa Harlowe, daughter of well-to-do, middle-class parents with social aspirations, is urged by her family to marry a man, Solmes, whom she finds repulsive. At the same time, her sister Arabella is being courted by an aristocrat, Robert Lovelace. Lovelace, attracted and fascinated by Clarissa, abandons his luke-warm courtship of Arabella and, after wounding the girl's aroused brother in a duel, turns his attention to Clarissa, in spite of her family's objections. Clarissa lets herself be persuaded; she goes off with Lovelace, who imprisons her in a brothel, where he eventually drugs and rapes her; she finally escapes, refuses the contrite Lovelace's offers of marriage, and eventually dies. Lovelace, repentant and haunted by his evil act, is killed in a duel by Clarissa's cousin, Colonel Morden.

Counterpointing and contrasting with these two major characters are Anna Howe, Clarissa's closest friend and confidante, and John Belford, Lovelace's closest friend. Around these four are a number of contrasting minor characters, each of whom contributes to the minutely recorded series of events and climaxes, events which in their barest forms verge upon melodrama, and at times even farce. Even so, the novel in its totality is greater than the sum of its parts: it has about it the ultimate power of Greek tragedy, and Clarissa herself, like the major characters of Greek drama, rises above the occasionally melodramatic or improbable sequences to attain a stature not seen in English prose fiction before, and seldom surpassed since.

Much of the power and the drama of *Clarissa* grows out of the author's effective use of contrast—between Clarissa and Anna Howe; between Lovelace and Belford; and between the country life of the upper middle class and the dark, rank side of urban England. This and the richness and variety of incident redeem the sometimes improbable events and lapses into didacticism and give the novel a sense of reality larger than life itself.

In the final analysis, the great strength of the novel is the creation of its two main characters. Clarissa, with her pride and self-reliance, "so secure in her virtue," whose feelings of shame and self-hatred are such that she begs Lovelace "to send her to Bedlam or a private madhouse" (no less a master than Henry Fielding praised Clarissa's letter after the rape as "beyond anything I had ever read"), could have degenerated into bathos or caricature but instead attains a level of intensity and reality unique in the novel prior to 1740.

Though Clarissa dominates the novel, Richardson is almost as successful with Lovelace, despite the fact that in the early portions of the novel he seems for the most part like Squire B., just another Restoration rake. His transformation, following his violation of Clarissa, grows and deepens: "One day, I fancy," he reflects, "I shall hate myself on recollecting what I am about at this instant. But I must stay till then. We must all of us have something to repent of." Repent he does, after his terse letter announcing the consummation of the rape: "And now, Belford, I can go no further. The affair is over. Clarissa lives."

Belford, like the reader, is horror-stricken. By the rape, Lovelace has acted not as a man, but an animal, and his expiation is, in its own way, much more terrible than Clarissa's, who at times somewhat complacently contemplates her own innocence and eventual heavenly reward. Lovelace remains a haunted man ("sick of myself! sick of my remembrance of my vile act!") until his death in a duel with Colonel Morden, a death which is really a kind of suicide. The final scene of the novel, and Lovelace's last words, "Let this Expiate!," are among the most memorable of the entire novel, and Richardson's portrayal of a character soiled and tarnished, an eternally damaged soul, is unforgettable.

As early as February, 1741, an anonymous correspondent had asked Richardson to write the "history of a Man, whose Life would be the path that we should follow." By the end of the decade, with *Pamela* and *Clarissa* behind him, and influenced by old friends, including Lady Bradshaigh, Richardson began thinking seriously about such a novel. Despite increasing ill health and the continuing demands of his business, he was soon immersed in the project, a novel designed to "present" the character of a "Good Man," and to show the influence such a character exerted "on society in general and his intimates in particular." Although he had at one time decided not to publish the novel during his lifetime, the first volumes of *Sir Charles Grandison* came out in 1753. Even before the seventh and last volume was in print the following year, some critics were stating their dissatisfaction with Sir Charles's "Unbelievable Perfection," a criticism Richardson repudiated in a concluding note to the last volume: "The Editor (that is, Richardson himself) thinks human nature has often, of late, been shown in a light too degrading; and he hopes from this series of letters it will be seen that characters may be good without being unnatural."

Subsequent critical opinion of the novel has varied widely, a few critics considering it Richardson's masterpiece, while many regard it as his least successful novel. *Sir Charles Grandison* differs dramatically from its predecessors in its concern with the English upper class and aristocracy, a world which Richardson freely acknowledged he had never known or understood: "How shall a man obscurely situated . . . pretend to describe and enter into characters in upper life?" In setting, too, the novel was a new departure, ranging as it does from England to Italy and including a large number of Italians, highlighted by Clementina, certainly the most memorable character in the novel. The conflict in Clementina's heart and soul, her subsequent refusal to marry Sir Charles because he is a Protestant, and her ensuing madness are as effective as anything Richardson ever wrote, and far more convincing than Sir Charles's rescue of Harriett Byron following her abduction by Sir Hargrove Pollexfen and their eventual marriage. Harriett, though not as interesting a character as either Pamela or Clarissa, shares with them one basic habit: she is an indefatigable letter-writer, perhaps the most prolific in the history of English prose fiction, at times sleeping only two hours a night and, when not admiring Grandison from afar, writing letters to him (not uncharacteristic of her style is her appeal to the clergyman who is supposed to marry her to Sir Hargrove: "Worthy man . . . save a poor creature. I would not hurt a worm! I love everybody! Save me from violence!").

Sir Charles himself is similarly less interesting than either Squire B. or Lovelace, and it is difficult today for even the most sympathetic reader to find a great deal to admire in the man who is against masquerades, dresses neatly but not gaudily, is time and time again described as a "prince of the Almighty's creation," an "angel of a man," and "one of the finest dancers in England." Most of the other characters, including the Italians (with the notable exception of Clementina), are similarly either unconvincing or uninteresting, except for two small masterpieces of characterization: Aunt Nell, Grandison's maiden aunt; and Lord G., Charlotte Grandison's husband, a gentle and quiet man, in love with his temperamental wife, often hurt and bewildered by her sharp tongue and brusque actions.

Horace Walpole is said to have written off *Sir Charles Grandison* as a "romance as it would be spiritualized by a Methodist preacher"; and Lord Chesterfield also dismissed it, adding that whenever Richardson "goes, *ultra crepidem*, into high life, he grossly escapes the modes." On the other hand, Jane Austen specifically "singled . . . [it] out for special praise," and Richardson's major biographers believe that in *Sir Charles Grandison*, his "surface realism and his analysis of social situations are at their height."

Whatever his weaknesses, Richardson was one of the seminal influences in the development of the novel. His impact upon his contemporaries and their immediate successors was profound, not only in England but on the Continent as well, and eventually on the beginnings of the novel in the United States. He popularized the novel of manners as a major genre for several decades, and his use of the epistolary method added another dimension to the art of narrative. Though his novels have frequently suffered in comparison with those of his major contemporary, Henry Fielding, in recent years a renewed interest and appraisal of Richardson and his work have placed him securely in the ranks of the major English novelists.

William Peden

Other major works

NONFICTION: *The Apprentice's Vade Mecum: Or, Young Man's Pocket Companion*, 1733; *Letters Written to and for Particular Friends, on the Most Important Occasions*, 1741; *A Collection of the Moral and Instructive Sentiments, Maxims, Cautions, and Reflexions, Contained in the Histories of Pamela, Clarissa, and Sir Charles Grandison*, 1755; *The Correspondence of Samuel Richardson*, 1804 (Anna Barbauld, editor).

Bibliography

Brophy, Elizabeth Bergen. *Samuel Richardson: The Triumph of Craft*. Knoxville: University of Tennessee Press, 1974. Rejecting the notion that Richardson's unconscious produced great novels in spite of the author—a view held by even his most recent biographers—Brophy examines Richardson's statements about fiction in his letters and his prefaces and postscripts to his novels. Having determined his theories about fiction, Brophy then compares these ideas with Richardson's practice. Two short appendices discuss the novelist's "nervous complaint" and conclude that he probably suffered from Parkinson's disease.

Carroll, John, ed. *Samuel Richardson: A Collection of Critical Essays.* Englewood Cliffs, N.J.: Prentice-Hall, 1969. Includes a dozen essays by leading scholars of Richardson and his age. Among these are Alan Dugald McKillop's discussion of Richardson's epistolary technique, A. M. Kearney and William J. Farrell on the various voices in *Pamela* and *Clarissa*, and Morris Golden on the relationship between Richardson's psyche and his characters.

Doody, Margaret Anne. *A Natural Passion: A Study of the Novels of Samuel Richardson*. Oxford, England: Clarendon Press, 1974. Seeks the antecedents of Richardson's fiction in seventeenth and eighteenth century drama, romance, religious writing, thought, and art. Doody shows how Richardson transformed these materials into fiction probing "man's relation to himself and his fate."

Downs, Brian W. *Richardson*. New York: E. P. Dutton, 1928. After a fifty-eight-page discussion of Richardson's life, Downs turns to his novels, which he praises for their psychological insight. Sets Richardson in his time but shows little sympathy towards his Puritan, middle-class values.

Eagleton, Terry. *The Rape of Clarissa: Writing, Sexuality, and Class Struggle in Samuel Richardson*. Minneapolis: University of Minnesota Press, 1982. A short but provocative Marxist reading of Richardson's greatest novel as myth, suggesting that it is far more subversive than its author intended.

Eaves, T. C. Duncan, and Ben D. Kimpel. *Samuel Richardson: A Biography*. Oxford, England: Clarendon Press, 1971. The definitive biography, based on fifteen years of research. Devotes three chapters to each of the novels and concludes with four excellent chapters on Richardson's personality, thoughts, reading, and achievements.

Golden, Morris. *Richardson's Characters*. Ann Arbor: University of Michigan Press, 1963. A psychological study of Richardson that sees in his characters aspects of himself. Suggests that while ostensibly Richardson supported morality, at least unconsciously he favored passion.

Kinkead-Weakes, Mark. *Samuel Richardson: Dramatic Novelist*. Ithaca, N.Y.: Cornell University Press, 1973. Seeking to understand Richardson's achievement and his appeal to nineteenth century writers such as Jane Austen and George Eliot, this study demonstrates Richardson's dramatic use of immediacy and explores the implications of his "writing to the moment."

McKillop, Alan Dugald. *Samuel Richardson, Printer and Novelist*. Chapel Hill: University of North Carolina Press, 1936. Long the standard biography, this study remains a good treatment of Richardson's life, which McKillop discusses in a lengthy appendix. The text itself focuses "on the origins, publication, and reception of" the three novels.

Watt, Ian. *The Rise of the Novel: Studies in Defoe, Richardson, and Fielding*. Berkeley: University of California Press, 1957. Contains excellent chapters on *Pamela* and *Clarissa*, praising the psychological depth of the characters. Analyzes Richardson's contribution to the development of English prose fiction and relates the novels to the social situation of their day.

Wolff, Cynthia Griffin. *Samuel Richardson and the Eighteenth-Century Puritan Character*. Hamden, Conn.: Archon Books, 1972. Examines Richardson's novels, especially *Clarissa*, as psychological and social studies, relating them to twentieth century psychology and eighteenth century Puritanism.

MORDECAI RICHLER

Born: Montreal, Canada; January 27, 1931

Principal long fiction

The Acrobats, 1954; *Son of a Smaller Hero*, 1955; *A Choice of Enemies*, 1957; *The Apprenticeship of Duddy Kravitz*, 1959; *The Incomparable Atuk*, 1963 (also known as *Stick Your Neck Out*); *Cocksure: A Novel*, 1968; *St. Urbain's Horseman*, 1971; *Joshua Then and Now*, 1980; *Solomon Gursky Was Here*, 1989.

Other literary forms

As a professional writer, spurning academic life for wider creative possibilities, Mordecai Richler has produced short stories, essays, articles, film scripts, television plays, and children's literature. Much of his work first appeared in prestigious magazines such as *The Atlantic*, *The New Yorker*, the *New Statesman*, and *Encounter*. Some of his individual stories, which often end up as chapters in his novels, have been collected in *The Street: Stories* (1969). A children's book, *Jacob Two-Two Meets the Hooded Fang* (1975), and two novels, *Joshua Then and Now* and *The Apprenticeship of Duddy Kravitz*, have been made into motion pictures, the latter winning the Golden Bear Award at the Berlin Film Festival in 1974. Richler's screenplay for this film was also nominated for an Academy Award and won a Screenwriter's Guild of America Award.

Achievements

Forsaking Canada for the more exciting atmosphere of Paris, Richler struggled with his work and lived in poor circumstances, publishing very few stories. Here, however, he met some significant figures of the new literary set who reacted favorably to his work; among them were Allen Ginsberg, Herbert Gold, and Terry Southern. After returning to Canada for a short while, Richler finished his first novel, *The Acrobats*. As is so often the case with Canadian writers, Richler preferred to publish outside his own country, where he felt more appreciated. His first effort was accepted by André Deutsch in London. In recent years, with his reputation secure, he has decided to publish with the Canadian house, McClelland and Stewart.

In order to make a living exclusively as a writer, Richler left Canada again. Still using his Canadian experience as the substance of his work, Richler was very productive in England, publishing stories and novels that met with much acclaim. Even his film scripts for *No Love for Johnnie* (1961), *Young and Willing* (1964), and *Life at the Top* (1965), which Richler considers inferior work for an often superficial medium, were positively reviewed. Richler twice has won Canada's foremost literary prize, the Governor General's Award, for *Cocksure* and *St. Urbain's Horseman*. Although he has achieved a certain notoriety for his searing portraits of Canadian life, he has finally gained acceptance as one of Canada's most distinguished novelists.

Biography

Mordecai Richler was born in Montreal, Canada, in 1931, in the heart of the Jewish ghetto. His father was a junk dealer and his mother was a housewife who has recently written a book about her life. Her father was a rabbi whose influence ensured an orthodox household. By turning away from orthodoxy at a young age, however, Richler ran into trouble at home, which perhaps accounts for some of his perceptive but acerbic reflections on family life. To further compound his problems as a youth, his parents were divorced when he was thirteen. As a response to the breakdown at home, Richler joined a Zionist labor group called Habonim and dreamed of settling in Palestine. Only later did he go to Israel as a journalist.

In his adolescent years, Richler attended Baron Byng High School, a predominantly Jewish school even though it was part of the Protestant school system. In his stories and novels it is transformed into Fletcher's Field High, and Richler peoples it with characters known to him as a schoolboy. After high school, Richler attended Sir George Williams University in Montreal (now Concordia University), since his grades were not good enough for McGill University. Although he returned to Sir George as writer-in-residence, the academic life did not appeal to him. He once remarked that "academe, like girls, whiskey, and literature, promised better than it paid." Rejecting a life of scholarship, Richler decided on the uncertain life of a free-lance writer in Europe, where he could develop his own style and not merely put a stamp of approval on someone else's.

After living in Paris for two years, where he published his first story in a magazine called *Points* and got his first taste of expatriate life, Richler returned to Montreal. There he joined the Canadian Broadcasting Company for a short time, earning enough money to complete his first novel, *The Acrobats*. The novel aroused more attention in England than in Canada, which perhaps convinced him that the richer literary heritage there would fuel his talents. For the best part of twenty years, then, Richler lived in England, producing many novels, short stories, and film scripts.

Although Richler needed this geographical and cultural change to gain an ironic and critical distance in his work, he used his Canadian experience as the basis of his fiction; he has said that the first twenty years of a writer's life determine the character of his writing and inform his imaginative vision. Even after many years in England, Richler never felt sufficiently integrated into English society to capture the essence of that particular culture. Feeling himself an outsider in England and cut off from the social context of Canada,

Richler returned to Montreal in 1972, where he continues to live with his wife and five children.

Analysis

In an article, "Why I Write," Mordecai Richler repeats the honest answer given by George Orwell to the same question: sheer egotism, aesthetic enthusiasm, political purposes, and historical impulse. These reasons, modified by Richler's unique perception, are clues to the form and content of his work.

Richler's egotistical desire to be talked about has, no doubt, been fulfilled, as he is the victim of attacks from both Jews and Protestants for what they consider to be unjust satirical portraits of their respective communities. He has even said that to be a Jew and a Canadian is to emerge from the ghetto twice, as a sense of self-consciousness and envy pervades both societies. His satire, however, even when confined by the geography of Montreal, is more universal than some critics have assumed, and this element has enhanced his status as a significant writer. Although Richler has never wanted to acquire the role of writer as personality (he avoids the talk-show circuit as much as possible and loathes being cast as the kind of figure Norman Mailer has become), his fierce attacks on provincialism, pretension, community arrogance, envy, and class economic superiority have marked him as a highly visible, eccentric, and often vicious outsider.

While there is a great deal of harshness in Richler's writing, it is not merely personal vindictiveness, but a narrative strategy of accurate observation informed by imagination; it is a grotesque comic style designed to emphasize the absurdity of the human condition and to mock those whose misdirected values merely cause suffering. In *The Acrobats*, Richler dissects a generation of hollow men who infest the corrupt world of Spain's festival time, in which a loss of belief is symbolized by *fallas*, empty wood and papier-mâché dolls. It is a nightmare world of confusion and fantasy which culminates in the death of antihero André Bennett. Without capturing the flavor and intensity of Hemingway's lost generation, Richler, in a limited way, sets the themes for his later novels by attacking all attitudes which he thinks are essentially destructive.

Richler has admitted to a certain sense of guilt prompted by the discrepancy between his life at home facing a blank page and the memory of his father going to work in his junkyard in subzero weather. Perhaps this recognition of the severity of ordinary life has given him the focus of his work, the precisely observed but critically and ironically rendered life of the common man fighting circumstances greater than himself.

Richler's intelligence, however, does not allow him to glorify uncritically his protagonists. The tension between what is and what ought to be is always present; the result is a controlled realism balanced by a satirical distance which allows fantasy, nightmare, and a morally grounded sense of the ridiculous. As George Woodcock has observed, Richler was influenced by the realism of André Malraux, Albert Camus, and Louis-Ferdinand Céline, but Richler himself has praised Evelyn Waugh as the greatest novelist of his time, and there is in his work much of the energy, sensibility, and bawdiness of American writers such as Philip Roth.

When Richler speaks of a political purpose, he follows Orwell's idea that a novelist should push the world in a certain direction, that in fact any serious novelist is therefore a moralist. Although many of his stories end tragically, there is still a sense that his characters exist not as victims of a cruel, impersonal fate, but as victims of their own and others' actions. The choices they make are important ones and often lead to disaster when they are not based on a consistent moral viewpoint. Norman Price in *A Choice of Enemies* recognizes that choices are significant, but no longer has the courage to make the difficult ones that confront his modern generation. He ends up complacently accepting values from his friends. In *The Apprenticeship of Duddy Kravitz*, Richler succeeds in making Duddy a partially sympathetic character, often a victim of powerful people even more ruthless than he is, but Duddy, blinded by ambition, is the indirect cause of his friend Virgil's paralysis from a motor accident. In his enthusiasm for the direct, specific attack, however, Richler's moral position often seems diffuse of simply confusing. Two of his novels, *St. Urbain's Horseman* and *Joshua Then and Now*, manifest a more coherent intention which makes the satire even more meaningful.

Much of the force of Richler's work comes from his observation and memory of life in the Montreal ghetto of his youth. Even novels such as *Cocksure* and *The Acrobats* are distilled through the experience of the expatriate Canadian trying to make sense of a less provincial foreign world. Richler has said that he feels rooted in Montreal's St. Urbain Street, and because that was his time and place, he has elected to get it right. To this end, Richler often writes about the same characters from Fletcher's Field High School as they experience life at different stages of intellectual and emotional growth. A peripheral character such as Jake Hersh, for example, in *The Apprenticeship of Duddy Kravitz* and *The Street*, will become the focus of *St. Urbain's Horseman*.

There is so much comic energy in *The Apprenticeship of Duddy Kravitz* that the reader can easily underestimate the social and moral implications of the work. Richler has stated that to a certain extent the reader should sympathize with Duddy, who must rise above the poverty of the St. Urbain ghetto to challenge and defeat powerful manipulators such as Jerry Dingleman, the Boy Wonder. The ambiguity of Duddy's character creates a problem of moral focus, however, in that some of his victories are at the expense of truly kindhearted people, such as Virgil Roseboro and Yvette.

There are certainly many reasons for Duddy's aggressive, almost amoral behavior. His mother died when Duddy was very young, leaving him without the female stability he needed at the time. His father, Max the Hack, who drives a Montreal cab and pimps on the side, lets Duddy fend for himself, as most of his affection and attention went to the older son, Lenny. Duddy remembers that his father wrote many letters to Lenny when he worked at a resort, but Max refuses to write to Duddy. Max also encourages Lenny to go to medical school and is proud of his achievements; he makes it obvious that he expects little from Duddy and does not perceive the extent of Duddy's ambition nor his loyalty to his family. Duddy is also often humiliated by the affluent university students with whom he works as a waiter at the Hotel Lac des Sables. Irwin Shubert, for instance, considers Duddy a social inferior and, using a rigged roulette wheel, cheats him out of three hundred dollars.

Although eliciting sympathy by explaining Duddy's situation, Richler undercuts a completely sympathetic attitude toward Duddy by detailing the results of his actions. His exploitation of the other students of Fletcher's Field High School leads even his friend Jake Hersh to believe that he makes everything dirty. Duddy's schemes to make money are clever enough; he works out a system to steal hockey sticks from the Montreal Canadians, but he does not realize that the blame rests on the stick boy, who is trying to earn money through honest, hard work. More seriously, Duddy, through a cruel practical joke, is responsible for the death of Mrs. Macpherson, the wife of one of his teachers. Later, as he tries to make his dream of owning land come true, Duddy rejects his lover Yvette, causes the paralysis of his friend, Virgil, from whom he also steals money, and alienates his grandfather, Simcha, who cares for him more than anyone else.

Duddy's relationship with Simcha provides both the moral tone and the narrative drive of the novel. Simcha, a man trusted but not loved by the elders of the St. Urbain ghetto for his quiet, patient integrity, is loved by his favorite, Duddy. Like many others of his generation, Simcha feels the weight of the immigrant's fear of failure and instills Duddy with the idea that a man without land is a nobody. For Simcha, this cliché is a more complex concept associated with the traditional struggles of the Jews and presupposes a sense of responsibility. Duddy misinterprets the implications of his grandfather's advice and perceives it as being a practical imperative to be gained at any cost, involving himself in many schemes—from importing illegal pinball machines to filming bar mitzvahs with a bizarre, alcoholic documentary director—in order to purchase land for commercial development.

For a short time, Duddy's plans misfire; he goes bankrupt and is unable to pay for the land he wants so badly. Upon hearing that the Boy Wonder, the ghetto "miracle" who has escaped his environment by drug peddling and other corrupt means, covets the same land, Duddy forges checks in Virgil's name to get enough money to make the purchase. In a closing scene, Duddy brings his family to see his property. By coincidence, the Boy Wonder arrives, and Duddy drives him away with verbal abuse. His father is more impressed with this act of defiance than with Duddy's achievement, and later, among his circle of friends, Max begins to create a legend about Duddy in much the same way as he created the legend of the Boy Wonder. Although his victory has been effected by deceit and victimization, Duddy's behavior seems vindicated; he smiles in triumph, unaware that he continues only under the spell of a shared illusion. The reader is left elated to a certain extent at the defeat of the Boy Wonder, yet sobered by the figure of Simcha, crying in the car, after having been informed by Yvette of Duddy's method of acquiring the land.

Unlike Duddy Kravitz, whose life is defined by the wealth he acquires, Jake Hersh of *St. Urbain's Horseman* is defined by the exploits of his cousin, Joey, the "Horseman" of the title. In his quest for certainty and identity in a world of confusion and moral ambiguity, Jake chooses a dubious model of behavior which eventually becomes an obsession. Much of the comedy and much of the human drama in the book come from the discrepancy between Jake's illusions of the Horseman and the reality of his own life.

Richler experiments with a cinematic style of flashbacks and flash-forwards, not only to create a sense of suspense, but also to show the role memory plays in developing a character. It is obvious that Jake is involved in some sort of sex scandal which threatens his married and professional life. As the trial progresses, the narrative is punctuated by the events in Jake's life which have led him to this degradation. In his youth, he wanted to escape the St. Urbain ghetto and the provincial nature of Canada itself. Typically, however, he leaves Canada to escape boredom only to find it everywhere.

Although Jake's loving relationship with his wife offers the promise of real stability, Jake seems to believe that only his cousin Joey leads a meaningful life, fighting injustice wherever he can find it. Specifically, he thinks Joey is the lone avenger riding after Joseph Mengele, the feared *Doktor* of the Nazi extermination camps. At first, Joey is simply the black sheep of the Hersh family, leaving home at a young age and returning periodically to disrupt the mundane lives of his relatives. Jake, who is eleven years younger than Joey, perceives him to be a hero and dismisses the accusations that he is just a criminal taking advantage of others for his own gain. Uncle Abe even tells Jake that the famed Horseman is more likely to blackmail Mengele than kill him.

By adulthood, Jake's fantasies and nightmares about his cousin assume mythic proportions, and he incorporates this mythology into his daily concerns, measuring himself against the Horseman he has created. Jake's consequent search for Joey in Israel and Germany uncovers the grim reality of Joey's fraud, drug smuggling, and disastrous love affairs, but Jake only rationalizes his negative impression; he places the Horseman's quest for "justice" beyond the sphere of ordinary moral culpability or human responsibility.

Jake reasons that he is a product of his generation, conceived in the Depression. He and others like him lived through the Spanish Civil War, World War II, the Holocaust, Hiroshima, the Israeli War of Independence, McCarthyism, the Korean War, and finally the Vietnam War. They were always the wrong age to be involved; they were merely observers, moral bystanders who could protest and give advice, but who were fundamentally impotent. Jake wants answers to his plight, but feels even more alienated from the important issues of his time because he is a case history of the Jewish intellectual born into the Canadian working class. He finds his generation and its concerns trivial and peripheral, easily susceptible, in his thinking, to the guilt induced by the "injustice collectors"—the prison-camp survivors and the starvelings of Africa.

These issues, these betrayals of age, are contrasted with the more personal betrayals of life: Jake's father rejects his marriage to a non-Jew; Luke Scott decides to choose a British director instead of Jake, his best friend, for his first major script; Jenny dismisses Jake as a lover because he is too young; and Harry Stein implicates Jake in the rape of a young au pair girl. Jake is no more capable of understanding these events than the historical events of more significant import.

After the trial, in which Jake is found guilty of indecent assault and fined, he receives word that the Horseman has been killed in a plane crash while smuggling cigarettes. He retreats to his attic and finds a gun hidden in the Horseman's saddle. It fires only blanks, its efficacy as illusory as the Horseman's exploits. Upon discovering this, Jake seems to have returned to reality, but later in his nightmare, he dreams that he is the Horseman extracting gold fillings from Mengele's teeth with pliers. He wakes up and changes the Horseman's journal to read "presumed dead." The irony is that Jake will probably continue to search for certitude and will live a tolerable life based on illusion; he does not realize that the love of his wife is the stable point which will exist despite the illusion.

There are many similarities between *St. Urbain's Horseman* and *Joshua Then and Now*: the time-schemes are not linear but shift backward and forward in a search for meaning which takes precedence over simple historical considerations; the characters are again graduates of Fletcher's Field High School who gain obvious material success, but who are not immune to even the minor ravages of time; the major issues of the world are always present, but private and personal issues dominate; and Joshua Shapiro, like Jake Hersh, tries to make sense of his own life in terms of facing the past. The important difference between the two novels is that Richler's attitude toward life in *Joshua Then and Now* is much more humane, and love is seen as the moral imperative that makes all other attitudes seem trivial.

Joshua Then and Now begins close to the present with Joshua in a cottage retreat suffering from multiple fractures incurred in a car accident. Because of hints of a sex scandal, he is guarded from the press by his father Reuben and father-in-law, Senator Stephen Hornby. Joshua reads many letters from his fans and colleagues who have scorned him for what they think is his atrocious behavior, but he is able to put this criticism into perspective. He believes this public display of disapproval is what he deserves for the roguish behavior of his youth. Reflecting on his life, he now is able to see clearly what was of real importance.

Joshua's background seems almost surreal; certainly it is more colorful than the lives of his friends in St. Urbain. Joshua's aspiration to be a sportswriter derived from his father, Reuben, who was a Canadian boxing champion. After his retirement from the ring, Reuben became an enforcer for a gangster named Colucci. As a youngster, Joshua had to suffer both his father's long absences and the resentment of the neighborhood over Reuben's involvement with Colucci. Joshua's mother, Esther, is an eccentric who bewilders him even more than his father. At Joshua's bar mitzvah, Esther has too much to drink and decides to let the young boys see her perform as an exotic dancer. She shocks them with the explicitness of her movements and even lets them fondle her. Later in life, she gets involved in pornographic movies and in running a massage parlor. It seems that Joshua's independent and sometimes improbable behavior is the logical result of his upbringing.

In trying to prolong his adolescence, Joshua becomes as ridiculous as his parents, and although his exploits seem harmless, they do have consequences; Joshua's fake letters about the novelist Iris Murdoch's homosexual activities, written to make money at the expense of the University of Texas, end up being made public, to Joshua's disgrace. The pranks that he plays to gain revenge on his enemies—taking labels off Pinsky's valuable wine bottles, defacing Jonathan Coles's original painting, and planting illegal currency at Eli Seligson's house—conclude with Joshua's injuring himself in a high-speed car chase. For Joshua, at least, these episodes are a learning experience; they are stages on his way to maturity.

Joshua has many friends from his youth who still get together as the "Mackenzie King Memorial Society," the name being an ironic comment on a prime minister whom they consider a fraud. As successful as they are, however, in their middle age they are susceptible to law suits, tax-evasion inquiries, bypass operations, hair transplants, and cancer. The struggle for material wealth and its attainment now seem inadequate as values. More important is Joshua's involvment with the WASP, country-club circle. After marrying Pauline, Joshua is introduced to Jane and Jack Trimble and Pauline's brother Kevin. Joshua marries above his social class, but he takes a resentful and superior attitude to his wife's friends and relatives. He does as much as he can to sabotage a group that he believes has all the advantages. Through the years, however, he sees the disintegration of the Trimble marriage, the dashed hopes of the senator, and the death of Pauline's dependent brother, which precipitates her madness, and realizes that, even with their pretensions, they were only trying to survive.

The echoes of the past are most vividly sounded when Joshua returns to Ibiza, Spain, to confront Mueller, a German, who had disgraced him more than twenty-five years before. To gain revenge on Mueller, Joshua leaves his wife at a crucial time in her life, when she needs his comfort to fight off impending madness. In Spain, he notices remarkable changes: the friends he had are gone; many of his former haunts have been destroyed; the road to Almeria, the route of the retreating Republican army, is now dotted with hotels, condominiums, and commercial signs; and more significantly, Mueller is dead, a victim of cancer. To cleanse himself of the past, however, Joshua pays a price. His wife is institutionalized; then, after a prolonged stay at the hospital she disappears. The novel ends with a loving reconciliation which suggests a change in Richler's perspective. Still on crutches as a result of his accident, Joshua recuperates at Hornby's cottage, accompanied by his children, the senator, and Reuben. In the final scene, Pauline returns, and Reuben sees Joshua in the vegetable garden without his cane, being supported by Pauline.

In *Solomon Gursky Was Here*, Richler has created his richest and most complex work, a one-hundred-fifty-year chronicle of the ambitious and conniving Gursky family (loosely based on the real-life liquor kings of Montreal, the Bronfmans), weaving back and forth in time from the ill-fated Franklin Expedition in the Arctic to the political uncertainties of modern times. Beneath the surface of what is essentially a mystery story, a search for the elusive but seemingly ubiquitous Solomon Gursky, Richler examines the greed and corruption of society, the nature of the Jewish and Canadian people, mythological forces of the past, and the tenuous but compelling hold of love. Although uncompromising in his satirical portrait of the characters, Richter nevertheless alludes to the positive creative power of those who strive for understanding, however difficult the quest may be.

At the center of the novel stands writer Moses Berger, son of failed poet L. B. Berger, who has sold out to the Gurskys. Because of his father, Moses hears of Solomon Gursky at an early age and becomes obsessed with the almost mythical nature of this character. The alcoholic Moses, more a follower than the leader that his name suggests, investigates stories and documents and uncovers clues about why Solomon decided to resist the purely materialistic interests of his brothers Bernard, the ruthless businessman who has built his fortune by bootlegging, and Morrie, his unctious partner. Moses discovers that Solomon's enigmatic grandfather, Ephraim, was a criminal once imprisoned on Botany Bay, by incredible ingenuity the only survivor of the Franklin Expedition, a shaman of Eskimos who taught them Yiddish, and an energetic profligate perplexing in his moral ambiguity. Ephraim is, however, both a comic manifestation and a serious vital force of Judaism, instilling imagination and realism in Solomon, his spiritual heir.

Moses' search for the "real" Solomon, then, is an attempt to reclaim his past as a Jew and participate in the redemptive value of this figure, who takes on the mythic qualities of the raven that insinuates itself into a diversity of situations to provoke the apathetic and the misguided. Although Moses cannot quite verify all the incarnations of the mysterious Solomon, he suspects that Solomon has influenced many of the nobler acts that occur: the attempt to take over Bernard's McTavish distillery, the creation of the Israeli Air Force, and the success of the raid on Entebbe. By trying to restore order in his own life, through research and the dogged pursuit of the truth concerning Solomon, Moses begins to understand that honest engagement, not exploitation of life, is a source of value and meaning. No one is spared in Richler's caustic view, but some can glimpse hope, however concealed it may be.

Richler has been praised widely for the richness of his comic vision and for his keenly observed, unsentimental portrait of the inhabitants of the Montreal ghetto. Through an imaginative extension of this vision, Richler has developed into a novelist of importance: his message has transcended the limited boundaries of St. Urbain Street to assume universal significance.

James C. MacDonald

Other major works

SHORT FICTION: *The Street: Stories*, 1969.

NONFICTION: *Hunting Tigers Under Glass: Essays and Reports*, 1968; *Canadian Writing Today*, 1970 (edited); *Shovelling Trouble*, 1972; *Notes on an Endangered Species and Others*, 1974; *The Great Comic Book Heroes and Other Essays*, 1978; *Home Sweet Home*, 1984.

CHILDREN'S LITERATURE: *Jacob Two-Two Meets the Hooded Fang*, 1975; *Jacob Two-Two and the Dinosaur*, 1987.

Bibliography

Darling, Michael, ed. *Perspectives on Mordecai Richler*. Toronto: ECW Press, 1986. A volume of essays devoted to reevaluating Richler's work using poststructuralist theory, close readings of individual texts, and innovative examinations of grammatical structure and symbolic patterns.

Dooley, D. J. *Moral Vision in the Canadian Novel*. Toronto: Clarke, Irwin, 1979. Discusses the artistic problem of Richler's attitude toward the character of Duddy Kravitz.

McSweeney, Kerry. *Mordecai Richler and His Works*. Toronto: ECW Press, 1985. McSweeney argues that, with his increasing technical ability, Richler abandons a more passionate and darker vision of humanity.

Ramraj, Victor J. *Mordecai Richler*. Boston: Twayne, 1983. A comprehensive look at Richler's life and work, but short on detailed analysis.

Sheps, G. David, ed. *Mordecai Richler*. Toronto: McGraw-Hill Ryerson, 1971.

A solid but standard collection of articles on Richler's work preceding his major achievements.

Woodcock, George. *Mordecai Richler.* Toronto: McClelland and Stewart, 1970. Presents a critical viewpoint emphasizing Richler's intellectual rather than intuitive approach to fiction. Also contains a brief biographical section.

CONRAD RICHTER

Born: Pine Grove, Pennsylvania; October 13, 1890
Died: Pine Grove, Pennsylvania; October 30, 1968

Principal long fiction

The Sea of Grass, 1937; *The Trees*, 1940; *Tacey Cromwell*, 1942; *The Free Man*, 1943; *The Fields*, 1946; *Always Young and Fair*, 1947; *The Town*, 1950; *The Light in the Forest*, 1953; *The Lady*, 1957; *The Waters of Kronos*, 1960; *A Simple Honorable Man*, 1962; *The Grandfathers*, 1964; *The Awakening Land*, 1966 (includes *The Trees, The Fields, The Town*); *A Country of Strangers*, 1966; *The Aristocrat*, 1968.

Other literary forms

Conrad Richter wrote fourteen novels, all of which were published by Knopf, but in addition to the longer fiction which Richter produced between 1937 and 1968, he also wrote short stories and a variety of nonfiction. He was nearly as prolific a short-story writer as he was a novelist, his earliest published story appearing in 1913. His first volume of collected short stories includes twelve stories under the title *Brothers of No Kin and Other Stories* (1924); nine more stories were collected in a volume entitled *Early Americana and Other Stories* (1936). Richter wrote short fiction throughout his career, producing more than thirty-one stories, most of which appeared in the *Saturday Evening Post*. Many of Richter's stories still remain uncollected, but a number were gathered in a collection entitled *The Rawhide Knot and Other Stories* (1978). Richter's nonfiction includes three book-length essays on his eclectic personal philosophy: *Human Vibrations* (1926); *Principles in Bio-Physics* (1927); and *The Mountain on the Desert* (1955). Six of Richter's novels have been adapted for motion pictures and television, and Richter himself worked periodically as a writer for Metro-Goldwyn-Mayer in Hollywood between 1937 and 1950, but found that writing for motion pictures was not his forte. His continuing popularity as a writer is reflected by the fact that at present, nearly sixteen years after his death, ten of Richter's books are still in print, yet to date, his notebooks, correspondence, and other papers that would make for scholarly appreciation and analysis of his craft as a writer remain to be published.

Achievements

Richter did not achieve widespread recognition during his long career as a writer despite the fact that he won the Pulitzer Prize for Fiction in 1951 for *The Town* and the National Book Award for Fiction in 1960 for *The Waters of Kronos*, beating out Harper Lee's *To Kill a Mockingbird* and John Updike's *Rabbit Run* among the competition. A reclusive man who spent much of his life in rural Pennsylvania and in the isolated mountains of New Mexico, Richter was not a colorful figure whose life drew attention to his work. Because much of his work appeared in serial form for popular and pulp magazines, he has been too hastily dismissed by academic critics. At his best, Richter is a historical novelist of the first rank. He re-creates the past, not as a historian would, but rather, by reproducing the actualities of frontier experience which are conveyed by fidelity to details and local expression. When Richter's purposes as an artist are more fully understood, it seems certain that critical assessments of his work will acknowledge the judgment of the general reader, with whom Richter continues to be popular.

Biography

Conrad Michael Richter was born in Pine Grove, Pennsylvania, on October 13, 1890. The eldest of three sons of a Lutheran minister, he grew up in several small rural Pennsylvania towns where his father had congregations. He came from mixed German, French, and Scotch-Irish blood. One of his forebears served with George Washington's Continental Army and another fought as a Hessian mercenary for the British. His grandfather, uncle, and great-uncles were preachers. Richter was brought up in bucolic surroundings. and he passed a happy boyhood in a score of central and northern Pennsylvania villages. In 1906, he was graduated from Tremont High School and during the next three years took a number of odd jobs—clerking, driving teams, pitching hay, and working as a bank teller. His first permanent job was as a reporter for the Johnstown, Pennsylvania, *Journal*, which he began at nineteen. His first published story, entitled "How Tuck Went Home," was written in 1913 while he was living in Cleveland, Ohio. In 1914, a second story, "Brothers of No Kin," was awarded a twenty-five-dollar prize for being one of the best stories of the year. In 1915, Richter was married to Harvena Maria Achenbach. Taking his bride West to find his fortune in a silver mine venture at Coeur d'Alene, Idaho, he made a short sojourn as a speculator in the mine fields. After returning East, where a daughter was born in 1917, Richter started writing children's literature and published a periodical for juveniles called *Junior Magazine Book*. Meanwhile, his short stories had been appearing in magazines such as *Ladie's Home Journal* and *Saturday Review*.

Richter's early work as a newspaper reporter and editor influenced his literary style. His sparse method of expression was a product of his journalistic training, and the typical length of his novels is about two hundred pages. In lieu of formal education, Richter, like many self-taught people, became a voracious reader. In an interview, he said, "All my life I have been a reader and one of my joys as a boy and young man was a good book in which I could lose myself." His reading was eclectic, ranging from the adventure writer W. H. Hudson to scientific authors such as Michael Faraday and G. W. Crele, whose theories of chemistry and physics influence Richter's later philosophical works. Ralph Waldo Emerson, Henry David Thoreau, and John Burroughs also helped shape his idealistic views on nature. The most important influence on his own writing came, however, from Willa Cather, whose pioneer characters and Western backgrounds provided the model for much of Richter's fiction.

In his early short fiction, Richter used the formulas of the popular literature of the period, which still abided by the conventions of the genteel tradition. The typical tale revolved around stock plots such as a case of mistaken identity, a rich youth's rehabilitation through hardships shared with the common people, a city girl coming to terms with country life, and so on. As might be expected, these stories used cardboard characters and were tailored to readers' moral and social assumptions. Richter's first stories were self-admitted "potboilers" from which he only expected to get a bit of money for his family. During the period between 1917 and 1928, when Richter was engaged in hackwriting and publishing for a living, he started to develop his ideas on "psychoenergics," as he called his theory of human personality. This theoretical interest led to three works, *Human Vibration*, *Principles in Bio-Physics*, and a privately printed monograph called "Life Energy." These essays contained the germ of another book-length essay that he published twenty-eight years later as *The Mountain on the Desert*, his fullest attempt to articulate his personal philosophy.

In 1928, Richter's wife's illnesses caused a move to the Southwest, an event that would have a major effect on his career as a writer and mark a turning point in his life. What had started as a misfortune would turn out otherwise. Stimulated by the culture and climate of New Mexico, Richter published a second volume of stories *Early Americana and Other Stories* and his first novel, *The Sea of Grass*.

The writer's material was enlarged. He had always taken the ingredients of his fiction from family memories and observations; when he moved to New Mexico, as he later wrote in his unpublished *A Few Personal Notes*, "The backlog of my material still came from first sources, fine old-time men and women, chiefly from New Mexico and Arizona, Texas and Indiana territory, who lived through many of the early days. . . ."

In 1940, Richter published *The Trees*, the first volume of a trilogy that would be completed with *The Fields* in 1946 and *The Town* in 1950. After the publication of his Southwestern novel *Tacey Cromwell* in 1942, Richter received his first literary award, the gold medal for literature given by the Society of Libraries of New York University. In 1944, an honorary Litt.D. degree was conferred upon him by Susquehanna University in recognition of a native son's attainments. During the decade of the 1940's, Richter also received the Ohio Library Medal Award for Literature.

In 1950, Richter returned to his native heath, Pine Grove, Pennsylvania, where he would remain for the rest of his life except for return trips to the

Southwest, and winters in Florida. In 1951, Richter won the Pulitzer Prize for Fiction for *The Town*. Although he wrote one more novel about the West, *The Lady*, most of Richter's remaining career was given over to the subjects with which he had started as a writer—the people and land of his birthplace. He completed his best-selling novel *The Light in the Forest* after his return home; like his later novel, *A Country of Strangers*, it was inspired by the beauty of the Eastern landscape and by the deeper sense of history one feels in the East. At the close of the 1950's, Richter was awarded his second honorary doctorate, this time by the university of his adopted state, New Mexico. In the early 1960's he completed two volumes of his projected Pennsylvania trilogy—*The Waters of Kronos* and *A Simple Honorable Man*. Richter won the National Book Award for the former; he was at work on the third volume of the trilogy when he died in 1968 at the age of seventy-eight. Since his death, two works have appeared: a novel, *The Aristocrat* and a book of stories, *The Rawhide Knot and Other Stories*.

Analysis

Conrad Richter's qualities as a writer are partly described by the title of one of his late novels, *A Simple Honorable Man*. Although the book is about his father, the same terms might be used to characterize Richter's fiction, which is simple, concise, and concerned with basic virtues. Thus, it is something of a paradox that Richter's novels and stories are underpinned by a rather complex theory of human life and history, and that these philosophical, quasi-scientific ideas provide a conceptual framework over which the characters, plots, and settings of his fiction are stretched like a covering fabric. Another major tendency of Richter's fiction is that it is intensely autobiographical, deriving from family traditions and experience. In his youth, Richter heard stories of frontier experiences from relatives who had been pioneers themselves. It was his fascination with the way things had been and his conviction that he could inspire his readers to cope with modern problems by showing how ordinary people in the past had overcome the adversities of their frontier that prompted him to become a historical novelist.

Equally important to Richter's development as a novelist, however, were the quasi-scientific philosophical principles which he developed long before his first novel was published. Thus, Richter is unlike most writers in that his fiction does not represent the developing and unfolding of a philosophy, but rather the extension of a belief system that was essentially static after being established. This being the case, it is important to grasp some of the rudiments of Richter's philosophy before discussing his longer fiction, for his themes as a novelist grow out of his philosophical notions.

It must be pointed out that despite their would-be scientific titles and vocabulary (*Human Vibration* and *Principles in Bio-Physics*), Richter's book-length essays lack the rigor of scientific methodology. At first glance, his theory of life seems to be based upon an odd merging of materialism and idealism. His first premise is that man functions in response to bodily cellular vibrations or "vibes" which are regulated by the reserves of psychical or physical energy. If energy abounds, man is in harmony with life. The ultimate expression of human harmony is compassion for one's fellow man. Other signs are charity, fortitude, and the confidence to prevail against hardship, a sense of unity with nature, a tendency toward betterment in history, and a quest for freedom. On the other hand, if energy sources are low, there is a lack of harmony in life. Conflict with nature, with other men, and with oneself all signify a deficiency of energy; other such manifestations are restless wandering, fruitless searching for intangibles, and historic change for the worse. Thus, as Richter explains it, human life and history are governed by mechanical laws.

Richter's second premise is based on quasi-scientific ideas. He holds that man responds in mind and body with "cellular energy" to outside stimuli. Activity causes the cells in one's body to overflow, revitalizing the weak cells. The process is like that of an electrical circuit in which there is a constant reenergizing while the operation continues. Therefore, constant use insures a steady power source, whereas disuse can cause the source to decline and lose power. In human terms, mental and physical exertion stimulates the release of energy and speeds up "energy transfer" through the cell structure.

Like many American autodidacts, Richter combined Yankee know-how and practicality with the visions of the crank philosopher. His "bio-physics" serves as a point of departure for accurate historical fiction about the actualities of pioneer life. By Richter's own admission, much of what he produced before he moved to New Mexico in 1928 was hack-writing for the pulp magazines, but there, led to new literary subjects, he launched his career as a serious author with a series of stories and novels; inspired by the grand surroundings of his Western residence and informed by extensive research and the philosophical themes which would run through his subsequent fiction, he produced his first novel.

The Sea of Grass was well-received on publication and is still highly regarded by readers and critics. The similarities between Richter's story of a strong-willed Southwestern pioneer woman and Willa Cather's *A Lost Lady* (1923) were quickly noted. The central idea of *The Sea of Grass* was sounded in a short story entitled "Smoke over the Prairie," published two years earlier in *Saturday Evening Post*. The novel is set in New Mexico during the last decades of the nineteenth century. It revolves around a feud between cattle ranchers, led by Colonel James Brewton, who use the open grasslands for grazing and growing numbers of farmers, called "nesters" by the cattlemen, who are supported by Brice Chamberlain, a federal judge. A subplot concerns a love triangle between Brewton, his wife Lutie, and Chamberlain, which ends with the tragic death of the son of Brewton and Lutie, whose paternity is uncertain, since it is implied that Chamberlain might well have been the boy's father.

The major theme is the decline of the grasslands, a historic change for the worse. The story is narrated as a reminiscence by Hal Brewton, a nephew of Colonel Brewton. He tells the story of an era that has already passed and thus conveys an aura of nostalgia which Richter himself apparently felt for these bygone days. In fact, Hal Brewton is actually a persona for the author and reflects his attitudes toward events. For this reason, Hal remains a one-dimensional character, yet his role as narrator serves to create an objective view of the material. Hal is involved in the events he describes but not so closely as to have his judgment obscured. He is a boy when the story starts and is the town doctor when the story ends twenty-five years later. The first part of the book is devoted to Lutie, a lively and lovely belle from St. Louis, who comes to Salt Fork, New Mexico, to marry the cattle baron Jim Brewton. The "Colonel," as he is called, has a battle going on with the nesters because he believes that the dry lands are doomed to be blown away if they are plowed. The marriage results in three children, but Lutie grows tired of her life as a rancher's wife and simply walks out, staying away for fifteen years. She had left thinking that her lover Brice Chamberlain would come with her, but he remains to support the cause of the farmers.

The title of the book implies that it is a story about the land, and it is indeed, for the basic conflict of the novel arises from how the land will be used. Yet *The Sea of Grass* also introduces the typical Richter hero and heroine in Colonel and Lutie Brewton. The Colonel embodies the best combination of idealism and pragmatism, but he is not complex. He reflects the virtues Richter admires—integrity and courage; he exercises his control over his world with sure authority. Lutie, on the other hand, is the first in a line of female characters in Richter's fiction who are not in harmony with their existence, and who achieve maturity only through hardship and suffering. When she returns to the Southwest, she has finally learned that she needs the sense of fulfillment that comes from the exertion required to survive on the sea of grass. *The Sea of Grass* is ultimately a novel in which the triumph belongs to the earth, for it is the land itself that finally, through a drought, defeats the persistent nesters and subdues Lutie's willful romanticism when her son is destroyed by the violence of the Southwest. Although *The Sea of Grass* is a lasting achievement, it has some of Richter's characteristic flaws as well. There is a thinness to the writing that gives the impression of a screenplay or an extended short story rather than a fully realized novel, a charge leveled with even more justification against Richter's next novel, *Tacey Cromwell*.

Tacey Cromwell was generally not as well-received as *The Sea of Grass*, perhaps because the heroine is a prostitute and the hero a gambler. Recalling his Idaho experience, Richter sets the plot of *Tacey Cromwell* in a mining town called Bisbee; his treatment of this setting reflects extensive research concerning life in early Western mining towns. He shows the ethnic diversity of the miners and the pretensions of the leading townsmen, who have risen from humble origins to positions of wealth and power. The plot of the novel is built around the conflict between the rough-and-ready immigrants and the new rich ruling class in town. The narrator is again a small boy, Wickers Covington, who is both an observer and a partial participant in the action, about which he reminisces as he tells the story after the fact.

The book begins with the runaway boy Wickers escaping from an uncle in Kansas who has mistreated him. Changing his name to Nugget Oldaker, he heads to Socarro, New Mexico, where his half brother Gaye Oldaker is living. He finds his kinsman in a house of tolerance called the White Palace, which is ironically named, for it is a place of prostitution. His brother's mistress is a prostitute named Tacey Cromwell. Fearing that an upbringing in a bordello would prejudice the lad's morals, the couple moves away to give Nugget a decent home. They relocate in a mining town in Arizona, where they settle down and start the climb to success. Tacey and Gaye never marry, but they remain something of a team. She shows incredible altruism toward her former lover, even after he leaves her and takes the richest woman in town as his wife. Tacey's conversion to respectability is hastened by the adoption of two children of a neighbor killed in a mine accident. The good woman of the town, however, take umbrage at the children being reared by even a reformed prostitute, and they bring legal action against Tacey, which results in her losing the children.

Undaunted by disappointment in love, community treachery, and sickness, Tacey starts a business as a dressmaker. At first she is boycotted by the priggish ladies, but one of her creations is worn at an annual ball by a lady who did not know or care about Tacey's reputation. The dress is a sensation, and her future as a dressmaker and designer is made overnight. Meanwhile, Gaye has been appointed territorial treasurer, a position he sought after being encouraged by Tacey. His wife, the haughty and puritanical Rudith Watrons, is drenched in a rainstorm that leads to a long illness and finally to her death. Nugget, who has grown up and become a mining engineer, returns to Bisbee, and one of the foster children taken from Tacey is restored to her. Thus, the novel ends with things returned to their original condition, but with the new harmony that hardship always hands to those who accept it in Richter's fictional worlds.

The novel also illustrates the conception of "westering," the process of evolution in which a region goes from frontier to community. Such a process, in Richter's conception, involves more than historical change. On the physiological and psychological levels, *Tacey Cromwell* depicts Richter's theory of altruism. Tacey's selfless assumption of guilt, both hers and her gambler-lover's, so that Gaye and his children might prosper, is close to the formula plot of the prostitute with a heart of gold used by Bret Harte in his Western fiction. Richter, however, has Tacey's sacrifice pay off, and she finally rises to respectability and eventual reunion with her lover and loved ones.

The Lady, Richter's ninth novel and his third with a Southwestern setting, was published fifteen years later in 1957. *The Lady* was better received by the critics and evidences Richter's increased competence as a writer. It is a stronger novel because the central character, Dona Ellen Sessions, is more fully developed than Tacey Cromwell. The plot is partly based on an actual case, an unsolved New Mexico mystery of the frontier period, that involved the disappearance and probable murder of a judge and his young son. The conflict in this book centers on the struggle between Spanish-American sheep-herders and Anglo-American cattle ranchers. The story is told by a narrator named Jud, who tells of events which happened sixty years before, when he was a boy of ten. He, like the juvenile narrators of *The Sea of Grass* and *Tacey Cromwell*, is both a participant and a witness. Jud is taken in by his cousin, the Territorial Judge Albert Sessions, after his own father has abandoned him. The judge's wife is the charming and arrogant "Dona Lady Ellen," as she is styled because of her noble Spanish and English bloodlines. She is the mistress of a giant sheep spread, inherited from her parents. In addition to breeding and wealth, she has acquired skills as a horseback rider and markswoman. The villain of the piece is her brother-in-law, a mercenary and unethical lawyer, Snell Beasley. The violent feud that is the focus of the book is begun when Beasley drives a cattle herd through her ranch; there is shooting that results in the death of some of the cattlemen.

The chain of events that leads to the disappearance of Judge Sessions and his young son Wily is set in motion. Thinking Dona Ellen is now vulnerable, Snell Beasley sets out to destroy her completely. She is forced to sell her once great ranch, and it seems that her humiliation is complete, yet in the final scene of the novel, poetic justice is served. In a buggy race between Dona Ellen and Snell, there is an accident and her adversary is killed; thus, the heroine gets her revenge in a somewhat melodramatic ending. Her victory underscores Richter's central themes of endurance in the process of "westering" and the mystic bond between people and landscape. It is fitting that Richter's last book about his adopted Southwest should be concluded with a glorification of the land which had inspired him to write the type of fiction that would be his forte—historical romances.

While working on his Southwestern novels, Richter began in the early 1940's his trilogy about the Pennsylvania-Ohio frontier, which was conceived from the first as a whole. The first novel of the trilogy, *The Trees*, is set in the late eighteenth and early nineteenth centuries; the novel unfolds the story of a typical pioneer family, the Luckett clan, whose frequent migrations through the great sea of woods that covers the Ohio Valley and the Allegheny mountains is the basis of the plot. In this novel, Richter vividly depicts the darkness of the forest floor as well as the moral darkness in the heart of man. The protagonist of *The Trees* is a "woods woman" named Sayward Luckett, a larger-than-life figure who is the focal character of the entire trilogy. She is married to Portius Wheeler, who, for reasons never explained, has abandoned his native New England, where he was educated as a lawyer, and has become a loutish and drunken backwoodsman. Although nearly all traces of culture and civilization have been erased from him by the time he is married to Sayward, she nevertheless prevents him from further decline, and he honors her by making a reformation.

In addition, *The Trees* tells how Sayward as a girl had wandered with her nomadic family, breaking away from that way of life to marry Portius and settle down. Richter intended that Sayward's experiences should reflect the whole pioneer experience of movement, settlement, and domestication. Using the span of one woman's life, the process of historical change in the Ohio Valley from hunters to farmers to town dwellers is reflected. Thus, like Richter's Southwestern novels, *The Trees* traces social evolution; it also resembles his Southwestern novels in being episodic, in having a strong heroine, and in its themes of hardship and endurance, ending in ultimate triumph. It differs most from the earlier books in that there is no boy-narrator; Richter's point of view is omniscient in the trilogy, and he uses more dialect in the dialogue. Further, in an effort to make his depiction of pioneer life more convincing, he uses folktales and superstitions in order to reflect the primitive way of life on the frontier.

The final two volumes of the trilogy, *The Fields* and *The Town*, continue the portrait of Sayward and depict the conquering of the land through the process of civilization. *The Fields* tells of Sayward's ten children and her husband's affair with the local schoolmarm, who bears him an illegitimate daughter. Sayward is devastated by Portius' unfaithfulness, yet she recovers from this crushing experience when she hitches a pair of oxen to a plow and begins to till the fields. She sees in the great brutes' tolerance and strength and in the permanence of the earth a prescription for her own survival.

The Town, though not any more successful artistically than the first two parts of the trilogy, was awarded the Pulitzer Prize in 1951, more for the entire series than for its concluding volume. *The Town*, which is set in pre-Civil War Ohio, deals mostly with the romance between Sayward's youngest son, Chancey, and her husband's illegitimate daughter, Rosa Tench. The love between the half brother and sister is marked by tragedy; she commits suicide following a balloon accident. The rest of the book completes Sayward's story. The conflict that fills out the plot is between mother and son: Sayward tries to make a pioneering man out of Chancey, but he refuses to accept her value system and goes off to edit a liberal newspaper in Cincinnati. The newspaper, which is supported by an unknown patron, publishes Chancey's socialist views, which are an affront to his mother. Just before her death, he learns that she was the secret benefactor who had supported his career over the years.

Chancey has to reexamine his philosophy in the light of this revelation. He concludes that his mother's doctrine of hard work and self-reliance is a better one than his own. Thus, Sayward dies at eighty having won her last victory, rescuing her baby son from the heresy of socialism; the puritan faith in work of the older generation remains superior to modern liberal social theory.

Thus, in his trilogy, Richter brings full circle the "westering" process in which wilderness gives way to farms and farms become towns—historic change for the better; that is the essence of the American experience. Yet as civilization conquers the wilderness, something is lost as well as gained. The frontier's hardships had tested men and honed their character. Modern Americans lack hardiness, vigor, and self-reliance, those qualities of mind and spirit which their ancestor's had in abundance, as the heroine of his Ohio trilogy so amply shows.

Richter produced some half-dozen minor novels on various historical subjects and themes, but the major achievements of his later career are *The Waters of Kronos* and its sequel, *A Simple Honorable Man*, the first two volumes of a projected trilogy which he did not live to complete. The former is regarded as one of Richter's highest artistic successes and won wide critical acclaim, earning the National Book Award for 1960. The book is one of Richter's most autobiographical. His main character, a man named John Donner, resembles Richter himself; the character's parents are very much like his family as well. *The Waters of Kronos* is an almost mystical story in which John Donner, an ill and aged man, returns from the West to his Pennsylvania hometown, which is covered by a man-made lake, to visit the graves of his ancestors. At the cemetery, he meets an old man, who takes Donner down a steep hill where, to his incredulous eyes, he finds his town just as it looked sixty years ago. The remainder of the plot is a reexamination of the scenes of his childhood and a reunion with friends and relatives. The journey into the past enables him to learn that what he has always feared is not true— that the gap between his faith and that of his father is not as wide as he once thought. He discovers that he is his father's spiritual son. His final realization from his return to the past is that they have both worshiped the same god in different ways. Having come to terms with his father's god in his novel, Richter's next book shows how he gains further understanding of his parents as a person.

A Simple Honorable Man describes the life of John Donner's father, Harry, who at age forty gives up a career in business for a lifetime of service to the Lutheran Church. Like *The Waters of Kronos*, this book is clearly autobiographical, but it is more than a nostalgic family history, for in this novel as in the previous one, Richter tries to come to grips with a number of philosophical problems. The novel emphasizes that the most important things in life are not social status, or power of office, or money, but altruistic service to others. Harry Donner's greatest satisfaction is not in putting money in the bank but in helping those who are in need.

The third volume of the trilogy, on which Richter was at work when he died, was intended to show, as the first two books had done, his reconciliation with his actual father, his final reconciliation with his spiritual father. The two volumes that he did complete are a fitting capstone to Richter's career as a writer. His personal struggles, reflected through those of the Donners, show him to be a man of spiritual and intellectual integrity. The order and lucidity of the narrative reveal his artistry; the restrained realism that characterizes his fiction mutes the sentimentality inherent in such materials, and even though dealing with personal subject of a moral nature, he never lapses into overt didacticism.

Except for *The Sea of Grass*, Richter's reputation will rest most firmly on the books written in the last stages of his career, especially *The Waters of Kronos*; nevertheless, he will probably continue to attract readers who admire exciting, concise, sometimes lyrical stories and novels about the early history of this country and the common people who experienced it.

Hallman B. Bryant

Other major works

SHORT FICTION: *Brothers of No Kin and Other Stories*, 1924; *Early Americana and Other Stories*, 1936; *The Rawhide Knot and Other Stories*, 1978.

NONFICTION: *Human Vibrations*, 1926; *Principles in Bio-Physics*, 1927; *The Mountain on the Desert*, 1955; *A Philosophical Journey*, 1955.

Bibliography

Barnes, Robert J. *Conrad Richter*. Austin, Tex.: Steck-Vaughn, 1968. A short and limited approach to Richter the writer. Opens with a brief biography and then follows with a survey of his fiction which used the Southwest as a setting—nine short stories out of seventy and three of his thirteen novels.

Edwards, Clifford D. *Conrad Richter's Ohio Trilogy*. Paris: Mouton, 1970. A good in-depth examination of Richter's Ohio Trilogy—*The Trees* (1940), *The Fields* (1946), and *The Town* (1950)—with a detailed analysis of the writer's philosophical and psychological themes.

Gaston, Edwin W., Jr. *Conrad Richter*. Rev. ed. Boston: Twayne, 1989. An excellent introduction to Richter, the man and the writer, and his work. Gaston scrutinizes Richter's life and philosophy as they resonate in all of his writings. Includes comprehensive notes, references, a bibliography, and an index.

Lahood, Marvin J. *Conrad Richter's America*. The Hague: Mouton, 1975. Lahood writes an appreciative, if not critical, summary of Richter's literary work. He avoids a chronological approach, devoting separate chapters to discussions of thematic subject matter.

Critical Survey of Long Fiction

Richter, Harvena. *Writing to Survive: The Private Notebooks of Conrad Richter*. Albuquerque: University of New Mexico Press, 1988. Richter's daughter offers an intimate look at personal notebooks by the writer dealing with the genesis of his literary work.

ELIZABETH MADOX ROBERTS

Born: Perryville, Kentucky; October 30, 1886
Died: Orlando, Florida; March 13, 1941

Principal long fiction

The Time of Man, 1926; *My Heart and My Flesh*, 1927; *Jingling in the Wind*, 1928; *The Great Meadow*, 1930; *A Buried Treasure*, 1931; *He Sent Forth a Raven*, 1935; *Black Is My Truelove's Hair*, 1938.

Other literary forms

Before Elizabeth Madox Roberts was a novelist, she wrote poetry, including children's verse—facts which explain much about her work as a novelist—and she continued to produce some poetry throughout her career. Her first collection of verse, privately printed in 1915, was *In the Great Steep's Garden*, a pamphlet consisting of a few short poems accompanying photographs. A second collection of poetry, *Under the Tree*, appeared in 1922, published by Huebsch, Inc., which soon became The Viking Press, publisher of Roberts' subsequent work. A revised edition of *Under the Tree* appeared in 1930, and a third collection of Roberts' poetry, *Song in the Meadow*, came out in 1940.

In addition, Roberts wrote short stories, which, like her poetry, found a ready market in leading magazines of the day. Her short fiction was collected in *The Haunted Mirror* (1932) and *Not by Strange Gods* (1941).

Achievements

Roberts' reputation as a writer furnishes an interesting case study in literary fashions and critical evaluation. Few novelists have begun their careers to such popular and critical acclaim as Roberts achieved with *the Time of Man* in 1926, acclaim that was renewed and confirmed by *The Great Meadow* four years later. With the 1935 publication of *He Sent Forth a Raven*, however, Roberts' literary reputation went into a precipitous decline. By her death in 1941, it had struck bottom. Since then, there have been intermittent attempts, including several book-length studies, to resurrect her reputation, frequently with highly inflated praise. Claims that she is among the half dozen or so great American novelists of the twentieth century do her as much disservice as does the vague "regionalist" label which her special pleaders decry.

Perhaps as a result of her early success and her relative isolation in Kentucky, Roberts seems likewise to have overestimated her powers: with talents along the lines of a May Sarton, Roberts was apparently encouraged to think of herself as another William Faulkner, with a little Herman Melville and Thomas Mann thrown in for good measure. Her style, so often termed "poetic," achieves some fine effects indeed, but at immense cost to the narrative flow of her novels. Her style is allied to her narrative focus, almost invariably the novel's female protagonist, whose perceptions and sentiments are spun out at length while the reader waits for something to happen. Little does happen, except that the heroines take long walks. The effect is somewhat reminiscent of an agrarian Virginia Woolf. Perhaps the reader is treated to such a subjective focus because Roberts' protagonists, however different, are to some extent alter egos of their author, whose own comments blend imperceptibly into their observations. The results of all this are slow-moving and sometimes flimsy plots, dimly realized characters (except usually for the protagonist), loss of authorial perspective, and tedium. As if these results were not unhappy enough, Roberts also had trouble dealing with ideas and with the overall plans for her novels.

Despite all these limitations and failings, Roberts is due for, and deserving of, a revival. Most readers will find her lighter novels, *A Buried Treasure* and *Black Is My Truelove's Hair*, still entertaining, and *The Great Meadow* possesses some epic qualities. All of Roberts' novels involve significant themes, and all deal incidentally with significant social issues, such as economic conditions, racism, and sexism. In particular, both feminists and antifeminists will find much of interest in Roberts' depiction of her female protagonists, in her treatment of male-female relationships, and in Roberts' own biography.

Biography

Elizabeth Madox Roberts' life was marked by a few salient facts. Descended from early settlers of Kentucky, she was the second of eight children born to Mary Elizabeth Brent and Simpson Roberts, Confederate veteran, teacher, grocer, and occasional surveyor/engineer. Roberts lived most of her life in Springfield, a small county-seat town on the southwestern edge of the Kentucky Bluegrass. She attended high school in Covington, Kentucky (1896-1900), and college at the University of Chicago (1917-1921; Ph.D. with Honors, English, 1921; David Blair McLaughlin Prize for prose, Fiske Poetry Prize, president of Poetry Club, Phi Beta Kappa), beginning college at the age of thirty-one because limited finances and ill health delayed her. She suffered from poor health much of her life. From 1910 to 1916, she made various stays with a brother and a sister in Colorado, in part to recuperate from what was possibly tuberculosis. At the height of her literary career, she experienced sever headaches and a skin rash, both possibly nervous in origin. During her last years, when she wintered in Florida for her health, she suffered severely from Hodgkin's disease (cancer of the lymphatic system), the eventual cause of her death.

Because of her ill health and perhaps her own disposition, Roberts led a quiet personal life, at times almost reclusive. She never married, though she always enjoyed a circle of friends, including friends from her Chicago years whom she later wrote and sometimes visited. In a sense, she never left the family circle, building her own house onto her parents' Springfield home when she came into money from her writing. She also enjoyed contacts and visits with her brothers and sisters. At heart, she was a solitary, introspective individual who guarded her privacy, growing a hedge around her backyard garden. Besides reading and writing, her favorite activities included listening to music, gardening, sunbathing, and taking long walks into secluded areas of the countryside (from which she returned to make voluminous notes).

These conditions of Roberts' life exercised strong influences, both positive and negative, on her writing career. Her family's proud pioneer heritage not only stimulated her imagination, but it also encouraged her to paint an overly idyllic picture of Kentucky's past and present. The sleepy farming region around Springfield was also a rich source of material—indeed, her prime source—but at the same time it effectively isolated her from literary circles which might have served to encourage, temper, and appreciate her efforts. These functions were served briefly by her stay at the University of Chicago. Her heady experience of Chicago, where literary circles flourished both inside and outside the university, filled her with ideas and propelled her into sustained literary production, but perhaps this hothouse experience also encouraged her to overreach herself as a writer.

The effects of Roberts' cirucmscribed personal life can also be detected in her fiction, particularly in her efforts to depict character and to describe male-female relationships, possibly also in her habitual narrative focus. To a great extent, Roberts' fiction provides an ironic counterpoint to her personal life. In most of her novels, the main narrative interest is her heroines' search for identity, worked out through the rituals of courting and mating: her heroines suffer their shipwrecks but eventually find safe harbor in marriage. The men in their lives are either grandfatherly, brutish, bucolic, or childishly vengeful; the heroines get advice from the grandfatherly ones, are hurt by the brutish ones, and marry either the bucolic or childishly vengeful ones. Fathers are frequently possessive, obstructing their daughters from marriage; one can only wonder about Roberts' relationship with her father, who refused her money for college and then had her underfoot for the rest of his life. To Roberts' credit, it must be said that in her novels, men, however unpromising, are absolutely vital to the scheme of things.

On the other hand, too, if Roberts' personal life had been less circumscribed, she might not have taken up writing at all. Writing became her means of achieving identity—and against stronger odds than any of her heroines had to face. However sickly and easily demoralized Roberts might seem, she had a vein of iron in her character that also came out in her heroines and in her themes. Even Roberts' ill health furnished her with potent material. Her heroines frequently develop by means of long illnesses and convalescences, from which they emerge born again, like a butterfly from its pupa. It was perhaps toward such a rebirth that Roberts was aiming in her writing.

Analysis

Although commentators on Elizabeth Madox Roberts like to describe her main theme in such terms as "the ordering of chaos" or "the triumph of spirit over matter," one need not be so high-minded and vague. A hardheaded Kentucky version of her major theme would be more specific: ownership of the land. This theme reflects an old, revered attitude in Kentucky, where in some parts even today one can be shot for trespassing. The theme also reflects an old, revered American (even Anglo-Saxon) attitude, a pioneer urge to settle and possess, if necessary by violence—an urge that today achieves its debased avatar in the mass media and advertising. In its gentler, more settled aspects, however, Roberts' theme embodies a Jeffersonian, agrarian vision of American democracy, the American dream of independence through ownership of the land. The theme eventually embodies a more universal vision, a vision of harmony with the land, a realization, serenely accepted, that those who possess the land are also possessed by it. Unhappily, whether expressed by Roberts or by other American writers whose characters want to own chicken farms or raise rabbits, the theme is a poignant reminder that many Americans have in actuality been vagabonds, whether the pioneer variety or today's rootless variety. In this sense, then, the theme embodies an idyllic but unrealized American dream; it was apparently Roberts' conviction, however, that this dream came very close to being realized in Kentucky.

In developing her theme, Roberts reveals the influence of her favorite philosopher, George Berkeley, the eighteenth century bishop who denied the existence of matter, holding that "things" exist only as "ideas" or "spirits" in the minds of God and man. Such a philosophy would seem, at first, to preclude any relationship with the land; on the contrary, it points to a divine immanence, to the spiritual nature of all "things," including the land. The philosophy also implies the worth of "subjective" truth, justifying Roberts' narrative focus on the lengthy observations of her protagonists. As a result of this focus, her novels are full of loving descriptions of the land, the flora and fauna, the weather. Held constantly before the reader, the land forms an immense backdrop or tableau against which human action is played out, a background so overwhelming at times that the characters seem to emerge out of it and then sink back into it.

Because of their closeness to the land, many of Roberts' characters exhibit a sameness: Mostly simple farmers, their lives governed by the imperatives of the seasons, crops, animals, they identify with the soil in their talk and in their impulses. Rather inarticulate, they have a blood-knowledge of the earth that requires little discussion. The continuity of their lives with the land is also reflected in their impulses to create life, to mate and procreate. To Roberts, these characters represent an ideal, a settled state, though to her readers they might seem too bucolic to be interesting.

The state of health represented by such characters is what Roberts' protagonists aspire to and her maladjusted characters lack. Like the bucolic characters, Roberts' protagonists seek to mate and procreate. The protagonists do not achieve their aims easily, though, having to reenact the archtypal struggle of their pioneer ancestors before they reach a settled state. When misfortune frustrates their desires, they get back in touch with the earth through the simple therapies of raising chickens, growing a garden, sunbathing, or taking rides in the country. Some end up marrying farmers. Such is the ultimate salvation of Theodosia, the highbred protagonist of *My Heart and My Flesh*, whose alienation from the land is an index of her initial maladjustment. Other unhappy characters in Roberts' novels are similarly out of touch with the land, such as Stoner Drake in *He Sent Forth a Raven* and the evil Langtry in *Black Is My Truelove's Hair*.

These patterns of behavior exhibited by her characters are the prime means through which Roberts' develops her theme, with examples of each pattern generally to be found in each of her novels. To some extent, however, each novel emphasizes a particular aspect of her theme, with *He Sent Forth a Raven* being Roberts' most ambitious effort to pull all her characteristic motifs together in a single work.

Although *The Great Meadow* was Roberts' fourth novel, it was apparently the first conceived. This is appropriate, since thematically *The Great Meadow* comes first among her novels. Set around the time of the American Revolution, it celebrates the early settlement of Kentucky, that other Eden, that paradise, that promised land. The epic qualities of this novel have led some commentators to compare it to Homer's *Odyssey* (c. 800 B.C.), though it could more appropriately be compared to Vergil's *Aeneid* (c. 29-19 B.C.). Like Latium, Kentucky has to be wrested from the "aborigines." The novel even has its epic heroine with a noble name, Diony, and noble progenitors, sturdy Pennsylvania Methodists and Quakers on her mother's side and Virginia Tidewater gentry on her father's. Diony is, in truth, the founder of "a new race," though before she marries and sets out for Kentucky, she has to get her father's permission (in typical fashion for Roberts' possessive fathers, he at first denies her).

After a slow start in Albermarle County, Virginia, the novel follows Diony, her husband, and a small party of settlers as they trek across the rugged Appalachians to Harrod's Fort, where they proceed to fight off the Indians and establish farms. The growth of their settlement corresponds to Diony's growth as a person, largely a development of awareness. A convinced Berkeleian who frequently quotes from the philosopher's works, she receives a real challenge to her beliefs when she is banged in the head with a tomahawk, but the tomahawk incident and the scalping of her mother-in-law are only smaller parts of the overall challenge represented by the alien wilderness. In the beginning, Diony had imagined God as a benevolent deity creating "a world out of chaos," but since everything which exists is a thought of God's,

He must also have created the wilderness, where wolves howl and savages prowl. Unlike Daniel Boone—or for that matter the Indians—Diony cannot feel at home in the wilderness; instead, she must remake the wilderness into her vision of home, a vision of a settled, orderly, agrarian society where the land is "owned."

Although Diony clings stubbornly to her vision of order, the wilderness does make her more tolerant of disorder. Even before she leaves for Kentucky, she has a "wilderness marriage . . . without law" (performed by a Methodist minister). Later, her experiences of hardship and deprivation at Harrod's Fort lead her to observe that "men wanted law to live by" but that women and babies "followed a hidden law"—that is, a law based on concrete, immediate human needs. This frontier tradition of making do the best one can, without too much scrupling about moral and legal niceties, serves Diony well at the end of the novel. Her husband, Berk Jarvis, goes off into the wilderness to seek revenge against the Indian, Blackfox, who has his mother's scalp. When Berk does not return in a year or so, he is presumed dead, and Diony marries Evan Muir, who had helped provide for her after Berk left. Then, three years after he left, Berk shows up. Faced with two husbands and a child by each, Diony exercises the frontier woman's option: she sends Evan away, takes Berk back, and then goes to bed for a good, sound sleep.

The same spirit of make-do morality also characterizes the settlers' relations with the Indians. Diony's mother, Polly, influenced by Quaker thought, not only opposes the slaveholding favored by the Tidewater gentry, but also opposes taking land from the Indians. At the dinner table where the men are enthusiastically discussing "the promise land" of Kentucky, Polly angrily announces that Kentucky "belongs to the Indians" and that white trespassers there will get "skulped." Quiet reigns while the men contemplate images of "battle, fire . . . rapine, plunder." These thoughts, however, dampen their enthusiasm only momentarily. Striking the table for emphasis, they argue that Kentucky, "a good country," belongs to those strong enough to take and hold it—that is, "the Long Knives." Later, the last term is revised to "civilized man." Apparently, the latter argument is the one Roberts favors, since the rest of her novel eulogizes the settlers' taking of Kentucky. For example, as Diony's party breaks through Cumberland Gap, Roberts describes them as marching forward, "without bigotry and without psalm-singing," to take "a new world for themselves . . . by the power of their courage, their order, and their endurance." Thus is a time-honored Kentucky tradition established.

If *The Great Meadow* celebrates the vision of this other Eden, *A Buried Treasure* and *Black Is My Truelove's Hair* celebrate the realization of the vision. Like all of Roberts' novels except *The Great Meadow*, they are set in early twentieth century Kentucky, roughly contemporaneous with the period of their composition. Both novels were expanded from shorter pieces and show the effects of padding and lengthening, but at the same time they are

Roberts' most entertaining novels and exhibit, in its purest form, her theme of living on the land. Generally light and pleasant works, they depict a pastoral scene where the land is the source of happiness and renewal.

A Buried Treasure differs from other novels in its comic tone and in its older protagonist, Philadelphia Blair. Philly's farmer husband, Andy, finds a pot of old gold and silver coins under a stump on their land, and the rest of the novel concerns their efforts to announce their find and at the same time protect it from thieves. The flimsy plot is complicated somewhat by Philly's machinations to slip away her cousin's daughter, Imogene (whose possessive father, Sam Cundy, will not let her wed), and marry her to Giles Wilson. In addition, a subplot, introducing experimentation with point of view and synchronous time, treats seventeen-year-old Ben Shepherd's search for his ancestors' graves. To a great extent, the whole novel is an extended pun on the meanings of "buried treasure." Ben Shepherd finds the graves of his ancestors, who naturally go all the way back to the pioneer settlers of Kentucky. Imogene marries her beau, a jolly young farmer who wears horseshoes. Philly becomes more aware of her deep love for Andy, particularly when he loans the widow Hester Trigg (who gives him cherry pie) his two pearls he got from the treasure pot and normally wears in a small sack tied around his lower abdomen. Both Philly and Andy become more aware of their love for the land, from whence the treasure pot came, put there perhaps by some ancestor. Despite an evil old hen that eats her own eggs, and the threat of two itinerant housepainters who are thieves, the novel ends happily in a communal ring dance out in the pasture under the moonlit sky of the summer solstice.

Compared to *A Buried Treasure*, *Black Is My Truelove's Hair* is somewhat less satisfactory. Its title drawn from an Appalachian ballad containing the line "I love the ground whereon he stands," *Black Is My Truelove's Hair* concerns a young woman, Dena Janes, who "loved too much" and whose first lover, the black-hearted Langtry, is untrue. A truck driver who brags that he has no home, Langtry takes Dena on the road, refuses to marry her, treats her brutally, and threatens to kill her if she ever loves another man. After six days, Dena flees home, walking most of the way. Beginning at this point (the affair with Langtry is told through brief flashbacks), the novel treats Dena's gradual rehabilitation in the rural community and her eventual engagement to marry the miller's son, Cam Elliot. Although received at first with leering remarks and invitations, Dena is not given the Hester Prynne treatment. Even on her way home from the Langtry affair, the distraught Dena maintains she has "a right to a life that makes good sense." Apparently the people of the community agree.

Dena restores herself with the help of time, a sympathetic sister, routine chores of gardening and tending animals, sunbathing, and the advice of the local oracle, the apple-grower Journeyman, who observes that Dena is like one of his overburdened apple trees, "destroyed by its own abundance." As

Dena recovers, the passage of time is marked by great to-dos over a strayed gander and a lost thimble; these comic commotions are supposed to be highly symbolic, but to the reader they may seem merely silly. The reader is also likely to find the ending anticlimactic. The fearsome Langtry shows up, gun in hand, but when he chases Dena into Journeyman's moonlit orchard and views her abundance, he shoots to miss. The story is resolved when Journeyman appears, destroys the gun, and buries it in the earth, leaving Dena free to go her own way.

While *The Great Meadow* and the pastoral novels emphasize the positive aspects of Roberts' theme, *The Time of Man* and her other novels emphasize negative aspects. Dealing with poor tenant farmers who move from place to place, *The Time of Man* shows the plight of people who live on the land but do not own it. They have, in effect, been reduced to beasts of burden. Laboring mainly for others, they receive only enough from their labors to insure their continuing usefulness, their subsistence. Their inability to escape from this cycle probably means that their children will continue it.

Although Roberts' subject raises weighty social issues, suggesting a novel along the lines of John Steinbeck's *The Grapes of Wrath* (1939), *The Time of Man* is not a novel of social protest. Instead, with Roberts' narrative focus on the mind of her protagonist, *The Time of Man* is more a *Bildungrsroman*, tracing the development of Ellen Chesser from a girl of fourteen to a woman in her mid-thirties.

The reader follows Ellen as she bounds about the woods and fields, joins a group of other teenagers, gets a boyfriend, loses her boyfriend, withdraws into her hurt, meets another man, marries him, has four children, is estranged from her husband when he is unfaithful, has a fifth child die, and is reconciled with her husband. In short, whatever her social status, Ellen's experience of life over a generation is typical of most people's; in this sense, then, her experience is representative of "the time of man"—experiences of beauty and love, disappointment and tragedy, all within the context of passing time. Her ability to hold her experiences within this context is the key to her appreciation of beauty and love and her endurance of disappointment and tragedy. This ability derives from her closeness to the land, her sense of the seasons and participation in the rhythms of the earth: her jaunts through the woods, her work in the fields and garden, her courtship and marriage, her children.

Ellen illustrates what the Indians knew—that one can live in harmony with the land without owning it. To this extent, the several moves she makes from farm to farm, first with her parents and then with her husband, are almost irrelevant. Still, Ellen is aware of the inequities and injustices of the landowner/tenant system, a carryover from slave plantations, with some landowners continuing to act as if they own their tenants. She is incensed when her husband, while she and the children starve, identifies with, even takes pride in, the richness and show of their arrogant landlord. Both she and her husband carry around a vision of having their own farm someday, in "some better country." Perhaps they are headed toward this vision when, at the end of the novel, after her husband has been wrongly accused of barnburning and run out of the country, they are on the road again.

Roberts' first novel, *The Time of Man* is judged by some critics to be her best. Her exposition of her heroine's mind and development is a consummate job, and the novel does include some recognition of social problems in "the great meadow" of Kentucky; many readers, however, will feel that Roberts dwells too long on Ellen's early years, so that the first part of the novel drags.

Roberts' other novels could all be called "novels of maladjustment," since they all show, in one manner or another, people who are out of touch with the land. Of these, *Jingling in the Wind*, which includes Roberts' only depiction of an urban setting, presents the most extreme case. There is much that Roberts finds artificial, even bizarre, in the city, such as neon advertisements that usurp the stars. In short, *Jingling in the Wind*, sometimes described as a satiric fantasy, is an outright attack on many trends of modern civilization. The loose plot concerns a couple of rainmakers, Jeremy and Tulip, who give up their unnatural profession in order to marry and have children. Usually considered Roberts' worst novel, *Jingling in the Wind* is interesting for its contribution to her grand theme.

Another novel of maladjustment is *My Heart and My Flesh*, centering around Theodosia Bell, a neurasthenic product of the wealthy landowning class. In this Faulknerian work exhibiting the results of Southern decadence, the protagonist gradually loses everything which has insulated her from contact with the land—her wealth, her boyfriends, her home, her grandfather and sottish father, even her feelings of racial superiority (she discovers she is a half-sister to three mulattoes in town, including one idiot). As a child, Theodosia is so out of place in the countryside that a pack of hounds attack her. As an adult, when disillusionment, poverty, and sickness have brought her down to earth, she moves in with the pack, even eats their food. Later she finds health and happiness by teaching in a country school, living in her pupils' homes and marrying a farmer. Thus, the pattern of rebirth through contact with the land is perfectly illustrated by Theodosia.

Conversely, a negative example is provided by Stoner Drake, the monomaniacal old man in *He Sent Forth a Raven*. The title's biblical reference to Noah, who trusted in God, provides a lucid contrast to Drake's blasphemous behavior. When his second wife dies, Drake vows never to set foot on God's green earth again. His anger hardening into inflexible principle, he keeps his word, never venturing from the house and managing his farm from a rooftop observatory, summoning workers and family members with blasts on a hunting horn or conch shell. The blasts symbolize not only his pathetic defiance of God but also his alienation from other people and the land. To Drake, of course, they symbolize command, and in his house he is an absolute dictator.

His rancorous behavior is self-punishing, but it also takes a toll on the people around him. For example, he prevents his daughter, Martha, from entertaining suitors. When one finally ventures a polite visit as a guest, Drake confronts him and Martha with loud, vile charges of fornication. The young man leaves, and Martha, thunderstruck, falls into fever and delirium, temporarily losing her hearing; when after some weeks it returns, the first things she hears are "the loud horn and the screaming of the swine." She thereafter reconciles herself to being a spinster and to banking the fires at night (so the house will not catch fire and her father burn up with it).

Standing in contrast to Drake is his granddaughter Jocelle, the novel's heroine, who takes a lesson from her aunt's fate. Growing up in the house with Drake and Martha, Jocelle manages to live a relatively normal life because she is free to roam the fields, sometimes even beyond the range of the horn. Like all of Roberts' female protagonists, Jocelle does suffer her traumas, but she is strong enough to bounce back. For example, when she is raped by Walter, Drake's nephew, Drake renews his ridiculous vow, but Jocelle eventually recovers from her shock. At the end of the novel, she is happily married and a mother, her husband the manager of the farm, while Drake sits before the fireplace and hardens into brittle senility, unable to remember the reason for his vow.

Harold Branam

Other major works

SHORT FICTION: *The Haunted Mirror*, 1932; *Not by Strange Gods*, 1941.
POETRY: *In the Great Steep's Garden*, 1915; *Under the Tree*, 1922, 1930; *Song in the Meadow*, 1940.

Bibliography

Adams, J. Donald. *The Shape of Books to Come*. New York: Viking Press, 1934. Adams was an early admirer of Roberts, and he compares her to Willa Cather and Ellen Glasgow. An interesting contemporary view of the novelist.

Auchincloss, Louis. *Pioneers and Caretakers: A Study of Nine American Women Novelists*. Minneapolis: University of Minnesota Press, 1965. Auchincloss offers a compact overview of the life and work of Roberts, whose best and most popular novel was her first, *The Time of Man*; she never wrote anything to equal it.

Campbell, Harry M., and Ruel E. Foster. *Elizabeth Madox Roberts: American Novelist*. Norman: University of Oklahoma Press, 1956. Full of information about Roberts' career, yet, poorly organized. Often dull to read, making this book unsuitable for any but the most dedicated students of Roberts.

McDowell, Frederick P. W. *Elizabeth Madox Roberts*. New York: Twayne, 1963. McDowell gives a useful critical overview of Roberts' works, including her poetry and short stories. Offers a short biography of her life, which was mostly spent in Springfield, Kentucky.

Rovit, Earl H. *Herald to Chaos: The Novels of Elizabeth Madox Roberts*. Lexington: University of Kentucky Press, 1960. A wonderful critique of Roberts' novels, probably the best one available. Rovit describes Roberts' style in a sensitive and perceptive manner and places her in the context of American, not simply Southern, literature.

SINCLAIR ROSS

Born: Shellbrook, Canada; January 22, 1908

Principal long fiction

As for Me and My House, 1941; *The Well*, 1958; *Whir of Gold*, 1970; *Sawbones Memorial*, 1974.

Other literary forms

The Lamp at Noon and Other Stories (1968) is a volume of ten short stories available in a New Canadian Library (McClelland and Stewart) paperback edition. A later collection, *The Race and Other Stories*, appeared in 1982. In addition to their intrinsic merit, the short stories are important as proving grounds for many of the plots, themes, and characters of Ross's novels.

Achievements

The fact that *As for Me and My House*, Ross's first novel and the one on which his reputation rested for many years, was published in the United States and not in his native land is indicative of his early struggle for recognition in Canada. Previously, he had published several short stories that gained little attention, perhaps because of their rather somber view of the human condition as reflected in the lives of the characters: Canadian prairie dwellers during the Depression. A few copies of *As for Me and My House* sold in Canada, but the reading public there was not interested in the Canadian West, a region apart from the rest of the world, and the merits of the novel went largely unappreciated until publication of the New Canadian Library paperback edition in 1957. Today, *As for Me and My House* holds a secure place among the classics of Canadian fiction. Like Mark Twain's *The Adventures of Huckleberry Finn* (1884) and F. Scott Fitzgerald's *The Great Gatsby* (1925), it is a parable by which a country can measure its imaginative life. In its complex rendering of humans struggling with inner conflict and the psychological effects of landscape and the elements, and in its richly resonant language, it surpasses the best of Frederick Philip Grove, the leading prairie realist before Ross, and it maps a fictional terrain that continued to be explored by Margaret Laurence, Rudy Wiebe, Robert Kroetsch, and others. Though his next two novels, *The Well* and *Whir of Gold*, fail to match the achievement of *As for Me and My House*, a renewing fourth novel, *Sawbones Memorial*, is of high quality.

In his best fiction, a sentence or two of Ross's lean, spare, honest prose can illuminate the life of an entire community. In his best fiction, too, Ross has the ability to identify with his characters and with their time and place.

Margaret Laurence once said that "he got his time and place in the prairies exactly right." Ross could not have asked for a more satisfying tribute.

Biography

A very private man, Sinclair Ross is reticent about his personal life and prefers to let his art speak for him. A few articles, interviews, and recollections of friends, however, make it possible to piece together at least the outward facts of his life.

Born January 22, 1908, in northern Saskatchewan, James Sinclair Ross was the third child of Peter and Catherine Ross, who met and married in Prince Albert, Saskatchewan, in 1897. Peter had been born on an Ontario farm to Scottish parents, and Catherine had been born in Scotland. When he was three, Ross's parents separated, his mother taking custody of him and his father taking the two older children. After the separation, Mrs. Ross found employment as a housekeeper on several farms. Ross assisted with farm chores and learned the vagaries of horses and men, as well as the daunting effects of landscape and climate on the prairie dwellers. He retained strong memories of his isolation in those years.

After he was graduated from high school in 1924, Ross went to work for the Royal Bank of Canada, his sole employer until his retirement in 1968. In 1933, the bank rewarded Ross's stints in several small Saskatchewan towns by sending him to Winnipeg, Manitoba, where he remained until 1946, except for World War II military service, and finally to Montreal. Upon retirement, he lived in Greece for three years and then moved to Spain in 1971. Culture and climate (he suffers from arthritis) influenced Ross's decision to live by the Mediterranean Sea. Competent in Spanish and French, somewhat less so in Greek, Ross reads the original versions of the literatures of these languages. Living abroad, he believes, has given him a stronger sense of his Canadian identity. Although the pattern of Ross's life is one of gradual withdrawal eastward from the pioneer prairies toward older, more cosmopolitan cultures, his true subject and setting remain the Canadian prairies, specifically rural Saskatchewan and its people.

Few of Ross's colleagues at the bank knew him as a writer, though he has always been a "compulsive scribbler," he says, despite having had "so little success." Given his isolation from any real literary community, some of Ross's determination to write, mostly at night after long days at the bank, must be credited to his mother, the strongest influence in his life and a model for some of the women in his fiction. Ever conscious of her moral and intellectual refinement (her father had studied theology at the University of Edinburgh, taught at Oberlin College in Ohio, and eventually been ordained a Unitarian minister), Catherine encouraged her young son to take piano lessons, experiment with oil painting, and read widely. In particular, Ross remembers reading Sir Walter Scott, Charles Dickens, and Thomas Hardy, whose *The Return of the Native* (1878) may well have influenced him, he says, though he has never been aware of any literary influences. For many years he had to support his mother as well as himself in the succession of small towns and cities to which she followed him, making it impossible to resign from the bank to devote his full energy to writing.

Ross's most productive period was the 1930's. Many of his best short stories were published then; one of them, "No Other Way," won third prize in a competition for unpublished writers. In 1941, *As for Me and My House* appeared. Ross had already destroyed the manuscripts of two earlier, unsatisfactory novels, and would later destroy another, a possibly autobiographical story of a Canadian soldier from Manitoba written during World War II.

Discouraged by the reception of *As for Me and My House*, Ross did not publish his second novel, *The Well*, until 1958, but it was greeted with even less enthusiasm than his first. *The Well* was influenced by his negative reaction to Montreal, where for twenty-two years the ascetic Ross lived largely within himself, avoiding the "literary swim," as he calls it. Much of his third novel, *Whir of Gold*, was also written in Montreal, then completed after retirement. Written in Europe, his fourth novel, *Sawbones Memorial*, is a forgiving reminiscence of the prairies as Ross knew them in the 1930's and 1940's. Bearing an obvious kinship to its predecessors, it is nevertheless a more mellow novel, striking a better balance between humorous detachment and bitterness, rejection, and grudging nostalgia. If his new awareness of his Canadian identity ensures continued psychic access to the time and place that is the strongest foundation of his art, Canadian literature and Ross's readers both stand to benefit.

Analysis

Despite his relatively small output and rather limited fictional world, Sinclair Ross succeeds in universalizing the human concerns of his novels. Drought, poverty, and the hardship and anxiety they cause are universal concerns, but life on the Canadian prairies in the 1930's and 1940's becomes in Ross's works a paradigm of the human condition everywhere. Moreover, at its most intense there is a characteristic mood in Ross's fiction, a synthesis of human isolation, claustrophobia, and threatening nature, that serves as his trademark, making his writing as distinctive and recognizable as that of his contemporaries Ernest Hemingway and William Faulkner.

"Most writers," Ross has said, "have only one or two themes that they constantly develop in their work." Actually, Ross has three: communication, or more often the failure of communication, in human relationships; the struggle to find an authentic self and live a fulfilled existence; and man's struggle against the land and the elements. In Ross's novels, man-woman relationships, in particular, are vitiated by a failure to communicate, or even a failure to attempt communication. In *As for Me and My House*, the Bentleys are isolated from each other by their emotional and psychological shortcomings. In *The Well*, a generation gap of attitudes and values separates the old farmer, Larson, and his young wife, Sylvia. In *Whir of Gold*, Sonny McAlpine's emotional immaturity and prairie Calvinist attitudes destroy his chances of happiness with the good-hearted prostitute, Madelaine. Among the prairie homesteaders, poverty, climate, physical toil, pessimism about the future, and a repressive Puritan morality are hardly conducive to romance.

Writing about women in Canadian and American prairie fiction, the novelist Robert Kroetsch asks, "How do you establish any sort of *close* relationship in a landscape—in a physical situation—whose primary characteristic is distance?" Thwarted in their attempts at closeness, Ross's women become domineering and manipulative (Mrs. Bentley), sexually aggressive (Sylvia), or maternal and possessive (Madelaine). Love becomes a power struggle. The women's superior social and intellectual backgrounds, or their emotional needs, cause them to treat their men as sons rather than lovers. As for the men in Ross's novels, Oedipal overtones—their failure in heterosexual love, their need for mothering women, the lack of adequate father figures in their youth, for example—are present in the principal male characters, and may conceal a latent homosexuality which Ross does not overtly confront until *Sawbones Memorial*. Indeed, Ross's men seem to have better rapport with animals than with other people, and the best-written passages in his later novels are those involving animals, especially horses. Horses serve as companions or as daring symbols of sexuality, independence, and the imaginative life.

For the artist, a recurrent figure in Ross's world of outsiders and misfits, the failure of communication is especially acute. The aspirations of the artist find little nourishment in prairie society, or—by implication—in Canada and North America as a whole. The failure of Ross's struggling painters and musicians to communicate their vision is symptomatic of the larger failure of the national imagination. In *As for Me and My House*, Philip Bentley's paintings are as stillborn as his first child. In *Whir of Gold*, Sonny McAlpine's musical ambition is blunted by prairie attitudes that burden him even in distant Montreal. In this respect, Sonny, like Philip, is a typical Canadian literary protagonist, incapable of great art or memorable literary heroism on account of the domination of a persistent puritanism. The failed artist as modern literary hero is a familiar type, best exemplified perhaps by James Joyce's Stephen Dedalus, but when the Canadian protagonist discovers he is in disagreement with the dictates of the system, whether religious, social, or other, his peculiar Calvinist-Puritan conditioning causes him to blame himself, internalizing the tension and engaging in painful and destructive soul-searching in an attempt to discover his deficiencies.

Philip Bentley's self-absorption and his unfinished pictures of headless figures and the false fronts of the town are a measure of the frustration of his search for meaning and significance in life. In this respect, Philip and the other artist-protagonists in Ross's fiction represent man's search in modern North America for an authentic existence, either by coming to terms with a repressive social, cultural, and natural environment (the Canadian way) or by overthrowing it entirely (formerly the American way). Ross's characters are locked into themselves and unable to find a means of escape. This in turn leads to a withholding of emotion and strained relationships devoid of real communication. The trap preventing self-realization in Canada has been called by Northrop Frye the "garrison mentality," the tendency of frontier societies to barricade themselves psychologically and culturally against the alien wilderness behind the ordered "civilized" propriety of a transported Eastern culture, rather than adapt to the new environment. The superficial Christianity that Bentley practices, for example, is inadequate to reconcile man with nature on the prairie; there are hints in *As for Me and My House* that a natural, pastoral paganism would be more helpful. Frozen in its own negations and reinforced in the Depression by an overwhelming sense of failure, Christianity engenders guilt and self-destructive behavior (in the turning to crime of the protagonists of *Whir of Gold* and *The Well*, for example), rather than encouraging self-realizing ambition, individualism, and instinct.

Indeed, by the time Ross came to write *The Well* and *Whir of Gold*, he felt that the real wilderness was in the human chaos of the modern city. The true prairie, as opposed to the garrison, was regenerative; it was the way to redemption and self-realization. Completely alienated from society, the criminal is the ultimate outsider, but in *The Well*, Chris Rowe, the small-time Montreal thug hiding out on a prairie farm, does find regeneration in nature, the courage to face punishment for his crimes, and probably an authentic existence within the community of prairie dwellers. Whereas in *The Well* a life in nature regenerates a young criminal, in *Whir of Gold*, his experience in the city almost destroys Sonny McAlpine. The keys to survival are his nostalgic recollections of his prairie upbringing, especially those involving his horse, which serve as an anchor of self and identity amid the disorientation and venality of Montreal.

Ross's third major theme, man's struggle with the land and the elements, probably derives from experience and observation as well as from his reading of the literary naturalists, especially Thomas Hardy. Moods are known to be affected by climate and geography, but on the prairies of Ross's novels, as on Hardy's moors, characters and their relationships seem to be deterministically influenced by wind, heat, drought, dust, rain, snow, and ice. The psychological and emotional toll these elements exact lead characters to regard nature as part of an indifferent, even hostile universe. Ross was also, however, the first of the Canadian prairie realists to go beyond this naturalistic treatment of the landscape; not only are his characters psychologically conditioned by the prairie, but they also project their own subjectivity onto the external environment. In effect, they interact with it, so that not only is character determined by external environment, but environment also becomes an extension of the mind. Its challenge can test and strengthen the endurance of those who survive, uniting them in the common struggle against it; it can be a regenerative sanctuary for an urban fugitive such as Chris Rowe.

The defeated ones find little in religion to sustain the human spirit, at least the version of it proferred by prairie Christianity. One of Philip Bentley's redeeming qualities is precisely that he cannot believe in deliverance through a faith reduced to hollow forms and meaningless rituals that hypocritically ignore the Christian virtues of charity and compassion. In a deeper sense, however, Ross is a religious writer in that the underlying concern of his fiction is man's struggle "with the implacable blunderings of Nature" in an indifferent universe. In the face of this daunting situation, Ross holds up rationalists and humanists, such as Mrs. Bentley and Paul Kirby in *As for Me and My House* and Doc Hunter in *Sawbones Memorial*, who stake their faith on human courage, reason, and idealism, "all the things that really are humanity," in Mrs. Bentley's words. Others, such as Sonny McAlpine and old Larson, find solace in the illusory world of the past, a youthful world of happiness and material and spiritual well-being, unthreatened by darker realities. If Ross's characters are escapist-dreamers, though, their dreams must sometimes be blown away, like the false fronts of Main Street in a wind storm, to reveal the reality in which a new, authentic self can be forged.

As a youth in Saskatchewan, Ross was encouraged by a United Church minister to enter the ministry rather than banking. Already skeptical about organized religion, although he taught Sunday school and played the organ in church, Ross "was not tempted in the least. But I began to think, 'Suppose I did, or someone else did who did not really believe in it, and felt trapped in the ministry.' That was the origin of *As for Me and My House*." Ross has revealed also that he once knew a minister whose plight resembled Philip Bentley's. Mrs. Bentley appears to have been based, at least in part, on Ross's mother, to judge by his recollections of her.

Like Ross's next two novels, *As for Me and My House* is the story of an inner quest for the authentic self. It thus belongs to a literary genre that includes works as diverse as John Bunyan's *The Pilgrim's Progress* (1678), Johann Wilhelm von Goethe's *Wilhelm Meister's Apprenticeship* (1795-1796), Henry David Thoreau's *Walden* (1854), and Walt Whitman's *Leaves of Grass* (1855). It is also kindred to a large number of Canadian works in which the search for personal and national identity is a dominant theme. Ross's ironic vision is nowhere better illustrated than in the fact that Bentley's search for an authentic self compels him to reject the church's way, which is to follow the teachings of Jesus Christ. Finally, he tears down the facade of his old self, but the new, authentic self must be forged in the secular, humanist crucible of art rather than in the empty chalice of the church. Sandra Djwa's perception of the "latter-day Puritanism of the psychological search for self," in a world where "Christianity has become a meaningless form without spirit, where people must learn to reject the false gods without before it it is possible to find the true God within and an authentic sense of direction," suggests the continuing contemporaneity of the book, if one thinks of the self-realization movements of the 1960's and 1970's.

As for Me and My House is a taut, intense, and bitter record of repressed, static lives in rural Saskatchewan in the 1930's. It deals with the Bentleys' year in Horizon, the fourth small-town prairie residence in twelve years for the thirty-five-year-old minister and his wife. Told in journal form by Mrs. Bentley, the book is an indictment of puritanical moral attitudes and cultural sterility. It is also bleakly pessimistic about the possibility of communication in human relationships, especially marriage. Outsiders by virtue of their position in the community and their parishioners' awareness that to them Horizon is merely a way station in a stultifying series of prairie pastorates, the Bentleys are estranged from the townsfolk as well as from each other. With no real vocation as a minister of the gospel, Bentley wants to believe he has some talent as a painter, but his daubing shows little evidence of this, mainly because his creativity is frozen by self-lacerating guilt arising from his clerical charade.

Embittered by his failure as a minister and twelve years of entrapment in drought and depression-ridden prairie towns, Philip seeks consolation through an adopted son whose natural father had abandoned him, but—in keeping with the melancholy pattern of discontinuity between the generations in Ross—societal pressure (the boy's Catholicism is unacceptable, as is his parental background) forces the Bentleys to give up their son. Philip lacks a natural father as well as a son. Having sired Philip illegitimately, his father died before he was born; Philip's own child was stillborn. Despite, or on account of, the scorn to which his illegitimacy subjected him, Philip followed his father's path, first into the ministry and then into art. He saw the church's offer of an education in return for a commitment to the ministry as a means of escaping humiliation, but planned to leave it quickly for a painting career. He is prevented from doing so by an inanition of the soul that arises from marital responsibilities, economic conditions, and guilt over abandoning his flock. Adultery seems briefly to offer a way out for Philip, but Mrs. Bentley soon learns of it, and the other woman dies giving birth to Philip's child. In what can be interpreted as a hopeful conclusion, though, the Bentleys adopt this child, and with the money Mrs. Bentley has saved, they leave Horizon for a city life as owners of a used bookstore. Their hope is that the bookstore will allow Philip time to pursue his painting without the crippling emotional and psychological burdens of the past.

The essence of Ross's achievement in *As for Me and My House* lies in the rich complexity of character and theme realized through brilliant manipulation of point of view and language. For almost three decades after the book's publication, it was assumed that Mrs. Bentley's reporting was accurate and that her point of view was reliable. Certainly, if the reader accepts the point of view of her journal, then the town and her husband both fail her. She is the long-suffering, supportive wife, the superior woman languishing in a cultural and domestic wasteland. As late as 1957, in his introduction to the New Canadian Library edition of the book, Roy Daniells called her "pure gold and wholly credible." If the reader accepts Ross's implicit invitation to read between the lines, however, Mrs. Bentley's self-indulgent meanness, her lonely pride, and her manipulation of Philip to satisfy her own ego are the reasons for her defeat and, to some extent, her husband's. The many inconsistencies and outright contradictions in her journal suggest that her single perspective is actually a source of considerable ambiguity in the book and of ambivalence on the reader's part. Several questions are raised: How accurate are her perceptions and assessments of her husband and the townspeople? How accurate are her perceptions of her own behavior and attitudes? Is the fact that the reader never learns her first name a clue to how *non*-revealing her journal is? In 1969, William H. New argued that the reader's ambivalence toward Mrs. Bentley arises not so much from uncertainty about her credibility as from Ross's ironically pitting the reader's viewpoint against hers in such a way that the reader comes to appreciate the depth and complexity of the narrator's situation, and Ross's control of his material. Through ironic use of symbols such as lamps, moths, Philip's study door, railroad tracks, and the false fronts of Horizon's main street, and through imagery involving gardens, horses, heat, dust, rain, snow and the prairie itself, Ross reveals Mrs. Bentley's journal to be an exercise in self-deception and evasiveness. In the final analysis, this book about communication and its failure informs the reader of the impossibility of taking sides, despite the human inclination to do so.

When *The Well* was published in 1958, Ross had been living in Montreal for twelve years. The new urban environment awakened an interest in the motivations of the criminal mind, while remoteness from the prairie prompted a realization of its regenerative potential. In *As for Me and My House*, Philip Bentley leaves the prairie to seek an authentic self in the city; in *The Well*, Chris Rowe flees the city and achieves authentic selfhood through his moral regeneration on the prairie. Apart from this about-face, the two novels bear a close kinship. Once more the setting is rural Saskatchewan; once more the characters fail to communicate and are claustrophobically trapped by the past as well as the present; once more they are psychologically conditioned by the prairie environment, while projecting their own subjectivity onto it; and once more there is discontinuity between the generations.

The Well is a story of three barren misfits whose lives converge in the little prairie community of Campkin in the 1940's. The central character, Chris Rowe, is a fatherless twenty-year-old criminal from Montreal whose petty larcenies have culminated in the shooting of an intended robbery victim whose

Critical Survey of Long Fiction

fate the novel leaves in doubt. Handsome, tough, and arrogant, Chris nevertheless has a potentially sensitive, gentle, nature which has been brutalized
by his urban upbringing. Fleeing on westbound trains to escape arrest, Chris
accepts an offer of farm work in Campkin, his intention being to maintain a
low profile for a while before resuming his westward flight. He soon finds
himself enmeshed, however, in a conflict for domination over him between
Larson, his employer, and Larson's wife, Sylvia.

Like Chris, Larson is pursued by the past. Ten years before, Larson's first
wife had died; his son, also named Chris, died soon after. Grief has warped
Larson's mind several degrees beyond eccentricity, despite outward symbols
of material success such as his Cadillac and new young wife. Pathetically
trying to relive the past, Larson makes a virtual shrine of the old homestead
he began with his first wife. Its chief icon is the well they dug together, a
symbol of their shared achievement and happy union. Larson also keeps a
horse with the same name as his dead son's horse, and he even imagines that
Chris Rowe is the dead son returned. He treats Chris as a surrogate son,
assuming he will take over the farm eventually and reestablish continuity with
the Edenic past. To the extent that Larson's aversion to the present stems
from his longing for the pretechnological past when farming offered pride of
individual accomplishment and close identity with the soil, Ross is sounding
a theme found in other prairie realists such as Grove and Laurence: the human
costs of increasing technology on the prairie farms. As usual, Ross's focus is
on the dynamics of one or two human relationships, but *The Well* can be read
as a work of social criticism that probes, as Robert Chambers, in his *Sinclair
Ross and Ernest Ruckler* (1975), states, "some neglected side effects of that
new prairie trinity: mechanization, mobility, and money."

Larson's wife, the voluptuous, ambitious Sylvia, had married Larson five
years earlier to escape the poverty and drudgery of life as a waitress in
Campkin. Partly because of a thirty-year age difference, there is neither love
nor communication between them; in fact, Sylvia's plan is to kill Larson and
abscond with his money. If Mrs. Bentley's designs for Philip are manipulative,
those of Sylvia for Chris are evil and predatory. Her fantasy is that the
adulterous relationship that quickly develops between them will make it easier
to coerce Chris into helping her murder Larson, stuff his body down the well,
and persuade the townspeople that he suddenly left on a train, as he often
talked of doing. After a judicious interval, the two would marry and retire to
California. In a lurid climax, Sylvia shoots her husband after wresting the gun
from Chris, whose loyalty to his new surrogate father prevents him from doing
so. Sylvia is eventually forced out of the house, never to be seen again. Larson
expires, but not before he has written a note indicting Sylvia, exculpating
Chris, and leaving the farm to him as well. Chris still faces uncertain punishment for the Montreal shooting, but the important thing is that he now has
the courage to do so. His refusal to be further tempted into crime by Sylvia,

coupled with his loyalty to Larson, is redemptive. Once free of the entra-
melling past, his best instincts released by the regenerative powers of nature
and the rhythms of farm life, Chris will have a chance to achieve authentic
selfhood, an end to alienation, and even community with the prairie dwellers.

If *As for Me and My House* is Ross's best novel, *The Well* is in many ways
his weakest. Ross has admitted his failure to "get inside" the criminal mind
to make Chris Rowe a sympathetic character. The ending is wildly melodramatic, as Ross has also acknowledged. "I would like to do it again and give
it a different ending," he has said. "I see now how it should be done." The
book suffers also from a thinness of texture, a lack of intensity and power,
attributable to Ross's decision to substitute the flat, banal language of barely
literate characters for the richly metaphorical prose of *As for Me and My
House*, and to the general lack of complexity of character, theme, and point
of view. In view of these flaws, the book's cool reception seems justified.

In two important ways, *Whir of Gold*, Ross's third novel, is a reverse image
of *The Well*. The latter is a Rousseauistic study of a victim of urban corruption
in Montreal whose innate goodness is brought out by the morally regenerative
life in nature; the former is a Hobbesian study of the nasty and brutish life
of a prairie youth in the same city. Again, a man and a woman compete for
domination of the young hero, but whereas in *The Well* the man is basically
decent, despite his misfortunes in life, and the woman grotesquely evil, in
Whir of Gold the reverse is true. In other ways, *Whir of Gold* resembles *The
Well* quite closely. Like Chris Rowe, Sonny McAlpine is arrogant, alienated,
and female-dominated. Like Chris, Sonny is drawn into crime. In common
with both of the earlier novels, *Whir of Gold* is concerned with entrapment,
the failure of communication, and the baneful influence of the past. Its conclusion is more pessimistic than those of Ross's previous novels. Indeed, Sonny
McAlpine's struggle and eventual defeat as a musician may represent Ross's
pessimistic answer to the question of whether Philip Bentley's move to the
city will really enable him to develop an authentic self. In the thirty years
between *As for Me and My House* and *Whir of Gold*, Ross seems to have
concluded that neither the rural nor urban environment in Canada is capable
of nourishing the artistic imagination.

The plot is simple and familiar, sometimes to the point of cliché. Determined to prove his superior musical talent and plagued by guilt over his
sensible choice of a career in popular rather than classical music in the Saskatchewan farm community where he was reared, the young, innocent Sonny
takes his clarinet to Montreal, but competition and commercialism in the
wicked city combine to thwart his ambitions. Out of money and hope, he is
contemplating retreat to the West when he meets Madelaine, a good-hearted
nightclub floozie as lonely as he. Mad, as she is called, is from Nova Scotia,
a place as remote in spirit from Montreal as is Saskatchewan. Comrades in
alienation, the two decide to live together in Sonny's skid-row rooming house

immediately after a first-night sexual encounter. More spontaneous and generous than other female characters in Ross's works, Mad nevertheless had comparable plans for her man. Once he is sexually involved with her, her idea is to return with him to Nova Scotia, where they will manage a restaurant, and live a simple, healthy life far from the psychological rat race and moral wasteland of Montreal. In effect, she tries to trap Sonny into domesticity, as Sylvia tried to trap Chris Rowe through her plot to kill Larson.

As Mad sees it, the chief obstacle to this scheme is Sonny's neighbor, Charlie, the only other character of consequence in the small, claustrophobic world of the novel. A small-time, street-mean crook, Charlie exploits Sonny's weaknesses (primarily, a self-destructive urge arising from the guilt he feels about wasting his musical talent) to involve him, against the vehement opposition of Mad, in robbing a jewelry store. In the robbery, Sonny is shot and is himself robbed of his share of the loot by Charlie. The relationship between Sonny and Mad is likewise doomed, as are most male-female relationships in Ross's novels. The protagonist's emotional immaturity causes him unconsciously to seek an Oedipal relationship, which Mad's need to mother conveniently satisfies. Because of his insecurity, however, Sonny is unwilling to risk commitment, treating Mad's mothering as a smothering possessiveness, and her praise of his sexual prowess as proof of his limited talent. Ross implies that Sonny's past background, specifically his repressive prairie puritanism, is largely responsible for both his lack of feeling for Mad and his guilt over his shabby treatment of her.

Sonny, it appears, was Mad's "whir of gold," a fleeting vision of happiness, beauty, and self-fulfillment. The book's title and central symbol derives from an incident in Sonny's childhood. Out of curiosity and cruelty, he once pursued and killed a flicker bird in an attempt to capture it. The bird's wings "flashed like a whir of gold, a gust of feathered light," before it died. Years later, his pursuit of a musical career leads to the deathly alienation of the criminal world, and his aborted relationship with Mad to the bleak realization, once she leaves, that he has rejected probably the best chance for happiness he will ever have. The whir of gold is a fragile thing, impossible to capture. To attempt to do so is to destroy it, and also to destroy oneself through its false promise of permanence.

Ross's deep pessimism about human relationships in *Whir of Gold* is presaged in much of his earlier fiction, where Puritan constraints conflict with the human instinct for beauty, imagination, freedom, and daring. Sonny has an innate predilection for these, but his farm upbringing and moral background have indoctrinated him with practicality, restraint, discipine, and caution, values dictated also by a prudent regard for the often hostile natural elements of the prairie. Not that beauty, imagination, freedom, and daring flourish in Montreal, but Sonny's failure there is partly a deterministic result of his projection of prairie attitudes onto the city, just as earlier Ross characters projected their fears onto the external prairie environment.

Unfortunately, *Whir of Gold* is not a powerfully realized novel. It does not make a profound or relevant statement about psychological repression and cultural alienation. In deferring to trends in popular fiction—inarticulate characters, limited lives, disjointed language, sordid settings—Ross denies it depth of meaning. Referring to the novel's "desperate brand of naturalism," Robert Chambers points out that "Ross's pages are covered with mundane and trivial things, as though the endless plates of bacon and eggs and all those nice hot cups of coffee will somehow cohere to underpin a work of art." The use of Sonny's first-person point of view weakens the novel further. Sonny is a vapid Candide, a vacuous Ulysses, and the other characters mere literary extensions of his personality. Ross professes an interest in the motivations of the criminal mind (though he admits he probably lacks sufficient insight), but Sonny is incapable of understanding Charlie's character or his own drift toward crime. Similarly, the forays into metaphorical language, so successful in *As for Me and My House*, seem artificially literary because they are inappropriate to Sonny's character. Again, *As for Me and My House* is rich in symbols, but the present novel has only two of any significance: the whir of gold and Sonny's horse, Isobel. Finally, the structure of the book is poorly balanced, with the central Sonny-Mad relationship starved for development in the second half because of Ross's increasing preoccupation with the robbery.

Apart from its successful interweaving of several perspectives in time, *Whir of Gold* did not advance Ross's reputation as a novelist any more than did *The Well*. In fact, it confirmed the uneasy doubts of some that Ross was a one-book author who had reached his peak in his first novel. Perhaps he was essentially a short-story writer, albeit a good one, lacking the technical resources or sustaining vision required of the novelist.

Sawbones Memorial reassured the doubters by proving convincingly that Ross was more than a one-book novelist, though its success is attributable in part to a form which utilizes the economy and precision of the short story. It succeeds also because in it Ross returns to the time and place he knows best, the Canadian prairies during the 1930's. Like *As for Me and My House*, it has a central intelligence who is perceptive and ironically detached. Unlike the two-or-three-person relationships he minutely dissects in earlier novels, Ross creates a large, diverse cast of thirty characters in *Sawbones Memorial*; and while the townspeople seem no less petty and narrow-minded than before, those on the side of life, a generous and enlightened few, dominate the action in his fourth novel. If, as Ronald Sutherland insists, a new Canadian literary hero has replaced the old, Doc Hunter must be counted a member of the new breed. Certainly his self-reliance, independence, and acceptance of life are preferable to Philip Bentley's intense struggle with his demons of guilt and self-doubt. Perhaps, as one reviewer stated, Ross himself "has stopped fighting life and come to terms with it." Perhaps the fact that the book was written in retirement in Europe, at several removes in time and space from Ross's Saskatchewan of the 1930's, explains the mellow, often humorous tone. In any case, the book is more hopeful than any of its predecessors, despite its return to some of Ross's familiar, depressing themes.

Sawbones Memorial is actually a collection of reminiscent vignettes depicting life in Upward, the small town that Doc Hunter has ministered to through forty-five years of pioneering, drought, and depression. The *raison d'être* of the vignettes is a ceremony held in April, 1948, to mark the doctor's retirement and the opening of the new Hunter Memorial Hospital. Accordingly, both reminiscing and looking to the future are in order. Though the action is limited to a few hours of the present, by the end of the novel Ross has roamed back and forth through four generations and several decades to lay bare the attitudes and preoccupations, the tensions and antagonisms, and the hypocrisies and prejudices of Upward's citizens.

Representing the full diversity of the community, the characters include farmers, storekeepers, teachers, ministers, and housewives, people old and young, living and dead, absent and present. They do not develop psychologically so much as they show the effects of time. Through the episodes in which they appear and reappear, they comment on the action, on Doc Hunter, and on one another. Occasionally, the same incident is retold by different characters, the contrasting viewpoints giving rise to comic or tragic irony. Little by little, the reader comes to know the characters. Doc Hunter's is the unifying point of view for those of the thirty characters whose stories constitute the book; conversely, the reader comes to know him through his shamanlike role in the lives of the other characters. The central character and intelligence, Doc is also the focus of attention at the gathering, as he has been the focus of the town's hopes and fears for over four decades. His own suffering, it is implied, broadens and deepens the efficacy of his mission as a doctor. It seems he was married too long to a frigid wife, and thus shares with other Ross protagonists an unfulfilled emotional life, though his experience has neither embittered him nor lessened his philosophical tolerance of human imperfection, of which there is God's plenty in Upward.

As with many fictional studies of small towns, from Winesburg, Ohio, to Peyton Place and beyond, Upward's appearance of respectability, especially its straitlaced attitudes concerning sexual morality, conceals a closetful of skeletons: rape, abortion, incest, murder, euthanasia, to name only a few. As the town's sole physician for almost half a century, Doc Hunter knows the contents of the closet better than anyone, a fact that gives pause to those who would prefer to forget their past in order to gossip more self-righteously. The more admirable characters, on the other hand, are often outsiders, defined as anyone who deviates from Upward's conventional standards of moral and social behavior. More so than Ross's earlier outsider-protagonist, these are very human characters whose struggles and triumphs the readers can share.

Sawbones Memorial is also more ambitious in form and conception than Ross's earlier novels. The large number of characters, the experimentation with multiple points of view, the reliance on dialogue, monologue, speeches, and flashbacks to convey information, reveal personality, and establish mood (much as in drama and film), are all new. The dialogue is especially remarkable in that each character is individuated through diction, idiom, intonation, or rhythm. (Ross has said that the idea of using nothing but the speech of his characters to construct a novel came to him as he overheard fragments of reminiscences at the opening of the Royal Bank's new head office in Montreal.) It is true that the book turns against two familiar themes, the failure of communication and the stultification of the spirit in the small prairie towns of Ross's time. The roots of man's alienation, whether personal or social, are still to be found in his agonized confusion over sexuality, but Ross deals with a larger range of human experience than before, including such timeless concerns as the nature of human evil and the evil of human nature, birth and death, youth and age, courage and cowardice, cruelty and compassion. For one day in time, at least, in the spring of 1948, these are reconciled as Doc Hunter speaks of retirement and the continuity symbolized by the new doctor's arrival. It is all beginning again, "just as it was all beginning that day" when he first arrived.

John H. Ferres

Other major works

SHORT FICTION: *The Lamp at Noon and Other Stories*, 1968; *The Race and Other Stories*, 1982.

Bibliography

Denham, Paul. "Narrative Techniques in Sinclair Ross's *As for Me and My House*." *Studies in Canadian Literature* 5 (Spring, 1980): 116-124. Denham's article, accompanied by useful source footnotes, illuminates Ross's enigmatic novel through a careful examination of its narrative techniques.

Djwa, Sandra. "No Other Way: Sinclair Ross's Stories and Novels." *Canadian Literature* 47 (Winter, 1971): 49-66. In her clear, readable essay, Djwa celebrates the stern, enduring characters of Ross's works as manifestations of an essentially "Canadian" personality. Enhanced by useful footnotes.

McMullen, Lorraine. *Sinclair Ross*. New York: Twayne, 1979. In the introduction (which provides new biographical insights), the separate chapters on Ross's works, and a brief conclusion, McMullen offers a thoughtful, invaluable assessment of Ross's achievement in his four novels and eighteen short stories.

Moss, John. "Mrs. Bentley and the Bicameral Mind: A Hermeneutical Encounter with *As for Me and My House*." In *Modern Times*. Vol. 3 in *The Canadian Novel*. Toronto: NC Press, 1982. Despite its pretentious title and Moss's sometimes arch tone, this study offers an interesting examination of Ross's most celebrated novel as a textual labyrinth with protagonist Mrs. Bentley as the guide.

Stuewe, Paul. "Some Neglected Alternatives: Ross, Buckler, MacLennan, Wilson, and Others." In *Clearing the Ground: English-Canadian Literature After "Survival."* Toronto: Proper Tales Press, 1984. Within the context of his spirited attack on Canadian criticism and its preoccupation with theme, Stuewe concisely discusses Ross's strengths as a writer by examining his four novels.

Williams, David, et al. "Opinions and Notes." *Canadian Literature* 103 (Winter, 1984): 156-186. Four essays by four different critics comprise this section devoted to Ross. The essays reassess Ross's best-known novel *As for Me and My House*, examine the importance of language in his works, explicate his "pioneer" fiction, and discuss the illusions contained in his short story "One's A Heifer," respectively.

PHILIP ROTH

Born: Newark, New Jersey; March 19, 1933

Principal long fiction

Letting Go, 1962; *When She Was Good*, 1967; *Portnoy's Complaint*, 1969; *Our Gang*, 1971; *The Breast*, 1972, revised 1980; *The Great American Novel*, 1973; *My Life as a Man*, 1974; *The Professor of Desire*, 1977; *The Ghost Writer*, 1979; *Zuckerman Unbound*, 1981; *The Anatomy Lesson*, 1983; *Zuckerman Bound*, 1985 (includes *The Ghost Writer*, *Zuckerman Unbound*, *The Anatomy Lesson*, and *Epilogue: The Prague Orgy*); *The Counterlife*, 1987; *Deception*, 1990.

Other literary forms

Five of Philip Roth's short stories are collected along with his novella *Goodbye, Columbus* in a volume bearing that title (1959). A number of his essays, interviews, and autobiographical pieces appear in *Reading Myself and Others* (1975). An unproduced screenplay, *The Great American Pastime*, was anthologized in 1968, and two of his works, *Goodbye, Columbus* and *Portnoy's Complaint*, have been made into films by others. In 1975, Roth began editing a series called Writers from the Other Europe for Penguin Books, to which he contributed several introductions. *The Facts: A Novelist's Autobiography* appeared in 1988.

Achievements

Ever since Roth's first published book, *Goodbye, Columbus*, won the National Book Award in 1960, he has been acclaimed as a leading Jewish-American writer along with Saul Bellow and Bernard Malamud. The grouping is somewhat misleading, as each of these novelists has a unique voice and an approach to contemporary issues that is peculiarly his own, and each of them has written novels that have no Jews at all in them. It is undeniable, however, that all three are vitally interested in the social and moral dilemmas facing modern people, particularly Jewish Americans. If Malamud once remarked, "All men are Jews," referring to the marginal nature of human existence, Roth believes that "All Jews are men"—that is, Jews have the same attributes, attitudes, and problems that other human beings have.

Like Bellow, Roth has become increasingly absorbed in the problematic nature of love relationships, not only between man and woman but also between father and son, brother and brother, neighbor and neighbor. In addition, he has taken as his special concern the relation between a writer and his critics, or between a writer and the society in which he lives. His fictional accounts of Jewish family relationships and illicit love affairs involving Jews in his early work made him notorious among the conservative Jewish establishment, although subsequently the notoriety seems to have died down. Readers have become either more accepting or less concerned with issues that once inflamed an older generation. In his later work, Roth has brilliantly presented the fascinating relationship between fiction and autobiography, using fictional surrogates, such as Nathan Zuckerman, to explore what he calls "counterlives," or the idea of an alternative existence to one actually lived.

Throughout his fiction, Roth exhibits the abilities of a master comedian. He has arguably the best ear of any contemporary writer, capturing the spoken voice in a wide variety of accents, intonations, and cadences, but his facility with dialogue has sometimes led critics to miss the serious undercurrents of his work. As a satirist, Roth works in a variety of modes, from the social (*Portnoy's Complaint*) to the political (*Our Gang*) to the literary and academic (*The Professor of Desire*). Whatever mode he adopts, he presents the objects of his satire or comedy in vivid and compelling fashion. Once referred to as preeminently a social realist (as in *Goodbye, Columbus*), he has transcended that mode successfully in such works as *The Counterlife* and *Deception*, which show him, as ever, both a consummate craftsman and a tireless experimenter with his medium.

Biography

Born in the Weequahic section of Newark, New Jersey, on March 19, 1933, Philip Roth learned very early what it was like to grow up Jewish in a lower-middle-class neighborhood of a large metropolitan area. His parents were Beth Finkel and Herman Roth, a salesman for the Metropolitan Life Insurance Company. After he was graduated from Weequahic High School in 1950, Roth worked for a while at the Newark Public Library and attended Newark College of Rutgers University. A year later, he transferred to Bucknell University. Although the family could ill afford the expense of a private college, Herman Roth determined that if his son wanted to go there, he would go. At Bucknell, Roth began writing stories and edited the school's literary magazine. He also had his first love affairs, from which he drew incidents (fictionally transformed, of course) for his subsequent novels. He received his B.A. in English, magna cum laude, in 1954, and he accepted a teaching fellowship at the University of Chicago for graduate work in English.

After receiving his M.A. in English from Chicago, Roth enlisted in the United States Army, but a back injury suffered during basic training resulted in an early discharge. He returned to Chicago to pursue doctoral studies in English but continued writing short stories, which had begun to get published as early as the fall of 1954 in small literary journals such as the *Chicago Review* and *Epoch*. Several of his stories were anthologized in Martha Foley's *Best American Short Stories* and in *The O. Henry Prize Stories*. These awards, the success of his first published volume, *Goodbye, Columbus*, a Houghton Mifflin Literary Fellowship, and a Guggenheim Fellowship persuaded Roth to abandon graduate work in English for a career as a creative writer.

While a graduate student and instructor at the University of Chicago, Roth met and later married his first wife, Margaret Martinson Williams. The relationship was never a happy one, and after a few years they separated, Margaret steadfastly refusing to agree to a divorce. Meanwhile, they spent one year of their marriage (1960) at the Writers' Workshop at the University of Iowa, where Philip served on the faculty. After his first full-length novel, *Letting Go*, was published in 1962, he became writer-in-residence at Princeton University. He later taught English literature at the University of Pennsylvania. His experiences as an academic provided much material for novels, many of which have a university setting or are otherwise peopled by academics.

The publication of *Portnoy's Complaint* in 1969, a year after his estranged wife was killed in an automobile accident, launched Roth's greatest notoriety, especially among the conservative Jewish community in America, and assured his fame as a novelist. He became an increasingly prolific writer, spending part of the year in his Connecticut home and part in London in an apartment near his writing studio. For years he has shared his life with the British stage and screen actress Claire Bloom, whom he married in April, 1990. In 1970 he was elected to the National Academy of Arts and Letters.

Analysis

While his early works clearly show the influence of his literary idols— Henry James, Leo Tolstoy, Gustave Flaubert, Thomas Wolfe, and Theodore Dreiser—Philip Roth came into his own as a novelist beginning with *Portnoy's Complaint*, which reveals a unique voice in American literature. His subsequent development parallels his growing interest in other Continental writers, such as Anton Chekhov, Franz Kafka, Fyodor Dostoevski, and particularly contemporary writers such as Milan Kundera, whose works Roth assisted the Czech writer in getting published in America. Roth's first novels are set squarely in his native land: in Newark, where he was born and reared; in the great Midwest, where he went to graduate school; and in New York and Philadelphia, where he lived, wrote, and taught literature at several universities. The protagonists of his later fiction travel abroad to Western and Eastern Europe and as far as Hong Kong. Roth's development as a novelist is thus the development, in part, of a growing cosmopolitanism along with a deepening interest in basic human concerns and predicaments.

Chief among those predicaments is the endless struggle between the id and the superego or, in less Freudian terms, between the drive for sensual gratification and the drive for moral uprightness. On the one hand, pulling at his protagonists (all but one of whom are men) is the powerful desire for sexual conquest; on the other is the almost equally powerful desire to lead a morally self-fulfilling and decent life. These drives, conflicting at almost every turn, nearly tear his protagonists apart. Even when, as at the end of *The Professor of Desire*, David Kepesh believes that he has at least achieved a reasonable equilibrium and found peace, a nagging unease enters the picture, upsetting his contentment and providing a presentiment of doom.

Indeed, Roth's heroes, if we can call such unlikely characters by that term, all seem doomed in one way or another. Their pervasive sense of disaster, however, does not destroy Roth's comedy; it deepens it. The sense of the absurd, of the incongruities of human experience, also pervades Roth's novels and is the source of much rich humor. Moreover, his protagonists usually are fully self-aware; they understand their predicaments with uncommon self-perception, if (more often than not) they are utterly baffled in trying to find a solution to or resolution of their dilemmas. Again, their awareness and frustration combine to make the reader laugh, though the reader must be careful not to let the laughter obscure or nullify the compassion that is also the character's due.

Roth's first full-length novel, *Letting Go*, sets out all these themes and influences. The principal character, Gabe Wallach, is an educated, sophisticated young Easterner of well-off middle-aged parents, who after a brief stint in the army pursues graduate studies in the Midwest. His mother has recently died, leaving her son with a heavy moral burden: not to interfere in the lives of others as she, regretfully, has done. It is a legacy Gabe finds almost impossible to live up to, until the very end, after he has nearly ruined the lives of several people close to him. Before that, he succeeds, however, in remaining aloof from his widower father, who is lonely and adrift and tries to persuade Gabe to return home. This is Gabe's only success, however, as eventually his father meets and marries a widow who helps him rediscover life's pleasures.

Meanwhile, Gabe has his affairs, none of which works out happily, and his friendships, especially with Paul and Libby Herz, whom he meets during graduate school in Iowa. Paul is a hardworking, highly principled young man who married Libby while they were still undergraduates at Cornell. Their mixed marriage—Paul is Jewish, Libby Catholic—is mainly the result of Paul's misguided sense of devotion and responsibility. Although the passion has long since gone out of their relationship, owing to Libby's poor health and neurotic disposition, Paul remains loyal. Together, they struggle with financial and other problems, including opposition from both sets of parents.

Gabe's life and the Herzes' intersect at various points, invariably with well-intentioned but almost disastrous consequences. At Iowa, Gabe tries to befriend the couple, offers various forms of assistance to them, and finds an unusual attractiveness in Libby, which culminates in little more than a kiss. Their affair, such as it is, focuses partly on Henry James's novel, *The Portrait of a Lady* (1881), which Gabe lends to Paul and Libby reads, finding in it the last letter Gabe's mother had written him when she lay dying. Both the novel and the letter help to form a bond between Gabe and Libby that endures.

Later, when Gabe is teaching at the University of Chicago, their relationship resumes when Gabe helps Paul get a job in his department.

Through Martha Reganhart, with whom Gabe has begun to live, Gabe finds someone who is willing to let her unborn baby be adopted by the Herzes. Paul and Libby have wanted a child and nearly had one, but poverty-stricken as they were, Paul persuaded Libby to have an abortion. The incidents surrounding that event are both comical and dreadful. Afterward, Libby's health never becomes robust enough for her to risk conceiving another child; hence, they hope to adopt one. The circumstances of trying to adopt a baby involve episodes best referred to as "deadly farce," including several in which Gabe intervenes on their behalf. At the same time, Gabe's relationship with Martha, a divorcee with two young children, deepens and then falls apart, largely the result of his inability to make a full and lasting commitment.

Gabe and Paul thus represent contrasting studies in personality. At the end, Gabe finally learns to "let go," the lesson his mother tried to teach him from her deathbed, but letting go for him means abandoning lover, friends, family, and career to become a wanderer in Europe, whence he writes Libby a final letter. Forwarded many times, an invitation to her adopted daughter's first birthday party arrives with no other message in it. This Gabe takes as "an invitation to be forgiven" for his nearly catastrophic interference in their lives. Gabe, however, feels unable to accept forgiveness—not yet, anyway. He is not "off the hook," he says, and does not want to be let off it, not until he can make some sense of the "larger hook" he feels he is still on.

The larger hook on which Roth's later protagonists wriggle is precisely the dilemma between commitment and freedom that they all experience. Thus, Alexander Portnoy finds himself torn between his desire to maintain his position as New York's Assistant Commissioner for Human Opportunity, a job of considerable responsibility as well as prestige, and his desire to enjoy the full sexual freedoms heralded by the 1960's. For a while he seems to manage both, until his affair with Mary Jane Reed develops into something else—Mary Jane's wish to get married. Her sexual adroitness—she is called "the Monkey"—has kept them together for more than a year, but this demand for full commitment proves too much for Alex, who abandons her in Athens during a trip to Europe in which they have experienced the ultimate of their sexual adventures. Alex flees to Israel, the land of his forefathers, only to find that when he tries to make love there he is impotent. The experience drives him to seek help from Dr. Otto Spielvogel, a New York psychiatrist.

The novel, in fact, is told as a series of confessions, or therapy sessions, and derives its title from the name Dr. Spielvogel gives to his patient's illness. "Portnoy's Complaint" is "a disorder in which strongly felt ethical and altruistic impulses are perpetually warring with extreme sexual longings, often of a perverse nature." The symptoms of the illness, Spielvogel believes, can be traced to the mother-child relationship, and indeed Portnoy's boyhood has

been fraught with problems, often hilarious ones as he recounts them, occa-
sioned by his stereotypical Jewish mother. Sophie Portnoy is a domineering,
overprotective mother who frequently drives her young son to distraction, as
he tries in vain to understand her demands upon him and her suffocating
affection. Jack Portnoy, his father, long-suffering (mostly from constipation)
and hardworking, seems unable to mitigate the family relationship, exacerbating Alex's quandary. No wonder he grows up as he does, afflicted with the
dilemma, or the condition, Dr. Spielvogel describes. By the end of the novel,
after the long unfolding of his tales of woe, all Alex hears from his therapist
is, "Now vee may perhaps to begin. Yes?"

In a sense, that *is* just the beginning. Roth tried hard to progress further in
his next "family" novel, *My Life as a Man*, which took him years to write.
Meanwhile, he wrote the pre-Watergate Nixon satire *Our Gang* and the satirical burlesque of American culture *The Great American Novel*, which takes
the great American pastime, baseball, as its focus and its vehicle. Yet it was
the fictionalized account of his marriage—or rather, the affair which turned
into marriage through a masterful trick—that really preoccupied Roth in the
years following *Portnoy's Complaint*. Roth invents not one fictional surrogate
but two: Peter Tarnopol, a writer, and Tarnopol's own fictional surrogate,
Nathan Zuckerman. The two "useful fictions" that precede "My True Story,"
or the novel proper, are Roth's early experiments with "counterlives" developed at greater length and complexity in his finest novel, *The Counterlife*.
They provide alternative, "possible" accounts of Peter Tarnopol's early life—
and, through Tarnopol's, Roth's.

Peter's problem is trying to discover how he ever got involved with Maureen, his wife of ten years, from whom he is finally separated but who refuses
to grant him a divorce. Related to this problem is the current one he experiences with his beautiful and dutiful lover, Susan Seabury McCall, a young
widow who provides Peter with apparently everything he wants; however, she
is essentially too submissive, too dull. One part of Tarnopol misses the excitement—no, the frenzy—that Maureen brought into his life, while another
part hates it. Though it does not follow a strict chronological sequence, the
novel becomes an account of his experience first with Maureen, then with
Susan, whom he finally also leaves and determines to give up, despite her
attempted suicide. Writing the novel in guarded solitude at an artist's colony
called Quahsay, Tarnopol retrospectively tries to understand his plight.

So does David Allen Kepesh in *The Breast*, another novel written during
this period when Roth was trying to compose *My Life as a Man*. Actually, it
is the sequel to *The Professor of Desire*, written a few years later. Like Portnoy, Zuckerman, and Tarnopol, Kepesh is a nice Jewish young man brought
up by caring parents in a sheltered Jewish environment, who early in life
experiences the pleasures of emancipation and of the flesh, first as a Fulbright
scholar living in London, then as a graduate student at Stanford University.

Like Tarnopol, he becomes the victim of a femme fatale, a woman who, like Maureen, has "lived." Helen Baird is a striking beauty, but more than her beauty, her experience living abroad as the lover of a Hong Kong millionaire attracts Kepesh. They become lovers and later, disastrously, husband and wife. Gradually, Kepesh sinks into the condition of becoming Helen's ser-vant, if not slave, until she flees once more to Hong Kong, hoping to reunite with her erstwhile lover. He will not have her, and David must rescue her, but in the process he becomes aware that their life together is over, and they get divorced.

David now moves back to New York, where he gets a job teaching comparative literature, meets Claire, a young schoolteacher, and falls in love with her. During this period he undergoes psychotherapy to "demythologize" his marriage to Helen; Dr. Klinger becomes Claire's advocate against David's brooding over Helen. During this period also, David's mother dies, and like Gabe Wallach in *Letting Go*, Kepesh has a widowed father on his hands. Yet the elder Mr. Kepesh is by no means as demanding as Dr. Wallach; on the contrary, he is delighted with his son's liaison with Claire (as he was not with the marriage to Helen) and hopes that they will marry. The novel ends as the young couple along with the elder Mr. Kepesh and a friend of his, a concentration camp survivor, spend a weekend in a bungalow in the Catskills, not far from where David grew up, and where he now ponders his future. He seems to have everything he wants or needs, but somehow he feels dissatis-fied, anxious, afraid that ennui will set in and destroy everything or that some other disaster will overtake them.

It does, but the disaster is hardly anything that David Allen Kepesh anticipates. About a year later, as his lovemaking with Claire has almost ceased, he turns into a six-foot, 155-pound breast. In *The Breast*, Roth partly follows Franz Kafka's "The Metamorphosis" (1915), an obvious, but not exact, source for this novella. Unlike Kafka, Roth tells the story from Kepesh's point of view, using the first-person narrator to convey something of the real anguish Kepesh feels and his amazement at his condition. If he was beset by a dilemma at the end of *The Professor of Desire*, his bafflement there is nothing to what he experiences now. Despite the aid and comfort that everyone—Claire, his father, Dr. Klinger—tries to give him, he remains at the end as bitterly confused and disturbed as ever, thoroughly unreconciled to his lot except as he vainly tries to persuade everyone that what has happened has not happened, that it is all a bad dream from which eventually he will awake, or that he has simply gone mad.

Roth's next novels form a trilogy to which he appends an epilogue, all under the title of *Zuckerman Bound*. Again, Roth borrows from autobiography to write his fiction, his own "counterlife." In *The Ghost Writer*, the first of the series which make up this *Bildungsroman*, or portrait novel, Nathan Zuckerman is at the beginning of a promising career as a writer. He has published a few short stories and is now staying at an artist's colony (Quahsay again), trying to write more. Since he is not far from the home of E. I. Lonoff, a writer he much admires, he visits and is welcomed by the older writer and his wife. Zuckerman is surprised by them in many ways: first by Lonoff's austere life as a writer, spent endlessly turning his sentences around, and then by Hope Lonoff's conviction that her husband would be better off without her. By birth and upbringing far different from him—she is a New England Yankee as opposed to his immigrant origins—she is temperamentally unsuited to the kind of life they have led for many years. She is convinced, moreover, that Lonoff would be better off living with a younger woman, like Amy Bellette, a former student from the nearby women's college where Lonoff teaches, who obviously adores him. Lonoff refuses, however, to entertain any such thoughts of abandoning Hope or realizing his fantasy of living abroad in a villa in Italy with a younger woman.

Nathan is persuaded to stay the night, especially after meeting Amy Bellette, who is also staying there on a brief visit. Nathan has his own fantasy that evening, that Amy is really Anne Frank, author of the famous diary, who has miraculously survived death camps. They fall in love, get married, and thus show his parents and other relatives that, despite what they may think from some of his stories, he is a good Jewish man, the worthy husband of the famous Jewish heroine. As a tribute to Roth's skill as a writer, the account of Amy's survival is quite credible; moreover, it shows Roth's understanding of compassion for the suffering in the death camps. At the same time, it supports Nathan Zuckerman's qualifications as a writer, justifying Lonoff's praise and encouragement of the young man.

Lonoff's belief in Nathan is borne out in *Zuckerman Unbound*, the second novel in the trilogy. By now Zuckerman is the author of several novels, including the notorious *Carnovsky*. This novel is to Zuckerman what *Portnoy's Complaint* was to Philip Roth, and *Zuckerman Bound* recounts experiences similar to those Roth most have had, such as the notoriety that involved mistaking his fictional characters for his real mother and father. Zuckerman is accosted in the streets, on the telephone, and apparently everywhere he goes by people who think they know him because they mistake his confessional novel for actual autobiography. Yet fiction and autobiography are at best distant relatives; for example, unlike Zuckerman's father, who is extremely upset by his son's novel and turns on him at his death, Roth's parents remained proud of their son's accomplishments and never took offense at what he wrote, notwithstanding the uproar in the Jewish establishment.

Zuckerman is beset by would-be hangers-on, such as Alvin Pepler, the Jewish marine, once a quiz-show winner but deprived of full fame by a scam reminiscent of the Charles Van Doren scandal. Zuckerman's brief affair (actually, no more than a one-night stand) with the Irish actress Caesara O'Shea is a comic treatment of the adventures attributed to Roth by columnists such as

Leonard Lyons, who insisted he was romantically involved with Barbra Streisand, though actually Roth at that time had not so much as met her. Finally, Zuckerman's trip to Miami with his brother, Henry, which ends with their estrangement on the way home after their father dies of a stroke, is totally different from actual events in Roth's life. All these incidents are, after all, "counterlives," imaginative renderings of what might have or could have happened, not what did.

Similarly, in *The Anatomy Lesson*, the third novel in the series, Roth borrows from incidents in his own life but fictionalizes them so that no one-to-one equivalence can be made. Now, some years later, Zuckerman is afflicted with a strange ailment that causes him intense pain, from which he gets temporary relief only from vodka or Percodan. He can no longer write, but four different women tend to his other needs, including his sexual ones. Among them are a young Finch College student, who also works as his secretary; his financial adviser's wife; an artist in Vermont who occasionally descends from her mountaintop to visit; and a Polish émigrée, whom Zuckerman meets at a trichological clinic (in addition to everything else, Zuckerman is losing his hair).

In despair of his life and his calling, Zuckerman decides to give up writing and become a doctor. He flies to Chicago, where he hopes his old friend and classmate, Bobby Freytag, will help him get admitted to medical school. En route on the plane and later from the airport, Zuckerman impersonates Milton Appel, a literary critic modeled on Irving Howe, who early praised Roth's work and then turned against it. In this impersonation, however, Zuckerman pretends that Appel is a pornography king, editor and publisher of *Lickety Split* and an impresario of houses of pleasure. The impersonation is triggered by Appel's appeal, delivered through an intermediary, to Zuckerman to write an op ed article on behalf of Israel.

Zuckerman as the porn king Appel provides plenty of material for those who like to see Roth as antifeminist but who thereby miss the point of his fiction. It is a tour de force, a persona adopting a persona—miles away from the real Roth. At his office in the hospital, Bobby Freytag reminisces with Zuckerman for a bit and then tries to talk him out of his scheme. Only the next day when, under the influence of too much Percodan and vodka, Zuckerman falls and fractures his jaw, does the healing begin, in soul as well as body. Zuckerman learns what real pain and loss are, as he walks the corridors of the hospital watched over by his friend, who also weans him from his drug addiction. At the end, Zuckerman is a chastened and more altruistic individual, though still deluded into thinking he could change into a more radically different person than he is.

The epilogue, *The Prague Orgy*, shows Zuckerman not as a doctor but as a famous novelist undertaking an altruistic mission on behalf of an émigré Czech writer whose father had written some excellent, unpublished stories in

Yiddish. Unfortunately, the Czech's estranged wife holds the stories but will not release them, and it is Zuckerman's task to fetch them. In the event, he manages to do so without having to sleep with her, despite her pleas, but the stories are immediately confiscated by the police, who then escort him out of the country (this is pre-1989 Czechoslovakia). Zuckerman thus learns to accept his limitations and to become reconciled to them. To become "transformed into a cultural eminence elevated by the literary deeds he performs" does not seem to be his fate, and he accepts that.

In *The Counterlife*, Nathan and his brother are briefly reunited, mainly so that Roth can explore alternative versions of a fate that first befalls one and then the other. The plot thus doubles back on itself more than once and is too complex for summary treatment. Despite its complexity, the novel is not difficult to follow and is full of surprises that intellectually stimulate as they also amuse the reader. Particularly interesting are the episodes in Israel, where Henry has fled to start a new life, bringing Nathan after him to discover what is going on. Much is going on, including a considerable amount of discussion from characters on the political left and right, with Nathan clearly in the middle. The latter part of the novel finds Nathan in London, married to a English divorcee with a child and trying to come to grips with British anti-Semitism, including some in his wife's family. Throughout the novel, Roth implicitly and sometimes explicitly raises questions about the nature of fiction and the characters that inhabit it.

He does so, too, in *Deception*, though in that novel, written almost entirely in dialogue, the experiment takes on a different form. Here, Roth drops his surrogate, Nathan Zuckerman; his main character, present in all the dialogue, is called Philip, who also happens to be a novelist who has written about a character named Zuckerman. Thus Roth seems here to speak in his own voice, though of course he does not, quite: He merely makes the partition separating him from his characters that much thinner, almost to the point of transparency, as when he takes on the critics who claim that when he writes fiction, he does autobiography, and vice versa. The novel is filled with discussions between "Philip" and his lover, who proves to be the woman Nathan married in *The Counterlife*; thus, much of the talk is naturally about fiction. Other characters, however, including several from central Europe, also appear to discuss personal and political issues. Again, the problem of British anti-Semitism appears.

Surveying the corpus of Roth's longer fiction, one may conclude that here is a novelist who rarely repeats himself, even as he reworks ideas, issues, dilemmas, or reintroduces characters and locales. This is the essence of the "counterlife" motif that has been present in Roth's work from the start but becomes explicit only later on, where its fascination has grown even as Roth's techniques and maturity as a writer have also grown.

Jay L. Halio

Other major works

SHORT FICTION: *Goodbye, Columbus*, 1959.

NONFICTION: *Reading Myself and Others*, 1975; *The Facts: A Novelist's Autobiography*, 1988.

Bibliography

Lee, Hermione. *Philip Roth*. London: Methuen, 1982. By a British author in Methuen's Contemporary Authors series, this monograph is a short, concise account of Roth's work up to and including *Zuckerman Unbound*. It contains a useful bibliography of Roth's uncollected stories and essays as well as his books, editions, essays and books about Roth, and an index.

Milbauer, Asher Z., and Donald G. Watson, eds. *Reading Philip Roth*. New York: St. Martin's Press, 1988. Borrowing its title from Roth's own collection of essays, this book begins with an informative interview with Roth and includes essays by writers such as Roth's friends Aharon Appelfeld and Milan Kundera. Most of the volume, however, contains fairly heavy readings of Roth's fiction by European and American critics such as Clive Sinclair, Martin Green, Sam B. Girgus, Donald Gartiganer, and Hana Wirth-Nesher. Indexed, but no bibliography.

Pinsker, Sanford. *The Comedy That "Hoits": An Essay on the Fiction of Philip Roth*. Columbia: University of Missouri Press, 1975. A witty, learned, and perceptive short book on Roth by a Jewish scholar who understands the language and structure of Roth's novels exceptionally well. No index or bibliography, but secondary references are footnoted.

_____ , ed. *Critical Essays on Philip Roth*. Boston: G. K. Hall, 1982. An outstanding collection of some of the best essays and reviews on Roth. It includes excellent essays by Mark Schechner, Sarah Blacher Cohen, and Morton Levitt, as well as a personal memoir by Theodore Solotaroff and the famous attack by Irving Howe called "Philip Roth Reconsidered." Contains an index but no bibliography.

Rodgers, Bernard F., Jr. *Philip Roth*. Boston: Twayne, 1978. This solid critical study by Roth's bibliographer contains a wealth of biographical and other information, along with clear and perceptive readings of the novels. Fully annotated and indexed, it also contains a "Select Bibliography" of both primary and secondary sources.

SUSANNA ROWSON

Born: Portsmouth, England; 1762
Died: Boston, Massachusetts; March 2, 1824

Principal long fiction

Victoria, 1786; *The Inquisitor: Or, Invisible Rambler*, 1788; *Mary: Or, The Test of Honour*, 1789; *Charlotte: A Tale of Truth*, 1791 (published in the United States as *Charlotte Temple*, 1797); *Mentoria: Or, The Young Lady's Friend*, 1791; *Rebecca: Or, The Fille de Chambre*, 1792; *Trials of the Human Heart*, 1795; *Reuben and Rachel: Or, Tales of Old Times*, 1798; *Sarah: Or, The Exemplary Wife*, 1813; *Charlotte's Daughter: Or, The Three Orphans*, 1828.

Other literary forms

Susanna Rowson was a prolific, well-rounded writer. Besides her ten works of long fiction, she produced three volumes of poetry: *Poems on Various Subjects* (1788), *A Trip to Parnassus* (1788), and *Miscellaneous Poems* (1804). Between 1794 and 1797, she wrote about seven dramatic works, most of which were probably performed but not published; the most popular of these was *Slaves in Algiers: Or, A Struggle for Freedom* (1794). She also composed the lyrics for numerous songs and contributed to the production of at least two periodicals: the *Boston Weekly Magazine*, for which she wrote articles on a wide range of subjects and apparently also served as editor between 1802 and 1805; and the *New England Galaxy*, which was founded in 1817 and for which Rowson wrote chiefly religious and devotional prose pieces. Finally, she wrote and had published six pedagogical works: *An Abridgement of Universal Geography* (1805); *A Spelling Dictionary* (1807); *A Present for Young Ladies* (1811); *Youth's First Step in Geography* (1818); *Exercises in History* (1822); and *Biblical Dialogues* (1822).

Achievements

Opinions of Rowson's achievements as a novelist have fluctuated widely since the nineteenth century. Earlier critics were high in their praises of the moral tendency of her work and her storytelling skills, while more recent estimates have tended to disparage both and to find her writing limited and ordinary.

Among the handful of Americans who wrote novels in the late eighteenth century, Rowson was both the most prolific and most coherent. As Dorothy Weil has shown, a well-developed system of aims and values emerges from all of Rowson's writings and gives her work notable unity and breadth. In particular, as Weil has demonstrated, Rowson's belief in the equality of the sexes and her concern with feminist issues and positive goals for women deserve wider recognition than they have received. In other respects, Rowson's novels are typical of the novelist's theory and practice in newly independent America and are interesting and revealing as a window on the nature of fiction in the late eighteenth century.

Biography

Susanna Haswell Rowson's remarkably full, active life began in Portsmouth, England, where she was born in 1762. Her mother died shortly after, and Rowson's first visit to America occurred when her father settled and married in Massachusetts and, in 1767, brought his daughter to join him, his new wife, and his three stepsons. Some of Rowson's experiences during this visit, including a shipwreck, appear later in *Rebecca*. By 1778, she was back in England, her father's apparently doubtful loyalty having led the fledgling American government first to confiscate his property and intern his family and him and then return them to England.

Rowson's initiative and independence soon showed themselves. By the time she was in her twenties, she had secured a position as governess in the family of the Duchess of Devonshire, beginning a life of service through teaching and writing; she also helped her father gain a pension, and she began publishing her fiction and poetry.

Rowson was twenty-four when her first novel, *Victoria*, appeared in London in 1786. The work's subtitle, a sign of her aims and interests as a novelist, declared that *Victoria* was "calculated to improve the morals of the female sex, by impressing them with a just sense of the merits of filial piety." Later in 1786, she married William Rowson, and though he was apparently an ineffectual person, they shared an interest in music and theater and remained married for thirty-eight years.

Between Rowson's marriage and her emigration to America in 1793, she wrote prolifically, publishing five novels and two books of verse. In 1792, following the failure of her husband's hardware business, the couple, along with Rowson's sister-in-law Charlotte, decided to join a theater company and tour the British Isles. The decision was fateful, because in 1793 they were seen by Thomas Wignell, an American who was recruiting players for the theater he was about to open in Philadelphia. Wignell took them to America in 1793, and thus began Rowson's American period, during which she blossomed both as a performer and as an educator amd moralist who attempted to serve others through many activities, including novel writing.

Rowson published her four-volume novel, *Trials of the Human Heart*, in 1795, and continued acting and writing in the theater until 1797. Then, once again, she turned her life and her career of service in a new direction. She opened a Young Ladies' Academy in Boston in 1797. Starting with only one pupil, she had one hundred and a waiting list within a year. She continued to instruct young women in her school until 1822, but she also continued to do so through her writing. She published the novels *Reuben and Rachel* and *Sarah* as well as another book of poetry, various songs and odes, and a theatrical piece. Her major works, however, were the six pedagogical books she wrote and published between 1805 and 1822 for use in her school.

All of this got done even as Rowson found time and energy for rearing several adopted children and for supporting church and charity, which included holding the presidency of Boston's Fatherless and Widow's Society. When she died on March 2, 1824, Rowson left in manuscript her final work, *Charlotte's Daughter*, the sequel to *Charlotte*; it was published posthumously in 1828.

Analysis

Benjamin Franklin certainly had neither women nor novelists foremost in his mind when he published his "Information for Those Who Would Remove to America" in 1782. Yet Susanna Rowson, who would remove to America a little more than a decade later, was exactly the sort of migrant Franklin would have wanted. America, he said, required useful members of society rather than persons "doing nothing of value, but living idly on the labour of others." Citizens of the new nation "do not inquire concerning a stranger, *what is he?* but *what can he do?* If he has any useful art, he is welcome; and if he exercises it and behaves well, he will be respected by all that know him."

Rowson understood the kind of labor Franklin meant, and the years she spent in America as writer and educator show that she cared about becoming a useful, respected member of society. Doing this as a novelist was no easy task, for while fiction might be popular among young readers, the "common verdict with respect to novels," as Noah Webster expressed it in 1788, was that "some of them are useful, many of them are pernicious, and most of them trifling."

Rowson responded by producing novels that consistently stress Franklin's service ideal, especially for the young women she saw herself addressing. "We are not sent into the world to pass through it in indolence," says one of Rowson's wise widows to the heroine of *Trials of the Human Heart*. "Life which is not serviceable to our fellow creatures is not acceptable to our Creator."

Such was the ideal that Rowson held up to the women for whom she wrote and that she herself sought to embody by writing novels that would be an honor to herself and a benefit to society. For many modern readers and writers of fiction, there may well be something objectionable about regarding novel writing as akin to useful arts of the kind Franklin mentions with approval in his prospectus—farming, carpentry, tanning, weaving, shoemaking, and the like—but Rowson and a few other scrupulous early American novelists were in effect trying to do just that: produce fiction that would be of direct, lasting benefit to its readers by helping them live happy, fulfilled lives.

Rowson's novels typically exhibit a clear moral purpose and an unmistakable connection between virtue and happiness. The strong didactic element which modern readers may find distasteful in Rowson and her contemporaries was in fact the essential finishing touch for many early American novelists. Of what use, these writers might have said, was an uncultivated field or undeveloped talent? Almost from the outset, Rowson stressed that the moral purpose of her fiction and the well-being of her readers were more important to her than financial or critical success.

Rowson realized, of course, that there were too many novels which were either trifling or pernicious, as Webster said, and did their readers no good. Her awareness was sharp enough that in *The Inquisitor* she offers a detailed summary of what she considered a typical "Modern Novel." To Rowson, the problem with such novels was that they were more likely to harm than improve the reader, mislead rather than enlighten. They tended to encourage vice and error by showing that they lead to happiness rather than suffering, thus making them attractive instead of repugnant to the unwary reader. Novels such as these, and writers such as Jean Jacques Rousseau and Johann Wilhelm von Goethe, were said to misuse the power of fiction by ennobling errant behavior such as suicide or adultery and charming the reader into accepting and even living by untruths made too attractive.

For Rowson and her contemporaries, fiction was never to make error noble and vice fascinating, deluding the reader and ultimately causing her unhappiness; it should have exactly the opposite psychological effect. Rowson would have agreed with what Columbia College student Daniel Tompkins, in 1794, called fiction's "true design and intent." Novels, he wrote in his journal, "are representations of men and things qualified to excite to the love of virtue and the detestation of vice." Such novels used the power of narrative and the feelings and imaginations of readers to move the reader away from vicious behavior and toward that which was virtuous and rewarding. As Rowson describes this process in her Preface to *Trials of the Human Heart*, she hopes to "awaken in the bosoms of . . . youthful readers a thorough detestation of vice, and a spirited emulation to embrace and follow the precepts of Piety, Truth, and Virtue."

At the heart of Rowson's novels, then, is her concern with what she likes to call the "true felicity" of her readers and her belief that virtue leads to happiness as surely as vice and error do not. In changing the reader for the better, the novels seek to be both moral and affective. They work through the feelings and imagination and end in well-rooted, satisfying behavior. A closer look at three representative novels of Rowson's will show how she tried to achieve these results.

As Dorothy Weil observes in her recent study of Rowson, *In Defense of Women* (1976), *Charlotte* (entitled *Charlotte Temple* in the American edition of 1797) is one of the wonders of American literature, primarily because of its immediate and long-lasting popularity. It was widely read upon its publication in America in 1797—about twenty-five thousand copies sold shortly after it appeared—and by the middle of the nineteenth century it had become the most frequently published popular novel in America. By 1905, it had gone through as many as two hundred editions, and in 1932, in his bibliographical study of Rowson, R. W. G. Vail claimed that more people had read *Charlotte* than any other work of fiction printed in America. Fueled by the novel's popularity, legends about the real-life identities of its main characters have flourished. In New York City's Trinity Churchyard, the grave of Charlotte Stanley, supposedly the model for the novel's heroine, now bears a slab with the inscription "Charlotte Temple."

The novel is also a revealing example of one kind of narrative by which Rowson tried to affect her readers as useful fiction was supposed to do. She does this by relating and having her readers imaginatively participate in one of the eighteenth century's favorite plots: the story of the causes and consequences of youthful error and delusion in which the heroine herself, and thus the reader, learns by bitter experience to love virtue and hate vice. Rowson also presents the heroine's learning process in a moral context of clearly stated values, thereby insuring that the nature of virtue and vice is well defined throughout.

The main events of the novel are easily summarized. Charlotte Temple is a fifteen-year-old student at a boarding school in Chichester, England; the year is 1774. One day, she meets Lieutenant Montraville, who, finding Charlotte attractive and eventually deciding that he loves her, persuades her to see him and then to accompany him to America. Although she doubts herself the moment she decides to go, Charlotte nevertheless leaves her friends and her parents behind and, in the company of her lover, his deceitful friend Belcour, and her evil teacher Madmoiselle La Rue, sails to America. Once there, Montraville falls in love with another woman even as Belcour deceives him into believing that Charlotte has been unfaithful; Montraville abandons her, though she is now pregnant with his child. Virtually alone and friendless, Charlotte has her baby and dies just after her distracted father has finally located her. Montraville kills Belcour in a duel and lives out his days married to the woman he loves but still sad and remorseful over his part in Charlotte's ruin. La Rue later dies in misery brought on by her life of dissipation.

This is the grisly narrative that Rowson attempts to make useful and instructive to the "young and thoughtless of the fair sex." She does this first by anchoring the events of the story in a context of contrasting values. In a novel designed to make virtue lovely and vice and error detestable, the reader should be very certain just what virtue and its opposites are. Among the important good people offered as attractive examples of the life of virtue are Charlotte's parents and Mrs. Beauchamp, her only real friend in America. These characters are distinguished by that active service to others that Rowson valued so highly. Each possesses a feeling heart and a generous hand, and each knows the exquisite satisfaction of comforting less fortunate fellow creatures. Moreover, these characters have given up fast-paced city life in favor of the simple, contented rural existence that befits men and women of feeling.

In contrast to such characters are the novel's bad people, especially La Rue and Belcour, who represent the false pleasures and values of selfishness. These clear contrasts between virtue and vice are established early in the novel and are regularly reinforced by a narrator who both relates and freely comments on the story. "Oh, my dear girls, for to such only am I writing," she says at one point in a typical utterance, "listen not to the voice of love unless sanctioned by parental approbation . . . pray for fortitude to resist the impulse of inclination when it runs counter to the precepts of religion and virtue."

The secret of fiction's power to further the happiness of readers lay not in static commentary and contrast, however, as much as in *process*—the learning process which the feeling reader would go through by participating imaginatively in the experience of the novel's heroine, Charlotte Temple. She is a poor deluded child who must learn by adversity that virtue leads to happiness, vice to misery. The novel is thus a psychological history of the causes and effects of error and vice, with Charlotte starting the novel as "an innocent artless girl" and ending "a poor forsaken wanderer" suffering "extreme agitation of mind" and "total deprivation of reason" as a result of her mistakes.

Rowson tries to show that Charlotte's basic problem is her inability to resist an impulse when it runs counter to the precepts of religion and virtue. Despite the fact that she was reared by exemplary parents, Charlotte falls, and she does so, Rowson shows, because she allows herself to come under the influence of bad people who disable her power to resist dangerous, delusive inclinations in herself—just what was said to happen to weak, unwary readers of pernicious novels. Charlotte thus ends as "the hapless victim of imprudence and evil counsellors," the "poor girl by thoughtless passion led astray."

Like bad novels, the evil counsellors who overwhelm Charlotte's discretion and good sense are capable of using appearances—particularly the power of language and dress—to disable and deceive. A sorceress possessed of the "art of Circe," La Rue convinces Charlotte to meet, and later to continue seeing Montraville against her own better judgment. Thus does Charlotte "forsake the paths of virtue, for those of vice and folly." Eloping to America with Montraville, becoming pregnant and then left abandoned "to die with want and misery in a strange land," the very opposite of a useful and respectable member of society, Charlotte is "held up as an object of terror, to prevent us from falling into guilty errors." The reader, Rowson would hope, sees and feels that deviation from virtue is "an object of detestation," and vice and error themselves as detestable as their opposites, embodied in happy characters, are desirable. The ideal reader is the "reader of sensibility" who will "acutely feel the woes of Charlotte" and therefore behave so as to avoid them.

Implicit in *Charlotte* is a pattern for a second type of useful novel which Rowson employed in *Mentoria*. As noted, the third-person narrator of *Charlotte* both relates and comments on the tale, making sure her readers understand its moral import and learn from it. In *Mentoria*, the nameless, wholly reliable preceptress of *Charlotte* becomes the story's main character. Her name is Helena Askham, and, in a series of letters to Lady Winworth's three daughters for whom she earlier was governess, Helena dispenses stories and lessons based on her own experience, which are designed to instruct young women on subjects of concern to them.

Like Charlotte, Helena combines humble origins with a good education. Unlike Charlotte, she is strong enough to resist impulses which run counter to the precepts of religion and virtue. She is able to do so because, sensitive and feeling though she is, she is also "endowed with discernment and sense far superior to the generality of young women of her age."

She shows her mettle early on when, placed in a situation very much like Charlotte's with Montraville, she is courted by Lady Winworth's son. Unlike Charlotte, who allowed the rhetoric and appearance of La Rue and Montraville to disable her judgment and excite errant, delusive hopes, Helena displays the control of feeling and pleasing inclination that is the mark of Rowson's strong women, and that enables her to stifle her rising passion for her suitor and reject him. Later, he does in fact marry someone closer to him in rank and fortune, and so does Helena, until her husband's death leaves her free to become governess and then mentor to the three Winworth children.

As this wise widow, a woman who, like the narrator of *Charlotte*, combines sensibility with strong good sense, Helena becomes the central character of *Mentoria*. The several stories she relates, therefore, are meant to do what the single story of Charlotte did: use the power of narrative as a memorable, striking means of instruction for young women, a way of making "a lasting impression on the minds of fair readers" and thereby of advancing their happiness.

For example, the life of Helena's friend Louisa Railton is offered as "a model by which every young woman who wishes to promote her own felicity, will regulate her conduct." The beauty of the virtue of filial piety is illustrated by Louisa's choosing, after her mother's death, "a low roofed mansion, scanty meals, and attendance on a sick peevish father, to the lofty apartments, plenteous table, and variety of amusements she might have enjoyed with Lady Mary," her rich relative. She thereby gains, however, "a contented happy mind, [and] serenity dwelt in her heart and cheerfulness beamed in her eyes. . . . She lived beloved by all and died universally regretted." Made desirable and attractive, and distinguished as in *Charlotte* from its selfish opposite, the virtue of filial devotion should impress the reader and prompt her to imitation. As Helena writes her pupils, "Be wise, my dear children, follow Louisa's example, so shall your lives be happy and your last moments peace." Helena continues to deal similarly with such topics as friendship, reputation, love, pleasure, and marriage, using the force of the striking instance to impress readers with the felicity of the virtuous life and the miseries of vice and error.

In *Trials of the Human Heart*, Rowson demonstrates a third type of "useful fiction." Her aim is to achieve the same effect as before—"to awaken in the bosoms of my youthful readers," as she says in the novel's Preface, "a thorough detestation of vice, and a spirited emulation, to embrace and follow the precepts of Piety, Truth and Virtue." Like *Charlotte*, *Trials of the Human Heart* is a story of adolescent initiation, but rather than involving the reader in the misfortunes of a heroine such as Charlotte whose imprudence is her undoing, Rowson offers the character of Meriel Howard, who is the undeserving victim of the cruelty or caprice of others and as a result suffers through what one character calls "some of the heaviest trials to which the human heart is incident"—four volumes' worth, in fact, related through letters exchanged among the characters.

Like other Rowson heroines, Meriel is artless and innocent at the start—having indeed spent much of her childhood in a convent—and she possesses a generous heart as well. As she writes her convent friend Celia, "I am weak as an infant, whenever a scene of distress or happiness meets my eye; I have a tear of sympathy for the one, and a smile of gratulation for the other." Thus endowed, Meriel leaves the convent and enters a world that ends up causing her far more distress than happiness.

The first incidents of the novel, when Meriel is about sixteen, are typical of the pattern of disappointed expectation that repeats itself in Meriel's life and occasions her learning and uttering many lessons about life. On her way home to Bristol, she thinks about the coming reunion with her parents, whom she has not seen for most of her childhood. "I pictured them to myself, as very amiable old people—and, in fancy, felt their embraces and kissed off the tears of joy I saw falling from their eyes." What she finds instead is a "suffering saint" of a mother, her settled melancholy the result of living with a husband who is cruel and unfeeling and a son notable for "frigid coldness." Meriel soon discovers that her father—who much later in the novel turns out *not* to be her father—is a freethinker and a hypocritical villain, concealing under the "mask of integrity and honour every vice which can disgrace human nature." Indeed, it was because of her father's vitiated morals that Meriel was originally placed in a convent. She now finds him ardently pursuing an adulterous affair; after she succeeds in breaking that up, she herself becomes the object of his amorous attention, an event one character describes as "too dreadful, too shocking to human nature, to wear even the face of probability."

Soon after, Meriel reflects that she no doubt has many more trials yet to endure, and she is absolutely right. In one episode after another, she—like her counterpart Rebecca, the heroine of the novel of the same name—attracts the compromising notice rather than the solicitude of married men and the venom rather than the pity of other women. As Meriel remarks later, looking back over her life, "how hard is my fate. Possessed as I am of a heart moulded to compassion, glowing with universal affection toward my fellow creatures, I am constantly thrown among people, whose every feeling is absorbed in self."

For Meriel as for the reader of this and virtually every other Rowson novel, the purpose of the heroine's experiences is to teach about truth and error— what Meriel calls the "useful lessons taught me in the school of adversity." Born to be the sport of fortune, Meriel learns that "this is a sad—very sad world to live in.—For if we love anything we are sure to lose it." The truly important lesson, however, follows on this. Having so painfully discovered the error of her innocent belief that "every heart glowed with humanity, friendship and sincerity toward each other," Meriel periodically entertains the opposite error. "What a world this is," she writes to her enviably placid convent friend. "Were it not impious, I could wish I had never entered it."

Despair is indeed impious, and the heroine, like the reader, learns that such feelings run counter to the precepts of religion and virtue. Unlike Charlotte, however, Meriel is capable of pulling back from harmful vice and error. The proper response to misfortune is, first, to bear up under it; one's duty, as Meriel says, is "to submit without repining, to the will of Him, who never lays on his creatures the rod of affliction but for some wise purpose." Second, one must serve, not retreat: "We are not sent into the world to pass through it in indolence," Meriel is told. "Remember, that life which is not in some measure serviceable to our fellow creatures, is not acceptable to our Creator." As Meriel and the reader learn, the suicidal response in any form is never appropriate. At the end of the novel, Meriel anticipates a happy marriage and hopes both to deserve and preserve her good fortune "by exerting the abilities with which I am amply endowed to chear the desponding heart, sooth the afflicted spirits and soften the bed of pain."

Like other Rowson heroines, Meriel has found the secret of happiness. For her readers, Rowson wanted nothing less. Living happily in the real world of human folly and disappointment is the ideal which her many novels and her own varied life embody. To have found so many ways to demonstrate that ideal is surely a tribute to her strength and her inventiveness.

Michael Lowenstein

Other major works

PLAYS: *Slaves in Algiers: Or, A Struggle for Freedom*, 1794; *The Female Patriot*, 1794; *The Volunteers*, 1795; *Americans in England*, 1796 (revised as *The Columbian Daughter*).

POETRY: *Poems on Various Subjects*, 1788; *A Trip to Parnassus*, 1788; *Mis-*

cellaneous Poems, 1804.

NONFICTION: *An Abridgement of Universal Geography*, 1805; *A Spelling Dictionary*, 1807; *A Present for Young Ladies*, 1811; *Youth's First Step in Geography*, 1818; *Exercises in History*, 1822; *Biblical Dialogues*, 1822.

Bibliography

Brown, Herbert Ross. *The Sentimental Novel in America, 1789-1860*. Durham, N.C.: Duke University Press, 1940. Although outdated in its designation of sentimentalists as "scribblers," Brown's study is notable for its discussion of Rowson's use of the reformed rake theme in several novels. Notes that Rowson critiqued the sentimental novel's formulaic qualities, and discusses the epistolary style of her novels.

Davidson, Cathy N. *Revolution and the Word: The Rise of the Novel in America*. New York: Oxford University Press, 1986. Davidson's superb interdisciplinary study of the eighteenth century "reading revolution" highlights commonplace responses to the extraordinarily popular *Charlotte Temple* and analyzes Rowson's complex characterization of the villain Montraville. Argues that Rowson's plots of "sexual crime and feminine punishment" expose society's double standard of justice. Rowson's other novels are briefly discussed.

Fiedler, Leslie A. *Love and Death in the American Novel*. Rev. ed. New York: Stein & Day, 1966. Although a classic study of the novel, Fiedler defines sentimentalism and specifically *Charlotte Temple* as "not literature" and "completely a woman's book"; he is equally mean-spirited in his denigration of Rowson's literary skills. The study has minor use for placing Rowson in the literary context of "Prototypes and Early Adaptations."

Loshe, Lillie Deming. *The Early American Novel*. New York: Columbia University Press, 1907. Significant biographical details support Loshe's contention that Rowson relied upon personal experience for many of her themes. This study is of most value, however, for placing Rowson's work in the context of the early sentimental novel: Unlike most authors of "domestic melodrama," Rowson developed realistic rather than romantic plots.

Spengemann, William C. *The Adventurous Muse: The Poets of American Fiction, 1789-1900*. New Haven, Conn.: Yale University Press, 1977. Spengemann argues that *Charlotte Temple* is a "pure" example of "the spirit of domesticity." Although he criticizes the emotionalism of Rowson's characterizations and her extravagant style, Spengemann acknowledges the value Rowson placed on factuality. Most useful for its discussion of the distinguishing features of American "domestic romances."

Vail, R. W. G. *Susanna Haswell Rowson, the Author of "Charlotte Temple": A Bibliographical Study*. Worcester, Mass.: American Antiquarian Society, 1933. Vail's comprehensive bibliography of Rowson's writings includes not only standard lists of editions of her various novels but also such de-

lightfully unusual features as the parts Rowson portrayed as an actress and
auction records that attest to her continuing popularity among collectors.
Brief biographical essays are also included.

Weil, Dorothy. *In Defense of Women: Susanna Rowson (1762-1824)*. University Park: Pennsylvania State University Press, 1976. An astute analysis
of Rowson's literary aspirations and accomplishments and of her extensive concern for the religious, moral, and intellectual education of young
women. Weil's text incorporates extensive excerpts from rarely published
works by Rowson and includes an excellent bibliography of primary and
secondary sources.

SALMAN RUSHDIE

Born: Bombay, India; June 19, 1947

Principal long fiction
Grimus, 1975; *Midnight's Children*, 1981; *Shame*, 1983; *The Satanic Verses*, 1988.

Other literary forms
The Jaguar Smile: A Nicaraguan Journey (1987) is a book of travel and political observations, written following Salman Rushdie's visit to Nicaragua in July, 1986, as guest of the Sandinista Association of Cultural Workers. Rushdie has also published several short stories; the best known is "The Prophet's Hair," which appeared originally in the *London Review of Books* in 1981 and has been reprinted in *The Penguin Book of Modern British Short Stories* (1987). A fable in the "Arabian Nights" style, *Haroun and the Sea of Stories* was published in 1990.

Achievements
Though furor and indignation followed publication of each Rushdie novel, each also received critical praise and rave reviews. *Midnight's Children* won the James Tait Black Memorial Prize, the English Speaking Union Literature Award, and the Booker Prize; it has been translated into twelve languages. Though *Shame* was banned in Pakistan, as *Midnight's Children* had been in India, it too received critical plaudits for its seriocomic portrait of Pakistani life. No writer since Jonathan Swift has aroused as much ire from so many sources, notwithstanding the notoriety of *The Satanic Verses*, which won the Whitbread Award as best novel of 1988. On February 14, 1989, the Ayatollah Ruhollah Musavi Khomeini, then spiritual leader of Iran, issued a *fatwā* (a proclamation concerning a matter of Muslim faith) that called for Rushdie's death as an enemy of Islam and sanctioned similar reprisals against those who published or distributed the book.

Rushdie's novels, actually modern picaresques, explore the tragicomic results of lost identity; they portray in bathetic, satirical style what he considers the consequences of living in cultures that have become mixed, distorted, and diluted through combinations of expediency, political ineptitude, and exploitive religion.

Biography
Ahmed Salman Rushdie was born in Bombay, India, on June 19, 1947, less than two months before the end of the British Raj. His father, Anis Ahmed Rushdie, and his mother, Negin Butt Rushdie, were Muslims with ties to the

region that would become Pakistan. The family did not at first join the Muslim exodus to Pakistan that began after partition in September, 1947. Even so, they became increasingly aware of their minority status as Muslims in a predominantly Hindu state.

Though the Rushdies were nominally Muslim, they also identified with India and with Great Britain. Rushdie's father had been educated in England, at the University of Cambridge, and had determined to rear his son and three daughters to appreciate their multicultural background. As a result, Rushdie had, from boyhood, access to a variety of works in his father's library. It became a recurring argument between father and son, however, that the boy did not make adequate use of this wealth of books. His private reading during boyhood was generally limited to an English translation of the *The Arabian Nights' Entertainments* (or *One Thousand Nights and a Night*). His mother, considered "keeper of the family stories," regaled young Rushdie and his sisters with a wealth of anecdotes on family history; he remembered them all, and would adapt many of them in his writings.

Rushdie was sent to the Cathedral School, a British-administered primary school with Anglican affiliation located in Bombay. Rushdie blossomed there under the guidance of dedicated English and Scottish masters who loved teaching and had remained after 1947 because they also loved India. It was thus with eagerness that the fourteen-year-old Rushdie journeyed to England in 1961 to become a student at Rugby School.

Ironically, it was at Rugby that Rushdie began to feel the consequences of his cosmopolitan upbringing. Though his masters were fair, Rushdie felt alienated from his British schoolmates. He encountered the normal ragging of every underclassman, but he also faced cruel pranks. Consequently, he became sullen and withdrawn.

Rushdie won a place at Cambridge, but he balked at attending. Since he had never confided in his parents about his troubles at Rugby, they could not understand why he refused to return to England. In 1964, the year before Rushdie had completed his studies at Rugby, his family had emigrated to Karachi, Pakistan. By 1965 the India-Pakistan war was raging. Father literally pushed son onto the airplane bound for London.

As it happened, Rushdie liked Cambridge, excelled there, and completed a master of arts degree with honors in 1968. He chose to read history rather than literature, and subsequently remarked that he was pleased he did so. It was at this time that he first read the works of Laurence Sterne, an author whose influence in his novels is clear.

Rushdie became interested in theater while at Cambridge, was a member of The Footlights, an undergraduate theatrical group, and for two years after having completed his studies acted at Oval House, a south London theater group that gave productions designed to attract the area's working-class population. By 1970, however, Rushdie had given up the idea of a career in the theater and accepted a position as copywriter for a London advertising agency. It was at this time that he wrote his first novel, never published, and written in what he later called "post-Joycean and sub-Joycean" style.

Grimus was Rushdie's first published novel, written while he was still working irregularly in advertising to provide an income. It was a commercial failure and never was published in the United States, but it was favorably reviewed in London's *The Times Literary Supplement* (January 21, 1975), and it attracted notice and the beginnings of an audience for Rushdie. It took several short stories and five years before Rushdie produced *Midnight's Children*.

Midnight's Children won rave reviews on both sides of the Atlantic, but it also offended a great many people, among them the family of Indira Gandhi, then Prime Minister of India. Rushdie made a public apology for the cutting satirical references to her and specific members of her family, but he made no changes in subsequent editions of the book. The affair was exacerbated by the fact that Rushdie's accusations coincided with the Indian army's assault on the Golden Temple of the Sikh Muslims. The assassination of Mrs. Gandhi in 1984 brought a tragic end to this series of events.

Having offended large numbers of Indians with *Midnight's Children*, Rushdie published *Shame*, his portrayal of the blood feuds that led to the deposing and execution of Pakistan's prime minister Zulfikar Ali Bhutto by his former protégé, Muhammad Zia al-Haq. The same pattern followed publication of this novel, but this time Rushdie had offended the Pakistanis, India's enemies. Again there were great commercial success and critical plaudits, but *Shame*, which Rushdie called *Midnight's Children*'s "anti-sequel," was denied publication in Pakistan just as *Midnight's Children* had been banned in India.

By 1985 Rushdie was sought after by every major publisher. Viking Penguin offered him an advance of $850,000 for rights to his work then in progress, leading to a rancorous break with Liz Calder, a new publisher. Everyone in publishing circles knew that the new book would cause a sensation, but no one, not even Rushdie, could have known that *The Satanic Verses* would make him a marked man. After February 14, 1989, with the Khomeini decree of death on his head, Rushdie's life came to resemble the plots of his novels. The threat of assassination caused him to close his London home and go into hiding. Viking Penguin received thousands of threatening letters. Bookstores that did not remove *The Satanic Verses* from sale were threatened with bombings. There were riots in Bombay; at least five people were killed and dozens injured in Islamabad, Pakistan; two Muslim leaders were killed in Brussels, Belgium, after they expressed opposition to censoring the book. Two bookstores in Berkeley, California, were firebombed, and a bomb blast in London, which killed the terrorist who had placed the bomb, was attributed to the anti-Rushdie campaign.

Rushdie's personal life was also unsettled. His relations with his father were never the same after the younger man left the Muslim faith, though there was a certain rapprochement before the elder Rushdie's death in 1987. Rushdie's family has always found his cutting anti-Muslim stance an embarrassment. Rushdie's first marriage to English publicist Clarissa Luard in 1976 ended in divorce. There was one child from this marriage, a son, Zafar. His second wife, American writer Marianne Wiggins, went into hiding with Rushdie following the Islamic *fatwā*.

Analysis

The average Western reader, ignorant of Islam and Hinduism, the 1947 partition of the Indian subcontinent and the creation of Pakistan, the India-Pakistan war of 1965, and the Pakistani civil war of 1974, will likely read Salman Rushdie's novels as bizarre entertainments. This is unfortunate, since each is a picaresque allegory into which the author has inserted details from his own life in order to prove that myth is history, today is yesterday, and the life of one person is integral to the history of nations. Rushdie masks events here and there and relentlessly mixes Persian and Hindu myths, but the hiatus in logic that this method creates is merely to prove his contention that an Anglo-Indian-Pakistani is a person with a hole in the body, a vital place in which there is nothing at all.

Midnight's Children is Rushdie's allegorical picaresque on the history of the modern state of India. Its narrator, Saleem Sinai, is one of those whose birth coincided with the hour and day India achieved independence: midnight, August 15, 1947. He and many others, including Jawaharlal Nehru, India's first prime minister, considered that these "midnight's children" were singled out, privileged by the hopeful hour at which they began their lives. Saleem discovers that he does indeed have special powers; he can, in his mind, summon all the other children born during the midnight hour of August 15, 1947, and when a boy he does so nightly, establishing the "Midnight Children's Conference," a forum he hopes will augur well for organizing the leaders of the new state.

Saleem's family is prosperous; they reside in one of Bombay's more affluent sections on an estate of homes once owned by an Englishman, William Methwold, who left India on the very day the Raj ended. Through a bizarre series of events (an accident at school that reveals that his blood type corresponds to neither parent and the subsequent confession of Mary Pereira, a nurse who had worked at the hospital at which Saleem was born), Saleem's family discovers that Mary had intentionally switched children, giving the Sinais a child of one of Bombay's poorest families. Only Saleem, through his telepathic powers, knows that the Sinais' real son, reared as a street urchin named Shiva, is actually an illegitimate child of the Englishman Methwold. Though the Sinais make no attempt to locate their own boy and do accept Saleem as their own, Saleem recognizes Shiva as his nemesis and realizes that Shiva may well destroy him.

All the children of midnight have some special talent or ability by virtue of their time and date of birth: Saleem's telepathic skills, Shiva's extraordinarily strong knees (which he uses to kill the Indian street entertainer he believes is his father), and the abilities of Parvati-the-witch, who seeks to use her talents only for good. All the children become caught up in the political machinations that follow upon India's independence and the creation of Pakistan. Saleem's family, aware that they are part of India's unwanted Muslim minority, emigrate to Pakistan. This event, plus the fact that Saleem no longer wishes to have any contact with Shiva, the rightful heir of the Sinais, ends Saleem's nightly summonings of the Midnight Children's Conference. Once in Pakistan, Saleem discovers that his telepathic powers do not work. He tries, instead, to develop his exceptional powers of smell, utilizing his huge nose to smell danger, injustice, unhappiness, poverty, and other elements of Pakistani life.

Saleem and his family become caught up in Pakistan's 1965 war with India. His former countrymen become his enemies, and all of his family are killed in the war, except his sister, who has taken the name Jamila Singer and become famous as a singer of patriotic songs. When the east wing of Pakistan secedes in 1973 and declares itself the independent state of Bangladesh, Saleem enlists in Pakistan's canine patrol, the Cutia, performing the function of a dog to sniff out traitors. Pakistan's devastating loss in the war leaves Saleem without a country. Ultimately, it is Parvati-the-witch who uses her magic to make him disappear and return him to India.

Saleem marries Parvati but is unable to consummate the marriage. Whenever he tries to do so, he sees the decaying face of Jamila, the woman who had been reared as his sister. Saleem had loved Jamila, but also had come to recognize that their nominal brother-sister relationship would not allow her to be his. Out of frustration, Parvati takes Shiva, now a major in India's army, as her lover. She gives birth to his child, named Aadam, whom Saleem acknowledges as his own son.

Shiva, the destroyer, supervises the slum clearance project that not only eliminates the Bombay quarter in which the magicians had lived but also kills Parvati and many of her magician colleagues who had refused to leave their homes. Saleem is one of those arrested and brought to Benares, the town of the widows. Here he is imprisoned, forced by Shiva to name and identify the skills of the children of midnight, and released only after having been forcibly sterilized. Oddly, those arrested as a result of Saleem's information do not blame him; they, too, are sterilized.

Much more happens in *Midnight's Children*. The novel is structured as a family history that reaches back to Saleem's grandparents and describes the political circumstances in India after World War I, through World War II and the end of the Raj, to the war with Pakistan and the Pakistani civil war. It is also highly mythic. Sinai, the surname of the narrator, masks the name of the Arabian philosopher Avicenna (Abu 'Ali al-Husain ibn 'Abd-Allah ibn Sina; 980-1037), who saw the emanations of God's presence in the cosmos as a series of triads of mind, body, and soul. The triads appear in the three generations of Sinais who appear in the novel, but the three religions of India—Hinduism, Islam, and Christianity—which also appear, do nothing to reverse the downward course of India's fortunes after 1947. Sin is the ancient moon god of Hadhramut, who acting at a distance can influence the tides of the world. He is represented by the letter S, and is as sinuous as the snake. Appropriately, Saleem discovers his son Aadam in the care of a master snake charmer, Picture Singh. Sinai is both the place of revelation, of commandments and the golden calf, and the desert of barrenness and infertility that is Rushdie's view of modern India.

Saleem's nose resembles the trunk of the elephant deity, Kali, who is the god of literature, and the huge ears of Saleem's son Aadam carry the motif into India's future. Shiva is the Hindu god of destruction and reproduction, a member of the trinity that includes Brama and Vishnu. The closing chapters of the novel find Saleem the manager of a Bombay pickle factory owned by his former nurse, Mary Pereira, the woman who had orginally exchanged him for the true son of the Sinais, underscoring the motif of absurd continuity, pickled history, and Saleem's huge nose, which is called a cucumber as often as it is an elephant's trunk.

The most savage satire of the book is reserved for Indira Gandhi, daughter of Nehru and, until her 1984 assassination, Prime Minister of India. Rushdie repeatedly cites the famous newspaper photograph in which her hair was white on one side, black on the other to symbolize hypocrisy. He ridicules Sanjay Gandhi, her son, now also dead, as the mastermind of India's slum clearance and birth-control plans. Specific members of Gandhi's cabinet appear in the novel with appendages to their titles, such as "Minister for Railroads and Bribery." Gandhi's campaign slogan "Indira is India, and India is Indira," which Rushdie often quotes in these contexts, thus becomes a dire prophecy. It is little wonder that distribution of *Midnight's Children*, published during India's state of national emergency, was prohibited. The novel also made Rushdie persona non grata in the country of his birth.

Shame is what Rushdie called his "antisequel" to *Midnight's Children*. It has picaresque and seriocomic elements that resemble those of the earlier novel, but its characters are Pakistanis, members of the power elite that had its historical counterpart in the circle of deposed prime minister Zulfikar Ali Bhutto and Bhutto's protégé, the man who engineered the coup and Bhutto's trial and execution, Muhammad Zia al-Haq. *Shame* created as much consternation in Pakistan as *Midnight's Children* had in India, with precisely the same result: the novel was banned in Pakistan, and Rushdie was considered subversive.

The title of *Shame* derives from the Urdu word *Sharam*, and it contains an encyclopedia of nuance the English barely suggests: embarrassment, discomfiture, indecency, immodesty, and the sense of unfulfilled promise. Rushdie thus explores here themes that are similar to those of his first novel. All the characters experience shame in one or another of these forms, as well as some its converse, shamelessness.

Shame also maintains the highly mythic, literary tone of *Midnight's Children*. Its unprepossessing hero is evocatively named Omar Khayyám Shakil, a paunchy doctor of great promise with the name of the Persian poet known for the twelfth century *Rubáiyát*, the erotic lyric poems, imitated in English by Edward FitzGerald in 1859. Rushdie's Omar is born in a crumbling house called Nishapur (also the town of the historical poet's birth), once the mansion of an Englishman, Colonel Arthur Greenfield, in a Pakistani backwater identified only as "Q," but perhaps Quetta.

The circumstances of Omar's birth are ambiguous. He has three mothers: Chhunni, Munnee, and Bunny Shakil. These three sisters all consider him their son, and none discloses which of them actually gave him birth; nor will they disclose the name of his father, though the reader learns that he is an Englishman. Omar's situation is thus a metaphor of the mixed cultural legacy Rushdie often describes. Indeed, Rushdie often speaks of himself as a man with three mothers: India, Pakistan, and England. The house in which Omar is reared is a labyrinth, a relic of the British Raj; its corridors lead to rooms unoccupied for generations, and Omar, who in his early boyhood is prohibited from leaving the house at any time, is frightened out of his wits when he ventures too far and sees that the water-seeking roots of a tree have punctured the house's outer walls. All of this is Rushdie's metaphorical description of the state of mind of a person with mixed and hostile origins: alienated, loveless, relentlessly, fearfully traversing the labyrinth of the mind, and feeling shame. Omar's only glimpse of the world outside Nishapur is through his telescope, appropriately since the poet for whom he was named was also an astronomer.

The novel is filled with a wealth of characters whose backgrounds are similarly symbolic and complex. Rushdie draws them together both through family relationships and through their individually shameful actions as well as their capacity to feel shame. For example, Bilquìs Kemal Hyder is a woman reared in Bombay, India, by her father, Mahound "the Woman" Kemal, owner of a motion-picture theater. The epithet regularly applied to her father is simultaneously an indication of his motherly solicitude for his daughter and a jibe at his having lost his masculinity by assuming the burden of child rearing. After her father dies in a terrorist bomb blast that also destroys his theater, Bilquìs is rescued by Raza "Razor Guts" Hyder, an ambitious young military officer who takes her as his bride and returns to the family home in Karachi, Pakistan, the country created by partition of the

Indian subcontinent. Thrust into an uncompromisingly Muslim environment, she finds herself shamed when she is unable to bear Hyder a son. Of their two daughters, Sufiya Zinobia Hyder and Naveed "Good News" Hyder, the first is perpetually childlike, the result of a mistreated case of meningitis. Bilquìs and Hyder's second daughter, "Good News," atones for her mother's relative infertility by bearing twenty-seven children.

The focus of *Shame* is the rise to power of Omar's companion in dissipation, Iskander "Isky" Harappa. Isky gives up drinking and womanizing in middle age, adopts the veneer of a devout Muslim, and seizes power after the loss of Pakistan's east wing. For a time he remains popular, assisted by his beautiful unmarried daughter, Arjumand "Virgin Ironpants" Harappa. Isky's wife, Rani Humayun Hyder, remains out of the limelight on the family's isolated estate, and weaves shawls that document all of her husband's acts of shame—a twist on the Penelope motif of Homer's *Odyssey* (ninth century B.C.). By the time Isky is hanged in a military coup, Rani has completed eighteen of them. (Rushdie enumerates the details of each in an angry excursus modeled on a Homeric epic catalog.)

Hyder then seizes power and encourages the trial and conviction of Harappa. A curious combination of circumstances causes Harappa's death, and Hyder orders the corpse hanged, ostensibly carrying out the court's sentence of execution. Hyder's increasing concern is, however, the deviant behavior of his daughter Sufiya Zinobia. Though well past twenty, she has the mental age of less than ten. Hyder accepts Omar Shakil's offer to marry her, made out of shame for his past womanizing and Platonic love for the young woman whose life he had saved. Sufiya Zinobia is, however, aware that some act about which she knows nothing regularly accompanies marriage. She twice escapes from the Hyder house, where she is literally imprisoned (recalling Shakil's own imprisonment in youth), allows herself to be raped at random by streetwalking men, then decapitates the men who have raped her. The villagers who discover these decapitated corpses create the legend of a wild white panther to explain the murders, but Hyder knows that his daughter is the killer and fears that she will eventually decapitate him.

When Hyder's downfall appears imminent, he, his wife Bilquìs, and Shakil escape to the closed mansion of Shakil's youth, and Shakil's three mothers give them sanctuary. Shakil quickly realizes, however, that the three old women plan to kill Hyder in reprisal for his having ordered the death of their younger son, Babar Shakil, for his terrorist involvements. This they do, though not before the accidental death of Bilquìs. Shakil dies soon thereafter, shot by Talvar Ulhaq, Hyder's son-in-law and former state police chief. The pantherlike figure of Sufiya Zinobia observes the carnage.

Rushdie's point, developed through these and other complexities of plot, is that shame and shamelessness develop through religious and political failure; the images of Islam and Pakistan that he invokes are filled with parricide and cruelty, but never genuine and simple love. That those who destroy one another are related by family as well as national ties merely compounds the tragedy and the shame.

The Satanic Verses is Rushdie's strongest indictment of politicized religion, mixed cultural identity, and insensitive, arbitrary officialdom. Its tone is allegorical, picaresque, satiric, and irreverent. Those who know details concerning the founding of Islam, British politics, and contemporary London will recognize the objections many have to the book; those unaware of these particulars will likely be puzzled by the novel's character and chronological shifts. They may even wonder why it has caused such consternation.

The novel begins with an explosion, a passenger airplane destroyed by a terrorist bomb as it flies over the English Channel. Only two passengers survive: Gibreel Farishta and Saladin Chamcha, two actors of Indian origin. Miraculously, they float to earth unharmed. Farishta, whose first name is that of the angel Gabriel, has made his reputation playing Krishna, Gautama Buddha, Hanuman, and other Indian deities in films known as "theologicals." Chamcha, a complete Anglophile, has achieved fame by doing commercial voice-overs in England, though his face is unknown to his admiring audience. With this as background, Rushdie establishes the figure of the angel Gibreel (in Islam associated with bringing Allah's call to Muhammad) and the apparently diabolical Chamcha, who has traded his ethnic identity for a pseudo-British veneer.

When they land, Chamcha discovers that he has grown horns under his very English bowler, as well as cloven hooves and a huge phallus—this despite his mild demeanor, elegant manners, and proper British appearance. Farishta (whose surname means "sweet") finds that he has a halo, despite his being an unconscionable womanizer. His very trip to England was a pursuit of Alleluia Cone, the British "ice queen" of Polish refugee parents. Cone is an internationally famous mountain climber who had conquered Mount Everest. Rushdie thus mixes the imagery of good and evil, angel and demon; this is an exponential motif of the entire novel. It follows that the British police arrest Chamcha as an illegal immigrant and brutalize him terribly. Farishta, however, because of his angelic appearance, remains free, having charmed the police and having refused to identify Chamcha.

The narrative then abruptly shifts to introduce Mahound, a blasphemous name for Mohammad, the founder of Islam. Edmund Spenser used the name Mahound in *The Faerie Queene* (1590, 1596) to represent a heathen idol reserved for oaths sworn by the wicked. Rushdie's Mahound profanely re-creates Mohammad's call from Allah through the angel Gabriel. Mahound, like Mohammad, is a businessman; he climbs Mount Cone and looks down upon the city of sand that Rushdie calls Jahilia, a fictive town that corresponds to Mecca. Mahound's pursuit of his destiny on Mount Cone corresponds to Gibreel's pursuit of mountain climber Alleluia Cone; his dream-filled sleeps as he awaits the angel Gibreel resemble the trancelike seizures, ever increasing in severity, of Gibreel Farishta.

Mahound's companions are described as the scum of Jahilia (Mohammad's were former slaves), and Rushdie puckishly names one of them "Salman." They have the habit, dangerous in a city built entirely of sand, of constantly washing themselves (a parody of Muslim ritual purification). The twelve whores of Jahilia (which means "ignorance" or "darkness"), reminiscent of Mohammad's twelve wives and known as "Mothers of the Believers," reside in a brothel called the Curtain. Translated as *hejab*, this can be associated with the curtainlike veil worn by pious Muslim women.

Abu Simbel, the name of the village flooded in the 1960's when Egypt constructed the Aswan High Dam, is the name given here to the ruler of Jahilia, a city also endangered by water. Because he recognizes Mahound as a threat to his power, Abu Simbel offers him a deal. If Mahound's Allah will accept a mere three of Jahilia's 360 deities into the new monotheistic religion, he will recognize it and give Mahound a seat on the ruling council. It will not be much of a compromise, Abu Simbel insists, since Mahound's religion already recognizes Gibreel as the voice of Allah and Shaitan (Satan) as the spirit the Quran records would not bow before Adam.

Mahound decides to compromise. He climbs Cone Mountain, consults with his Gibreel, then returns to Jahilia to announce the new verses: "Have you thought upon Lat and Uzza, and Manat, the third, the other? . . . They are the exalted birds, and their intercession is desired indeed." These are the so-called Satan-inspired inclusions of the goddesses of motherhood (Lat), beauty and love (Uzza), and fate (Manat) as daughters of Allah, which the Quran rejects as heresy. Mahound later publicly recants this heretical insertion and flees to Yathrib (the ancient name for Medina), corresponding to the historical account of the *hegira*, Mohammad's flight from Mecca to Medina. Gibreel reappears to announce: "It was me both times, baba, me first and second also me." One can draw implications that Islam was founded by rationalizing good and evil, that its founder was both a sincere mystic and a power-hungry entrepreneur, and that Gibreel, an actor who specializes in impersonating deities, had given at least one bravura performance that changed history.

Rushdie goes on to recount a masked sardonic version of the holy war to establish Islam, continuing to blur the distinction between ancient and modern times. A bearded, turbaned imam in exile in London (which he considers Sodom) is in exile from his homeland, called Desh. When a revolution begins in Desh and overthrows the corrupt empress, named Ayesha (ironically also the name of Mohammad's favorite wife), Gibreel (perhaps the angel, perhaps the actor Farishta, perhaps one and the same) flies the imam to Desh on his back in time to see the carnage. This episode can be interpreted as the recall to Iran of the Ayatollah Khomeini, in exile near Paris until the overthrow of the Shah. When the revolution succeeds, Ayesha metamorphoses into the mother goddess, Al-Lat, she whom Mahound had falsely named a daughter of Allah in the satanic verses.

In a parallel sequence, an epileptic peasant girl, also named Ayesha, arouses the lust of a landowner named Mirza Saeed, whose wife is dying of breast cancer. As Moses led the Israelites out of Egypt, so Ayesha, who declares that her husband the archangel Gibreel has told her to do so, leads the entire village, including Saeed's wife, on a pilgrimage by foot to Mecca. She declares that the Arabian Sea will open to admit them (recalling the parting of the Red Sea in Exodus); butterflies mark their privileged status, and they are Ayesha's only food (recalling the manna of the Israelites). All that the unbelievers see as they watch the pilgrims is their disappearance into the Arabian Sea. The implication remains that Ayesha parts the sea for those who believe; to everyone else, the entire enterprise ends as a cult suicide.

Much more happens in *The Satanic Verses*. London, called "Ellowen Dee-owen" by Farishta, is beset by ethnic antagonisms. Its police and most whites are brutal racists; its Indians are rogues or displaced mystics. Still, nothing in Rushdie's novel is what it appears to be, and that is his point. Empires and religions alike arise from a combination of noble and sordid motives. It is impossible to admire or hate anything unreservedly; there is evil even in that which appears absolutely good, and, conversely, one can explain evil in terms of good gone awry. Such relativism is hardly new, but the notoriety *The Satanic Verses* has received has obscured the author's point. What is clear is that *The Satanic Verses* is the logical sequel to ideas Rushdie began to develop in *Midnight's Children* and *Shame*, as well as an allegory that strains narrative and religious sensibilities to the breaking point.

Robert J. Forman

Other major works

NONFICTION: *The Jaguar Smile: A Nicaraguan Journey*, 1987.
FABLE: *Haroun and the Sea of Stories*, 1990.

Bibliography

Appignanesi, Lisa, and Sara Maitland, eds. *The Rushdie File*. Syracuse, N.Y.: Syracuse University Press, 1990. A survey of critical reaction to *The Satanic Verses*. Contains a chronology of events following the novel's publication, extracts from several interviews with Rushdie, the text of the Khomeini *fatwā*, reprints of representative articles from Europe and the United States, and a series of reflections on religion, censorship, Islam, toleration, and the relation between truth and fiction.
Mortimer, Edward. "*Satanic Verses*: The Aftermath." *The New York Times Book Review*, July 22, 1990, 3, 25. A discussion of the right to publish

offensive literature. Mortimer concludes that genius and literary worth can mitigate such offense and allow publication. Mortimer believes that *The Satanic Verses* is, indeed, a work of genius and not, as some have claimed, an unreadable novel published to provoke controversy. He does, however, suggest that an author's self-imposed censorship has its place in the writing of fiction.

Pipes, Daniel. *The Rushdie Affair: The Novel, the Ayatollah, and the West*. New York: Birch Lane Press/Carol Publishing Group, 1990. This volume also recounts the controversy attending publication of *The Satanic Verses*, though it examines the question from the Muslim point of view. It suggests that the valid arguments of many against publication were lost in the wake of the Khomeini *fatwā* that decreed Rushdie's death, in effect giving credence to the wild Muslim stereotype held by many Westerners. It also contains information on the historical founding of Islam, which will be helpful to readers of *The Satanic Verses* who are without this background.

Rushdie, Salman. "Salman Rushdie." Interview by John Haffenden. In *Novelists in Interview*, edited by John Haffenden. New York: Methuen, 1985. Conducted following the success and controversy of *Shame*, this interview concentrates on Rushdie's background and contains insights into his early life in Bombay and Karachi, his schooling at Rugby School and Kings College, Cambridge, and his experiences as actor, advertising copywriter, and aspiring author.

Weatherby, W. J. *Salman Rushdie: Sentenced to Death*. New York: Carroll & Graf, 1990. A sensationally written biography of Rushdie that focuses on his difficulties with his family (particularly his father) and his disputes with publishers and agents, fellow writers, and wives. It offers an essentially negative portrait of a brilliant but insecure and ruthlessly ambitious man.

J. D. SALINGER

Born: New York, New York; January 1, 1919

Principal long fiction
The Catcher in the Rye, 1951.

Other literary forms
Little, Brown and Company has published three collections of J. D. Salinger's short fiction: *Nine Stories* (1953), *Franny and Zooey* (1961), and *Raise High the Roof Beam, Carpenters, and Seymour: An Introduction* (1963). An unauthorized paperback collection of his stories in two volumes, apparently published by an unidentified source in Berkeley, California, *The Complete Uncollected Short Stories of J. D. Salinger*, was issued in 1974. It provoked Salinger's first public statement in some years, denouncing the collection, which was suppressed by the copyright holders. There has been one film adaptation of his work, produced by Samuel Goldwyn and adapted by Julius J. and Phillip G. Epstein from Salinger's "Uncle Wiggily in Connecticut," renamed *My Foolish Heart* (1950) and starring Susan Hayward and Dana Andrews. Salinger was so upset by the screen version that he has since banned all further adaptations of his work into any other medium.

Achievements
In the post-World War II years, Salinger has been unanimously acclaimed by both the literate American youth and the critical establishment. His only novel has sold steadily since its publication, and not only does it still generate high sales, but it also generates intense discussion as to its appropriateness for classroom use. Although his productivity has been slow, his popularity both in terms of sales and critical articles and books written about him has continued unabated since the early 1950's.

The Catcher in the Rye has been cited as one of the most read and influential postwar novels and has entered the culture as a statement of youth's view of the complex world. The novel has been translated into German, Italian, Japanese, Norwegian, Swedish, French, Dutch, Danish, Hebrew, Czechoslovakian, Yugoslavian, and Russian, and has been highly successful. In Russia, possession of a copy of *The Catcher in the Rye* is something of a status symbol for young intellectuals. Although there have been problems in translating the particularly American idiom into foreign languages, the story somehow touches a nerve that cuts across cultural and global lines. The novel has also been favorably compared to Mark Twain's *The Adventures of Huckleberry Finn* (1884) in terms of its portrayal of the "phoniness" of society, the coming of age of a young man, and its use of colloquial language.

Salinger's reputation, paradoxically, has been aided by his refusal to give interviews or to be seen in public. Under his cloak of secrecy, critics and magazine writers have pursued him relentlessly, trying to discover his thoughts, concerns, and approaches to literature and writing. Partly as a result of their speculation, more has been written about Salinger than any other postwar author. Since 1953, all of his short fiction has appeared exclusively in *The New Yorker*. He is said to be working on a novel about the fascinating Glass family, whose members have appeared in most of his work since the publication of *The Catcher in the Rye*.

Biography

Jerome David Salinger was born in New York, New York, on January 1, 1919, the second child and only son of Sol and Miriam (Jillich) Salinger. Since the details on Salinger and his parents' life is clouded, one can only assume that this date is correct. Salinger's father was born in Cleveland, Ohio, and has been noted as being the son of a rabbi, but he drifted far enough away from orthodox Judaism to become a successful importer of hams and to marry a gentile, the Scotch-Irish Marie Jillich, who changed her name soon after to Miriam to fit in better with her husband's family.

Salinger attended schools on Manhattan's upper West Side, doing satisfactory work in all subjects except arithmetic. He probably spent most of his summers in New England camps like most sons of upper-middle-class New York families; he was voted the "most popular actor" in the summer of 1930 at Camp Wigwam in Harrison, Maine. When he reached high school age, he was placed in Manhattan's famed McBurney School, a private institution, where, although interested in dramatics, he flunked out after one year. In September of 1934, his father enrolled him at Valley Forge Military Academy in Pennsylvania.

During his two years at Valley Forge, Salinger did satisfactory, but undistinguished, work. He belonged to the Glee Club, the Aviation Club, the French Club, the Non-Commissioned Officers' Club, and the Mask and Spur, a dramatic organization. He also served as literary editor of the academic yearbook, *Crossed Sabres*, his senior year. He is credited with writing a three-stanza poetic tribute to the academy that has since been set to music and is sung by the cadets at their last formation before graduation. Although not yet the recluse that he would later become, Salinger began to write short stories at that time, usually working by flashlight under his blankets after "lights out." Astonishingly, he also appeared interested in a career in the motion-picture business, either as a producer or a supplier of story material. He was graduated in June of 1936.

It is unclear what Salinger did after graduation, but he enrolled at least for the summer session of 1937 at Washington Square College in New York. Salinger, in one of his rare interviews, has mentioned that he spent some time in Vienna, Austria, and Poland learning German and the details of the ham importing business; it is not clear if his father accompanied him or not, but his trip probably occurred before Adolf Hitler's *Anschluss*, possibly in the fall of 1937.

On his return, Salinger enrolled at Ursinus College, a co-educational institution sponsored by the Evangelical and Reformed Church at Collegeville, Pennsylvania, not far from Valley Forge. Although he remained only one semester, he wrote a humorous and critical column, "The Skipped Diploma," for the *Ursinus Weekly*. He returned to New York and enrolled in Whit Burnett's famous course in short-story writing at Columbia University. It has been noted that Burnett was not at first impressed with the quiet boy who made no comments in class and seemed more interested in playwriting. Yet Salinger's first story, "The Young Folks," was impressive enough to be published in the March, 1940, issue of *Story*, edited by Burnett.

After publishing in a magazine famous for discovering new talent, Salinger spent another year writing without success until, at age twenty-two, he broke into the well-paying mass circulation magazines with a "short, short story" in *Collier's* and a "satire" in *Esquire*; he even had a story accepted by *The New Yorker*, which delayed publication of "Slight Rebellion off Madison," until after the war. This story proved to be one of the forerunners to *The Catcher in the Rye*.

During 1941, he worked as an entertainer on the Swedish liner *M. S. Kungsholm*. Upon his return to the United States, he wrote to the military adjunct at Valley Forge, Colonel Milton G. Baker, to see if there was some way that he could be inducted into the service, even though he had been classified as 1-B because of a slight cardiac condition. After Selective Service standards were lowered in 1942, Salinger was inducted and attended the Officers, First Sergeants, and Instructors School of the Signal Corps. He also reportedly corrected papers in a ground school for aviation cadets. He applied for Officers' Candidate School but was transferred to the Air Service Command in Dayton, Ohio, and wrote publicity releases. Finally, at the end of 1943, he was transferred to the Counter-Intelligence Corps. He also conducted a long correspondence with Eugene O'Neill's daughter Oona (later the last Mrs. Charles Chaplin).

He continued to write whenever he found the opportunity, publishing again in *Collier's*, *Story*, and at last in the well-paying and highly celebrated *Saturday Evening Post*. One of the *Saturday Evening Post* stories marks the first mention of the character Holden Caulfield. Salinger also sent Whit Burnett two hundred dollars from his earnings from the "slicks" to be used to encourage young writers and be applied to future writing contests for college undergraduates, such as the one won by Norman Mailer in 1941.

After training in Tiverton, Devonshire, he joined the American Fourth Division and landed on Utah Beach five hours after the initial assault wave on D-Day. He served with the Division through five European campaigns as a special agent responsible for security of the Twelfth Infantry Regiment. There is an unsupported story that Salinger had an audience with author and war correspondent Ernest Hemingway, who shot off the head of a chicken either to impress Salinger or to demonstrate the effectiveness of a German Luger. This incident has been used to explain why Salinger has written about Hemingway in a bad light in his stories and has Holden Caulfield in *The Catcher in the Rye* detest Hemingway's *A Farewell to Arms* (1929). There are also reports that during the war Salinger married a French woman, Sylvia, who was a doctor, possibly a psychiatrist. The two returned together to the United States after the war, according to biographer Ian Hamilton, but the marriage did not last long.

After the war, Salinger decided to make a living by selling stories to the so-called "slicks," publishing again in the *Saturday Evening Post* and *Collier's*, which issued "I'm Crazy" in its Christmas issue. "I'm Crazy" featured the long-delayed debut of Holden Caulfield, who had been mentioned as missing in action in several of Salinger's wartime stories. *Mademoiselle*, *Good Housekeeping*, and *Cosmopolitan* also published Salinger's work. *Cosmopolitan* featured a short novelette, "The Inverted Forest," an involved, obscure allegory of an artist, his possible muses, and his fate. During part of this period, Salinger lived with his parents but also kept a Greenwich Village apartment to entertain various young women. He also, supposedly, began to develop an interest in Zen Buddhism that is illustrated in his stories following publication of *The Catcher in the Rye*, especially the Glass family saga, but there is no suggestion that he actually converted to Buddhism.

After the disastrous film version of "Uncle Wiggily in Connecticut" and stories in *Harper's* and *World Review*, he settled down with a contract to produce stories exclusively for *The New Yorker* and has published exclusively for that magazine since. At that time, Salinger was also his most public: he lived in Tarrytown, New York, and even visited a short-story class at Sarah Lawrence College. Although he seemed to enjoy the conversation and interaction, he never repeated it. It was during that period that he decided to avoid all public appearances and concentrate his efforts on writing.

The Catcher in the Rye finally made its appearance on July 16, 1951, although years earlier Salinger submitted, had accepted, and then withdrew a much shorter version. It was not the immediate hit that time suggests, but it did gain Salinger enormous critical praise and respect. The novel was successful enough to cause Salinger to have his picture removed from the dust jacket of the third edition and all subsequent editions; annoyed by the letters, autograph seekers, and interviewers that sought him, he apparently sailed to Europe to keep his composure and avoid publicity.

In 1952, Salinger moved to Cornish, New Hampshire, where he has lived since. He often visited nearby Dartmouth College, where he met his future wife, Claire Douglas, at a cocktail party in Manchester, New Hampshire. He fraternized with high school students in the area, attending high school basketball games and entertaining them at their parties. In November, 1953, he granted Shirley Blaney an interview for the high school page of the Claremont, New Hampshire, *Daily Eagle*. He reputedly became upset when the interview was printed prominently on the editorial page. At that point, he ceased entertaining the students and built a fence around his home that still stands.

In 1955, he returned to print in *The New Yorker* with the publication of "Franny," the first of the Glass Family series that occupied all of his forthcoming stories. He supposedly dedicated it to his new bride, whom he married in Barnard, Vermont, on February 17, 1955. On December 10 of that year, the Salingers became the parents of their first child, Margaret Ann; on February 13, 1960, his only son, Matthew, was born. Since then, Salinger has concentrated his efforts on rearing his family and documenting the Glass family. Little has been heard or read from Salinger since the 1965 publication of "Hapworth 16, 1924" in *The New Yorker*. He was divorced from his wife in November, 1967.

The reclusive Salinger, dubbed "the Greta Garbo of American letters" by *People Weekly*, was thrust into the media limelight in the mid-1980's because of disputes over the content of a biography being published by Ian Hamilton. Thwarted in his quest for an interview with Salinger, Hamilton had nevertheless stumbled onto two valuable—and hitherto untapped—research sources: collections of Salinger letters in Princeton University's Firestone Library and the library of the University of Texas. Galleys of Hamilton's book were slipped to Salinger by a book dealer in 1986, and Salinger immediately protested the use of his unpublished letters. Attempts at compromise failed, and Salinger filed suit against Hamilton and his publisher, Random House. Eventually, a U.S. Court of Appeals ruling decreed that the letters were indeed Salinger's property and could not be quoted, or even paraphrased, without his permission. The Supreme Court declined to hear an appeal, and Salinger returned to his seclusion. Hamilton's book *In Search of J. D. Salinger*, minus the content of the letters but filled out with a detailed account of the controversy, was finally published in 1988.

Analysis

J. D. Salinger's characters are always extremely sensitive young people who are trapped between two dimensions of the world: love and "squalor." The central problem in most of his fiction is not finding a bridge between these two worlds but bringing some sort of indiscriminate love into the world of squalor: to find a haven where love can triumph and flourish. Some characters, such as the young, mixed-up Holden Caulfield, adopt indiscriminate love to aid them in their journey through the world of squalor, while others, such as Seymour Glass, achieve a sort of perfect love, or satori, and are destroyed, in Seymour's case by a bullet through his head. Each of these characters is metropolitan in outlook and situation and is introverted: their battles are private wars of spirit, not outward conflicts with society. The characters' minds struggle to make sense of the dichotomy between love and squalor, often reaching a quiet peace and transcending their situation through a small act.

Frederick L. Gwynn and Joseph L. Blotner, in *The Fiction of J. D. Salinger* (1958), offer an analysis of Salinger that claims he is the first writer in Western fiction to present transcendental mysticism in a satiric mode, or simply to present religious ideas satirically. Although much has been made of Salinger's Zen Buddhism, the stories do not seem to be about applying Buddhist principles to modern life, nor do they present a clear and coherent statement of what these principles entail or signify. Holden Caulfield does not react as a Buddhist would, nor does he seek consolation from Buddhism. The Glass family may mention Buddhism, but because of their acquaintance with all religions and their high intelligence and hyperkinetic thirst for knowledge, Salinger suggests they they have picked and chosen aspects from various religions and created a composite of them all. If anything, Salinger's characters seem to move toward a "perfect" Christian ideology—indiscriminate love.

The normality of the characters in Salinger's stories is a primary attraction for readers. Holden Caulfield is no better or no worse than any young high school boy; he is merely a bit more articulate and honest in his appraisals, more open with his feelings. Even though the Glasses are brilliant, they are not cerebral or distanced from the reader because of their brilliance; and all the characters live in the same world and environment as the readers do. Their moments of pain and delight are the same as the readers', but Salinger's characters articulate these moments more naturally and completely.

Another element that draws readers into Salinger's world is his use of satire. The satire not only touches upon the characters' descriptions and reactions to the world, but also touches on the characters themselves. Holden Caulfield's confrontation with Maurice, the brawny elevator operator/pimp, shows not only the ridiculousness of the antagonist but also Holden's stupidity for attempting to reason with him. Even if he does not realize it, Holden does many of the things that he tells readers he hates. He is critical enough, however, to realize that these things are wrong.

All of Salinger's work has also a strong focus on the family; it is held as an ideal, a refuge, and a raft of love amid a sea of squalor. Although the family does not provide the haven that Salinger suggests it might be, it is through coming home that the characters flourish, not by running away. Holden Caulfield, in *The Catcher in the Rye*, never realistically considers running away, for he realizes that the flight cannot help him. At the critical moment his family may not be ready to grant him the salvation that he needs, but it is his only security. If the world is a place of squalor, perhaps it is only through perfect love within the family unit that an individual can find some kind of salvation. It is important to notice that the family unit is never satirized in Salinger's fiction.

The basic story of *The Catcher in the Rye* follows the adventures of sixteen-year-old Holden Caulfield, during a forty-eight-hour period after he has been expelled from Pencey, the latest in a long line of expulsions for Holden. After a few confrontations with various fellow students at Pencey, he goes to New York City, his hometown, to rest before confronting his parents with the news. During the trip he tries to renew some old acquaintances, has an adventure or two, and tries to come to grips with the headaches that he has been having lately. Eventually, after two meetings with his younger sister, Phoebe, he returns home. At the book's opening, he is somewhere in California recovering from an illness (it is not clear if it is physical or mental) and has reconciled himself to his lot by returning to the bosom of his family. The entire story is told through the first-person narration of Holden, who uses adolescent phrasings and profanity as he tries to reconstruct his "crazy" period of the previous year.

Holden Caulfield is a normal sixteen-year-old, no better and no worse than his peers, except that he is slightly introverted, a little sensitive, and willing to express his feelings openly. His story can be seen as a typical growing process. As he approaches and is ready to cross the threshold into adulthood, he begins to get nervous and worried. His body has grown, but his emotional state has not. He is gawky, clumsy, and not totally in control of his body. He seeks to find some consolation, some help during this difficult time but finds no one. The school cannot help him, his peers seem oblivious to his plight, his parents are too concerned with other problems (his mother's nerves and his father's business activities as a corporate lawyer). His girl friend, Sally Hayes, is no help, and his favorite teacher merely lectures him drunkenly. The only people with whom he can communicate are the two young boys at the museum, the girl with the skates at the park, and his younger sister Phoebe: all of them are children, who cannot help him in his growing pains but remind him of a simpler time, one to which he wishes he could return. Eventually, he does cross the threshold (his fainting in the museum) and realizes that his worries were unfounded. He has survived. At the end of the book, Holden seems ready to reintegrate himself into society and accept the responsibilities of adulthood.

Through Holden's picaresque journeys through New York City, he grows spiritually. He slowly begins to recognize the "phoniness" around him and the squalor that constantly presses down on him. Although he castigates himself for doing some of the phony things, lying especially, Holden does realize that what he is doing is incorrect: this understanding sets him above his fellows; he knows what he is doing. Holden never hurts anyone in any significant way; his lies are small and harmless. Conversely, the phony world also spins lies, but they are dangerous since they harm people. For example, Holden mentions that Pencey advertises that it molds youth, but it does not. He is angry with motion-pictures because they offer false ideals and hopes. Yet, his lies help a mother think better of her son. Like Huck Finn, he lies to get along, but not to hurt, and also like Huck, he tries to do good.

By the end of the book, Holden has accepted a new position—an undiscriminating love for all mankind. He even expresses that he misses all the people who did wrong to him. Although not a Christ-figure, Holden does acquire a Christlike position—perfect love of all mankind, good and evil. He is not mature enough to know what to do with this love, but he is mature enough to accept it. In this world, realizing what is squalor and what is good, and loving it all is the first step in achieving identity and humanity: compassion is what Holden learns.

Recalling all the suffering and pain that he has witnessed, Holden develops a profound sense of the human condition and accepts Christ's ultimate commandment. In the passage regarding Holden's argument with his Quaker friend, Holden argues that Judas is not in hell because Jesus would have had the compassion and love not to condemn Judas to hell. Also, Jesus did not have time to analyze who would be perfect for his Disciples; thus, they were not perfect and would have condemned Judas if they had had the chance. In this discussion, Holden points out his own dilemma, not having time to analyze his decisions, and his belief in the perfect love that he embraces at the end of the book. Although not a would-be saint, Holden does become a fuller human being through his experiences.

The title symbol of the novel comes from Holden's misreading of a line from a song. His wish, as expressed to his sister, is that he wishes to be a catcher in the rye, standing beneath a cliff waiting to catch any child that falls over the cliff: he wants to spare children the pain of growing up and facing the world of squalor. He also wishes to provide some useful, sincere activity in the world. The catcher-in-the-rye job is a dream, a hope, and a job that Holden realizes is impractical in the world as it is. Only by facing the world and loving it indiscriminately can anyone hope to live fully within it and have any hope of changing it.

In the novel, Holden is also constantly preoccupied with death. He worries about the ducks freezing in the winter, the Egyptian mummies, and his dead brother Allie. He cries to Allie not to let him disappear. This symbolizes Holden's wish not to disappear into society as another cog in the great machine, and his wish not to lose what little of himself he feels that he has. To Holden, the change from childhood to adulthood is a kind of death, a death he fears because of his conviction that he will become other than he is. This fear proves groundless by the end of the book. His name also provides a clue: Holden—hold on. His quest is to hold on to his adolescent self and to save other children from the pain of growth. His quest fails, but his compassion and the growth of his humanity provide him with better alternatives.

In terms of sex, Holden is often puritanical. His trouble lies in the fact that he begins to feel sorry for the girls he dates, and he has too much compassion for them to defile their supposed virtue. This problem ties in with his compassion: he tries to see people as they are and not as types. He looks quickly and may make rash judgments, but once he talks to or acquaints himself with someone, he sees him or her as an individual. His mentioning of the boring boy he knew in school who could whistle better than anyone is the perfect example: Holden cannot help but confront people as individuals. Again, this shows his growing compassion and indiscriminate love. He sympathizes with the girl's position, which is a very mature quality for a teenager, and with anyone's position once he gets to know that person.

The Catcher in the Rye also reflects the art of a maturing author. Although there is no indication that Holden will become a novelist, there are clues scattered throughout the novel that he has an artistic sensibility. His sensitivity, his compassion, his powers of observation, and his references to himself as an exhibitionist are several such clues.

Later, Salinger more fully develops the contrast between squalor and love in the world and reintroduces various elements of his Caulfield family saga in his grand design of charting the story of the Glass family. The compassion, the satire, the heights of perfect love, the love of the family unit, and the use of brilliant conversational language that characterized Salinger's great novel, *The Catcher in the Rye*, will continue to set his fiction apart.

Domenic Bruni

Other major works

SHORT FICTION: *Nine Stories*, 1953; *Franny and Zooey*, 1961; *Raise High the Roof Beam, Carpenters, and Seymour: An Introduction*, 1963.

Bibliography
Belcher, William F., and James W. Lee, eds. *J. D. Salinger and the Critics* Belmont, Calif.: Wadsworth, 1962. This collection of critical essays could function as a casebook for Salinger study. Part 1 contains thirteen essays exclusively on *The Catcher in the Rye*; the smaller part 2 covers his stories and contains general studies. Suggests topics for essays and includes a bibliography.

French, Warren. *J. D. Salinger.* New York: Twayne, 1963. This good general study offers a detailed introduction to Salinger and analyzes all of his work published by 1963. Includes an annotated bibliography.

Gwynn, Frederick L., and Joseph L. Blotner. *The Fiction of J. D. Salinger.* Pittsburgh: University of Pittsburgh Press, 1958. This tiny book provides capsule introductions to Salinger's fiction and is most useful in its discussion of his early stories. Contains a short bibliography.

Laser, Marvin, and Norman Furman, eds. *Studies in J. D. Salinger: Reviews, Essays, and Critiques of "The Catcher in the Rye" and Other Fiction*. New York: Odyssey Press, 1963. Although the collection concentrates on *The Catcher in the Rye*, it includes four explications of "For Esmé—with Love and Squalor," a section on censorship of *The Catcher in the Rye*, some negative evaluations of Salinger's work, and some suggested writing topics.

Lundquist, James. *J. D. Salinger*. New York: Frederick Ungar, 1979. Discusses Salinger's work as exhibiting four stages of development: alienation resulting from World War II, isolation ended through "Zen-inspired awakening," Zen art applied to the short story, and philosophical experimentation. Especially strong on Salinger's later work, the book also contains an exhaustive bibliography.

JAMES SALTER

Born: New York, New York; June 10, 1925

Principal long fiction
The Hunters, 1957; *The Arm of Flesh*, 1961; *A Sport and a Pastime*, 1967; *Light Years*, 1975; *Solo Faces*, 1979.

Other literary forms
Dusk and Other Stories (1988) is a collection of short stories, many of which were published earlier in such journals as *The Paris Review*.

Achievements
James Salter is a novelist who has never reached a large or wide audience for his delicately plotted and precisely written novels, although he has received much critical praise. The most noticeable aspect of his novels is a search for an Edenic world or a perfect moment. His protagonists fail to achieve or sustain that moment, but they prove themselves worthy of the quest. Also noteworthy are his careful observation and his polished and occasionally lyrical style.

Biography
James Salter was born on June 10, 1925, in New York City. He attended Georgetown University and was graduated from West Point. After graduation, Salter became a U.S. Air Force pilot and served on active duty from 1945 until 1957. His first novel, *The Hunters*, drew directly on that experience as it describes Air Force fighter pilots in the Korean War. In 1961, his next novel, *The Arm of Flesh*, returned to the milieu of fighter pilots, but its protagonists are a lost pair of pilots in peacetime in a troubled Germany. In 1967, Salter published a novel called *A Sport and a Pastime*, set in the very different world of the French bourgeoisie; it deals with two young lovers and stresses the inevitability of fate. In 1975, he published an ambitious and different type of novel: *Light Years* is an analysis of the breakup of a supposedly perfect marriage, done in the manner of F. Scott Fitzgerald. In *Solo Faces* Salter returned to his studies of aloof warriors who live by a very specific code. This time the area of action is not that of fighter pilots but mountain climbing. Salter settled in Aspen, Colorado.

Analysis
James Salter's primary concerns are the achievement of perfection and the integrity of the individual. He is more interested in how people live than in what success they achieve. Salter's novels stress that whatever perfection is

achieved is in any case transitory. Age or death destroys skills and whatever grace his characters discover or embody. This reality does not mean that the struggle is useless; it is part of the human being's glory to struggle for something higher in the face of imperfect human nature.

The Hunters, Salter's first novel, draws upon his Air Force experience. The hero is Cleve Saville, a veteran pilot who has come to Korea to fly Air Force jets against the Russian MIGs. As an experienced pilot, Cleve is also called upon to train an unsuccessful flight of young pilots. Cleve's first conflict is with Lieutenant Sheedy. Sheedy is good at self-promotion; he makes a number of dubious claims about shooting down Russian MIGs. His wingman is very cooperative, supporting claims that cannot be confirmed by film. The commander of the squadron, Colonel Dutch Imil, is eager to accept these dubious claims, because they enhance his reputation and that of the group. The conflict comes to a head when Cleve overhears Sheedy rewriting the description of a kill in order to get the Distinguished Flying Cross rather than a lesser Air Medal. This represents a violation of the code of the warrior by which Cleve lives: what is important is to strive for excellence within the group; any attempt to grab glory, deserved or not, is unacceptable. True glory is, for Cleve, within oneself.

In Korea Cleve meets an old friend, Captain Abbot, who was a very successful pilot in World War II but has now lost his nerve. He claims malfunctions with his plane and scrubs nearly every mission. As a result, Abbot is sent to Japan to an office job, where he can retain his rank if not his integrity. Cleve is sympathetic toward Abbot, but he knows that he cannot give him the courage he needs to continue to be a fighter pilot; it must come from within.

Cleve works at teaching the young pilots in his flight the calm professionalism that is needed in a good pilot. He becomes a father figure to all these pilots but one: Lieutenant Pell.

Though Pell is only a newly trained fighter pilot, he has great confidence. Cleve has noticed that overconfidence in Pell's brash overtures to a Japanese woman while he waited to be shipped to Korea. Cleve reprimanded Pell at that time, but Pell had not paid much attention. The real problem comes when Pell begins to be successful in shooting down MIGs while his leader, Cleve, has yet to shoot down his first airplane. Pell's success comes because he often leaves the formation to go after Russian airplanes on his own. Cleve reprimands him and brings the matter to Imil, but Imil refuses to do anything that would jeopardize his "kill rate."

While Cleve is on leave in Tokyo having an idyllic encounter with the daughter of a Japanese painter, he receives news that someone in his flight has been shot down. Upon returning, he finds that Daughters died because Pell left him unprotected and went off on his own to gain the glory of another kill. Yet Imil refuses to ground a man with five kills, an ace.

The climax of the book comes when Cleve shoots down the enemy's ace, "Casey Jones," while he and his wingman, Hunter, are very short of fuel. After this victory, Cleve barely manages to glide his airplane to a landing, but Hunter does not make it. Back at the base, Cleve is unable to support his claim of having downed Casey Jones, because the film did not run and his dead wingman was the only witness. Suddenly, Cleve reverses the situation by claiming that Hunter shot down Casey Jones and that he was a witness to it. Cleve is proud of his accomplishment but does not need the recognition that would come with such a victory. He has kept a pledge to Hunter that he would get a MIG before he left Korea; for Cleve, meeting commitments and personal integrity are more important than public glory.

Cleve dies in the last chapter, but that is really a denouement rather than a climax, for he has succeeded in living by the code of the warrior. Salter's philosophy of heroism owes much to Ernest Hemingway. His style is also rather similar to Hemingway's, although Salter avoids the mannerisms of the earlier writer.

Light Years is a very different novel from *The Hunters*, more in the tradition of Henry James or F. Scott Fitzgerald than that of Hemingway. Viri is a successful architect, but he longs for a greater creative achievement; he envies such great architects as Christopher Wren and Stanford White, but he realizes that their accomplishments are beyond him. His wife, Nedra, is the center of the marriage: she arranges the meals, parties, and outings that make their life outwardly enviable. There always seems to be an amusing friend—Viri and Nedra are hardly ever alone—and their superb food and wine are described in loving detail, as is their stately Victorian house on the Hudson River.

When Nedra must visit her dying father in Altoona, Pennsylvania, she observes the broken windows and empty warehouses that signify a very different life-style. She does sincerely grieve at the death of her father, but her call to Viri is telling: she bemoans the badly designed hospitals of the area. Clearly, Nedra's life is more style than substance. The visit raises anxieties, reminding her of her very different origins; the good life she enjoys with Viri seems not a natural but an invented one.

Soon the façade of Viri and Nedra's "perfect" marriage is peeled back further. Nedra is having an affair with Jivan, and Viri is attracted to another woman. Nedra does not seem to consider her affair a threat to the marriage, and Viri apparently accepts it, although he is not pleased by it. Nedra holds that the way one lives one's life is more important than traditional bonds and legal connections.

The turning point of the book seems to come near the middle rather than the end. Nedra and Viri's friend Arnaud is mugged and beaten in New York City. He recovers physically from the beating but not psychologically, for he has experienced the darkness outside Eden and can no longer participate in the round of parties and dinners, wine, chocolate, and pears. A cloud has fallen upon Eden.

Viri and Nedra go to Europe, a trip that should be the culmination of their perfect life but instead proves its destruction. Nedra suddenly announces, "I don't want to go back to our old life." Outwardly beautiful as their marriage may be, it has become a lifeless routine. They are divorced in the fall (another echo of a lost Eden) and go their separate ways.

Exhilarated by the possibilities of a new life, Nedra returns to Europe and stays for a while at Davos, Switzerland. She meets a Mr. Pall there but does not stay; continuing her search for perfection, she feels a kind of "pagan happiness." The climax of that search is her attempt to join a theatrical company. She is rejected because of her age, but she has a brief affair with the director, Richard Brom. He assures her: "You'll find your new life." She knows, however, that "these are her last days. She will never find them again."

Viri decays very quickly after Nedra leaves. The house that once held a kind of perfection now feels dark and gloomy. He visits friends, but that is only a reminder of a better past. Finally, he sells the house and goes to Europe.

Nedra has taken an apartment and is serene although her health is failing. She talks often to her daughter Franca; she had earlier encouraged Franca to search for the life that has eluded her. Now she says that love is only an illusion; it does not last. She dies like her father did: "suddenly in the fall of the year."

The novel ends with Viri. He has married an Italian girl, but it is more a capitulation than a love match. Revisiting the house on the Hudson, he finds it "terrible." At the end he sums up the fall from Eden: "It happens in an instant. It is all one long day, one endless afternoon, friends leave, we stand on the shore."

Solo Faces has another uncompromising protagonist: Rand, a mountain climber and a man of few words. He is involved with a woman, Louise, but she is less important to him than his quest to climb mountains. When he meets another climber, Cabot, he decides to leave his job and woman and go to France.

In Chamonix, Rand—his first name, Vernon, is only mentioned near the end of the book—waits for the weather to clear, although he does a few easy climbs with an Englishman, Bray. When Cabot arrives in Chamonix, the serious climbing and testing begin. Rand and Cabot decide to climb the Dru, a very difficult mountain. On the climb, Cabot is hurt when a rock slide smashes his face. Rand manages to reassure him and finally to drag him to the summit where he can be rescued, but now Cabot cannot bear to climb with Rand, for Rand has seen his weakness. Cabot has used climbing as an attempt to achieve fame and fortune; Rand, on the other hand, sccs climbing as an activity to be practiced for its own sake.

Soon after, Cabot is leading an assault upon a famous mountain, the Eiger. Significantly, Rand is excluded, and the climb is like an attack upon an enemy. Cabot takes camera crews along to record this event in order to profit from the climb—a complete violation of the code by which Rand lives. Cabot also drives his men beyond what they are capable of achieving; one of the party, Bray, falls to his death as a result of Cabot's ambition.

Rand's great moment in climbing is in direct contrast to that of Cabot. When he hears that an Italian climbing party is caught on the Dru with some injured climbers, he hastily collects a group and climbs the mountain under very difficult conditions to rescue them. The guides of Chamonix have taken an easier and more roundabout direction, and Rand's party arrives first. As a result of this heroic deed, he becomes famous. He resists for a while, refusing to talk to reporters, but finally the machine of publicity overcomes his reticence. He goes to Paris, where he lives with Catherin, but now he is noticed in restaurants; he is a celebrity. Yet celebrity is a very passing state and quickly fades. Once more, Rand leaves a loving woman and returns to his quest in Chamonix.

Rand, now a legend, makes solo climbs on mountain after mountain. Rumors about his activities and accomplishment circulate, and his name is spoken reverently. Rand ignores all of this to concentrate on what he must do: climb as well as he can. He chooses the most famous climb of all, the Walker, for a solo ascent. The climb is difficult, but he continues until he reaches a limit, a line he cannot cross. There is a moment when he cannot go on, cannot climb higher. In this failure, "something had gone out of him."

The rest of the book is a long denouement after the climax on the Walker. Returning to the United States, he meets with Cabot, who has fallen from a mountain in the Tetons; he is in a wheelchair, although there is nothing physically wrong with him. Rand attempts to get him out of the wheelchair by goading and pushing him. Rand knows that one cannot give up, even if he has lost the magical power he once possessed; it is as heroic to live well in defeat as it is to live well in victory.

In the last section of the novel, Rand is living in Mexico. Certain that man is only a "fake," no matter how strong or heroic he may seem, he struggles to maintain his integrity, to live out the time given to him. He returns to California and to Louise as the novel ends. Rand has taken his quest as far as he could and must now live in a diminished world.

Salter writes for the most part in a minimalist manner, with few adjectives or needless passages. Yet he is fond of physical description of places and, oddly, of characters' teeth. Lyrical, poetic passages mark important moments in each narrative. These passages are, perhaps, too frequent in *Light Years* and weaken the novel. In *Solo Faces*, he manages to reserve them for a few crucial moments; in that context, they are very effective.

James Salter's most persistent theme is the quest for whatever perfection this earth holds. That flawless moment can be achieved only briefly, if at all, but each of his protagonists is compelled to take up the quest. The end may be death or despair, but that does not matter. What matters is the attempt, the uncorrupted quest.

James Sullivan

Other major work
SHORT FICTION: *Dusk and Other Stories*, 1988.

Bibliography
Bourjaily, Vance. "Different Points of View." *The New York Times Book Review*, August 5, 1979, 11. Bourjaily is impressed by *Solo Faces*, which he finds to be a "beautifully fashioned and satisfying novel." He finds some problems, however, in the withheld point of view and in shifts of point of view. He is also critical of the final scene between Rand and Cabot.
Broyard, Anatole. "Ending in the Middle." *The New York Times*, June 25, 1975, 41. Broyard contrasts the effective plot and style of *A Sport and a Pastime* to the slim narrative and bloated style of *Light Years*. He especially finds the characters in *Light Years* to be less interesting and their problems unconvincing.
Dowie, William. "A Final Glory: The Novels of James Salter." *College English* 50 (January, 1988): 74-88. A thematic study of all Salter's fiction. Dowie, bemoaning the neglect of this novelist, sees the search for glory as the central theme of Salter's writing. Includes a brief bibliography.
Miller, Margaret Winchell. "Glimpses of a Secular Holy Land: The Novels of James Salter." *The Hollins Critic* 1 (February, 1982): 1-13. Another thematic study of Salter's fiction. Miller focuses on the paradise or "secular holy land" Salter's protagonists achieve for a short time. She also touches on his experimental technique, which she describes as "oblique."
Rorem, Ned. "The Artistry of James Salter." *Book World*, March 6, 1988, 1-2. Rorem finds a musical style to permeate Salter's writing: "tune-like phrases with their repetition and variation." He also identifies a melancholy running through these novels. Rorem praises Salter highly and compares him to such writers as Flannery O'Connor and John Cheever.

WILLIAM SAROYAN

Born: Fresno, California; August 31, 1908
Died: Fresno, California; May 18, 1981

Principal long fiction

The Human Comedy, 1943; *The Adventures of Wesley Jackson*, 1946; *Rock Wagram*, 1951; *Tracy's Tiger*, 1951; *The Laughing Matter*, 1953 (reprinted as *The Secret Story*, 1954); *Mama I Love You*, 1956; *Papa You're Crazy*, 1957; *Boys and Girls Together*, 1963; *One Day in the Afternoon of the World*, 1964.

Other literary forms

Despite his many novels, William Saroyan is more famous for his work in the short story, the drama, and autobiography. Each of these areas received emphasis at different stages in his career. In the 1930's, he made a spectacular literary debut with an avalanche of brilliant, exuberant, and unorthodox short stories. Major early collections were: *The Daring Young Man on the Flying Trapeze and Other Stories* (1934), *Inhale and Exhale* (1936), *Three Times Three* (1936), and *Love, Here Is My Hat and Other Short Romances* (1938). *My Name Is Aram* (1940), a group of stories detailing the experiences of Aram Garoghlanian growing up in a small California town, marks the culmination of his short-story artistry.

Most of Saroyan's plays and his productions on Broadway were concentrated in the years between 1939 and 1942. *My Heart's in the Highlands* was produced by the Group Theatre in April, 1939. His second major production, *The Time of Your Life* (1940), was awarded both the Pulitzer Prize and the New York Drama Critics' Circle Award and is still considered Saroyan's best play. *Hello Out There* (1942), a one-act play, is also regarded as a fine drama.

In 1951, Saroyan and Ross Bagdasarian published a very popular song, "Come On-a My House." Saroyan also wrote several television plays, including an adaptation of *The Time of Your Life*. Starting with *The Bicycle Rider in Beverly Hills* (1952), Saroyan composed extensive memoirs, including *Here Comes, There Goes, You Know Who* (1961), *Not Dying* (1963), *Days of Life and Death and Escape to the Moon* (1970), *Places Where I've Done Time* (1972), *Sons Come and Go, Mothers Hang in Forever* (1976), *Chance Meetings* (1978), and *Obituaries* (1979).

Achievements

A thorough evaluation of Saroyan's achievement as a writer has yet to be made. By the age of twenty, he had already decided his role in life was to be that of a professional writer, and throughout his remaining fifty years he dedicated himself to that vocation, publishing voluminously in all literary forms, with the exception of poetry. The sheer bulk of his work and his admission that much of it was done merely to earn money have worked against him. Further, his frequent arguments with his critics and his increasingly difficult personality left him with few strong critical advocates. Currently, his literary reputation is quite low.

Saroyan's lasting literary achievement is in the area of the short story, where he expanded the genre by linking narrative form to the essay and infusing his work with a highly individual vision of poetic intensity. Many of his stories feature a character modeled on Saroyan, a writer-persona who, though often obsessed with his own ideas and feelings, is vitally alive to the world of his immediate experience. Several of the most successful stories concern childhood experiences in an ethnic, small-town environment modeled on Saroyan's Fresno. Saroyan impressed his early readers with his rediscovery of the wondrous in the texture of ordinary American life. *The Saroyan Special: Selected Stories* (1948) is a collection of his best stories. *My Name Is Aram* delineates with some beautiful character portraits Saroyan's sense of the poetic interplay of values in the ethnic community.

Saroyan's plays oppose the vitality of personality and individual dreams to the force of social institutions and the threats of war. In their sense of improvised movement, his plays were a deliberate challenge to the strictly plotted productions of the commercial theater.

Starting in the mid-1940's, Saroyan turned his attention to longer fiction, writing over the next two decades a series of novels concerned with marriage and divorce. Apparently inspired by his own experiences, the books become increasingly skeptical about romantic love and reflect Saroyan's growing cynicism about the man-woman relationship while retaining his fondness for the charm of childhood.

Saroyan's longer fiction grows gradually out of those short stories concerned with growing up in a small town. *My Name Is Aram*, a story collection moving toward novelistic unity, leads directly to *The Human Comedy*, where Saroyan finally succeeds in making a novel out of his childhood material. While *The Adventures of Wesley Jackson* must be regarded as a failed attempt to write in the picaresque mode, *Rock Wagram* is a surprisingly mature handling of the thematic scope provided by the novel form. Whereas *The Adventures of Wesley Jackson* presents marriage as an idyllic goal for the solitary man, *Rock Wagram* focuses on the crushing effect of the title character's failed marriage. Several shorter book-length works—*Tracy's Tiger*, *Mama I Love You*, and *Papa You're Crazy*—seem more tied to Saroyan's earlier material in their confinement to the perspectives of childhood and youth and, for the most part, are limited in theme and story situations. Saroyan's other novels—*The Laughing Matter*, *Boys and Girls Together*, and *One Day in the Afternoon of the World*—are deliberate forays into social areas where relationships are often intense and events are somber in their finality. Like *Rock Wagram*, each of these books centers on a male's struggle with marriage, death, and divorce. The last novel, *One Day in the Afternoon of the World*, features a character who at last seems to have acquired the wisdom to deal with such personal crises. Though his longer fictions are professionally wrought, Saroyan's achievements in the novel form are limited.

The mood of the later novels is picked up and carried to greater extremes in Saroyan's memoirs, a series whose loose formats encourage the author to reveal, often in free associations, his deep anxiety about his relationship to his society. Saroyan's memoirs, generally his weakest works, become increasingly preoccupied with death, the significance of his literary achievements, and with his struggle to ward off a bitterness that he occasionally admits but wants to deny.

Biography

So much of William Saroyan's work—especially his fiction—is drawn from the circumstances of his life that it has a biographical dimension. He was born in 1908, in Fresno, California, the city where he died on May 18, 1981. The child of Armenian immigrants, he faced his first hardship when, at his father's death in 1911, he was placed for four years in the Fred Finch orphanage in Oakland. During these years, his mother worked in San Francisco as a maid, finally gathering the money to move back to a house in Fresno with her four children. Here Saroyan lived from age seven to seventeen, learning Armenian, acquiring an irreverence for the town's chief social institutions, the church and the school, and working as a newspaper boy and as a telegraph messenger to help support the family. At fifteen, he left school permanently to work at his Uncle Aram's vineyards. In 1926, he left Fresno, first to go to Los Angeles, then, after a brief time in the National Guard, to move to San Francisco, where he tried a number of jobs, eventually becoming at nineteen, the manager of a Postal Telegraph branch office. In 1928, determined to make his fortune as a writer, he made his first trip to New York. He returned to San Francisco the following year, somewhat discouraged by his lack of success. In the early 1930's, however, he began to write story after story, culminating with his decision in January, 1934, to write one story a day for the whole month. That year, *Story* published "The Daring Young Man on the Flying Trapeze," and suddenly Saroyan stories were appearing in many of the top periodicals. His first book of stories was published that year, and the following year he had enough money to make an ethnic return, a trip to Soviet Armenia.

Except for a few months in 1936 spent working on motion pictures at the Paramount lot, Saroyan spent the majority of the 1930's in San Francisco. By 1939, he had shifted his activities to drama, writing and producing plays on Broadway. After *The Time of Your Life* won both the New York Drama Critics' Circle Award for the best play of 1939 to 1940 and the Pulitzer Prize, Saroyan made headlines by rejecting the Pulitzer on the grounds that he was opposed to prizes in the arts and to patronage. More controversy followed when he wrote *The Human Comedy* as a screenplay for M-G-M, then argued about directing the film and tried to buy his work back for twenty thousand dollars, more than he was paid for it. At that time he was also, in a letter to *The New York Times*, publicly denouncing the Broadway theater.

Even though he had pacificist sympathies, Saroyan was inducted into the United States Army in October, 1942, serving until 1945. His most traumatic experience in the 1940's, however, was his marriage to Carol Marcus, which lasted from 1943 to 1949, and which was resumed briefly from 1951 to 1953, before a final divorce. The couple had two children, Aram and Lucy.

In the 1950's, Saroyan began to write more long fiction, much of it dealing with marital difficulties. In addition, in 1951, he was the coauthor of a hit song, "Come On-a My House," and in the late 1950's, he began writing television plays. From 1952 to 1959, he lived in a Malibu beach house, an environment which encouraged him to work very steadily. During this time, he lived a less public existence and, feeling monetary pressure because of his gambling and his huge income tax debt, he increasingly developed a reputation as a difficult personality.

In 1960, after some travel about the world, he settled in a modest apartment at 74 Rue Taitbout, Paris. The following year he was briefly a writer-in-residence at Purdue University. By 1962, he arranged to buy two adjacent houses in Fresno and thereafter alternated living between Fresno and Paris. He spent most of the last fifteen years of his life working on various volumes of memoirs. Five days before his death he called the Associated Press to give this statement: "Everybody has got to die, but I have always believed an exception would be made in my case. Now what?" After much success (much money earned by writing, much money lost by gambling), much international travel, much controversy, much fame, and much obscurity, William Saroyan died of cancer in his hometown, Fresno, in 1981.

Analysis

William Saroyan's work habits were a major determinant (for better or worse) of his unique literary effects. He regarded writing as work, something that required disciplined effort, but also as an activity whose chief characteristic was the free play of the mind. As he explained his practice, Saroyan would often give himself assignments, a story or a chapter a day (or so many hours of writing), but would seldom work from a detailed organizational plan. Uncomfortable with mulling over possible styles, attitudes, narrative directions, he would often prefer to plunge into writing, fueled by coffee and cigarettes, hoping that whatever got down on paper would inspire the story to "take off on its own." Whatever relationships would be worked out would be those of deep structure, drawn from his inner being rather than from rhetoric.

At times he would begin with a "theory" or abstract idea. (For example, the theory stated at the end of "War" is that hatred and ugliness exist in the heart of man.) The act of writing itself was to clarify and refine the idea for the writer. In "Myself upon the Earth," the writer's own situation, his dead father, and his attitudes toward the world begin to weave into the free connections that substitute for a conventional plot. Thematically, the apparently undisciplined becomes the true discipline as the dedication expressed in an attitude toward life—toward humanity—is transformed through the narration into a dedication to art.

There are obvious difficulties with this method of composition. "The Man with His Heart in the Highlands" begins in the course of its improvisation to split in two; when Saroyan puts it into the form of a full-length play, the theme of the importance of acceptance in forming the new American community is finally seen as a basic articulation in the material. Saroyan also acknowledged revision as an important stage in the writing process, but much of his work suffers from a lack of objectivity, the ability to see his own work clearly and revise it accordingly.

While the act of writing was for Saroyan both a kind of thinking and a performance, the materials of his art were usually the materials of his life. Much in the manner of Thomas Wolfe (an early influence), Saroyan's fiction was often drawn directly from his experience. A letter to Calouste Gulbenkian (in *Letters from 74 Rue Taitbout*, 1969) shows how Saroyan drew in detail on his external experience and his frame of mind for most of the content of "The Assyrian." Writing, he came to believe, was connected with "noticing" life and with the sense that life itself was theatrical. Although Saroyan acknowledged that the process of writing had to discover form in its materials and that the writer had to be transformed into a character framed by his art, the sense of witnessed scene and character in his best work lends a necessary solidity to his creative exuberance.

The favorite writer-personas in Saroyan's early fiction were poet-philosophers in the manner of Walt Whitman; American wiseguys (the young grown suddenly smarter about the ways of the world than their elders); or combinations of the two. His later long fiction featured the writer as a veteran of life, sometimes bitter but with his own philosophic resignation, a mode of stoic humility about what he might be able to accomplish. Saroyan's typical themes—the advocacy of love and a condemnation of war and violence—are less important than the way in which he plays the narrator (usually a writer) against the narrator's circumstances. In the most deep-seated manifestation of this paradigm—the ethnic boy responding to his American environment—Saroyan associates the ethnic self in the ethnic community with naturalness, lack of self-consciousness, true being, and dignity of person. The American environment, while it promises opportunity with its training and its competitive games, also has institutions which seem to specialize in modes of restriction, punishment, and prejudice.

The ethnic responds to his environment with a complex involvement and detachment. On the one hand, he is willing, even eager, to be assimilated; on the other hand, however, he is always aware of a kind of existence that has no adequately defined relationship to the American world of conventional social fact. The ethnic's psychological relationship to the world recalls Whitman's democratic paradox of man being intensely individual and at the same time like everyone else. In Saroyan's fiction, there is at times an emphasis on the individual's alienation—as when the protagonist in "The Daring Young Man on the Flying Trapeze" feels "somehow he had ventured upon the wrong earth" and the central character in "1,2,3,4,5,6,7,8" feels the room he is living in is not a part of him and wants a home, "a place in which to return to himself." Invariably, however, the ethnic family and its small-town environment expand quite naturally for Saroyan into a version of the democratic family of man.

This sense of communal home, however, is not easily preserved—as Saroyan's novels with their marital catastrophes and lonely protagonists repeatedly demonstrate. From the beginning, the fate of Saroyan's ethnic was complicated by the fact that his deepest allegiance was to a national community that no longer existed. In an early story, "Seventy Thousand Assyrians," the Assyrian states, "I was born in the old country, but I want to get over it . . . everything is washed up over there." Though Saroyan could be sympathetic to such practicality, he tried to achieve, often with a deliberate naïveté, a poetic point of view that would embrace both existence in the old community of family values (which was a basic part of his being) and existence in the practical new world (which offered the only opportunity for becoming).

From the perspective of Saroyan's writer-persona, the world outside is continually new, funny, sometimes strange, often wonderful, a place of innocent relationships and suspended judgments. A recurring situation in his work has someone who is apprehended for theft trying to explain that he is not guilty because his value system is different from that of his accusers. On the one hand, Saroyan believes in an attitude of joyful acceptance: here he sees man "on the threshold of an order of himself which must find human reality a very simple unavoidable majesty and joy, with all its complications and failures." On the other hand, he imagines, like Whitman, a more somber mystic vision based on "the joyous sameness of life and death." In this mysterious crucible, life is fate, perhaps only glimpsed fully when "drawing to the edge of full death every person is restored to innocence—to have lived was not his fault." Saroyan's basic impulse is to preserve, recapture, and restore the innocence that the world has lost that state of being which sees experience only as a fantastic fate which serves ultimately to redeem the primal self.

Like Sherwood Anderson's *Winesburg, Ohio* (1919) and William Faulkner's

The Unvanquished (1938), *My Name Is Aram* is a book that falls midway between short-story collection and novel. The stories are separate and distinct, but they all concern the small-town experiences of the same boy, Aram, with his Armenian relatives. There is little sense of sequence but rather an accumulated manifestation of the potential wisdom in this world. Saroyan emphasizes the preservation of innocence, the warding off of the absolute element in the values of the adult culture. Aram and his friends turn social rituals into human games, and in the course of their experiences demonstrate that the many social failures in these stories have really two constituents, the innocent immediacy of the experience (its essential value) and the cultural "truths" and judgments applied to it. Through vital participation in their world, Aram and his friends begin to negotiate its preconceived ideas.

The setting, the characters, and the young man's perspective which predominate in *The Human Comedy* all have their sources in Saroyan short stories. The background is World War II, and the California small town has accordingly become "the home front." In the book's basic drama, the innocence in this environment—its vulnerable children, young people, and women and its emotional closeness—must come to terms with death and its finalities.

Within the context of the small-town milieu, the novel focuses primarily on the Macauley family and most often on Homer Macauley, a fourteen-year-old telegraph messenger boy. As Homer delivers telegrams announcing the deaths of soldiers, he finds himself getting caught up psychologically in the shock of the family reactions. On his first such delivery, to Rosa Sandoval, the woman responds with an eerie, calm hysteria in which she confuses Homer with her dead son and begins to think of both as little boys. Feeling at first both compassion and an urge to flee, Homer gradually arrives at an awareness of the meaning of death. With the help of his mother (whose husband has recently died), he fights through feelings of loneliness and isolation toward the idea that death and change afford perspectives for redeeming the values of innocence, love, and life itself.

The ideal of the community dominates the book. The novel implies in its moments of crisis and healing—Homer becoming briefly transformed into the son of another woman; Tobey taking the place of the dead Marcus in the Macauley family—that mankind is a single family. Though the fact of death and the awareness of death are constant threats to the individual, the book, as the allusions to Homer's *Odyssey* (c. 800 B.C.) imply, is about to return home, the coming back from the ugly realities of the outside world to the love and security which the family of man can provide.

The book seems intent on assuring its readers that despite economic tribulations, the discontent of restless desire, the anxiety connected with competition, and the confining tendency of its institutions, the community is an active, positive force. A working out in the rhythms of experience of the differences between people—age, sex, degrees of formality—invariably shows positive contrasts. The many relationships Homer has with older people are all thematically active ingredients for dramatizing the closeness of the community. *The Human Comedy* insists—perhaps too facilely at times—on the capacity of the American community to regulate the experience of life and the encounter with death.

The Adventures of Wesley Jackson may be Saroyan's worst novel. It is marred by two closely related problems, an uncertain grasp of form and a confusion about its issues. Saroyan's indiscriminate use of his own military experience takes the novel hopelessly out of control. Evidently attempting to give himself ample latitude with the novel form, Saroyan chose to employ the picaresque form, referring in his comments on the novel to Mark Twain's *The Adventures of Huckleberry Finn* (1884). Unfortunately, Wesley is much too introverted to be an effective picaro of any kind. He is intended to be a nonconformist, but, except for a few anti-Army establishment opinions, his personal idealism and prosaic earnestness only serve to make him seem as remote from the realities of Army life as from the realities of war. Lacking a feeling for the actual operations of the Army, the book meanders haphazardly from the bureaucratic to the personal, from one location to another, from family concerns to writing ambitions, succeeding finally in giving the impression of an Army journal rather than a picaresque novel.

At times the book develops an antiwar theme; at times the theme seems to be the pettiness of the Army bureaucracy. No one theme, however, is developed consistently. Wesley's self-absorbed narration does provide some shaping by turning the officers into bad fathers (cruel figures of authority), the women into sympathetic (though vague) images, and his fellow soldiers into boys, sometimes naughty but basically innocent. In sporadic, almost desultory, fashion the first part of the book features Wesley's search for his father, the essentially good man who has been displaced and ignored by organized society. The last part of the book becomes concerned with Wesley's search for a son (actually a search for a woman to bear him a son). Were Wesley's narration less limited, less egotistical, these thematic threads might have made firmer connections.

The split structure of *Rock Wagram*—approximately half the novel taking place in September, 1942, and half in February, 1950—emphasizes the drive of Rock Wagram (pronounced Vah-GRAM) to be married to Ann Ford and his resultant puzzled desperation when that marriage fails. The chronological gap, by omitting the marriage and Rock's military experience, accents the negative quality of this part of his life. Yet by leaving out the specific difficulties that are so much a part of his later depression, the novel makes Rock's psychology a problematic frame for understanding events instead of using the events of the past to put his psychology in an understandable perspective. At times, the failure of the marriage seems explained by Ann's frivolous, lying character. At other times, the failure seems to grow out of Rock's ethnic assumption that man must become involved in a family existence.

Rock Wagram explores the tensions between man as individual and man as social animal. In his motion-picture career, Rock has become successful as an individual star, but his acquaintance with Ann Ford kindles his memories of certain values from his Armenian background, particularly the notion that a man is not complete until he had founded his own family, been husband to his wife, father to his children. Unhappily for him, Ann turns out to be like so many other characters whose departures from their true natures disturb him; her lies signify to him that she is refusing to be herself, hoping for something better. Earlier Rock has met a series of males rebelling against their heritage: Paul Key, the Hollywood producer who hates being a Jew; Sam Schwartz, Paul's nephew, who devotes himself to becoming the image of success; and Craig Adams, the completely assimilated Armenian. Although these men are denying both their heritage and their own individuality, they are better adapted to the world of casual social relationships than he, and the book raises doubts about the possibilities of a deeply authentic existence.

Rock chooses to see his life—and the life of man—as involving continual adjustment to a Shavian life force, a power which, once he begins to perceive it through his Armenian ethnic environment, becomes his ultimate guide to true being. To get in tune with this force, he tries to be uninhibited in his social relationships, to go with the flow of events, to pay attention to his circumstances and to the people he is with, and to be, as he puts it, "a good witness" to his own experience and to his world.

Part of Rock's effort to live in terms of true being is a half-conscious cultivation of strategies toward death. His reaction to the death of his brother Haig is rage; at the death of his friend Paul Key, he affects a Hemingwayesque stocisim; and to his mother's death, he responds by plunging deeply and intensely into his subjective nature. In spite of all attempts to come to terms with the reality of death, he seems at last depressed, left with a sense of being part not only of a dying culture, but also of a dying world. As he goes back to acting at the end of the narrative, his feeling for his art is one of obligation rather than enthusiasm for an individualized expression of himself. Yet, as the humor in his last statement indicates, he is finally not without hope in probing his lonely situation for its satisfactions.

The laughter of *The Laughing Matter* is that of black comedy. From the time Swan Nazarenus announces to her husband that she is pregnant with another man's child, *The Laughing Matter* moves powerfully but erratically toward what seems an almost self-indulgently gruesome ending. The story line is captive to the emotional tensions and explosions of Evan Nazarenus as he attempts to sort out a future direction for himself, Swan, and their two children, Red and Eva. As he resorts successively to drink, violence, a return to family harmony, an abortion, and more violence, the problem-pregnancy tends to be obscured by his confusing attempts at solution. Since his personality is never clarified in the characterization, and since he often gives the impression of running aimlessly about the countryside, Evan becomes progressively less sympathetic in his shifting relationship to people and events.

The accompaniment to the mad rhapsody of his behavior is more carefully controlled. The children are innocent victims, becoming increasingly aware that something is wrong and even acting out some of the tensions themselves. The Walzes, a neighbor couple, have their own fights, and Evan's brother, Dade, who has, after years of domestic turbulence, lost his family entirely, conveniently defines one possible outcome.

Complicating the question of what to do is the issue of who is to blame. In one scene between Evan and Dade, the two brothers—who often speak in an old-country tongue—review their ethnic fate as heads of families, Evan wondering what they as males have done wrong. Evan debates whether he ought to be more feminine, more kindly, or strive to retain his masculine pride in the face of what may be an essential challenge to his person. His solution, the abortion, is less an act of harsh morality (as he later views it) than the result of a desire to begin again, to regain a kind of innocence by reversing events.

The ironies and the deaths pile up so rapidly at the conclusion that they achieve only a blurred effect. The fact that so much violence results from simple ignorance begins to make the characters comic rather than tragic, and this may have been the prompting behind Saroyan's title. When Evan accuses the wrong man as the adulterer (pushing the poor lonely man toward suicide), and when he shoots and kills his brother Dade under the mistaken notion that they have been responsible for Swan's death from abortion, Evan seems more the incompetent than the grief-stricken victim. His own death in an auto accident may have been meant to suggest that the whole chain of events was merely a series of accidents, but this must be weighed against the remarks of the doctor who explains to Dade that Swan committed suicide and that she had evidently had a strong death wish for several years. For all its masculine madness, this book begins and ends by pointing an accusing finger at the woman.

Boys and Girls Together is a realistic study of a husband-wife relationship that moves with an understated satire toward black humor. The husband, Dick, is a writer who finds that his current domestic relationship has made it impossible for him to work, thus heaping financial strain upon his already turbulent marriage to Daisy. In the course of their sporadic fighting, the couple discovers greater and greater depths of incompatibility. Dick comes to the conclusion that she is ignorant, trivial, and selfish; Daisy accuses him of being egotistical and immature. Were it not for the two children (Johnny, five, and Rosey, two and a half), the writer, who is a family man, would undoubtedly leave.

As this account of a few days in their lives demonstrates, what keeps the marriage together is their socializing with other couples. The slight story line follows the meeting of Dick and Daisy with two other couples for a few days of fun in San Francisco. Though only casual friends, all the couples have common characteristics: In each instance, the husband has achieved prominence in the arts; in each case, the husband is many years older than the wife; and in each instance, the difference in age seems part of the strain on the marriage. Before all six can get together, the oldest husband, Leander, dies of a heart attack, an episode witnessed by Oscar Bard (the actor) and his wife, and by Leander's wife Lucretia. Dick and Daisy arrive soon after the attack and seem generally ineffective in preventing the scene from sliding from seriousness to farce. Dick eventually begins to act as satiric observer, commenting on Oscar's egotistical discomfort and on Lucretia's performance as grieving widow. The scene has its climax in Oscar's long speech on the difficulties of their kind of marriage. While he begins by pointing out realistically that the women they have married are not for them, he finally comes to the conclusion that it is sexual attraction that gives the necessary life to all partners in such marriages and which makes them continue to put up with each other. Dick does not disagree. Soon the survivors are planning a trip to Reno as another distraction from the harsh realities around them. Earlier, Dick had resented it when his wife teased him about being a fool for sex. In the last part of the novel, his understated satiric vision outlines them all as characters in a sexual farce.

If all of William Saroyan's writing can be regarded as his attempt to understand and define his position in the world, his long fiction must be seen as his deliberate recognition of the crueler circumstances in that world—death, the failure of love, divorce, the recalcitrant details of life itself. His own marital troubles undoubtedly inspired the novels of the 1950's and 1960's with their fragmented families, and while the intently masculine perspective in these books reveals a serious but virtually unexamined reverence for love and marriage, it also demonstrates the author's own very personal irritation with wives. In nearly all of his novels, the formal problem tends to be the male protagonist's varied reactions to his situation. In *Rock Wagram* and *The Laughing Matter*, Saroyan is successful in focusing these reactions by means of intense emotional pressures, but his confusion about final blame for the marital breakdown makes a fictional closure difficult. With *Papa You're Crazy* and *Mama I Love You*, he moves to the detachment of the child's point of view but is still uncertain about the extent to which the world's facts ought to—and must—impinge on the individual family member. (To what degree, for example, does the particular existence of the parent doom or mold the life of the child?) In *Boys and Girls Together* and *One Day in the Afternoon of the World*, Saroyan gets mixed results from mining the attitudes of his male protagonists for a perspective that would be both a consistent and legitimate interpretation of their marital situations. In Saroyan's long fiction, as well as in his other writing, both his strengths and his weaknesses derive from his insistent emotional presence.

Walter Shear

Other major works

SHORT FICTION: *The Daring Young Man on the Flying Trapeze and Other Stories*, 1934; *Inhale and Exhale*, 1936; *Three Times Three*, 1936; *The Gay and Melancholy Flux: Short Stories*, 1937; *Little Children*, 1937; *Love, Here Is My Hat and Other Short Romances*, 1938; *The Trouble with Tigers*, 1938; *Three Fragments and a Story*, 1939; *Peace, It's Wonderful*, 1939; *My Name Is Aram*, 1940; *Saroyan's Fables*, 1941; *The Insurance Salesman and Other Stories*, 1941; *Forty-eight Saroyan Stories*, 1942; *Some Day I'll Be a Millionaire: Thirty-four More Great Stories*, 1944; *Dear Baby*, 1944; *The Saroyan Special: Selected Stories*, 1948; *The Fiscal Hoboes*, 1949; *The Assyrian and Other Stories*, 1950; *The Whole Voyald and Other Stories*, 1956; *William Saroyan Reader*, 1958; *Love*, 1959; *After Thirty Years: The Daring Young Man on the Flying Trapeze*, 1964; *Best Stories of William Saroyan*, 1964; *The Tooth and My Father*, 1974.

PLAYS: *The Hungerers*, 1939; *Three Plays: My Heart's in the Highlands, The Time of Your Life, Love's Old Sweet Song*, 1940; *A Special Announcement*, 1940; *Subway Circus*, 1940; *The Ping-Pong Game*, 1940; *Jim Dandy: Fat Man in a Famine*, 1941; *Three Plays: The Beautiful People, Sweeney in the Trees, Across the Board on Tomorrow Morning*, 1941; *Razzle-Dazzle*, 1942; *Get Away Old Man*, 1943; *Don't Go Away Mad and Two Other Plays*, 1949; *The Slaughter of the Innocents*, 1952; *The Cave Dwellers*, 1957; *Once Around the Block*, 1959; *Sam the Highest Jumper of Them All: Or, The London Comedy*, 1960; *Settled Out of Court*, 1960 (adaptation with Henry Cecil); *The Dogs: Or, The Paris Comedy and Two Other Plays*, 1969.

NONFICTION: *The Time of Your Life*, 1939; *Harlem as Seen By Hirschfield*, 1941; *Hilltop Russians in San Francisco*, 1941; *Why Abstract?*, 1945 (with Henry Miller and Hilaire Hiler); *The Twin Adventures: The Adventures of William Saroyan*, 1950; *The Bicycle Rider in Beverly Hills*, 1952; *Here Comes, There Goes, You Know Who*, 1961; *A Note on Hilaire Hiler*, 1962; *Not Dying*, 1963; *Short Drive, Sweet Chariot*, 1966; *Look at Us: Let's See: Here We Are*, 1967; *I Used to Believe I Had Forever: Now I'm Not So Sure*, 1968; *Letters from 74 Rue Taitbout*, 1969; *Days of Life and Death and Escape to the Moon*, 1970; *Places Where I've Done Time*, 1972; *Sons Come and Go, Mothers Hang in Forever*, 1976; *Chance Meetings*, 1978; *Obituaries*, 1979; *Births*, 1983.

CHILDREN'S LITERATURE: *Me*, 1963; *Horsey Gorsey and the Frog*, 1968.

Bibliography

Calonne, David Stephen. *William Saroyan: My Real Work Is Being*. Chapel Hill: University of North Carolina Press, 1983. A good introduction to Saroyan's work. Calonne balances his examination of Saroyan's short stories, plays, novels, memoirs, and essays. Includes excellent notes, a bibliography, and an index.

Floan, Howard R. *William Saroyan*. New York: Twayne, 1966. The first important study of Saroyan, whose work is divided into four periods distinct in genre and tone. Floan concentrates on the first two periods (1934-1943) when Saroyan wrote his best short stories and plays.

Foster, Edward Halsey. *William Saroyan*. Boise, Idaho: Boise State University, 1984. A very short look at Saroyan, his Armenian background, his concept of good literature, and his enduring popularity. Foster touches only on Saroyan's most important work.

Kherdian, David. *A Bibliography of William Saroyan*. San Francisco: Roger Beacham, 1965. A limited and dated bibliography which brings together all the original writings of Saroyan appearing in book form. A very few periodicals and newspaper accounts are arbitrarily included.

Lee, Lawrence, and Barry Gifford. *Saroyan: A Biography*. New York: Harper & Row, 1984. A vivid biography of Saroyan that concentrates on the writer. Its unusual three-part structure opens at the height of his career (1940-1950), shifts to his roots and early literary struggles (1908-1939), and concludes with his last years (1950-1981).

MAY SARTON

Born: Wondelgem, Belgium; May 3, 1912

Principal long fiction

The Single Hound, 1938; *The Bridge of Years*, 1946; *Shadow of a Man*, 1950; *A Shower of Summer Days*, 1952; *Faithful Are the Wounds*, 1955; *The Birth of a Grandfather*, 1957; *The Small Room*, 1961; *Joanna and Ulysses*, 1963; *Mrs. Stevens Hears the Mermaids Singing*, 1965; *Miss Pickthorne and Mr. Hare: A Fable*, 1966; *The Poet and the Donkey*, 1969; *Kinds of Love*, 1970; *As We Are Now*, 1973; *Crucial Conversations*, 1975; *A Reckoning*, 1978; *Anger*, 1982; *The Magnificent Spinster*, 1985; *The Education of Harriet Hatfield*, 1989.

Other literary forms

A poet as well as a novelist, May Sarton has published a considerable number of volumes of verse. Her *Collected Poems, 1930-1973* appeared in 1974. She has also written a fable, *Miss Pickthorne and Mr. Hare*; an animal fantasy story, *The Fur Person: The Story of a Cat* (1957); several volumes of autobiography, including *I Knew a Phoenix: Sketches for an Autobiography* (1959), *Plant Dreaming Deep* (1968), and *A World of Light: Portraits and Celebrations* (1976); and several journals of her life in Nelson, New Hampshire, and York, Maine.

Achievements

It was after World War II, with the novel *The Bridge of Years* and the poems collected in *The Lion and the Rose* (1948), that Sarton's reputation began to grow. Her novels have met with a mixed response from critics and reviewers, sometimes condemned for awkward or imprecise style, an odd charge against a practicing poet. Even Carolyn Heilbrun, Sarton's defender, admits that confusing shifts of viewpoint occur in her fiction. On the other hand, Sarton's honesty in presenting human problems, seeing them from varied perspectives, has generally been acknowledged. In some ways, novels such as *Mrs. Stevens Hears the Mermaids Singing* and *Crucial Conversations* are dramatized debates about art, feminine culture, interpersonal relationships, tradition, and memory. Sarton has also been accused of sentimentality and preciousness, and she has tried to shift her style to a more direct, less self-conscious one since the early 1970's, perhaps answering critics of *Mrs. Stevens Hears the Mermaids Singing*, who saw it as too arch, too knowing. She has tended to take current issues or fashions such as the Vietnam War, death-and-dying, feminine consciousness, and Jungian psychology as material for her novels. Autobiographical material frequently enters into her fiction, particular characters being reinvoked in various works and especially types such as authoritarian women, supportive women, and rebellious young people.

Sarton has complained of the lack of serious critical scrutiny of her work and has expressed disappointment as well at her failure to achieve a large popular success. She has been stereotyped as a woman's writer, presumably creating slick plot situations, overdramatic dialogue, and conventional characters in romantic duos or trios. Some of these charges are true; she herself, noting the difficulty of supporting herself by her work even as late as the 1970's although she is a prolific and well-established writer, has spoken of the difficulties of being a single woman writer not sustained by a family or a religious community. Nevertheless, she continues to affirm the possibility of self-renewal, commenting: "I believe that eventually my work will be seen as a whole, all the poems and all the novels, as the expression of a vision of life which, though unfashionable all the way, has validity." The recent surge of interest in her work, particularly among feminist scholars, would seem to confirm Sarton's hopes.

Biography

May Sarton was born Elèanore Marie Sarton in Wondelgem, Belgium, on May 3, 1912. Her mother, Mabel Elwes Sarton, an English designer who worked at Maison Dangette, Brussels, was a determined craftsperson and an uncompromising seeker of high standards. Her father, George Sarton, pampered by his Belgian upper-middle class family after losing his mother early, was an active socialist who did mathematical studies at the University of Brussels before settling into his life's work as a major historian of science; he founded the leading journal in the field, *Isis*, in 1912. He was a methodical scholar who even after his day's scholarly labors would make notes in the evening concerning recent research by other scholars. May's mother compromised her talents for her husband's career, but Mrs. Sarton's gift of "refashioning things magically" inspired her daughter's own verbal artistry.

One close friend of her mother was Céline Dangotte Limbosch or "Mamie," whose home near Brussels Sarton has recalled as the one place in the world which would not change and whose traits appear in the heroine of *The Bridge of Years*. Her husband, Raumond Limbosch, a poet who never published his poems, also figures in that novel as a philosopher.

Sarton's earliest years were spent in Belgium, but with the coming of World War I, the family fled to England. In 1915, the Sartons went to America, staying briefly in New York before settling in Washington, where the Carnegie Institute gave support to Mr. Sarton's projected history of science. May's mother founded Belgart, specializing in handmade fashion apparel. May's father's somewhat informal appointment at Harvard University led the family to Cambridge, Massachusetts, in 1918. There, young May attended Shady Hill School, a Spartan institution run by an educational innovator, Mrs. Ernest Hocking, wife of a well-known philosopher, who combined the study of philosophy with poetry. Miss Edgett, an imaginative math teacher, inspired Sarton to be a poet, but Sarton also received encouragement from a family friend in Cambridge, Edith Forbes Kennedy. Edith was the inspiration for a character, Willa MacPherson, in *Mrs. Stevens Hears the Mermaids Singing*, whose friendship and encouragement push young Hilary Stevens along on her poetic career. School plays also awakened Sarton's interest in drama.

In 1919, the family briefly returned to settle their affairs in Belgium. For a short time, Sarton attended the Institute Belge de Culture Française, which she later attended for a year at age twelve. The institute was presided over by Marie Closset, who published poetry as "Jean Dominique," and two other women. Literature was taught from great works, and memorization was required. Sarton spent that year with the Limbosches while her parents were in Beirut so that her father could learn Arabic for his research. The literary atmosphere and general culture which she encountered there influenced Sarton greatly.

A 1926 graduate of Cambridge Latin High School, Sarton recalls attending Boston Repertory Theater, reading poems with friends, and feeling revolutionary about Henrik Ibsen during these years. Her parents had settled into Channing Place, Cambridge, which was the center of Sarton's life until her parents' deaths. Sarton spent two years wanting to be an actress, doing summer stock in Gloucester before joining Eva LeGallienne's Civic Repertory Theater in 1929. She spent three years with the theater company; from 1931 to 1932, Sarton was in Paris working as director of the company's apprentices. While in Paris, she became friends with Aurélian-Marie Lugné-Poë, a founder of Theatre de L'Oeuvre, a theater which brought many new plays to France. Lugné-Poë appears as a director in *The Bridge of Years*. Although he thought Sarton had more talent as a writer, he was willing to help her improve her acting skills. Their unsuccessful romantic relationship parallels that which occurs in *A Shower of Summer Days*, whose heroine goes to a country home in Ireland to overcome a love affair.

When LeGallienne ran out of money, Sarton, together with Eleanor Flexner and Kappo Phelan, kept the Apprentices Theater going, settling in Dublin, New Hampshire, and appearing elsewhere on tour. That venture failed after two years, a considerable shock for Sarton which turned her in the direction of writing fiction. In the following year, she wrote several short stories, none of which sold. In June, 1936, she went to Cornwall, England, first staying with Charles Singer, the historian of science, and then moving to London. She met Elizabeth Bowen, who was to become a friend over the next several decades and was the subject of passionate feelings; Juliette and Julian Huxley, at whose apartment over the London Zoo she spent a month; and Virginia

Woolf. She also met James Stephens, the Irish poet, and became a particular friend of S. S. Koteliansky, editor and mentor of various writers, including Katharine Mansfield. From 1936 to 1940, Sarton visited Belgium each spring, and for decades she could not decide whether she was European or American. She began writing poetry at the age of twenty-six. Wanting funds and having no settled career, she returned to the United States in 1939 to read her poetry at various colleges. Despite feeling "the inward disturbance of exile," she felt the love and friendship of many different people.

During the years of World War II, she worked for the Office of War Information in the film department. In 1943, she set up poetry readings at the New York Public Library to provide cultural experience for wartime workers. She returned to England in 1944 to visit her friend Elizabeth Bowen, who also visited Sarton whenever she was in the United States. With *The Bridge of Years*, Sarton's novel-writing began again in earnest. Novels and other fiction and volumes of poetry have appeared at close intervals since. Her early poetry won her the Gold Rose for Poetry and the Edward Bland Memorial Prize (1945).

Sarton supported herself by teaching, serving as Briggs-Copeland instructor in composition at Harvard from 1950 to 1952, poet-in-residence at Bryn Mawr from 1953 to 1954, and lecturing on poetry at Harvard, the University of Iowa, the University of Chicago, Colorado College for Women, and Wellesley and Beloit colleges. In 1953, she met Louise Bogan, whose calm and order she valued considerably, though Bogan, poetry editor of *The New Yorker*, did little to forward Sarton's career. Other novels appearing in the early 1950's earned Sarton a Guggenheim Fellowship from 1954 to 1955. Her reputation had grown with *A Shower of Summer Days*, though the critical reception, as with later novels, was mixed.

The Birth of a Grandfather came at a turning point in Sarton's life: her mother had died in 1950 after a long illness and her father died quite suddenly in 1956. The family home in Cambridge was sold, and Sarton moved in October, 1958, to an old house equipped with a barn and thirty-six acres in Nelson, New Hampshire, a small village. *The Small Room*, a novel dealing with women training women as intellectual disciples in the atmosphere of a small women's college, was written there. It also introduced a lesbian love affair between Carryl Cope, a brilliant but flinty scholar, and Olive Hunt, a benefactor of the college. *Mrs. Stevens Hears the Mermaids Singing*, which was written at a time of gloom because of worries over her financial situation, was at first refused publication because it depicted a lesbian affair, and the publishers required excisions before the book was accepted.

Kinds of Love, *As We Are Now*, *Crucial Conversations*, and *A Reckoning* explore various marital or amatory dilemmas along with the problem of being feminine and an artist. During this period, Sarton settled briefly in Ogunquit, Maine, and then in York, Maine, in an old house on the coast, writing further volumes of poetry, autobiographical sketches, and journals. Her abiding love for animals is reflected in *The Fur Person*, a story about a gentleman cat's adventures.

Sarton's career reflects her conviction that "art must become the primary motivation for love is never going to fulfill in the usual sense." Increasingly, she has taken her stand as feminist: "We [women] have to be ourselves." Her own sexual orientation seems to have grown partly out of her isolation as a woman and a writer and her sense that marriage and family would detract from her creativity. Despite her age, she continues to be an active and indeed prolific writer.

Analysis

Based upon Sarton's student years in Belgium and memories of her own family, *The Bridge of Years* centers on a Belgian family, Paul and Melanie Duchesne, and their three daughters, during four segments of their lives. These periods, besides accounting for personal growth in the major characters, also demarcate the stages of political change after World War I: optimism in the immediate postwar period; the decline of public morale and search for political solutions to the Depression of the 1930's; the fear of renewed European conflict attendant upon the rise of Hitler; and the outbreak of that conflict as liberal, humanitarian values come under attack with World War II. The novel is, perhaps, Sarton's most complex work, partly because the prototypes of the main characters were close to Sarton's own experience and the themes were motivated by intellectual friendships established in Europe prior to World War II.

Melanie Duchesne, a designer of furniture, a stickler for fine craftsmanship, a courageous and optimistic woman whose country home is a model of stability, is based upon Sarton's mother and her long-time friend, Céline Limbosch. Paul, the temperamental philosopher who cannot express his thoughts, is partly based on Raymond Limbosch and partly on George Sarton, May's father, especially in his need for an ordered existence and exact routine. Paul's breakthrough into true philosophical statement under the pressure of the war is, as much as anything, Sarton's own search for authentic expression. Her father's leftist socialism and critical intelligence are reflected in Pierre Poiret, the university-student son of close friends of the Duchesnes'. The immemorial Bo Bo, the stiff but protective Teutonic nursemaid, is a portrait of Sarton's childhood governess.

Of the daughters, Colette, the youngest, is the poet, a romanticist living in a fairy world, Sarton's view of herself as a child. Solange, who becomes a veterinarian, has the patient skill with animals that Sarton herself possesses. The eldest daughter, Françoise, with her long affection for Jacques Croll, a fatigued soldier from World War I, believes that art is everything, turning herself inward when Jacques, maneuvered by Melanie, marries a local girl.

Françoise feels compromised when Jacques tips her a wink as he walks down the church aisle with his bride. Her resulting emotional breakdown, and the awareness that art cannot be everything when "life [is] lived near the point of conflict," reflect Sarton's own emotional turmoil in the 1930's as she sought to become an artist.

Paul Duchesne's skepticism about the perfectibility of the human spirit is tempered by his German friend, the intellectual Gerhard Schmidt, who sees the need for individual effort to resist tyranny. After escaping from his home-land during Hitler's purge of intellectuals, he goes to fight with the Loyalists in Spain while his son, Hans, hypnotized by the Nazis, becomes a storm-trooper. This opposition of father and son is repeated in the case of Emile Poiret, a pious Catholic floral illustrator with a sense of cosmic presence in things, and his antireligious son, Pierre. The novel presents facets of the European response to the breakdown of democratic civilization in the 1920's and 1930's and, at a more personal level, reflects the idea that some persons must extend themselves in love if civilization is to continue.

The question of who one is, especially in the context of generations and of change, is a continuing concern of Sarton. It is presented through the dramatic, carefully staged scenes of *The Birth of a Grandfather*, in which the omniscient author moves among the characters, heightening the effect by the questions which they ask themselves. The interior speculation is in the style of Henry James, though the consciousness attributed to a given character does not always seem consistent with his personality or inner life. This novel begins at the Maine island retreat of the wealthy and established Wyeth family. Tom Dorgan, a Boston Irish Catholic, is romantically involved with Betsy Wyeth, Frances and Sprig Wyeth's daughter. In contrast to these young lovers, Lucy, Frances' sister, is undergoing a divorce. It is Frances, the major char-acter, and her husband, Sprig, from the middle-aged generation, whose pain-ful readjustment to marriage and to age form the basis of the plot.

The older generation includes Uncle Joe, an urbane retired diplomat, Aunt Jane, a wise old woman capable of immersing herself in others, and Gran-Quan, Sprig's father, a man consumed by dramatic self-pity over the death of his wife and constantly supported by his sister, Jane. The Wyeths' son, Caleb, is reluctantly in the heart of family matters, biding his time until he gains independence from them. Appropriately enough, a major scene is the family's Fourth of July celebration on a nearby island. The fireworks are, for Frances, like moments of purity amid darkness, but they also herald the sudden death of Aunt Jane and the breaking up of Gran-Quan's private world and descent into insanity. Betsy and Caleb see their parents in new ways: Frances represents human frailty, and Sprig is seen as one sheltered from the pains of life.

The second part of the novel, "Ice Age," set in Cambridge, Massachusetts, shows the threat that tension and obligation bring to family unity. Tom and

Betsy have married, and a child is on the way. This potentially joyful event threatens Sprig, who cannot accept the loss of direction in his life, which has settled into traditional philanthropy and conservation of the family wealth. By contrast, his friend Bill Waterford, who treats life with saving grace, calmly announces his impending death from cancer. Bill's life has had a sense of purpose. Two dinner scenes set forth two perspectives: in one, Hester, Sprig's sister, sees Sprig and Frances trying vainly to avert the emotional threat of Caleb's demand to be allowed to go alone to Greece for a year. In another, Tom Dorgan, innocently holding forth on the coming prospect of family life, exacerbates the conflict of generations, but he also sees that the Wyeths can admit to being wrong and remain loyal to each other. Caleb puts aside his immediate demand for independence, recognizing his father's own imprisonment in his reticence and sense of responsibility.

Coming to terms with Caleb leaves Sprig uncertain about his love for his wife, and a visit to Bill provokes the question of what real life is. Bill's wife, Nora, warns him that one may fail to exercise one's talents out of fear of freedom and power, a question which Sarton has explored in various ways in probing the nature of the artist. Caleb's destination, Greece, awakens other echoes in Sprig, reminding him of the Greek scholarship for which he had once wished; Sprig then realizes his potential for continued growth.

In part three, the grandfather is reborn, both in the sheer physical sense of the new grandchild and in meeting the meaning of his own life. Sprig must surrender his friendship with Bill, and he must test his own talent, no longer relying on Bill's support. Frances wonders whether she has not turned self-detachment into a prison; the answer comes with the realization that birth and death, the march of ongoing generations, has significance. This insight strikes her when, while visiting Bill, she encounters his nearly exhausted wife, Nora; a seemingly unsuitable marriage has worked because Bill was able to give of himself. Upon the departure of Caleb, to whom Sprig has given financial independence so that Caleb may try what he has wanted, Sprig himself turns to translating Greek plays as a self-imposed test. He acknowledges also that he has loved himself rather than Caleb in their relationship. With new honesty and willingness to assume self-defined responsibility, Sprig reconnects to the exuberance of his youth. He and Frances reaffirm their faithfulness, and love wins out as absolute value.

Sarton uses imagistic motifs such as the current in the Charles River or the isles of Greece to suggest important ideas in the novel. The shifting omniscient viewpoint highlights dramatic intensities, but it is used at times without strong motivation or without a careful build-up of character. It also can turn into undisguised narrative commentary. Moral implications do come through in catchwords such as "escape" and "freedom," which reverberate through the novel. Occasionally, moral judgements become banal. The novel has shown Sprig's life as empty of personal demands upon himself and his resistance to his children as a fearful reaction to his own aging, but the moral tends to blunt the focus.

Coming roughly at the middle of Sarton's career, *Mrs. Stevens Hears the Mermaids Singing* is the author's most intense study of the feminine artist. Here, too, the style received mixed reviews, one critic praising the music of the prose, another objecting to the fussiness and humorlessness of the writing. What one critic found to be a well-done presentation of the mystery of the creative impulse, a second found to be "an embarrassing probing of art" and "acute self-consciousness," and a third found the novel's characters "muse-chasers who believe themselves to be delicate vessels of talent." Carolyn Heilbrun, in noting that the novel deals with the poet Hilary Stevens' escape from the passivity of a feminine destiny, sees Sarton as aware that "the real artist is not the fantasy creature imagined by women trapped in domesticity." Art comes, as Hilary insists, at the expense of every human being, the self and the self's ties with other people.

The plot interweaves Hilary's initiation of Mar Hemmer, a potential poet recovering from an intense relationship with a man, with her reveries as she is being interviewed about her own poetic development. Mar, despite his lack of emotional proportion, helps her to see her own life in perspective. Married to an unstable war veteran in England, Hilary began to write poetry after his sudden death. An intellectual friend, Willa MacPherson, encourages her to continue writing poetry and provides one night of passionate sexual exploration. Another friend, however, creates self-doubt, which Hilary identifies with the masculine force in herself. She knows that she can preserve her artistry only by caring about life, which does not necessarily mean sparing others from pain. As Hilary later points out to Mar, poetry and feeling are connected only if the poet understands that "true feeling justifies whatever it may cost." One cannot anesthetize the pain of life.

Philippa Munn, Hilary's proper girlhood governess with whom she is infatuated, plays the role which Sarton's own teachers did in her youth. Poetry diffuses sensuality, Hilary learns; it creates a moment of revelation, not simply of indulgence. As Hilary's wise physician tells her as she lies in the hospital recovering from a breakdown over her husband's death, she must write poems about objects and about a person to whom she can fasten herself deeply, but she should not confuse love for someone with poetry. Poetry can become "passionate decorum" in which love is presented as a mystique; what gives strength to poems is form.

Mrs. Stevens Hears the Mermaids Singing mixes the Platonic tradition of poet as maker whose creations surpass his own conscious understanding with an Aristotelian stress on the formal artifact which has its own laws of being and is autonomous. The notion of the poet as rapt by emotional experience lies also within the Platonic tradition of poetry as ecstasy. The events making up the life of Hilary Stevens have parallels with Sarton's own life, and the novel is a justification of that life. The presentation of the poet as a solitary individual misunderstood by the world also reflects Sarton's Romanticism.

As the heroine of *A Reckoning*, Laura Spelman, resident of an upper-middle-class Boston suburb, faces terminal cancer, she interprets her growing "death-wish" as a return to the Jungian "house of gathering." It is a world of timeless personages; Sarton had been reading Jung before writing the book. She had also become more concerned with feminism and more open about lesbianism. As Laura is alienated from her own body, she works to resolve her unexamined passions by assessing her life. She comes, according to one critic, to an "understanding of life as an amalgam of human relationships, culture, and the natural world."

The novel also shows Harriet Moors, a budding novelist and lesbian, trying to put her life into art, an issue complicated by the opposition of her lover to any fiction that might hint at the truth of their liaison. It seems that not only marriage but also a binding lesbian attachment is fatal to art: Harriet Moors will have to suffer the loss of her lover as the price of continuing with her art.

Laura has to sort out her feelings for her mother, Sybille, a woman of dazzling power whose beauty and charm have oppressed her daughters. Jo, Laura's sister, after her mother had interrupted Jo's passion for a woman, had fled into the sterile intellectuality of academic life. Daphne, Laura's other sister, has become insecure and emotionally dependent. Laura has found escape in marriage. The destructive Sybille is a less flattering version of Céline Limbosch, of whom Sarton has said that she forced friends into decisions they did not wish to make and attacked their authentic being. Even in her senility in a nursing home, Sybille is someone about whom her daughter treads warily. Earlier in her life, Laura had had an intense friendship with Ella; the reader may strain, in fact, to realize it was a lesbian affair. Harriet Moors's visits for advice on her novel rekindles in Laura her memories of Ella. She comes to realize that if love is painful, then art is mutilating. Yet in dying, Laura finds positive answers in music and in poetry. The final reckoning is instigated by Laura's warm and helpful Aunt Minna, whose reading aloud to Laura forces her to consider that "journey into being a woman" and what women are meant to be. Women are locked away from one another in a man's world, she decides. Marriage may be normal destiny, but for those living intensely, a mystical friendship is the hope—of women for women, of men for men. Sybille, according to Ella, feared "the tenderness of communion."

Laura's loss of lonely autonomy is convincingly presented, but the master image, that of weaving a pattern, is imposed rather than dramatized. Ella's appearance at the end does not really complete the final weaving of the pattern by mystical friendship; the scene reminds the reader of sentimental fiction often found in women's magazines. Clearly, too many issues have come within the compass of the heroine's last months. Death may force its victims to focus their lives and aspirations, but the last days of Laura Spelman are not deeply and plausibley linked to her life as a married woman and parent or even to her efforts to approach art. As in *Mrs. Stevens Hears the Mermaids Singing*, reminiscence plays a key role. Whole scenes are recalled in dramatic form, but the very selectivity of memory and its often self-serving quality may raise questions about the honesty and sheer structural relationship between what Laura recalls and what she really was—a Boston upper-middle-class housewife with delusions of creativity, the kind of thing against which Sarton herself has warned. Finally, the linkage of femininty and artistic creation is sidetracked by the lesbian issue. *A Reckoning* lacks the strengths of Sarton's best work: thematic depth, balanced characters, organic use of imagery, adequate plot development, and motivated action. The final reckoning with May Sarton must be deferred.

Roger E. Wiene

Other major works

PLAY: *Underground River*, 1947.

POETRY: *Encounter in April*, 1937; *Inner Landscape*, 1939; *The Lion and the Rose*, 1948; *The Land of Silence and Other Poems*, 1953; *In Time Like Air*, 1957; *Cloud, Stone, Sun, Vine: Poems, Selected and New*, 1961; *A Private Mythology*, 1966; *As Does New Hampshire and Other Poems*, 1967; *A Grain of Mustard Seed: New Poems*, 1971; *A Durable Fire: New Poems*, 1972; *Collected Poems, 1930-1973*, 1974; *Selected Poems of May Sarton*, 1978; *Halfway to Silence*, 1980; *Letters from Maine*, 1984; *The Silence Now*, 1989.

NONFICTION: *I Knew a Phoenix: Sketches for an Autobiography*, 1959; *Plant Dreaming Deep*, 1968; *Journal of a Solitude*, 1973; *A World of Light: Portraits and Celebrations*, 1976; *The House by the Sea*, 1977; *Writings on Writing*, 1980; *Recovering: A Journal*, 1980; *At Seventy: A Journal*, 1984; *After the Stroke: A Journal*, 1988; *Honey in the Hive: Judith Matlock, 1898-1982*, 1988.

CHILDREN'S LITERATURE: *Punch's Secret*, 1974; *A Walk Through the Woods*, 1976.

MISCELLANEOUS: *The Fur Person: The Story of a Cat*, 1957.

Bibliography

Bloin, L. P. *May Sarton: A Bibliography*. Metuchen, N.J.: Scarecrow Press, 1978. In two parts, the first listing Sarton's poetry, novels, nonfiction, essays, and articles. The second part lists secondary sources, including book reviews. A conscientious compilation of sources that is most useful to the Sarton scholar. The author acknowledges Sarton's assistance in putting together this work.

Curley, Dorothy N., Maurice Kramer, and Elaine F. Kramer, eds. *Modern*

American Literature. 4 vols. 4th ed. New York: Ungar, 1969-1976. A collection of reviews and criticisms of Sarton's poems and novels, the latest entry being 1967. Includes criticism on *Mrs. Stevens Hears the Mermaids Singing*, considered an important book and which the author says was most difficult to write. The supplement has reviews on Sarton's *Collected Poems*.

Evans, Elizabeth. *May Sarton*. Rev. ed. Boston: Twayne, 1989. In this volume in Twayne's United States Authors series, Evans upholds Sarton as a writer who speaks for women, insisting they claim their own identity; hence, her increasing popularity among feminists. An interesting addition to this somewhat standard criticism is an appendix of letters of Sarton's to her editor while writing *Mrs. Stevens Hears the Mermaids Singing*. Selected bibliography.

Grumbach, Doris. "The Long Solitude of May Sarton." *The New Republic* 170 (June 8, 1974): 31-32. Grumbach draws together Sarton's philosophy, in particular the serenity of her writing in the face of her declared "traumas." Noting that critics have often ignored Sarton, Grumbach says: "Hers has been a durable fire . . . her small room seem to make most male critics uncomfortable." An article well worth reading.

Martin, Lucy L. "May Sarton: Poetry (Life) Is a Discipline, Not a Self-Indulgence." *Maine Tribune*, June 20, 1975, pp. 22-23. Martin writes of Sarton's intention to enhance life, not sentimentalize it. Proposes an interesting theory on why Sarton was ignored by critics: that the lack of explicit sexuality in her work and her views of love as a "heroic demand" made her unappealing to critics. Provides criticism on *Mrs. Stevens Hears the Mermaids Singing*, which Martin considers an inspiration to women.

Sibley, Agnes. *May Sarton*. New York: Twayne, 1972. Obviously a must for criticism on Sarton, because there is so little of book-length size written about her—despite her prodigious output. This study discusses Sarton's poems, from *Encounter in April* in 1937 to *A Durable Fire*, published in 1972. Sibley has grouped novels under two themes that she considers relevant to Sarton: "detachment" for the early novels and "communion" for the later ones.